Essential Psychopathology and Its Treatment

THIRD EDITION

A NORTON PROFESSIONAL BOOK

Essential Psychopathology and Its Treatment

THIRD EDITION

Jerrold S. Maxmen, M.D.

Nicholas G. Ward, M.D.

Mark D. Kilgus, M.D., Ph.D.

W. W. Norton & Company

New York • London

For information about permission to reproduce selections from this book, write to Permissions, W. W. Norton & Company, Inc., 500 Fifth Avenue, New York, NY 10110

For information about special discounts for bulk purchases, please contact W. W. Norton Special Sales at specialsales@wwnorton.com or 800-233-4830

Manufacturing by Courier Westford
Book design by Jonathan Lippincott
Production manager: Leeann Graham

Library of Congress Cataloging-in-Publication Data

Maxmen, Jerrold S.
  Essential psychopathology and its treatment / Jerrold S. Maxmen, Nicholas G. Ward, Mark D. Kilgus. — 3rd ed., rev. for DSM-IV-TR.
     p. ; cm.
  "A Norton professional book."
  Includes bibliographical references and index.
  ISBN 978-0-393-70560-7 (hardcover : alk. paper)   1. Psychology, Pathological.   2. Psychiatry.   I. Ward, Nicholas G.   II. Kilgus, Mark D. III. Title.
     [DNLM: 1. Mental Disorders—diagnosis.   2. Mental Disorders—therapy. 3. Psychopathology. WM 141 M464ea 2009]
  RC454.M3 2009
  616.89—dc22   2008051235

ISBN: 978-0-393-70560-7

W. W. Norton & Company, Inc., 500 Fifth Avenue, New York, N.Y. 10110
www.wwnorton.com
W. W. Norton & Company Ltd., Castle House, 75/76 Wells Street, London W1T 3QT

1 2 3 4 5 6 7 8 9 0

Contents

Acknowledgments

It is a testimony to the careful authorship of Jerrold Maxmen that so much of his original work is still included in this latest revision. It is often easier to demolish a house and start over than to extensively remodel an old one. Yet some houses are designed and constructed so well that they would be irreplaceable. Such fondness for Jere's classic text and its persistent relevance have made it worthy of an update. Some chapters have been more thoroughly revised than others, depending upon how the new evidence generated during the last 12 years has changed our view of the "essentials."

The work of revision was distributed among the faculty of the Department of Psychiatry and Behavioral Medicine at the Carilion Clinic in Roanoke, Virginia. These superb clinicians and teachers are acknowledged in the List of Contributors. Special recognition is warranted for those colleagues who have authored one of the three new chapters: Vishal Anand, Kim Oram, Bill Rea, and especially for Andy Pumariega and George Rekers, my long-time mentors and friends.

Creating a book is much like the birth of a child—we hope that this child is as attractive to you as it is to those who labored over it this past year. We would desire that our child not require immediate correction. However, please provide comments and suggestions for the next edition to the parents at mkilgus@carilion.com.

—Mark D. Kilgus, M.D., Ph.D.
Chair, Department of Psychiatry and Behavioral Medicine
Carilion Clinic
1st Floor Administrative Suite
2017 South Jefferson Street
Roanoke, VA 24014

List of Contributors

FELICITY ADAMS, M.D., a child and adolescent psychiatrist in the Department of Psychiatry and Behavioral Medicine at the Carilion Clinic, serves on the faculty for both the Carilion Clinic Psychiatry Residency Program and the Child and Adolescent Psychiatry Fellowship. (Chapters 21 & 23)

VISHAL S. ANAND, M.D., a forensic psychiatrist, served on the faculty for both the Carilion Clinic Psychiatry Residency Program and the University of Virginia School of Medicine. He currently practices with the Department of Veterans Affairs in Austin, Texas. (Chapter 8)

KIMBERLY BARNETT ORAM, PSY.D., a clinical psychologist, is Assistant Professor of Counseling Psychology at Trinity International University, Florida. (Chapters 8 & 18)

TRACEY CRISS, M.D., an adult psychiatrist in the Department of Psychiatry and Behavioral Medicine at the Carilion Clinic, serves on the faculty for both the Carilion Clinic Psychiatry Residency Program and the University of Virginia School of Medicine. (Chapter 13)

DAVID A. DOWNS, JR., M.D., a geriatric psychiatrist, is Section Chief for St. Albans Hospital in the Department of Psychiatry and Behavioral Medicine at the Carilion Clinic Radford campus. (Chapter 10)

WILLIAM S. ELIAS, M.D., a neurologist in the Carilion Clinic Department of Medicine, is former director of the Carilion Sleep Center, where he continues to practice sleep medicine. He is on the faculty for the Carilion Clinic Psychiatry Residency Program. (Chapter 20)

BENJAMIN T. GRIFFETH, M.D., an adult psychiatrist, is the Associate Program Director for Curriculum with the Carilion Clinic Psychiatry Residency Program and serves on the clinical faculty for the University of Virginia School of Medicine. He is head of emergency psychiatry at the VA Medical Center in Salem, Virginia. (Chapter 24)

DAVID W. HARTMAN, M.D., an adult psychiatrist, is Section Chief for adult outpatient psychiatric services in the Department of Psychiatry and Behavioral Medicine at the Carilion Clinic. He serves on the faculty for the Carilion Clinic Psychiatry Residency Program and for the University of Virginia School of Medicine. (Chapter 22)

ANN E. HEDBERG, M.D., an adult psychiatrist and anesthesiologist, serves as Associate Program Director for the Carilion Clinic Psychiatry Residency Program in the Department of Psychiatry and Behavioral Medicine. (Chapters 2 & 3)

BUSH KAVURU, M.D., a geriatric psychiatrist and psychosomatics specialist in the Department of Psychiatry and Behavioral Medicine at the Carilion Clinic, serves on the faculty for the Carilion Clinic Psychiatry Residency Program. (Chapter 1)

J. THOMAS NOGA, a geriatric psychiatrist, serves on the faculty for the Carilion Clinic Psychiatry Residency Program and is Director for Medical Education at Catawba State Hospital. (Chapters 4 & 12)

ANDRES J. PUMARIEGA, M.D., a child and adolescent psychiatrist, is Chair for the Department of Psychiatry at Reading Hospital and Medical Center in Pennsylvania. He is Professor of Psychiatry at Temple University School of Medicine. (Chapters 7 & 19)

WILLIAM S. REA, M.D., an adult and addictions psychiatrist, is Section Chief for adult inpatient psychiatric services in the Department of Psychiatry and Behavioral Medicine at the Carilion Clinic. He serves on the faculty for the Carilion Clinic Psychiatry Residency Program and as site psychiatry clerkship director for the University of Virginia School of Medicine. (Chapters 6 & 11)

ANURADHA REDDY, M.D., M.P.H., a child and adolescent psychiatrist in the Department of Psychiatry and Behavioral Medicine at the Carilion Clinic, serves on the faculty for both the Carilion Clinic Psychiatry Residency Program and the Child and Adolescent Psychiatry Fellowship. (Chapters 17 & 23)

GEORGE A. REKERS, PH.D., TH.D., a clinical child and adult psychologist, is Distinguished Professor of Neuropsychiatry and Behavioral Science Emeritus at the University of South Carolina School of Medicine. He is a Fellow of the American Academy of Clinical Psychology, and a Diplomate in Clinical Psychology of the American Board of Professional Psychology. (Chapters 8 & 18)

RICHARD W. SEIDEL, PH.D., a clinical psychologist, is the Director of Research and Education for the Department of Psychiatry and Behavioral Medicine at Carilion Clinic and serves on the faculty for the Carilion Clinic psychiatry and family medicine residency training programs, for the Department of Psychology at Virginia Tech, and for the University of Virginia School of Medicine. (Chapters 5 & 9)

DAVID B. TRINKLE, M.D., a geriatric psychiatrist, is Section Chief for geriatric psychiatry in the Department of Psychiatry and Behavioral Medicine at the Carilion Clinic. He serves as medical director for the Carilion Clinic Center for Healthy Aging, program director for the Carilion Geriatric Psychiatry Fellowship, and on the clinical faculty for the University of Virginia School of Medicine. (Chapter 10)

SACHINDER VASUDEVA, M.D., an adult psychiatrist, is the medical director of the Center for Traumatic Stress at the VA Medical Center in Salem, Virginia, and serves on the faculty for the Carilion Clinic Psychiatry Residency Program. (Chapter 14)

GEBREHANA W. ZEBRO, M.D., board certified in both internal medicine and psychiatry, is Section Chief for the consultation and liaison service in the Department of Psychiatry and Behavioral Medicine at the Carilion Clinic. (Chapter 15)

Preface

Until recently, psychiatric diagnosis was ridiculed by social critics and downplayed by most professionals: At best, diagnoses were meaningless categories; at worst, denigrating labels. But in 1980, psychiatric diagnosis suddenly became the cornerstone for *all* clinical practice. During the 1970s, major developments in psychiatric epidemiology and drug therapy spurred the development of something American psychiatry never had: a clinically useful nosology. (A "nosology" is a system for naming and classifying diseases.) In July 1980, the American Psychiatric Association published this nosology as the third edition of the *Diagnostic and Statistical Manual of Mental Disorders*, or *DSM-III*.

This volume became the 20th century's greatest advance in psychiatric diagnosis. Instead of merely tinkering with old categories or adding nosological blubber, *DSM-III* introduced major conceptual and practical shifts and, for the first time in making diagnoses, favored scientific evidence over theoretical speculation. The respect of *DSM-III* for rigorous scientific thought has spread throughout clinical practice. Psychotherapy, once a strictly intuitive affair, is now researched with standards similar to other sciences. Since *DSM-III*, meetings of mental-health professionals have undergone a mind-boggling transformation: Participants now ask such once ill-mannered questions as "Where's the evidence?" and "What are the data?" No longer are things true simply because Professor X says so. Today, diagnostic common sense necessitates proof. Scientifically, *DSM-III* had its deficiencies, but these stemmed far more from gaps in scientific knowledge than from inadequacies in *DSM-III* itself.

These deficiencies, real and dubious, motivated a 1987 revision (*DSM-III-R*), a 1994 update (*DSM-IV*), and a 2000 text *revision* (*DSM-IV-TR*); all presented clinical and scientific advances. *DSM-IV-TR* is also intended to be a cross-cultural and political advance. In much of the world, a diagnostic system called ICD (International Classification of Diseases) is used for psychiatric diagnosis. The most recent version, ICD-10, was released in 1993, and clinical modifications were added in 2007 (ICD-10-CM). *DSM-IV-TR* attempts to be harmonious with ICD-10, so that when clinicians from different countries discuss a particular diagnosis, they are really talking about the same disorder or disease.

Some people consider a *scientific* psychiatry to be a dehumanized psychiatry. We could not disagree more. As long as therapists treat *people*-with-illnesses, instead of *illnesses*-that-happen-to-be-in-people, clinical practice necessitates artistry, intuition, philosophy, ethics, and science—each with its own contribution. The distinct contribution of science is that, when properly conducted, it yields the most likely predictions, and therefore affords patients the greatest chance of receiving treatments most likely to work. Offering patients anything less is hardly humanistic.

There is, of course, far more to proper clinical assessment than diagnosis, and any clinician who evaluates a patient's condition *solely* in terms of whether it meets *DSM-IV-TR* criteria is gravely misinformed and shows a disturbing misunderstanding of the diagnostic process. Proper clinical assessments must address the patient's context, including his or her family, friends, upbringing, genetic patterns, physical health, current stressors, psychodynamics, and so on. Still, good care begins with accurate diagnosis.

DSM-III (now *DSM-IV-TR*) is the first nosology widely applied by *all* mental-health disciplines. This is fortunate, for the essentials of psychopathology should be understood not just by psychiatrists, but by physicians, psychologists, nurses, social workers, psychotherapists, and counselors. In 2004, conservative estimates established that diagnosable mental disorders afflict greater than one out of every four adults, or nearly 58 million Americans (Kessler et al., 2005). Nearly half of these individuals meet criteria for two or more mental disorders. Mental disorders are the leading cause of disability in the United States and Canada. Aside from the emotional toll, these disorders annually cost the nation over $200 billion in lost earnings and many billions more in direct health care expenditures. These amounts are similar to those for heart disease and cancer. Of all patients with mental disorders, about half are treated by primary-care physicians, a quarter by mental-health professionals, and another quarter go untreated. Thus recognizing and healing psychopathology is an everyday task for every helping professional. *Essential Psychopathology and Its Treatment* presents the current evidence and collective thinking of experts. Although stressing the new, the book does not abrogate the old. Time-tested concepts and practices are included. But psychiatric diagnosis is open to question as a dynamic and evolving endeavor. When Robert Spitzer, the chief architect of *DSM-III*, was asked, "What happens if a clinician doesn't want to diagnose using *DSM-III* criteria?" he replied, "Then don't! It's a free country. *People* wrote *DSM-III*, not God."

Essential Psychopathology and Its Treatment is a "no-nonsense" book. Many psychiatric texts are written as if students were idiots, not to be "subjected" to anything more than the "most basic facts." As for concepts, forget it! "Everybody knows" that students are "antipsychiatry," and therefore, to prevent students from being turned off to psychiatry, these texts should be as simpleminded as possible. Again, we disagree. This text will not pander. Diagnostic psychopathology is essential to clinical evaluation, and if students don't wish to learn the subject and know it well, they might wonder why they are choosing to provide inferior care.

The "essential" in *Essential Psychopathology and Its Treatment* does not refer to the "essence" of psychiatry or to "all the psychiatry you'll ever need to know." Reality dictates that in psychiatry, as in everything else, choices must be made—choices that eliminate some good stuff in the process. For better or worse, the "essential" in *Essential Psychopathology and Its Treatment* reflects these choices: Some information is *relatively* more critical than other information. To save space, smaller type is used for less important material, and fewer references are cited. The downside of this "essential trimming" is that major works in diagnostic psychopathology don't appear, significant details are omitted, and controversial material is mostly excluded.

In this book, people with *major* mental disorders are called "patients" instead of "clients." Referring to patients with *severe* mental disorders as "clients" is not only euphemistic, but may unwittingly trivialize the burden of having a disorder such as schizophrenia. Calling these people "patients" is purely descriptive and certainly no sign of disrespect. It is not intended as a reference to a strictly traditional medical model of care. "Patient" is derived from the Latin word *patiens*, meaning "one who endures" or "one who suffers," and the actual definition of "patient" does not itself connote passivity. In contrast, those who seek help for problems other than serious mental disorders (e.g., adjustment reactions, marital difficulties) are often called "clients." "Client" originates from the Latin root *cliens*, which means "follower" and suggests dependency rather than empowerment. This book employs "he" and "she" randomly, except when discussing a mental disorder more common in men or women. Any resemblance between the pseudonyms we've assigned to patients in case examples and to actual individuals with the same name is purely coincidental.

This text aims to be concise, to give students of all ages and levels of experience a brief, relatively jargon-free, and readable blend of the newest and most fundamental information in this rapidly evolving field. We hope that

Essential Psychopathology and Its Treatment fascinates students about the subject and encourages them to question whatever they read, to pursue the topic further, to chuckle every now and then, and most of all, to help their patients. We intend this to be a teaching text that assists with discovery and not just a compendium of information on psychopathology. Hopefully it reads as well and is as thoroughly integrated as previous editions.

A word of caution: Do yourself a big favor and avoid self-diagnosis. With "medical student's disease," future physicians "catch" diabetes while studying medicine, cancer while studying surgery, and schizophrenia while studying psychiatry. Everybody has some features of a mental disorder, but that hardly means one has a mental disorder. Hemophiliacs bruise, but everyone who bruises isn't a hemophiliac. The same applies to mental disorders. If you are concerned that you, or a loved one, has a mental disorder, consult an expert.

References

American Psychiatric Association. (2000). *Diagnostic and statistical manual of mental disorders*, 4th ed., text rev. Washington, DC: American Psychiatric Association.

Kessler, R.C., Chiu, W.T., Demler, O., & Walters, E.E. (2005). Prevalence, severity, and comorbidity of twelve-month DSM-IV disorders in the National Comorbidity Survey Replication (NCS-R). *Archives of General Psychiatry*, 62(6), 617–627.

National Institute of Mental Health, available online at www.nimh.nih.gov.

World Health Organization. (2004). The World Health Report 2004: Changing History, Annex Table 3: Burden of disease in DALYs by cause, sex, and mortality stratum in WHO regions, estimates for 2002. Geneva: Author.

Essential Psychopathology and Its Treatment

THIRD EDITION

Diagnostic
Psychopathology

1

Psychopathology

Such is man that if he has a name for something it ceases to be a riddle.

—I. B. Singer, "Property"

At 58, Amy's life stopped. Although cancer-free for 5 months since her mastectomy, she remained paralyzed by depression and insomnia. Amy had withdrawn from family and friends, quit work, become addicted to sleeping pills, and contemplated suicide. Once a film buff, now she hid in bed ruminating about "it" (she was afraid to say *cancer*). Diligently, she attempted relaxation exercises to overcome insomnia, yet she was unable to concentrate—the harder she tried, the more she failed, and the less she slept. Her demoralization was pervasive.

After all, the reasons for her symptoms were understandable and Amy "knew" that only time could heal her. To be sure, having cancer and a mastectomy is an understandable reason for sadness and insomnia. But this thinking misses the point: Amy had an additional problem—a mental disorder called "major depressive disorder."

Only after Amy's psychopathology was recognized and the proper antidepressant medication prescribed did her life return to normal. She still worried about her mastectomy—who wouldn't?—but she worried as a "normal" person, not as a depressed one. Now, at least, she could get her mind off the cancer. Without major depression impeding her concentration, she was able to perform the relaxation exercises, stop taking sleeping pills, sleep well, socialize, and return to work. No matter how "understandable" her symptoms, Amy was helped only *after* her major depression was diagnosed.

Critics would charge that to diagnose Amy's condition is to label and thus to dehumanize her. Yet it was only after a therapist recognized that Amy was suffering from more than the normal postmastectomy demoralization that her humanity returned. Explained Amy, "For months I'd assumed that there wasn't *really* anything wrong with me, and that if I only had the 'right' attitude, I'd feel fine. After all, other women get over their mastectomies. Why couldn't I? It had to be my fault—or so I thought. As soon as I learned that there really *was* something wrong with me, and that it had a name, my self-blame vanished. At last, something could be done: My depression could be treated. But you can't treat what you can't name." When used with clear goals in mind, psychiatric diagnosis avoids the pitfalls of labeling, the meaninglessness of academic exercise, and the distortions of an arrogant clinician's ego. Indeed, when diagnostic evaluation is thus abused, the culprit is the therapist, not the process.

THE PURPOSES OF A PSYCHIATRIC DIAGNOSIS

Psychiatric diagnosis serves two main purposes (Spitzer, 1976). The first is to *define clinical entities* so that clinicians have the same understanding of what a diagnostic category means. Patients with a particular (medical or psychiatric) diagnosis need not exhibit identical features, although they should present with certain cardinal *symptoms* (e.g., diminished interest in pleasurable activities, insomnia, diminished concentration, or thoughts of suicide in major depression). The disorder should have a similar *natural history*—a typical age of onset, life course, prognosis, and complications. A diagnosis should reflect the *etiology* and *pathogenesis* of the condition. *Etiology* refers to the origins of a disorder; *pathogenesis* refers to its course of development. Although the same disorder can arise in more than one way, a diagnostic category should indicate whether the disorder consistently runs in families, is genetically transmitted, is initiated by psychosocial forces, and is exacerbated or aggravated by specific biological and environmental conditions.

The second goal of psychiatric diagnosis is to *determine treatment*. Having diagnosed Amy's condition as "major depression," the clinician knew to provide antidepressants; if the diagnosis had been unhappiness and insomnia, she would not have prescribed antidepressants but rather psychotherapy and sleep aids. Diagnosis not only influences biological treatments but also shapes the choice of particular psychotherapies.

How well a diagnosis defines a disorder and guides treatment depends on its validity and reliability. When a diagnostic category represents a genuine entity—that is, when patients with the same diagnosis have similar clinical features, natural histories, etiologies, pathogeneses, and responses to treatment—the category is said to have high *validity*. The more clinicians agree on a diagnosis when examining the same patient, the greater its *interrater reliability*. It is possible for a diagnostic category to have high validity without reliability, and vice versa. For example, a professor could conceive of the "Abominable Snowman syndrome" with very specific diagnostic features. It then would be easy to get clinical agreement (high reliability) on who did or did not fit the diagnosis—but the diagnosis itself is meaningless (low validity) as a syndrome. The diagnostic category of "codependent personality" exemplifies the reverse situation: Such people probably exist and share clinical features, history, etc. (high validity), but the diagnostic criteria are so vague or varied that clinicians have trouble agreeing on who has it (low reliability). Prior to the *DSM-III* diagnostic manuals, the standard joke was that if 10 psychiatrists examined the same patient, they would come up with 12 different diagnoses—another example of very low reliability!

DEFINING PSYCHOPATHOLOGY

Who in the rainbow can draw the line where the violet tint ends and the orange tint begins…so with sanity and insanity.

—Herman Melville, *Billy Budd*

Psychopathology is defined as the *manifestations* of mental disorders. (It also refers to the *study* of mental disorders—their problems, causes, and processes.) Psychopathology involves *impairments*, *deviance*, and *distress*, but not all impairments, deviance, and distress are psychopathological. Being ugly (not gorgeous), inefficient (not active), and thoughtless (not considerate) are all impairments, but they do not constitute psychopathology. Being an atheist, punker, crook, or drag queen is deviant, but not psychopathological. Being starved, broke, or lonely is distressing, but not psychopathological.

Distinguishing psychopathology from normality is usually easy, although on occasion it can be difficult. Critics argue that because the line between psychopathology and normality is hazy, psychopathology is a myth. That's nonsense. Day and night clearly exist, even though at dusk it is hard to know which it is. Psychopathology is no less real for its relativity. The definition of a mental disorder in the *DSM-IV-TR* does not suggest that there are sharp distinctions between psychopathology and normality or between different mental disorders. According to *DSM-IV*-TR mental disorders must produce clinically significant *impairment* or *distress* in one's personal, social, or occupational life. Biological changes may or may not be involved. *DSM-IV-TR* states:

… each of the mental disorders is conceptualized as a clinically significant behavioral or psychological syndrome or pattern that occurs in an individual and that is associated with present distress (e.g., a painful symptom) or disability (i.e., impairment in one or more important areas of functioning) or with a significantly increased risk of suffering death, pain, disability, or an important loss of freedom. In addition, this syndrome or pattern must not be merely an expectable and culturally sanctioned response to a particular event, for example, the death of a loved one. Whatever its original cause, it must currently be considered a manifestation of a behavioral, psychological, or biological dysfunction in the individual. Neither deviant behavior (e.g., political, religious, or sexual) nor conflicts that are primarily between the individual and society are mental disorders unless the deviance or conflict is a symptom of a dysfunction in the individual, as described above. (pp. xxxi)

DSM-IV-TR classifies *mental disorders*; it does not classify *individuals* with mental disorders. Patients who receive the same diagnosis are not the same in every important respect. Just as the only similarity among diabetics is having symptoms of diabetes, the only similarity among people with schizophrenia is having symptoms of schizophrenia, such as delusional thoughts, hallucinations or catatonic symptoms. Otherwise, some people with schizophrenia are delightful, some obnoxious, some brilliant, and some stupid. When, for the sake of brevity, a patient with schizophrenia is called a "schizophrenic," it should be done with the understanding that a disorder is an attribute of a person and never his or her totality.

Many terms resemble "mental disorder." A *syndrome* refers to any cluster of signs and symptoms. Clinicians often use *mental disease* and *mental illness* as synonyms for mental disorder, especially for the more severe ones clearly involving biological changes, such as schizophrenia and bipolar disorder. Technically, this usage is inaccurate. In medicine, *disease* refers to the specific physical disturbances of a condition, whereas *illness* refers to the total experience of a condition, including physical disturbances. In DSM-IV-TR, diagnostic categories are always called *disorders*.

Laypeople often use terms such as *insanity* and *nervous breakdown* to mean mental disorder. Neither term has psychiatric meaning. *Insanity*, which is a legal term (the definition of which varies among states), establishes a defendant's lack of criminal responsibility due to a mental disorder or defect. *Nervous breakdown* is a popular term for any severe incapacitation due to emotional or psychiatric difficulties.

The term *problems in living* is often a euphemism for mental disorder. To have a mental disorder is surely a problem in living, but it is far more than that, and to equate the two is to err in categorization and to trivialize the pain of mental disorders. "Problems in living" connote the difficulties of everyday life: losing a job, squabbling with children, undergoing a divorce, fearing rejection, evading the bill collector, and dealing with low self-esteem. Problems in living can be miserable, yet they are vastly different in magnitude and type from mental disorders. Problems in living consist of "*issues*," whereas mental disorders consist of psychopathology.

Symptoms, Signs, and Issues

Psychopathology manifests as *symptoms* and *signs*. Symptoms are experienced subjectively, cannot be observed, and must be reported by the patient; signs can be observed and documented objectively. Symptoms include pain, hallucinations, appetite loss, paranoid thinking, and anxiety, whereas signs include phobic behavior, restlessness, weight loss, and paranoid speech. Depressed mood is a symptom, crying a sign; chest pain is a symptom, heart failure a sign. Mental-health professionals sometimes ignore this distinction and refer to signs as symptoms. For literary convenience, this book does likewise, except when lumping them together clouds clinical thinking.

People may have a symptom (e.g., anxiety, insomnia) without having a mental disorder. By itself, a symptom rarely constitutes a mental disorder. A symptom only reflects a mental disorder when it is a part of a specific symptom constellation. Most symptoms exceed the boundaries of routine experience; unlike issues (or problems in living), symptoms are not everyday occurrences. Everybody contends with issues, only some with symptoms. Patients with mental disorders have both symptoms *and* issues, whereas clients with problems in living have only issues.

Issues contain ideas; symptoms do not. However, just as mail transmits ideas, symptoms can express issues. The ideas patients communicate when they manifest symptoms reflect the issues concerning them. For instance, two men with the severe mental disorder of major depression may have the symptom of overwhelming hopelessness. The first, an elderly, devout Catholic, insists he is hopeless "because I sinned 20 years ago by cheating on my wife." The second, a young up-and-coming actor, feels equally hopeless because "I'm not a star." Both patients have psychopathology—that is, hopelessness—yet, because their issues are so different, each expresses hopelessness quite differently.

As very broad generalizations, *biological factors* primarily cause symptoms, whereas *psychosocial factors* primarily determine issues. Because most symptoms usually arise from an altered *brain*, biological therapies usually correct them; because issues mainly derive from an altered *mind*, psychosocial therapies usually rectify them. Since patients with mental disorders present with both symptoms and issues, their treatment frequently involves medication as well as psychotherapy. Since clients with problems in living present with issues but not symptoms, they only receive psychotherapy. Psychological symptoms such as negative thinking in depression or panic reactions in panic disorder fall in-between these two: They often stem from a combination of psychological and biological causes and are effectively treated by medication and/or psychotherapy.

Phenomenology is the aspect of psychopathology that deals with a person's consciously reported experiences (Jaspers, 1923/1972). Phenomenological investigation focuses on the form of experience, i.e., the *way* in which the content is experienced, while the content itself is of secondary importance (Burgy, 2008). It is also a branch of philosophy that posits that behavior is determined not by an objective external reality, but by a person's subjective perception of that reality. Phenomenology is an important aspect of both existential and descriptive psychiatry. From a phenomenological point of view, psychopathology is the study of the nature and evolution of psychiatric symptoms.

TWO DIAGNOSTIC APPROACHES

There are two major approaches to diagnostic psychopathology. The first is called *descriptive* because diagnoses are based on relatively objective phenomena that require nominal clinical inference; these phenomena include signs, symptoms, and natural history. The second is called *psychological* because diagnoses are based primarily on inferred causes and mechanisms. The psychological approach also considers descriptive phenomena, but as merely superficial manifestations of more profound underlying forces.

The descriptive approach focuses on the *what* of behavior, the psychological on its *why*. Amy's case illustrates the common mistake of confusing the two. *What* was wrong (major depression) had been ignored because people focused on *why* things were wrong (having cancer and a mastectomy). Failing to distinguish the *what* from the *why* of psychopathology is the novice's first big mistake. An example: A hallucinating, disheveled youth, convinced he was Jesus Christ, told beginning medical students that his parents stifled his creativity, poisoned his food, and stole his Nintendo. Once he left the room, the students were asked, "What do you think is wrong with him?" "Nothing," they replied, "the problem is that he has lousy parents." Yet, even assuming he has dreadful parents (the why), he is no less delusional and hallucinatory (the what).

Both descriptive and psychological approaches are valuable, since each addresses a different aspect of psychopathology. Take a delusion. The descriptive approach would detail its characteristics: Is it fixed? Vague? Paranoid? Circumscribed? The psychological approach would focus on inner mechanisms (e.g., projection), which might produce the delusion.

Emil Kraepelin (1856–1926) is virtually synonymous with descriptive psychiatry— sometimes called "Kraepelinian psychiatry"—because he devised the first major psychiatric nosology based on descriptive criteria (Kraepelin, 1915/1921). Examining thousands of delusional and hallucinating patients, he divided those without obvious brain damage into two groups according to prognosis and age of onset. The first he diagnosed as "dementia praecox": *dementia* referred to the progressively downhill course of the disorder and *praecox* referred to the appearance of symptoms during the teens or twenties. He diagnosed the second group as "maniacal depression"—today called "bipolar disorder." These patients typically returned to normal and were initially hospitalized in their 30s and 40s. Thus, in creating a descriptively-based nosology, Kraepelin added natural (or longitudinal) history to current (or cross-sectional) symptoms. His textbook is *the* classic in descriptive psychiatry, and his approach has dominated European psychiatry to this day.

The psychological approach was launched by the Swiss psychiatrist Eugen Bleuler (1857–1939). In *Dementia Praecox, or the Group of Schizophrenias* (1911/ 1950), Bleuler introduced the term *schizophrenia* to signify the disorder's basic defect of splitting of psychic functions—that is, disorganization and incongruency between thought, emotion, and behavior (not a split or multiple personality, as popularly believed). Bleuler believed that these splits gave rise to the fundamental symptoms of schizophrenia: flat or inappropriate *affect*, profound *ambivalence*, *autism*, and disturbed *associations* of thought—the "4 A's." These splits are inferred psychological mechanisms of causation and thus fundamentally different from Kraepelin's observed, descriptive criteria.

Until *DSM-III* (1980), the psychological approach dominated American psychiatry, largely because it dovetailed with Freudian thought, which has always enjoyed more popularity in the United States than anyplace else. Indeed, Bleuler's psychological approach paved the way for diagnoses based on psychoanalytic criteria, such as "poor ego boundaries," "oral regression," "polymorphous perversity," "projection," and "primary process." The more psychiatrists focused on these inferred phenomena, the more they recognized that *everybody* had them to various degrees. This belief helps to explain three key differences between psychological and descriptive diagnoses.

First, the psychological view holds that, as a price for civilization, everyone has some degree of psychopathology; with the descriptive approach, only a minority has psychopathology. Second, psychologically derived diagnoses follow a *unitary model*, in which there is essentially one mental disorder whose name is a matter of degree, not type—from the least severe to the most: neuroses, personality disorders, manic–depression, and schizophrenia. As in physical medicine, the descriptive approach follows a *multiple model*, in which disorders are distinct and numerous. Third, the psychological view often considers patients to have more severe psychopathology than does the descriptive view. Patients diagnosed as "neurotic" by psychological criteria might have "no mental disorder" by descriptive criteria, whereas those diagnosed as "schizophrenic" by psychological criteria might be diagnosed as "manic" or "depressive" by descriptive criteria.

THE DESCRIPTIVE REVIVAL

A purely psychological approach pervaded *DSM-I* (1952), the first official psychiatric nomenclature for the United States. All *DSMs*, or *Diagnostic and Statistical Manual of Mental Disorders*, are created by the American Psychiatric Association. *DSM-I* diagnoses were loosely defined and emphasized psychological etiologies in the terminology (e.g., "schizophrenic reactions," "paranoid reactions," and "psychoneurotic reactions").

The main reason for writing *DSM-II* (1968) was to rectify *DSM-I*'s failure to conform to the World Health Organization's *International Classification of Diseases*. *DSM-II* eliminated "reactive" from most diagnostic labels, thereby inching away from an etiologically based nosology. *DSM-II* suffered from low interrater reliability. The "U.S./U.K." study (Cooper et al., 1972) showed that, unlike the descriptively oriented British psychiatrists, American psychiatrists frequently reached different diagnoses after observing the same videotape of the same patient being interviewed by the same psychiatrist. *DSM-II*'s diagnoses also lacked validity: The categories did not define disorders having predictable symptoms, natural histories, or responses to treatment.

> In trying to be flexible, *DSM-II*'s diagnostic categories were often vague, idiosyncratic, and susceptible to bias. For example, studies revealed that patients with the same clinical features would receive the more benign diagnosis of manic–depression if they were Caucasian but the more ominous diagnosis of schizophrenia if

they were African-American. Without objective diagnostic standards, a nosology based on inferred psychological phenomena often said more about the clinician's orientation than about the patient's attributes. In theory, the chief virtue of the psychological approach was that it indicated a disorder's cause, but since the etiologies of most mental disorders were unknown, American psychiatry was moving away from the psychological tradition and returning to Kraepelin.

Additional factors contributed to this descriptive revival and to the emergence of *DSM-III*. Different classes of medications were discovered that alleviated or eliminated symptoms of one disorder but not another. As a result, correct diagnosis became essential for choosing the correct medication. Researchers increasingly applied the same scientific methods (e.g., standardized interviews, double-blind conditions, matched controls, statistical proof) used in other branches of medicine to study mental disorders. Data began to show which mental disorders ran in families, which had predictable life courses, which afflicted various populations, which improved with specific therapies, etc. To ensure that they were studying patients with similar disorders, researchers devised explicit, readily verifiable, and specific diagnostic criteria, which, after adjustment for clinical purposes, became *DSM-III*'s most distinctive innovation.

The latest nosology, *DSM-IV* (1994) and its text revision (TR) in 2000 continue the descriptive approach of *DSM-III* and *DSM-III-R* (1987). Changes in criteria that have occurred with the two revisions since *DSM-III* have been based largely on field testing of diagnostic criteria for validity, reliability, and stability. Each diagnostic manual is a work in progress that incorporates changes based on new information.

DSM-III THROUGH *DSM-IV-TR* INNOVATIONS AND LIMITATIONS

Beginning with *DSM-III*, there are seven major departures from the earlier diagnostic manuals:

1. Whenever possible, *scientific evidence*, not theoretical hypotheses, determines diagnostic categories.
2. A *descriptive* rather than psychological approach is the foundation for diagnosis. Consequently, *DSM-IV-TR* employs a largely nonetiological framework and a multiple rather than a unitary nosological model.

3. Diagnoses are defined by clearly delineated, objective, and readily verifiable criteria.

4. The diagnostic definitions of DSM-IV-TR recognize that most patients with the same mental disorder do not have identical clinical characteristics. Patients usually share one or two core features, but beyond that, have a variety of different symptoms that are all consistent with the disorder. Thus, DSM-IV-TR diagnoses often require some core diagnostic criteria, but offer a choice among others.

5. DSM-IV-TR presents multiaxial diagnosis, allowing separate listings for the personality disorders, contributing medical diagnoses, etc.

6. Technical terms are defined.

7. DSM-IV was extensively field-tested prior to publication.

To illustrate some of these innovations, Table 1-1 contrasts DSM-II and DSM-IV-TR definitions of what is essentially the same kind of moderate depression: DSM-II calls it a "depressive neurosis," DSM-IV-TR, a "major depressive disorder, recurrent."

Whereas DSM-II indicates only that depressed patients are depressed, DSM-IV-TR specifies the symptoms of this type of depression and shows how major depression differs from normality (criteria A–C) and from other mental conditions (criteria D–E). Because DSM-IV-TR criteria (e.g., decrease in appetite, insomnia) are relatively objective and explicit, they are far easier for clinicians to identify and agree on; in contrast, DSM-II's inferred psychological mechanisms (e.g., internal conflict) produce a much lower interrater reliability. Whether or not DSM-IV-TR criteria for a major depression are optimal or valid can be disputed; yet because they are precise, when a therapist states that "patient X meets DSM-IV-TR criteria for major depressive disorder," clinicians know what is meant.

Despite the exactness of DSM-IV-TR criteria, their application still necessitates clinical judgment. In criterion "A" for depressive episode, for instance, how much sleep loss (#4) constitutes "insomnia"? How much diminished interest or pleasure is "marked" (#2)? In practice, as clinicians gain experience, they develop internal norms to answer such questions. In addition, both recent history—e.g., two-week requirement in criterion "A" for an episode—and past history—two or more episodes in criterion "A" for major depressive disorders, recurrent—are included. DSM-II says nothing about time.

In regard to etiology, DSM-IV-TR is largely atheoretical. Except in obvious cases (e.g., "cocaine abuse," "adjustment reaction"), its diagnostic criteria are free of etiological considerations—be they biological, psychoanalytic, social, or behavioral. In contrast, DSM-II requires an internal conflict or major loss to define depressive neurosis.

TABLE 1-1

DSM-II and DSM-IV-TR Definitions of a Moderate Depression

DSM-II: DEPRESSIVE NEUROSIS

This disorder is manifested by an excessive reaction of depression due to an internal conflict or to an identifiable event such as the loss of a love object [i.e., a person] or cherished possession.

DSM-IV: MAJOR DEPRESSIVE DISORDER RECURRENT

A. The presence of two or more Major Depressive Episodes.

Note: To be considered separate episodes, there must be an interval of at least 2 consecutive months in which criteria are not met for a Major Depressive Episode.

B. The Major Depressive Episodes are not better accounted for by Schizoaffective Disorder and are not superimposed on Schizophrenia, Schizophreniform Disorder, Delusional Disorder, or Psychotic Disorder Not Otherwise Specified.

C. There has never been a Manic Episode, a Mixed Episode, or a Hypo Manic Episode. **Note:** This exclusion does not apply if all of the manic-like, mixed-like, or hypo manic-like episodes are substance or treatment induced or are due to the direct physiological effects of a general medical condition.

DSM-IV-TR: MAJOR DEPRESSIVE EPISODE

A. Five (or more) of the following symptoms have been present during the same 2-week period and represent a change from previous functioning; at least one of the symptoms is either (1) depressed mood or (2) loss of interest or pleasure.

Note: Do not include symptoms that are clearly due to a general medical condition, or mood-incongruent delusions or hallucinations.

(1) depressed mood most of the day, nearly every day, as indicated by either subjective report (e.g., feels sad or empty) or observation made by others (e.g., appears tearful). **Note:** In children and adolescents, can be irritable mood.

(2) markedly diminished interest or pleasure in all, or almost all, activities most of the day, nearly every day (as indicated by either subjective account or observation made by others)

(3) significant weight loss or weight gain when not dieting (e.g., a change of more than 5% of body weight in a month), or decrease or increase in appetite nearly every day. **Note:** In children, consider failure to make expected weight gains.

(4) insomnia or hypersomnia nearly every day

(5) psychomotor agitation or retardation nearly every day (observable by others, not merely subjective feelings of restlessness or being slowed down)

(6) fatigue or loss of energy nearly every day

(7) feelings of worthlessness or excessive or inappropriate guilt (which may be delusional) nearly every day (not merely self-reproach or guilt about being sick)

(8) diminished ability to think or concentrate, or indecisiveness, nearly every day (either by subjective account or as observed by others)

(9) recurrent thoughts of death (not just fear of dying), recurrent suicidal ideation without a specific plan, or a suicide attempt or a specific plan for committing suicide

(*continued*)

TABLE 1-1
Continued

B. The symptoms do not meet criteria for a Mixed Episode.

C. The symptoms cause clinically significant distress or impairment in social, occupational, or other important areas of functioning.

D. The symptoms are not due to the direct physiological effects of a substance (e.g., a drug of abuse, a medication) or a general medical condition (e.g., hypothyroidism).

E. The symptoms are not better accounted for by Bereavement, i.e., after the loss of a loved one, the symptoms persist for longer than 2 months or are characterized by marked functional impairment, morbid preoccupation with worthlessness, suicidal ideation, psychotic symptoms, or psychomotor retardation.

Note. From *DSM-II*, p. 40; *DSM-IV*, pp. 327, 345.

DSM-III adopted, and DSM-IV-TR continues, a *multiaxial* system, so that a diagnosis could reflect more than a primary clinical syndrome, such as schizophrenia or phobic disorder. DSM-IV-TR uses five axes, as described in Table 1-2. Axes I–III are required; axes IV and V are optional.

The major reason DSM-III introduced *multiaxial* diagnosis was to underscore the distinction between mental and personality disorders or traits. *Personality*, or *character*, refers to a person's longstanding, deeply ingrained patterns of thinking, feeling, perceiving, and behaving. Everybody has personality *traits*,

---

TABLE 1-2
DSM-IV-TR *Multiaxial Diagnostic System*

DIAGNOSTIC AXIS	CONTENT	EXAMPLE
I	Clinical disorders	Major depressive disorder, recurrent
	Other conditions that may be a focus of clinical attention	
II	Personality disorders	Obsessive–compulsive personality disorder
III	General medical conditions	Diabetes
IV	Psychosocial and environmental problems	Problems with primary support group; divorce
V	Global Assessment of Functioning (GAF): currently and at highest level the past year	Current GAF: 55 Highest GAF last year: 80

which are prominent behavioral features and not necessarily psychopathological. In contrast, only some people have *personality disorders*—that is, when personality traits are so excessive, inflexible, and maladaptive that they cause significant distress or impairment. Mental disorders (Axis I) tend to be more acute, florid, and responsive to treatment than personality disorders (Axis II), which are more chronic, consistent, developmental, and resistant to treatment. When patients manifest both mental and personality disorders, the multiaxial system helps clinicians focus on the diagnostic and therapeutic differences between the disorders.

Despite its many advances, *DSM-IV-TR* is not diagnostic dogma but a *guide*. Remember—before *DSM-IV-TR* was published, many were already formulating *DSM-V*. Controversies rage over whether some of *DSM-IV-TR's* diagnostic categories describe genuine disorders in people or are nothing more than meaningless labels on paper. Nosologies other than *DSM-IV-TR* do exist, and on occasion this text will draw on them.

Although *DSM-IV-TR* diagnoses have improved treatment planning, they remain insufficient, partly due to their variable validity. Yet, even if totally valid, no psychiatric (or medical) diagnosis would be sufficient by itself to establish the treatment. Other factors must be considered: the patient's ability to introspect, his or her defenses, family relationships, current stressors, compliance with therapy, etc. Clinical evaluations that ignore such factors in favor of checklists of *DSM-IV-TR* criteria cannot lead to effective treatment plans, because they overlook that it is patients, not diagnoses, who are being treated. This text certainly stresses diagnosis, but clinical assessment clearly entails more than a diagnosis.

AN OVERVIEW OF PSYCHIATRIC EPIDEMIOLOGY

Psychiatric epidemiology is the science that studies the frequency and distribution of mental disorders within various populations. By identifying the presence or absence of a mental disorder in a specific group, defined by age, sex, race, socioeconomic class, inpatient status, health, diet, other illnesses, etc., the epidemiologist compiles clues about a disorder's etiology, pathogenesis, prevention, and treatment.

Most often cited are measures of *incidence* and *prevalence*. For a specific time interval and population, incidence refers to the number of *new* cases, whereas *prevalence* refers to the number of *existing* cases. These terms are usually expressed as percentages and calculated as follows:

$$\text{Incidence Rate} = \frac{\text{Number of persons developing the disorder}}{\text{Total number of persons at risk}} \text{ / Per unit of time}$$

$$\text{Prevalence} = \frac{\text{Number of persons with the disorder during a period of time}}{\text{Total number of persons in the group}}$$

If 2,000 new cases of a disorder arise in 1 year in a population of 100,000, the *incidence* rate is 2% (2,000/100,000). *Prevalence* reflects how widespread a disease or disorder is during a specified period of time, which can vary from a moment (called "point prevalence"), to 1 year ("1-year prevalence"), to a lifetime ("lifetime prevalence").

Incidence and prevalence can convey very different pictures of a disorder's frequency. Treatment does not affect incidence (new cases), but it *does* affect prevalence (existing cases). Prevention may reduce incidence (and consequently prevalence). Unlike incidence, prevalence is a factor of a disorder's duration, frequency of recovery, and death rate. That's why acute disorders generally have a higher incidence than point prevalence, whereas it is just the reverse for chronic disorders. For example, if an average person gets three colds per winter, the 6-month incidence rate may be over 90%; however, the point prevalence rate for a cold may only be 20%. For AIDS, a long-lasting illness, the point prevalence rate (existing cases) is much higher than the 6- or 12-month incidence rate (new cases).

The frequency of a mental disorder varies enormously, depending on how the disorder is defined, which populations are polled, and which assessment instruments are employed. For instance, pre-*DSM-III*, mental disorders were defined so variously that older surveys generated prevalence rates from 11 to 81%.

The value of an epidemiologic study depends on the sensitivity and specificity of its diagnostic instruments. A test is *sensitive* when it accurately detects the *presence* of a disorder in a person who *has* the disorder. A test is *specific* when it accurately detects the *absence* of a disorder in a person who does *not have* the disorder. Remember when a "handwriting expert" would examine a person's writing and then say, "Underneath you have feelings of insecurity"? Of course he has some feelings of insecurity! Who doesn't? This test demonstrates high sensitivity but low specificity.

More accurate epidemiologic investigations resulted from a major advance in defining mental disorders. Feighner et al. (1972) first listed specific signs and symptoms as diagnostic criteria. Called the "Feighner criteria," they were used primarily by researchers. Adding duration, severity, and life course, Spitzer and colleagues (Spitzer, Williams, & Skodal, 1980) refined Feighner's criteria into the Research Diagnostic Criteria (RDC). These two diagnostic tools led to the more clinically oriented *DSM-III.*

The Feighner and RDC approaches developed *structured interviews* that greatly facilitated data collection. A series of preset, standardized questions systematically determined if the subject met specific diagnostic criteria. Two structured interviews widely applied in research are the "Schedule for Affective Disorders and Schizophrenia" (SADS) and the *DSM-III*-based "Diagnostic Interview Schedule" (DIS).

Using the DIS, researchers from the National Institute of Mental Health (NIMH) interviewed almost 20,000 adults to establish the 1-year and lifetime prevalence of 30 mental disorders (Robins & Regier, 1991). The major concern regarding this project, known as the Epidemiologic Catchment Area (ECA) study, was that it may not have been a true national sample. This concern was addressed in the newer National Comorbidity Survey (NCS) in which 8,098 adults were interviewed to establish 1-year and lifetime prevalence of 17 "common" mental disorders (Kessler et al., 1994). The NCS used *DSM-III-R* diagnoses and an improved version of the DIS that had more thorough lists of symptoms than the ECA. The NCS yielded much higher rates of mental disorders than the ECA. Trained clinicians interviewed a subset of the respondents and found that most of the diagnoses were accurate.

The ECA and NCS reported that mental disorders had affected 20–30% of adult Americans during the preceding year and 32–50% of them throughout life. The primary focus of the ECA and the NCS studies was upon making categorical assessment of mental disorders without regard to severity. To address this limitation, the NCS Replication study (NCS-R) was conducted between 2001 and 2003. The NCS-R surveyed 9,282 respondents 18 years and older from across the United States, using *DSM-IV* criteria, a substantially expanded interview process, and a broader range of mental disorders. Unfortunately, there is not much epidemiological information about childhood mental disorders and longitudinal studies are needed to understand the association between childhood mental disorders and adult mental disorders (Kessler, 2008).

Table 1-3 is based on the NCS-R findings and shows the lifetime prevalence of some of the common mental disorders. About 46.4% of respondents in the study had history of at least one mental disorder. Among the mental disorders, anxiety disorders (28.8%) are the most common followed by impulse control disorders (24.8%) and mood disorders (20.8%). The most common

TABLE 1-3

Lifetime Prevalence of Mental Disorders in Percent by Age in Years

MENTAL DISORDERS	ALL AGES	18–29 YRS.	30–44 YRS.	45–49 YRS.	≥60 YRS.
Any Disorder	**46.4** (26.2)	52.4	55.0	46.5	26.1
Any Anxiety Disorder	**28.8** (18.1)	30.2	35.1	30.8	15.3
Panic disorder	**4.7** (2.7)	4.4	5.7	5.9	2.0
Agoraphobia without panic	**1.4** (0.8)	1.1	1.7	1.6	1.0
Specific phobia	**12** (8.7)	13.3	13.9	14.1	7.5
Social phobia	**5** (6.8)	13.6	14.3	12.4	6.6
Generalized anxiety disorder	**5.7** (3.1)	4.1	6.8	7.7	3.6
Posttraumatic stress disorder	**6.8** (3.5)	6.3	8.2	9.2	2.5
Obsessive–compulsive disorder	**1.6** (1.0)	2.0	2.3	1.3	0.7
Separation anxiety disorder	**5.2** (0.9)	5.2	5.1		
Any Mood Disorder	**20.8** (9.5)	21.4	24.6	22.9	11.9
Major depressive disorder	**16.6** (6.7)	15.4	19.8	18.8	10.6
Dysthymia	**2.5** (1.5)	1.7	2.9	3.7	1.3
Bipolar I–II disorders	**3.9** (2.6)	5.9	4.5	3.5	1.0
Any Impulse-Control Disorder	**24.8** (8.9)	26.8	23.0	–	–
Oppositional-defiant disorder	**8.5** (1.0)	9.5	7.5	–	–
Conduct disorder	**9.5** (1.0)	10.9	8.2	–	–
Attention-deficit/hyperactivity	**8.1** (4.1)	7.8	8.3	–	–
Intermittent explosive disorder	**5.2** (2.6)	7.4	5.7	4.9	1.9
Any Substance Abuse Disorder	**14.6** (3.8)	16.7	18.0	15.3	6.3
Alcohol abuse	**13.2** (3.1)	14.3	16.3	14.0	6.2
Alcohol dependence	**5.4** (1.3)	6.3	6.4	6.0	2.2
Drug abuse	**7.9** (1.4)	10.9	11.9	6.5	0.3
Drug dependence	**3.0** (0.4)	3.9	4.9	2.3	0.2
Two or More Disorders	**27.7** (5.8)	33.9	34.0	27.0	11.6

(Twelve-month prevalence in parentheses)

Adapted from Kessler et al., 2005a, 2005b

individual mental disorder was major depressive disorder. There was a general trend of higher prevalence among the middle age groups followed by a decline in the oldest. Of the 12-month prevalence estimates of the NCS-R, 22.3% were classified serious, 37.3% moderate, and 40.4% mild. Among disorder classes, mood disorders had the highest percentage of serious cases (45.0%) and anxiety disorders the lowest (22.8%). That almost half of all Americans suffer or have suffered from some type of mental disorder is startling and underscores the need for all health care professionals to understand the essentials of psychopathology. Most mentally ill patients are treated by non-psychiatrists including general practitioners, internists, nurses, psychologists, social workers, and counselors.

Because people who have one disorder frequently (about 60% of the time) have two or more disorders (not mutually exclusive), the total percentage for classes of disorders in Table 1-3 is less than the sum of each separate disorder. Having coexisting or multiple diagnoses is referred to as comorbidity or co-occurring disorders. Factors leading to erroneous assumptions of true comorbidity include symptoms arising from the same underlying cause; diagnostic procedures failing to discriminate; diagnostic criteria not discriminating; higher-order pattern of the same diagnostic entity; incorrect placement of the border between the normal and pathological or between disorders (Achenbach, 1991).

References

Achenbach, T. M. (1991). "Comorbidity" in child and adolescent psychiatry: Categorical and quantitative perspectives. *Journal of Child and Adolescent Psychopharmacology, 1,* 271–278.

American Psychiatric Association. (1952). *Diagnostic and statistical manual of mental disorders,* 1st ed. Washington, DC: American Psychiatric Association.

American Psychiatric Association. (1968). *Diagnostic and statistical manual of mental disorders,* 2nd ed. Washington, DC: American Psychiatric Association.

American Psychiatric Association. (1980). *Diagnostic and statistical manual of mental disorders,* 3rd ed. Washington, DC: American Psychiatric Association.

American Psychiatric Association. (1994). *Diagnostic and statistical manual of mental disorders,* 4th ed. Washington, DC: American Psychiatric Association.

American Psychiatric Association. (2000). *Diagnostic and statistical manual of mental disorders,* text rev. Washington, DC: American Psychiatric Association.

Bleuler, E. (1950). *Dementia praecox, or the group of schizophrenias.* New York: International Universities Press. (Original work published 1911)

Burgy, M. (2008). The concept of psychosis: Historical and phenomenological aspects. *Schizophrenia Bulletin, 34,* 1200–1210.

Cooper, J.E., Kendell, R.E., Gurland, B.J., Sharpe, L., Copeland, J.R.M., & Simon, R. (1972). *Psychiatric diagnosis in New York and London.* New York: Oxford University Press.

Feighner, J.P., Robins, E., Guze, S.B., Woodruff, R.A., Winokur, G., & Munoz, R. (1972). Diagnostic criteria for use in psychiatric research. *Archives of General Psychiatry, 26,* 57–63.

Jaspers, K. (1972). *General psychopathology.* Chicago: University of Chicago Press. (Original work published 1923)

Kessler, R.C., Berglund, P., Demler, O., Jin, R., Merikangas, K.R., & Walters, E.E. (2005a). Lifetime prevalence and age-of-onset distributions of DSM-IV disorders in the National Comorbidity Survey Replication. *Archives of General Psychiatry, 62*, 593–602.

Kessler, R.C., Chiu, W.T., Demler, O., & Walters, E.E. (2005b). Prevalence, severity, and comorbidity of 12-month DSM-IV disorders in the National Comorbidity Survey Replication. *Archives of General Psychiatry, 62*, 617–627.

Kessler, R.C., McGonagle, K.A., Ahzo, S., Nelson, C.H., Hughes, M., Eshleman, S., et al. (1994). Lifetime and 12-month prevalence of DSM-III-R psychiatric disorders in the United States: Results from the National Comorbidity Survey. *Archives of General Psychiatry, 51*, 8–19.

Kessler, R.C., & Wang, P.S. (2008). The descriptive epidemiology of commonly occurring mental disorders in the United States. *Annual Review of Public Health, 29*, 115–129.

Kraepelin, E. (1921). *Clinical psychiatry: A text-book for students and physicians.* Translated and adapted from the 7th German Edition by A. Ross Diefendorf. New York: Macmillan. (Original work published 1921)

Melville, H. (1924). *Billy Budd.* London: Constable and Company Ltd.

Robins, L.N., Helzer, J.E., Weissman, M.M., Orvaschel, H., Gruenberg, E., Burke, J.D., et al. (1984). Lifetime prevalence of specific psychiatric disorders in three sites. *Archives of General Psychiatry, 41*, 949–958.

Robins, L.N., & Regier, D.A. (Eds.). (1991). *Psychiatric disorders in America: The Epidemiologic Catchment Area study.* New York: Free Press.

Schizophrenia Bulletin Advance Access Published online on January 3, 2008. © The Author 2008. Published by Oxford University Press on behalf of the Maryland Psychiatric Research Center.

Spitzer, R.L. (1976). More on pseudoscience in science and the case for psychiatric diagnosis: A critique of Rosenhan's "On being sane in insane places" and "The contextual nature of psychiatric diagnosis." *Archives of General Psychiatry, 33*, 459–470.

Spitzer, R.L., Williams, J.B.W., & Skodal, A.E. (1980). DSM-III: The major achievements and an overview. *American Journal of Psychiatry, 137*, 151–164.

2

Assessment

Would a patient with severe stomach pain undergo surgery or be given medication without first obtaining an evaluation? Hopefully not. Yet in psychiatry, this questionable procedure had been the norm: Many patients had chosen and received specific treatments without being formally assessed or diagnosed. The unitary model of mental illness rendered diagnosis almost academic and, since there was basically one "decent" treatment—psychoanalytic psychotherapy—the "prescription" was a foregone conclusion. If performed at all, assessments blended imperceptibly into psychotherapy. Today, however, the growing number and efficacy of contemporary biological and psychosocial treatments demands that *every* patient must receive a formal diagnostic assessment (evaluation) *before* treatment begins.

Assessment may be defined as *a time-limited, formal process that collects clinical information from many sources in order to reach a diagnosis, to make a prognosis, to render a biopsychosocial formulation, and to determine treatment.* This definition emphasizes that assessment is a specific task that is distinct from therapy. Indeed, some superb therapists are poor diagnosticians, and vice versa. Clinicians continue to reassess patients as treatment proceeds, but the *formal* assessment ends before *formal* treatment begins.

The patient interview is usually the principal source of data, but it is not the only source. Information can be gathered from friends, family, physical examinations, laboratory tests, psychological studies, staff observations, standardized interviews, and brain-imaging techniques. Patient interviews generally require 1–3 hour-long sessions, although for patients with impaired concentration, sessions should be shorter and more frequent. Conversely, for healthier outpatients, the initial meeting can be 90 minutes.

The primary objective of these initial interviews is to obtain information that will determine the patient's diagnosis, prognosis, psychodynamics, and treatment. These interviews should also make the patient feel comfortable, foster trust, and develop the expectation that psychiatric treatment will help. With these ingredients, a therapeutic alliance can begin to form.

How a clinician seeks, selects, and organizes all the facts, figures, and fears that patients present is no easy task. The art of asking the right questions is an important skill. Essential for mastering this task is finding a standardized format; flexibility and following patients' leads are fine, chaos is not. As when learning to play the piano or to dance, students learn the basic formal aspects before improvising. Psychiatric assessment typically consists of eight steps (though the sequence for *conducting* and *reporting* these steps varies, to some extent): (1) obtaining a *history*, (2) evaluating the patient's *mental status*, (3) collecting *auxiliary data*, (4) summarizing *principal findings*, (5) rendering a *diagnosis*, (6) making a *prognosis*, (7) providing a *biopsychosocial formulation*, and (8) determining a *treatment plan*. Table 2-1 outlines these steps and presents a method for reporting the formal assessment.

Whether oral or written, the report given to the patient should be clear, succinct, and systematic. Although the exhaustively detailed history, or *anamnesis*, is still used in psychoanalysis, most patients will benefit more from a briefer history, since it is more likely to be read. A major challenge in reporting a patient's evaluation is to convey the germane data in the fewest words. Chapter 9 illustrates a recorded assessment.

THE HISTORY

Taking the patient's history begins with eliciting *identifying information* about the patient, followed immediately by his or her *chief complaint* (CC). The identification data include the patient's age, sex, marital status, occupation, religion, race, and if pertinent, nationality, ethnic group, and sexual orientation. The CC is a sentence or two describing the *patient's*, not the therapist's, view of the main problem, preferably in the patient's exact words. If the patient's CC is senseless (e.g., "I need a new dress"), the therapist can add his or her own version of the CC (e.g., for 3 weeks the patient heard auditory hallucinations).

History of Present Illness

The history of the present illness (HPI) consists of the major symptoms, issues, and events that brought the patient to treatment. For each major problem, the HPI chronicles when it began, what initiated or exacerbated it, what escalated

TABLE 2-1

An Outline of the Psychiatric Assessment

I. HISTORY

    A. Identifying information

    B. Chief complaint

    C. History of present illness

    D. Past psychiatric and developmental history (Table 2-2)

    E. Family psychiatric and medical history

    F. Medical history and physical examination

II. MENTAL STATUS EXAMINATION

    A. Appearance

    B. Behavior (including impulse control)

    C. Speech

    D. Emotion

        1. Mood

        2. Affect

        3. Mood congruency

    E. Thought processes and content

        1. Word usage

        2. Stream of thought

        3. Continuity of thought

        4. Content of thought

    F. Perception

    G. Attention

    H. Orientation

        1. Time (date, time of day)

        2. Place

        3. Person

    I. Memory

        1. Immediate

        2. Recent

        3. Remote

    J. Judgment

    K. Intelligence, information, and abstraction

    L. Insight

III. AUXILIARY DATA

    A. Interviews with relatives and friends

    B. Complete medical history and physical examination

(continued)

TABLE 2-1

Continued

   C. Laboratory tests (Table 2-3)

   D. Standardized interviews

   E. Psychological tests (Table 2-4)

   F. Brain-imaging studies

IV. SUMMARY OF PRINCIPAL FINDINGS

V. DIAGNOSES (*DSM-IV-TR*)

   A. Axis I: Mental disorder

   B. Axis II: Personality disorder/trait

   C. Axis III: General medical conditions

   D. Axis IV: Psychosocial and environmental problems

   E. Axis V: Global Assessment of Functioning (GAF)

VI. PROGNOSIS

VII. BIOPSYCHOSOCIAL FORMULATION (**p**redisposing, **p**recipitating, **p**erpetuating, and **p**rotecting factors that provide an understanding of the patient and present illness)

VIII. PLAN

   A. Additional data gathering (e.g., interviews, tests, consultations)

   B. Treatment goals (immediate, short-term, long-range)

   C. Treatment plan

      1. Immediate management

      2. Short-term interventions

      3. Long-term therapies

---

or diminished its severity, what problems concurrently existed, what effect it had on the patient's functioning, how the patient tried to resolve it, when it ended, why it ended, and the patient's subjective view of it. When a problem emerged gradually, estimate the time of onset. If the patient has had the same disorder repeatedly, the history should start with the most recent episode.

Any and all "entrances" and "exits"—that is, people or events entering a patient's life (e.g., a newborn) or exiting from it (e.g., a child leaving for college)—are noted. Changes are always important to identify, even ostensibly good ones. For instance, after obtaining a long-desired promotion to vice-president of a major corporation, a man became severely depressed—now he bossed his former peers, traveled in a faster social crowd, and faced a wife demanding fur coats.

The therapist should ask why the patient has come for help *now*. A 37-year-old single designer sought treatment for, as she said, "an inferiority complex." When asked why she had come for treatment at this particular time, she answered that a friend suggested it. By pursuing the "Why now?" question, the therapist discovered that the day after the patient's mother had married her fifth husband, the patient had wondered, "What's wrong with me?" That is when the patient had followed the friend's advice to seek help.

The clinician should never assume that the patient's use of a technical term is the same as his or her own: Patients will say *anxiety* but mean *depression*, *paranoia* but mean *embarrassment*, *nervousness* but mean *hallucinations*. If a clinician is at all unsure of what a patient means by a word, the patient should be asked to describe it more fully or to give an example.

During intake interviews, clinicians notoriously avoid asking about three immediate and critical issues: (1) drug and alcohol use, (2) suicidal tendencies, and (3) violent or homicidal tendencies. The reasons for this avoidance vary. Without realizing it, a therapist may avoid inquiring about these problems because, if they do exist, the therapist might not know how to intervene— it's "safer" not to ask in the first place! A therapist may also fear that such questions would embarrass the patient. This embarrassment, however, is the therapist's more than the patient's. Most patients expect clinicians to ask "embarrassing" questions—it's the clinician's job—and if the clinician doesn't, some patients will feel that the clinician is being slipshod or not taking their case seriously. In any event, tactfully posed questions rarely offend patients.

Be sure to ask about present and past use/abuse of alcohol, drugs, and prescription medications. Don't assume that the middle-class suburban homemaker in front of you would never use all those terrible substances. Anyone can. Regarding prescription drugs, an easy question is, "Have you ever used more than the amount prescribed?" Obtain drug names, amount, duration used, and frequency, ask about use of IV drugs, whether needles were shared, and finally, complications and problems related to drug/alcohol use, such as periods of abstinence/sobriety, withdrawal symptoms, lost jobs, etc. Many patients with alcohol problems, when asked if they are alcoholic, respond with "No, I only drink beer," or "No, I only get drunk on weekends." A careful, compassionate approach works best.

Suicide must be evaluated, or at least considered, with *every* patient. Suicide is the 11th leading cause of death in the United States, but among youth it has become tied with cancer as the 2nd most frequent cause of death. More people die from suicide than from homicide. Officially, about 30,000 Americans kill themselves each year, but suicide is underreported. If there is any question of suicide, the clinician *must* ask. The questions can be posed in a progressive manner, starting with passive suicidal ideation: "Have you ever felt that you would be better off dead, that if you died tomorrow, it wouldn't matter?" If the answer is yes, then active suicidal ideation can be determined by inquiring, "Have you thought about harming or perhaps killing yourself?" Questioning patients about committing suicide does *not* make people commit suicide or "introduce suicidal thoughts into their head." A patient who has been depressed, miserable, anxious, and without sleep, when asked, "Have you considered suicide?" will not respond, "Gosh, doctor, that's a good idea, I never thought of that. Thanks for the suggestion." Most potentially suicidal patients are relieved when a therapist raises the subject. Contrary to myth, people who talk about suicide *do* commit suicide. Because 80% of those who killed themselves previously mentioned their problem to somebody, clinicians should take these patients seriously.

The risk of suicide escalates as the patient's suicidal *thoughts* intensify and become more frequent. Almost everyone has had fleeting suicidal thoughts; only the suicidal ruminate about it. More dangerous is when the patient has a *plan*, especially if he or she has settled on one plan, can detail it, and has begun implementing it. People who *attempt* suicide are more likely to commit suicide; the more serious the past attempt, the greater the risk of eventual suicide. A patient is at greater risk of suicide if a past attempt involved a more lethal (in the patient's, not the clinician's, mind) method, occurred after long planning rather than impulsively, did not allow much chance of discovery afterward, and was not prefaced by a signal for help.

Almost 95% of patients who attempt or commit suicide suffer from a mental disorder: 80% of them have depression, 10% have schizophrenia, and 5% have delirium. Alcohol, especially in conjunction with depression, increases the rate of death; 15% of alcoholics commit suicide. Patients abusing drugs also kill themselves; the frequency depends on the specific drug, with IV-use being especially high. Hopelessness is an experience common to many with mental disorders. Significant hopelessness is a strong predictor of ultimate suicide (Beck, Brown, Berchick, Stewart, & Steer, 1990).

The suicide rate is greatest for men over 45 and for those between the ages of 15 and 24. Although females engage in three times more suicide attempts, men are four times more likely to complete suicide. Gun availability certainly helps; firearms kill 66% of U.S. teens versus 6% in Great Britain. The major risk factors for suicide are being male, older, unemployed, unmarried, living alone, having a chronic illness, substance abuse, and at least one major psychiatric diagnosis. Additional risk factors include a threatened financial loss, an absence of any religious affiliation, a recent loss or death (a particularly higher risk factor for alcoholics), a family history of suicide, and suddenly giving away prized possessions (Motto, Heilbron, & Juster, 1985). One can remember the risk factors for suicide with the mnemonic "**SAD PERSONS**." The letters stand for **S**ex (male gender), **A**ge (older), **D**epression, **P**revious suicide attempt, **E**thanol abuse, **R**ational thinking loss (psychotic), **S**ocial supports (lacking), **O**rganized plan, **N**o spouse, and **S**ickness (chronic medical illness).

Menninger (1938) observed that patients who commit suicide do so from three, not one, possible wishes: the wish to die, the wish to kill, and the wish to be killed. Many people might want to die, yet few are prepared to kill, and even fewer, to be killed; the latter two require a degree of violence, anger, and physical pain that only the "truly" suicidal could endure. Impulsive and angry people who are depressed have a higher risk for suicide and homicide.

Knowing all of these risk factors only tells you the statistical risk of suicide in the future. They can help predict the chances of suicide in the next year or two, but won't necessarily tell you what this particular patient will do in the next few days or week. Two more personal questions can help. Assuming that the patient hasn't recently made an attempt, ask, "You have been feeling suicidal, but you haven't acted on it—what stopped you?" Answers that suggest low risk include, "I'm a mother, and I would never leave my children with a legacy of suicide. I could never do that," or "My religious beliefs [or values] would never let me commit suicide. I don't believe in it." A high-risk answer would be something to the effect of, "So far, I've been chicken, but I'm working up the courage." A second helpful question to ask is, "Why do you want to live?" Patients who are trying to conceal their suicidal feelings often can deny feeling suicidal but have a harder time making up believable reasons for living. They might say, "Because my parents don't want me to kill myself" (a high-risk answer) instead of, "I'm smart and kind. I want to see what I can do to help people" (a lower-risk answer).

The presence of violent tendencies in a patient must always be evaluated. Never assume that the mild-mannered "Clark Kent" patient in front of you would not hurt a fly. Asking, "How do you handle your anger?" is a benign introductory probe that then can be followed with, "Have you ever broken things or hurt others when you were angry?" Violent tendencies tend to be expressed via two broad patterns: ongoing suppression or repression punctuated by sudden eruptions; and routine, regular outbursts of anger and destructive behavior. Some individuals are regularly violent toward a certain person or persons (such as a spouse), but to no one else and are probably safe on voluntary inpatient units.

The history of the present illness often ends with ascertaining "significant negatives"—those symptoms, issues, experiences, or events that have *not* occurred, even though they frequently accompany problems like those of the patient. For example, significant negatives for a severely depressed patient might include a denial of suicidal thoughts, the absence of recent losses, an unchanged libido, and no family history of bipolar disorder. When significant negatives are omitted from the report, other professionals cannot tell whether these negatives are truly absent or the interviewer simply forgot to ask about them.

Past Psychiatric History

The developmental history can be integrated with past psychiatric history (PH) or social history or presented separately (whichever is clearer.) The PH describes previous episodes in the patient's life that resemble or differ from the current episode, including each episode's duration, treatment, and outcome. The PH presents the patient's longstanding personality traits and characteristic ways of dealing with problems. In setting treatment goals, it helps to determine the patient's highest level of functioning during his or her life *and* during the past year. The patient's level of functioning prior to the onset of the current episode is sometimes called *baseline functioning* and is an important reference point in deciding if the patient is better (i.e., back to normal for him or her).

Social and Developmental History

The social history can begin with the present by elaborating on "identifying information." It should include information on the present family situation, residential setting, occupation, and financial status. Although an exhaustive developmental history is usually unnecessary, it is valuable to cover the highlights, especially when they illuminate the present illness. Table 2-2 lists possible topics in the developmental history, though it is not a comprehensive outline. Two quick ways to elicit critical information is to ask the patient (1) to name the three or four crucial turning points in his or her life, and (2) to describe the most significant or memorable event during each developmental period.

It is also important to ask if there is a history of physical, sexual, or emotional *abuse*. If there is, do not assume that the patient is devastated. A majority of people who have been abused function normally as adults. Also do not assume that questions about abuse will somehow damage the patient. The questioner's level of comfort with these questions is often the key to establishing rapport. Ask the patient in a gentle, accepting way. For example, "Many people with emotional problems were abused as children and as adults. Has that happened to you?" If the patient becomes very hesitant, she or he can be told, "Does talking about this right now make you too uncomfortable? You don't have to talk about it right now. You can wait until you feel ready."

TABLE 2-2

The Developmental History

I. PRENATAL

—Pregnancy: Planned? Desired?

—Health of mother

—Complications during pregnancy and birth

—Full-term?

II. INFANCY to ADOLESCENCE

—Physical illnesses

—Temperament (especially compared to siblings and social attachments): Shy? Friends? Family Relations?

—Developmental milestones: Walking, talking, reading, grades, menstruation, puberty?

—Education: Furthest grade level completed? Learning problems?

—Family: Stable? Abusive? Neglectful?

—Earliest and most vivid memories?

—Symptoms or phobias: Enuresis? Nightmares? Cruelty to animals? Fire-setting? Oppositional behavior? Drug or alcohol misuse? Identity problems?

—Sexuality and gender identity: Orientation? Development?

III. EARLY and MIDDLE ADULTHOOD

—Occupations: First job? Dates of each job? Repeated performance patterns? Likes and dislikes? Work disabilities? Discrepancies between ability, education, and present work? Ambitious? Current job and economic circumstances?

—Military service: Combat experience? Type of discharge? Disability benefits?

—Social: Dating? Recreation? Activities?

—Family of origin: Separated from? If so, when and how?, If not, why not? Feelings toward them?

—Marriage: When? Why? How many? Quality of relationship? Quality of sex life? Money—who manages it? Disputes over? "Faithfulness"? Divorce?

—Children: Dates of miscarriages, including abortions; names, dates of birth, personalities of, and feelings toward, children?

—Religion: Its effect, if any, on the patient? Conversion? Exacerbates or alleviates psychiatric problems? Spiritual beliefs?

—Legal problems: Previous arrests, current charges, felonies, prison term?

—Standards: Moral, political, social, atheistic, ethical?

VI. LATE ADULTHOOD

—The "seven losses": How the person prepares for, adapts to, or surmounts each of them:

    (a) loss of work (unemployment)

    (b) loss of financial security (insecurity)

    (c) loss of familiar surroundings, including home and community (dislocation)

    (d) loss of physical health and ability to function (incapacitation)

    (e) loss of mental abilities (incompetence)

    (f) loss of people, especially spouse (isolation)

    (g) loss of life (death)

Note. This table suggests topics for inquiry; it is not a comprehensive outline of development.

Family History

Some clinicians prefer to put information about family functioning in the social developmental history and reserve the category of family history (FH) for family psychiatric problems.

In modern psychopathology all data regarding a family history of mental disorders is of great importance. Special emphasis should be placed on first-degree relatives. Ask about the past presence of alcoholism, drug abuse, antisocial behavior, depression, schizophrenia, "nervous breakdowns," suicide, and psychiatric treatment. Because diagnoses by professionals (especially before 1980) were based on criteria different from those in *DSM-IV-TR*, and because laypeople do not employ diagnostic terms in the way professionals do, therapists should place little weight on diagnoses ascribed to family members and rely more on the ill relative's objective characteristics (such as speaking incoherently or being hospitalized). In general, patients underreport psychiatric diagnoses in family members (Andreasen et al., 1986). A family member with major depressive disorder or generalized anxiety disorder is more likely to report the same disorder in relatives than a member who does not have this diagnosis (Kendler et al., 1991). Since response to medication is genetically transmitted, to some extent, if a mentally ill relative received medication, the clinician should inquire about the type, duration, and results.

Through a *genogram* (McGoldrick & Gerson, 1985) or a traditional narrative, the clinician indicates the "dramatis personae" and how they are related, employed, and involved with the patient. A full genogram can be quite time-consuming and may not be completed on the initial interview. The FH specifies with whom in the family the patient lives (if anyone), who the patient sees the most, trusts the most, and depends on the most in a crisis. A description of routine family functioning may include information about who plays which roles in the family, who manages the money, who sets the day-to-day rules, and who makes decisions. Family snapshots are valuable as much for how they are selected and discussed as for what they portray. Then, considering the family as a system—that is, as a totality in which each member's actions affect all others—how does the patient normally perpetuate or try to alter the family patterns, and how does the family as a whole contend with crises?

The FH documents how the patient's family members have influenced and been influenced by the patient's illness. The clinician's opinion about these influences is reported in the biopsychosocial formulation; only the opinions of relatives, whether "correct" or not, are reported here. How relatives (or friends) have tried to solve the patient's difficulties should also be mentioned.

In gathering the FH, the clinician should note if information from family members varies depending on whether the patient is present. Although the clinician should never assume that one family member speaks for all, many families will present a united front, unless the therapist explicitly asks each member to state his or her own view of the problem. Finally, psychiatric crises are highly traumatic for family members; avoid drawing derogatory conclusions about family members' typical behavior based on how they act during a crisis.

The Medical Assessment

The medical assessment consists of the patient's medical history, a physical examination, and laboratory tests (Table 2-3). The chief goals of this stage of psychiatric evaluation are (1) to detect medical causes for psychiatric symp-

---

TABLE 2-3
Laboratory Tests for Psychiatric Assessment

A. Frequently ordered screening tests:
   1. Complete blood count
   2. Urinalysis (protein, glucose, microscopic exam for bacteria, blood cells)
   3. Electrolytes (sodium, potassium, bicarbonate, chloride, phosphate, calcium, and glucose)
   4. Hepatic and renal function tests
   5. Thyroid function tests (T-4 and TSH)
   6. Toxicology screen of urine (and blood alcohol, if indicated)
   7. Urine pregnancy test (women of childbearing potential)
   8. Serum albumin, total protein (nutritional status)

B. Relatively inexpensive, low-yield tests:
   1. Sedimentation rate (Westergren)
   2. Skin testing (for infectious diseases)
   3. Stools for occult blood
   4. EKG
   5. Chest and skull x-rays
   6. B-12 and folate levels (geriatric)
   7. FTA-ABS (98% sensitivity) or MHA-TP (95% sensitivity) for neurosyphilis (not VDRL or RPR, insensitive for tertiary syphilis)

C. With evidence of cognitive or neurological disorders:
   1. EEG (including sleep tracings)
   2. CT or MRI scan
   3. Lumbar puncture (CSF protein, glucose, cells, gram stain cultures)
   4. HIV testing

D. Serum levels of psychotropic drugs (when appropriate)

---

toms, (2) to identify physical states that may alter how psychiatric medications are prescribed, (3) to discover previously undiagnosed medical diseases (which are disproportionately high among psychiatric patients), (4) to alert therapists to substance abuse, and (5) to monitor blood levels of various psychotropic agents.

Most internists agree that there is no such thing as a "routine" lab test. Too often they are ordered on a "you never know what might be wrong and anyway the patient has a good lawyer" basis. Clinical judgment, not a standard checklist, should determine which tests are ordered. The only consistently underutilized tests in psychiatry are urine drug screens (which need to be obtained within 48 hours of ingestion of most drugs in order to be effective). High blood levels in patients who are mildly intoxicated indicate drug tolerance. In a young, well-nourished adult who has no health complaints or risk factors, none of the other lab tests should be regarded as routine. The gamma-glutamyl transferase (GGT) is the most sensitive of liver function tests and can detect early signs of alcoholism. However, it is often *too* sensitive, detecting something abnormal when nothing is wrong. Careful interviewing about alcoholism has been shown to detect this disease more efficiently than any lab test. Furthermore, lab tests should be ordered on the basis of presumed diagnosis. For example, a patient with significant unexplained anxiety may need to be evaluated for hyperthyroidism; an elderly depressed patient who is eating poorly might be evaluated for malnutrition.

Whether the medical assessment should be done by the patient's psychiatrist or family physician depends on several factors, one being who is the most qualified to perform it. In most cases, the family practitioner or internist is the first choice. All psychiatric inpatients are required to receive a complete medical assessment, but whether all outpatients should receive one remains controversial. Commonly used guidelines for requesting a medical assessment are: any patient with signs of cognitive impairment (see Chapter 10), psychosis, or incapacitation; all patients over the age of 50 should have a medical examination once a year; those under 50, every 3–5 years. Clinicians of mental- and medical-health disciplines may wish to have all new patients fill out a questionnaire, such as the "Medical–Psychiatric History Form" (Figure 2-1).

THE MENTAL STATUS EXAMINATION

The mental status examination (MSE) describes the patient's appearance, behavior, speech, emotions, and cognitive and perceptual processes. (Perhaps the term *psychological status* would more aptly describe this part of the evalua-

FIGURE 2-1
Medical–Psychiatric History Form

Instructions: Please complete this form and return it to your therapist at your next appointment. By doing so, you will provide important diagnostic information while freeing up time with your therapist for other matters. If you are unsure about a question or are unable to answer it, don't worry about it: Simply place a question mark ("?") next to it and move on. Everything you indicate will be held in the strictest confidence.

PATIENT DATA
Name _____ Today's date _____
Street address _____
City _____ State _____ Zip _____
Telephone <home> _____ <work> _____
Business street address _____
City _____State _____ Zip _____
Occupation _____Age ____ Birth date _____
Person to contact in case of emergency: Name _____
Relation _____ Telephone _____
City _____State _____ Zip _____

MEDICAL HISTORY
Your physician's name _____
Street address _____ City _____
State _____ Zip _____ Telephone ( ) _____
Are you allergic to any drugs? Yes ( ) No ( ). If so, to which ones:
_____
Do you have any other allergies? Yes ( ) No ( ). If so, to what:
_____
Are you pregnant? Yes ( ) No ( ). Do you smoke? Yes ( ) No ( ).
When was your last EKG? _____ Was it normal? yes ( ) no ( ).
When did your physician last examine you? _____

Have you been treated for any of the following:
AIDS, or acquired immune deficiency syndrome, or HIV positive ( )
Alcohol abuse ( ), alcoholism ( )
Anemia ( )
Asthma ( ), hay fever ( )
Cancer ( )
Diabetes ( )
Drug abuse or addiction ( )
Epilepsy, seizures, or convulsions ( )
Fainting spells, lightheadedness, or dizziness ( )
Gastrointestinal problems ( )
Glaucoma ( )
Heart murmur or disease ( )
Hepatitis, liver disease, or jaundice ( )
High blood pressure [hypertension] ( )
Kidney disease ( )
Lung disease, pneumonia ( )
Migraine ( )
Rheumatic fever ( )
Serious injury or accident ( )
Stroke ( )
Thyroid problems ( )
Tuberculosis (TB) ( )
Ulcer ( )
Uncontrolled bleeding ( )
Venereal disease ( )
Other ( ) If so, what?

FIGURE 2-1
Medical–Psychiatric History Form (continued)

Please list any (prescription or over-the-counter) medication that you are currently taking and reason.

_____

_____

Please list any street drugs that you have taken in the past.

_____

Have you ever been treated for a psychiatric illness such as anxiety, depression, insomnia, mania, psychosis?
Yes ( ) No ( )
If yes, what were you treated for? _____ Who treated you (name and address)?

_____

Have you ever taken any psychiatric medication? Yes ( ) No ( ) If yes, please list them.

_____

Hospitalization: List all your hospitalizations both medical and psychiatric.

Type of Illness/Operation	Hospital	Year

Alcohol use?_____ How many days per month?_____ Average amount in a day?_____
Have people ever annoyed you by criticizing your drinking?_____
Have you ever felt bad or guilty about your drinking?_____
Have you ever tried to cut down on your drinking?_____
Have you ever had a drink first thing in the morning to steady your nerves or get rid of a hangover?

_____

Smoking?_____ How much per day?_____
Age began smoking?_____ Age stopped smoking?_____
Usual weight?_____lbs. Recent loss or gain?_____ Weight at age 20_____
Average hours of sleep at night?_____

SYMPTOM LIST
PLACE A CHECK (✔) in front of any of the following that are, or have been, a problem for you. DOUBLE
CHECK (✔✔) the main problems for you.

_____ **Rashes, color change**	_____ **Ear trouble, infection**
_____ Itching	_____ Hearing loss, ringing in your ears
_____ Warts, moles	_____ Eye problems
_____ Eczema, lumps, hives	_____ Nosebleeds
_____ Very dry skin	_____ Stuffy nose, sinus trouble, hayfever
_____ Excessive sweating	_____ Sore throats
_____ Bleeding or bruising from minor injury	_____ Hoarseness
_____ Anemia	_____ Dental or gum problems
_____ Lymph node or gland swelling	

FIGURE 2-1
Medical–Psychiatric History Form (continued)

_____ **Enlarged or painful breasts**

_____ Breast lumps

_____ Discharge from nipples

_____ **Shortness of breath**

_____ Cough, chest colds

_____ Bringing up sputum or blood

_____ Wheezing, asthma

_____ Chest pain, pleurisy

_____ TB or exposure to TB

_____ Fever, sweats, chills

_____ Pneumonia

_____ **Chest pain, tightness, pressure**

_____ Fast or irregular heartbeat

_____ Trouble breathing when lying down

_____ Waking short of breath

_____ Swelling of feet or ankles

_____ Previous heart trouble

_____ Murmurs or rheumatic fever

_____ High blood pressure

_____ Poor circulation, varicose veins

_____ Blood clots

_____ **Pain or burning on urinating**

_____ Trouble starting or stopping urine

_____ Blood or pus in urine

_____ Frequent urinating

_____ Waking to urinate (# times/night___)

_____ Sores or discharge

_____ Gonorrhea or syphilis

_____ **Trouble swallowing**

_____ Poor appetite

_____ Gas, cramps, pains

_____ Heartburn, indigestion

_____ Nausea, vomiting

_____ Constipation, diarrhea

_____ Blood in stool or black stool

_____ Yellow jaundice, hepatitis

_____ Hemorrhoids

_____ Gall bladder problems

_____ Hernia

_____ **Pains in joints, arthritis**

_____ Swollen joints

_____ Back pain, neck pain

_____ **Head injury, concussion**

_____ Headaches

_____ Dizziness, fainting

_____ Convulsions, seizures, fits

_____ Shaking, tremor

_____ Weakness, paralysis

_____ Numbness, tingling

_____ Difficulty walking, coordination

_____ Depression, anxiety

_____ Poor sleeping

_____ Nervousness, tension

_____ Trouble thinking, remembering

_____ Crying, upset, worrying

_____ Sexual problems

_____ **Cancer**

_____ Diabetes

_____ Goiter, thyroid problem

FOR WOMEN ONLY:

_____ Irregular or frequent periods

_____ Very heavy periods

_____ Spotting between periods

_____ Painful periods

_____ Vaginal discharge or itching

Age your first period started_____

Number of days between periods _____

Number of pregnancies_____

Living children _____

Number of miscarriages_____ abortions_____

Date of last period_____

Date of last cancer smear (PAP)_____

Did your mother take any hormones while she
was pregnant with you? Yes (   ) No (   )

Don't know (   )

tion.) Whereas the psychiatric history is a *subjective* account given by the *patient* about *past* events that *have not been witnessed* by the therapist, the MSE is an *objective* report of the patient's *current* mental state as *observed* by the therapist. Although history of the patient can usually be reconstituted at future times, the MSE provides a profile of the patient that can be obtained only in the present moment. Because it is collected firsthand, the MSE is the most reliable part of the assessment; consequently, *every* patient's mental status must be ascertained.

There are two types of MSEs: *informal* and *formal*. Clinicians gather the informal MSE while taking a history; for most patients, these observations will suffice. The *formal* MSE is given to all patients with possible organic or psychotic disorders; to his or her informal observations, the therapist adds a series of standardized questions that assess memory, thought processes, attention span, and so on.

In reporting an MSE the clinician should present concrete illustrations to justify every conclusion. It is not sufficient to state that a patient is delusional; report the content of the delusions: "The patient is convinced that penguins read his mind." Saying that a patient has a depressed mood is a conclusion and, as such, requires experienced substantiation: "The patient moved slowly, cried throughout the interview, and never laughed. The patient also said that he felt sad most of the time."

This last statement illustrates how some information in the MSE could fit into a variety of categories. Should the description of this forlorn patient belong in the category of "Appearance," or "Behavior," or "Speech," or "Emotion," or should it be split among all of them? No single answer exists. *Where* information is reported is less important than *how* it is reported: It should be well organized, coherent, and clear.

This section on the MSE, as well as the glossary of signs and symptoms at the end of the book, presents much of the language of psychopathology. Although technical terms do give professionals a shorthand for communication, they can also be abused. Jargon can mislead one into a false sense of knowledge and expertise. To know the definition of catatonia does not mean that the clinician knows anything else about catatonia. In reporting the assessment, descriptions in nonjargony language are often more informative and less ambiguous than professional terminology.

At the same time, technical terms are not mere words; they also represent concepts, and so when terms are used carelessly, concepts get muddled. For instance, when clinicians interchange the terms "shame" and "guilt," they're missing an important conceptual distinction: Shame is an *interpersonal* phenomenon involving embarrassment; guilt is an *intrapsychic* phenomenon involving the violation of one's conscience or superego. Given this different focus, when therapists overlook this distinction, assessment and treatment suffer. As Wittgenstein (1958) observed, "Philosophical problems arise when language goes on a holiday" (p. 3).

Once acquired, a professional vocabulary can shape how a professional thinks. That is to be expected—and cautioned against as well. Terms become mental categories, and being human, clinicians will fit their observations into these categories and tend to adjust their observations when they don't quite fit. With a clinical vocabulary, one is more likely to see the world *solely* through the lens of psychopathology. People no longer forget things, they "repress" them; shy persons are now "schizoid"; people aren't even people— they're "objects." The dangers far exceed the rudeness of "psychobabble" and "psychoanalyzing" everybody: To view people only in terms of their psychopathology is to ignore all their other qualities—and that is not only bad manners, it's bad psychiatry. Therapists do not treat psychopathology, but *people* with psychopathology.

Appearance

This section of the MSE reports how the patient looks: clothes, posture, bearing, grooming, apparent age, etc. Clothes are a type of language; what people wear is a form of communication. The patient's degree of alertness should be described (is the patient in a coma, a stupor with clouded consciousness, or alert?). "Palm reading" may reveal if the patient is frail, a hard laborer, or a nail-biter. Shaking hands with the patient at the outset of the interview does more than convey respect: It provides data. Is the patient's handshake crushing, firm, or weak? Are the palms sweaty? Are the hands rough or smooth?

Behavior

This category on behavior refers to the patient's motor activity: gait, gestures, stereotyped movements, other muscular movements such as twitches or tics, and impulse control. Psychomotor agitation and retardation, including extreme manifestations such as catatonia, are described here. Problems with impulse control refer to how the patient handles immediate aggressive, sexual, and suicidal wishes. If difficulties with impulse control arise during the interview (as opposed to only being reported in the history), they also should be reported here. Examples: A patient smashes the clinician's desktop with a fist when the interview is interrupted by a telephone call; a patient dashes from the office on hearing a distressing comment.

Speech

This category describes the manner (volume, rate, coherence) but not the content of speech. Speech can be loud, rapid, pressured, slowed, soft, hesitant, slurred (i.e., dysarthria), monotonous, latent, etc. Latency—a delay in responding and initiating speech—often occurs in depressed patients. Pressured or rapid speech that cannot be interrupted is a cardinal sign of mania. Slightly pressured speech can occur with anxiety. Reporting of foreign or regional accents also occurs here.

Mood and Affect

The phenomenology of emotion is discussed psychiatrically in terms of *mood* and *affect*: Mood is a pervasive and subjectively experienced feeling state; affect refers to instantaneous, observable expressions of emotion. In psychopathology, affects are overt and moods are covert. *Moods are what people tell you they feel, and affects are what you see them feeling.* Moods influence how people feel about themselves and their world; affects do not. People complain about their moods, but not about their affects. Moods persist, affects don't. It is useful to ask patients to characterize their mood on a scale from 1 to 10 (from saddest to happiest).

In reality, distinguishing moods from affects can be difficult. For example, is anger a mood or an affect? It could be either, and which it is doesn't matter all that much unless there is incongruence. *What does matter is that the clinician provides clear, specific descriptions of the patient's emotions.* "He states that he feels angry while smiling and appearing calm" (incongruent or inappropriate). "She cries one moment and laughs the next" (labile). "His expression never varies" (flat). "She says she feels 'like an emotional robot . . . the living dead.'" "When first mentioning his wife, he pounded the table." As in this last example, what is occurring or being discussed during an emotional display may be worth reporting.

A normal range of affect is labeled "broad." Other affective ranges include "flat," "blunt," "constricted," "labile," and "inappropriate." A normal mood is called "euthymia." Moods can also be high or low. On the up side, as one gets higher, moods go from "elevated," to "euphoric," to "expansive." On the down side, "dysphoria" is any mood the patient finds unpleasant, including anxiety, apprehensiveness, dysthymia, and irritability. "Dysthymia" is used throughout this text to mean the *symptom* of depression, as distinguished from the various *syndromes* of depression. *Relatedness* refers to the ability to express warmth and interact with the interviewer. *Mood-congruency* refers to whether a patient's behavior, affect, delusions, and hallucinations are consistent with his stated mood. If he constantly smiles while talking about his sadness and losses, his affect is incongruent with his stated mood. A depressed person who believes that she is evil and that Satan has destroyed her soul has a mood-congruent delusion. If she believes that extraterrestials have programmed her to infiltrate the FBI, she has a mood-incongruent delusion.

Thought Processes and Content

Since no one can directly know another's thought processes, therapists must infer them from patient's speech and behavior. A patient may *say* that he is God, which doesn't necessarily mean he *thinks* so; the style and context of delivery will determine if the assertion is deceptive or delusional. Whenever pathological thought is reported, the clinician should also include examples.

Psychiatrists traditionally used the term *thought disorder* to describe any communication arising from pathological thought processes. However, because the term is so nonspecific, *DSM-IV-TR* discourages its use in favor of more descriptive categories: word usage, stream of thought, continuity, and content.

1. *Word usage* includes abnormalities such as neologisms and word approximations. Neologisms (e.g., "I need a flame to binkle my bed") are most often seen in schizophrenia. Word approximations (e.g., "I know the time by the thing that goes around") may be a sign of brain disease.

2. *Stream of thought* refers to the quantity of thoughts (e.g., overabundant, slowed). When the patient's speech is restricted to a few words or syllables, it is called "poverty of speech" and should be described in the speech section of the MSE. This description should be distinguished from "poverty of *content* of speech," which is discussed below. Interruption of a train of speech before a thought has been completed is called "thought blocking." These blockages can last seconds to minutes and may suggest a psychotic process.

3. *Continuity of thought* refers to the associations among ideas. Some of the disturbances in this category are always pathological, such as clanging, echolalia, perseveration, and "word salad." When a patient has improved moderately, the flight of ideas will make much better sense. For example, a psychotic patient who was with a group of other patients talking about being abandoned by their families, said, "I've slept in trees before. Sleeping in trees is uncomfortable. Family trees are the worst."

4. *Content of thought*, when disturbed, can result in delusions, overvalued ideas, illogical thinking, and magical thinking. Delusions in which the patient experiences her actions, thoughts, feelings, and perceptions as not her own or

somehow imposed on her are called Schneiderian first-rank symptoms (FRS), after Kurt Schneider, who first identified the phenomenon. Common examples include experiencing thought insertion or broadcasting, thought removal, and getting special messages from the TV or radio. Although no longer considered pathognomonic of schizophrenia, FRS are often found in schizophrenia and are sometimes observed in mania. A sign or symptom is *pathognomonic* if it exists in only one disorder.

Illogical thinking is another disturbance in thought content. One patient wrote: "People's bodies conform to the shape of their clothes so that my mother's body must be a rectangle because she's wearing a chemise and when my brother wears bell-bottoms, his legs become large, double-edge razors." This patient also said that by getting dressed, he could induce his father, via telepathy, to take a shower (delusional and magical thinking.) A psychology student who says, "I put a textbook by my pillow and learn by osmosis" is also demonstrating magical thinking; however, this conviction is probably not delusional, but instead an overvalued idea or a joke.

Whereas in poverty of speech the patient utters only a few words or syllables, in poverty of *content* of speech the patient's words are sufficient and individual sentences may even make sense, but the total communication remains meaningless. (Although usually pathological, this phenomenon may also be observed in political speeches and bureaucratic reports!) For example, when asked what religion meant to him, a patient replied: "All that church stuff. Amazing Grace, Amazing Grace. 'I know that my redeemer liveth, and that he shall stand at the latter day upon the earth.' (Job 19:25) It is personal, very personal. I understand what you mean, you who live in God's grace."

Incoherence is a general, but often useful, term to describe incomprehensible speech in which the specific type of disturbed thinking is difficult to identify, or in which there is a mixture of the thought disturbances mentioned above. Incoherence describes the response of a patient who was asked, "Do you fear anything specific?":

> That's just it. A doctor told me not to put a stamp on me. The Secretary of the Treasury is not part of it. People say to you, "Isn't it too bad that you're sick." It feels like I was very obstreperous. I couldn't communicate at any level. My inside couldn't make sense of my outside. All the anxieties, and all the (*pause*), and all the rococo themes of psychiatric uh, uh, uh (*pause*) illness played back upon me again and again.

Obsessions, which are persistent, unwanted *thoughts*, are another type of disturbed content. Because compulsions are "senseless" repeated *deeds*, they are behaviors, but since they arise from obsessions, the two can be reported together.

Perception

This category describes fundamental abnormalities in the five senses: hearing, seeing, touching, tasting, and smelling. These abnormalities, which include hallucinations, illusions, depersonalization, derealization, and déjà vu, are often, but not always, psychopathological. Technically, dreams are hallucinations, but they are not reported as perceptual disturbances. Most people have brief experiences with derealization, depersonalization, and déjà vu.

Although some patients will readily admit when they are hallucinating, many will not. Patients may be hallucinating when their eyes dart from side to side, when they stare at nothing, or when they seem preoccupied, as if they were listening to voices. Ask, "Do you see or hear things that other people do not?" Because some patients will refer to their own thoughts as voices, the clinician should ask if the voices come from inside or from outside their head. If from the inside, ask if the voice is the patient's or someone else's.

In general, only auditory and visual hallucinations occur in psychiatric disorders, whereas these and olfactory, tactile, and other hallucinatory phenomena occur in disorders caused by drug use or medical conditions. The hallucinations of patients with mood disorders tend to be mood-congruent; those of people with schizophrenia, mood-incongruent.

Attention and Concentration

Attention is the ability to sustain a focus on one task or activity. Impaired attention—distractibility—can usually be detected during a routine interview by observing if a patient's focus is frequently directed to unimportant or irrelevant external stimuli. If attention seems impaired and its immediate cause is unclear (e.g., due to anxiety, hallucinations, or to other psychotic preoccupations), formal clinical testing should be performed.

In the most widely used test, referred to as the "serial 7's," the patient is asked to subtract 7 from 100 without stopping as far as possible. The patient's educational background or infrequent use of mathematics, however, may interfere with performance. A more informative test is the "serial 1's," in which the patient is asked to "count backward by 1's from 57 and stop at 22." Because it requires no math skills, this is a purer test of concentration, and by noting if the patient stops at 22, the clinician also tests immediate memory.

Orientation

As patients become progressively disoriented, they are unable to indicate the current time, then their current location (place), and last, their own name. To test for orientation to time, the clinician ascertains if patients can identify the date, the day of the week, the time of day, or how long they have been hospitalized. Failing these questions, patients are asked to identify the season and part of the day (e.g., morning, afternoon, evening). Therapists may be astonished to discover a seemingly normal patient who, when asked directly, says the current year is 1953.

Disturbances in orientation, memory, and judgment usually suggest the presence of cognitive dysfunction, which may arise from substance abuse or from medication toxicity (especially possible with tricyclic antidepressants and phenothiazines that have anticholinergic side effects, as well as the hypnoanxiolytics that have sedative side effects). Impaired orientation very rarely occurs in schizophrenic, paranoid, psychotic, or mood disorders, but more commonly in dissociative disorders and dementing illnesses. Impaired memory and judgment may occur in each of these disorders.

Memory

In the MSE, memory is categorized as *remote, recent,* or *immediate.* Remote memory refers to many years ago, recent memory to the past several days to months, and immediate memory to the past several minutes. When people begin to lose their memories, immediate memory usually goes first, remote memory, last.

> Remote and recent memory can be assessed by how well patients recall historical and current events. Immediate memory is best evaluated by formal testing: For example, clinicians name three single-word objects (e.g., *book, umbrella, elephant*), and then have patients immediately repeat the words to ensure they registered. Clinicians then tell patients that in 5 minutes, they will be asked to repeat the three objects. Most patients can recall two out of three; one or zero suggests organic factors.

Sensing their failing memory and disorientation, many patients with neurological dysfunction feel embarrassed and try to conceal the loss by *confabulating.* One example: A 63-year-old professor with a slow-growing brain tumor had become adept at bluffing by using his charm to hide his inability to remember simple facts. When asked to name the year, he replied, "The year, well, it is the year of our discontent. Who cares about the year? It's but time, and time is relative."

Judgment

This category evaluates patients' abilities to exercise judgment in dealing with social situations, which includes acting appropriately during the interview and understanding the consequences of their actions. Although judgment is largely assessed by observing patients during the interview, if the clinician remains uncertain about the evaluation, patients can be asked what they would do in hypothetical situations: "What would you do if you found a stamped, addressed envelope lying on the street?" or, "What would you do if you were the first one in a theater to see a fire?" Asking a patient to provide three wishes may help assess judgment but may also reveal projected information that improves the clinician's understanding and provides further support for the diagnosis.

Intelligence and Information

The only precise measure of intelligence comes from an IQ test, such as the Wechsler Adult Intelligence Scale (WAIS). IQ tests were originally developed to predict school performance, and they do this fairly well. However, they *don't* do as well when used for other purposes, such as to predict a person's ability to fix a car, run a company, or win a Nobel prize. Because there are different forms of intelligence and no one global entity, IQ intelligence can be thought of as "scholastic potential." By definition, IQ is whatever an IQ test measures, the average IQ being 100. Most people reading this book will not know anyone in their personal lives with an IQ below 90. The diagnosis of mental retardation requires a tested IQ of below 70. High IQ scores may reflect the cultural enrichment of a person's inborn biological potential.

The assessment of intelligence includes examining the patient's general fund of information, which is why intelligence and information are usually linked in the MSE. Both are affected by culture, education, performance anxiety, and psychopathology, especially the presence of delirium or dementia. Because the initial interview can only reveal gaping deficits, intelligence can be tested clinically by having patients perform simple math (e.g., "multiply 7 × 12") or by having them read something and then tell the examiner what it meant. Performing simple calculations involving money is correlated with intelligence (e.g., "How much change would you get back if you purchased an item for $6.32 with a 10-dollar bill?"). Evaluating patients' information resources involves questioning their general knowledge and awareness of current events. Such questions should be geared to the patient's background: "Who wrote Hamlet?" "Who won last week's election for governor?"

Another important aspect of intelligence is the ability to abstract—that is, to think symbolically, to generalize, and to conceptualize. This ability is frequently absent with a functioning IQ under 90 or with schizophrenia. Patients' behavior during the interview usually provides enough data to determine their ability to abstract. If there is any reason to question this ability, especially with evidence of psychosis or organicity, two clinical tests should be performed. Before describing these specific tests, a cautionary note: Too much stock should not be placed in any single answer or on clinical tests in general, since at best they are only rough measures of patients' abilities. They do, however, provide some relatively objective data. (Whenever formal clinical testing is done, clinicians should record not only their conclusion—e.g., "the patient's similarities were concrete"—but also what the patient actually said.)

The first test of abstractive ability determines whether patients can recognize *similarities*. Questions are asked such as, "What is the similarity between a poem, novel, and sculpture?" Or, "What is the similarity between a table, desk, and chair?" To the latter question, a properly abstracted answer would be, "They are all furniture." A concrete answer would be, "All are made of wood"; even more concrete would be, "I don't see any similarity." A bizarre answer would be, "They're all more human than humans."

The second test involves patients' abilities to interpret *proverbs*. Ideally, the proverbs given to patients should contain words and ideas within the parameters of their educational and cultural backgrounds, and *not* be ones that have been heard many times before. If patients already know the proverb, asking what it means may test prior learning but not the capacity to abstract. An example: "The opera's not over till the fat lady sings." An abstract response would be, "Nothing is resolved until everybody does their thing." A concrete response would be, "An opera is never finished until a fat woman sings." A bizarre response would be, "Fatso opera singers like sex." A personalized response would be, "I'm not fat!"

Insight

In the MSE *insight* refers to patients' awareness of their chief problem. A delusional patient who claims she came for treatment to get the telephone company to stop the ringing in her ears lacks insight. The insight continuum ranges from (1) a complete denial of illness, to (2) a dim and fleeting admission of illness, to (3) an awareness of illness but with accusations that others are causing it, to (4) an intellectual recognition of problems and their origin within, to (5) a convincing awareness of the disorder and its internal sources. The patient's level of insight is a rough predictor of how much he will cooperate with treatment and benefit from insight-oriented psychotherapy; the latter can be predicted further by offering the patient several interpretations during the assessment, not for therapeutic purposes, but to see how he reacts to an interpretation.

AUXILIARY DATA

Information gathered outside the patient interview is considered auxiliary data; typically, this auxiliary data constitute a tenth to a third of the information needed to determine the patient's diagnosis and treatment. Sometimes with uncooperative or very disorganized patients, outside information is central. As discussed already, two major sources of auxiliary data are interviews with friends or relatives and results from the medical assessment. In addition there are specialized tests and procedures.

Psychological and Neuropsychological Tests

Psychological tests are most often used to quantify personality, intelligence, and the presence, degree, and type of neuropsychological brain dysfunction. Psychological tests can add valuable information that complements the interview. The best tests are *objective* measurements that utilize standardized questions, scoring, and interpretation. The reliability and validity of psychological tests vary. These tests, like laboratory tests, should not be used routinely but to address *specific* questions, the answers to which may alter the patient's treatment. (Patients must not be intoxicated or going through drug withdrawal at the time of testing.) Specific clinical questions might be: "What is the patient's IQ?" "How tenuous is the patient's contact with reality?" "Which conflicts most trouble the patient?" "How much control does the patient have over aggressive impulses?" "Does the patient have neuropsychological (e.g., frontal lobe) impairment? If so, which functions are affected and to what extent?" Table 2-4 outlines the most commonly used psychological tests.

Most psychological tests were developed before *DSM-IV-TR*, and some still reflect a psychological, rather than descriptive, diagnostic approach. As a result, patients are more likely to be diagnosed as schizophrenic and borderline by psychological tests than by *DSM-IV-TR* criteria. With these reservations in mind, the clinician should formulate specific questions and then ask the test-

TABLE 2-4
Psychological Tests

I. *Achievement tests.* Also known as "proficiency tests," they try to measure the outcome of systematic education and training.

II. *Aptitude tests.* They try to measure potential ability in specific areas, such as music, medicine, and accounting.

III. *Intelligence tests.* These tests include the WAIS-R, commonly used for adults, and the Wechler Intelligence Scale for Children (WISC). The Stanford–Binet is sometimes used. In addition to measuring IQ, the tests can detect psychotic and organic impairments. The WAIS and WISC yield verbal (which also includes arithmetic), performance (spatial abilities), and full-scale scores. Education tends to affect the verbal more than the performance score; in dementia, performance often declines more than verbal.

IV. *Personality tests.* These assess personality traits and are of two general types:

    A. *Structured.* In these largely quantitative tests, the patient's response is compared to a "right" or "normal" response. The Minnesota Multiphasic Personality Inventory (MMPI) is the most widely used objective personality test. It has 550 true–false questions covering a wide range of subject matter (e.g., "I like parties and socials"; "I'm afraid of the germs on doorknobs"). It also has validity scales, which measure tendencies to portray oneself in a favorable or pathological manner, and measures of defensiveness.

    B. *Projective.* In these largely qualitative tests, there is no "correct" answer, only the subject's projections. Projective tests include the Rorschach ("inkblot"), the Thematic Apperception Test (TAT), and the figure drawing test.

V. *Neuropsychological tests.* These tests, such as the Halstead–Reitan Battery and a variety of scales from the WAIS and WISC, specifically evaluate brain impairment, determining if cerebral damage exists and whether it is diffuse or localized. Many tests can be used to assess specific types of brain functioning:

    A. Abstract reasoning and problem-solving

    B. Memory

    C. Orientation

    D. Perceptual (auditory, visual, tactile), motor, tactile–spatial, visuomotor, and visuospatial tasks

    E. Language (receptive and expressive)

    F. Flexibility of thinking and speed of response

    G. Attention and concentration

---

ing psychologist whether they can be answered. The choice of tests is the psychologist's, not the referring clinician's.

Amytal Interviews

Although popularly known as "truth serum," amytal does not make people tell the truth; some patients even confabulate while receiving it, and malingerers can continue to malinger. Consequently, amytal interviews have little place in the routine assessment. On occasion, they may be helpful in retrieving lost memories, in differentiating neurological from psychiatric disorders (Ward, Rowlett, & Burke, 1986), in distinguishing schizophrenic from mood disorders, and in unblocking a stuck psychotherapy. They will not help in detecting a malingerer. Polygraphy (lie detection), which relies upon continuous physiological monitoring to infer an accurate response to questioning, has some limited clinical applications (e.g., assessment of sex offenders).

Neuroendocrine Batteries

At present, most psychiatrists believe that these neuroendocrine tests lack the sufficient sensitivity and specificity to be useful and valid in the routine assessment.

SUMMARY OF PRINCIPAL FINDINGS

After the history, MSE, and auxiliary data are reported, the clinician's next task is to highlight the major findings in a paragraph or two. This summary must indicate if there is an immediate threat to life (via suicide, assaultiveness, or homicide) and does *not* include the patient's diagnosis, prognosis, biopsychosocial formulation, or treatment plan. These are all conclusions (of sorts) based on the findings summarized in this section.

References

American Psychiatric Association. (2000). *Diagnostic and statistical manual of mental disorders*, 4th ed., text rev.. Washington, DC: American Psychiatric Association.

Andreasen, N.C., Rice, J., Endicott, J., Reich, T., & Coryell, W. (1986). The family history approach to diagnosis. *Archives of General Psychiatry, 43*, 421–429.

Beck, A.T., Brown, G., Berchick, R.J., Stewart, B.L., & Steer, R.A. (1990). Relationship between hopelessness and ultimate suicide: A replication with psychiatric outpatients. *American Journal of Psychiatry, 147*, 190–195.

Center for Disease Control. (April 4, 2008). *National Vital Statistics Reports*, Vol. 56, number 10.

Kendler, K.S., Silberg, J.L., Neale, M.C., Kessler, R.C., Heath, A.C., & Eaves, L.J. (1991). The family history method: Whose psychiatric history is measured? *American Journal of Psychiatry, 148*, 1501–1504.

McGoldrick, M., & Gerson, R. (1985). *Genograms in family assessment*. New York: Norton.

Menninger, K. (1938). *Man against himself*. New York: Harcourt, Brace & World.

Motto, J.A., Heilbron, D.C., & Juster, R.P. (1985). Development of a clinical instrument to estimate suicide risk. *American Journal of Psychiatry*, 142, 680–686.

Ward, N.G., Rowlett, D.B., & Burke, P. (1986). Sodium amylobarbitone in the differential diagnosis of confusion. *American Journal of Psychiatry*, 135, 75–78.

Wittgenstein, L. (1958). *Philosophical investigations* (2nd ed.). Translated by G.E.M. Anscomb. New York: Macmillan.

Zimmerman, M. (1994). *Interview guide for evaluating DSM-IV psychiatric disorders and the mental status exam*. Psych Products Press.

3

Diagnosis and Prognosis

Di-agnostic?...Lessee...agnostic means "one what don't know"...an' di is a Greek
prefix denotin' two-fold—so the di-agnostic team don't know twice as much as an
ordinary agnostic...right?

—Pogo, *New York Post,* August 11, 1966

On the publication of *DSM-III*, its chief architect, Robert Spitzer (Spitzer et
al., 1980, p. 151), began summarizing its major accomplishments by citing
this unimpeachable source: Pogo knows that diagnostic labels may imply more
knowledge than actually exists. Despite increased reliability and validity, the
diagnostic categories of *DSM-III* are not eternal truths, but they are state-
of-the-science hypotheses. Further revisions—*DSM-III-R, DSM-IV,* and now
DSM-IV-TR—are proof that these diagnostic categories are not immutable.
They are to be used with caution, but used nonetheless, for unless the clinician makes the correct diagnosis, no effective treatment can be launched and
no accurate prognosis can be estimated.

Considering that *DSM-IV-TR* entails over 200 diagnoses, making a diagnosis has become an increasingly complex task, if only because the number of
diagnoses has skyrocketed. In 1840 there was but one psychiatric diagnosis:
idiocy (or insanity). In 1880 there were seven: mania, melancholia, monoma-
nia, paresis (syphilis of the brain), dementia, dipsomania, and epilepsy. Over
the next 100 years, the number of psychiatric diagnoses has risen at an average
rate of two per year. Because the interval between *DSM-IV-TR* and *DSM-V,*
the next major revision, has been extended to 2012, the *DSM-IV-TR* was published to correct factual errors and update information.

DEFINITIONS

Differential diagnosis is the process of choosing the correct diagnosis from
conditions with similar features. Traditionally, differential diagnosis began

with two general questions: (1) Was the patient's condition caused by a known medical condition or a drug? (2) Was it a psychosis, nonpsychosis, or personality disorder? In large measure, the first question addresses an *etiological* distinction; the second, a *descriptive* distinction.

Disorders caused by general medical conditions were originally called *organic mental disorders*. This term was dropped in DSM-IV because it implies that other psychiatric disorders do not have a biological basis. The remaining disorders were called "functional disorders" because no organic cause was known, and the prime etiology was assumed to be psychosocial. Because research on schizophrenia, manic depression, and other so-called functional disorders has revealed a strong biological component, the term *functional* has been eliminated. The term *primary mental disorder* is used to separate these from "Mental Disorder due to a General Medical Condition" or "Substance-Induced Mental Disorder."

Psychosis exists when reality testing is grossly impaired; *reality testing* is the ability to evaluate the external world objectively and to distinguish it from inner experience. Delusions, hallucinations, and massive denial are indicative of impaired reality testing and, therefore, of psychosis. Minor distortions of reality are not considered psychotic, such as a person who experiences transitory derealization or a man overestimating his attractiveness to women. Psychosis is usually inferred when a patient's behavior is grossly disorganized, characterized by incoherent speech, "senseless" violence, and total inattentiveness to the environment. Psychosis may be experienced as distressful and alien (i.e., ego-dystonic) or as an acceptable and integral part of the self (i.e., ego-syntonic).

Neurosis, a nonpsychotic and ego-dystonic syndrome, can be very disabling, but in general does not paralyze the individual's functioning or violate social norms. Reality testing and personality organization remain intact. It is purely a descriptive term, without etiological or theoretical associations. *Neurotic process* is primarily driven by anxiety and expressed through unconscious defense mechanisms that are believed to produce neurotic symptoms (e.g., dysphoria, obsessions, compulsions, sexual dysfunction, panic, phobias). This terminology is no longer featured in the DSM-IV-TR but still used by some health care professionals.

Personality disorders are longstanding conditions, beginning in adolescence or early adulthood, and characterized by inflexible and maladaptive patterns of sufficient severity to cause either clinically significant functional impairment or subjective distress. Unlike psychoses and neuroses, personality disorders are *always* chronic, even though their intensity may fluctuate. As a rule, they are nonpsychotic and ego-syntonic, but exceptions exist. Exemplifying the rule is antisocial personality disorder, a nonpsychotic state in which the patient doesn't mind his thievery, but his victims do. Two exceptions are the painful shyness seen with avoidant personality disorder and the transient psychosis of the borderline personality disorder. The rages of borderline personalities may be distressing to themselves and others but are usually ego-syntonic because they are considered acceptable and integral parts of the individuals.

TWO BASIC DIAGNOSTIC PRINCIPLES

DSM-IV-TR stresses two fundamental principles: *parsimony* and *hierarchy*. The principle of parsimony recommends that clinicians seek the single most elegant, economical, and efficient diagnosis that accounts for *all* the available data; when a single diagnosis is insufficient, the fewest number of diagnoses is sought. The principle of hierarchy is that mental disorders generally exist on a hierarchy of syndromes, which tend to decline in severity: Medical or pharmacological > psychotic > mood > anxiety > somatic > sexual > personality > adjustment > no mental disorder. Thus, when a patient's symptoms could be attributed to several disorders, but are entirely explainable by the most severe disorder, the most parsimonious diagnosis belongs to the disorder in that more severe category. The "decision tree" in Figure 3-1 illustrates how these two principles guide differential diagnosis. In essence, a decision tree is an algorithm, or flow chart, which uses branching logic to home in on the most likely diagnosis.

Without the use of these principles, the diagnosis of a patient with auditory hallucinations, persecutory delusions, apprehensiveness, and somatic preoccupations could range from schizophrenia to a paranoid personality, generalized anxiety, and somatoform disorder. *With* these principles, there is but one diagnosis—schizophrenia—because it is the highest ranking disorder on the hierarchy that accounts for *all* the symptoms. However, more than one diagnosis is sometimes justified. If this person has other clusters of symptoms that are not completely explained by the diagnosis of schizophrenia, then the clinician would proceed down the decision tree in Figure 3-1. For example, if this person also has panic attacks during remission, then panic disorder might be added to the diagnosis.

The decision tree is also a guide to understanding the organizational structure in *DSM-IV-TR* and to establishing hierarchical treatment priorities. A patient with substance abuse, a mood disorder independent of substance abuse, and an avoidant personality disorder is likely to be treated in a hierarchical fashion, with the substance abuse being the first priority of treatment.

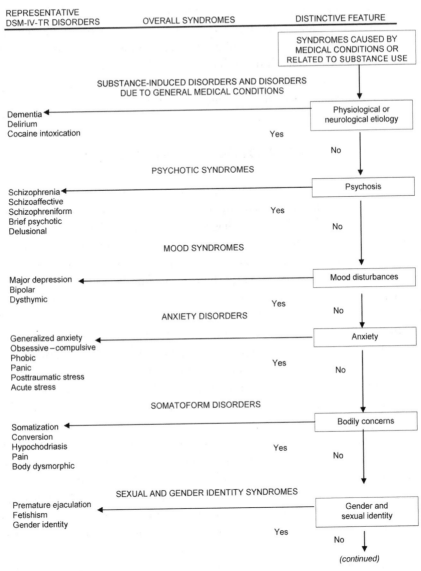

FIGURE 3-1
An Overview of Differential Diagnosis

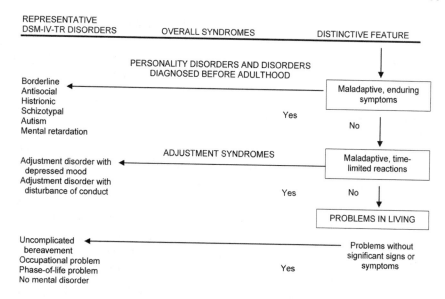

FIGURE 3-1
An Overview of Differential Diagnosis (continued)

Note. In placing the differential diagnosis of DSM-IV-TR's 200+ categories into a manageable perspective, this overview contains some inaccuracies and oversimplifications. The left column presents sample DSM-IV-TR diagnoses. The middle column lists general syndromes, which are clusters of signs and symptoms. The right column indicates the most distinctive overall feature of each syndrome. Some syndromes (such as sleep, impulse, dissociative, eating, and factitious disorders) do not fall neatly into this hierarchy and for simplicity are omitted.

SEVEN STEPS FOR PSYCHIATRIC DIAGNOSIS

Among the several perfectly good ways of reaching a diagnosis is the following procedure involving seven somewhat overlapping steps.

1. *Collecting data:* Performed during the assessment (Chapter 2).

2. *Identifying psychopathology:* Performed during the assessment (Chapter 2).

3. *Evaluating the reliability of data:* Not all information is equally reliable, and not all informants are equally reliable. Present information is more reliable than past information, since memories fade and current moods often color past recollections. Information garnered during a crisis must be evaluated cautiously. Signs are more reliable than symptoms, because signs can be observed. Objective findings are more reliable than intuitive, interpretive, and introspective findings. Observations such as "The patient seems to be concealing a depression" or "I'm feeling manipulated by the patient" may be true and worth pursuing, but they are far less useful in making a reliable diagnosis than

more readily verifiable observations, such as crying, slow gait, and incoherence.

4. *Determining the overall distinctive feature*: The clinician should try to identify the patient's most prominent symptom cluster, such as those listed in the righthand column of Figure 3-1. If one general category of distinctive features does not stand out, pick two; the next two steps will resolve uncertainty.

5. *Arriving at a diagnosis*: Following the principles of parsimony and hierarchy, the clinician systematically considers every *DSM-IV-TR* mental disorder that exhibits the patient's overall distinctive feature. This task is not easy: *DSM-IV-TR* lists over 200 diagnoses, which are divided into 16 general categories for Axis I, and one for Axis II; all 17 are summarized in Table 3-1.

6. *Check diagnostic criteria*: The clinician should confirm the diagnosis by verifying if the patient's characteristics meet the *DSM-IV-TR* diagnostic criteria for the disorder. To demonstrate: Table 3-2 lists *DSM-IV-TR*'s criteria for generalized anxiety disorder. (Note how criteria D and F illustrate the principle of hierarchy.) Criterion D illustrates that generalized anxiety disorder (GAD) is at the bottom of the anxiety disorder hierarchy (some have even referred to GAD as a "wastebasket diagnosis"). Criterion F illustrates the hierarchy of other disorders above GAD. It is not a rigid hierarchy; a person with alcohol abuse and/or a mood disorder can have a diagnosis of GAD if the symptoms are present after the person has been abstinent for a few months and not in the midst of the mood disorder.

These criteria are guides, not laws. A patient, for instance, might well have a genuine generalized anxiety disorder even if her condition does not quite match *DSM-IV-TR*'s definition. The six symptoms listed under criterion C do not include "an exaggerated startle response" or "nausea and diarrhea," and yet these commonly occur in generalized anxiety disorder. If a patient's condition only approximates the criteria, the clinician can write: "The patient meets *DSM-IV-TR* criteria for generalized anxiety disorder, but has had only 5 months of excessive anxiety and worry and only two symptoms in criterion C." By using *DSM-IV-TR* as a reference point, clinicians speak the diagnostic language of their colleagues, while not being locked into its use. If clinicians have reason not to use *DSM-IV-TR*, they should specify which criteria are being used (e.g., Feighner, RDC).

7. *Resolve diagnostic uncertainty*: If at this stage, one diagnosis (per axis) does not suffice, or if some evidence is inconsistent with other data, or if the diagnosis remains unclear for any reason, the most likely culprits are (a) inadequate data, (b) premature closure, (c) atypical presentations, or (d) multiple disorders.

TABLE 3-1

DSM-IV-TR *General Diagnostic Categories*

AXIS I

1. *Disorders Usually First Diagnosed in Infancy, Childhood, or Adolescence*

   This category includes most, but not all, of the disorders that arise before adolescence, such as attention-deficit disorders, and autism. These disorders, although present early, sometimes are not diagnosed until adulthood and may be an attenuated form.

2. *Delirium, Dementia, and Amnestic and Other Cognitive Disorders*

   These disorders are temporary or permanent dysfunctions of brain tissue caused by neurological diseases, general medical conditions, or chemicals.

3. *Mental Disorders Due to a General Medical Condition*

   These mental symptoms are thought to be due to the direct physiological consequences of a general medical condition. This category underscores the importance of a thorough medical examination as part of the diagnostic process, and primarily refers to catatonic disorder and personality changes that are caused by a general medical condition. This section does not include disorders such as major depression and panic disorder that are listed elsewhere but are caused by a general medical condition. In these cases they are listed under the appropriate disorder, e.g., mood disorder due to a general medical condition.

4. *Substance-Related Disorders*

   This category refers to the maladaptive use of drugs and alcohol. Mere consumption and recreational use of substances do not constitute disorders. This category necessitates an abnormal pattern of use, as with alcohol abuse and cocaine dependence. It includes side effects of medication and toxic exposure. The term "substance" can refer to drugs of abuse or medications or toxins.

5. *Schizophrenic and Other Psychotic Disorders*

   The schizophrenic disorders are characterized by active psychotic symptoms for at least 1 month (e.g., grossly disorganized behavior, nonmood-congruent delusions and hallucinations) and by at least 6 months of behavioral deterioration. The delusional disorders are characterized by delusions in the absence of other psychotic symptoms. In general, these patients are less impaired than those with schizophrenia. This section also includes a grab-bag of psychotic disorders that usually have a briefer course and better prognosis than delusional and schizophrenic disorders. This category includes schizophreniform disorder, brief psychotic disorder, and schizoaffective disorder.

6. *Mood Disorders*

   The cardinal feature of these disorders is disturbances of mood. Patients may or may not have psychotic symptoms; when they do, delusions and hallucinations are usually mood-congruent. These disorders include major depression, bipolar disorder, dysthymic disorder, and cyclothymic disorder.

7. *Anxiety Disorders*

   These disorders are characterized by physiological signs of anxiety (e.g., palpitations) and subjective feelings of tension, apprehension, or fear. Anxiety may be acute and focused (panic disorder) or continual and diffuse (generalized anxiety disorder). This category also includes phobic, obsessive–compulsive, and posttraumatic stress disorders.

(continued)

TABLE 3-1
Continued

8. *Somatoform Disorders*

   These disorders are dominated by somatic symptoms that resemble physical illness but cannot be fully accounted for by disease or a pathophysiological mechanism. The symptoms are not produced intentionally, and there must be strong evidence that psychological factors have an important role in their genesis. This category includes somatization and (hysterical) conversion disorders, hypochondriasis, pain disorder, and body dysmorphic disorder.

9. *Factitious Disorders*

   In these disorders (e.g., Munchausen syndrome), physical or psychological symptoms are produced voluntarily for no apparent (or ulterior) motive other than being ill. Malingering is differentiated from factitious disorders in that the individual has an ulterior motive other than taking on the sick role (secondary gain).

10. *Dissociative Disorders*

    These disorders all feature a sudden, temporary alteration or dysfunction of memory, consciousness, identity, and behavior, as in dissociative amnesia, fugue, identity disorders, and depersonalization disorder. These disorders may also have a gradual onset and become chronic.

11. *Sexual and Gender Identity Disorders*

    This category includes sexual desire and arousal disorders, orgasm disorders, sexual pain disorders, gender identity disorders, and paraphilias (in which bizarre imagery or acts are required for sexual excitement, e.g., necrophilia).

12. *Eating Disorders*

    These disorders involve significant problems in regulating eating. Included are anorexia nervosa and bulimia nervosa. These disorders involve disturbances in perception of body shape and weight along with inappropriate compensatory behaviors such as binge eating, induced vomiting, laxatives, and starvation.

13. *Sleep Disorders*

    This category covers problems with sleep regulation and the dyssomnias, including primary insomnia, primary hypersomnia, narcolepsy, breathing-related sleep disorder, and circadian rhythm sleep disorder. Also included are problems that occur during sleep (the parasomnias): nightmares, sleep terrors, and sleep walking disorders.

14. *Impulse-Control Disorders Not Elsewhere Classified*

    These disorders involve failure to resist an impulse, drive, or temptation to perform an act that is harmful to the person or others. These disorders of impulse control include pathological gambling, kleptomania, pyromania, trichotillomania, and intermittent explosive disorder.

15. *Adjustment Disorders*

    These relatively mild disorders occur within 3 months of a clearly identifiable psychosocial stressor. Disorders are classified according to the predominant symptom, such as adjustment disorder with depressed mood or adjustment disorder with disturbance of conduct.

TABLE 3-1

Continued

16. *Other Conditions That May Be a Focus of Clinical Attention*

This category covers psychological factors affecting a medical condition, medication-induced movement disorders, marital and other relational problems, or problems related to abuse or neglect.

AXIS II

17. *Personality Disorders*

These disorders are patterns of personality traits that are longstanding, maladaptive and inflexible, and cause either impaired functioning or subjective distress. Examples include borderline, schizoid, and avoidant personality disorders.

Note. From *DSM-IV-TR,* p. 685.

Inadequate data may reflect missing information that clarifies the diagnosis, once obtained. For instance, *DSM-IV-TR*'s brief psychotic disorder must be "at least 1 day and no more than 1 month" in duration, but the patient, previously normal, manifested psychotic symptoms every 3 or 4 days and then returned to normal. Additional data solved the puzzle of this intermittent psychosis: When the patient's urine tested positive for amphetamines, his diagnosis was changed to substance-induced psychotic disorder. Sometimes data are inadequate because the therapist has not talked to the right people. After conducting 2 months of stalemated couples treatment, the therapist insisted on seeing the couple's 5-year-old daughter as part of a family assessment. Until then, Mother and Father had colluded in a secret, which in pure childhood innocence, their daughter revealed when she asked, "How come Daddy stumbles around every night after he comes home?"

Premature closure amounts to "to jumping the diagnostic gun," without proper differential diagnosis. A common trap is the "5-minute diagnosis": After interviewing a patient for 5 minutes, the therapist "unconsciously" reaches a diagnosis and then inadvertently distorts, converts, and selectively seeks information that confirms this initial diagnosis. Call it human nature, but *every* clinician is prone to see what he or she wants to see. What distinguishes the skilled professional is the willingness to double-check a diagnosis by repeating the previous six steps.

A clinician in training diagnosed a patient in the emergency room as having a major depression. The diagnosis seemed obvious: The patient's face was blank, his

TABLE 3-2

DSM-IV-TR *Criteria for Generalized Anxiety Disorder*

A. Excessive anxiety and worry (apprehensive expectation), occurring more days than not for at least 6 months, about a number of events or activities (such as work or school performance).

B. The person finds it difficult to control the worry.

C. The anxiety and worry are associated with three (or more) of the following six symptoms (with at least some symptoms present for more days than not for the past 6 months). **Note:** Only one item is required in children.

    (1) restlessness or feeling keyed up or on edge

    (2) being easily fatigued

    (3) difficulty concentrating or mind going blank

    (4) irritability

    (5) muscle tension

    (6) sleep disturbance (difficulty falling or staying asleep, or restless, unsatisfying sleep)

D. The focus of the anxiety and worry is not confined to features of another Axis I disorder, e.g., the anxiety or worry is not about having a Panic Attack (as in Panic Disorder), being embarrassed in public (as in Social Phobia), being contaminated (as in Obsessive–Compulsive Disorder), being away from home or close relatives (as in Separation Anxiety Disorder), gaining weight (as in Anorexia Nervosa), having multiple compaints (as in Somatization Disorder), or having a serious illness (as in Hypochondriasis), and the anxiety and worry do not occur exclusively during Posttraumatic Stress Disorder.

E. The anxiety, worry, or physical symptoms cause clinically significant distress or impairment in social, occupational, or other important areas of functioning.

F. The disturbance is not due to the direct physiological effects of a substance (e.g., a drug of abuse, a medication) or a general medical condition (e.g., hyperthyroidism) and does not occur exclusively during a Mood Disorder, a Psychotic Disorder, or a Pervasive Developmental Disorder.

Note. From *DSM-IV-TR,* p. 476.

---

gait slow, his movements agitated; he felt sad and lonely. He even *said* he was depressed. Yet soon after the patient was admitted, the trainee was called by a supervisor who said that the patient's diagnosis was Parkinson's disease, not depression. The clinical error was that he saw a depressed-looking person and stopped thinking: He assumed that the patient was depressed, did not perform a systematic differential diagnosis, and only saw what he expected to find.

Although *atypical presentations* cause diagnostic confusion, some patients simply do not conform to classic textbook descriptions. For instance, patients with major depression usually feel sad, yet some don't feel sad at all, but complain primarily of bodily aches and pains. Another advantage of using *DSM-IV-TR* decision trees is that they often detect these atypical cases.

Multiple diagnoses—that is, more than one diagnosis per axis—may be indicated after first attempting to ascribe a patient's symptoms to a single diagnosis. Just as medical patients can have more than one disorder, so can psychiatric patients.

If a diagnostic uncertainty persists, the clinician should use the most applicable *DSM-IV-TR* label: "diagnosis deferred," "unspecified mental disorder," "[specify class of disorder] not otherwise specified" or "specific diagnosis (provisional)." Finally, the patient may have "no mental disorder," a most underutilized diagnosis.

MULTIAXIAL DIAGNOSIS

In 1947, multiaxial diagnosis was first proposed in Sweden but not adopted. Five years later Danish psychiatrists officially adopted a biaxial system that separated symptoms from etiology. After two decades of promotion by the World Health Organization, the concept surfaced in United States in 1975, when John Strauss suggested a multiaxial approach with an axis for social functioning. In 1980, *DSM-III* incorporated multiaxial diagnosis in order to clarify the complexities and relationships of biopsychosocial difficulties and thereby facilitate treatment planning. *DSM-IV-TR* uses five axes:

Axis I: Clinical syndromes (e.g., mental disorders); developmental disorders; other conditions that may be a focus of clinical attention

Axis II: Personality disorders/traits; mental retardation

Axis III: General medical conditions/symptoms that pertain to current problem

Axis IV: Psychosocial and environmental problems

Axis V: Global Assessment of Functioning (GAF)

The main advantage of separating Axes I and II is to prevent the typically more florid presentations of Axis I mental disorders from overshadowing, or becoming confused with, the more chronic and subtle Axis II personality disorders. Distinguishing between these axes may clarify what therapy can reasonably accomplish, given that treatment is more likely to alleviate Axis I than Axis II disorders. Therapists (and clients) who fail to separate mental from personality disorders are frequently disappointed, however unjustifiably, when only the former remits with brief treatment. Where uncertainty exists, clinicians may choose to add "provisional" after the diagnosis on any axis.

Axis III lists only general medical conditions that are "potentially relevant to the understanding or management of the case." It is unfortunate that some nonphysicians are reluctant, or believe it is inappropriate, to list an Axis III diagnosis, since a patient's diagnosis should be complete. When writing an Axis III diagnosis, many nonphysicians like to add the source of this diagnostic information parenthetically (e.g., the patient's doctor, the patient, the chart). For example:

Axis I: Panic disorder
           Psychological factors affecting physical condition
Axis II: Dependent Personality Disorder (Provisional)
Axis III: Crohn's disease (Dr. Sachar)
Axis IV: Occupational problem (job loss, acute)
           Problems with primary support group (failing marriage, chronic)
Axis V: Global Assessment of Functioning = 65

In its dry way, Axis IV attempts to include all of Shakespeare's "slings and arrows of outrageous fortune." It lists the psychosocial and environmental problems that may affect prognosis of mental disorders on Axes I and II. Stressors may involve jobs, finances, living situations, health, social support, family conflicts, and negative life events (Table 3-3). Even "positive" stressors should be listed, if they are problematic. For example, a job promotion brings higher financial reward (good news!) but longer hours at the office, more travel, and increased responsibility (bad stressful news!). All relevant problems should be listed, including those that *contributed to* the disorder(s) and those that *resulted from* the disorder(s). In general, this list is confined to problems in the past year. However, earlier problems should be listed if they clearly contribute to the present diagnosis or have become a focus of treatment; for example, post-traumatic stress disorder, rape, childhood sexual and physical abuse, or combat experience could all be listed. Problems that have become the primary focus of treatment should be recorded not only in Axis IV but also in Axis I (See Table 3-4, "Other Conditions That May Be a Focus of Clinical Attention"). For example, if the therapy only focuses on "bad hair" and it really is bad, it might be listed in Axis I. However, the astute clinician in this situation might consider body dysmorphic disorder instead.

Axis V indicates the patient's current overall level of social, psychological, and occupational functioning. Physical functioning and limitations are not included here but may be listed in Axis IV. The Global Assessment of Func-

TABLE 3-3
DSM-IV-TR *Axis IV Classification*

The following problem categories may be noted on Axis IV; each is followed by a list of examples.

Problems with primary support group, such as death of a family member; health problems in family; disruption of family by separation, divorce, or estrangement; removal from the home; remarriage of parent; sexual or physical abuse; parental overprotection; neglect of child; inadequate discipline; discord with siblings; birth of a sibling

Problems related to the social environment, such as death or loss of friend, inadequate social support, living alone, difficulty with acculturation, discrimination, adjustment to life cycle transition (e.g., retirement)

Educational problems such as illiteracy, academic problems, discord with teachers or classmates, inadequate school environment

Occupational problems such as unemployment, threat of job loss, stressful work schedule, difficult work condition, job dissatisfaction, job change, discord with boss or coworkers

Housing problems, such as homelessness, inadequate housing, unsafe neighborhood, discord with neighbors or landlord

Economic problems such as extreme poverty, inadequate finances, insufficient welfare support

Problems with access to health care services, such as inadequate health care services, transportation to health care facilities unavailable, inadequate health insurance

Problems related to interaction with the legal system/crime, such as arrest, incarceration, litigation, victim of crime

Other psychosocial problems, such as exposure to disasters, war, or other hostilities; discord with nonfamily caregivers (e.g., counselor, social worker, physician); unavailability of social service agencies

Note. From *DSM-IV-TR*, p. 31.

---

tioning (GAF) scale is generally recommended for rating Axis V (Tables 3-5 and 3-6 for adults and children, respectively).

Usually this rating is done to ascertain the patient's level of functioning in the present. This current rating, together with the Axis I diagnosis, help clinicians decide if patients should be hospitalized immediately or live in a group home. Clinicians may also want a rating of patients' highest level of functioning in the past year, which helps to determine prognosis and treatment (since patients who previously functioned at a higher level usually recover at a higher level). To illustrate: With everything else being the same, and with Tom and Jerry being equally delusional—one's certain he's a cat, the other, a mouse—if

TABLE 3-4

DSM-IV-TR *Other Conditions That May Be a Focus of Clinical Attention*

Mental- and medical-health professionals see many people with emotional or behavioral difficulties that are *not* mental disorders but problems in living. In addition, psychological factors affecting "medical conditions" or "medication-induced movement disorders" are also encountered. Though mainly a classification of mental disorders, *DSM-IV-TR* also catalogues and briefly describes these problems. For some problems in living, such as uncomplicated bereavement or occupational problems, patients themselves seek help; for other problems in living, such as malingering or adolescent antisocial behavior, people other than patients request professional consultation. Since an individual can have a mental disorder *and* a problem in living yet only want assistance for the latter, if the problem in living is not a manifestation or consequence of the mental disorder, the problem in living should be specified on Axis I. For instance, an agoraphobic may seek help for academic problems, but not phobia.

This table names and sketches these *DSM-IV-TR* "other conditions," which are referred to as "V" codes. If the *other condition* is not a primary focus of treatment but is a significant psychosocial or environmental problem, it should be listed under Axis IV. For example, a client may be illiterate but requesting treatment for panic disorder. The illiteracy would be classified under Axis IV as an educational problem.

Abuse or neglect problems refer to severe mistreatment of one individual by another. Subtypes include *physical* or *sexual abuse* of a *child* or *adult* or *neglect of a child*. This is coded differently if the focus of attention is on the perpetrator or on the victim.

Academic problem refers to school or learning difficulties not due to a specific developmental, mental, or medical disorder. Examples include the student with poor study habits or the serious underachiever.

Acculturation problem refers to a problem involving adjustment to a different culture (e.g., following migration).

Adult antisocial behavior refers to rule-breaking or law-breaking by those without a mental disorder, such as occurs in conduct, antisocial personality, and impulse control disorders. Examples include many, but not all, thieves, mobsters, and dope dealers.

Age-related cognitive decline is an objectively identified decline in cognitive functioning consequent to the aging process that is within normal limits given the person's age. Individuals with this condition may report problems remembering names or appointments or may experience difficulty in solving complex problems. This category should be considered only after it has been determined that the cognitive impairment is not attributable to a specific mental disorder or neurological condition.

Bereavement refers to a normal reaction to the death of a loved one. Chapter 10 describes uncomplicated bereavement and how it differs from depression.

Borderline intellectual functioning refers to those seeking help with problems that arise primarily from having IQs of 71–84. Borderline intellectual functioning is easily missed in the presence of another mental disorder, such as schizophrenia or panic disorder, and it may also be hard to distinguish from mental retardation (see Chapter 20).

TABLE 3-4

Continued

Childhood or adolescent antisocial behavior refers to isolated acts of rule-breaking or law-breaking by youth; when it is a pattern, the person may have a conduct or impulse-control disorder.

Identity problem refers to uncertainty about multiple issues relating to identity, such as long-term goals, career choice, friendship patterns, sexual orientation and behavior, moral values, and group loyalties.

Malingering refers to the voluntary and deliberate production of false or grossly exaggerated physical or psychological symptoms to achieve a goal; the person wants this goal, and its attainment is understandable in view of the person's circumstances and not just his or her psychology. Malingering may involve evading the draft or playing hooky; it may also serve more respectable ends, such as feigning illness while being held by terrorists. Two caveats: First, malingerers *do* get sick. Second, some malingerers who are ostensibly faking an illness may actually be doing so as a face-saving way to get help with a genuine illness. Malingering should be differentiated from *somatoform* and *factitious disorders*, and should be considered if: (1) medicolegal issues are involved, e.g., workman's compensation, malpractice, "pain and suffering" cases; (2) inconsistent or contradictory information is given in the history; (3) marked discrepancies are noted between history and objective findings; (4) there is lack of cooperation with diagnostic evaluation; (5) patient adamantly refuses to be hypnotized, to have an amytal interval, or a polygraph; (6) patient demonstrates treatment noncompliance; or (7) there are indications of antisocial personality disorder.

Medication-induced movement disorders include **neuroleptic-induced parkinsonism, dystonia, akathisia** or **tardive dyskinesia, neuroleptic malignant syndrome, medication-induced postural tremor, medication-induced movement disorder NOS** (e.g., movement disorder or malignant syndrome not caused by a neuroleptic or tardive dystonia), and other medication-induced disorders such as **adverse effects of medication NOS,** e.g., hypotension, priapism, and cardiac arrhythmias.

Noncompliance with medical treatment refers to noncompliance with an important aspect of the treatment for a mental disorder or a general medical condition. The reasons for noncompliance may include discomfort resulting from treatment (e.g., medication side effects), expense of treatment, decisions based on personal value judgments or religious or cultural beliefs about the advantages and disadvantages of the proposed treatment, maladaptive personality traits or coping styles (e.g., denial of illness), or the presence of a mental disorder (e.g., schizophrenia, avoidant personality disorder). This category should be used only when the problem is sufficiently severe to warrant independent clinical attention.

Occupational problems refer to work difficulties that do not result from a mental disorder, such as job dissatisfaction or uncertainty in choosing careers.

Phase-of-life problem refers to difficulties that primarily arise in response to major developmental turning points (i.e., crises, "passages"), such as puberty, separating from parents, starting a career, "midlife crises," and retirement.

(*continued*)

TABLE 3-4

Continued

Psychological factors affecting medical condition refers to psychological or behavioral factors that affect a general medical condition by adversely affecting its course (e.g., exacerbations, prolonged recovery), adding a health risk (e.g., overeating in diabetes, high salt intake with hypertension), causing stress-related physiological responses (e.g., bronchospasm in asthma or chest pain in coronary artery disease), or interfering with treatment (e.g., irregularly taking medication, improper wound care). The psychological factors must have a clinically significant adverse effect on the medical conditions and "there must be reasonable evidence (direct causality is not required) to suggest an association between the psychological factors and the medical condition." Subtypes:

Mental disorder affecting ... [*indicate the general medical condition*]; includes Axis I or II disorders (e.g., major depressive disorder complicating the treatment of diabetes).

Psychological symptoms affecting ... [*indicate the general medical condition*]; include psychological symptoms that do not meet full criteria for an Axis I disorder (e.g., anxiety in irritable bowel syndrome or peptic ulcer disease).

Personality traits or coping style affecting ... [*indicate the medical condition*]; includes traits that are subthreshold for Axis II disorders or represent another pattern that has been demonstrated to be a risk factor for certain illnesses (e.g., type A, pressured, hostile behavior for coronary artery disease).

Maladaptive health behavior affecting ... [*indicate the general medical condition*] (e.g., a "couch potato" lifestyle, overeating, unsafe sex).

Stress-related physiological response affecting ... [*indicate the general medical condition*] (e.g., stress-related worsening of blood pressure or coronary pain).

Relational problems refer to a pattern of interaction that is associated with clinically significant impairment in individual or family functioning or the development of symptoms in one or more individuals involved in the relationship. Subtypes include: parent–child, partner, sibling, or NOS (e.g., coworker, neighbor) relational problem, or relational problem related to a mental disorder or general medical condition.

Religious or spiritual problem refers to distressing experiences that involve loss or questioning of faith, problems associated with conversion to a new faith, or questioning of spiritual values that may not necessarily be related to an organized church or religious institution.

TABLE 3-5

DSM-IV-TR *Axis V Classification: Global Assessment of Functioning (GAF)*

Consider psychological, social, and occupational functioning on a hypothetical continuum of mental health–illness. Do not include impairment in functioning due to physical (or environmental) limitations. **Note:** Use intermediate codes when appropriate, e.g., 45, 68, 72.)

100 | **Superior functioning in a wide range of activities, life's problems never seem to get out of hand, is sought out by others because of his or her many positive qualities. No symptoms.**

90 | **Absent or minimal symptoms** (e.g., mild anxiety before an exam), **good functioning in all areas, interested and involved in a wide range of activities, socially effective, generally satisfied with life, no more than everyday problems or concerns** (e.g., an occasional argument with family members).

80 | **If symptoms are present, they are transient and expectable reactions to psychosocial stressors** (e.g., difficulty concentrating after family argument); **no more than slight impairment in social, occupational, or school functioning** (e.g., temporarily falling behind in school work).

70 | **Some mild symptoms** (e.g., depressed mood and mild insomnia) **OR some difficulty in social, occupational, or school functioning** (e.g., occasional truancy, or theft within the household), **but generally functioning pretty well, has some meaningful interpersonal relationships.**

60 | **Moderate symptoms** (e.g., flat affect and circumstantial speech, occasional panic attacks) **OR moderate difficulty in social, occupational, or school functioning** (e.g., few friends, conflicts with peers or co-workers).

50 | **Serious symptoms** (e.g., suicidal ideation, severe obsessional rituals, frequent shoplifting) **OR any serious impairment in social, occupational, or school functioning** (e.g., no friends, unable to keep a job).

40 | **Some impairment in reality testing or communication** (e.g., speech is at times illogical, obscure, or irrelevant) **OR major impairment in several areas, such as work or school, family relations, judgment, thinking, or mood** (e.g., depressed man avoids friends, neglects family, and is unable to work; child frequently beats up younger children, is defiant at home, and is failing at school).

30 | **Behavior is considerably influenced by delusions or hallucinations OR serious impairment in communication or judgment** (e.g., sometimes incoherent, acts grossly inappropriately, suicidal preoccupation) **OR inability to function in almost all areas** (e.g., stays in bed all day; no job, home, or friends).

20 | **Some danger of hurting self or others** (e.g., suicide attempts without clear expectation of death, frequently violent, manic excitement) **OR occasionally fails to maintain minimal personal hygiene** (e.g., smears feces) **OR gross impairment in communication** (e.g., largely incoherent or mute).

10 | **Persistent danger of severely hurting self or others** (e.g., recurrent violence) **OR persistent inability to maintain minimal personal hygiene OR serious suicidal act with clear expectation of death.**

0 | Inadequate information.

Note. The GAF Scale is a revision of the GAS (Endicott J., Spitzer R.L., Fleiss, et al. [1976]: The Global Assessment Scale: A procedure for measuring overall severity of psychiatric disturbance. *Archives of General Psychiatry, 33,* 766–771). This is a revision of the Health–Sickness Rating Scale (Luborsky, L. [1962]: Clinicians' judgments of mental health. *Archives of General Psychiatry, 7,* 407–417). In *DSM-IV-TR,* p. 34.

TABLE 3-6

Children's Global Assessment of Functioning (GAF) Scale

Rate the patient's most impaired level of general functioning for the specified time period by selecting the lowest range which describes his/her functioning or best matches the individual's symptom severity, **whichever is worse**. Within the selected 10-point range, determine whether the individual is functioning at the higher or lower end of that range (e.g., 35, 58, 62). Rate actual functioning regardless of treatment or prognosis. The examples of behavior provided are only illustrative and are not required for a particular rating. Specified time period: 1 month

91–100

Superior functioning in all areas (at home, at school, and with peers); involved in a wide range of activities and has many interests (e.g., has hobbies or participates in extracurricular activities or belongs to an organized group such as Scouts, etc.); likeable, confident; "everyday" worries never get out of hand; doing well in school; no symptoms.

81–90

Good functioning in all areas; secure in family, school, and with peers; there may be transient difficulties and "everyday" worries that occasionally get out of hand (e.g., mild anxiety associated with an important exam, occasionally "blow-ups" with siblings, parents, or peers).

71–80

No more than slight impairment in functioning at home, at school, or with peers; some disturbance of behavior or emotional distress may be present in response to life stresses (e.g., parental separations, deaths, birth of a sib), but these are brief and interference with functioning is transient; such children are only minimally disturbing to others and are not considered deviant by those who know them.

61–70

Some difficulty in a single area, but generally functioning pretty well (e.g., sporadic or isolated antisocial acts, such as occasionally playing hooky or petty theft; consistent minor difficulties with schoolwork; mood changes of brief duration; fears and anxieties which do not lead to gross avoidance behavior, self-doubts); has some meaningful interpersonal relationships; most people who do not know the child well would not consider him/her deviant but those who do know him/her well might express concern.

51–60

Variable functioning with sporadic difficulties or symptoms in several but not all social areas; disturbance would be apparent to those who encounter the child in a dysfunctional setting or time but not to those who see the child in other settings.

41–50

Moderate degree of interference in functioning in most social areas or severe impairment of functioning in one area, such as might result from, for example, suicidal preoccupations and ruminations, school refusal and other forms of anxiety, obsessive rituals, major conversion symptoms, frequent anxiety attacks, poor or inappropriate social skills, frequent episodes of aggressive or other antisocial behavior with some preservation of meaningful social relationships.

TABLE 3-6
Continued

31-40

Major impairment in functioning in several areas and unable to function in one of these areas, e.g., disturbed at home, at school, with peers or in society at large; persistent aggression without clear instigation; markedly withdrawn and isolated behavior due to either mood or thought disturbance; suicidal attempts with clear lethal intent; such children are likely to require special schooling and/or hospitalization or withdrawal from school (but this is not a sufficient criterion for inclusion in this category).

21-30

Unable to function in almost all areas, e.g., stays at home, in ward, or in bed all day without taking part in social activities or severe impairment in reality testing or serious impairment in communication (e.g., sometimes incoherent or inappropriate).

11-20

Needs considerable supervision to prevent hurting others or self (e.g., frequently violent, repeated suicide attempts) or to maintain personal hygiene or gross impairment in all forms of communication, e.g., several abnormalities in verbal and gestural communication, marked social aloofness, stupor, etc.

0-10

Needs constant supervision (24-hr. care) due to severely aggressive or destructive behavior or gross impairment in reality testing, communication, cognition, affect, or personal hygiene.

Note. From Shaffer et al. (1983).

before becoming ill Tom had a solid marriage, good job, and satisfying hobbies, whereas Jerry did not, then after recovery Tom would probably function better than Jerry. Treatment goals should reflect these different expectations.

PROGNOSIS

In different ways, each *DSM-IV-TR* axis sheds light on prognosis. A patient's prognosis or outcome is a product of several factors: (1) the natural course of the particular disorder; (2) the patient's highest prior level of functioning (see above); (3) the duration of the present illness (the longer the duration, the bleaker the outlook); (4) the abruptness of onset (the more acute the onset, the better the prognosis); (5) the age of onset (the earlier in life, the poorer the outcome); (6) the availability of effective treatments; (7) the patient's compliance or adherence with treatment; and (8) the presence of a supportive social network.

It is worth noting that how disturbed a patient is during an acute episode is *not* always a good predictor of long-term outcome. A 20-year-old patient who has deteriorated over a period of 6 years from schizophrenia and who now displays social withdrawal and flat affect has a far worse long-term prognosis than a 50-year-old patient who functioned well until a month ago, when she became acutely manic, insisted she was the reincarnation of Queen Victoria, threw 100-dollar bills out the window, and spoke nonstop. Clinicians should be clear about *which* prognosis they are determining: Is it for a short-term (e.g., posthospitalization) or a long-term (e.g., a year after discharge) outcome? Is it for an Axis I or an Axis II disorder? Is it a forecast of something more specific, such as relapse, suicide, assault, social functioning? When clinicians dispense prognostic information to patients and their families, they should describe these various types of outcomes instead of indicating a single, and less meaningful, prognosis.

WARNINGS ABOUT *DSM-IV-TR*

Rote memorization of *DSM-IV-TR* criteria is a long and pointless endeavor to be avoided; the learning of specific criteria occurs most effectively through clinical experience. However, when this text presents a disorder, students should still examine its *DSM-IV-TR* criteria in order to (1) obtain an overall picture of the disorder, (2) learn its defining characteristics, (3) become familiar with its common symptoms, (4) understand the meanings of the technical terms that describe it, and (5) learn which features differentiate it from other *DSM-IV-TR* disorders.

DSM-IV-TR is based on a categorical approach to diagnosis. As in medicine, this type of approach works best for disorders that have homogeneous characteristics and clear boundaries differentiating them from other disorders. A stroke and a myocardial infarction are examples of such discrete medical categories. This categorical approach does not work as well for disorders that exist on a continuum—those that can be better described by dimensions and have great variability within the diagnostic category. Anemia and vitamin deficiency are medical examples of dimensional-continuum types of disorders. Because the diagnosis of anemia depends on a hematocrit (a red blood cell count), what count constitutes anemia is always open to debate. Some people function normally with "low" hematocrits, whereas others with "low-normal" do not. Diagnosing psychopathology presents the same problems, since every disorder has both categorical and dimensional aspects. Autistic disorder is an example of a diagnosis that seemed to fit a pure categorical approach relatively easily (language impairment). However, with the increased recognition of higher-functioning forms of autism and Asperger's disorder, perhaps the dimensional approach is better suited to the spectrum of pervasive developmental disorders (PDD) that share some degree of impairment in social relatedness. Many other disorders have continuous dimensional qualities. For example, antisocial personality traits might range from a persistent breaking of parking laws (a not uncommon quality in the general populace) to killing with no remorse (a much rarer characteristic). How to establish hyperactivity in attention-deficit/hyperactivity disorder is equally difficult. Where do you set the bar? In response to the dimensional complexities in a categorical approach, the task force on *DSM-IV-TR* recommends:

> In *DSM-IV*, there is no assumption that each category of mental disorder is a completely discrete entity with absolute boundaries dividing it from other mental disorders or from no mental disorder. There is also no assumption that all people described as having the same mental disorder are alike in all important ways. The clinician using *DSM-IV* should therefore consider that individuals sharing a diagnosis are likely to be heterogeneous even in regard to the defining features of the diagnosis and that boundary cases will be difficult to diagnose in any but a probabilistic fashion. This outlook allows greater flexibility in the use of the system, encourages more specific attention to boundary cases, and emphasizes the need to capture additional clinical information that goes beyond diagnosis. (p. xxxi)

References

American Psychiatric Association. (2000). *Diagnostic and statistical manual of mental disorders*, 4th ed., text rev. Washington, DC: American Psychiatric Association.

Endicott J., Spitzer R.L., Fleiss, J.L., & Cohen, J. (1976). The Global Assessment Scale: A procedure for measuring overall severity of psychiatric disturbance. *Archives of General Psychiatry, 33*, 766–771.

Feighner, J.P., Robins, E., Guze, S.B., Woodruff, R.A., Winokur, G., & Munoz, R. (1972). Diagnostic criteria for use in psychiatric research. *Archives of General Psychiatry, 26*, 57–63.

Luborsky, L. (1962). Clinicians' judgments of mental health. *Archives of General Psychiatry, 7*, 407–417.

Shaffer, D., Gould, M.S., Brasic, J., Ambrosini, P., Fisher, P., Bird, H., et al. (1983). A children's global assessment scale (CGAS). *Archives of General Psychiatry, 40*(11), 1228–1231.

Spitzer, R.L., Williams, J.B.W., & Skodal, A.E. (1980). *DSM-III*: The major achievements and an overview. *American Journal of Psychiatry, 137*, 151–164.

4

Etiology

In general, *etiology* refers to the *origins* of a disorder, whereas *pathogenesis* refers to *all the mechanisms* that ultimately produce it. In this chapter, the term *etiology* encompasses pathogenesis and includes everything that has caused the patient's presenting difficulties. At the turn of the 20th century, the most prevalent mental illness was general paresis (i.e., syphilis of the brain). Other common psychiatric disorders were "myxedema madness" (a type of hypothyroidism), the epilepsies, and psychoses due to vitamin deficiencies and brain infections. As soon as the cause for each of these conditions was discovered, the job of treatment shifted to physicians *other* than psychiatrists, such as internists and neurologists.

Indeed, a major reason *DSM-III* (and now *DSM-IV-TR*) switched to a nosology based on descriptive instead of on etiological criteria was because the etiology of most mental disorders is idiopathic. (*Idiopathic* refers to unknown causation, whereas *iatrogenic* refers to physician-induced illness such as drug side effects). Exceptions exist, as when a disorder's etiology is both obvious and inherent to its definition, such as the role of amphetamines in amphetamine intoxication, or the role of psychosocial stressors in producing a posttraumatic stress disorder. Otherwise, *DSM-IV-TR* eschews all etiological hypotheses — biological as well as psychosocial.

Although the precise etiologies of most mental disorders are largely unknown, more is understood about etiology today than ever. Most dramatic have been advances in psychobiology and epidemiology; less heralded (but equally important) has been the growing appreciation of how intrapsychic, familial, and social influences interact with biology to produce mental disorders. Etiology can be attributed to either genetic influences or environmental influences or the interaction of genetic and environmental influences.

A complete psychiatric assessment, or "workup," includes the detailed history, comprised of personal history, family history, physical examination, a medical review of systems, and mental status examination, culminating in a case formulation, and finally the *DSM-IV-TR* diagnosis, with prognosis included if possible. Thus through the formulation the clinician has an opportunity to explain his or her thinking process and rationale for the conclusions represented succinctly in *DSM-IV-TR* diagnoses, even if provisional. The case formulation should discuss predisposing, precipitating, protective, and perpetuating factors in relation to the etiology and pathogenesis of the disorder. One approach to organizing the formulation is to use the *biopsychosocial model* wherein the patient's present illness is discussed in terms of biological, psychodynamic, cognitive, emotional, and behavioral aspects, as well as familial and interpersonal etiologies (see Engel, 1977).

Etiology is generally sought not only to explain the origin of illness or disease in a particular patient but also to generalize to all patients who present similarly. This allows for development of reliable diagnostic criteria and invites the study of mechanisms of illness that then pave the way to rational design of therapeutic interventions. Due to the uncertain etiology generally associated with psychiatric disorders and their symptoms, when in the clinical setting with an actual patient the clinician may be less concerned with the precise nature of etiology than with making a reliable diagnosis and formulation that fits the history and examination data and then supports and guides the clinician toward case-specific, individualized treatment planning. The initial assessment mandates a complete history to catalogue the precise sequence of facts particular to the individual case—facts about the individual from prenatal to the present time as well as facts about the individual's environment, all of which we must place in the context of the patient's chief complaint and his or her personal narrative or interpretation of such facts. Throughout the process it is prudent to keep separate these many facts from the patient's interpretations of them (and our own, for that matter). Determination of etiology must therefore be based on factual information from reliable historical sources and reliable observations; it cannot otherwise be satisfactorily ascertained. Since reliable facts and evidence are not always available, the establishment of more precise etiology in many cases may need to be suspended or presumed until such facts can be discovered. In the meantime, available evidence is used to support what is called a presumptive, or working, diagnosis. After available data sources have been surveyed and data have been organized according to reliability and apparent relevance to the individual, the diagnostician engages in a process known as differential diagnosis that involves comparing and contrasting several possible diagnoses to determine which of them most closely fits all the available detail and time course of the evidence.

McHugh and Slavney (1998) provide an excellent text for the student of psychiatry to acquire an appreciation for common etiological categories that psychiatric caregivers encounter in their patients. The student can learn to appreciate the characteristics and unique properties of the *disease perspective* (e.g., dementia syndromes or manic–depressive disorder), the *dimensional perspective* (e.g., mental retardation syndromes, personality disorders), the *behavioral perspective* (e.g., pathological gambling, alcoholism), or the *life story perspective* (e.g., adjustment disorder with depression, conversion disorder). Appropriate discussions of etiology will follow naturally once the clinician identifies the type of disorder.

The Dimensions of "Causation"

To speak of "*the* cause" of a mental disorder is naive; it is akin to patients who enter treatment and say, "I want to get to the *root* of my problem." This "root myth" assumes that a single factor has caused the problem and that unearthing it will result in cure. Unfortunately, there is no such thing as *the* root to a problem; at most, there are roots, with many sprouting, variegated phenomena. Formulations, therefore, should consider diverse etiological influences. For example, many teenagers begin smoking to feel grown up. But what *initiates* a disorder usually differs from what *perpetuates* it. So, if these individuals are still smoking when they reach 30, the reason is no longer to feel like an adult; at this point, they are smoking from habit. What originates and maintains a problem may also differ from what *exacerbates* it; for example, stress may rekindle a smoking habit in somebody who previously had stopped.

Another factor in causation is *predisposition* (or risk). At the present time this concept is generally cast in terms of a susceptibility gene or set of genes that becomes activated under certain stressors or conditions, such as exposure to a microbe, toxin, antigen, emotional trauma, irradiation, or an injurious physical environment.

Many mechanisms might lead to a pathological cascade of gene expression or biological transformation that leads to a complex and highly pleiotropic phenotype such as the phenomenon we observe clinically as "schizophrenia." While we observe from clinical histories that schizophrenia takes place over time, there are data to support the idea that the disease process may be initiated as early in development as prenatally or within the first trimester of development. Several lines of evidence point to and support this hypothesis, which is aptly called the *neurodevelopmental hypothesis*. Many experimental animal models have shown that insults of many types during this early period of neurodevelopment can lead to aberrant gene expression and subsequently abnormal brain development and brain function later in life. In a recently published epidemiological study of children born in Denmark from 1955 to 1975, a higher incidence of schizophrenia was found in those born by mothers who had lost a first-degree relative in their first trimester. It is not known whether an emotional trauma in itself leads to other pathological events that start the cascade toward schizophrenia. It seems likely that such a pathological insult acts through known mechanisms such as hypoxia, hypoglycemia or hyperglycemia, hypercortisolemia, alcohol or drug-induced brain injury, malnutrition, hippocampal maldevelopment (as in primary seizure disorder), and many others.

A predisposition may be "disorder-*specific*" (e.g., a gene producing a vulnerability to a particular disorder) or "disorder-*nonspecific*" (e.g., broken families during childhood produce a vulnerability to many mental disorders). When determining causation, clinicians should be careful to delineate these four levels (the 4 **P**'s): predisposition, initiation (precipitation), exacerbation (provocation). and perpetuation. Many theories of mental illness are originally proposed as initial causes of a disorder, whereas subsequent data indicate that these theories are more relevant to what maintains (perpetuates) or aggravates (provokes) a disorder.

> For instance, the hypothesis that "double-bind communication" causes schizophrenia has been largely refuted, yet growing evidence shows that double-bind communication and high-expressed emotion in the environment can trigger a relapse to psychotic symptoms with about the same likelihood as discontinuing medication (Hogarty et al., 1974). An example of double-bind communication would be "for a fat kid, you are pretty good looking."

Clinicians should also distinguish between what is *inherent* to a disorder and what is a *consequence* of it. Both factors feed into one another and may profoundly affect the patient. The importance of this distinction becomes apparent by carefully examining the sequence of events. For example, one may presume that a job loss caused a severe depression, whereas a careful history demonstrates that the patient's depressive symptoms of low energy, indecisiveness, and poor concentration caused the job loss. Causes can be categorized as (1) necessary and sufficient, (2) necessary but not sufficient, or (3) facilitating or predisposing but neither necessary nor sufficient.

Few diseases have causes that are necessary and sufficient; one example is Huntington's chorea, a progressive and fatal dementia, in which having the autosomal dominant genetic mutation of the *huntingtin* gene on chromosome 4 is all that is needed to produce the illness. Alcoholism illustrates the second type; although alcohol is necessary for the disorder, other factors are required to produce it, since not everyone who drinks becomes an alcoholic. These other factors may include stressful environments and comorbid predisposing genes, such as the short-form allele of the serotonin transporter promotor gene, which also predisposes to anxiety (Herman et al., 2003). Many causes fall into the third category; for example, loss of parents during childhood or physical or sexual abuse in childhood may contribute to psychopathology later in life. Such events are neither necessary nor sufficient, however, to produce the psychopathology we may observe in clinical settings. Conversely, the harmful effects of a disorder may be reduced or prevented by rectifying the facilitating or predisposing causes (e.g., poverty, stress), even when they are not necessary or sufficient causes. And we must remember that there are very likely protective factors that lend remarkable resilience or even relative immunity from some disorders in some individuals in spite of traumatic events or harsh environments.

Because mental disorders have multiple rather than singular causes, and because some of these causes are facilitating or predisposing, *multicausality* has been misconstrued as *omnicausality*: that is, anything can cause anything, as long as there is a tenuous connection. If a passive father has a schizophrenic son, then passive fathers are deemed a cause of schizophrenia. This line of thinking is nonsense; it's like saying that milk is a cause of schizophrenia because a person with schizophrenia drank milk. Omnicausality falters because it equates a *casual* with a *causal* association between two events—a confusion that can only be clarified by studying the matter with scientific *controls* (Goodwin & Guze, 1989).

Some diagnostic categories, such as schizophrenia, consist of not one but several psychiatric entities that all share similar cardinal features. The entities may be defined by the most prominent symptom, as in the various *subtypes* of schizophrenia (paranoid, catatonic, etc.). Each subtype may involve different etiological factors. Conversely, entities that present with the same clinical picture may have arisen via different etiological routes. For instance, genetics clearly produces some depressions, but not others; many antihypertensive medications induce some major depressions, bereavement triggers others, and "learned helplessness" causes others. The reason these depressions may present with the same symptoms is because, no matter what their origins, at some point a specific series of changes was launched within the brain—that is, a "final common pathway" that produced the characteristic symptoms of major depression.

Symptoms and *issues*, although related, are of a different order. Symptoms may be reported such as hallucinations or insomnia, whereas issues contain the meaning of symptoms and reflect how patients cope, how they feel toward authorities, and so on (see Chapter 1).

For 15 years a middle-aged man occasionally had the delusion that people were sneaking itching powder into his food. Since his divorce of 20 years ago, homosexual urges had frightened him. When he felt close to another man—or to use his words, "got the itch for somebody"—his delusion would arise. The man's symptom was a delusion; many patients have delusions. The man's issues about itching powder and homosexuals were idiosyncratic; they derived from his life experience, were symbolically meaningful to him, and erupted in circumstances stressful for him.

Symptoms have *form* whereas issues have *content*. For instance, two patients may present with major depression; both complain of severe guilt, hopelessness, and insomnia. Their symptoms are the same, yet their issues vary. The first patient, a young, successful TV executive, insists that her sleeplessness stems from her being "a total failure," while the second, a retired Baptist postal clerk, is sure his sleeplessness is a punishment from God. Both patients suffer from the biologically induced insomnia of major depression. Yet the issues the patients bring to their insomnia— that is, what it means to them and how they deal with it—differ according to their life experiences.

In general, biology determines symptoms and psychosocial influences shape issues. How a particular patient expresses signs and symptoms of a mental disorder greatly depends on his or her personalty traits and biological constitution. When drunk or "stoned," some people may giggle, some babble, some dance, some cry, some withdraw, some get the munchies, and others become violent. They all have a drug-induced mental state, yet how it manifests varies according to the individual's constitutional traits. The same holds for medical illness. For example, coronary patients cope with heart attacks in many different ways depending on their personality. Arthur Kleinman (1988) makes a similar distinction for all medical disorders: There is a *disease* that may be caused by a virus, bacteria, etc., with *symptoms*, such as fever and abdominal pain; and there is the *illness* and with it, *illness behavior*—going to a doctor, having a shaman exorcise the demon, or trying to make spiritual sense out of the fever-induced hallucinations.

Like intoxication, mental disorders tend to amplify personality traits. During a major depression, a lifelong worry-wart frets nonstop, a chronically suspicious man becomes paranoid, and a mild hypochondriac becomes a severe one. Consequently, the cause of a patient's behavior can never be fully attributed to either psychology *or* biology. Both are responsible for behavior, albeit in different ways—a truism recognized long ago by Hughlings Jackson, the Father of English neurology: "There is no physiology of the mind anymore than there is a psychology of the nervous system." As long as people have minds *and* brains, it is hard to imagine how one could function without the other!

Given that mental disorders neither overpower personality nor make it disappear, being mentally ill or taking LSD, PCP, or alcohol neither explains nor justifies committing antisocial acts. Mental illness is no excuse for bad manners. Statements such as "Peter beat up Sally because he was drunk" or "Darlene's schizophrenia caused her to drown her child" imply that the patient/criminal is not responsible for the act, as if the drug or the mental illness *made* him or her commit the crime. Being schizophrenic *per se* does not make one violent. Being acutely psychotic may diminish normal social restraints or magnify preexisting violent tendencies, but that's quite different from dissociating the person from his or her crime by totally blaming the illness. It is akin to the old defense, "The devil made me do it."

Volition

"Volition" refers to the act of willing. How much a patient "wills" or determines his or her behavior during a mental disorder may be difficult to discern. The first question is "Can people fake mental illness?" The answer is "Yes, but not for long." If there are any doubts, try it! Actors can fake madness for 3 hours a night and twice on Wednesdays and Saturdays, but not much longer. Only those with mental disorders can pace for hours, shadow-box for days, and dwell on rotting bladders and stinking bowels. It's too exhausting to sustain. Nor can one hallucinate at will, except with the help of certain chemicals or a sensory-isolation chamber.

Nevertheless, the question of people faking mental illness stubbornly persists, partly because some patients seem to respond to the environment according to what's "convenient" or "necessary." When clinicians must decide whether to permit a floridly psychotic inpatient to attend the funeral of a loved one, they find that most patients pull themselves together, go to the funeral, and do just fine. How come? Because, like the intoxicated, the mentally ill can still modify their behavior depending on the situation and the severity of their illnesses. When a tipsy student receives a telephone call from his parents, he can "get his act together," as long as the call is not too long and he is not too drunk. Likewise, if they are not too ill and not required to act "properly" for too long, people with mental illness are often able to "normalize" their behavior. Therefore, highly disturbed psychiatric patients are not helpless automatons, for they can exert some control over their disorder.

Conversely, just as being intoxicated makes it extremely difficult to perform routine tasks, so does being mentally ill. Like everyone else, people with mental illness must contend with problems in living, but unlike everyone else, they must do so with the added burdens of psychiatric symptoms. Interviewing for a job is hard enough; feeling certain that the interviewer is Satan doesn't help. Writing a term paper can be stressful, but imagine trying to do so with racing thoughts and taunting hallucinations. Mental illness makes everything harder. Simple chit-chat isn't easy when you're sure a bomb is going to explode in your stomach. Given all their symptoms, what amazes many clinicians is not how poorly people with mental illness do, but how well.

Explaining versus Understanding

In the formulation the clinician should seek to understand as well as to explain the patient's difficulties. Unfortunately, many clinicians are unaware of the difference between "explaining" and "understanding." In this context, *understanding* is not being used in the *explanatory* sense of "I understand *why* Jim hates his mother," but rather in the *descriptive* sense of "I understand *how* Jim hates his mother."

To explain something is to view it from the outside; to understand it is to view from within. Explaining relies on logic and intellect, understanding on experience and empathy. Explanations should be objective, whereas understandings can only be subjective. Explanations address the "why" of behavior, understanding, the "what." For different reasons, both explaining and understanding are crucial for clinical care. One is not better than the other; they are simply different.

Clinicians often say they are understanding (*verstehen*) when actually they are explaining (*erklaren*). Consider Karen, a psychiatric inpatient who was convinced she had no legs. When her psychiatrist went on vacation, she walked up to the staff and complained, more intensely than ever, of having no legs. Every time this occurred, her substitute therapist replied, "You're walking, so that proves that you have legs. But even so, you're obviously worried about having no legs because your doctor is on vacation." Karen was infuriated; she claimed that the staff "doesn't understand me." The staff responded, "But we do understand: Your psychiatrist has gone away, and you're understandably upset." Patient and staff were talking past each other. The patient accurately felt that she was being "explained away." The staff mistakenly believed that they were showing understanding, when they were actually giving a correct explanation. Another psychiatrist demonstrated empathic understanding when he said to Karen, "You must feel like a paraplegic. It's frightening to feel you have no control over your legs, or that they don't work properly, or that they don't belong to you. No wonder you're upset!" Feeling that somebody was finally on her "wavelength," Karen was ready to consider the explanation about her therapist's absence.

It's not that clinicians never understand their patients; to various degrees, they all do. Yet to the degree that clinicians do understand, it's more a product of their being *people* than of their being *professionals*. Therapists are inherently no better or worse than anyone else at understanding people. Indeed, a good novelist reveals a thorough understanding of a character's psychology without using a single psychological term. The ability to understand can be improved with experience and training, but it doesn't originate in the reading of books or articles.

In contrast, by learning etiological theory, clinicians are far more adept at explaining behavior. They can learn how the unconscious does this and how the id does that; they can learn how the brain's chemicals affect this and how the person's environment affects that. Both explanation and understanding are important, and both belong in the formulation. The following sections introduce explanatory theories, since they, unlike understandings, lend themselves to didactic presentations.

Neurons and Neurotransmitters

The fundamental unit of biologically derived behavior is the nerve cell or *neuron*. The brain has at least 100 billion neurons; each neuron consists of a microscopic *cell body* (or "head") that trails off into an *axon* (or "tail") with an extremely narrow width but a length of up to several inches or feet. By definition, axons transmit electrical impulses *away* from the cell body, whereas *dendrites* transmit them *toward* it. Electrical impulses originate in cell bodies and run through these axons, until they are conveyed to hundreds, or even thousands, of other nerve cells.

Although in very close proximity, neurons are anatomically separate from one another. Therefore, to reach a nearby neuron, electrical impulses do not travel over continuous tissue, but flow across the spaces between neurons. As illustrated in Figure 4-1, this passage is accomplished by chemicals called *neurotransmitters*, which transmit messages over these tiny spaces called *synaptic clefts*.

Neurotransmitters are synthesized inside the neuron and actively transported to the axon's end or *presynaptic terminal*; from here, neurotransmitters "swim" (diffuse) across the synaptic cleft and bind onto *receptors* that are located on the surface (membrane) of adjacent dendrites or cell bodies. By doing so, neurotransmitters can trigger or inhibit the receptor's ability to fire. The nerve cell acts like a wet sponge: When it fires, it releases its fluids of neurotransmitters; when not firing, it expands and reabsorbs them.

Whether a nerve cell fires mainly depends on the quantity and arrangement of neurotransmitters reaching its receptors at any instant. Other deter-

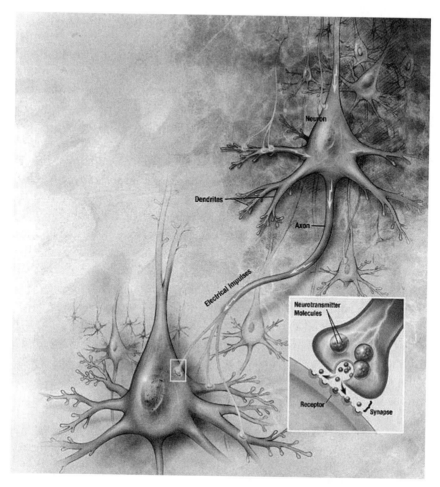

FIGURE 4-1
The Neuron, Synapse, and Neurotransmitters
National Institutes of Health

mining factors include (1) variations in the rate of synthesis and release of a neurotransmitters from the first cell; (2) increases and decreases in the sensitivity and numbers of the receptors on the second cell; and (3) inhibition of the first cell's ability to reabsorb neurotransmitters, thereby increasing their concentration at the second cell's receptors. Drugs also exert effects. In pharmacology, *agonists* are substances that enhance or potentiate the firing of a neuron, whereas *antagonists* are drugs that block or reduce the effects of an agonist.

Many types of receptors have been discovered, including some for benzodiazepines, marijuana, and opiates. Endorphins, opiate-like peptides synthesized in the brain, bind to opiate receptors to mediate the perception of pain. The jogger's "high" has been attributed to a buildup of these endorphins. Most receptors are affected by one type (or subtype) of neurotransmitter. Symptoms of mental disorders appear to arise from changes in these receptor–neurotransmitter systems. The most influential neurotransmitters and their receptor properties are discussed further in Chapter 6 and include dopamine, norepinephrine, serotonin, acetylcholine, glutamate, gamma-aminobutyric acid, and endorphins. Dopamine and norepinephrine are *catecholamines*; serotonin is an *indoleamine*. Table 4-1 lists the major neurotransmitters and their primary precursors (major chemical antecedents), primary metabolites (major breakdown product), and brain source.

Although a great deal more research is needed before it is clear how neurotransmitters contribute to mental disorders, some of the more widely touted hypotheses are as follows: Schizophrenia seems to involve excessive activity in the dopamine receptor systems. The "catecholamine hypothesis" of depression holds that a functional underactivity of norepinephrine causes severe depression, whereas a functional overactivity of this neurotransmitter causes mania. Other theories contend that depression stems from a high ratio of acetylcholine to catecholamine (e.g., dopamine or norepinephrine), whereas mania erupts with the ratio reversed. Sleep and perhaps mood are affected by changes in the serotonin receptor system. When stimulated, GABA receptors inhibit neurons and induce calm; thus, anxiety increases when this system becomes less active. Abrupt opiate (and sometimes tobacco) withdrawal apparently accelerates the firing of norepinephrine from the *locus coeruleus*—a densely populated area of neurons that produces most of this neurotransmitter. Theories are many, and continually growing as to basis of mental disorders.

Psychoneuroendocrinology

The field of *psychoneuroendocrinology* studies the influence of hormones in the central nervous system and, as such, seeks to explain their interrelationships with receptors, neurotransmitters, and the resultant functioning (thoughts, motivations, emotions, and behaviors). Unlike neurotransmitters, which act close to their locus of origin, *hormones* are produced by glands, secreted into the bloodstream, and often act far away from their locus of origin. Until recently, psychoneuroendocrinology focused on hormonal actions outside the brain. Now, more sophisticated technologies have made it possible to study the *pituitary*, a "window" into the brain, by examining how neurotransmitters, hormones, and the brain interact to produce mental disorders.

The *hypothalamus* is located directly above the pituitary gland; considerable psychoendocrine activity transpires along this "hypothalamic–pituitary

TABLE 4-1
Neurotransmitters: Precursors, Metabolites, and Origins

NEUROTRANSMITTER	PRIMARY PRECURSORS	PRIMARY METABOLITES	PRIMARY ORIGINS
Dopamine (DA)	Tyrosine → L-DOPA → DA	Homovanillic acid (HVA)	Nucleus accumbens, ventral tegmental area, hypothalamus, substantia nigra
Norepinephrine (NE)	Tyrosine → L-DOPA → DA → NE	Methoxyhydroxy-phenyl-glycol (MHPG)	Locus coeruleus, lateral tegmental field
Serotonin (5-HT)	Tryptophan → 5 hydroxy L tryptophan (5-HTP) → 5-HT	5-Hydroxyindole-acetic acid(5-HIAA)	Raphe nuclei
Acetylcholine (Ach)	Choline + Acetyl-CoA → Ach	Choline, acetate	Pontomesencephalo-tegmental complex, basal optic nucleus of Meynert, and medial septal nucleus
Gamma-aminobutyric acid (GABA)	Glutamate → GABA	Succinate	All levels of CNS, including hypothalamus, hippocampus, cerebral cortex, and cerebellar cortex
Glutamate (Glu)	Glutamine → Glu	α-Ketoglutarate	Cortex, thalamus, basal ganglia, amygdala, hippocampus
Histamine (H)	Histidine → H	Histidine	Posterior hypothalamus, various tubero-mammillary nuclei
Endorphins	Pro-opiomelanocortin (POMC) → endorphin + ACTH	Inactive peptides	Pituitary, hypothalamus

axis." For example, the biological or vegetative signs of depression (e.g., disturbances in sleep, appetite, sex) are partially mediated in the hypothalamus, the chief connecting station where neurotransmitters and hormones affect each other. An underactive thyroid can cause depression, and too much thyroid hormone can induce depression, mania, or psychosis. Conversely, during cases of major depression and anxiety disorders, the adrenal glands may release ex-

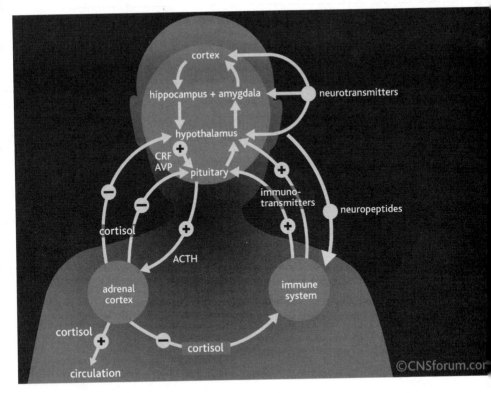

FIGURE 4-2
Hypothalamic–Pituitary–Adrenal Axis

cessive amounts of cortisol. The amygdala, which plays an important role in mediating emotional states (anxiety, fear) and emotional aspects of memory, is also intimately connected with the hypothalamus. Figure 4-2 traces the hypothalamic–pituitary–adrenal pathway.

Technology and Etiology

Throughout history, etiological knowledge has been only as advanced as the methods available to study it. For example, psychodynamic etiologies have always reflected the patients and the society that were investigated. Freud revealed the pathogenic power of repressed sexuality in a sexually repressive society; Jung's patients were not sexually inhibited but religiously troubled, and his theories focused on philosophical, cosmic, and religious themes. Adler, not surprisingly, uncovered the inferiority complex when dealing with ambitious, middle-class patients (Wender & Klein, 1981).

More recently, an explosion in biomedical technology has uncovered alterations in the brain's anatomy, chemistry, and physiology that were previously undetectable. Introduced in 1973, *computerized tomography* (CT) provides a two-dimensional anatomical image by contrasting the specific gravities of various brain tissue. Even newer is *magnetic resonance imaging* (MRI), in which images reflect the chemical properties of tissues by measuring the resonances of a particular atom (e.g., phosphorus) within those tissues. At present, functional MRI (fMRI) can help to correlate metabolic defects with behavior, and unlike the CT scan, it can more accurately distinguish brain tissues (e.g., white matter vs. gray matter, a tumor vs. normal brain tissue, a multiple sclerosis plaque vs. white matter). *Positron emission tomography* (PET) measures the metabolic activity of a compound (e.g., glucose) at various sites in the brain. By labeling a psychotropic drug, such as haloperidol, PET can measure the number and alterations of dopamine receptors. Magnetic resonance spectroscopy (MRS) can measure local variations in molecular species important to metabolism of neurotransmitters. Magnetic encephalography (MEG) can map magnetic field variations. Electroencephalography (EEG) mapping is also useful.

This new tecnology is helping to invalidate the traditional Cartesian distinction between *organic* and *functional* disorders by demonstrating that many "functional" disorders involve changes in fine neuronal tissues and in cerebral ventricles; altered glucose metabolism and neurochemical changes are also coming to light. Because the organic–functional distinction has little basis in fact, *DSM-IV-TR* has dropped this distinction.

Environmental Biology

"Environmental biology," our neologism, might be described as the study of the two-way relationship between environment and biology in the production of mental disorders. Three of these relationships deserve comment: (1) biological effects from the environment, (2) psychosocial trauma-inducing biological changes, and (3) genotypes and phenotypes.

Biological Effects from the Environment

Environmental stress and psychosocial stress are *not* synonymous, since the environment can also generate biological stress. Conditions during pregnancy and afterward, viruses, drugs, malnourishment, physical abuse, or premature birth may produce mental disorders in children or, at least, predispose them to one. For example, in comparison to normals, people with schizophrenia have a higher rate of birth complications.

Light—both natural and artificial—appears to be another biological (or physical) force, the absence of which contributes to mental disorders. Patients with seasonal mood disorders may become depressed every fall and winter and recover every spring and summer. These patients' depressions improve with prolonged exposure to bright artificial light. The antidepressant effect of light is given further credence by the finding that people are more likely to have depressions the farther they live from the equator (Rosenthal et al., 1984).

Psychosocial Trauma-Inducing Biological Changes

Biological changes do not necessarily have biological origins; they may be generated psychosocially. Kandel (1983), for instance, has demonstrated how environmental stress can alter the brain's anatomy and biochemistry to produce avoidance behavior (a model of anxiety). He uses the marine snail *Aplysia* in his research, because it has a relatively simple nervous system with large and easy-to-visualize brain cells. (The *Aplysia* weighs up to 4 pounds, consists of only 20,000 cells, and has the largest neurons in the animal kingdom—up to 1 mm in diameter. Whereas a simple human behavior typically involves hundreds of thousands of brain cells, simple behaviors of an *Aplysia* involve less than 50.) By conditioning the *Aplysia* and then photographing its neurons, Kandel recorded the actual anatomical changes in a brain cell caused by a specific stressful environment.

> The brain matures in interaction with the environment, and, once developed, it continues to be influenced by the environment. Being continually unable to cope—"learned helplessness"—can induce biological changes resulting in depression. As another example, patients with advanced Parkinson's disease who can hardly walk will nonetheless race to the exit if they are in a movie theater that catches on fire. They *do* have brain disease, yet how their diseased brains functions depends on the environment.

Genotypes and Phenotypes

Having a gene, and having it produce visible effects, are two different things. The gene structure itself is the *genotype*; how this gene is expressed—that is, if it becomes manifest—is the *phenotype*. If there is a gene (or genotype) for an ulcer, whether it develops into an ulcer (the phenotype) depends on environmental factors such as diet, stress, infection, and smoking. Because of this interrelationship, to ask whether a mental disorder is caused by genes *or* environment is naive. When a person inherits the genotype for a mental disorder, how the person's environment affects that gene determines the degree, form, and existence of the disorder. Genetic theory is not equivalent with behavioral predestination. If a person inherits the genotype for a mental disorder, other "protective" genes or biological and psychosocial interventions can still alleviate or prevent it.

The Genetics of Mental Disorders

Genetic factors are prerequisites for most, but certainly not all, cases of schizophrenia and manic–depression, and somewhat less, for major depression. Heredity partly contributes to panic and obsessive–compulsive disorders, but appears to be less implicated in generalized anxiety disorders. These conclusions derive mainly from research on twins and adoptees.

Twin Studies

By comparing identical or *monozygotic* (MZ) twins with fraternal or *dizygotic* (DZ) twins, investigators attempt to assess the relative contributions of nature and nurture in causing certain mental disorders. Identical twins have identical genes; the genes of fraternal twins are like those of any other pair of siblings. A *concordance rate* for a phenotype is the percent of twins who both exhibit the same phenotype. Because MZ and DZ twins usually share a similar environment, the difference in concordance rates between MZ and DZ twins largely reflects genetic influences.

For example, on average the concordance rate for schizophrenia among MZ twins averages 45%; this means that when one twin of an MZ pair has schizophrenia, 45% of the time the other twin does also. In contrast, DZ twin-pairs have a concordance rate of about 10% for schizophrenia. (If one sibling has schizophrenia, other siblings have a 10% chance of developing schizophrenia.) The statistically significant difference between 45% and 10% suggests that genes transmit schizophrenia. At the same time, these figures also demonstrate an important role for nongenetic factors. If genes alone were involved, one would expect a 100% concordance rate; that is, if one member of an MZ pair had schizophrenia, then the twin would also have schizophrenia. But it's not; it's only about 45%.

Geneticists attribute this 55% difference to *penetrance*, a term used to account for why the genotype does not become the phenotype 100% of the time. Penetrance may occur because the abnormal genes were too weak to express or were impeded by other genes; spontaneous genetic mutations, viral infections, and in utero difficulties may also explain penetrance.

Concordance rates of identical twins might be altered if they were treated differently from fraternal twins. However, two findings do not support this contention. First, MZ twins who were physically dissimilar showed the same concordance rates as those who looked the same. Second, identical twins who grew up with everybody (themselves included) assuming that they were fraternal twins showed concordance rates of identical twins.

Adoption Studies

To further clarify the nature–nurture question, various studies of adoptions have been conducted. The first major adoption studies of mental disorders occurred in 1963. They were conducted in Denmark, because the government had a register of every adoption, including those infants who were separated from their biological parents when less than 3 months old and then legally adopted.

As illustrated in Figure 4-3, one method of using these records for research purposes is to compare the biological and adoptive parents of adult adoptees with schizophrenia. Because biological parents gave away the child so early in life, their psychosocial influence on the adoptee with schizophrenia was probably nil; only genetic influences would persist. Therefore, if schizophrenia were genetically transmitted, the biological parents should have a much higher incidence of schizophrenia than the adoptive parents. On the other hand, if

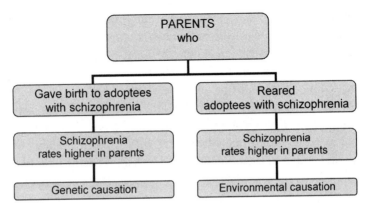

FIGURE 4-3
Comparison of Schizophrenia Frequency between Biological and Adoptive Parents

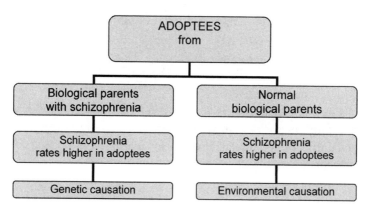

FIGURE 4-4
Comparison of Schizophrenia Frequency between Adoptees

schizophrenia were produced psychosocially, just the opposite should occur. The results were striking: Repeatedly, the adoptee's biological parents were schizophrenic, whereas the adoptive parents were "normal."

In another adoption strategy (Figure 4-4), children of biological parents with schizophrenia were reared by adoptive parents and contrasted to a matched control group of adoptees whose biological parents had no family history of mental disorders. Once again, genetic interpretations prevailed, since schizophrenia-like disorders were far more common among the offspring of parents with schizophrenia than among those of "normal" parents. These and similar findings have provided overwhelming evidence that genetic factors play a major role in the etiology of schizophrenia.

Subsequent research has suggested that what is genetically transmitted may not be a single gene for schizophrenia, but a gene, or genes, for "schizophrenia-spectrum disorders." Besides schizophrenia, this spectrum may include several disorders that are similar, but not identical to, schizophrenia, such as the schizotypal personality and schizoaffective disorders. Similarly, the concept of *genetic spectrum disorders* also may apply to other syndromes. For example, investigators are pursuing genes for "depressive-spectrum disorders," which may contribute to the etiology of major depression, bipolar disorder, substance dependence, and anxiety disorders.

Finally, even when genes are implicated, this concept of spectrum disorders underscores the need to specify *what* is being inherited. Is it a predisposition to one disorder or to a number of possible disorders? Is it a particular trait, such as shyness or the inability to synthesize information? Or is it a vulnerability to certain psychosocial stressors, such as a chaotic family life, loss, or intense emotions? Some of these answers may involve psychosocial influences.

Psychosocial Theories

Numerous psychological and social factors influence the course of a mental disorder, and the many ways in which they do so can be divided into seven general models: developmental, defense mechanisms, intrapsychic conflict, stress, behavioral, family systems, and sociocultural.

> Some important models are not mentioned partly because their direct application to diagnostic psychopathology has (as yet) been limited. These include (1) the *existential* model, which focuses on the purpose and meaning of life, (2) the *humanistic* model, which concentrates on fulfilling or actualizing one's potential, (3) Piaget's *cognitive* model, which portrays the stages of development of a child's thought processes, and (4) Kohlberg's *moral* development model, which applies the stages of cognitive development to moral reasoning.

Developmental Models

Three developmental models are of particular etiological significance: Freud's *psychosexual*, Erikson's *psychosocial*, and Bowlby's *attachment* models. Each model presents a series of overlapping stages (or "passages") and claims that an "arrest" or "crisis" at any stage may induce associated psychopathology. A developmental *crisis* is not a catastrophe or an emergency; it is the normal developmental challenge posed by each psychosocial stage, which becomes a "necessary turning point, a crucial moment, when development must move one way or another, marshalling resources of growth, recovery, and further differentiation" (Erikson, 1968, p. 16). One stage builds upon the previous (epigenetic), and regressions to an earlier stage of functioning may occur. Since each stage provides a new perspective that is foundational for the next, it is not possible to skip ahead. It is not expected that one would function at the highest achieved stage at all times. Sometimes psychopathology represents completely aberrant development versus delays or arrest of normal developmental stages. Successful interventions assist the patient in getting "unstuck" or onto the normal developmental trajectory. Tables 4-2 and 4-3 outline the psychosexual and psychosocial models of development respectively.

Bowlby considered "attachment behaviors" to be those observable actions of a child that facilitate closeness to the primary caregiver, usually the biologi-

TABLE 4-2

Freudian Psychosexual Development

AGE (years)	STAGE	RESOLUTION SUCCESSFUL	PATHOLOGICAL
0-1	ORAL Primary gratification from mouth, lips, and tongue	Self-reliance; self-trust; trust in others; capacity to give and receive without dependence and envy	Needy; demanding; dependent on others for self-esteem; pathological optimism or pessimism; jealousy; immature and image distorting [narcissistic]*
1-3	ANAL Primary gratification from sphincter control; aggressive, sadistic, and libidinal impulses	Autonomy; independence; capacity to cooperate	Excessive orderliness, stubbornness, and willfulness; miserly; heightened ambivalence; obsessive-compulsive [immature and neurotic]
3-6	PHALLIC Primary gratification from genital area; oedipal issues	Basis for sexual identity; drives constructively redirected; superego established	Castration fear in boys, penis envy in girls; failure to identify with same-sexed parent; neurotic disorders [neurotic]
6-12	LATENCY Relative quiescent sexual drives	Integration and consolidation of prior psychosexual gains; basis for love, work, and play	Lack of, or excessive, inner controls; poor sublimation; precociousness; premature closure of personality; neurotic disorders [neurotic]
12-18	GENITAL Reawakening of libidinal drives; sexual maturation	Full and satisfying genital potency; consolidation of prior accomplishments [mature]	Any of the above problems; impaired ability to love and work; neurotic disorders [neurotic]

*The general class of defense mechanisms, as categorized by Perry and Cooper (1989), Vaillant (1971), and Vaillant et al. (1986), is shown in brackets. (See specific defenses in Table 4-4.)

cal mother. In theory, this attachment behavior serves the evolutionary purpose of protecting the child from predators. "Maternal bonding" refers to the mother's attachment to the child. Disturbances in attachment and bonding may produce insecurity, anxiety, dysthymia, distrust, fear of loneliness, etc. A significant loss during childhood, usually of a parent, may be of special etiological significance, especially in depression (Gardner et al., 2005).

TABLE 4-3
Eriksonian Psychosocial Development

AGE (years)	PERIOD	TASKS	VALUES
0-1	Infancy	Trust vs. mistrust	Hope
1-3	Toddler	Autonomy vs. shame	Will and doubt
3-6	Preschool	Initiative vs. guilt	Purpose
6-12	School-age	Industry vs. inferiority	Skill and competence
12-20	Adolescence	Identity vs. identity diffusion/confusion	Fidelity
20-30	Young adulthood	Intimacy vs. isolation	Love
30-65	Adulthood	Generativity vs. stagnation	Care
65+	Late adulthood	Integrity vs. despair/disgust	Wisdom

Development does not stop with adolescence; it continues through life. The patient's presenting problems may result not only from an immediate precipitant, but also from a phase-of-life, or developmental, crisis. A 40-year-old man may be fired and develop acute, overwhelming anxiety. Losing his job is clearly the primary precipitant, yet why he was fired and why he is *that* devastated may be secondary to a "midlife (psychosocial) crisis."

Intrapsychic Conflict

Freud divided the *topography* of the mind into three levels: the *unconscious*, whose mental content is rarely in awareness; the *preconscious*, the mental content of which is not immediately in awareness, but can be readily recalled by conscious effort; and the *conscious*, the mental content of which is in awareness. Freud also proposed three psychic *structures*: the *id*, which harbors instinctual sexual and aggressive drives; the *superego* or conscience; and the *ego*, which mediates between these psychic structures and between the person's inner needs and the environment. Defense mechanisms are ego functions. Intrapsychic conflict involves struggles between these various levels and structures of the mind. Although the Freudian structural model is an attempt to "understand" complex inner workings of mental life, as shared by a particular patient, it falls short of objectively "explaining" those workings. Despite being rather vague and abstract, it is an empirical and practical tool that can, when carefully employed, assist patients in understanding and managing their suffering.

Defense Mechanisms

Sometimes called "coping mechanisms," defense mechanisms are relatively involuntary patterns of feelings, thoughts, or behaviors that arise in response to a perceived internal or external psychic danger in order to reduce or avoid conscious or unconscious stress, anxiety, or conflict. Whether a defense mechanism is adaptive depends on the defense and the circumstance. For example, projection is generally not adaptive, whereas sublimation is generally adaptive; denial is usually maladaptive, but when the person is dealing with an overwhelming, acute stress, denial may help to maintain psychic equilibrium. Table 4-4 describes the major defense mechanisms and categorizes them from the least to the most mature: "immature," "image-distorting," "neurotic (intermediate)," and "mature." Immature and image-distorting defenses are primitive and usually pathological.

Stress

The body's response to any demand for adaptation is called *stress*, and the demand, a *stressor*. By itself, stress is neither good nor bad: Without stress, people stagnate or atrophy; with too much stress, however, they become overwhelmed. A stressor can be acute or chronic. When it is acute and severe, people react in a series of steps, as depicted in Figure 4-5; these reactions may be normal or pathological, but even when normal, they may temporarily impair functioning. One need only recall the morning the Challenger exploded or 9/11 to remember how most people immediately reacted with either "outcry" or "denial." Chronic stressors, such as a failing marriage, though less severe at any one moment, may eventually "wear a person down" and lead to a deteriorating mental state.

Behavioral

Traditionally, the behavioral (or learning) model focused exclusively on how identifiable environmental forces influence the production of observable behaviors. This model has expanded to include "inner behaviors" that are environmentally induced, yet nonobservable, such as thoughts and feelings. Cognitive–behavioral and rational–emotive therapy approaches use this expanded model, and some behaviorists are attempting to integrate psychodynamic with behavioral principles. Even still, behaviorism focuses on how the environment creates, shapes, changes, or alters the frequency of a behavior. A behavioral formulation would indicate whether the patient's difficulties are/

TABLE 4-4
Defense Mechanisms

Acting-out is the direct expression of impulses without any apparent reflection, guilt, or regard for negative consequences. Whereas "acting-*up*" is a lay term for misbehavior, acting-*out* is a misbehavior that is a response to, and a way of coping with, stress or conflict. After breaking up with his girlfriend, a teenager acts-out by impulsively overdosing. [Immature]

Altruism is demonstrated when people dedicate themselves to the needs of others, partly to fulfill their own needs. [Mature]

Denial is the lack of awareness of *external* realities that would be too painful to acknowledge. It differs from repression (see below), which is a denial of *internal* reality. Denial operates when a woman says, "I'm sure this lump in my breast doesn't mean anything." [Immature] Denial may be temporarily adaptive or more extreme and pathological. For example, the same woman says, "I don't really have a lump in my breast." [Image-distorting]

Devaluation is the demeaning of another or oneself by the attribution of exaggerated negative qualities. By constantly ridiculing his competence, a patient devalues a therapist to avoid facing her sexual feelings toward him. [Image-distorting]

Displacement is the discharge of pent-up emotions, usually anger, onto objects, animals, or people perceived as less dangerous than those that originally induced the emotions. A man comes home after a bad day at work and kicks the dog. [Neurotic]

Fantasy is the excessive retreat into daydreams and imagination to escape problems or to avoid conflicts (also called "autistic fantasy" or "schizoid fantasy"). [Immature]

Humor is the use of irony or amusing, incongruous, or absurd associations to reduce what otherwise might be unbearable tension or fear. An example: the character of Hawkeye Pierce in M*A*S*H, or Seinfeld. [Mature]

Idealization is the unwarranted praise of another or oneself by exaggerating virtues. "Better" to idealize a spouse than to see the jerk for what he is and be a very lonely divorcée. [Image-distorting]

Identification is the unconscious modeling of another's attributes. It differs from role modeling and imitation, which are conscious processes. Identification is used to increase one's sense of self-worth, to cope with (possible) separation or loss, or to minimize helplessness, as with "identification with the aggressor," as seen in prisoners who may assume the mannerisms of their guards. [Immature]

Intellectualization is the overuse of abstract thinking, which, unlike rationalization (see below), is self-serving only in its aim to reduce psychic discomfort. Alcoholics use intellectualization when they quibble over the definition of alcoholism as a way of avoiding their drinking problem. [Neurotic]

Introjection is the incorporation of other people's values, standards, or traits to prevent conflicts with, or threats from, these people. Introjection may also help a person retain a sense of connection to a lost loved one, as when people adopted John Kennedy's accent after his death. [Immature]

Isolation of affect is the compartmentalization of painful emotions from the events associated with them, thus allowing the experience or recollection of an emotionally traumatic situation, without the anxiety customarily or originally experienced. A soldier may kill without experiencing the terror or guilt he would otherwise feel. [Neurotic]

TABLE 4-4
Continued

Projection is the unconscious rejection of unacceptable thoughts, traits, or wishes by ascribing them to others. [Image-distorting when delusional; immature otherwise]

Rationalization is the self-serving use of plausible reasons to justify actions caused by repressed, unacceptable emotions or ideas. Psychotherapist: "I charge a high fee so that therapy will be meaningful to the patient." [Neurotic]

Reaction formation prevents the expression or experience of unacceptable desires by developing or exaggerating opposite attitudes and behaviors. "The lady doth protest too much." [Neurotic]

Regression is retreat under stress to earlier or more immature patterns of behavior and gratification. On hearing terrible news, an adult begins sucking his thumb. [Immature]

Repression is the exclusion from awareness of distressing feelings, impulses, ideas, or wishes. Repression is unconscious, suppression (see below) is conscious. A man is unaware that he resents his more successful wife. [Neurotic]

Somatization (hypochondriasis) is an excessive preoccupation with physical symptoms in response to psychologically stressful situations. [Immature]

Splitting is the viewing of oneself or others as all good or all bad, as opposed to being a mixture of positive and negative attributes. In splitting, the person frequently alternates between idealization and devaluation. [Image-distorting]

Sublimation is the gratification of a repressed instinct or unacceptable feeling by socially acceptable means. Better a surgeon than a sadist. Better a therapist than a voyeur. [Mature]

Suppression is the conscious and deliberate avoidance of disturbing matters: A basketball player is penalized for a foul but he suppresses his anger and soon scores a goal. [Mature]

Turning against the self occurs when the person takes a hostile thought or impulse aimed at another and inappropriately redirects it inward. Less distress is experienced by blaming, hurting, or even mutilating the self than by feeling guilty for being furious at the other person. [Immature]

Undoing is the use of behavior or thoughts to cancel or eradicate the effect of a previous act or thought associated with a painful idea, event, or emotion. After arranging a murder, Lady Macbeth washed her hands, which had no blood on them, and said, "Out, out damn spot." [Image-distorting when delusional; otherwise neurotic or mature, depending on circumstances]

were encouraged (through *positive or negative reinforcement*) or punished by the environment. Often the internal (intrapsychic) environment of the person's thoughts provides its own reinforcement and punishment.

Family Systems

In this model the family is viewed as a *system*, which is a complex of interacting elements. Systems theory holds that one cannot fully understand a system

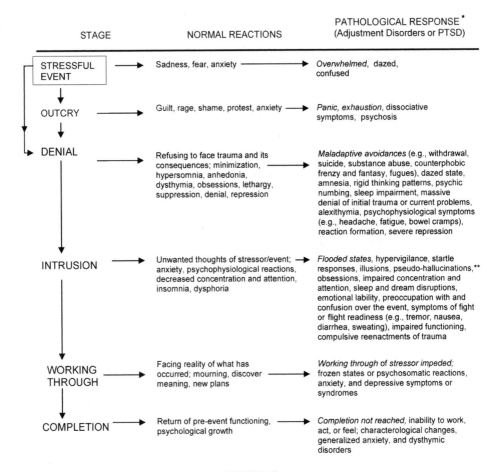

FIGURE 4-5
Sequential Responses to Trauma

Modified from Horowitz (1985).

*Pathological variations also include unusually intense or prolonged "normal" reactions. *Main features are italicized.*
**Pesudo-hallucinations are fantasized reactions in which people intensely experience something as real, despite intellectually knowing otherwise. These may be the "felt presence" of a dead grandfather or an "out-of-body" experience.

(e.g., organization, family, person) by examining only its parts. What happens in one part of a system eventually reverberates and affects the others; no person is an island. In the family systems model, the patient's behavior is viewed less as the product of an intrapsychically induced mental disorder and more the result of intrafamilial disturbances. This approach does not necessarily deny the existence of mental illness but suggests that the confluence of forces within the family maintains, exacerbates, and perhaps even initiates it.

Sociocultural

The pathogenic role of social, cultural, political, economic, religious, racial, and gender aspects are often given short shrift, partly because ideology tends to overwhelm the few facts that exist. Sociologists examine these matters, but usually lack training in psychopathology to place them in context, whereas mental-health professionals usually lack sociological sophistication. Therefore, clinicians should be especially careful when attributing mental pathology to social pathology (or even social normality). On the other hand, when specific social factors are responsible, their influence (for good or ill) should be recorded in the patient's biopsychosocial formulation.

References

Crain, W.C. (1985). *Theories of development: Concepts and applications* (2nd rev ed.) Englewood Cliffs, NJ: Prentice-Hall.

Engel, G.L. (1977). The need for a new medical model: A challenge for biomedicine. *Science,* 196(4286), 129–136.

Erikson, E.H. (1968). *Identity: Youth and crisis.* New York: Norton.

Gardner, K.L., Thrivikanan, K.V., Lightman, S.L., Plotsky, P.M., & Lowry, C.A. (2005). Early life experience alters behavior during social defeat: Focus on serotonergic systems. *Neuroscience,* 136(1), 181–191.

Goodwin, D.W. (1985). Alcoholism and genetics: The sins of the father. *Archives of General Psychiatry,* 42, 171–174.

Goodwin, D.W., & Guze, S.B. (1989). *Psychiatric diagnosis.* Oxford: Oxford University Press.

Herman, A.I., Philbeck, J.W., Vasilopoulos, N.L., & Depetrillo, P.B. (2003). Serotonin transporter promoter differences in alcohol consumption behavior in a college student population. *Alcohol,* 38(5), 446–449.

Hogarty, G.E., Goldberg, S.C., Schooler, N.R., & Ulrich, R.P. (1974). Drugs and sociotherapy in the aftercare of schizophrenic patients: II. Two-year relapse rates. *Archives of General Psychiatry,* 31, 603–608.

Horowitz, M.J. (1985). Disasters and psychological responses to stress. *Psychiatric Annals,* 15, 161–167.

Kandel, E.R. (1983). From metapsychology to molecular biology: Explorations into the nature of anxiety. *American Journal of Psychiatry,* 140, 1277–1293.

Kleinman, A. (1988). *The illness narratives: Suffering, healing, and the human condition.* New York: Basic Books.

Kohlberg, L., Levine, C., & Hewer, A. (1983). *Moral stages: A current formulation and a response to critics.* Basel, NY: Karger.

McHugh, P.R., & Slavney, P.R. (1998). *The perspectives of psychiatry* (2nd ed.). Baltimore: Johns Hopkins University Press.

Perry, J.C., & Cooper, S.H. (1989). An empirical study of defense mechanisms. *Archives of General Psychiatry, 46,* 444–452.

Rosenthal, N.E., Sack, D.A., Gillin, J.C., Lewy, A.J., Goodwin, F.K., Davenport, Y., et al. (1984). Seasonal affective disorder. *Archives of General Psychiatry, 41,* 72–80.

Sadock, B.J., & Sadock, V.A. (2005). *Kaplan and Sadock's comprehensive textbook of psychiatry* (8th ed.). Philadelphia: Lippincott, Williams & Wilkins.

Vaillant, G.E. (1971). Theoretical hierarchy of adaptive ego mechanisms. *Archives of General Psychiatry, 24,* 107–118.

Vaillant, G.E., Bond, M., & Vaillant, C.O. (1986). An empirically validated hierarchy of defense mechanisms. *Archives of General Psychiatry, 43,* 786–794.

Weiner, H. (1985). Schizophrenia: Etiology. In H.I. Kaplan & B.J. Sadock (Eds.), *Comprehensive textbook of psychiatry* (4th ed., pp. 651–680). Baltimore: Williams & Wilkins.

Wender, P.H., & Klein, D.F. (1981). *Mind, mood, and medicine: A guide to the new biopsychiatry.* New York: Meridan.

5

Treatment

The most important factor in deciding treatment is the patient's diagnosis. Other factors—psychological, medical, sociocultural, ethical, intellectual, financial—influence the choice and conduct of treatment, but except for emergency interventions, no treatment should begin without a diagnosis. Conversely, although diagnosis may serve other ends, its chief purpose is to help determine treatment. Therefore, when clinicians debate a patient's diagnosis, it is important to know how a change in diagnosis will alter the patient's treatment.

WHAT DO TREATMENT PLANS INCLUDE?

Every patient should have a *treatment plan*—that is, an organized program of one or more treatments for helping him or her achieve specified objectives. The clinician should indicate the type, amount, focus, goals, and timing of each treatment.

1. The *types* are numerous and varied by the model of the provider and the needs of the patient. The variants include, but are not limited to, individual, couple, family, or group psychotherapy, and medication. Each of these modalities has a number of options based on psychodynamic, cognitive, and/or behavioral principles. Furthermore, in acute situations, the type of treatment may be very short-term and straightforward, such as recreational therapy, medication, "suicide precautions," "seclusion room," "school consultation," and so on. The specific interventions should be specified in the treatment plan.

2. The *amount* of treatment refers to its frequency and duration. Will psychotherapy sessions occur once or twice a week? Will therapy continue for 6 weeks or 6 months? The dose, frequency, and duration of medication should also be indicated.

3. The *focus* refers to the specific problem(s) that treatment will address. Treatment does not, and cannot, concentrate on everything; choices and priorities must be set. Is it better to focus on a patient's alcoholism or depression? Should the etiological focus be on childhood trauma, ongoing familial problems, or precipitating stressors?

4. The *goals* (or objectives) of each treatment should be specified; otherwise, clinicians and patients cannot know *where treatment is going, when it should end*, and *whether it has succeeded*. A goal of "helping the patient function better" is too vague, because it does not specify the areas in which the patient should function better. To report that risperidone is being prescribed to "treat the patient's schizophrenia" borders on poverty of content. Is the goal to eliminate hallucinations or to stop the patient from telling everyone about his hallucinations? Is it to stop delusions, elevate mood, diminish agitation, increase social interactions, make it possible to leave the hospital, or function at work? No medication should be prescribed without first specifying its target symptoms and functions.

At times, the objectives are clear but unrealistic: "To help the patient enjoy her (thoroughly obnoxious) mother." In establishing goals, two generalizations should apply: (a) the briefer the treatment, the less ambitious the goals; and (b) the more recent the problem, the fuller and faster it will improve with treatment.

> Outlining treatment goals *on paper* helps clinicians sharpen their awareness; if they can't articulate the goals clearly, they don't really know what the goals are. Discussing goals with patients before treatment begins helps patients make a more informed judgment about entering treatment and reduces unrealistic expectations of therapy. Furthermore, having agreed upon goals up front helps develop the therapeutic relationship, a critical piece of the therapeutic process. Overexpectations of therapy may be the greatest preventable cause of malpractice suits. When patients and therapists explicitly agree on the goals of treatment, both are also more likely to be on the same "wavelength" during treatment. Clearly delineating goals also minimizes the possibility of other providers working at cross purposes, as when an individual psychotherapist tells a teenager "to liberate himself from parental domination," while the family therapist tells his parents "to set limits on their kid." This may also mean contacting (with an appropriate release of information) other professionals involved in the patient's care, such as physician or counselor.

5. The *timing* of therapies—that is, when and in what sequence—generally follows these guidelines: Treatment should rectify biological changes before psychosocial influences, symptoms before issues, acute crises before chronic

problems, and psychoses before neuroses. Psychotic patients should receive supportive psychotherapy; only later, when nonpsychotic, can they benefit from other forms of psychotherapy. The hierarchy of *DSM-IV-TR* diagnoses listed in Figure 3-1 can also be used as a guide to determine which diagnosis/problem should be treated first.

> Treatments cannot happen all at once, nor should they. For instance, patients with severe major depression view all information in the worst possible light; they use insights not for self-improvement but for self-punishment. During insight-oriented psychotherapy, a very proper 55-year-old woman recalled a long-forgotten affair from 30 years earlier. But instead of using this insight to unburden herself of a long-repressed guilt (as would "normal" people), she berated herself: "This proves I'm a whore and deserve to die." Like most severely depressed patients, she could benefit from insight only *after* antidepressant medications had alleviated her symptoms.

One model that has helped inform clinicians on how to match their approach to their patients' timing is the transtheoretical model or stages of change model (Prochaska, Diclemente, & Norcross, 1992). This model (Figure 5-1) argues that patients vary in how ready, willing, and able they are to engage in treatment. For example, one person may have recently been told

Stage of Change	Characteristics
Precontemplation	Not currently considering change: "Ignorance is bliss"
Contemplation	Ambivalent about change: "Sitting on the fence"; not considering change within the next month
Preparation	Some experience with change and are trying to change; "testing the waters," planning to act within 1 month
Action	Practicing new behavior for 3–6 months
Maintenance	Continued commitment to sustaining new behavior post 6 months to 5 years
Relapse	Resumption of old behaviors: "Fall from grace"

Figure 5-1
Prochaska's Stages of Change

that she has a drinking problem and needs help, but she is not convinced there is a problem (precontemplation stage). Another may have just gotten his third DUI and lost his job because he failed a drug test at work—this individual, hopefully, sees he has a significant problem and is ready to engage actively in a treatment plan (action stage). This approach argues that clinicians need to recognize these differences and adjust *their* approach to help patients advance through the stages toward lasting behavior change.

> The inpatient treatment of anorexia nervosa further illustrates the importance of timing and the tailoring of interventions. These self-starving young females (see Chapter 19) are admitted when their weight has become medically precarious; since 10–15% of these patients who are hospitalized die prematurely, regaining weight is a medical necessity and the first goal of treatment. Yet, on first meeting these patients, clinicians are often struck by their "goodie two-shoes" personae that belie significant levels of distress and self-doubt. Furthermore, the disorder often appears during or following a time of stress, such as going away to college. Clinicians are tempted to explore those areas right away, but when immediately addressed, patients usually become so distressed, they actually lose weight. Only after their weight is stabilized can patients benefit from examining these issues.

THREE LEVELS OF TREATMENT

Psychiatric treatment occurs in three levels: biological, psychosocial, and moral–existential. First, if needed, the psychiatrist prescribes medication to rectify *biological* abnormalities. Second, the therapist facilitates psychotherapies to address *psychosocial* problems. Third, the therapist uses the clinician–patient relationship to demonstrate that he or she values the patient as a person, moving into the *moral–existential* dimension of therapy (Abroms, 1983).

This three-level model holds that biological and psychosocial treatments are both valuable, albeit in *different* ways. To argue that talk therapy is better than drug therapy (or vice versa) is pointless; they serve different functions. Group therapy frequently helps diabetics cope with their illness, yet nobody would suggest that such groups regulate blood sugar; conversely, insulin regulates blood sugar, yet nobody would suggest it helps diabetics cope with their illness. Just as group therapy and insulin help patients with diabetes in different ways, so do psychotherapies and biotherapies help patients with mental disorders. Excellent therapists can have very different interests (e.g., psychoanalysis, medications), but still appreciate that each treatment serves a distinct purpose.

In general, biological therapies eliminate or alleviate *symptoms*, such as the insomnia of a person with depression, the delusions of a person with schizophrenia, or the spending sprees of a person in a manic state. In contrast, psychosocial therapies usually address *issues*, such as coping with a job loss, a failed marriage, a medical condition, or a psychiatric disorder. When used properly, biological and psychosocial therapies do not impede but *facilitate* one another. Repeated evidence has shown that medications do not increase patient's passivity, decrease motivation, or diminish involvement in psychotherapy. Correctly medicated patients gain more from psychotherapy. Wildly hallucinating people with schizophrenia feel so bombarded by stimuli that they cannot focus sufficiently to benefit from psychotherapy; once medicated, they can.

Conversely, psychotherapies can accomplish what drugs cannot. They can teach patients about their mental disorders—their symptoms, dangers, causes, and precipitants. Psychotherapies can alert patients to situations that are likely to trigger another episode of illness (e.g., Marlatt & Gordon, 1985), help patients understand what their conditions mean to them (e.g., Ellis, 1975), and improve patients' willingness to adhere to the psychiatric treatment plan, such as taking medication. They can also facilitate social adjustment, interpersonal relationships, and leisure-time pleasures and occupational skills, as well as heighten self-esteem, guide ambition, and promote well-being. Finally, psychotherapeutic investigation can reveal how previous experiences affect current difficulties. A patient who cannot figure out why terrible things keep happening to her—why people are rude to her, why men avoid her, why nobody will hire her—can be shown why these events happen, what she can do about them, and how she can regain control over her life.

The moral–existential aspects of therapy do not involve particular treatments or occur during specified periods. Instead, they prevail throughout therapy, pervading both biological and psychosocial treatments. To quote Abroms (1983), moral–existential interventions involve the "realm of pure value, where the ultimate aim is integrity of the person. . . . [They entail] moral qualities of trust and gratitude, of loyalty and devotion, and above all, of respect . . . the therapist becomes firm in the resolve to stand by the patient, even to tolerate a measure of moral failure" (p. 744). While therapists may not condone their patients' behaviors and choices, they accept patients for who they are. Once patients fully understand what their choices are, they must make an existential decision. Sometimes they may decide not to change, or at least not at this time. Therapists must learn to accept such decisions.

OVERALL GUIDELINES FOR SELECTING TREATMENTS

Treatment selection should be based primarily on pragmatic, rather than on etiological, considerations. Some of the major difficulties of linking treatment with an etiological theory are as follows: (1) The cause of most mental disorders is unknown. (2) The treatment must then be consistent with the theory, which may determine what can and cannot be treated. For example, Freud's early feelings about schizophrenia excluded this illness from the scope of psychoanalytic therapy. (3) A total commitment to any single etiological theory and its accompanying treatments limits the therapist's range of interventions. (4) The goals of therapy often become the fulfillment of a theory rather than what the patient actually needs or desires. (5) Even if the etiology of a disorder were known, therapies addressing it are unlikely to rectify the patient's current disorder. For example, a man who is chronically depressed because he was deprived (or depraved) as a child might find that further insight into his childhood cannot alter the many self-destructive patterns that he has developed over the years. When theory prevails over pragmatism, a therapist may insist that a patient who feels and functions substantially better has not "really" improved because the patient has not accepted the origins of his problem and that, as long as he continues to "resist," he will never improve. In other words, the patient can't get better unless he "buys" the therapist's theory.

To serve up pragmatically based treatments, one should follow (Bill) *Tilden's Law*: "Never change a winning game." If a treatment works, don't change it; if a treatment doesn't work, do change it. Tilden's law does not mean that clinicians should alter treatments every time patients have setbacks, but it does mean that if patients fail to improve following an ample trial with a particular treatment, another treatment should be tried. For example, even if a patient "should" respond to antidepressant medications, if she doesn't, she doesn't, and a different treatment should be attempted. Or, if a patient has failed to improve after three trials of insight-oriented psychotherapy with three different therapists, chances are that a fourth trial of insight-oriented therapy won't help; however, another treatment, such as behavioral, cognitive, or drug therapy, might help.

When pragmatically chosen treatments are based on *scientific evidence* instead of on intuition or theory, they have the greatest chance of being effective. For instance, studies show that if a patient's biological relative has improved with a particular drug, so will the patient. "Scientific," however, is not synonymous with "biological"; although medications are more amenable to scientific investigation, hundreds of well-controlled, quantified studies have evaluated psychotherapy. Furthermore, meta-analytic studies, such as the seminal work of Smith, Glass, and Miller (1980), have shown a robust effect for psychotherapeutic interventions (more recently, Anderson & Lambert, 1995; McDermut, Miller, & Brown, 2001; Shadish et al., 2000).

> Scientific studies of social relations can also guide the treatment of patients. For example, before discharging inpatients, staff must decide how much patients should change their lives during the immediate posthospital stage. One investigation (Breier & Strauss, 1984) indicated that the answer was "very little." This research reported that discharged psychotic patients go through two stages: First, a period of *convalescence*, in which they mainly see themselves as "ex-patients" and maintain contacts with hospital staff and former patients. During the second stage of *rebuilding*, these patients view themselves more as members of society and less as "ex-patients"; key relationships are formed with people in the community instead of with former hospital associations. In general, patients fare much better when therapy fosters stability during the convalescence stage and does not encourage patients to make changes until they enter the rebuilding stage.

As the mental health field has continued to expand, and as health care costs have skyrocketed, pressure has increased to provide evidence-based treatments. These are interventions that, firstly, have demonstrated "efficacy," meaning that they work under relatively ideal conditions. Secondly, the treatments are judged "effective" because they work in real-life settings where people's lives are more complicated. Clinicians and patients need these solutions—that is, ones that generalize to daily practice. A number of resources exist to aid practitioners in determining *which* treatments to use *when* (e.g., Barlow, 2001). Furthermore, major professional organizations, as well as some governmental agencies, have published evidence-based practice guidelines that are available on the Internet—examples include the American Psychiatric Association (www.psych.org), the American Psychological Association (www. apa.org), the American Academy of Child and Adolescent Psychiatry (www. aacap.org), and the National Institute on Drug Abuse (www.nida.nih.gov).

Acutely psychotic patients benefit most from psychotherapeutic contacts that are relatively simple, clear, and brief. These patients are frequently overwhelmed by external stimuli, have trouble distinguishing reality from fantasy, often confuse their outer with their inner world, and have short attention spans. Thus, insight-oriented therapies rarely help, but frequently harm, the acutely psychotic person; reality testing is more beneficial. If a patient says, "I'm the worst sinner on earth," the therapist can empathize with the patient's emotional state but still test (or clarify) reality: "I understand that you feel miserable, but what evidence do you have that your sins are worse than others' sins?" Sessions should be shorter and more frequent: A patient in an extremely psychotic state, with a short attention span, may profit more from five, 10-minute contacts a day than from the classical, once-a-day, 50-minute hour.

Acutely ill patients should also be discouraged from making any important life decisions, especially if the decisions are irreversible. This does not mean that therapists should run their patients' lives, nor that *all* patients in therapy should place major decisions on hold. Therapists should intervene only when a patient's judgment is severely impaired by a mental disorder.

> Every axis in *DSM-IV-TR* highlights a key issue for planning treatment. In setting treatment goals, clinicians distinguish between Axes I and II, since diagnoses on Axis I usually respond more readily to treatment than those on Axis II. Treatment plans address the stressors in Axis IV and use the level of functioning on Axis V for determining treatment goals.
>
> Axis III disorders should not be overlooked. Many people with physical illnesses also suffer from psychiatric disorders. For example, the lifetime prevalence of depression for persons with diabetes is approximately 25%, for coronary heart disease 26%, while the current prevalence for cancer has been estimated as high as 42% (Popkin & Tucker, 1994).

PSYCHOPATHOLOGICAL CLUES

During assessment, clinicians should sprout antennae for seven psychopathological clues that facilitate both biological and psychosocial treatments.

1. *Locus of responsibility*: Patients who always view others as responsible for their difficulties—so-called "externalizers"—do poorly in psychotherapy and are less cooperative in taking medication. Patients can change themselves much more readily than they can change others.

2. *Habitual view of "helping" figures*: How patients feel about other helping figures—doctors, nurses, teachers, parents—may predict how they will behave toward the therapist. Some patients are highly suspicious of helping figures. The paranoid wonders, "What's the *real* reason this therapist claims he likes me and wants to help?" With suspicious patients, therapists should keep a safe psychological distance to prevent what patients might experience as phony intimacy. These patients are also allergic to interpretations that are too frequent or probing, viewing them as too intrusive and the therapist as "playing with my head." Conversely, for patients who view helping figures as omnipotent, unending sources of gratification and dependency, therapists should avoid becoming swamped by their needs by limiting phone calls and not scheduling too many sessions at the outset of treatment (sessions can always

be added). The objective is to provide a structure for the therapeutic relationship that is experienced as safe enough for making changes in thoughts, feelings, and behaviors.

3. *Defense mechanisms and coping patterns*: Patients who rely on more immature defense mechanisms, such as projection and massive denial, are more likely to *not* benefit from, and to be harmed by, insight-oriented psychotherapy. Because past behavior is the best predictor of future behavior, therapists should ask, "How have you handled major problems and stresses in the past?" Therapists can then decide if patients have used avoidance, denial, overcompensation (i.e., reaction formation), or intellectualization. These responses often predict "flights into health," in which patients dramatically improve after several sessions and want to stop therapy; this first blush of relief quickly pales as they discover that their old problems remain.

4. *Therapist-patient relationship*: Treatment is not just about the medication, or the treatment technique, or even the specific disorder being treated. There are a number of "common" or "nonspecific" factors that cut across treatments that influence outcomes. One important variable is the ability of the patient and provider to form a supportive and respectful working relationship (Norcross, 2002; Safran & Moran, 2000). Some patients will be unable to form a productive therapeutic relationship, such as those with severe personality disorders. Based on where they fall using the stages of change model, others may not yet be ready to engage in the therapeutic process. Either way, therapists need to be aware of and evaluate the ability of the therapist and patient to form a good working relationship.

> If the patient or therapist is unsure if psychotherapy holds promise, the clinician may recommend an initial *trial period* of (roughly) six weekly sessions. Each party can see if the "chemistry" between them is likely to be therapeutic. A formal trial period allows both parties to begin therapy without feeling committed to ongoing treatment. As long as therapists do not make patients feel as if they are "on trial," a trial period allows each person a graceful way to terminate treatment. This approach is particularly helpful with certain male patients who are fearful of establishing a dependency relationship such as therapy and are quite uncomfortable talking about their feelings. Furthermore, given that the average number of therapy sessions is five (Hanson et al., 2002), a six-week trial is likely to provide enough time to agree upon what to do next.

5. *Following the affect*: By noting what is being discussed when the patient's affect changes abruptly, the therapist can discern, from among many issues, the ones of prime import to the patient. For instance, a man claims he's gotten over a divorce yet breaks down and weeps when mentioning his

former wife. Usually nonverbal, these telltale affective signals may be sub-tle—a tear is shed, a gaze averted, a leg moved, a body tensed. Therapists can gain considerable information by sensitively pursuing any topic that suddenly triggers an intense affect.

6. *Listening for the associations*: When patients jump to apparently unre-lated topics, or when they keep returning to the same topic, that topic deserves attention. To illustrate: While continually harping about his daughter's failure to apply to medical school, a 65-year-old man kept raising the topic of his own retirement. Initially, the connection between these two concerns was unclear; but exploring the association revealed the man's rage at his daughter for "giv-ing up." Realizing this, he stopped being angry at his daughter and could more objectively consider retirement.

7. *The therapist as "emotional barometer"*: How a therapist feels toward a patient is often, though not always, a reliable indication of how most people feel about the patient. If the therapist is constantly irritated by a patient, even if the therapist doesn't know precisely how or why, the patient is probably irritating. (If the therapist is irritated by *all* her patients, then the problem lies with the therapist, not the patient. In psychoanalytic terms, this is called *countertransference* and it means the therapist might need therapy.) The thera-pist's reactions to a patient are not irrelevant feelings but germane clinical data. For instance, when a paranoid patient emotionally attacks a therapist, the patient may be conveying, however unconsciously, how he always feels under attack in the "real" world. In many cases, the therapist picks up the patient's feelings. The task is to use these feelings as data about what the patient is experiencing, what the world looks like through his eyes. It may also help the therapist deal with her irritation to recognize that being irritating is the best strategy the patient has come up with to manage his distress/fears in interpersonal situations.

A SUMMARY OF PSYCHIATRIC TREATMENTS

Despite the ever-increasing number of therapies—in reality, the commonly used treatments of any enduring importance have not changed very much over the years. These treatments are listed in Table 5-1 and briefly described below.

BIOLOGICAL THERAPIES

Biological therapies are the subject of Chapter 6.

TABLE 5-1

Modern Psychiatric Treatments

I. BIOLOGICAL THERAPIES

  A. Medication

    1. Antipsychotics (e.g., chlorpromazine, haloperidol, risperidone)

    2. Antidepressants

      a. Tricyclics (TCAs) and multicyclics (e.g., imiprimine, amitriptyline)

      b. Selective serotonin reuptake inhibitors (SSRIs; e.g., fluoxetine, sertraline, paroxetine, fluvoxamine)

      c. Serotonin and norepinephrine reuptake inhibitors (SNRIs; e.g., venlafaxine)

      d. Monoamine oxidase inhibitors (MAOIs; e.g., phenelzine)

      d. Atypical (e.g., trazodone, bupropion, venlafaxine)

    3. Mood stabilizers (e.g., lithium, carbamazepine, valproic acid, and calcium channel blockers)

    4. Hypnoanxiolytics (e.g., benzodiazepines)

      a. Antianxiety agents (e.g., diazepam, alprazolam)

      b. Hypnotics (e.g., flurazepam, temazepam)

      c. Atypical anxiolytics—azapirones (e.g., buspirone)

      d. Atypical hypnotics (e.g., zolpidem)

  B. Electroconvulsive therapy (ECT), transcranial magnetic stimulation (TCMS), and vagal nerve stimulation (VNS) primarily used for severe depression. (ECT is also used for refractory mania and schizophrenia.)

  C. Phototherapy

II. PSYCHOSOCIAL THERAPIES

  A. Individual treatments

    1. Insight-oriented therapy (psychodynamic/psychoanalytic)

    2. Cognitive therapy

    3. Behavioral therapy

    4. Supportive therapy/counseling

  B. Group treatments

    1. Psychotherapy

    2. Psychoeducational

    3. Self-help (e.g., Alcoholics Anonymous, Recovery)

  C. Couple and family treatments

    1. Couple therapy

    2. Family therapy

III. Specialized treatment techniques

    1. Hypnosis

    2. Biofeedback

    3. Relaxation

IV. NO TREATMENT

PSYCHOSOCIAL THERAPIES

This text defines psychosocial therapies as the informed and systematic application of techniques based on established psychological principles by professionals who are trained and experienced to understand these principles and to apply these techniques to modify maladaptive feelings, thoughts, and behaviors.

With so many psychosocial treatments (and so many defended passionately), one can easily overlook their similarities. Both explicitly and implicitly, psychosocial treatments all involve a contract and a degree of rapport and trust between a supposed expert and a patient or client with emotional or behavioral problems. Whether or not the patient has symptoms, all treatments seek to combat demoralization by restoring the patient's sense of mastery. Furthermore, they all derive from a particular theory or set of principles in which both parties have some faith; the commonality across therapies is that they all work to change a person's thoughts, feelings, and behaviors to improve functioning. Most therapists are not exclusive practitioners of one particular school of therapy, but instead combine approaches depending on the patient's needs.

In preparing patients for psychotherapy—whichever particular treatments are utilized—two questions should be answered before therapy is formally begun: (1) Are there realistic goals that can be reached? (2) What is this therapy all about; how should I act and how will you act? The activity of agreeing on realistic goals can be therapeutic in itself. The patient may feel better now that this "great blob of bad feeling" is being sorted out with somebody who seems to understand and has information and tools to help. Almost all patients have unspoken misconceptions about therapy that can be corrected. At this stage, unrealistic expectations such as "I really want to learn how to change my mother" or "You are wise, just tell me what to do" can be dealt with before they undermine the therapy. A patient may come to agree on a preliminary framework such as "I can only change myself" or "I am not here to attain enlightenment but rather to control my negative thoughts." Later, more specific goals can be established. Preparing patients for what to expect in therapy has been shown to reduce the duration of therapy and result in better outcomes (Yalom, 2005). Too often patients are told to say whatever comes to mind, only to find that talking about the weather and baseball scores wasn't the idea. Patients need to be educated on how they can get the most out of treatment and what they can expect from the therapist.

Individual Psychotherapies

There are four basic types of psychotherapies that involve a single patient: insight-oriented psychotherapy, cognitive-behavioral, behavioral, and supportive therapy. (For clarity, the distinctions between these therapies drawn below are somewhat overstated.)

• *Insight-oriented psychotherapy.* There are two primary forms of insight oriented psychotherapy: *psychoanalysis* and *psychodynamic psychotherapy.* For *psychoanalysis* "free association" is the cardinal rule—that is, without self-censorship, the patient should say whatever comes to mind, including dreams, fantasies, early memories, current experiences, or feelings about the analyst (i.e., transference). Psychoanalysis aims to heal by uncovering as much as possible about how the patient's mind functions. The approach is physically and verbally structured to foster an environment untainted by the analyst—she adopts a position of nondisclosure and is emotionally and behaviorally neutral toward anything offered by the patient. Consequently, the patient reclines on a couch; the analyst sits behind the patient so that no nonverbal signals influence the patient's free associations. By deliberately acting as a "blank screen" and not as a "real person," the analyst assumes that everything the patient attributes to her are projections of the patient rather than qualities of the analyst.

Psychoanalysis requires three to five meetings a week. It is prescribed for "problems in living," and for mild to moderate depression, anxiety, and obsessiveness, which does not interfere with more than one of the three main areas of functioning: familial, occupational, and recreational. The patient must be bright, introspective, usually under the age of 50, a good abstract thinker, nonpsychotic, and can pay out-of-pocket for four sessions per week for a period of at least two or three years. For most, this treatment is an expensive luxury. It is like having a car that isn't running quite right overhauled, when a tune-up might have been enough.

In *psychodynamic psychotherapy*, clinicians also address the patient's difficulties by relying on insight—bringing unconscious or unclear material into sharp awareness. In comparison to psychoanalysis, the patient sits face-to-face with the therapist, has one or two sessions a week, does not free associate, and pays more attention to the realities of current life than to dreams and childhood recollections. The patient should be nonpsychotic, introspective, intelligent, and capable of abstract thought. Psychodynamic psychotherapy is therefore best used for problems in living, neurotic symptoms, and ego-dystonic character traits.

Interpretation is the hallmark of this form of treatment, but the therapist is more active and directive in gathering information and offering interpretations (Malan, 1995). In Malan's model, the clinician makes an interpretation by articulating the coping strategy (or defense) that the person is currently using, the anxiety it tries to prevent, and the underlying hidden feeling (or unconscious impulse). This intrapsychic conflict or pattern manifests itself often in the relationship with the therapist, as well as past and present significant others. Once the patient understands, i.e., has insight into his feared emotions, the fear is reduced and he is able to cope more effectively.

Like psychoanalysis, successful psychodynamic therapy does not eliminate every problem or bestow "perfect mental health." Problems are inherent to the human condition, and perfect mental health does not exist. By therapy's end, however, the patient should have developed more realistic and flexible ways of dealing with and reconciling personal needs and environmental demands; psychic pain, especially when the patient produces it "unnecessarily," should be reduced; the patient should leave with an understanding of why "bad things" were happening and how to avoid similar pitfalls in the future; and lastly, the patient should have acquired a framework for continued self-reflection and problem solving.

• *Cognitive therapy.* "Cognition" means "the process of knowing or perceiving." Cognitive theory assumes that patients' faulty evaluations of the data they take in through their senses produce pathological moods—anxiety, depression, worry, guilt, etc. In cognitive therapy, whether a glass is half empty or half full all depends on one's glasses (rose-tinted or gray?).

The cognitive therapist identifies the habitual ways in which patients distort information (Beck, Rush, Shaw, & Emery, 1979). They make mountains out of molehills, project their own fears onto others, or see things in the worst possible light. These patterns, which are called "automatic thoughts," are accompanied by "automatic emotions" such as dread, worry, and tension. The cognitive therapist teaches patients to recognize their distressing emotions, the situations that produce them, and their usual patterns of automatic thoughts. The work is then to generate "disputing beliefs" that view the information in a more rational and accurate way (Ellis, 1975, 1984).

For example, a combat veteran feels guilty because "I should have prevented Jack from jumping up to return fire. If I had, he wouldn't have been killed." The "irrational belief" is the vet's expectation that he "should" have been able to apply the knowledge he gained only after the death of his buddy to save him. A rational, disputing belief might be "Given the circumstances and what I knew at the time, I did the best I could, and Jack's death was a tragedy, but not my fault." Incorporating these new beliefs decreases distress and increases self-confidence, thereby allowing a person to try new behaviors; they are frequently and effectively combined with behavioral techniques such as relaxation training or exposure treatments (*cognitive–behavioral therapy*). Cognitive therapy is used most often to treat mild to moderately severe depressions, anxiety, panic attacks, and phobias (e.g., Beck et al., 1979; Chambless & Ollendick, 2001). Throughout the typical 10–25 weekly sessions, patients record episodes at home that led to troublesome feelings and thoughts, and at the following session, the cognitive distortions creating them are examined.

As an example, a student social worker entered cognitive therapy for a moderate depression that intensified when she started her placement on a psychiatric inpatient service. A typical exchange between her and the therapist:

PATIENT: [Situation] On my very first day on the ward, a patient asked me if his medication should be changed. I freaked.

THERAPIST: When you were freaking, what did you think about?

PATIENT: [Automatic thoughts] I felt like an idiot. That I can't even answer a simple question, and if I can't do that, then maybe I shouldn't be a therapist. [automatic emotions] I felt terrible, filled with shame and guilt.

THERAPIST: [Pointing out a more rational thought] But you're a social work student, not a trained physician. Why should you know about this medication?

PATIENT: [Automatic thought] Maybe, but then the patient asked me when he'd be discharged and I felt like a fool for not knowing the answer.

THERAPIST: In retrospect, do you believe your feeling was justified?

PATIENT: [Rational thought] No. That's silly! Why should I know when he'd be discharged—I had just arrived on the ward 2 hours earlier. He's not even my patient!!

[Note: Behind this is a more global thought that will resurface in other situations and need to be disputed: "I should know everything. If I don't, that means I'm stupid and everybody will think I'm stupid."]

• *Behavior therapy.* Any treatment that attempts to alter quantifiable behavior by systematically changing the environment that produces the behavior is behavior therapy. Generally speaking, changed behaviors are believed to lead to changed feelings and beliefs. There are two primary schools of behavior therapy, one based on classical conditioning (Pavlovian) and one based on operant conditioning (Skinnerian). In Pavlov's original experiments, meat powder (the unconditioned stimulus, or UCS) was placed in a dog's mouth, thereby causing the dog to salivate (the unconditioned response, or UCR). Then Pavlov rang a bell when the meat powder was applied. After a number of trials, the bell *alone* (now a conditioned stimulus, or CS) was able to elicit the salivation (a conditioned response, or CR).

Classical conditioning spawned the anxiety-reducing therapies of systematic desensitization and prolonged exposure, or flooding. The concept is that the brain sees something in the environment as a threat that in reality is not as dangerous as is feared (or not dangerous at all—either way, it's a CS). The brain reacts with fear, a CR, to prepare the person to respond to the perceived danger (e.g., the fight/flight response). As the exposure continues, the brain recognizes that there is no actual threat present, the CS loses its power to generate anxiety, and the fear extinguishes.

In *systematic desensitization*, treatment proceeds from the least to the most anxiety-producing stimuli. The patient is first taught muscle relaxation skills. Then a hierarchy of fears is constructed; as a simplified example, a person with a fear of snakes might find a color picture of snakes mildly distressing, a rubber snake more so, and a live snake terrifying. The therapist has the patient create a relaxed state and then presents the picture. Once the patient can view the picture with little anxiety, the therapist moves up the heirarchy. Consequently, over time the fear, in this case of snakes, lessens (Wolpe, 1958).

> If the patient is phobic about cats, the therapist might say after the patient relaxes, "Picture a cat 100 yards away—that is, the full length of a football field." Once the patient can do this without becoming tense, the therapist might say, "Now imagine this cat 75 yards away." This progressive desensitization process is continued so that, after the patient is able to imagine touching a cat, she may be exposed to cats in photos, and then to cats in real life (*in vivo*). It is this *in vivo* step that is critical for success. In fact, some patients can skip the progressive relaxation step and go straight to the *in vivo* part when accompanied by a trusted person.

Flooding, by contrast, does not gradually expose the patient to the fear-provoking stimulus, but instead presents the feared object or situation "all at once" for a prolonged period of time. In using flooding, a child with a school phobia would be taken to school (often kicking and screaming) and be maintained in that environment against his will. After a couple of days the child realizes that he has no option but to attend school and that he has survived being at school. The result is desensitization to his fear and restoration of daily functioning. While this process is the "opposite" of systematic desensitization, the result is the same in that exposure to the feared situation leads to decreased anxiety.

Operant conditioning is a process of systematically rewarding and reinforcing positive behaviors. An *operant* is a behavior shaped by its consequence.

Positive reinforcement is a procedure that uses consequences for increasing operant behaviors. For example, by repeating a routine, a stand-up comic learns which jokes elicit laughs and which do not: The audience's laughter, which is a consequence, positively reinforces certain jokes, which become operants.

> With her behavior therapist, a person with bulimia may discover that bingeing and vomiting reduce anxiety or boredom, thus reinforcing the harmful behaviors. The behavior therapist helps the patient find other activities that reduce anxiety or boredom (e.g., taking a warm shower, going for a walk, calling a friend). Substitution of the benign activities helps reduce the frequency of binges.
>
> Token economies are programs that systematically apply operant conditioning. They are used most often to prepare chronically hospitalized patients with schizophrenia or mental retardation for living in the community. When these patients display adaptive behaviors, they receive tokens, which they can exchange for desired goods (e.g., candy) and privileges (e.g., watching TV). This positive reinforcement supposedly conditions patients to perform adaptive behaviors (operants) in response to society's natural rewards (e.g., praise) without needing tokens.
>
> The distinctions between behavior therapies and psychotherapies are more semantic than real, more professional than clinical. Psychotherapies emerged from a medical (and thus, psychiatric) tradition, whereas behavior therapies have their origins in experimental psychology. In any effective therapy new behavior always changes feelings, and vice versa. To varying extents, all psychotherapies address behavior, and all behavior therapies address feelings. As the fields of behaviorism, psychoanalysis, and even psychobiology increasingly influence each other, techniques are often called "behavioral" more from tradition than from anything else.

• *Supportive psychotherapy/counseling.* Whereas psychodynamic psychotherapy stresses insight, supportive psychotherapy emphasizes advice, education, persuasion, reason, and other appeals to conscious processes to alleviate current and practical life difficulties. This is generally what is meant by the term *counseling.* The therapist supports the patient's more mature defenses and adaptive capacities and discourages immature defenses and maladaptive behaviors. To benefit, patients need not be particularly introspective, intelligent, or able to think abstractly, but they do need to have a willingness to change, to examine themselves, and to show up for usually one to four sessions a month.

During an acute psychosis, supportive psychotherapy is the verbal therapy of choice; it provides reality testing, emotional comfort, and help in distinguishing between sensible and senseless ideas, feelings, and actions. After an acute episode, supportive psychotherapy can show patients how to prevent a relapse by avoiding situations that are likely to precipitate symptoms. For instance, after enduring several bouts of major depression, many patients become so adept at identifying the earliest symptoms that they can avert a full-fledged (9–12 months) relapse by calling their psychiatrist, resuming medication, and examining their concerns with the help of professional perspective.

Short-term therapy. This is a time-limited treatment (usually 8–20 sessions) that focuses on a clearly delineated problem that has erupted recently (within the past 2 months) and the goals of which are specified and agreed on from the outset. There are numerous models of short-term therapy, including behavioral, cognitive, interpersonal, and insight-oriented. These therapies often focus on the same goals and problem areas but differ in the type and timing of interventions (Bloom, 1992; Ursano & Hales, 1986).

Depending on whether it suppresses or provokes anxiety, short-term psychotherapy may stress support or insight. When supportive, short-term psychotherapy helps people get over acute problems and maintain the psychological status quo. When educational, patients may learn about thoughts and behaviors that interfere with their functioning and how to replace them with more adaptive ones. An example: A patient puts off responding to a complaint, and the complainer gets increasingly angry. In educational therapy, the patient learns how to respond to the complaint, which makes her less anxious and less likely to delay responding. When combined with other biological or psychosocial treatments, this therapy becomes part of a crisis intervention program. Insight-oriented short-term psychotherapy typically examines a "focal conflict"—a recent and well-defined wish that conflicts with the person's enduring traits. Marty suddenly faces a focal conflict when he meets a woman and must choose between Mom or marriage. Anxiety-provoking short-term psychotherapy would focus on this choice, but not on other related yet more peripheral issues in Marty's life, such as his painfully low self-esteem. The brevity of this therapy helps keep the patient more intensively focused.

Group Treatments

Homo sapiens are one of the most social creatures on the planet, and therefore relationships are the source of much of the joy of human existence. However, the opposite is also true—stress, distress, and unhappiness often result from interpersonal problems. Over the years, multi-person interventions, such as group psychotherapy and psychoeducational groups, have been created as modalities to treat these interpersonal problems effectively.

• *Group psychotherapy.* More than any other treatment, group therapy is ideally suited to address *interpersonal* difficulties. Methods vary, but generally patients learn how they affect others and practice better ways of relating to people. Irvin Yalom (2005), perhaps the most well-known pioneer of group psychotherapy, has described 11 therapeutic factors in group treatment (Table 5-2). The group offers a safe environment in which to try new behaviors. Once confident enough, patients can try out the new behaviors in the "real" world, and then go over the results in the group to further refine their skills. A typical group session lasts 60–90 minutes, occurs once a week for outpatients (three to five times a week for inpatients), has 6–10 members, and is led by one or two therapists.

Group psychotherapy differs from (1) *encounter groups*, which help "normal" people engage in consciousness raising and self-actualization, and (2) *T-groups* (the *T* stands for *training*), which teach normal people how groups function (group process) by having them participate in a group.

Surveyed patients claim that groups help most by giving them a sense of belonging and by showing them they are not the only ones in the world facing difficulties. However, patients with psychosis and people who are extremely

---

TABLE 5-2

Yalom's Curative Factors of Group Treatment

- *Instillation of hope*—faith that the treatment mode can and will be effective.
- *Universality*—demonstration that we are not alone in our misery or our "problems."
- *Imparting of information*—didactic instruction about mental health, mental illness, psychodynamics, or whatever else might be the focal problem of the group.
- *Altruism*—opportunity to rise out of oneself and help somebody else; the feeling of usefulness.
- *Corrective recapitulation of primary family group*—experiencing transference relationships growing out of primary family experiences, providing the opportunity to relearn and clarify distortions.
- *Development of socializing techniques*—social learning and development of interpersonal skills.
- *Imitative behavior*—taking on the manner of group members who function more adequately.
- *Catharsis*—opportunity for expression of strong affect.
- *Existential factors*—recognition of the basic features of existence through sharing with others (e.g., ultimate aloneness, ultimate death, ultimate responsibility for our own actions).
- *Direct advice*—receiving and giving suggestions for problem-solving strategies.
- *Interpersonal learning*—receiving feedback from others and experimenting with new ways of relating.

Note. Adapted from Yalom, 2005.

---

sensitive to personal slights or to feelings of persecution are likely to panic or become further disorganized if the group becomes too intense. Narcissistic, paranoid, or rigidly moralistic patients generally do poorly in therapy groups and are quickly ostracized by other patients.

- *Psychoeducational groups.* These groups provide patients with specific information and/or skills to improve their ability to function in their various life roles. An assertiveness training group, for example, would teach members about different styles of behavior—passive, assertive, and aggressive. Group members would then pick problematic situations and practice using assertive skills in the group. Between sessions, members apply the lessons learned in their real lives. They then review their experiences in the group and continue to refine their skills via this feedback loop.

- *Self-help groups.* Self-help groups provide a vehicle for people with a common problem to come together to receive support, share information, and get feedback. These groups are very popular and can be found for a wide range of medical, psychological, and social problems. They are not led by professionals. Interestingly, the advent of the Internet has spawned a new generation of cyberspace self-help groups.

The most recognized self-help groups are probably those for drug and alcohol recovery. Alcoholics Anonymous, Narcotics Anonymous, and Alanon are well established in many parts of the world as a method to promote recovery. Some providers criticize these groups for their dubious efficacy, evangelistic nature, lack of trained leadership, and avoidance of scientific scrutiny. Nonetheless, many self-help groups assist patients who are alcoholics and drug addicts, whom many therapists don't like or can't help.

Couple and Family Treatment

In many instances the interpersonal issues reside within the family. When the difficulties are between spouses, meeting with both partners for couple therapy may provide an effective intervention. If the family includes children or there are others who are part of the family, then treatment may be expanded to work with the additional members. Such an approach usually views the family as a system, meaning that by changing any part (the relationship between two people, or even one person's behavior), the larger system can be changed. Further adding to the treatment arsenal, group and family therapies may be combined to create a multiple family group therapy.

- *Couple therapy.* Couple therapy focuses on improving the relationship between two partners. Neither party is therefore considered the patient. The goal is to improve each person's satisfaction with the relationship. There are typically two focal points in this work: communication and conflict resolution. Enhancing communication requires paying specific attention to the intent and the impact of the communication (Gottman, 1999). This requires partners to ask one another their perception of a communication, and to attend to both verbal and nonverbal messages. Each partner then has the opportunity to clarify. This technique is sometimes referred to as "active listening." For example, when the wife says "You never listen to me!", the husband may conclude that he's not doing a good enough job (e.g., fixing the sink, watching the children). If he asks if she means he's not doing enough tasks, the husband may learn that his wife is actually seeking emotional support and not a new sink in the kitchen. He can then specifically provide what she wants. Thus increased skill in transmitting and receiving messages accurately can lead to increased satisfaction in the relationship.

The other primary focus is conflict resolution, sometimes called negotiation. Many people are uncomfortable in managing disagreements and resort to short-term coping strategies to reduce their immediate discomfort. As an illustration, imagine a husband and wife disagreeing over whether to have joint or separate bank accounts. The husband wants separate, but the wife thinks that's unfair because she is only working part-time. As the debate heats up, both people become more rigid in their positions, and soon the husband starts yelling over the top of his wife's voice. She responds by walking out and slamming the door. What began as a problem for the couple to solve soon became an exercise in each person fighting to reduce his or her immediate distress—he bellowed, and she walked out. These coping methods may well reduce discomfort temporarily, but they not only don't solve the original problem, they also can create additional dissatisfaction in the overall relationship. Therapy teaches partners how to identify (1) guidelines for interacting during a disagreement (e.g., not yelling or walking out), (2) the goals of their interaction (e.g., solving the bank account question), and (3) the tools they need, such as problem-solving skills, to address the problem (Emery, 1994).

• *Family therapy.* Like couple work, family therapy seeks to improve communication and conflict resolution skills to reduce stress and increase adaptive functioning. There are many models of family therapy (Nichols, 1984) in which the focus is on the family as a dysfunctional system. Thus there is no single patient and the unit of treatment is the family itself. One of the more common approaches is structural family therapy (Minuchen, 1974). This model focuses on family members' alliances and boundaries. For example, suppose the mother confides in her daughter that "Your dad isn't that interested in me" instead of dealing directly with her husband to improve the marriage. The husband/father resents this arrangement and pulls further away from both, thereby reinforcing the dysfunctional structure. Treatment would focus on moving the parents closer together as partners and removing the daughter from the marriage and into the role of their child.

Every family, like every relationship, has a structure or set of rules. Not surprisingly, major life changes in the family can require an adjustment or recalibration of how people interact. Times of transition, such as a child moving into adolescence and pushing for more independence, create potential issues that families sometimes need help in navigating. Family therapy, using tools such as role-playing inside and homework outside the sessions, can help family members get (back) in synch with one another.

• *Multiple family group therapy.* This format of group therapy generally consists of four to seven families meeting with two or more therapists for 60–90 minutes. These families typically have a hospitalized relative on the same unit. The meetings occur once or twice a week and usually include the hospitalized patients. In many respects, multiple family group therapy offers something other treatments cannot: It affords relatives a chance to see that they are not alone in the world, to share mutual problems with a uniquely sympathetic audience, to learn how other families cope with similar problems, and to feel more hopeful by observing other patients' improvement. Conversely, this group format enables inpatients to see what other patients' families are like; as a result, when patients talk to one another outside of the multiple family group—informally or in group therapy—they can speak with firsthand knowledge of their families.

With the above treatments, a convenient distinction is made between "counseling" and "therapy." Couple and family *counseling* is used if the psychopathology mainly resides within the patient, or if the couple or family had been functioning normally but now is doing poorly as a result of a crisis. If the psychopathology is enduring and resides within the couple or family, couple or family *therapy* should be used. Changes in behaviors and interpersonal interactions are the goal.

Whether or not the family has played a major role in producing the disorder, counseling is based on the assumptions that there is a patient with a mental disorder who disrupts the family members, and who, in turn, may act "neurotically," unwisely, or harmfully. Family members are not viewed as victimizers. In a sense, everybody is a victim. Counseling usually helps family members to solve problems, to minimize psychological trauma to other family members, and to deal more constructively with the patient's disorder. Family members, for example, might learn to stop telling a depressed member to "pick yourself up by your bootstraps," but that it *is* okay to ask her to do a few chores or join the family on an outing.

In family therapy, clinicians consider the real patient to be the entire family even though the family may implicate a single member (usually the most vulnerable) as the *identified patient*. In this view, the family is as much an unwitting victimizer as a victim. Therapy tries to rectify distorted communications and relationships within a couple or a family as a means of helping the entire family, including the identified patient.

Specialized Treatments

In addition to the psychological treatments that rely on talking with the patient to change their thoughts, feelings, and/or behavior, therapists sometimes augment their treatment by incorporating specialized techniques that can help improve symptoms. Three of the more common tools include hypnosis, biofeedback, and relaxation training.

• *Hypnosis.* Hypnosis is a state of hypersuggestibility in which the patient is relatively oblivious to everything except the hypnotist's voice. Hypnosis is *not* sleep but a form of intense, restricted alertness. The "power" of hypnosis lies within the subject, not the hypnotist. When a person says "You can't hypnotize me," he is correct. Psychological (and probably neurological) variables affect patients' ability to enter a trance (Pettinati et al., 1990). The hypnotist cannot "control" the patient. Most people have experienced hypnosis without realizing it. In driving long distances at night on a highway, the driver will "glaze over" and then suddenly jerk awake to attention. When "glazed over," the driver is in a light hypnotic trance, focused on the road and oblivious to everything else.

Although the public often views hypnosis as a magic potion that, without any time or effort, will remedy every human affliction, its clinical efficacy is far more limited. Mental-health professionals also have become enamored with hypnosis, particularly since the attention the work of Milton H. Erickson received in the 1980s. Nonetheless, hypnosis can be helpful in treating habits such as overeating and smoking. When psychotherapy with a patient becomes "stuck," hypnosis can be used to accelerate information-giving. Hypnosis is generally ill-advised for patients who are currently or potentially psychotic.

• *Biofeedback.* An electronic instrument informs the patient about changes in one or more physiological variables that she does not normally perceive, such as brain-wave activity and blood pressure. A patient with tension headaches, for example, can identify tension in her facial muscles by the sound of beeps from a biofeedback machine, which reflect the degree of this tension. She then experiments with different mental activities (e.g., fantasizing lying on a beach, deep breathing, humming "Ooooooooommmm") to see which decreases the frequency of beeps, indicating diminished facial tension and headaches. Biofeedback is mainly used to treat psychophysiological disorders such as tension headaches and hypertension.

• *Relaxation training.* Relaxation techniques such as "progressive muscle relaxation" allow a patient to systematically contract each muscle group in his body and then fully relax it. These exercises, which resemble meditation techniques, can reduce anxiety and induce sleep. They are also used in conjunction with behavioral techniques such as systematic desensitization. Relaxation training can also engage the imagination through the addition of guided imagery. In this version of the exercise, the therapist verbally guides the patient through a pleasant and relaxing experience while the patient uses his imagination to visualize it.

NO TREATMENT

"All that's therapy isn't therapeutic." This dictum of Thomas Detre's receives too little attention. All treatments, including psychosocial treatments, have side effects. Abraham Kardiner (1977) wrote, "Freud was always infuriated whenever I would say to him that you could not do harm with psychoanalysis. He said, 'When you say that, you also say that it cannot do any good. Because if you cannot do any harm, how can you do good?'" (p.69) Clinical experience confirms Freud's observation: An upsurge of repressed thoughts or primitive feelings can exacerbate psychotic, neurotic, and affective symptoms. Patients can become overly dependent on therapists or "addicted" to therapy; they may substitute therapists for friends and therapy for living. For some patients, insight becomes an excuse to avoid change, while others misuse it as punishment, not learning. Thus, in devising treatment plans, clinicians should weigh a therapy's potential hazards and benefits, and for certain patients conclude that "no treatment" is the prescription of choice.

Sometimes no treatment is the best treatment, not because therapy would harm, but because it would most likely fail. Many patients with psychosomatic problems are not helped by therapy, nor are those with personality disorders (especially antisocial personality disorder). Too often, somaticizing patients emerge from therapy "psychologizing" their problems—and newly equipped with a whole new list of symptoms and issues. The same often applies to the "unmotivated" and to those seeking compensation, disability, or a lawsuit. (Clinicians should think twice when explaining a failed treatment as due to the patient, who was "unmotivated." The patient may be unmotivated, but after all, it is at least part of the therapist's job to motivate—that's what makes a treatment successful!) Some people, such as those seen during bereavement or an acute crisis, will improve without therapy if they have supportive friends. Thus, don't assume that every patient needs, or will benefit from, treatment, and don't forget that a failed treatment hurts more than no treatment.

DOES THERAPY WORK?

Strange how people say "I don't believe in psychiatry." No one says, "I don't believe in surgery." That's because everyone knows that surgery helps sometimes, but not at other times: It depends on the patient, the illness, the goals of surgery, and the surgeon. The same holds true for psychiatric treatment: Whether it helps depends on the patient, the disorder, the goals of treatment, and the therapist.

Also strange is asserting "I don't believe in psychiatry" as if it were a matter of theology, as in "I don't believe in God." Patients should evaluate their therapy by trusting their own judgment, not as a question of faith. They can ask themselves if, given reasonable expectations and sufficient time, treatment seems to be helping or not.

What is meant by the assertion "I don't believe in psychiatry"? Surely people do believe that psychoactive drugs can treat some problems, and surely they believe that talking to a relatively neutral, objective, and skilled professional who's uninvolved in the patient's personal life can affect how the patient views herself and the world.

To ask "Does psychotherapy work?" is akin to asking "Does a restaurant work?" No one would compare McDonald's with Chez Andre's Exclusive French Cuisine. Each is splendid at what it does. The same is true for psychotherapy. It does what it does, as long as what's expected of it is appropriate, and as long as the therapist, like the restauranteur, knows her stuff. And just as whether a restaurant "works" depends on who's making the judgment, so too with therapy. In evaluating if a patient has improved, who's the best judge? The patient? The therapist? A researcher? A family member? A friend? There is an abundance of research on the effects of psychotherapy, and the overall conclusion is that approximately two-thirds of people improve in the short term from psychotherapy (Shadish et al., 2000; Smith et al., 1980).

Therefore, the proper question is not "Does psychiatry work" but "Which treatments work for which disorders, in which patients, toward which goals, under which conditions, and according to whom?" In evaluating if a particular therapy is effective, valid research now compares the effects of an active treatment (e.g., cognitive therapy, fluoxetine) with an inactive or placebo treatment (e.g., supportive contact, placebo pill). The patients, and when possible the clinicians, are "blind" to (uninformed about) which treatment is active or, if it's medication, which treatment the patient is receiving. When only patients are blind, it is called a single-blind study; when both clinicians and patients are kept uninformed, it is a double-blind study. In the pages that follow, as we consider specific psychopathologies and clinical syndromes, results from this type of experimental research are presented. Nevertheless, as mentioned previously, although our scientific evidence in psychiatry is growing, it is also still just emerging.

References

Abroms, E.M. (1983). Beyond eclectism. *American Journal of Psychiatry, 140,* 740–745.

Anderson, E.M., & Lambert, M.J. (1995). Short-term dynamically oriented psychotherapy: A review and meta-analysis. *Clinical Psychology Review, 15,* 503–514.

Barlow, D.H. (Ed.). (2001). *Clinical handbook of psychological disorders.* New York: Guilford Press.

Beck, A.T., Rush, A.J., Shaw, B.F., & Emery, G. (1979). *Cognitive therapy of depression: A treatment manual.* New York: Guilford.

Bloom, B.L. (1992). *Planned short-term psychotherapy.* Boston: Allyn & Bacon.

Breier, A., & Strauss, J.S. (1984). The role of social relationships in the recovery from psychotic disorders. *American Journal of Psychiatry, 141,* 949–955.

Chambless, D.L., & Ollendick, T.H. (2001). Empirically supported psychological interventions: Controversies and evidence. *Annual Review of Psychology, 52,* 685–716.

Ellis, A. (1975). *A new guide to rational living.* North Hollywood, CA: Hal Leighton.

Ellis, A. (1984). Rational–emotive therapy. In R. J. Corsini (Ed.), *Current Psychotherapies* (3rd ed.). Itacsa, IL: Peacock Press.

Ellis, A., & Grieger, R. (1977). *Handbook of rational–emotive therapy.* New York: Springer.

Emery, R.E. (1994). *Renegotiating family relationship: Divorce, child custody, and mediation.* New York: Guilford.

Gottman, J.M. (1999). *The marriage clinic: A scientifically-based marital therapy.* New York: Norton.

Hanson, N.B., Lambert, M.J., & Forman, E.M. (2002). The psychotherapy dose: Response effect and its implications for treatment service delivery. *Clinical Psychology: Science and Practice, 9,* 329–343.

Kardiner, A. (1977). *My analysis with Freud.* New York: Norton.

Luborsky, L. (1984). *Principles of psychoanalytic psychotherapy.* New York: Basic Books.

Malan, D.H. (1995). *Individual psychotherapy and the science of psychodynamics* (2nd ed.). London: Hodder Education.

Marlatt, G.A., & Gordon, J.R. (Eds.). (1985). *Relapse prevention.* New York: Guilford Press.

McDermut, W., Miller, I.W., & Brown, R.A. (2001). The efficacy of group psychotherapy for depression: A meta-analysis and review of the empirical research. *Clinical Psychology: Science and Practice, 8,* 98–116.

Minuchen, S. (1974). *Families and family therapy.* Cambridge, MA: Harvard University Press.

Nichols, M.P. (1984). *Family therapy: Concepts and methods.* New York: Gardner Press.

Pettinati, H.M., Kogan, L.G., Evans, F.J., Wade, J.H., Horne, R.L., & Staas, J.M. (1990). Hypnotizability of psychiatric inpatients according to two different scales. *American Journal of Psychiatry, 147,* 69–75.

Popkin, M.K., & Tucker, G.J. (1994). Mental disorders due to a general medical condition and substance induced disorders. *DSM-IV Sourcebook,* 243–276.

Prochaska, J.O., DiClemente, C.C., & Norcross, J,C. (1992). In search of how people change: Applications to addictive behaviors. *American Psychologist, 47,* 1102–1114.

Safran, J.D., & Moran, J.C. (2000). *Negotiating the therapeutic alliance: A relational treatment guide.* New York: Guilford.

Shadish, W.R., Matt, G.E., Navarro, A.N., & Phillips, G. (2000). The effects of psychological therapies under clinically representative conditions: A meta-analysis. *Psychological Bulletin, 126,* 512–529.

Smith, M.L., Glass, G.V., & Miller, T.I. (1980). *The benefits of psychotherapy.* Baltimore: Johns Hopkins University Press.

Ursano, R.J., & Hales, R.E. (1986). A review of brief individual psychotherapies. *American Journal of Psychiatry, 143,* 1507–1517.

Wilkins, W. (1973a). Client's expectancy of therapeutic gain: Evidence for the active role of the therapist. *Psychiatry, 36,* 184–190.

Wilkins, W. (1973b). Expectancy of therapeutic gain: An empirical and conceptual critique. *Journal of Consulting Psychology, 40,* 69–77.

Wolpe, J. (1958). *Psychotherapy by reciprocal inhibition.* Palo Alto, CA: Stanford University Press.

Yalom, I.D. (2005). *The theory and practice of group psychotherapy* (5th ed.). Basic Books: New York.

To obtain information about any self-help group, contact the National Self-Help Clearinghouse, Graduate School and University Center of the City University of New York, 365 5th Avenue, Suite 3300, New York, NY 10016, or on the Web at www.selfhelpweb.org.

6

Psychopharmacology

For centuries people have tried to establish how the brain, with its physical and neurochemical processes, gives rise to perception, sensation, motion, emotion, and thought. The functional systems of the brain most important in psychopathology include the limbic system, the prefrontal cortex, the amygdala, the basal ganglia, and the thalamus. The limbic system, a series of deep brain structures encircling the middle brain, is responsible for regulating emotion (Figure 6-1). The functional disturbance of brain cells in this system underlies many psychiatric disorders. This chapter intentionally simplifies some aspects of psychopharmacolgy in order to establish a solid foundation for the begin-

FIGURE 6-1
Deep Brain Structures

ning or nonmedical student, and to share useful metaphors for the purpose of providing education to our patients on this topic. Understanding improves retention and adherence to treatment.

As introduced in Chapter 4, the brain is composed of nerve cells, or neurons, that communicate with each other across short gaps called *synapses* (see Figures 4-1 and 6-2). The axons of neurons with cell bodies in one part of the brain may stretch into an adjoining or distant part of the brain to affect neurons there. Neurons make chemicals that allow them to communicate with one another and thereby control body movements, thoughts, feelings, and actions. When the neuron activates, it releases chemicals called *neurotransmitters* into the synapse. These, and other chemicals with similar molecular structures, bind to receptors on the receiving neuron (like a key into a lock) and stimulate or modulate its electrical activity. The chemical key can unlock the receptor completely (agonist) or lock it completely (antagonist) or partially lock or unlock it. The transmitted chemical message then creates an electrical

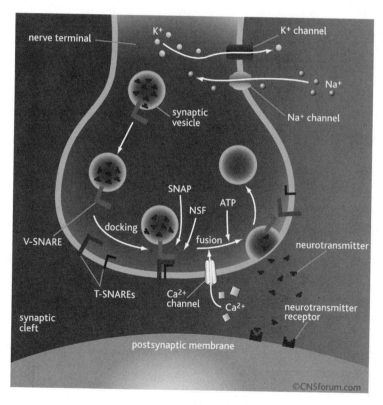

FIGURE 6-2
The Synapse and Neurotransmission

charge (depolarization) that travels down the entire length of the receiving neuron. It is through this electric flow down an axon that information is conducted. As the brain matures, the axon becomes coated with a fatty substance (myelin) that serves as insulation to improve the efficiency of the signal. This process of myelination (which continues from birth into the 20s) explains how we become more thoughtful and less impulsive as we age. We can imagine the harm at the cellular level that huffing gasoline (or other organic solvents) can have in the developing brain—it literally dissolves the myelin sheath and contributes to a short-circuiting of the electric impulses (an "irritable brain"). At birth we have the largest number of neurons we will ever possess, and then careful pruning occurs especially in the first two decades. Incorrect pruning and altered neuron migration in the course of development are suspected mechanisms in schizophrenia.

Activation of a single neuron would be expected to have little effect in the brain. However, activation of whole tracts of neurons lead to phenomena such as motor activity, sensation, or even thought. After the neurotransmitter has been released into the synapse, it is inactivated either by enzymatic breakdown or a reuptake process in which it is "vacuumed" up by the releasing neuron (specifically, reuptake inactivation through presynaptic receptors). A collection of nerve cell bodies of the same neurotransmitter type (e.g., dopamine) is referred to as a nucleus (e.g., nucleus accumbens).

Seven major neurotransmitters are currently known to have an effect on perception, motor activity, sensation, emotion, attention, and cognition: These are acetylcholine, glutamate, gamma-aminobutyric acid, dopamine, serotonin, norepinephrine, and endorphins. Neurons are usually dedicated to producing one primary neurotransmitter. All of these transmitters are necessary for the smooth functioning of the brain, and all of them interact in complex ways. For example, endorphin-releasing neurons modulate GABA neurons, which in turn modulate dopamine-releasing neurons in the main reward pathway in the brain. In another example, serotonin downregulates dopamine (this is the pathway by which some antidepressants may actually worsen ADHD symptoms). A similar result occurs when the release of glutamate through agonism at the NMDA receptors, causes reduced levels of dopamine. In Figure 6-3, we see interactions of three transmitters. If a person is at a romantic dinner with a new love interest, dopamine and serotonin rise, leading to pleasurable feelings. If a waiter drops a tray, startling the individual, anxiety might suddenly spike decreasing the immediate pleasure.

Each of the neurotransmitters seems to have a different major function. Several of them modulate the function of other neurotransmitters. All of the neurotransmitters are necessary in exact proportions for maximal functioning

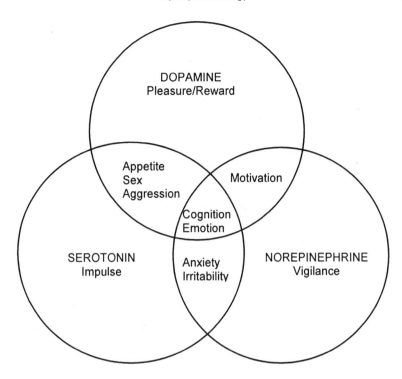

FIGURE 6-3
Overlapping Functions of Monoamine Neurotransmitters

of the central nervous system. These neurochemical interactions must occur in a balanced way for normal functioning. Having too much or too little may be related to an inherited biological predisposition or environmental factors. In the course of daily living, demands are made on these neurochemical pathways, and, if these demands are persistent or excessive, they may exhaust their capabilities and alter or shut down functioning (i.e., mental breakdown). Another environmental factor is the availability of the raw materials in the diet to manufacture the neurotransmitters. The building block for serotonin is tryptophan, an essential amino acid, which may be lacking in the diets of strict vegetarians.

Stressors, in essence, pull on the chain of neurochemicals and cause it to break at the weakest link. Certain individuals may have been born with relative deficiencies in neurotransmitters or receptors (weak links) that predispose them to breaking even under minimal stress. In such cases, treatment involves increasing the chemical suspected to be deficient (fortify the link) and relieving the stress on the chain through various types of psychosocial therapies (previously discussed). Someday we may be able to scan the brain and determine the exact cause of the imbalance, but for now we surmise which neurochemical to address based upon the clinical presentation (more on this topic later). An important consideration in treatment is that neurochemistry (and response to medications designed to restore balance) varies across the life cycle by age and ethnic group. Many medications that are prescribed to restore balance are metabolized in the liver by an enzyme system called cytochrome P450. This system has over two hundred variations of enzymes. Because people of Asian descent have lower levels of the cytochrome P450 system than do people of northern European extraction, lower doses of psychotropic medications would be needed for the same clinical effect. The same applies to older adults, who generally metabolize drugs more slowly.

The body tends to maintain itself in a stable state of neurotransmitters, a state called *homeostasis*. This tendency toward stability applies to both healthy and pathological neurotransmitter states. The brain, once depressed, will maintain the neurotransmitters and receptors in the depressed state. Waiting for neurotransmitters to reset may take years; historically, people were placed in asylums (meaning "peace") where the cares of the world were removed with the hope that under less stressful conditions (relaxed chain), the neurophysiology would be rebalanced.

MAJOR NEUROTRANSMITTERS

As mentioned earlier, seven major neurotransmitters are of particular interest in psychiatry: acetylcholine, glutamate, gamma-aminobutyric acid, dopamine, serotonin, norepinephrine, and endorphin. As each is considered, it is important to understand that they interact in complex ways.

Acetylcholine

Acetylcholine is present in both the peripheral and the central nervous systems. In the peripheral nervous system it is an excitatory neurotransmitter that stimulates muscle fibers to fire. In the central nervous system it has a more complex role: Although it is somewhat involved in excitatory activity, it is also involved in synaptic plasticity, learning, and short-term memory. Disorders associated with acetylcholine function include Alzheimer's disease, and some of the medications used to treat this problem directly affect acetylcholine function.

FIGURE 6-4
Distribution of Acetylcholine Receptors Throughout the Brain

There are two types of acetylcholine receptors: nicotinic receptors in the peripheral nervous system, and muscarinic receptors in the peripheral as well as central nervous systems. Muscarinic receptors are *metabotropic*, meaning that they affect neuronal functioning indirectly through signal transduction on ion channels, rather than directly through the ion channels themselves. These receptors influence second messenger systems and account for synaptic plasticity.

There are relatively few cholinergic receptors in the brain. The site of greatest acetylcholine synthesis in the brain is the interpeduncular nucleus (near the substantia nigra in the midbrain). Patients with Alzheimer's disease sometimes, but not always, show reductions in cholinergic neurons in Meynert's nucleus (Figure 6-4).

Glutamate

Glutamate is the most pervasive excitatory neurotransmitter in the brain (Figure 6-5). It could be thought of as the accelerator that drives brain function. Glutamate is necessary for thought, learning, and motor activity. An excess of glutamate can be associated with seizures. There is some evidence that chronic use of alcohol followed by detoxification leads to a relative excess of

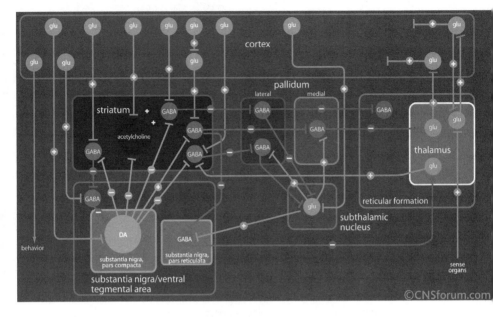

FIGURE 6-5
Glutamate Pathways in the Brain

glutamate; one medication (acamprosate) used for alcohol dependence is a glutamate receptor modulator.

The primary brain glutamatergic pathways are those that connect the thalamus and the cortex, those going from one part of the cortex to another, and the extrapyramidal pathway (i.e., connections between the cortex and striatum). Other glutamate connections exist between the cortex, substantia nigra, subthalmic nucleus, and pallidum. Glutamate-containing neuronal terminals are very common in the brain, accounting for almost 50% of all neurons.

Gamma-aminobutyric Acid

GABA is the primary inhibitory neurotransmitter in vertebrates. It could be thought of as the brake that helps slow down cerebral function. GABA receptors are *ionotropic*, meaning that their activation directly affects potassium or chloride ion channels in the neuron. Relative lack of this inhibitory neurotransmitter can result in seizures. Many drugs of abuse substitute for natural GABA. Alcohol, benzodiazepines, and barbiturates all fall into this category. When a person uses these substances for a long period of time, the brain downregulates production of GABA. If the person abruptly stops using the external substance, the relative lack of a "brake" compared to the "accelerator" of glutamate can lead to withdrawal seizures. GABA is also profoundly involved in anxiety regulation.

GABAergic inhibition is seen throughout brain structures, including in the hippocampus, hypothalamus, and cerebral and cerebellar cortices (Figure 6-6).

Dopamine

Dopamine activates one of five types of receptors in the central nervous system and has an important role in cognition, motor activity, reward, muscle tone,

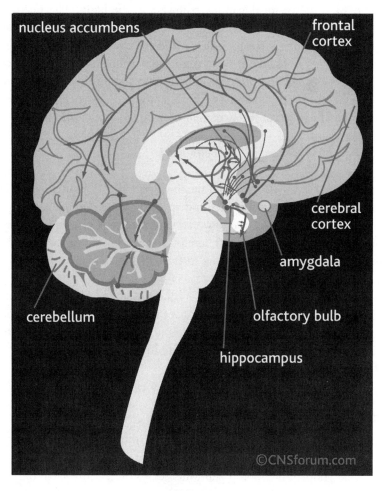

FIGURE 6-6
Major GABA Pathways in the Brain

sleep, mood, attention, and learning. Most of the higher-level effects of dopamine are modulated by the D1 or D2 receptors. Insufficient dopamine in the basal ganglia leads to Parkinson's disease; insufficient dopamine in the frontal cortex can contribute to attention-deficit disorder. Dopamine is the major neurotransmitter involved in the primary reward system of the brain. This system is deeply engaged in the reinforcement of motivated behavior, including pursuit of food, pleasure, and sex. It is this part of the brain that is "hijacked" by drugs such as cocaine and amphetamines, which substitute for dopamine. A major category of drugs, most commonly used to treat schizophrenia, and psychosis in general, are the antipsychotics. Most of these seem to have some effect on the dopaminergic system.

There are three major dopamine pathways in the brain. The first extends from the ventral tegmentum to the mesolimbic forebrain (Figure 6-7) and is responsible for cognition, reward systems, and emotional behavior. The second extends from the substantia nigra to the caudate nucleus putamen (neostriatum) and is associated with movement and sensory stimuli. The final pathway extends from the hypothalamus to the pituitary and is concerned with neuronal/hormonal control of the hypothalmic–pituitary endocrine system.

Serotonin

Serotonin (5-HT) is a neurotransmitter involved in the regulation of mood, anxiety, aggression, sleep, appetite, and sexuality. There are several types of serotonin receptors; all except one work via a secondary message or system in the neuron. Diminished levels of serotonin have been associated with violence. Many medications used in the treatment of anxiety and mood disorders modulate serotonin levels.

The principal nuclei for serotonin are the rostral and caudal raphe nuclei. Axons from the rostral raphe nuclei project to the cerebral cortex, limbic regions, and the basal ganglia. Serotonergic nuclei in the brainstem give rise to descending axons, some of which terminate in the medulla, while others descend the spinal cord (Figure 6-8).

Norepinephrine

Norepinephrine is a chemical that functions locally within the brain as a neurotransmitter, and can also function as a hormone in the peripheral vascular system. Like dopamine, norepinephrine seems to be involved in reward, arousal, and mood regulation. Deficiencies in norepinephrine function in the brain can lead to depression and to attention-deficit disorder.

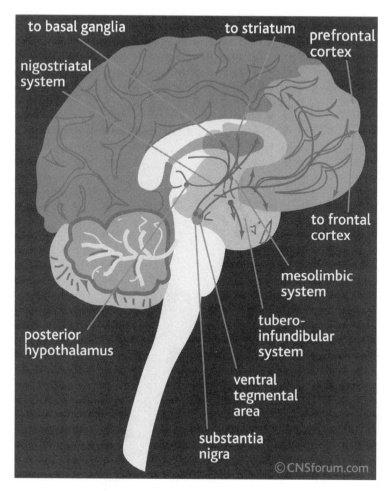

FIGURE 6-7
Major Dopamine Pathways in the Brain

The primary noradrenergic nuclei are the locus coeruleus and the caudal raphe nuclei. The ascending axons from the locus coeruleus project to the frontal cortex, thalamus, hypothalamus, and limbic system. The locus coeruleus is very actively involved in symptoms of withdrawal from drugs of abuse. Nerves projecting from the caudal raphe nuclei rise to the amygdala and descend to the midbrain (Figure 6-9).

Endorphin

Endorphins are peptide neurotransmitters that work as natural painkillers and as antianxiety transmitters. Endorphin receptors on GABA neurons diminish

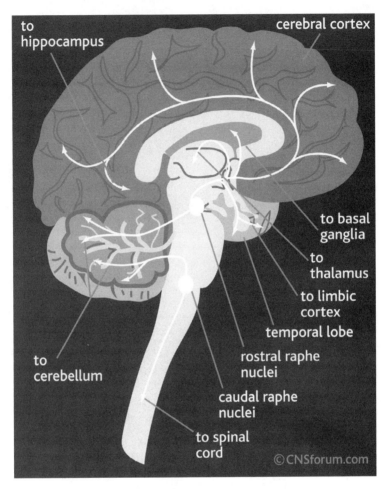

FIGURE 6-8
Major Serotonin Pathways in the Brain

their inhibition of dopamine neurons, causing opioids to activate the reward
system, leading to addiction.

Much of the action of drugs used in psychiatry and neurology can be explained by their effects on neurotransmitter systems. Some medications—for
example, some of the selective serotonin reuptake inhibitors—are highly pref-
erential to which type of receptor they affect. These are sometimes called
"clean" medications. Other medications—for example, the tricyclic antidepressants—affect multiple receptors and are sometimes called "dirty" medica-

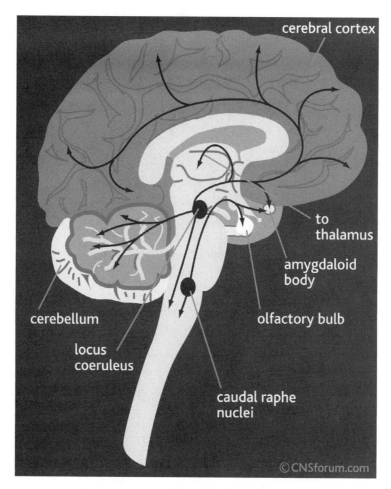

FIGURE 6-9
Major Norepinephrine Pathways in the Brain

tions. Although both types of medications may have side effects that could be intolerable to a given person, there are a broader range of possible side effects in a given individual with dirty medications.

It is important to realize that multiple neurotransmitter systems can be involved in a psychiatric illness. For example, dopamine, serotonin, and nor-epinephrine are all involved in the modulation of mood and anxiety. As a result many medications that are originally developed for treatment of a partic-ular illness (e.g., antidepressants for depression) are applied in the treatment of other illnesses (e.g., antidepressants for anxiety disorders and obsessive–compulsive disorder). Before describing how various categories of drugs affect various neurotransmitter systems, it is helpful to understand two subfields of study: pharmacodynamics and pharmacokinetics.

Pharmacodynamics and Pharmacokinetics

Pharmacodynamics is the study of what a drug does to the body, whereas *pharmacokinetics* is the study of what the body does to a drug. *Pharmacodynamics* is discussed under each section of psychiatric medication. Pharmacokinetics, however, can be discussed in more general terms. (In this text the terms "drug" and "medication" are used interchangeably.)

A drug must have some means of getting into the body to be effective. Most drugs commonly used are given orally, but some can be given by injection or by transdermal patch and initially bypass the liver ("first pass") to deliver more of the parent drug to the target. Other drugs are actually inactive compounds themselves ("pro-drugs") that are then transformed into active compounds by the body.

Because of the presystemic elimination by the liver, higher concentrations of medications are required orally than intravenously to achieve the same pharmacological effect. Some drugs have very poor oral bioavailability. For example, buprenorphine has little absorption if you swallow it in pill form. However it is rapidly and effectively absorbed if nebulized in a nasal spray or if the pill is given sublingually. Ingesting food may interfere or improve absorption, depending on the medication. Various preparations of medications are developed for the purpose of improving pharmacodynamics for an intended therapeutic effect or to improve side effects by either increasing or delaying absorption. For example, a medication may be mixed with a waxy substance and delivered in a pill so that it slowly erodes in the gut and is absorbed over many hours instead of all at once (sustained or extended release). This may be of value in providing once-daily dosing instead of having to remember multiple doses during the day (i.e., increases compliance). Other drugs can be given in an injectable form that is released slowly over a period of weeks. These so-called "depot" drugs are especially useful in psychiatric conditions such as schizophrenia for which compliance with taking drugs consistently each day is poor.

The FDA allows generic drugs (i.e., drugs that go by the chemical name of their active ingredient) to have 80–120% of the bioavailability of the brand-named medication. Brand names are given to medications by the company that initially developed the drug; the patent (and exclusive rights to market) lasts an average of 7 years before other companies can make the generic equivalents.

Once a drug is absorbed, it is distributed throughout the body. In part this distribution depends on factors such as its ability to dissolve in water versus in lipids, its ability to cross the blood–brain barrier, and whether the drug binds to protein in the bloodstream. For example, valproate is entirely protein-bound within the vascular space and unavailable to the brain unless its blood level exceeds 50 μg/ml. Because older adults typically have a greater proportion of body fat (and less water), the volume of distribution in the body will increase.

Once the drug has been distributed throughout the body, it exerts both therapeutic and nontherapeutic effects. The therapeutic effects, of course, are the reason to prescribe the drug. The nontherapeutic effects are side effects and may range from trivial to life-threatening. All medications have side effects. Fortunately, the FDA must approve all pharmaceuticals prior to their marketing; the results of this agency's extensive testing for safety and efficacy on approved medications are summarized in the *Physician's Desk Reference* (PDR). These include potentially adverse effects in a "black box warning" (so-called because of the surrounding black border in the PDR). A frequently reported measure of relative medication safety is the therapeutic index. This is the ratio of the lowest concentration of a medicine that causes toxicity to the lowest concentration that produces the desired therapeutic effect. TCAs, lithium, and opiates are examples of medications with low therapeutic indices (i.e., more dangerous).

The actual effects of drugs occur on the cellular level at receptor sites. The major neurotransmitters mentioned above bind to these receptors, which are located on neurons and other cells in the body. The therapeutic effect for psychotropic medications would obviously take place in neurons, whereas side effects can occur on any cell (including neurons) that has a receptor to receive this medicine. For example, there are serotonin receptors in the gut as well as the brain, and some of the gastrointestinal side effects of SSRIs result from effects on these receptors. When drugs attach to receptors in the central nervous system, they may stimulate an electric impulse, partially stimulate, or inhibit activity (agonists, partial agonists, and antagonists, respectively). In general, agonism at a presynaptic receptor will decrease neuronal activity, and agonism at a postsynaptic receptor will increase it.

The body begins metabolizing drugs as soon as they are absorbed. Some drugs are broken down enzymatically in the synapse or other extracellular space, some in the liver, and some excreted via the kidneys. It is important to know whether a drug has metabolites (breakdown products) that themselves have either therapeutic or nontherapeutic effects.

Most psychotropic drugs undergo two phases of metabolic reactions mediated by enzymes. In the first phase, drugs are oxidized, reduced, and hydrolyzed into intermediate metabolites. The second phase further breaks down these intermediate products, through glucouronidation and acetylation, into water-soluble metabolites that can be excreted by the kidneys. Some medication is already very water-soluble (e.g., lithium and gabapentin) and can be directly excreted renally, especially if the molecule is a small one. A few medications (equivalent to intermediate metabolites) undergo only phase II metabolism (e.g., lorazepam and oxazepam) and require less enzymatic work prior to excretion. This is important to understand when treating patients with compromised liver function (e.g., the patient with a cirrhotic liver needing alcohol detoxification with benzodiazepines).

As mentioned above, a major oxidative enzyme system involved in breaking down many psychotropic drugs is the cytochrome P450 system, located in the endoplasmic reticulum of hepatocytes. The system comprises well over 200 isozymes and varies remarkably from individual to individual. Many psychiatric drugs are not only substrates broken down by this system but also inhibit certain of the isozymes. For example, cimetidine, fluvoxamine, and grapefruit juice all inhibit certain enzymes (3A3/4) and cause elevated blood levels of drugs broken down by the system if given concurrently. Medications can work in the other direction by inducing these same isoenzymes; for example, phenytoin, carbamazepine, and rifampin, prescribed over time, lead to increased enzyme levels (3A3/4) with consequent decrease in the blood levels of the drugs (autoinduction). The clinician must be aware of potential and known drug–drug interactions.

The half-life of a drug is the time needed for the amount of drug in the body, or drug concentration, to fall by 50%. Clinically the term refers to the time required for half of the active ingredient to be metabolized to an inactive form or eliminated from the body. After four or five half-lives the amount of active drug remaining in the body is negligible (< 5%). It is important to note that many intermediate metabolites are active, in that they may attach to receptors and have clinical effects. The half-life of active metabolites often exceeds (and is never shorter than) the half-life of the original drug. *Pro-drugs* are medications that do not have any therapeutic activity until they are metabolized—that is, the metabolites are the active drug.

The absorption, action, and metabolism of drugs change throughout the life cycle. Generally children and adolescents are more sensitive to medications than adults and metabolize them faster per body weight. As we grow older, especially over the age of 60, our ability to break down drugs begins to deteriorate. Some drugs show markedly elevated blood levels in older adults at doses commonly given to younger people.

PSYCHOTROPIC MEDICATIONS

At first glance, the use of psychotropic medications may appear confusing because a medication that is labeled for one condition is used in multiple conditions. For example, the tricyclic antidepressant imipramine is used as a treatment not only for depression but also for generalized anxiety disorder, panic disorder, social phobia, and bedwetting.

When psychiatrists choose medications, they often do so on the basis of a drug's therapeutic receptor action rather than the category of drug. When several medications are likely to be equally effective, medication choice is often based upon side effect profiles. A medication that is initially approved by the FDA for a particular category, say, valproate for epilepsy, may become established through common use as effective for other illnesses, such as bipolar disorder.

In the remainder of this chapter it may help to look at Tables 6-1 and 6-2 that show, respectively, where particular categories of drugs have their effects (either activation or inhibition) and the effects of receptor activation or blockade. We are able to predict likely side effects and therapeutic benefits based on the receptor-binding profiles of any medication. Many psychotropics affect more than one type of receptor either directly, by binding, or indirectly, by modulating other neurons ("dirty drugs," as described above). Because patients may present with multiple symptoms associated with different neurotransmitter systems, some manufacturers combine two different medications (e.g., Symbyax, a combination of olanzapine [an antipsychotic] and fluoxetine [an antidepressant]) with different receptor targets into one preparation in order to restore balance—essentially creating a dirtier drug. The second-generation antipsychotics hit several receptors in addition to dopamine and yet are better tolerated—so cleaner may not be better in every case. Another example: By influencing serotonin *and* norepinephrine, serotonin norepinephrine reuptake inhibitors (SNRIs) may be more versatile antidepressants.

Antidepressants

There are multiple categories of antidepressants. Most of them seem to exert their benefit either by inhibiting monoamine oxidase, the enzyme that breaks down serotonin, dopamine, and norepinephrine, or by inhibiting reuptake inactivation by the releasing neuron. We will separate these drugs into classes based on which neurotransmitters they affect.

Although antidepressants begin to raise the levels of the neurotransmitters in the synapse within several hours of administration, it may take anywhere

TABLE 6-1

Receptor Effects of Psychotropic Drugs

	DA	NE	5-HT	GABA	GLU	END	HIST	A-ADREN	B-ADREN	ACH
Tricyclic antidepressants		+ to +++	+ to +++				– – –	– – –		– – –
Monoamine oxidase inhibitors (MAOIs)	++	+++	+++				– –	– –		– –
Selective serotonin reuptake inhibitors (SSRIs)	+/–		+++							
Selective norepinephrine reuptake inhibitors (SNRIs)	+/–	++	+++							
Dopamine/norepinephrine reuptake inhibitors (DNRIs)	+ to ++	++								
Stimulants	++ to +++	++ to +++			+					
Typical antipsychotics—high potency	– – – –						– – – –	– – – –		– – – –
Typical antipsychotics—low potency	– – – –						– – –	– – –		
Atypical antipsychotics—high potency	– – – –		+ to ++				– – –	– – –		
Atypical antipsychotics—low potency	– – – –		+ to ++				– – –	– –		– – – –
Hypnoanxiolytics (sedative/hypnotics)				+++						
Opioid antagonists						– – – –				
Lithium			+ to ++							
Anticonvulsant mood stabilizers							– – –	–		
Clonidine, guanfacine									++	

DA = dopamine; NE = norepinephrine; 5-HT = serotonin; GABA = gamma-aminobutyric acid; GLU = glutamate; END = endorphin; HIST = histamine; A-ADREN = alpha-adrenergic; B-ADREN = beta-adrenergic; ACH = acetylcholine.

+ = weak agonist; ++ = medium agonist; +++ = strong agonist; – = weak antagonist; – – = medium antagonist; – – – = strong antagonist

TABLE 6-2

Clinical Effects with the Associated Neurotransmitters/Receptor Conditions

	DOPAMINE	NOREPINEPHRINE	SEROTONIN (5-HT)	GAMMA-AMINOBUTYRIC ACID	GLUTAMATE	ENDORPHIN MU	HISTAMINE	ALPHA-ADRENERGIC	BETA-ADRENERGIC	ACETYLCHOLINE
Antidepressant	++	+++	+++							
Antianxiety	−	−	+++	+++						
Obsessive–Compulsive			− − −							
Antipsychotic (reduction in positive symptoms)	− − −									
Antipsychotic (improvement in negative symptoms)			++							
ADHD	++									
Reduction in cravings	+++			+		−			++	
Sedation	−		++				−			
Weight gain			++				− −			
Lightheadedness							−	−		
Cognitive slowing				++		+	−			−
Constipation, blurred vision, dry mount										− −
Nausea	−		+++	− − −						−
Irritability	++	++	−	− − −	++		− to +			
Hypotension								− −	+	
Tachycardia								− − −	−	− −

+ = weak agonist; ++ = medium agonist; +++ = strong agonist; − = weak antagonist; − − = medium antagonist; − − − = strong antagonist.

from 2 to 8 weeks to see their full benefit. Ultimately there are changes in the number of receptors and second-messenger systems that seem to coincide with therapeutic effect. Generally the recommendation is to continue treatment with antidepressants for at least a year following remission of the depression. Sudden discontinuation may cause flu-like symptoms. There are many serotonin receptors in the gastrointestinal tract, which explains the initial nausea and at least some of these withdrawal effects. Serotonin syndrome, in which the body must cope with excessive amounts of serotonin both in the central nervous system and peripherally, is a potentially life-threatening condition with symptoms of tachycardia, diaphoresis, mydriasis, hypertension, rhabdomyolysis, and hyperthermia. Not all drugs that increase serotonin are psychiatric ones. For example, tramadol, an analgesic, also raises serotonin, as do the herbs St. John's wort, yohimbine, and boswellia. Ecstasy or MDMA, a so-called "club drug," acts as a hallucinogen and stimulant but also increases serotonin levels. Ecstasy abusers sometimes take fluoxetine prior to ingesting the ecstasy, because fluoxetine inhibits the cytochrome enzyme that breaks down the abused drug. By using these two drugs together, they increase the risk of serotonin syndrome.

Tricyclic Antidepressants

Tricyclic antidepressants (TCAs), beginning with amitriptyline and imipramine, revolutionized the treatment of depression. These "dirty" medications are serotonin and norepinephrine reuptake inhibitors. They delay or prevent the releasing nerve cell from reuptake inactivation of the neurotransmitter. As a result, the serotonin or norepinephrine has a greater effect on the target neuron. Tricyclic antidepressants generally work in approximately two-thirds of depressed people.

There are three problems with this category of medication. First, because they have effects not only on those neurotransmitters but also on histamine (H-1), cholinergic, and alpha-adrenergic receptors, they carry a high rate of side effects that reduce their tolerability. Side effects include weight gain, sedation, constipation, blurred vision, and mild cognitive slowing. Remembering that we advise depressed patients to continue the medication for a year, it is understandable that the side effects could be burdensome.

Second, tricyclic antidepressants interact in complex ways with other commonly prescribed medications. These drugs–drug interactions can raise severe problems that can be difficult to predict. Many TCAs are metabolized by cytochrome P450-2D6.

Tricyclics affect sodium channel transmission in the heart. This is the mechanism that allows the heart muscle to recover after each beat. An overdose on as little as a week's worth of medication can result in a fatal cardiac arrhythmia. Given that a substantial number of depressed people experience suicidal thoughts and the fact that it takes a few weeks for a full antidepressant response, the practitioner must exercise caution to *not* provide patients with an instrument for suicide by overdose.

Tricyclic antidepressants are also used for anxiety disorders, panic disorder, and obsessive–compulsive disorder. In nonpsychiatric illnesses they are used in enuresis, sleep disorders, and pain medicine. They are used in pain medicine because they bolster serotonin and norepinephrine. There are two types of pain transmission in humans: acute sharp pain is mediated by endorphin neurons ("fast pain tracts"), and chronic, nagging pain is mediated by serotonin neurons ("slow pain tracts").

All antidepressants work in approximately two-thirds of depressed individuals. Head-to-head comparisons have largely been unconvincing. However, among individuals with "melancholic depression," clomipramine has shown a clear advantage. A melancholic depression is one in which the individual simply cannot experience pleasure and often suffers extreme neurovegetative signs of depression.

Heterocylic antidepressants such as trazodone, nefazodone, and maprotiline are similar to the tricyclics, for all practical purposes. Nefazodone is rarely used because of hepatic toxicity. Trazodone is now used most commonly as a sleep aid because of its combined serotonergic and antihistaminic actions.

Selective Serotonin Reuptake Inhibitors

The introduction of fluoxetine under the brand name of Prozac in 1986 largely revolutionized the treatment of depression. As a category these selective serotonin reuptake inhibitors (SSRIs) are much safer in overdose than the TCAs are. Previously primary-care physicians with limited experience with tricyclics would refer depressed patients to psychiatrists for treatment. Because of the stigma of mental illness, many people simply would not go.

With fluoxetine and the other SSRIs, the front line of treatment for depression could be moved from the psychiatrist's office to that of the primary-care doctor. Fluoxetine and its successors have become among the most widely prescribed medications in the history of the world. As a category all of these medications work in a very specific way by inhibiting reuptake inactivation of serotonin. The drugs in this category share more similarities than differences.

The primary differences involve with whether the drug affects enzymes in the liver that break down other drugs. These enzymes, called the cytochrome P450 system, have many slight variations and are highly variable from person to person. Roughly speaking, the SSRIs may be divided into two groups: one with little cytochrome interaction and one with more. The group with little cytochrome interaction includes sertraline, citalopram, and escitalopram. The group with more cytochrome interactions includes fluoxetine, paroxetine, and fluvoxamine. Other drugs, ranging from something as simple as the over-the-counter cough medicine dextromethorphan to asthma drugs, antibiotics, and cardiac drugs, may be broken down by the same cytochrome system. As a result caution must be exercised to not prescribe an SSRI that might have problematic interactions with other drugs. Most SSRIs are highly protein-bound and range from about 46% (escitalopram) to 98% (sertraline).

Roughly speaking, each of the SSRIs leads to improvement in about two-thirds of depressed people. Further study has shown their utility in the treatment of generalized anxiety disorder, panic disorder, obsessive–compulsive disorder, social phobia, and bulimia.

In children and young adults use of the SSRIs may lead to an increase in suicidality in a small subgroup. However, this slight possibility must be balanced against the risk of suicide in untreated depression. Since the FDA required that all SSRIs be labeled with a caution of possible severe complication (the "black-box warning") in 2004, the number of prescriptions for this category of drugs for children and adolescents has markedly dropped. Regrettably, this decline has led to an increase in the number of completed suicides. In prescribing any medication, the risks and benefits of NOT treating must be balanced with those of treating the illness.

Mirtazapine, which acts indirectly on both serotonin and norepinephrine, is effective in treating depression but has a very high incidence of weight gain (also because of antihistaminic receptor activity). About 17% of patients on this medication gain more than 10 kilograms. Mirtazapine in low doses is fairly sedating and has found a useful niche in inducing sleep while augmenting antidepressant response with another medication.

Selective Serotonin Norepinephrine Reuptake Inhibitors

Some drugs slow reuptake inactivation of more than one neurotransmitter. For example, *venlafaxine* and *duloxetine*, as selective serotonin norepinephrine reuptake inhibitors (SNRIs) both inhibit reuptake inhibition of serotonin and norepinephrine. Both affect serotonin at any dose. Venlafaxine affects norepinephrine only at doses of 150 mg or above. Duloxetine affects both serotonin and norepinephrine throughout its dosage range. However, tolerability of the two drugs is markedly different. Both drugs cause nausea in the immediate release form in roughly a third of patients because of serotonin receptors in the gut. Venlafaxine is available in an extended release form that significantly reduces the incidence of nausea. Duloxetine is not. On the other hand, duloxetine has been demonstrated to be of value in certain types of neuropathy, specifically that caused by diabetes. Venlafaxine has the lowest protein binding of any antidepressant and has few cytochrome interactions.

Selective Dopamine Norepinephrine Reuptake Inhibitors

Bupropion is the prototypical member of this class. It inhibits reuptake of both dopamine and norepinephrine. It is an effective antidepressant. However, in some vulnerable individuals, boosting norepinephrine seems to increase anxiety—this is a not uncommon side effect of this drug. Interestingly, because the final reward pathway for addiction seems to involve dopamine, bupropion has been demonstrated to be helpful in alleviating nicotine and stimulant addiction. Unfortunately, bupropion may lower the seizure threshold more than other antidepressants. Most antidepressants have an incidence of seizures of about 1 in 3,000, but bupropion has an incidence of 1 in 1,000. One confounding variable is that this medication was field-tested at higher than currently recommended doses in a cohort of females with bulimia who undoubtedly had some electrolyte abnormalities that may have lowered the seizure threshold. In addition, patients with bulimia may show cerebral dysrhythmias in up to 15% of people with the disorder. For this reason bupropion is contraindicated in patients who have a preexisting seizure disorder or who have an active eating disorder.

Reboxetine is an antidepressant similar to bupropion without the increased risk of seizures, but it is not available in the United States. Atomoxetine, an approved antidepressant in Europe, is used in attention-deficit disorder because of its ability to increase norepinephrine.

Monoamine Oxidase Inhibitors

This category of drugs acts by inhibiting monoamine oxidase, the second catabolic pathway for dopamine, norepinephrine, and serotonin. Monoamine oxidase is also important in metabolizing stimulants and a nonessential toxic amino acid called tyramine. If a person on a monoamine oxidase inhibitor (MAOI) eats tyramine-containing food, the tyramine can cause extremely high blood pressure, with resulting stroke or myocardial infarction. Tyramine is a byproduct of a bacteria-metabolizing protein and is present in many aged foods, including aged cheese and soy sauce. Patients on MAOIs must very carefully exclude these foods from their diet.

There are two types of MAO in the body, type A and type B. Type A is found both intracerebrally and extracerebrally and is responsible for breaking down tyramine. Type B is found in the brain only and is the one with psychotropic effects.

Currently three MAOIs are available in the United States. Two of them, tranylcypromine and phenelzine, are irreversible, nonselective MAOIs. Once they bind to monoamine oxidase, the enzyme is permanently inactivated. New monoamine oxidase molecules are inactivated by the presence of the drug in the body. Because they bind to both A and B, dietary precautions are necessary.

A third MAOI, selegiline, is a reversible type B inhibitor. In low doses it works to help with depression, and no dietary precautions are necessary in the lower doses. This medication has been used in treating Parkinson's disease and is now available in a transdermal patch.

When a depressive episode has not responded to two adequate trials of different antidepressants, it is considered to be *treatment refractory*. Techniques used in this situation include electroconvulsive therapy or other pharmacological options. For example, two antidepressants might be used at the same time, or a potentiator added. A potentiator is a drug that, by itself, may have no antidepressant action but which, when added to an antidepressant, improves the efficacy. Examples include low-dose thyroid hormone, lithium, buspirone, and atypical antipsychotics.

Antipsychotics (also called Neuroleptics)

Ancient literature from India refers to the use of Indian snake root (*Rauwolfia serpentina*) as an antipsychotic. In fact, one of the active chemicals in it, reserpine, has some weak antipsychotic properties.

Typical Antipsychotics

Chlorpromazine was the first modern drug synthesized specifically for treatment of psychosis in 1950. It was the prototype of a class of antipsychotics that are now called *typical* antipsychotics. All antipsychotics tend to block D2 receptors in the dopamine pathways in the brain. Excessive dopaminergic activity in the mesolimbic system has been associated with psychosis; too little results in poor attention, little pleasure, parkinsonism (poverty of movement), tardive dyskinesia, and neuroleptic malignant syndrome. The typical antipsychotics are nonspecific in their dopamine blockade and are associated with a fair amount of side effects, decreasing their tolerability. The side effects include extrapyramidal or parkinsonian symptoms (imbalance between dopamine and acetylcholine) such as restlessness, increased muscle tension, or muscle spasm (dystonic reaction). Long-term use can also cause a potentially permanent movement disorder called *tardive dyskinesia*. In this disorder an individual has ongoing involuntary movements, often of the mouth and tongue, of which he or she is not aware. These movements can be socially disabling. In some cases, when the involuntary movements spread to the trunk, they can interfere with walking, balance, and even breathing. Tardive dyskinesia seems to occur much more with typical antipsychotics than with the newer atypical ones.

Acute extrapyramidal side effects (EPS) can be alleviated with the use of anticholinergic medication. However, this treatment is ineffective with tardive dyskinesia.

Typical antipsychotics are commonly divided into low-potency and high-potency classes. The potency does not refer to the effectiveness of the medication but rather to the number of milligrams necessary to achieve therapeutic effect. Chlorpromazine, thioridazine, and prochlorperazine are low-potency medications with doses usually in the several-hundred-milligram range. The low-potency medications typically have antihistaminic, alpha-adrenergic, and anticholinergic side effects and are also fairly sedating.

High-potency antipsychotics include haloperidol, fluphenazine, trifluoperazine, and perphenazine; dosing is typically in the 5–60 mg range. These medications have less sedating side effects but are more likely to cause EPS. This effect is partly due to the fact that low-potency antipsychotics often carry their own anticholinergic actions that would tend to alleviate acute EPS.

Two of the high-potency atypical antipsychotics, haloperidol and fluphenazine, are available in a long-acting intramuscular depot form. These depot medications are especially useful to stabilize people with psychosis who have had a history of poor or erratic compliance.

Atypical Antipsychotics

The category of atypical (second-generation) antipsychotics was led by the prototype clozapine. Approved by the FDA in 1989, clozapine, like many other members of this class, exerts serotonin action as well as dopamine receptor blockade. However, each of the atypicals has a somewhat different spectrum of effect on receptor subtypes, leading to different side effect profiles. As noted

in Chapter 12, schizophrenia carries both positive symptoms such as hallucinations or delusions and negative symptoms such as apathy, poor social awareness, abulia (paralysis of will), and anhedonia (absence of pleasure). In many
ways these negative symptoms are more incapacitating over the long run than
positive symptoms. The atypical antipsychotics, led by clozapine, showed remarkable improvements in alleviating the negative symptoms of schizophrenia, which are not shown by the typical antipsychotics.

Clozapine was very helpful in allowing many patients with chronic schizophrenia to leave long-term hospitals and be treated in the community. Unfortunately, it has significant side effects. The most serious is agranulocytosis, a
potentially fatal lack of infection-fighting white blood cells. In a person with
agranulocytosis a strep throat may be fatal. Agranulocytosis occurs in about
1% of patients on the drug in the first 3 months. Thereafter, the incidence
falls over time to less than 0.01% after a year. For this reason patients on
clozapine have their white blood cell counts monitored frequently. Clozapine
is also associated with weight gain, which tends to be a class effect of the
atypicals, and development of metabolic syndrome or diabetes mellitus.

During the 1990s several other atypical antipsychotics were introduced.
Olanzapine and quetiapine have similar effects to clozapine but without the
risk of agranulocytosis. However, they are also associated with significant chances
of weight gain and development of metabolic syndrome. Risperidone has less
sedating effect but is more likely to raise prolactin levels; elevated prolactin
levels may be associated with galactorrhea.

The newest atypical antipsychotics are aripiprazole and paliperidone. Aripiprazole has a partial agonist binding pattern to the dopamine receptors,
which seems to help prevent some extrapyramidal symptoms. It also is weight
neutral.

Ziprasidone is an effective antipsychotic that does not have weight gain as
one of its side effects. However, it does have a side effect of slightly affecting
repolarization of the heart muscle and prolongation of the QTc interval on
the electrocardiogram (EKG). This is usually not clinically significant but can
become so if the patient has natural conditions that prolong this interval or is
on other drugs that do so.

Some of the newer atypical antipsychotics have received FDA indications
for conditions other than psychosis. For example, olanzapine and quetiapine
are useful in the stabilization of bipolar disorder. There is growing evidence
that as well as antipsychotic properties, this category of drugs also has mood
stabilizing, antianxiety, and antidepressant properties.

In older patients with dementia-related psychosis, the drugs in this category
markedly increase the risk of cerebrovascular accident.

Hypnoanxiolytics

Benzodiazepines are the prototypical drugs in this class and have their effect as agonists on the GABA system, duplicating the calming, sedating, and muscle-relaxing effects of GABA. With chronic use of benzodiazepines the brain downregulates production of GABA and benzodiazepine use tends to increase gradually. Remembering that GABA is the major inhibitory neurochemical balancing glutamate, if the benzodiazepine is abruptly discontinued, there is insufficient GABA to balance the glutamate. The patient then experiences anxiety, tremor, and perhaps even seizures. Because of the abuse potential and the life-threatening withdrawal associated with benzodiazepines, they should be used with caution and over as short a period of time as possible. Benzodiazepines are ideally suited for the very short-term treatment of anxiety. For example, a patient just diagnosed with cancer and facing major surgery within a few days would be an ideal candidate.

Individual members of the class of benzodiazepines have more in common than they differ. All of the members of the class have strong antianxiety action. However, they differ in how rapidly absorbed and metabolized they are. Alprazolam, one of the shortest-acting members of this class, reaches a peak blood level very quickly and for that reason is useful for treating an acute panic attack. However, its abuse potential is among the highest for that very reason of the rapid peak and fast decline. The rapidity with which a benzodiazepine reaches its peak blood level is highly correlated with its abuse potential. A benzodiazepine such as alprazolam or triazolam is highly abusable because as its blood level rapidly climbs, the person gets a noticeable "buzz." The fast decline causes withdrawal symptoms, and the discomfort provides the negative reinforcement to "take another pill."

Some of the benzodiazepines (diazepam, chlordiazepoxide, clorazepate) have short half-lives (2–6 hours) and rapid absorption but are broken down into a metabolite (nordiazepam) that has a very long half-life of 96 hours. These benzodiazepines carry a risk of a very gradual buildup of sedation, incoordination, and cognitive problems because of increasing levels of nordiazepam. They are metabolized by cytochrome P450-3A4 enzymes. Table 6-3 provides dosage equivalents and half-lives of various benzodiazepines.

Other Antianxiety Medications (Anxiolytics)

As indicated above, antidepressants, acting through different receptors, are used successfully to treat most anxiety disorders over the long term. Unlike the hypnoanxiolytics, which have an immediate effect, the antidepressants take

TABLE 6-3
Benzodiazepine Doses, Half-Lives, and Active Metabolites

DRUG	EQUIVALENT DOSAGE (mg)	HALF-LIFE (hours)	ACTIVE METABOLITE HALF-LIFE (hours)
Alprazolam*	0.5	6–12	N/A
Chlordiazepoxide	10.0	5–30	36–200
Clonazepam*	0.5	19–50	N/A
Clorazepate	2.5	1–2	36–200
Diazepam	5.0	4–12	36–200
Flurazepam	15.0	2.3	30–100
Loprazolam	0.5	6–12	6–12
Lorazepam*	0.5	12	N/A
Oxazepam*	15.0	5–15	N/A
Temazepam*	10.0	8–15	N/A
Triazolam*	0.25	1.5–5	N/A

*No active metabolites.

a couple of weeks for a therapeutic effect (right about the time that tolerance would start to be a problem with benzodiazepines). Sometime antihistamines, such as hydroxyzine, are prescribed acutely for their antihistaminic effect, presumably. Buspirone is a nonaddictive antianxiety agent that works as a 5-HT1A partial agonist (a presynaptic receptor for serotonin). In addition, buspirone has some partial agonist properties on postsynaptic dopamine receptors. Although it has been shown to be more effective than placebo in treating generalized anxiety disorder, it may take 6 weeks to see a result; when effective, it is typically prescribed at doses higher than 40 mg per day. For this reason it is less commonly used in treatment of anxiety disorder than the SSRIs. One area in which buspirone may have a niche is in the augmentation of the other antidepressants, including SSRIs.

There are other categories of hypnotics (sleep agents) that, although they work on the GABA system, have somewhat less abuse potential than the benzodiazepines or barbiturates. These include zolpidem, zaleplon, and eszopiclone. Because melatonin rises during the nighttime and induction of sleep, a novel medication (ramelteon) has been developed that is a melatonin agonist and has no abuse potential. However, ramelteon is broken down by cytochrome P450-1A2 and therefore must be used with caution or not at all when a person is taking fluvoxamine, a potent inhibitor of this enzyme.

Lithium

In the 19th century lithium was used to treat gout. Lithium carbonate, a naturally occurring mineral salt, is an unusual medication because of its chemical simplicity. After absorption into the body the lithium ion can readily displace sodium or potassium at some receptors. The exact mechanism of lithium's action in psychiatric disorders is still being elucidated. The mechanism probably involves working postsynaptically at G-proteins and other secondary messenger systems (inhibits inositol function) to change intracellular homeostasis. Since the late 1940s lithium has been used as the well-documented treatment for bipolar disorder because it is effective in treating not only depression but mania. Most importantly, it is used for maintenance treatment of bipolar disorder because it is effective in preventing relapse to depression or mania. Lithium is the only medication that has been consistently shown to decrease the risk of suicide in people taking it.

Lithium is excreted unchanged via the proximal tubule of the kidneys. The usual blood level targeted for lithium is 0.6–1.1 mEq/liter. It becomes toxic at blood levels above 1.5 mEq/liter. In the toxic range it can cause acute renal or cerebellar damage. Over time in a small proportion of people lithium can be nephrotoxic even in therapeutic doses. Because lithium is used in maintenance treatment of people with bipolar disorder, it is important to follow their renal function, with creatinine clearance tests, over time. Other drugs that affect renal function may elevate blood levels of lithium. Another potential long-term side effect to lithium is thyroid suppression, with about 5% of people on lithium developing iatrogenic hypothyroidism.

Mood Stabilizers/Anticonvulsants

Multiple anticonvulsants have been shown to be effective in treatment of bipolar disorder, especially rapid cycling. Some of them, such as valproate, topiramate, gabapentin, and tiagabine, enhance GABA function via various mechanisms. Valproate seems more effective than lithium in mixed bipolar states and rapid cycling. It is metabolized by the liver with no active metabolites. It does have serious and potentially fatal side effects which fortunately are rare; these include toxic hepatitis, hemorrhagic pancreatitis, aplastic anemia, and thrombocytopenia. Carbamazepine inhibits voltage-dependent sodium channels. It also has the possibility of causing aplastic anemia and idiosyncratic hepatitis. Oxcarbazepine is an analogue of carbamazepine with somewhat less risk of aplastic anemia. Tiagabine and gabapentin are less potentially toxic than the prior mentioned medications; however, so far studies have been more equivocal at demonstrating their effectiveness in bipolar disorder.

Another anticonvulsant, lamotrigine, works by inhibiting glutamate and voltage-gated sodium channels. It has FDA approval for treatment of bipolar depression. An unfortunate but rare side effect of the medication is development of Stevens–Johnson syndrome, a potentially fatal allergic reaction involving gross inflammation of the skin and mucous membranes. A person with this syndrome in its more severe forms can look like someone with second-degree burns all over the body and in the mouth and throat. The risk of Stevens–Johnson syndrome with lamotrigine is markedly elevated if the person is already on either carbamazepine or valproate. Despite this risk, lamotrigine is a valuable tool in the treatment of bipolar disorder.

Stimulants

Stimulants are drugs that function as agonists on dopamine and/or norepinephrine receptors, usually through the transporter system. They increase alertness, decrease fatigue, and sharpen attention and concentration. All of the members of this class have significant abuse potential. Amphetamine, the prototype of this class, was first synthesized in 1887 but not used medically until 1929, when a pharmacologist named Gordon Alles tried it on himself. It was sold as an inhaler under the brand name Benzedrine as a decongestant from the mid-1930s and was widely used by soldiers during the Second World War to increase alertness. From the late 1930s it was marketed in oral form as the first antidepressant.

Other similar members of this class include methylphenidate and dextroamphetamine. Drugs in this class are used to treat narcolepsy, but their most common use is in treating attention-deficit disorder in children, adolescents, and adults alike. While in normal individuals the psychostimulants may cause anxiety and difficulty focusing attention as a dose-dependent side effect, in people with attention-deficit disorder the stimulants have a paradoxical antianxiety and calming effect. Amphetamine is excreted unchanged in urine over a period of several days. Normally about 30% is excreted within 1 day. Acidifying the urine increases this to 75%, and alkalinizing it reduces it to 1%.

In addition to significant abuse potential (as the structure similar to cocaine) there are other significant potential problems with stimulants. For example, they generally increase heart rate and pulse and lower the seizure threshold.

There are multiple stimulants available on the market today. Some of them are mixtures of various amphetamine salts (e.g., Adderall) with different absorption profiles leading to extended benefit. Concerta and Metadate are sustained-release forms of methylphenidate.

Anti-Alzheimer Drugs

Accessing memory and the higher executive functions of the mind such as reasoning and social judgment requires the functioning of all neurochemicals. For example, depression in older adults due to a serotonin deficit can cause a clinical presentation that is difficult to distinguish from senile dementia of the Alzheimer's type (SDAT). This pseudodementia of depression, unlike SDAT, is completely reversible with treatment of the mood disorder. Even in people with true Alzheimer's, their cognition can be partly improved by treating any coexisting mood disorder.

The main neurotransmitters involved in Alzheimer's disease are acetylcholine (ACH) and, to a lesser extent, glutamate (GLU). Part of the primary pathology in SDAT is deterioration of ACH function. ACH pathways important for memory gradually show decreasing amounts of the neurotransmitter. At the same time GLU pathways show some abnormalities of neuronal function. These two fact have led to separate treatments for SDAT.

Acetylcholine is primarily broken down by a synaptic enzyme called *cholinesterase*. The primary category of anti-Alzheimer medication is that of *cholinesterase inhibitors*. By incapacitating cholinesterase, these drugs—donepezil, tacrine, and rivastigmine—allow brain levels of acetylcholine to rise. All three drugs are approved for use in moderate to severe Alzheimer's disease. Donepezil and rivastigmine are also approved for mild SDAT. None of the drugs reverses the course of SDAT, but for at least the first several months of treatment, cognitive decline is slowed. There is some data suggesting that these drugs delay the need for placement of these patients in nursing homes.

Treatment of SDAT via the glutamate pathway is exemplified by use of memantine. In Alzheimer's disease excessive accumulation of calcium in glutamate neurons leads to neuronal damage over time. This mechanism is called *excitatory amino acid neurotoxicity*. Memantine modulates a particular glutamate subreceptor (N-methyl-D-aspartate, or NMDA). Memantine is an NMDA antagonist with a low to moderate affinity for the receptor. Blocking NMDA receptors with memantine slows intracellular calcium accumulation and thereby diminishes further nerve damage. Memantine has been shown to have an efficacy similar to the cholinesterase inhibitors in moderate to severe SDAT but has failed to distinguish itself from placebo in treatment of the milder stages of the illness.

One symptom of Alzheimer's disease is an increase in aggressive and even violent behavior by sufferers. This aggression, more than cognitive decline, forces families to place relatives in nursing homes or dementia units because the patients cannot be maintained at home. Memantine has more of an antiaggressive effect than the cholinesterase inhibitors and delays the point at which the patient must be institutionalized for his or her own safety as well as that of the caregivers.

Memantine and donepezil together have been shown to be more effective than either alone, probably because of their independent but complementary modes of action.

Many people with dementia become more paranoid and even psychotic as the illness progresses. The initial approach to this condition is reassurance, reinforcement of reality testing, and reorientation. In those patients with more severe forms of psychosis, treatment with an antipsychotic becomes necessary. As a class atypical antipsychotics have been effective in treating dementia-related psychosis but significantly raise the risk of stroke. Preliminary research shows a similar risk from the typical antipsychotics. This risk must be balanced against the risks of not treating the psychosis.

Herbals and Nonpharmaceuticals (Food Supplements)

These are not to be confused with over-the-counter medications that similarly do not require a physician's prescription, but unlike herbals and food supplements, are pharmaceuticals closely monitored by the FDA. Herbals et al. do not go through rigorous field testing any more than would the produce in grocery stores. There are few double-blind or placebo-controlled studies supporting their effectiveness, and even where those studies exist with the purported active ingredient, there is no way to be certain that the product being purchased has the ingredient in the advertised concentration. They are not consistently assayed for potency, nor are they studied for harmful contaminants. What is being purchased may not be pure and may have thousands of chemicals mixed in that, at best, do nothing and, at worst, are toxic (e.g., tryptophan and eosinophilia myalgia syndrome). This is not to say that these herbals might not have some beneficial effect (in fact, a substantial percentage of today's pharmaceuticals are derived from plants and most of the others that are synthesized are based on variations from chemicals extracted from herbals). It is the unregulated preparations that pose potential danger to the unsuspecting consumer. Also, herbals and the many compounds contained within may interact unfavorably with other medications.

References

MD Consult. (2008). Elsevier, Inc. Available online at www.mdconsult.com.

Physicians' Desk Reference. (2008). Montvale, NJ: Thomson PDR. Available online at www.pdrhealth. com.

7

Systems-Based Practice

Systems-based practice is defined as awareness of, and responsiveness to, the larger context and system of health care, as well as the ability to call effectively on other resources in the system to provide optimal health care. Systems-based practice includes the abilities to (1) work effectively in various health care delivery settings and systems relevant to clinical specialty; (2) coordinate patient care within the health care system relevant to clinical specialty; (3) incorporate considerations of cost awareness and risk–benefit analysis in patient care and/or population-based care, as appropriate; (4) advocate for quality patient care and optimal patient care systems; (5) work in interprofessional teams to enhance patient safety and improve patient care quality; and (6) participate in identifying systems-based errors and in implementing potential systems-based solutions.

Systems-based practice has been defined as a core competency in medicine through a joint initiative of the Accreditation Council for Graduate Medical Education and the American Board of Medical Specialties. This initiative defined core competencies that cut across all specialties in medicine. These include patient care, medical/clinical knowledge, practice-based learning and improvement, interpersonal and communication skills, professionalism, and systems-based practice. These core competencies are now a major focus for residency training and board certification, and have also been adopted by the Joint Commission for the Accreditation of Health Care Organizations for the evaluation of physician competency for hospital credentialing.

DELIVERY OF CLINICAL SERVICES

There are aspects of clinical service delivery within systems-based practice that are unique to psychiatry and to the needs of people with mental illness. These include clinical needs, provision of support, normalization of care environment, and recovery and resiliency needs.

Clinical needs include diagnostic services, pharmacotherapy, psychotherapy of different modalities, case management, and different levels of care and intensity (ambulatory, intensive outpatient, day treatment, mobile crisis, intensive community-based services, group homes, residential programs, acute inpatient services, dual-disorder treatment for people with mental illness and substance abuse or developmental disorders).

Support needs for patients and families include care management, housing, finances, education/vocation, respite, family support, consumer and family education, recreation/socialization, and assistance with independent living skills.

Needs for normalization of the care environment include using the least restrictive environment of care, community integration, teaching daily living skills to achieve independence and self-sufficiency, freedom from discrimination and stigma, and facilitation of family and peer connections/relationships.

Recovery and resiliency needs include promotion of strengths while addressing needs, instilling hope for a meaningful life and assisting the individual in achieving it, and identifying natural resources and coping skills in dealing with adversity.

COST AND FUNDING OF SERVICES

There is generally a lack of insurance parity for psychiatric and mental health services, with much more restricted coverage for psychiatric disorders. A disproportionate share of funding for mental-health services has been traditionally borne by government, which had funded long-term state hospitals for the seriously mentally ill and more recently funded public mental-health services through Medicaid and Medicare. With the advent of effective pharmacotherapy, more people were released from long-term institutions, but the infrastructure for support in communities was not adequately provided, leading to homelessness and high rates of rehospitalization as well as of incarceration and placement in state custody. During a time in the 1970s and 1980s private insurance coverage for mental-health services was liberal, but this led to major overuse of high-cost institutional (inpatient and residential) services. These developments culminated in concerns both by advocates that people with mental illnesses were being reinstitutionalized, and by insurers that the cost of care was skyrocketing.

In the late 1980s behavioral managed care "carveouts" (separate companies to manage mental health benefits) became an approach used by insurers to control costs, mainly through tightly restricting the use of hospitalization and extended outpatient psychotherapy, leading to increased fragmentation of care as a result. Managed care was first adopted by private health plans but then spread to Medicaid- and even Medicare-funded programs. At the same time, public mental-health programs began to experiment with different approaches to the delivery of intensive community-based services for more seriously ill individuals as a way to maintain them in their communities and prevent rehospitalization, institutionalization, or homelessness. More recently, these community-based services have incorporated increased roles for patients (now termed *consumers*) and for family members, as these parties have advocated both for greater funding for care and for a greater role in the self-determination of their or their family member's care.

ORGANIZATION OF MENTAL HEALTH SERVICES

Mental-health and psychiatric services are organized across various service sectors that, at times, overlap. These include the private, academic, state hospital, and community mental-health sectors. The private sector includes not-for-profit and for-profit institutions, which can be freestanding (i.e., solely psychiatric or mental health), or part of broader medical institutions. These institutions serve patients covered by private or public insurance plans, with only a few being exclusively private. They can either focus solely on inpatient, residential, or outpatient care, or they can comprise continuums of care that include different levels of care intensity and restrictiveness (e.g., acute inpatient units, longer-term residential programs, partial hospital programs, intensive outpatient clinics, and outpatient clinics). Some institutions are operated by, or closely affiliated with, medical schools and/or are part of academic medical centers. There are still remnants of the large state hospitals for the severely mentally ill that dominated state-funded systems, but these are mostly downsizing or being closed as more and more patients are "deinstitutionalized" into community-based services.

There has always been, and continues to be, a strong community-based sector of independent private practitioners, including psychiatrists, psychologists, and other licensed mental-health professionals, delivering outpatient services for people with mild to moderate mental health needs who have insurance or the ability to pay out of pocket. In the 1960s, as part of federal enabling and funding legislation, hundreds of community mental-health centers were developed in the United States to provide care for people with mental illnesses closer to their own communities, both for the poor and in underserved regions. These were largely modeled after child guidance clinics, which developed in the 1920s to care for children and youth with behavioral problems coming to the attention of juvenile courts or child welfare agencies. Community mental-health centers enjoyed much support during the 1960s through 1980s, but suffered from federal budget cuts. As the funding system shifted to Medicaid and Medicare funding of public mental-health services, many of these community mental-health centers evolved into not-for-profit entities, providing outpatient and intensive community-based services. Many of these programs now include more comprehensive community outreach services or are co-located in schools, welfare offices, detention centers or jails, and developmental disorders programs.

The mental-health system interacts with a number of other service systems to comprise the overall system of care for people with mental illnesses or emotional disturbances. These include medical, educational/vocational, criminal/juvenile justice, and welfare services.

Medical Service System (Primary Care, Community Hospitals, Tertiary Medical Centers)

Medical illness is often comorbid with psychiatric disorders, with high rates of depression and anxiety disorders particularly seen in people with chronic medical illnesses such as diabetes, cancer, and heart disease. Psychiatric consultation services are commonly found in tertiary medical centers and in many community hospitals, particularly those with integrated psychiatric services. However, the primary-care sector and ambulatory specialty medical sectors are largely cut off from psychiatric or mental-health services. Many barriers exist in obtaining mental-health service referrals for ambulatory primary-care patients, including separate physical locations, different insurance systems (medical and behavioral), lack of referral relations between sectors, and poor communication of critical information. Another component of the medical service sector where there is a high prevalence of need but significant shortages and barriers, is comprised of facilities serving older adults (nursing home and assisted living facilities). Older adults not only face high rates of dementia but also high-prevalence levels of depressive and anxiety disorders. There is an increasing interest in, and practice models for, the provision of integrated as well as consultative mental-health services in primary-care clinics, health maintenance organizations, nursing homes, and assisted living facilities to serve these increasing needs.

Educational/Vocational Service System

The educational and vocational systems face the impact of increased educational demands for average students or workers, due to the increased technological and informational demands on our society. In addition, the increasing needs of people with learning disorders and serious emotional disturbances are placing added burdens on schools and vocational agencies. These challenges occur in the context of underfunding of service, and this lack of funding is especially felt in the area of special education services. Many school districts and state vocational programs actively avoid the mandates of federal laws such as the Individuals with Disabilities Education Act (IDEA) and Section 504 of the Americans with Disabilities Act, which outlines requirements for accommodations of mentally ill/emotionally disturbed children and adults in schools and workplaces. The avoidance of these laws results in an underidentification of people with covered disabilities. A recent salutary development in the area of interagency systems of care for children is a renewed interest in school-based services, coordinated services for people with developmental disabilities, and integrated vocational services in intensive community treatment programs.

Criminal/Juvenile Justice Service System

Studies have documented high rates of psychopathology among youth in the juvenile justice system, with estimates of approximately 50–70%, and among adults in the criminal justice system, with rates of 20–40%. Mentally ill individuals are often arrested due to their propensity to abuse substances and display aggressive or disruptive behaviors. There is also disproportionate representation of poor and minority populations, especially of African-Americans and Latinos, among people referred into juvenile or criminal justice. This lopsided representation reflects the adversity faced by these populations as well as the lack of culturally competent services in mental health and other agencies. Individuals going into juvenile and criminal justice underutilize mental-health services over their lifetime when compared to cohorts in other systems. The poor level of services within juvenile justice facilities also deprives inmates of adequate services, with racial bias further preventing access to services. In spite of similarities in their populations, the justice and mental-health systems have significant differences in their orientations and philosophies (with the former having more of a community safety and punishment orientation, except for some rehabilitation focus in juvenile justice). Areas of natural collaboration between these systems occur in the diversion of mentally ill or emotionally disturbed individuals and their treatment after entering these systems. Multisystemic therapy (MST) and community-based systems-of-care programs for youth, assertive community treatment (ACT) for adults, mental-health courts, and drug courts have all resulted in significant reductions in detention or jail, rates of arrest and incarceration, and treatment costs.

Welfare

Children and adults served in the welfare system have extremely high mental-health needs, with prevalence rates estimated at about 50% for both children and for their mothers, yet they are significantly underserved with respect to mental-health services. Already traumatized by the conditions of abuse and neglect that led to removal from their homes, children placed in foster care and women in welfare programs are confronted with the additional traumas of the loss of relationships, multiple relocations, uncertainty about their future, and the difficult task of establishing new positive attachments and embarking on new lives. A high percentage of these individuals are also of racial/ethnic minority backgrounds, in need of culturally competent services. In addition to having trauma-related disorders, these individuals are also at high risk for disruptive behaviors and substance abuse, and have greater difficulties in functioning at home, work, school, and their communities—placing them at high risk for additional failed placements and services. The welfare system also faces significant challenges posed by the legal system, lack of resources, and legislation. These challenges include an increasing orientation toward family reunification (over 90% of abused children are returned to their families), under-enforcement of protective orders for battered women, lack of adequate numbers and quality of foster homes, and increasing welfare-to-work requirements for poor women with children. Several models have effectively addressed the needs of children and parents served in the welfare system, including in-home intervention for abused or at-risk infants/toddlers and their families, visiting nurse programs for abused infants, family preservation and intensive in-home mental-health programs, and co-located mental-health services in welfare to work. The implementation of trauma-focused therapies in schools and community programs also addresses the needs of these populations.

PHILOSOPHIES OF CARE

Two predominant philosophies underlying systems-based practice have evolved, one addressing services for children and the other addressing services for adults.

Community Systems of Care Principles

The systems-of-care model for children's mental health is guided by a core set of principles. These principles were first outlined under the Child and Adolescent Service Systems Program (CASSP) initiative that set up the state-level offices for child mental health across the United States in the 1980s. The key principles include access to a comprehensive array of services, treatment individualized to the child's needs, treatment in the least restrictive environment possible (with full utilization of the resources of the family and the community), full participation of families as partners in service planning and delivery, interagency coordination, the use of case management for coordination of services, no ejection or rejection from services due to lack of "treatability" or "cooperation" with interventions, early identification and intervention, smooth transition of youth into the adult service system, effective advocacy efforts, and the provision of nondiscriminating, culturally sensitive services.

Recovery Principles

Under these principles, mental-health recovery is seen as a journey of healing and transformation that enables a person with a mental-health problem to live a meaningful life in a community of his or her choice while striving to achieve his or her full potential. The 10 fundamental values of recovery-oriented services are (1) self-direction, (2) individualized and person-centered care, (3) empowerment (presenting a range of care options and participating in all care decisions), (4) holistic perspective (services address an individual's whole life, including mind, body, spirit, and community), (5) nonlinear perspective (recovery not seen as a step-by-step process but one based on continual growth, occasional setbacks, and learning from experience), (6) strengths-based approach (focuses on valuing and building on the multiple capacities, resiliencies, talents, coping abilities, and inherent worth of individuals), (7) peer support (by other consumers, sharing effective coping strategies), (8) respect, (9) responsibility, and (10) hope (providing essential and motivating message of a better future).

Models and Evidence-Based Practices

A number of models for organized interagency systems of care have been developed in the United States through the Comprehensive Community Mental Health Services for Children and Their Families Program, funded by the Center for Mental Health Services. This center has funded over 80 model sites serving over 80,000 children since 1994. These programs involve the multiple child-serving agencies in addition to mental health, as well as family and youth participation. Children and youth in these systems-of-care programs have shown significant results in improved child behavior and functioning, fewer contacts with law enforcement, increased stability in living situation, improvements in child and family strengths and resources, reduced caregiver strain, and improved family function. Preliminary results demonstrate reduced cost of care within these programs when indirect cost offsets are considered, such as child welfare, juvenile justice, educational, and general health costs.

A number of community-based interventions for children and youth that have shown promise include school-based interventions, mentoring programs, family support and education programs, wilderness programs, crisis mobile outreach teams, time-limited hospitalization with coordinated community services, and family support services. Studies involving these modalities have demonstrated significantly better outcomes than traditional outpatient or residential services. These include reduced levels of externalizing and internalizing symptoms, improved family functioning, reduced utilization of more restrictive services, and improved cost-effectiveness. Additionally, a number of in-home preventive parent–child interventions with infants and young children have demonstrated long-term effectiveness in reducing child abuse as well as adverse behavioral and academic outcomes. Multisystemic therapy (MST) is one model that combines home-based, wraparound, and cognitive–behavioral interventions within a systemic context. It has been evaluated with youth at risk of detention/incarceration and at risk of psychiatric or substance abuse hospitalization, with significant results in reducing out-of-home placement, externalizing problem behaviors, rates of recidivism, and costs of treatment.

The model that has emerged that exemplifies the community-based system approach for adult services is the assertive community treatment (ACT) team model. This model serves a group of people with serious mental illnesses at high risk for recidivism, using an integrated team of mental health, substance abuse, and vocational therapists, a psychiatrist, nurses, and peer counselor. The team takes responsibility for the patient's care and delivers whatever care is needed (e.g., psychotherapy, support services) in the community to ensure that the patient is able to function in the community and live a meaningful life. The ACT programs have been successful in reducing hospitalizations, homelessness, incarceration, and in improving function in the community. Also available are various evidence-based community practices—for example, intensive case management, family psychoeducation, integrated dual-disorders treatment (mental health and substance abuse), supported employment, and disease management—that involve community systems-of-care approaches and have demonstrated outcomes in improving function for people with serious mental illnesses in the community.

CLINICAL PRACTICE

In addition to the clinical skills of diagnostic assessment, medical assessment, treatment planning, pharmacotherapy, different forms of psychotherapy, and implementation of specialized treatments (e.g., as electroconvulsive therapy, biofeedback, hypnosis, behavioral therapy), mental-health professionals working in broader systems of care must master a number of additional skills, including consultation, advocacy, cultural competence, interdisciplinary systems coordination, and quality improvement.

Consultation

Mental-health consultation is the process of interaction between two professionals: one who is a specialist (consultant) and one who invokes the consultant's help (consultee) in a current work problem that is believed to be within the realm of the specialist's competency. It may include management of one or more clients of a counselor or planning of a program for these clients (Caplan, 1999). Successful consultative work requires several ingredients: (1) a clarity of roles and responsibilities for the consultant, (2) clear expectations for the consultation, (3) clarity of communication (and attunement to lines of communication/hierarchy), (4) clarity of roles and priorities among all players in the system, (5) attunement to the priorities and mandates of the organization, and (6) respect and utilization of the skills of other professionals in the system. The three A's of *ability*, *affability*, and *availability* are also important in being a successful consultant. There are different types of consultative relationships:

• *Case-based consultation* includes both client-centered consultation, where the focus is on the client and/or provider in order to serve the need of a specific patient(s), and consultee-centered consultation, where the focus is on the skills/knowledge of the consultee as opposed to the client (analogous to supervision).

• *Administrative-based consultation* is consultee-centered, where the focus is the professional and his or her skills, or program-centered, where the focus of the evaluation and recommendations is the program, often regarding administrative issues.

- *Internal consultation* (often called *mental-health collaboration*) involves shared responsibility for the case, and the consultee agrees to respect the advice of the consultant because of the sharing of responsibility and expertise.

- *Liaison-based consultation* is an ongoing relationship developed with a consultee and/or specialty team. The liaison clinician is still seen as external to the team but approximates becoming a team member, while bringing in objective perspectives and external resources on either cases or programmatic issues. The liaison clinician uses his or her knowledge of the relations and interactions in the team to leverage ongoing improvement and change in team members' function.

Advocacy

The Institute of Medicine (2001) endorsed the empowerment of patients and their families in the "new rules" for a 21st-century health care system. These rules emphasize the points that (1) care is based on continuous healing relationships (most notably, family relationships), (2) care is customized according to the patient's and family's needs and values, (3) the patient (or family, in the case of minors) is the source of control, (4) knowledge is shared with patients and families and information flows freely, and (5) transparency in the care process is necessary. The president's New Freedom Commission on Mental Health (2003) also endorsed family-driven care.

Patient-centered, family-driven care implies that families must take a central role in defining their care. They have a primary decision-making role in the care of themselves (or with parents, their children), as well as the policies and procedures governing care for all children in their community. This role includes choosing supports, services, and providers; setting treatment goals; designing and implementing programs; monitoring outcomes; partnering in funding decisions; and determining the effectiveness of all efforts to promote the mental health and well-being of children and youth. In patient-centered and family-driven care, patients and families are given accurate, understandable, and complete information, which is necessary to set goals and to make choices for service planning. Patients, families, providers, and administrators embrace the concept of sharing decision making and responsibility for outcomes. Families, consumers, and their organizations engage in peer support activities to reduce isolation, gather and disseminate accurate information, strengthen their voices, and provide direction for decisions that impact funding for services, treatments, and supports. Efforts to change community attitudes focus on removing barriers and discrimination created by the stigma associated with mental illness. Experiential expertise coming from the lived experience of the patient and his and her family is seen as equally valid as professional expertise (from formal education, training, practice-based learning, and scientific literature).

Clinicians have a responsibility to advocate on behalf of, and with patients and their families at both the clinical level and at the systems level. They also have an advocacy responsibility toward their patients and families regarding both their psychiatric care as well as their education about the broader system. Furthermore, they have a responsibility to empower the patient and family in the development of the services plan and in making the critical choices on treatment selection—with the rare exception being when the patient's life is endangered by the direction proposed by the patient and family. Clinicians should advocate for patient and family support services, which are formal and informal supports that enable patients and their families to make use of treatment. These may include some financial supports, respite care, peer counseling, referral information, and other nontraditional services.

At the systems level, clinicians should advocate for sufficient resources for safe and effective service delivery in their communities, but also to have patients and family members sit on oversight, policy-making, and quality improvement bodies for mental-health care organizations. Clinicians should also collaborate with consumer and family organizations, which often promote and sustain patient and family supports and advocacy at the local, state, and national levels, and serve as sources of considerable information for both professionals and family members. Major family/consumer organizations include the National Alliance for the Mentally Ill, Mental Health America, the Federation of Families for Children's Mental Health, and many disorder-specific organizations. Such organizations have played instrumental roles in preserving federal research and services funding in the face of threatened funding cuts, and are pushing for legislation that establishes parity in insurance coverage of mental disorders with physical illnesses.

Cultural Competence

The United States is becoming an increasingly diverse nation, especially with the growth of minority groups with non-European origins. By the year 2050, the United States will no longer have a numerical "majority" racial/ethnic population, and this will happen by 2030 for those under 18 years of age. Increasing immigration into the United States means that currently over 40 million Americans were not born in this country. This demographic and cultural shift has significant implications for mental-health services. Cultural values and beliefs influence normal human development (at the physical, psychological, cognitive, and social levels), family development, and the development of protective factors/strengths. Culture also impacts on mental illness at various levels: biologically (e.g., genetic polymorphisms and variations in medication metabolism found in different populations); in terms of the explanatory models used for understanding illness, disease, and psychopathology (based on science, religion, spiritual beliefs, or even interpersonal factors, including stigma of mental illness); and in relation to help-seeking expectations and service-utilization patterns.

The principle of cultural competence is an integral aspect of the philosophy of community-based systems of care (Cross et al., 1989). It proposes that practitioners in systems of care develop the necessary attitudes, skills, and knowledge base to serve minority and culturally diverse children and families in their communities. It also proposes that practitioners develop policies and procedures within these systems to remove any barriers to the accessing of services and to make these services more responsive to the values of diverse communities. The systems-of-care approach is congruent with the cultural values of ethnic minority populations, which first emphasize strong extended family involvement in the life of the individual and the use of natural community resources in dealing with emotional and physical problems.

Guidelines for evaluating cultural competence skills, published by the Center for Mental Health Services, operationalize elements of cultural competence at both the clinical and systems levels. Important applications of cultural competence include linguistic competence and support for linguistic minorities; special approaches to engagement, assessment, and diagnosis (particularly taking into account culturally specific symptom expressions, the cultural context of symptoms, and special stressors such as immigration trauma, acculturation stress, and community violence); treatment planning that involves the family and minority community; and treatment approaches that are adapted to the cultural values and beliefs of the patient and have an evidence base with that specific population. It also involves systems-wide applications of cultural competence, including cultural competence planning for the system (i.e., identifying the population distribution for an area being served and the special cultural needs); governance that reflects the diversity of the area served; services that are culturally appropriate; quality assurance and improvement and information systems oriented to examining disparities and cultural needs; and staff training and development oriented to developing cultural competence in practitioners.

Interagency/Interdisciplinary Care Planning and Systems Coordination Skills

Clinicians need knowledge and skills in a number of areas to promote inter-agency and interdisciplinary coordination of care. Most of these skills are deployed in interdisciplinary and interagency teams that assemble to coordinate care for multineed patients receiving services from multiple professionals and agencies. The knowledge and skills needed include *knowledge* of community resources, agencies and their legal and operational mandates, the skills and strengths provided by different human services professionals, *skills* in leadership, communication, collaboration, and systemic assessment and intervention. The latter often involve carefully outlining the structure and lines of authority and relations in an organization, and evaluating how clinicians can most effectively advocate and consult for their patients or population of patients.

Wraparound Model

One established model for interdisciplinary and interagency planning is the wraparound process involving a care-planning team. This type of approach is most often seen in children's systems-of-care programs, and in treatment or care planning programs for youth with complex needs and their families. The wraparound model prioritizes family voice in the process of developing a team of people with complementary strengths committed to improving the mental health of the child or youth. The team is facilitated by a care coordinator, who may also have had experience with raising a child with complex needs. This complementary approach to the usual medical model involves the following stages:

Pre-meeting preparation of the family establishes the initial engagement and provides mutual orientation as well as safety planning and developing a shared vision for services and outcomes by the family with a care coordinator and, when available, a family partner (a peer counselor with personal experience with a child with emotional disturbance/mental illness).

Pre-meeting preparation of all team members is necessary to discuss provider hopes and concerns for their work with the family, to review a summary of history and other information on the child's status ahead of time, with family informed consent, and for preliminary conversations between professionals to help them sort out their own interface issues without further burdening the family when the team meeting occurs.

In the actual *team meeting*, (1) family members identify the domains to be addressed (e.g., housing, employment, transportation, school, or legal, emotional, or behavioral concerns); (2) needs and strengths in the youth, family, and community for the domain chosen are identified; (3) options are generated to meet the needs, ideally building on strengths; and (4) a plan of care is developed, settling on the best options and identifying *who* will do *what* by *when*.

Weekly to monthly *follow-up meetings* continue for the youth and family team until the family's vision is achieved or the family chooses to withdraw, and the team follows the youth through different levels of care to provide continuity. A care coordinator is responsible for tracking outcomes from the plan of care and supporting accountability; if progress is not made, the assumption is that the plan of care was flawed, not that the youth or family or provider is to blame.

Quality Improvement

As systems of care move toward greater accountability and a stronger evidence-base, quality improvement becomes an integral function. Quality improvement should not only evaluate and improve effectiveness and efficiency of services, but assure consumer (youth and family) satisfaction and, foremost, promote and assure safety in care delivery.

Skills

An ongoing orientation toward improvement implies that clinicians are never satisfied with the quality of their care and its outcomes (clinical and functional), and that they always seek to improve not only the effectiveness of their practices but also the process of care in terms of efficiency (cost and time) and effectiveness (improving access and reducing errors). Important skills in participating in and implementing quality improvement approaches include planning skills, analytic skills (especially the use of tools for analyzing processes of care, e.g., "wish-boning" and flow diagrams), outcome evaluation skills (some of these border on clinical research skills), data management and analysis skills, communication and collaboration skills, and financial analysis skills. Clinicians need to balance cost and quality considerations in pursuing quality improvement projects or programs, keeping in mind the classic triangle of *cost, quality,* and *access* and how these interact in care delivery. Staff and patient involvement in problem identification, analysis, solution identification, and policy and procedure development is critical to the success of any safety or quality improvement program.

Patient Safety

Patient safety is an important component of quality improvement and self-analysis by mental-health-care organizations on issues involving significant risk (e.g., medication interactions; identification of, and intervention in, cases involving suicidal and aggressive risk; management of substance detoxification and comorbid medical conditions; side effects from procedures such as seclusion and restraint and electroconvulsive treatment). Rule 6 of Recommendation 4 in the Institute of Medicine's (2001) *Crossing the Quality Chasm* is that "safety is a systems property" (p. 8). The Hippocratic Oath ("Above all else, do no harm") belongs not just to the individual physician, but to the system of care as a whole.

Patients and families often interact with multiple individuals and agencies concurrently and are therefore key to addressing safety issues and concerns. Coordinated, respectful, and collaborative communication between system partners can promote safe and effective care. Systems that do not communicate adequately, that communicate in a conflicted manner, and/or that give patients and families contradictory requirements can augment distress in the family, causing harm. Clinicians have a leadership responsibility to model collaborative, respectful interactions with system partners to help reduce the harm that "system stress" causes to families. Patients and families, as experts in their life experience, also provide invaluable information on the physiological and psychological responses to interventions used with their children. Failure to listen to families in this regard can, in itself, become a safety issue.

The first rule of *Crossing the Quality Chasm* is "Care is based on continuous healing relationships." Supporting the capacity of families to promote healing and continuous support for patients maximizes the impact of continuous healing relationships. Disrupted attachments, when occasioned by multiple placements in out-of-home settings, can be harmful to the health of patients and to family function. Short-term emergency response (e.g., repeated hospitalizations or acute residential treatment), although necessary for safety, must be balanced against long-term harm caused by disrupted attachments. Also, the episodic nature of much of mental-health care in fragmented systems of care contributes to a discontinuity of providers that can create safety issues. Care can be enhanced and harm reduced by promoting engagement with needed clinical and support services in systems of care on a continuous basis.

References

American Academy of Child and Adolescent Psychiatry, Work Group on Community-Based Systems of Care. (2007). *System-based practice: Modules for teaching systems-based practice.* Washington, DC: American Academy of Child and Adolescent Psychiatry.

Caplan, G. (1970). *The theory and practice of mental health consultation.* London, UK: Tavistock.

Caplan, G. (1999). *Mental health consultation and collaboration.* Long Grove, IL: Waveland Press.

Cross, T., Bazron, B., Dennis, K., & Isaacs, M. (1989). *Towards a culturally competent system of care.* Washington, DC: CASSP Technical Assistance Center, Georgetown University Child Development Center.

Elpers, J. (2000). Public psychiatry. In B. Sadock & V. Sadock (Eds.), *Comprehensive textbook of psychiatry* (Vol. II, pp. 3185–3199). Philadelphia: Lippincott, Williams & Wilkins.

Four Racial Ethnic Panels. (1999). *Cultural competence standards for managed mental health services for four underserved/underrepresented racial/ethnic groups.* Rockville, MD: Center for Mental Health Services, Substance Abuse and Mental Health Administration, U.S. Department of Health and Human Services.

Huffine, C., & Anderson, D. (2003). Family advocacy development in systems of care. In A.J. Pumariega & N.C. Winters (Eds.), *Handbook of community systems of care; The new child and adolescent community psychiatry* (pp. 35–65). San Francisco: Jossey Bass.

Institute of Medicine. (2001). Formulating new rules to redesign and improve care. In Institute of Medicine Committee on Quality of Health Care in America (Ed.), *Crossing the quality chasm: A new health system for the 21st century* (pp. 61–89). Washington, DC: National Academy Press.

Institute of Medicine. (2002). *Unequal treatment: Confronting racial and ethnic disparities in health care.* Washington, DC: National Academies Press.

Lieberman, R., Kopelowicz, A., & Smith, T. (2000). Psychiatric rehabilitation. In: B. Sadock & V. Sadock (Eds.), *Comprehensive textbook of psychiatry* (Vol. II, pp. 3218–3245). Philadelphia: Lippincott, Williams & Wilkins.

New Freedom Commission on Mental Health. (2003). *Achieving the promise: Transforming mental health care in America.* Final Report. Rockville, MD: U.S. Dept of Health and Human Services, No. SMA-03-3832.

Osher, T.A., & Osher, D. (2002). The paradigm shift to true collaboration with families. *Journal of Child and Family Studies, 11,* 47–60.

Pumariega, A.J. (2003). Cultural competence in systems of care for children's mental health. In A.J. Pumariega & N.C. Winters (Eds.), *Handbook of community systems of care: The new child and adolescent community psychiatry* (pp. 82–106). San Francisco: Jossey Bass.

Pumariega, A.J., Diamond, J., England, M., Fallon, T., Hanson, G., Lourie, I., et al. (1996). *Guidelines for training towards community-based systems of care for children with serious emotional disturbances.* Washington, DC: American Academy of Child and Adolescent Psychiatry.

Pumariega, A.J., Nace, D., England, M.J., Diamond, J., Mattson, A., Fallon, T., et al. (1997). Community-based systems approach to children's managed mental health services. *Journal of Child and Family Studies, 6*(2), 149–164.

Pumariega, A.J., Rogers, K., & Rothe, E. (2005). Culturally competent systems of care for children's mental health: Advances and challenges. *Community Mental Health Journal, 41*(5), 539–556.

Ruiz, P. (2003). Systems-based practice core competencies. In S. Scheiber, T. Kramer, & S. Adamowski (Eds.), *Core competencies for psychiatric practice* (pp. 109–118). Washington, DC: American Psychiatric Press.

Stein, L., & Santos, A. (1998). *Assertive community treatment of persons with severe mental illness.* New York: Norton.

Steinberg, D.S., & Yule, E. (1985). Consultative work. In M. Rutter & H. Lionel (Eds.), *Child and adolescent psychiatry: Modern approaches* (2nd ed., pp. 914–926). Boston: Blackwell Scientific.

U.S. Office of the Surgeon General. (2001). *Mental health: Culture, race, and ethnicity. A supplement to Mental health: A report of the surgeon general.* Rockville, MD.: U.S. Department of Health and Human Services, Substance Abuse and Mental Health Services Administration, Center for Mental Health Services, National Institutes of Health, National Institute of Mental Health.

Walker, J.S., & Bruns, E.J. (2006). Building on practice-based evidence: Using expert perspectives to define the wraparound process. *Psychiatric Services, 57,* 1579–1585.

Winters, N.C., & Terrell, E. (2003). Case management: The linchpin of community-based systems of care. In A.J. Pumariega & N.C. Winters (Eds.), *Handbook of community systems of care: The new child and adolescent community psychiatry* (pp. 171–200). San Francisco: Jossey Bass.

Winters, N.C., & Pumariega, A.J. (2007). Work group on community-based systems of care, committee on community psychiatry, and work group on quality issues practice parameters for child mental health in systems of care. *Journal of the American Academy of Child and Adolescent Psychiatry, 46*(2), 284–299.

8

Legal, Ethical, and Multicultural Issues

Ethics and law are not the same, but they often interrelate. In managing their professional work with patients, health care providers' primary focus should be patients' well-being and best interest. However, it may be difficult at times for professionals to ascertain what action or decision will best benefit the patient. In addition, practitioners also must consider what is in the best interest of society or persons directly involved with the patient.

LEGAL ISSUES

The law regulates specific aspects of psychiatric practice in a manner distinct from other forms of medical practice, because of the issues surrounding autonomy and safety that are often encountered. Importantly, such laws often vary considerably between jurisdictions. It is essential that all clinicians seeking to work with individuals suffering from psychiatric disorders familiarize themselves with the relevant laws. Some specific areas of psychiatric practice that are regulated by the legal system, either in the form of specific state or federal laws or through judicial case rulings, include involuntary hospitalization and involuntary treatment. Other areas similarly regulated include informed consent, confidentiality, duty to warn and/or protect a potential victim that might be in danger, capacity to provide informed consent for psychiatric treatment and surrogate decision making, admission and treatment of minors, reporting of abuse and/or neglect, and standards of care.

Mr. Smith is a 35-year-old unmarried Caucasian male who was diagnosed with schizophrenia, paranoid type, at the age of 22. At the time, he was in college and doing well academically but had started to become increasingly withdrawn from his friends and family. Those close to him began noticing that he appeared increasingly suspicious, making remarks about being followed and recorded by members of the Secret Service. He gradually stopped attending hockey practice and a book club, and his grades started to slip. One evening, his college roommate Adam arrived home to find Mr. Smith attempting to disassemble the microwave oven while it was still plugged into the wall outlet. When his roommate attempted to intervene, Mr. Smith became acutely agitated, started making angry remarks about hidden transponders, and threw a chair across the room. His roommate called the police, and Mr. Smith was escorted to the emergency room of the university hospital, where he remained extremely agitated and continued to make paranoid statements. He was admitted to the inpatient psychiatric service on an involuntary commitment status. During the hospitalization, a diagnosis of schizophrenia, paranoid type, was confirmed based on history obtained from multiple sources. He was stabilized on an antipsychotic medication, which almost completely dissipated his delusional thinking, and he was discharged in stable condition.

Mr. Smith did well for about a month after his discharge, but then stopped taking his medication and started to become paranoid again. He also developed auditory command hallucinations telling him to kill his college principal, because he was the leader of the secret conspiracy to kill Mr. Smith. Mr. Smith described these hallucinations to his roommate Adam and told Adam that he would likely kill his principal "before he gets me killed." Adam again contacted the police, and Mr. Smith was escorted back to the hospital emergency room and readmitted to the inpatient psychiatric service. Upon admission, he denied any urges to harm himself or others but did present as agitated and refused to accept any medication. He was again admitted on an involuntarily committed status and a request for authorization of medications by force was submitted to the court. At a judicial hearing, it was determined that Mr. Smith lacked capacity to make his own treatment decisions because he did not appreciate the fact that he suffered from a mental illness, and hence involuntary treatment was authorized. Treatment with antipsychotics was instituted and Mr. Smith appeared to improve. However, he remained somewhat suspicious and did appear somewhat preoccupied with internal stimuli, even though he consistently denied hallucinations and any urges to harm himself or anyone. Meanwhile, Adam, who had been unable to visit Mr. Smith in the hospital due to his college schedule, left two messages for Mr. Smith's attending physician requesting a call back to discuss Mr. Smith's status prior to admission. Five days after admission, Mr. Smith's attending physician deemed that Mr. Smith no longer met criteria for continued involuntary hospitalization, even though he remained mildly psychotic, and Mr. Smith was discharged per his own insistence.

Three days after discharge, Mr. Smith shot and killed his college principal, Mr. Jones. He was arrested and charged with second-degree murder. At the time of arrest, he was noted to be muttering to himself about having "done God's will," but was unable to receive any antipsychotic medication for the first 48 hours of his incarceration due to lack of availability and the absence of a psychiatrist on the medical unit of the jail. He continued to make psychotic remarks when he first met with his court-appointed attorney, Mr. Black. Mr. Black had much concern about Mr. Smith's mental state and petitioned the court to have Mr. Smith evaluated for competency to stand trial. Mr. Smith was found incompetent to stand trial and was committed to a forensic psychiatric hospital for restoration to competency. Following restoration of competency to stand trial after 3 weeks of inpatient treatment, he collaborated with his attorney and successfully mounted an insanity defense. This led to his incarceration in the state forensic psychiatric hospital for 5 years, followed by continued hospitalization in the state civil forensic hospital for another 2 years. He was eventually released to the community.

In the year following the murder, Mr. Smith's family filed a malpractice lawsuit against the attending physician and the hospital where Mr. Smith had been admitted. The suit alleged that the attending physician failed to follow the standard of care by not obtaining appropriate collateral information when making a decision about Mr. Smith's readiness for discharge and not having conducted an adequate risk assessment. During initial depositions, the attending physician testified that he had indeed contacted Adam and had not been able to elicit any additional information of concern. However, he acknowledged that there were no entries in the medical record to substantiate his testimony. Adam testified that he never heard back from the attending physician. The family of Mr. Jones also filed suit, alleging that the attending physician failed to take reasonable steps to warn or protect Mr. Jones from a potentially dangerous patient. Both suits were settled out of court for an undisclosed amount.

Following his release from the state civil hospital, Mr. Smith has been stable and relatively free of psychiatric symptoms. He has, however, been unable to procure work because of his past criminal and psychiatric history. He has applied for Social Security disability benefits, but his application has been denied.

The case above illustrates some of the various ways in which the law interfaces with the practice of psychiatry. This interface can be conceptualized as consisting of at least three separate elements: (1) the legal regulation of the practice of clinical psychiatry, (2) the specialized application of psychiatric expertise to answer legal questions in legal contexts (both civil and criminal), and (3) the diagnosis and treatment of psychiatric disorders in the correctional system.

Involuntary Hospitalization

Individuals known to suffer from, or suspected to suffer from, psychiatric disorders may be admitted to inpatient psychiatric units against their will if certain conditions are met. The state's ability to detain psychiatric patients involuntarily stems from two primary legal principles: *parens patriae* (i.e., the state's obligation to protect individuals from the consequences of their own limitations) and "police powers" (i.e., the state's right to protect society from the acts of potentially dangerous persons). Historically, psychiatric patients were confined to institutions for indefinite periods while receiving little treatment. Over the past several decades, there has been considerable evolution in society's views on the balance between protecting the civil rights of psychiatric patients and protecting the community from potential harmful acts that such individuals might commit.

State laws now vary considerably with regard to (1) the criteria that must be met before involuntary hospitalization can be considered, (2) the process that must be followed in order to involuntarily hospitalize an individual, and (3) the duration of time the individual can be held without judicial review. As a general matter, most states require that individuals be deemed to suffer from a psychiatric disorder that renders them at high risk of harm to themselves or others, and/or their ability to provide for their basic needs is significantly compromised. The precise language used in the relevant legal statutes may significantly influence whether or not an individual meets the criteria for involuntary hospitalization; for example, a requirement that an individual pose an "imminent danger" to self or others is a much higher threshold relative to the requirement that the individual simply be at risk for significant deterioration in psychiatric status. Most states allow clinicians to place a time-limited hold on a patient (typically a matter of days), during which a judicial proceeding can be scheduled. At such a proceeding, a trier of fact (i.e., a judge or magistrate) determines whether the initial commitment and/or continued hospitalization is legally justifiable. Germane to such a legal determination is testimony by a treating psychiatrist or other mental-health professional relating to the individual's psychiatric disorder, current mental status, degree of risk for harmful behavior in the near term, and ability to provide for basic daily needs in a safe manner. Most states allow such individuals to retain independent psychiatrists (typically at their own expense) to testify at such hearings. Testimony by significant others is also permitted in most instances.

A generally accepted principle is that psychiatric patients must be treated in the "least restrictive alternative" available; that is, involuntary commitment is the last resort after patients have refused the opportunity to voluntarily agree to be hospitalized. An additional issue that arises in some states is the patient's capacity to consent to voluntary hospitalization. That is, individuals who are willing to be hospitalized must have a rational understanding of the reasons for hospitalization and the implications of that hospitalization. If the individual lacks such an understanding, involuntary hospitalization may need to be considered, even though the patient is agreeable to hospitalization, in order to allow for judicial review and ensure that the patient's legal rights are being protected to the appropriate degree. It is important to note that involuntary hospitalization does not, in most instances, automatically provide legal authorization for involuntary treatment (e.g., administration of scheduled medications).

Involuntary Treatment

Most jurisdictions allow for emergency use of medications or physical restraints to manage situations involving physical aggression or imminently dangerous behavior by patients, without the need to obtain judicial authorization. However, ongoing scheduled treatment with psychotropic medication over a patient's objection requires that the treating clinician obtain advance judicial authorization by following a legal protocol prescribed by a jurisdiction or agency. Historically, commitment to a psychiatric institution was deemed to authorize involuntary treatment. Recent shifts in the criteria for civil commitment toward a "dangerousness" standard led to the recognition of the distinction between the goals and rationale for hospitalization versus forced treatment. Furthermore, the law has come to recognize that committed patients are not necessarily incompetent in a broad sense.

Currently, jurisdictions adopt one of two approaches to involuntary psychiatric treatment. Some courts afford wider authority to mental-health professionals to force treatment in psychiatric settings based upon professional judgment, with relatively little oversight by the legal system. Such a model reduces delays inherent in the legal process and allows for more timely treatment. This model is often opposed by legal professionals and some patient advocates for not offering enough protection to patient rights. Other jurisdictions require a court to make a decision about a patient's decisional capacity with regard to consenting to (or refusing) psychiatric treatment. A legal finding of incompetence results in the court's application of the *substituted judgment* principle, i.e., an opinion that includes prescription of those treatments that the patient would have elected to accept if competent. From a practical perspective, treatment refusal in an inpatient psychiatric setting must first be approached clinically by addressing issues such as the therapeutic relationship and reasons for the refusal. Common reasons for treatment refusal include adverse effects from medications or denial of illness (Hoge et al., 1990; Guthiel & Appelbaum, 2000). Negotiation may be appropriate in some situations, and recruiting significant others to assist may be helpful. If such measures are unsuccessful, or if there are concerns about the patient's capacity to make an informed choice to accept or refuse psychiatric treatment, then the process prescribed by applicable law must be followed. Discharge from inpatient care is appropriate only if treatment refusal cannot be overcome through clinical and legal means, and if the patient is deemed to not meet criteria for commitment. Certain states have legal provisions that allow for forced outpatient treatment ("outpatient commitment"). The success of such programs varies considerably.

Informed Consent

The doctrine of informed consent, well recognized in law, has evolved considerably in recent decades, shaped by historical, social, and cultural forces (Appelbaum et al., 1987; Schwartz & Roth, 1989). It is essential that informed consent be obtained from the patient before any treatment is initiated. Essential elements of such consent include *disclosure, voluntariness,* and *competency.* At a minimum, *disclosure of information* that is essential for the patient to make a reasoned and informed choice includes the indication for the treatment proposed, the potential risks and benefits of such treatment, alternatives to the proposed treatment, and potential consequences if the proposed treatment is not administered. *Voluntariness* refers to a consent that is free from coercion or threat. While this issue may often be straightforward, certain treatment situations (e.g., patients admitted involuntarily to locked psychiatric units) may unintentionally but inherently involve an element of coercion. Attempts must be made to minimize such effects. As a matter of law, adults are presumed competent unless adjudicated otherwise, whereas minors are presumed to lack capacity.

When consent is being obtained from patients suffering from active psychiatric disorders, it is particularly important to assess the elements of *competency.* These include an understanding and appreciation of the necessary information, an adequate reasoning process, and the evidencing of a choice. It is important to note that suffering from a psychiatric disorder does not, per se, render a patient incompetent to make treatment decisions. Individuals may retain the capacity to make certain treatment decisions but not others, and any evaluation of competency must be decision specific rather than global. A related principle of the "sliding scale" requires higher levels of competency to make decisions about treatments that carry a higher risk–benefit ratio.

Some situations do not require clinicians to obtain informed consent. *Psychiatric emergencies*—situations wherein there is an imminent danger of serious harm to the patient or to others—permit the administration of treatment that is essential only to prevent such harm. With *incompetent patients*, relevant law must guide the process of obtaining consent from surrogate decision makers, and attempts must be made to involve the patient in the decision-making process to the degree possible. A patient may choose to *waive the right* to make his or her own decision. Such a scenario warrants careful exploration and discussion with the patient. A clinician may wish to withhold information about a treatment option on the grounds that provision of certain information to the patient in the process of obtaining informed consent may be harmful to the patient. This so-called *"therapeutic privilege"* is no longer recommended except under very specific and limited circumstances (e.g., if the disclosed information would prompt suicidal behavior).

Special considerations apply when informed consent is to be obtained for certain types of mental health treatment (e.g., electroconvulsive therapy or psychotherapy), certain patient populations (e.g., older adults), or certain contexts (e.g., participation in clinical research) (Schwartz & Mack, 2003). Finally, it is important to recognize that obtaining informed consent is an ongoing process that is engaged in, with the patient, during the course of treatment, rather than a single event in time.

Confidentiality

Without first obtaining appropriate authorization from the patient, clinicians are ethically bound to hold confidential (not disclose to most third parties) information obtained in the course of evaluating or treating him or her. This principle is the cornerstone of the psychotherapeutic relationship. Such disclosure may occur without prior authorization, in most instances, to other care providers within the same system of care, to consultants, or to other staff members intimately involved in the care of the patient. Most jurisdictions allow for exceptions to confidentiality in any circumstance where a typical patient–clinician relationship is not established (e.g., forensic or independent evaluations). Also, emergency situations usually allow for disclosure of the minimum amount of confidential information necessary to conduct an assessment and provide immediate management. There are laws mandating that abuse or neglect be reported and that the safety of third parties, the public, or the patient takes precedence over confidentiality. Group and marriage/family therapies present special challenges with regard to confidentiality, as information is disclosed with multiple parties present. Practitioners who work with minors should have specialized training with their patient population and related state laws regarding parental or guardian rights to information.

Privilege refers to the patient's right to prevent the professional information from being presented as testimony in a legal proceeding. In many states, the patient or the patient's legal guardian holds the privilege in patient–practitioner communication. Privileged communication is not subject to disclosure except under conditions prescribed by law or regulation, i.e., practitioners should not disclose patient information unless the right to confidentiality is waived by the patient or where mandated or permitted by law, as discussed above. Practitioners should be aware of their state's specific laws regarding provider–patient privilege. Ethical practitioners discuss the limits of confidentiality with patients, describing any specific applicable exceptions, at the outset of a professional relationship.

When child, elder, or dependent-adult abuse is suspected, most states require reporting to a government agency, which necessitates breaking confidentiality. Practitioners should stay current in their detailed knowledge of their state's current laws regarding reporting of abuse. For example, some states require that a practitioner report suspected abuse of an individual even if the practitioner knows that another professional has already made a report on that patient. In addition, mental-health professionals are typically required by law to break confidentiality, if necessary, in order to intervene when there is clear and imminent danger posed by patients to themselves or others. Furthermore, health care providers may be required by a court order to disclose certain patient information.

Most states permit or require health care providers to breach confidentiality in order to protect patients from harming themselves and to warn or protect other persons threatened by them; these practices are required to implement the moral principle of compassion toward the suicidal patient and to implement the principles of compassion and fairness to persons threatened by a patient. With regard to suicidal patients specifically, it is standard to consider the least intrusive protective measures necessary to ensure patient safety. Protective measures may include contacting a patient's family members, even if the patient does not agree, or arranging for the potential involuntary psychiatric hospitalization of a patient for a period of stabilization and treatment. As indicated above, arranging for involuntary psychiatric hospitalization should be done judiciously and within the purview of state law. With regard to threatened dangerous behavior toward others, a practitioner may have the duty to notify law enforcement authorities and warn identified potential victims. Predicting future dangerousness is not an exact science, and health care providers cannot be expected to perfectly predict violence. However, in such situations, providers should be able to show that they exercised reasonable professional judgment in comparison with their peers. Thus, timely consultation with other professionals can be a highly valuable risk-management strategy. Obviously, direct threats of violence should be taken very seriously and should likely trigger a warning. It is also very important to promptly create a written clinical record with careful documentation of any reasoning behind clinical decisions and related actions, including written documentation of the content of conversations with colleagues.

Health Insurance Portability and Accountability Act

The Health Insurance Portability and Accountability Act (HIPAA) was passed by Congress in 1996 to promote standardization and efficiency in the health care industry. This promotion involves the electronic transmission of health information for facilitating communication. In addition, the act was intended to give patients more rights and control over their health information by limiting its use and requiring providers to establish policies and procedures to protect the security of health information. All health care providers are ethically and legally obliged to be familiar with the specific requirements of HIPAA, which are typically taught at specific trainings that providers are required to attend by their health care institution employers.

The Duty to Warn and/or Protect

The case of *Tarasoff v. Regents of the University of California* brought into sharp focus the issue of warning a potential victim of one's patient of threats made by the patient against the individual, or taking steps to prevent such threats from being carried out (Ewing & McCann, 2006). Jurisdictions vary considerably in whether or not they impose a "Tarasoff Duty" on clinicians, and if so, precisely under what circumstances such a duty attaches, or how it might be satisfied. From a practical perspective, a thorough clinical risk assessment is key. For outpatients deemed to be at imminent risk of harm to others, hospitalization is usually necessary and also sufficient to satisfy such requirements in most instances. Inpatients should be stabilized to the point that they no longer pose a threat to identified others prior to discharge. A written or verbal warning may be indicated in circumstances where an outpatient is deemed imminently dangerous to another individual but cannot be restrained in a timely fashion. All warnings must involve disclosure of the minimal amount of confidential information necessary to convey the concern and must be carefully documented in the patient's medical record, including a clear rationale for having issued the warning.

Malpractice

Malpractice suits against mental-health professionals were considered rare historically but have become increasingly frequent. Some common reasons for malpractice lawsuits against psychiatrists include allegations of failure to adequately evaluate and manage risk of suicidal behavior or violence, to adequately monitor and manage adverse effects from psychopharmacological agents, to appropriately diagnose or treat a psychiatric disorder, and to appropriately supervise trainees (e.g., residents or medical students). In order for an individual to successfully bring a suit of malpractice against a clinician, all the following elements must be established: (1) There must have been a *duty* to provide care to the plaintiff. Such duty may sometimes be deemed to have been established by the giving of advice in informal settings. (2) There must have been a *dereliction* of such duty by failure to follow the established standard of care, i.e., providing care less than that expected from ordinary practitioners in the specialty. Some jurisdictions are now requiring that a physician provide that level of care that is expected from a *competent* (rather than average) practitioner in the community, thereby raising the standard of care. (3) The plaintiff must have developed *damage*, or an adverse event or outcome. (4) There must be a *direct* relationship between the alleged negligence and the occurrence of harm to the plaintiff. This fourth point is often the most difficult element of malpractice to establish due to the potential contribution of other factors.

All health care providers are at risk for being accused of, and/or sued for, malpractice and should carry adequate professional liability insurance. Measures that may reduce the risk of malpractice suits include engaging patients in the decision-making process to the extent possible obtaining second opinions and consultations when dealing with complex issues or those that involve subspecialty expertise; maintaining a positive therapeutic relationship with patients and their families and attempting to address negative outcomes within the therapeutic relationship when appropriate and documenting patient encounters completely, precisely, and in a timely fashion. Fostering positive therapeutic relationships, of which open communication and attention and sensitivity to patients and their behavior are characteristic, generally reduces risk of being sued by recipients of services. Patients are generally hesitant to fault the practitioner who consistently applies the moral principles of fairness, integrity, and compassion in mental-health care. Practicing ethically and responsibly is basic to more specific risk-management strategies. Professional organizations can provide information regarding risk-management strategies; continuing education courses can be taken in risk management and are required by some state licensing boards upon license renewal.

Expert Witness (Consultation to the Court)

Distinct from the legal regulation of clinical practice is an area of practice involving the application of psychopathological knowledge in legal contexts, either criminal or civil, to answer specific legal questions. This constitutes "forensic psychiatry" or "forensic psychology" defined in its strictest sense. Questions requiring expertise in psychopathology frequently arise in both the criminal and civil arenas of law. Attorneys, judges, insurance companies and other administrative bodies frequently solicit expert opinions, in the form of a written report and/or oral testimony, to resolve legal conflicts. Clinicians who participate in such proceedings do so at their own discretion, based on interest, training, and certification.

Participation in such activities involves adherence to certain principles that are distinct from clinical practice. For example, the opinions that result from such examinations are not typically confidential to the same degree as other clinical records are, since they are generated for the purpose of informing a specified individual or agency. It is essential for the "examinee" to understand this limitation to confidentiality in advance. The examinee must also understand that participation in such examinations will not result in the creation of a typical clinician–patient relationship, i.e., the clinician performing the examination functions as an agent of the individual or organization that is retaining his or her services rather than an advocate for the examinee, as would be expected in a typical diagnostic or therapeutic relationship. It stems from this that examinees must understand that the opinions generated may not necessarily be "helpful" to their case, and may result in punishment, denial of benefits, or a finding of liability. In order to avoid ethical dilemmas and conflict of interest issues, it is essential that a treating clinician not render forensic opinions with regard to his or her own patient. It is of paramount importance that clinicians seeking to undertake forensic examinations always strive for objectivity to the extent possible and not fall prey to the biases and coercive forces that are inherent in working in an adversarial system of justice.

An important starting point in conducting any forensic examination involving mental illness is to fully understand and delineate the question(s) that the clinician is being asked to answer. It is important that the clinicians have expertise and experience in the issue that is being addressed, and resist the tendency to address issues that fall beyond their area of clinical expertise, or to answer questions that are primarily legal rather than clinical. Commonly requested forensic evaluations in criminal court include evaluations of *competency to stand trial*, of a defendant's mental state at the time of the offense to assist in determining whether the defendant should be held *criminally responsible* for the alleged offense, and of other competencies, such as competency to confess or competency to be sentenced or executed. Commonly requested forensic evaluations in civil contexts include evaluations of psychiatric disability in a variety of contexts (e.g., worker's compensation benefits, Social Security Disability or private insurance), of a plaintiff in a personal injury lawsuit where emotional harm or psychic damages have been alleged, and of civil competencies such as testamentary capacity, ability to manage funds, or need for a guardian of person.

Competency to Stand Trial

Competency to stand trial (CST) evaluations are among the most commonly requested forensic psychiatric and psychological evaluations in criminal court. The case of *Dusky v. United States* (1960) first provided criteria for competency to stand trial, describing them as "whether he [the defendant] has sufficient present ability to consult with his lawyer with a reasonable degree of rational understanding and whether he has a rational as well as factual understanding of the proceedings against him." Miller (2003) has described the necessary capacities as including a cognitive element (i.e., the capacity to comprehend relevant legal concepts and procedures) and a volitional element (i.e., the capacity to utilize information appropriately in one's own defense and to function effectively in the legal environment). To try an individual who does not have such capabilities deprives the defendant of "due process of law" and casts doubt on the fairness of the criminal justice system. Mental illnesses, such as psychotic disorders or intellectual disability may interfere with such capacities, rendering the defendant incompetent to stand trial. Clinicians (usually a psychiatrist or psychologist), in addition to evaluating such competencies, may be required to opine on whether the condition underlying such incompetency is treatable, i.e., whether the individual can be "restored" to competency. Evaluations of CST are "here and now" functional evaluations, based on the defendant's current abilities. It follows that CST may change with time.

Criminal Responsibility/Insanity Defense

In most states criminal defendants may mount a defense to the effect that they were mentally ill at the time of an alleged crime and hence should not be held accountable for their actions. The concept of excusing criminal behavior on the basis of mental illness has a long historical tradition in English case law, with a variety of definitions or "tests of legal insanity" having applied over the centuries. The current definition of legal insanity in most U.S. jurisdictions stems, in part or in whole, from the famous *McNaughten* case. Broadly speaking, most insanity tests require the individual to have suffered from a serious mental disorder or intellectual disability that results in the satisfaction of one or both of two "prongs" of insanity: (1) a *cognitive* element—i.e., inability to understand or appreciate the nature of the act committed, or an inability to recognize that the act was wrong, either from a legal or a moral viewpoint; and (2) a *volitional* element—i.e., an inability to control one's behavior or conform one's behavior to what is legally or morally correct. The outcome of the evaluation will depend in large part on the specific definition of legal insanity that is applicable in the jurisdiction where the crime occurred. Unlike an evaluation of CST, an evaluation of criminal responsibility is a retrospective evaluation. The evaluator must utilize multiple sources of data (e.g., defendant interview, review of witness accounts and transcripts, police reports, medical and mental-health records) to reconstruct the defendant's mental state at the time of the crime and then reach conclusions relevant to the applicable legal criteria. An actual finding of whether or not the defendant was sane at the time of the crime is a legal determination that is made by the trier of fact (judge or jury), based in part upon a written report or oral testimony provided by the mental-health expert.

Evaluation of Psychiatric Disability

Individuals with psychiatric disorders may, in some instances, be rendered unable to perform one or more work-related functions that may impair their ability to work. In this regard it is important to recognize the difference between the concepts of impairment (i.e., the loss of a certain body part or bodily function) and disability (i.e., the inability of an impaired individual to meet certain social or occupational demands). For example, a depressed individual may suffer from low motivation and concentration and is hence impaired— unable to adequately focus on complicated graphics—which in turn disables him from his usual occupation that requires such ability.

The definition of disability varies considerably depending upon the agency granting disability benefits. The Social Security Administration requires that the individual be unable to engage in any "substantial gainful occupation," whereas a private insurance company may require only that the individual be unable to perform his or her usual occupation. Exclusions may exist with regard to conditions that are eligible for consideration; for example, worker's compensation carriers typically require that the disabling condition have developed in the course of work.

The role of a forensic psychiatrist or psychologist is to understand the relevant definition of disability and then perform a detailed evaluation focusing not only on symptoms and diagnostic issues but also on the specific functions that the individual is, or is not, able to perform. Such requests often include questions about recommended treatment, prognosis for recovery, and whether or not the individual has reached the point of "maximum medical improvement" (MMI)—that is, the point at which the impairment is well stabilized such that no further improvement can be expected over the next year, even with additional treatment.

Evaluation of Emotional Harm in Personal Injury Litigation

Forensic psychiatrists and psychologists are often called upon to render expert opinions in the course of personal injury litigation in cases where emotional or psychological harm is alleged. Questions posed for the examining clinician include whether or not the plaintiff suffers from a mental disorder or condition, the causal link of such a disorder to the alleged act or negligence that is the focus of the suit, and the degree of impairment that has resulted (used in the evaluation of damages or monetary compensation that the plaintiff will be awarded).

Documentation

Thorough and timely documentation of patient encounters is an essential practice in medicine and important for purposes of clinical care as well as risk reduction. The actual format utilized for documentation may vary depending upon institutional requirements (e.g., availability of electronic medical records) and personal style. However, attention to *timeliness, completeness, clarity, brevity,* and *professionalism* is sure to improve documentation across practice settings.

Timeliness. A record of an encounter should be created as soon as is reasonably possible following the patient contact or other clinical event. Records of high-risk situations must be created immediately after adequate interventions have been made. Progress notes and other documentation may be required by law, by managed-care companies, and by other third parties. Ethically, it is standard practice to keep accurate and timely records of all mental-health assessment, treatment interventions, and patient contacts.

Completeness. The components of a medical note will vary depending upon the nature of the encounter. For office visits, date and time of visit, duration of visit, encounter code and diagnostic code (if applicable), a description of relevant history, objective findings, investigational results (if appropriate), current medications, comorbid conditions, a summary impression, and proposed plan should all be included. Emergency visits or inpatient encounters may also need to include an expanded section on risk assessment. If collateral contacts are made, these should be described.

> According to Corey, Corey, and Callahan (2007), the minimum information typically described by law to be contained in mental-health records includes the following: patient identifying information, signed informed consent for treatment, releases of information obtained, types of services provided, precise times and dates of appointments made and kept, chief complaints and pertinent history, intake sheet, objective findings from the most recent physical examination, documentation of referrals for health care, reports of diagnostic procedures and tests, determined diagnosis, prognosis and significant continuing problems or conditions, treatment plans with specific target problems and goals, signed and dated progress notes, and termination and discharge summaries (p. 172). Progress notes typically address categories of information such as current symptoms and changes in symptom patterns, patient functional status, social support resources and utilization of social support, response to treatment, treatment recommendations, medication changes with clear justification, homework or assignments, use of alternative or complementary treatments, referral information, diagnosis, and treatment plan.

Clarity. It is essential to clearly describe the basis of diagnoses and conclusions and the reasons that certain interventions were made. In many instances, it is equally important to include which other interventions were considered and why they were not deemed to be necessary. When documenting assessment and treatment, it is important that written records be legible, descriptive, and objective. The *Clinician's Thesaurus* (2005) by Edward Zuckerman is a helpful resource for finding appropriate language for use in mental health care documentation.

Brevity. While describing one's thinking and reasoning is of paramount importance, it is equally important to keep the narrative succinct. It is reasonable to acknowledge uncertainty when this exists, while avoiding undue conjecture.

Professionalism. Describe clinical impressions based upon historical or objective facts, without resorting to the use of pejorative labels, expressing provider frustration, or blaming the patient. It is prudent to remember that the created record is permanent and assume that it will eventually be available to the patient for review. The information in health care records is legally accessible by patients in most, if not all, states and it is good practice to assist patients in understanding any record that they will review. Explaining diagnostic classifications as representing clusters of behaviors or symptoms may be especially helpful in decreasing confusion and errors in patient interpretation of recorded information. Records may also be introduced as evidence in criminal and civil legal proceedings, including malpractice litigation. Other professionals involved with the patient currently or in the future may read the clinical record. Keeping accurate records assists practitioners in organizing clinical information, monitoring progress, and communicating treatment.

Some third-party payers allow for an accessible record of essential clinical information, while permitting a second set of psychotherapy process notes kept in a separate file that is kept confidential from the third party. But it is the health care provider's responsibility to be aware of all legal and third-party policies (which can change frequently) regarding psychotherapy process notes. Some providers elect to omit any specific reference to especially sensitive or potentially damaging clinical information from all of their written records and write notes in more general diagnostic terms.

Practitioners should consult their specialty's code of ethics and relevant law regarding the time periods required for retention of records and when it is permissible to destroy old health care records. Practitioners must also consult ethical code and law when planning for the safekeeping and handling of health care records in the event of provider incapacitation or death.

Emergency Medical Treatment and Labor Act

In 1986 Congress enacted the Emergency Medical Treatment and Labor Act (EMTALA). This act requires most hospital emergency departments and ambulance services (all that accept payment from the U.S. Department of Health and Human Services Centers for Medicare and Medicaid Services under the Medicare program) to provide emergency treatment, as needed, to any and all persons regardless of insurance coverage, ability to pay, citizenship, or legal status. Thus, EMTALA essentially enforces the moral principle of compassion. Such hospitals must perform a medical screening examination to determine whether an emergency medical condition is present for all individuals requesting emergency care. Examination and treatment cannot be delayed because of any insurance or payment issues. In addition, those for whom emergency care is provided must be treated until the condition is resolved or stabilized. Furthermore, if the hospital cannot treat the condition, the hospital must transfer the patient to another hospital that has the ability to treat the condition. According to the nondiscrimination clause in EMTALA, this second hospital is required to accept the patient if it has the specialized capability and capacity.

The greatest impact of EMTALA is that everyone in need of urgent medical care is now legally guaranteed to receive it. Therefore, all mental-health care providers should recognize that any patient in need of urgent evaluation for immediate psychiatric hospitalization can be transported by their family members or ambulance to the nearest hospital emergency room where they will receive such an evaluation and care, if necessary, regardless of ability to pay for that service. However, there are criticisms (generally based on the moral principle of fairness) ranging from arguments that EMTALA is incomplete to complaints regarding cost pressures on hospitals and related financial ramifications.

ETHICAL AND CULTURAL ISSUES

Ethics refers to moral principles that are embraced and used to guide behavior. In Western societies there is a general consensus that a decision or action is ethical if it simultaneously implements the universal moral principles of *fairness*, *integrity*, and *compassion*. These principles underlie the core ethics of the mental-health professional: *nonmaleficence* (integrity), *beneficence* (compassion), and *justice* and respect for *autonomy* (fairness). Ultimately based on these moral principles and core values, codes of ethics delineating required ideal standards for the conduct of practitioners are adopted by organizations that regulate health care professions. Most of these codes and other resources on this subject can be accessed through the website www.centerforethical practice.org.

Managed Care

With the expectation of improving their incomes, unlicensed mental-health professionals in the mid-1970s strongly lobbied to obtain state licensure in order to become eligible for third-party reimbursement. However, mental-health practitioners were surprised when third-party payment sources began closely regulating mental-health care practices through managed care in order to control rising costs. The benefit of managed care has been that more people have access to mental-health care benefits. In addition, having strict standards for practicing mental-health treatment protects the public. The disadvantage is that practitioners have less control over decision-making in the provision of services. Treatment decisions may be more related to financial concerns than to the actual quality of care.

Having a third party involved in the therapeutic relationship obviously raises ethical questions. For example, diagnoses must "qualify" for third-party payment, and the payer may even impose requirements regarding the nature and amount of treatment that fits the given diagnosis. Thus, practitioners may find themselves in the position of trying to fit presenting problems into a diagnosis that will elicit reimbursement and then develop a treatment plan that fits, according to the managed-care company, with this diagnosis. Of course, this third-party control over treatment factors leads to specific concerns regarding the termination of treatment. In short, providers are ethically bound to not abandon their patients (the principle of compassion) and are responsible for providing competent care (the principle of integrity), yet practitioners may be working under the treatment limitations imposed by managed care (often a violation of the principle of fairness).

Additional concerns that extend from third-party involvement in the therapeutic relationship pertain to confidentiality and informed consent. As discussed previously, there are important limitations to confidentiality that involve ensuring the safety of the patient and others with whom the patient is involved. In addition, patients are able to consent to the release of their confidential clinical information in specific ways for the purpose of coordination of treatment between providers. However, the managed-care environment has greatly impacted the confidentiality rights of consumers of health care, sometimes without consumers' full realization, requiring providers to release patient information in order for mental-health services to be authorized and reimbursed. With the participation of managed care, informed consent, which involves fully informing patients about pertinent clinical issues to enable them to make informed decisions about their treatment choice, must now also include information regarding the complicating role of the third party in the therapeutic relationship. And, because managed care requires that a diagnosis be assigned, patients should be informed that a diagnosis can become a permanent part of their medical history, possibly impacting future health and life insurance costs and eligibility and even employment opportunities. Obtaining fully informed consent from patients at the outset of mental-health services demonstrates respect for patient rights and acknowledges patients' autonomy in making health care decisions for themselves. When informed of the risks to confidentiality that accompany third-party reimbursement, some patients will elect to forfeit third-party payment benefits and pay for mental-health services themselves to maintain greater confidentiality; therefore, mental-health care providers do well in applying the moral principles of compassion and fairness by informing patients of this option and letting them consider the risk–benefit ratio to using their health insurance for a mental-health condition.

The managed-care environment of mental-health care creates challenges that must be appropriately managed by practitioners. In addition, this environment begs reflection regarding how to best educate mental-health consumers regarding their role in their own treatment and payment for mental-health care, because their choice of practitioner and the nature of the treatment received are strongly influenced by third-party payment sources. Providers may be burdened with the need to actively seek authorizations for their clinical services and for potential further treatment options necessitating referrals for their patients, often with no billable reimbursement for the professional time required by these duties.

At times, especially during occasions of patient crisis, practitioners acting ethically may choose to provide low- or no-cost services. Pro bono services, however, are not cost-free for the provider. Practitioners may also bear the burden of obtaining additional training in time-limited or brief treatment models. Federal regulations, laws, and insurance companies can create a dilemma for providers who are required by their profession's ethical code to provide pro bono services when needed, but simultaneously prohibited by law from charging patients differently (e.g., charging the indigent nothing, but others a fee) for the same mental-health service. In such a case, the law must be followed, while creatively and compassionately working out a way for the patient to receive the needed mental-health services. In serving indigent patients, providers need to be aware of federal third parties and insurance company policies that may make it illegal or impermissible to tell patients that they will waive deductible or co-pays that third parties require be billed to them. In such cases, providers may maintain integrity in following the law together with their compassion for their patients by choosing not to send indigent patients' unpaid accounts to collection. However, to stay within the law, providers cannot tell the patients in such cases that they do not enforce payment of billed co-pays.

Dual/Multiple Relationships

The concept of dual or multiple relationships refers to having more than one role with a person, such as when someone serves as both psychotherapist and professor for a graduate student. The concept may also refer to having a relationship or role with an individual who is close to a patient, such as having a patient's spouse as a business partner or dating a patient's relative. Generally, avoiding dual or multiple relationships is necessary for maintaining the integrity of the professional mental-health care relationship.

Small rural communities tend to be especially challenging with regard to preventing multiple relationships and handling them when they inevitably occur. When practicing in small communities, it is important to address concerns up front and on an ongoing basis with patients. It is likely to be helpful to directly acknowledge and discuss with patients in advance any known contacts that might occur outside the health care relationship. Indeed, it may be helpful when working in any practice environment to discuss with patients general guidelines for handling spontaneous contacts, should they occur. For example, a practitioner and patient might decide that if an unplanned contact occurs, the practitioner will not acknowledge the patient unless first approached by the patient. This agreement respects the privacy of the patient and the patient's social boundaries. A patient may want to introduce his or her spouse, but choose not to acknowledge the presence of a therapy relationship when in the company of a friend or business partner.

Of course, it is important to realize that the acceptability and even therapeutic value of multiple relationships may vary between cultures and situations. Thus, practitioners are urged to learn about the unique cultures and individuals with whom they work in order to provide the most ethical and therapeutic care possible. In addition, community counseling, which emphasizes the use of various community resources to assist patients, may require helpers to balance multiple professional roles.

Mental-health care providers should be aware that social contact of any kind with a patient may impact the therapeutic relationship. Thus, the practitioner must be open to exploring this impact and must be responsible for initiating such discussion, when appropriate, during the treatment process. Of course, social contact with a patient can vary from running into a patient at the grocery store to interacting for business purposes to attending social functions in common to having a romantic relationship.

Pursuing a business partner relationship of any kind with a current or former patient is not considered ethical by codes of ethics and by many states' professional regulations, and could result in disciplinary action by the professional licensing board. Sexual relationships with either current or former patients are clearly unethical and also illegal in most states. Although less clear than with regard to sexual relationships, developing friendships with patients or taking friends on as patients also raises ethical and clinical concerns, threatening the integrity of the therapeutic relationship. For this reason, many practitioners wisely avoid mixing friendship with mental-health care provision. In addition, complications are likely to occur when bartering for services takes place. Ethical practitioners rarely accept bartering agreements and only under certain extraordinary circumstances and with much forethought. Remember, it is the responsibility of the provider of mental-health care services to maintain appropriate professional boundaries regardless of patient behavior. Situations such as those noted above have the potential to create problems for both patient and provider, and mental-health care providers are generally wise to avoid them when possible. Keeping professional boundaries in health care relationships helps practitioners maintain objectivity and good judgment. This stance protects patients and keeps the proper focus of the relationship on treatment issues.

When avoidance of a dual role is not possible or the professional finds that a dual role has arisen unexpectedly, it is important to manage the situation and relationships with great care, attempting to protect the patient from harm. There is an inherent power differential in the health care relationship, and the patient's well-being must be of primary importance to ensure that exploitation does not occur. It is wise to seek peer consultation or supervision when grappling with ethical concerns, especially those involving dual/multiple relationships.

Conflicts of interest ("dual agency") arise when the practitioner's other relationships create a situation where his or her allegiance is divided and may conflict with the patient's best care. For example, as discussed above, a clinician may work for a managed-care company whose policies are designed to reduce services. Another example might be a clinician initiating involuntary commitment to a psychiatric unit in a hospital for which she works. Many such conflicts present themselves on a regular basis in clinical practice. The onus is upon clinicians to ensure that patient care is not compromised and to avoid relationships that would jeopardize their integrity in this regard.

Although it is often necessary to individualize treatment, professional boundaries should be carefully maintained. For instance, *boundary crossings* may occur when personal information is disclosed after carefully weighing the risks, benefits, and alternatives to achieve the desired therapeutic goal. The motivation for such a disclosure must be effective treatment versus any personal gain for the clinician. At no time should the patient–therapist relationship serve as a means for meeting the psychological, social, or physical needs or desires of the clinician. These are clearly *boundary violations* that exploit patients and are never appropriate.

Multiculturalism and Spirituality in Ethical Care

Rooted in the moral principles of fairness and compassion, professional codes of ethics require mental-health providers to be sensitive to cultural, religious, and spiritual issues important to their patients (Sperry, 2007). The multicultural world in which we live adds complexity for health care professionals who are trying to practice in an ethical manner. Applying the commonly known basic ethical dictums in health care fields, "First, do no harm" (nonmalefi- cence), "Promote good" (beneficence), and justice, is not as simple as it might initially seem. An intervention that would "do no harm" and "promote good" for an individual from one cultural background might harm or create the possibility for harm for a person from another culture. For example, encourag- ing an Anglo person from middle-class America to stop worrying so much about what others think of him or her might be helpful within the context of treatment. However, this "encouragement" might have a much different im- pact on an Asian-American individual who values community more highly than independence. To take this a step further, should the Asian-American patient really take this suggestion to heart and begin to make changes based on it, persons in his or her social support system may not respond very positively to these changes. Because social support is widely known to be a cornerstone of good mental health, this intervention might not be as helpful as intended. This brief example is but one illustration of the complexity of health care intervention in a pluralistic world. Practitioners must be knowledgeable re- garding the general cultural characteristics of the populations with which they work, while closely attending to their patients in order to understand them as unique individuals.

As required by the principles of fairness and compassion, ethical health- care professionals will honor and protect patients' civil rights to make their own decisions regarding their therapeutic goals; and patients' goals will differ according to culture, subculture, or value system. As long as patients' treatment goals are within the law, do not threaten harm to self or others, and are both clinically reasonable and achievable, the health care professional must work in accordance with patients' goals.

Science and religion both strongly influence worldview (*Weltanschauung*) and have been intertwined throughout history. Prior to the 1800s, Judeo- Christian doctrine provided the most common framework for interpreting and perceiving reality in Western culture. As the scientific method gained promi- nence as the standard for study even outside the natural sciences, science and religion were increasingly viewed as separate entities. Religion was relegated to the private lives of individuals. Modern psychology seemed to bring about a parallel internal split within the Western individual between the psychologi- cal and spiritual aspects of the self. Paradoxically, as public and private life with regard to science and religion became increasingly separate, 20th-century technological advances placed diverse peoples with diverse worldviews increas- ingly in contact. Perhaps this increased exposure to different others moved the evolution of thought toward the postmodern realization that an individual's perspective impacts his or her perception of reality. Indeed, the lenses through which individuals view and understand themselves and their worlds became center-stage.

Related to these changes came an increased focus on multicultural concerns and contextual factors in the application of psychology. Science realized that healing and illness occur and are perceived through the internal and external contexts of the individual. One such context is religious/spiritual experience. Sperry (2007) noted the recent new practice of incorporating spirituality into the therapeutic realm as adjunctive therapy or as a strengths-based resource. Clinicians and patients may share meaningful spiritual dialogue despite differences in their personal spiritual choices. Common elements for connection include such concepts as meaning, mindfulness, morality, and community.

Along with these advances, modern medicine employed new technologies that have vastly increased knowledge in neuropsychiatry. There had always been debate regarding the relationship between body and mind, and this new knowledge seemed to "weigh in" on the monist camp's belief that all reality is material. The other side of this debate, dualism, purports that mind and matter substantively differ. But, even if the mental-health care provider is a monist, believing that mind emerges out of matter, one cannot ignore the importance of the patient's perception regarding spirituality or religion. For example, in the United States, empirical studies indicate that a minority of mental-health care providers report theistic beliefs, whereas the majority of the nation's population affirms belief in God (94%), in the deity of Jesus Christ, and in answered prayer (Steere, 1997). Ethical clinical practice respects the spiritual convictions of the patient and refrains from denigrating or undermining the patient's spiritual commitments. Sperry (2007) makes the case that the ethically required process of incorporating sensitivity to the significance of a patient's spirituality in mental-health care needs to involve a spiritual assessment. While not a standardized protocol, the following four questions are quite useful in eliciting key information (Koenig & Pritchett, 1998): (1) Is religion or spirituality important to you? (2) Do your religious or spiritual beliefs influence the way you look at your problems and the way you think about your health? (3) Would you like me to address your religious or spiritual beliefs and practices with you? (4) Are you part of a religious or spiritual community? When patients express reluctance or opposition to receiving mental health services from a clinician who does not share their cultural identity and/or religious beliefs, the ethical clinician will attempt referral to a provider who shares the patient's worldview and/or cultural perspective.

It is incumbent upon treatment professionals to explore and clarify their own values, as it is now widely accepted that these will impact the therapeutic relationship and work. Sue and Sue outline the moral and professional responsibility of mental-health care professionals to develop (1) increased awareness and handling of the biases, stereotypes, and assumptions that are elemental in their work; (2) increased awareness of cultural differences in values and worldview; and (3) appropriate, diversity-sensitive intervention strategies (as cited in Corey et al., 2007).

> Any one professional cannot be expected to work well with all patients. Yet, it seems important that practitioners view persons holistically and understand mental illness in a multidimensional and contextual fashion. Multiple components, including psychological, social, biological, and spiritual factors, influence the definition of, development of, maintenance of, and recovery from mental illness. Influencing these factors are key elements of diversity such as gender, age, socioeconomic status, and sexual, cultural, race/ethnic, and religious identities. Because mental illness does not occur in a vacuum, interventions that are insensitive to diversity issues may be unhelpful, toxic, or oppressive. Corey et al. (2007) implore counselors to not impose their own personal value system on mental-health care consumers "as the criteria for how all patients should think and act." They later distinguish between having strong convictions and imposing those convictions on others.

Though the prevalence of mental illness around the world suggests that all cultures, races, and societies are vulnerable, mental-health care services have not been equally accessible to all in need. Persons from minority groups tend to underutilize mental-health care services and often terminate services early. In many of these cases the barrier is not access but rather educational and cultural factors. Regardless, justice—a basic ethical value—may not be served in the allocation of scarce or limited resources in such situations.

Ethics of Nontraditional Treatment

In general, the principle of integrity, the professional codes of ethics, and even governmental regulations require that clinical interventions offered by the practitioner be within the standards of care for the profession, conforming to conventional clinical procedures. Public interest in nonconventional treatments in mental-health care has been increasing since the 1990s (Lake & Spiegel, 2007). The integration of conventional and nonconventional mental-health care is not simple, yet it seems to be increasingly in demand as consumers of mental-health care become aware of and seek more treatment options and may have preferences and perspectives that differ from those of the health care providers. Nonconventional mental-health treatments themselves—arising from non-Western and native healing traditions—are diverse, ranging from self-healing prayer, meditation, yoga, and other "centering" exercises, to the use of herbs for the treatment of anxiety or depressed mood to treatments based in Chinese medicine (Sperry, 2007). Perhaps the increasingly global nature of our world (discussed above) is related to this rise in interest level, as people learn about practices common or known in other cultures. Lake et al. (2007) propose that this rise in interest is fueled by constraints that are placed on conventional treatments by biotechnological advances. The biomedical model of mental illness focused attention so greatly on the brain and nervous system as explaining all behavioral problems that other aspects of persons and mental illness were neglected. For example, compared to the shorter sessions with mental-health professionals approved by the managed-care environment, nonconventional practitioners tend to spend longer periods of time with their patients. Perhaps people are responding to the therapeutic nature of the practitioner–patient relationship itself.

Because current consumers of health care may seek treatments other than conventional methods based in Western health care or may obtain conventional *and* nonconventional treatments simultaneously, health care providers do well to become more familiar with nonconventional treatments. Today, health care practitioners are likely to encounter patients from diverse spiritual and ethnic traditions. It seems that relevant treatment would have to consider diversity factors that have been identified above as important in culturally sensitive mental-health care. Community workers need to be aware of cultural factors that may be instrumental in contributing to patients' problems or resources that might help alleviate or solve patients' problems; in many cultures individuals with problems are more likely to put their trust in traditional healers. For these reasons, counselors need to be aware of indigenous healing systems and be willing to work collaboratively with them when it is to the benefit of the patient. In addition, people often come together around spiritual and other diversity-related practices and activities; and social support is generally encouraged, as it widely accepted as a cornerstone of mental health. However, with the legitimate emphasis upon evidence-based practice, mental-health professionals have an ethical obligation to engage in the clinical research necessary to establish that they are doing no harm and, indeed, truly providing benefit with any nontraditional treatments. Also, there are times when clinicians must understand cultural factors and practices in order to effectively change them for patients' benefit.

The guidelines of the Federation of State Medical Boards (FSMB; 2002) recognize that persons seeking treatment have a right to explore any methods of their choosing. Yet, nonconventional treatments vary in cost and availability and the quality and quantity of research and clinical and anecdotal evidence backing them. Admittedly, some current conventional treatments were once considered non-conventional but later supported as efficacious by new evidence revealed through inquiry and well-designed investigations. FSMB guidelines recognize that a comprehensive discussion of the risks and benefits of all treatments is in the best interest of patients. Detailed documentation of such conversation is necessary and further guidelines regarding documentation related to integrative treatment are provided by the FSMB. Shared decision-making is one way of reducing liability. The FSMB has passed guidelines for practitioners who provide nonconventional treatments and for those who provide conventional treatments.

The Professional Person

Ethical professional judgment must simultaneously incorporate the universal moral principles of *fairness, integrity,* and *compassion;* an ethical violation is likely if the mental-health practitioner leaves out any one of these three principles in making a decision about his or her professional conduct in any specific situation. However, it must be acknowledged that in trying to provide quality care that is in the best interest of the patient, no matter how much forethought and planning has taken place, mental-health care professionals will inevitably come across situations in which the appropriate ethical course of action is ambiguous at best. Consulting with colleagues during such times is invaluable. Thus, it is important to nurture ongoing connections with other mental-health care professionals.

In addition, practicing mental-health care can be emotionally taxing. Personal self-care and stress management skills are extremely important for practitioners. Furthermore, ethical professional helpers face the mixed emotional bag of ongoing self-exploration and personal development, in that being with patients triggers reactions, and working well with them requires self-awareness. For this reason, pursuing counseling or psychotherapy can be immensely helpful, both personally and professionally, for mental-health care providers. Change and growth are certainly challenging and can even be experienced as painful at times. Mental-health care professionals usually find their work to be both rewarding and stressful. Perhaps these are truly two sides of the same coin, as taking responsibility in relationships with others and with the self is the path leading to both.

References

Appelbaum, P.S., Lidz, C.W., & Meisel, A. (1987). *Informed consent: Legal theory and clinical practice.* New York: Oxford University Press.

Corey, G., Corey, M.S., & Callahan, P. (2007). *Issues and ethics in the helping professions* (7th ed.). Belmont, CA: Thomson Brooks/Cole.

Dusky vs. United States. (1960). 362 US 402.

Ewing, C.P., & McCann, J.T. (eds.). (2006). Prosenjit Poddar and Tatiana Tarasoff: Where the public peril begins. *Minds on trial: Great cases in law and psychology* (pp. 57–67). New York: Oxford University Press.

Federation of State Medical Boards. (2002). *Model guidelines for physician use of complementary and alternative therapies in medical practice.* Available at www.fsmb.org/pdf/2002_grpol_ Complementary_Alternative_Therapies.pdf.

Gutheil, T.G., & Appelbaum, P.S. (2000). *Clinical handbook of psychiatry and the law* (3rd ed.). Philadelphia: Lippincott, Williams & Wilkins.

Hoge, S.K., Appelbaum, P.S., Lawlor, T., Beck, J.C., Litman, R., Greer, A., Gatheil, T.G., & Kaplan, E. (1990). A prospective, multicenter study of patients' refusal of antipsychotic medication. *Archives of General Psychiatry, 47,* 949–956.

Josephson, A.M., & Peteet, J.R. (2004). *Handbook of spirituality and worldview in clinical practice.* Washington, DC: American Psychiatric Publishing.

Koenig, H., & Pritchett, J. (1998). *Religion and psychotherapy.* In H. Koenig (Ed.), Handbook of religion and mental health (pp. 323–336). San Diego, CA: Academic Press.

Lake, J.H., & Spiegel, D. (2007). *Complementary and alternative treatments in mental health care.* Arlington, VA: American Psychiatric Association.

Miller, R.D. (2003). Criminal competence. In R. Rosner (Ed.), *Principles and practice of forensic psychiatry* (2nd ed., pp. 186–212). New York: Wiley.

Schwartz, H.I., & Mack, D.M. (2003). Informed consent and competency. In R. Rosner (Ed.), *Principles and practice of forensic psychiatry* (2nd ed., pp. 97–106). New York: Wiley.

Schwartz, H.I., & Roth, L.H. (1989). Informed consent and competency in psychiatric practice. In A. Tasman, R.E. Hales, & A.J. Frances (Eds.), *Review of psychiatry* (Vol. 8, pp. 409–431). Washington, DC: American Psychiatric Association.

Sperry, L. (2007). *The ethical and professional practice of counseling and psychotherapy.* Boston: Pearson Education.

Steere, D. (1997). *Spiritual presence in psychotherapy: A guide for caregivers.* New York: Brunner/ Mazel.

Zuckerman, E.L. (2005). *Clinician's thesaurus: The guidebook to conducting psychological interviews and psychological reports* (6th ed.). New York: Guilford Press.

9

Sample Case History: Sherlock Holmes

In *The Seven-Per-Cent Solution*, Nicholas Meyer (1993) revealed that Sigmund Freud had evaluated Sherlock Holmes, yet not until now has Freud's initial writeup of the case come to light. Quite remarkably, Freud's presentation illustrated the standard approach used 100 years later!

IDENTIFYING INFORMATION

2 June 1891

The patient, Mr. Sherlock Holmes, is a 41-year-old, white, single, Protestant private detective, referred for cocaine misuse, depression, and bizarre behavior by his friend and colleague, Dr. John H. Watson. (*Informant*: Quotations are from the patient, while all other information, unless specified to the contrary, is from Dr. Watson, a reliable historian.)

CHIEF COMPLAINT

"I have applied all my will to banishing this [cocaine] habit and I have not been able to do so. . . . Once a man takes the first false step, his feet are set forever on the path to his destruction."

HISTORY OF PRESENT ILLNESS

The patient was apparently well until 24 April 1891, when late at night he snuck through the back door of Watson's home, appearing agitated, perspiring, gaunt, and pale. His eyes roved restlessly, but nothing seemed to register. He started to close and bolt every shutter in the room, but suddenly stopped and began to pace until Watson persuaded him to sit. Holmes then launched into a rambling story that people with air guns were after him because he had penetrated the defenses of a Professor Moriarty, an ex-university professor of mathematics with "incredible mental prowess and hereditary diabolic tendencies." He insisted that Moriarty is the "Napoleon of crime, the organizer of half the evil in the world, and the center of a web of malefactors."

After an hour of standing, sitting, and pacing, Holmes's excited speech slowed into inarticulate mutterings, followed by whisperings. He slept for 2 hours and awoke with a blank stare. He did not recognize the name Moriarty when it was mentioned, but insisted that before he slept he was discussing an entirely different subject. Although earlier Watson had mentioned that his wife was away, Holmes requested that she be thanked for an excellent dinner (which had never been eaten).

The next day, Holmes would not admit Watson to his room, fearing he was Moriarty in disguise. Holmes questioned Watson about items that only Watson would have known. Once inside, Watson noted that there were new shutters of heavy iron and new locks on the doors. Holmes rambled on about Moriarty.

Later that day, Watson was approached by Professor Moriarty, who taught math at a small school but had privately tutored Holmes and his older brother Mycroft when both were children. Moriarty claimed that for the previous 5 weeks, Holmes had been harassing him by standing outside his house all night, dogging his footsteps, telling his superior that he was a master criminal, and sending him telegrams with warnings such as, "Your days are numbered." The professor was contemplating legal action to prevent this harassment, but was dissuaded from doing so by Watson's reassurances.

Mrs. Hudson, Holmes's landlady of many years, told Watson that around the end of February, Holmes began spending his days locked in his study-bedroom; he would barricade the doors, bolt the shutters, see no one, and refuse all meals. Late at night, he'd sneak out to spy on the professor.

Watson believes that Holmes has episodically snuffed cocaine for at least 5 years, but that only recently has this use escalated to where it totally impairs occupational and social functioning. He now intravenously injects himself with unknown (but increasing) amounts of a 7% solution of cocaine three to four times a day. Holmes only makes wild accusations about Moriarty during cocaine intoxication; at other times on cocaine Holmes becomes grandiose, saying such things as, "It is very dangerous for me to leave London for any length of time. It generates in the criminal classes an unhealthy excitement when my absence is discovered." He denies and conceals his cocaine use, but without his usual meticulousness and caution—syringes are left in open drawers, his shirt sleeves are rolled up, thereby exposing puncture marks, etc.

Two weeks ago, at Watson's insistence, Holmes stopped taking cocaine, and within a day, felt extreme despair, gloom, and boredom—extreme even for Holmes. He has stopped working on any other case, believing that no other criminal in Europe is clever enough to bother with. He has lost all interest in his usual activities, has no appetite, has shed 10 pounds, looks pale, and stays in bed most of the day. Watson has never heard Holmes speak of suicide. Being concerned about his worsening state, Dr. Watson, in collusion with Mycroft Holmes and Professor Moriarty, tricked the patient into leaving London for treatment here in Vienna.

PAST HISTORY—DEVELOPMENTAL, PSYCHIATRIC, DRUG AND ALCOHOL, AND FAMILY

Little is known about the patient's early childhood. His mother was involved in an illicit love affair, which Holmes's father discovered. He then shot her to death. Moriarty, then Holmes's tutor, was the one who told the patient the news. There is no information as to his behavior prior to, or immediately after, this catastrophe. Sherlock was an intelligent child and went through college with high grades. His income derives from family landholdings and a thriving detective practice.

Watson thinks that the patient's father died years ago, but knows nothing of the circumstances. The patient's sole living relative is his older brother Mycroft, who is also a bachelor. Watson claims that Mycroft is even more intelligent, reclusive, and eccentric than he, living in London's highly traditional Diogenes Club, the main qualifications for membership of which are shyness and misanthropy, and whose main distinction is that members' chairs are positioned back-to-back so that nobody speaks with another. Watson is unaware of any mental illness in the family.

Watson describes the patient as a "deeply private person, whose reclusivity reaches major proportions" at times and who behaves "as a 'thinking machine,' impassive, aloof, and austere and not in direct contact with the sordid realities of physical existence." Holmes once observed, "Watson, I am a brain." Nonetheless, Watson contends that underneath this bravado, Holmes is a deeply compassionate man who regards his emotions as interfering with his mental processes. He tries, Watson maintains, to suppress his emotions by indulging in intellectual pursuits, such as chemical experiments and violin improvisation for hours on end, or by practicing shooting at the walls of his room. Except for a brief attraction to Irene Adler, women have been conspicuously absent in the patient's life.

Watson considers Holmes to be an ill-mannered eccentric, who is easily bored when not confronted with an interesting problem to solve. Holmes confirmed this by saying, "I abhor the dull routine of existence, I loathe stagnation." On occasion, he becomes demoralized, sad, and hopeless; he lacks energy, sleeps 10–12 hours a day (normally he sleeps under 5 hours a day), socially isolates himself, and has lost interest in everything. These depressive periods occur once or twice a year, last from several days to weeks, but no longer than 2–3 months. Some of these periods end when Holmes gets a new and challenging case, some end for no apparent reason, and some because Holmes binges on cocaine for a week or two. When confronted with an interesting problem, he would stop using cocaine, but return to it when bored or depressed. Except for some prior experimentation with morphine injections, Holmes has not used any drug except cocaine.

MEDICAL HISTORY AND PHYSICAL EXAMINATION

Although a physical exam was not performed, the patient was observed to be malnourished, had dilated pupils, puncture marks on both arms, and a weak pulse.

Mental Status Examination

[Formal testing not performed.]

Appearance: Gaunt, sallow, malnourished, tired-looking, and appears to have lost weight. He continues to wear his only double-visored hat indoors.

Behavior: Enters office slowly, weak handshake, dry palms, and sits throughout the 80-minute consultation. His movements are a bit slow, although when speaking of Moriarty, he becomes fidgety and speaks with more animation.

Speech: He says very little and only speaks when asked a direct question. His speech is hushed, moderately slow, but not slurred.

Emotion: Patient says that he is despondent, has no interest in things, and that nothing brings him pleasure. His facies is glum, his general look, bored. His affect and mood are appropriate to what is said. There are no signs of anxiety.

Thought processes and content: During the middle of the interview, he says that he thinks I am Moriarty in disguise, and that his brother and Watson have concocted a sinister plot to deliver him into the clutches of his enemies. Yet, when confronted, Holmes abandons this idea and apologizes. When asked if he still believes that Moriarty is a master criminal, he says he would rather not discuss the matter. Despite these apparently overvalued ideas, there is no evidence of actual delusions, ideas of reference, incoherence, phobias, obsessions, or compulsions. His thinking is goal-directed. He denies suicidal ideation.

Perception: Although not specifically tested, there are no indications of a perceptual disturbance.

Attention: His mind seems to wander on occasion, but not while speaking.

Orientation: Knows the date, time, place, his name, Watson's name, and my name.

Memory: Excellent immediate, recent, and remote memory.

Judgment: No apparent functional disturbance.

Intelligence, information, and abstraction: Extremely high.

Insight: On confrontation, he admits to cocaine addiction and acknowledges that it is a serious problem.

DIAGNOSIS

Axis I: 292.84 Cocaine abuse; substance-induced mood disorder
            292.0   Cocaine withdrawal (Provisional)
            296.30 Major depression (Provisional)
            296.80 Bipolar disorder (Provisional)
Axis II: 301.40 Obsessive–compulsive personality disorder (Provisional)
            Schizotypal personality disorder (Provisional)
            Paranoid personality disorder (Provisional)
Axis III: None
Axis IV: Psychosocial and environmental problems: None elicited
Axis V: Global Assessment of Functioning (GAF)
Current: GAF 35; impairment in reality testing and impairment in mood, judgment
            Highest in past year: GAF 70; excellent work functioning, but few relationships

PROGNOSIS

Guarded prognosis for cocaine abuse, especially in view of (1) the disorder's natural course and the patient's (2) history of depressive symptoms, (3) current reluctance to abandon cocaine, and (4) characteristic unwillingness to place himself under the care of others.

BIOPSYCHOSOCIAL FORMULATION

The patient's heavy cocaine abuse produces grandiose, persecutory, and over-valued ideas and agitation. Holmes's particular choice of cocaine may partly serve to self-medicate an underlying depression (especially given his unusual intolerance of boredom), and partly due to his attraction to the sense of sharp-ened intellect cocaine affords. Stopping cocaine brings on, and/or aggravates, depressive symptoms, especially dysthymia, anhedonia, hypersomnia, psycho-motor retardation, and social isolation. Why the patient's use of cocaine sharply increased late last February remains unclear, since no precipitant has been identified.

The diagnosis of cocaine abuse is firm. In addition, in light of current information, the patient's symptoms strongly suggest a mood disorder, even though they frequently fall short of meeting *DSM-IV-TR* criteria. The episodes lasting 2 weeks after cocaine use strongly suggest a substanced-induced mood disorder. Because his depressive symptoms are episodic, a dysthymic disorder is highly unlikely, whereas a major depression is a distinct possibility. Slightly more probable would be bipolar disorder, since his periods of enormous en-ergy, even when not on cocaine, resemble hypomania, and his hypersomniac depressive intervals suggest bipolar depression. Because we lack information, a family history of mood disorder or substance abuse is impossible to make. In view of his longstanding meticulousness, perfectionism, excessive use of logic and intellect at the expense of emotion, and mild self-righteousness and suspiciousness, an obsessive–compulsive personality disorder should be consid-ered. A schizotypal or paranoid personality disorder should also be considered. The patient's belief in having a "sixth sense" for criminals, his odd appearance, always wearing his special hat, and his frequent social anxiety support a schizo-typal diagnosis. His brother Mycroft probably has a schizotypal personality disorder—a disorder that has strong genetic components. The patient's para-noid ideas and the social anxiety that tends toward paranoia support a paranoid diagnosis. However, the patient's ability to have close friends other than rela-tives, the appropriateness of being suspicious as a professional detective, and the variability of his overvalued ideas (which may fluctuate with cocaine use) argue against a diagnosis of schizotypal or paranoid personality disorder.

Psychodynamically, *repression*, supplemented by other defenses, appears to have played a major role in shaping Holmes's preoccupations and behavior. His *repressed* rage at his father for killing his mother seems to have been *dis-*

placed onto Moriarty, the man who informed Holmes of the murder. *Introjecting* rage intended for his father may have compounded Holmes's depression. His repressed rage at his mother's unfaithfulness and her subsequent "abandonment" of young Sherlock may have contributed to his disinterest in women—his viewing them as untrustworthy, immoral, and undependable. By *sublimation*, Holmes excelled in detective work "to punish the wicked and see justice done."

PLAN

1. Withdrawal from cocaine.
2. Observation; look for hidden cocaine use.
3. Evaluation of mood and personality disorders.
4. Evaluate unconscious, or "automatic," thoughts for irrational beliefs that may trigger substance use and consider use of cognitive therapy to replace with "rational beliefs."
5. Consider use of behavioral techniques to reduce anxiety and tension, such as progressive muscle relaxation.
6. Encourage involvement with social supports—friends and family.
7. Encourage involvement in pursuits that usually bring him pleasure, such as violin playing, attending Wagnerian opera, chasing criminals.
8. Next appointment: Tuesday, 16:00.

—Sigmund Freud, M.D.

Reference

Meyers, N. (1993). *The seven-per-cent solution.* New York: Norton.

MENTAL DISORDERS

10

Delirium, Dementia, Amnesia, and Other Cognitive Disorders

"Like trees, we grow old from the top," says Gore Vidal's Emperor Julian. Although most would agree, they're barking up the wrong tree: Dementia—or what is commonly called "senility"—is *not* inherent to aging, but a set of illnesses that strikes 15–20% of elderly Americans. To assume that with age certain disease states are natural and inevitable, stereotypes the older adults and causes many curable dementias to go untreated. Dementia is most simply defined as "mental deterioration." While there are definite changes in cognition associated with aging, the development of serious impairment of cognitive function that results in loss of function, loss of self-care ability, emotional distress, and behavioral disturbance is not a normal result of aging alone.

The DSM-IV-TR term *cognitive disorder* is used in this chapter to describe what was formerly called *organic brain syndrome*. The term *organic* was dropped because it implies a false dichotomy between physical and mental disorders. The cardinal symptoms of cognitive disorders are recent memory impairment, disorientation, poor judgment, confusion, and a general loss of intellectual functions. Also common are psychotic symptoms, including hallucinations, paranoia, delusions, and illusions. Emotional reactions such as depression, anxiety, fear, and irritability frequently occur, as do personality changes and behavioral disturbances, including agitation and aggression. The cognitive disorders are proven (or reasonably presumed) to be produced by medical, neurological, and/or biochemical alterations in the brain's structure or function. Overall, as our population lives longer the rates of dementia are increasing. The remaining lifetime risk of any dementia, including Alzheimer's disease, for women who live to be at least age 55 is 21%. Thus more than one in five American women who live to be at least age 55 can expect to develop dementia in their remaining lifetime. Remaining lifetime risk of dementia for men is 14%, or one in seven men who live to be at least age 55. One in 5 women and 1 in 6 men who reached 65 years of age developed dementia.

This chapter examines three types of cognitive disorder: *delirium*, whose primary characteristic is a clouding of consciousness (a reduced awareness of the environment); *dementia*, whose chief feature is a deterioration of intellectual functions; and *amnestic disorders*, whose cardinal symptom is memory impairment.

Two other types of cognitive disorder, *intoxication* and *withdrawal*, are discussed in Chapter 11. Other disorders caused by a *general medical condition* or *substance abuse*, such as psychotic disorder and anxiety and mood disorders, are discussed in related chapters.

DELIRIUM

Clinical Presentation

Delirium—from the Latin *delirare*, meaning to rave, to be crazy—is characterized by a clouding of consciousness, disorientation, and recent memory loss. These signs arise abruptly (e.g., from several hours to days), fluctuate wildly, often become worse at night or in the dark (i.e., "sundowning"), and rarely persist for more than a month. Often appearing frightened and agitated, patients with delirium frequently have illusions, hallucinations (in any of the five senses, but vision most commonly), incoherent speech, and disrupted sleep–wake cycles. The *DSM-IV-TR* diagnostic criteria for delirium are listed in Table 10-1.

Disorientation to time usually comes first: At midnight, the patient may say it's noon or that the year is 1948. As delirium worsens, the patient becomes disoriented to place (e.g., thinks he's at a country club when he's sitting in his bedroom), and later to people (e.g., misidentifies her spouse). Immediate memory dwindles first, followed by intermediate (10-minute), and then remote memory. If either disorientation or recent memory loss is absent, the diagnosis of delirium is doubtful. Lucid intervals, with symptoms often becoming worse at night, are usually diagnostic of delirium. It is important to remember that unlike chronic dementias, delirium is sudden in onset, fluctuates with lucid intervals, and has a high frequency of visual hallucinations. Complicating this presentation, however, is the fact that anyone with limited "brain reserve capacity," such as those with dementia, is more predisposed to the occurrence of delirium.

Clinical Course and Complications

Any time there is a sudden, unexplained behavioral change or psychosis, delirium must be suspected. Early detection of delirium is extremely important

TABLE 10-1

DSM-IV-TR *Criteria for Delirium*

Common Criteria for Delirium

A. Disturbance of consciousness (reduced clarity of awareness of the environment) with reduced ability to focus, sustain, or shift attention.

B. Change in cognition (such as memory deficit, disorientation, language disturbance) or the development of a perceptual disturbance that is not better accounted for by a preexisting, established, or evolving dementia.

C. The disturbance develops over a short period of time (usually hours to days) and tends to fluctuate during the course of the day.

Additional Criterion for Delirium Due to a General Medical Condition

D. There is evidence from the history, physical examination, or laboratory findings that the disturbance is caused by the direct physiological consequences of a general medical condition.

Additional Criteria for Substance Intoxication Delirium

D. There is evidence from the history, physical examination, or laboratory findings of either (1) or (2):

    (1) the symptoms in Criteria A and B developed during Substance Intoxication.

    (2) medication use is etiologically related to the disturbance.

Note: This diagnosis should be made instead of a diagnosis of Substance Intoxication only when the cognitive symptoms are in excess of those usually associated with the intoxication syndrome and when the symptoms are sufficiently severe to warrant independent clinical attention.

Additional Criterion for Substance Withdrawal Delirium

D. There is evidence from the history, physical examination, or laboratory findings that the symptoms in Criteria A and B developed during, or shortly after, a withdrawal syndrome.

Note: This diagnosis should be made instead of a diagnosis of Substance Withdrawal only when the cognitive symptoms are in excess of those usually associated with the withdrawal syndrome and when the symptoms are sufficiently severe to warrant independent clinical attention.

Additional Criterion for Delirium Due to Multiple Etiologies

D. There is evidence from the history, physical examination, or laboratory tests that the delirium has more than one etiology (e.g., more than one etiological general medical condition, a general medical condition plus Substance Intoxication or medication side effect).*

Note. From *DSM-IV-TR,* pp. 136, 141, 143, 146–147.

*This is a common diagnosis in older adults because frequently more than one medication, medical condition, or infection is at play.

because it can lead to death. Delirium usually arises quickly, from several hours to days, depending on its cause. The onset may be dramatic, as when patients begin thrashing about, tearing out IVs, or fighting. When the onset is subtle and the symptoms are exaggerations of normal personality traits, delirium may go undetected. For instance, a normally perfectionistic physician recovering from heart surgery started to cuss at nurses for not washing their hands. Initially the staff said, "Everybody knows doctors make the worst patients," and missed the delirium, until his behavior became frankly psychotic. At first, patients with delirium may simply appear a bit confused, mistake a night nurse for a relative, or not find their rooms. Nurses' and families' reports may be the first clue to a delirium when they describe a calm patient by day and a confused one by night. Frequent, around-the-clock mental-status testing is often needed to detect a delirium.

Accidents are common in delirium; the patient may fall out of bed or step in front of a truck. The longer delirium continues, the greater the chance of permanent brain damage. Delirium greatly increases both mortality and morbidity; it rarely persists for over a month—by then, the patient is either diagnosed as demented or dead. If delirium has a protracted course, a review of the diagnosis and consideration of a more permanent and chronic condition should be entertained. The one exception here is persisting delirium and cognitive impairment due to chronic alcoholism. There have been many cases where ongoing abstinence, usually through placement or in state psychiatric hospitals, over the course of 12 months or more, has allowed the slow but often full recovery of brain function, even in older adults.

Etiology and Pathogenesis

Most patients with delirium have an underlying medical, surgical, chemical, or neurological problem; it may be an infectious disease, drug intoxication or withdrawal, congestive heart failure, fluid and electrolyte imbalance, or stroke. Sometimes the first sign of a medical illness will be a delirium. Drug-induced delirium is most often secondary to anticholinergic toxicity. Psychotropic drugs, especially tricyclic antidepressants and low-potency antipsychotics, frequently cause delirium because of their substantial anticholinergic properties. Hypnoanxiolytic agents (e.g., lorazepam, alprazolam) can also cause delirium. Older adults are especially susceptible, because they are highly sensitive to anticholinergics and hypnoanxiolytics. Fortunately, most of the newer antidepressants (SSRIs, SNRIs, mirtazepine, and bupropion) are not anticholinergic. Unfortunately, several drugs for blood pressure, heart malfunction, ulcers, emphysema, allergies, and inflammation have significant anticholinergic effects. Other commonly prescribed drugs and over-the-counter medications are frequently overlooked because they are thought to be benign; for example, diphenhydramine (Benadryl), which in overdoses creates the perfect example of "anticholinergic delirium." Others include antibiotics, (ciprofloxacin [Cipro], levofloxacin [Levaquin], and related agents), drugs used to treat urinary incontinence, some drugs used for acid reflux, and certainly opioid pain medications. Delirium is often multifactorial!

Another cause of delirium is sensory isolation, which can occur in intensive and cardiac care units (ICU/CCU psychoses). The monotony of a strange and unfamiliar setting may cause patients to see walls quiver, mistake technological noises for human voices, hallucinate taps on their shoulders, etc. The extent to which patients' deliria stem from sensory isolation or from the disease, medical complications, and treatment that brought them to an ICU or CCU is often unclear and varies depending on the circumstances.

The most common causes of delirium in hospitalized older adults are urinary tract infections, pneumonia, drug interactions, fever, heart failure, postoperative states, other pulmonary conditions, and environmental change. Delirium is a marker of "brain reserve capacity," and recent evidence suggests that those with recurrent delirium are at greater risk of developing Alzheimer's disease and other dementias. Close monitoring, therefore, of a patient's cognitive status following episodes of delirium is indicated.

Differential Diagnosis

Accentuated *normal personality traits* are part of patients' past history and persist in aging with minimal fluctuation, whereas personality in delirium often shows wild fluctuations between normal (during lucid intervals) and abnormal/out of character (during confused intervals). Unlike *dementia*, delirium is characterized by an abrupt onset, a fluctuating course, and a clouding of consciousness. Sometimes the strokes in vascular dementia cause abrupt deterioration, but they almost always have accompanying neurological deficits. When delirium is superimposed on dementia, it appears as a sudden, unexplained worsening with much fluctuation.

When *schizophrenia* erupts, the patient's hallucinations and apparent confusion can resemble a delirium, but the patient will not show the disorientation, memory loss, and diurnal pattern seen in delirium. It is unusual for visual hallucinations to be present early in the course of schizophrenia. *Generalized anxiety disorder* and delirium may both present with agitation, yet the former is without disorientation, confusion, or memory loss.

Substance-induced delirium can usually be determined by history from the patient, family, or friends, or by direct detection of the offending agent or agents. Withdrawal-related delirium can be more difficult to detect than delirium from intoxication. A good example is delirium from alcohol withdrawal. By the time an individual in alcohol withdrawal becomes delirious, it is likely alcohol will no longer be detectable (3–5 days postdrinking). History-taking, usually from family or friends, as well as keeping this condition in the differential diagnoses, are vital.

There is a growing body of evidence supporting a relatively new form of dementia, *diffuse Lewy body dementia* (DLBD). DLBD may be the second most common form of dementia and is closely related to Alzheimer's disease but involves a much more rapid loss of cholinergic neurons. DLBD often resembles delirium. Cognitive loss is mild in early DLBD, but sudden episodes of confusion, parkinsonism, disorientation, and visual hallucinations, with a return to fairly good lucidity, are common. Falls and a marked intolerance to antipsychotics are also common; the latter may help differentiate DLBD from delirium and other dementias. Unlike delirium, no clear underlying medical cause is easily identified in DLBD, from which patients "just recover" back to their baseline until another episode occurs.

Management and Treatment

The first priority is to keep the patient alive and to medically stabilize him or her; a close second is to prevent brain damage; third is to prevent the patient from inflicting self-harm. A thorough history from family, friends, past caregivers, and charts may reveal similar confusional periods with a known cause (e.g., hypoglycemia in diabetes or drug overdose) that immediately suggests a present cause and possible treatment. Quickly identifying a delirium and then referral to a physician to determine its cause are critical to these goals. Careful nursing care is also essential and often lifesaving. Because medically hospitalized patients with delirium may fall out of bed, wander off, trip, break bones, develop concussions, rip out IVs, hurl IV bags, and so on, these patients often need constant observation and sometimes physical restraints. Restraint use is somewhat paradoxical. Restraints frequently cause problems, including injury; however, there is often no alternative to provide for patient safety and, equally important, maintenance of interventions such as IVs and airways essential for treatment. Foley catheters should be viewed as a restraint, as they are well proven to act as such. Clearly, a patient-specific and thoughtful assessment for the use of any restraint must be made and then performed correctly. The proper use of restraining devices and techniques is important and a staff-training issue.

Patients with delirium should be frequently oriented. Health care professionals' contacts with the patients should be brief and numerous (e.g., 3 minutes four times an hour), always telling the patient the date, the place, the staff member's name, and what he or she is doing. The patient should be reassured as to her safety and repeatedly oriented. Pictures of family members, a clock, and a calendar showing the date should be visible to the patient. The best treatment for an ICU psychosis is removal from the ICU. If that is medically unsafe, all the above measures should be taken.

Before the underlying cause of the delirium is rectified, the patient may be helped initially by small doses of antipsychotic drugs (e.g., haloperidol 0.5–2 mg or ziprasidone 10–20 mg IM). Some (Wells & McEvoy, 1982) claim that antianxiety agents (e.g., lorazepam 1–2 mg IM) are as helpful and safe as antipsychotics. Other authors (Goodwin & Guze, 1989) opine that many patients with delirium become even more agitated and disorganized on antianxiety drugs; they therefore recommend antipsychotics. Often, both are given together. If one is managing an alcohol withdrawal delirium, there is an evidence-based protocol available (Mayo-Smith, 1997) but doses need to be reduced for the elderly. The most important aspect of this treatment is to keep the patient safe while not further complicating the delirium. Antipsychotics can cause dystonia and/or neuroleptic malignant syndrome, but their benefits and risks in treating delirium are well established. The newer second-generation or "atypical" antipsychotics (including ziprasidone, olanzepine, aripiprazole, quetiapine, and risperidone) are less likely to manifest side effects but are not available in an intravenous delivery form. Anxiolytics can cause disinhibition or excess sedation; older adults should receive one-half to one-third of these hypnoanxiolytic doses. They may benefit most from benzodiazepines (e.g., oxazepam or lorazepam) that are not conjugated into other medically active compounds, have a relatively short half-life and accumulate less. If it is clearly an anticholinergic delirium (e.g., benadryl overdose), physostigmine is sometimes used to achieve an immediate though occasionally short-lived lucid period in someone experiencing severe and frightening visual hallucinations and subsequent agitation (Stern, 1983). Case reports have suggested that symptoms of delirium and frequency of recurrence of delirium can be improved by cholinesterase inhibitors (e.g., doxeprazil, rivostigmine, galantanine) (Wengel et al., 1998).

More important than the choice of drug is the dose: Too little, and the delirium worsens and becomes more dangerous; too much, and more delirium, coma, and respiratory depression may follow. Errors on either side of this delicate balance can lead to death, but it is probably better to err on the side of too little. More of a drug can always be given, but not *less*! If the initial doses mentioned above are insufficient or wear off, they may be repeated hourly, as long as the patient is checked before each new dose is administered.

In summary, a thorough evaluation of each patient with delirium is necessary, and treatment should be individualized according to the specific situation and unique needs. Treatment is closely monitored and well coordinated with all involved professionals.

DEMENTIA

Clinical Presentation

Dementia—from the Latin *demens*, meaning "out of one's mind"—is characterized by a loss of intellectual abilities, especially memory, judgment, abstract thinking, and language skills, together with marked changes in personality and impulse control. Most dementias begin gradually (months to years). Unlike delirium, dementia occurs without a clouding of consciousness. Table 10-2 lists *DSM-IV-TR* diagnostic criteria for dementia.

Initially, there is *memory loss* for recent events: Ovens are left on, keys misplaced, conversations forgotten. Later, episodes of getting lost while driving in once familiar locations begin; questions are repeated because the question and the answer are quickly forgotten. Retained, and often dwelled on, are details from childhood and other long-term memories. *Personality changes* are often intensifications or exact opposites of preexisting character traits. A gregarious grandfather retreats to a corner and daydreams. A mildly suspicious and self-righteous woman begins calling the police every night, accusing her neighbors of performing abortions in their basements. *Impaired judgment* and *poor impulse control* are common: Patients may start speaking crudely, exhibit genitals, or shoplift. A normally cautious businessman has three car accidents in 6 months because he impulsively passes cars on hills and swerves back and forth between lanes "to get ahead of the traffic."

Intellectual abilities deteriorate. Patients may have trouble naming objects (agnosia). They may have difficulties understanding language (aphasia); speech becomes stereotyped, slow, vague, and filled with irrelevant detail as these patients increasingly are unable to concentrate, to follow conversations, or to distinguish the germane from the trivial; words are misused, chosen more by sound than by sense. Patients cannot perform simple motor tasks (apraxia); driving, cooking, handling money, and using tools become too complicated. They find it hard to draw a simple house, copy the placement of four matchsticks, or assemble blocks. The patients themselves lack insight into their condition (*anosognosia*—reduced awareness of symptoms; *anosodiaphora*—lack of concern about the consequences of symptoms). Often the severity of these

TABLE 10-2
DSM-IV-TR *Criteria for the Dementias*
Alzheimer's, Vascular, Substance-Induced, Multiple Etiologies or Due to a General Medical Condition

Common Criteria Persisting for the Dementias

A. The development of multiple cognitive deficits manifested by both

 (1) memory impairment (impaired ability to learn new information or to recall previously learned information)

 (2) one (or more) of the following cognitive disturbances:

   (a) aphasia (language disturbance)

   (b) apraxia (impaired ability to carry out motor activities despite intact motor function)

   (c) agnosia (failure to recognize or identify objects despite intact sensory function)

   (d) disturbance in executive functioning (i.e., planning, organizing, sequencing, abstracting)

B. The cognitive deficits in Criteria A1 and A2 each cause significant impairment in social or occupational functioning and represent a significant decline from a previous level of functioning.

C. The deficits do not occur exclusively during the course of a delirium.

Additional Criteria for Dementia of the Alzheimer's Type

D. The course is characterized by gradual onset and continuing cognitive decline.

E. The cognitive deficits in Criteria A1 and A2 are not due to any of the following:

 (1) other central nervous system conditions that cause progressive deficits in memory and cognition (e.g., cerebrovascular disease, Parkinson's disease, Huntington's disease, subdural hematoma, normal-pressure hydrocephalus, brain tumor)

 (2) systemic conditions that are known to cause dementia (e.g., hypothyroidism, vitamin B_{12} or folic acid deficiency, niacin deficiency, hypercalcemia, neurosyphilis, HIV infection)

 (3) substance-induced conditions

F. The disturbance is not better accounted for by another Axis I disorder (e.g., Major Depressive Disorder, Schizophrenia).

With Early Onset: if onset is at age 65 years or below
With Late Onset: if onset is after age 65 years

Additional Criteria for Vascular Dementia (formerly known as multi-infarct dementia)

D. Focal neurological signs and symptoms (e.g., exaggeration of deep tendon reflexes, extensor plantar response, pseudobulbar palsy, gait abnormalities, weakness of an extremity) or laboratory evidence indicative of cerebral vascular disease (e.g., multiple infarctions involving cortex and underlying white matter) that are judged to be etiologically related to the disturbance.

(*continued*)

TABLE 10-2
Continued

Additional Criteria for Dementia Due to Other General Medical Conditions

D. There is evidence from the history, physical examination, or laboratory findings that the disturbance is the direct physiological consequence of one of the general medical conditions listed below.

Dementia due to HIV disease, head trauma, Parkinson's disease, Huntington's disease, Pick's disease, or Creutzfeldt–Jakob disease.

Dementia due to a general medical condition not listed above, e.g., normal-pressure hydrocephalus, hypothyroidism, brain tumor, vitamin B_{12} deficiency, intracranial radiation).

Additional Criterion for Substance-Induced Persisting Dementia

D. There is evidence from the history, physical examination, or laboratory findings that the deficits are etiologically related to the persisting effects of substance use (e.g., a drug of abuse, a medication).

E. The deficits do not persist beyond the usual duration of Substance Intoxication or Withdrawal.

Additional Criterion for Dementia Due to Multiple Etiologies

D. There is evidence from history, physical examination, or laboratory tests that the disturbance has more than one etiology (e.g., head trauma plus chronic alcohol use, Dementia of the Alzheimer's Type with the subsequent development of Vascular Dementia).

Note. From *DSM-IV-TR*, pp. 147–171.

---

symptoms is not recognized by others until the patient is observed in a new place (where inability to learn new information is a tip-off), or until the spouse dies and family members become aware, for the first time, of how sick their parent is. Initially they blame this deterioration on grief but then realize it has been going on much longer.

In response to these impairments, patients most commonly use denial and seem not to notice these major problems; less commonly, they become ashamed, anxious, demoralized, irritable, and dysthymic; hypochondriasis increases; energy and enthusiasm decline. Some patients display "catastrophic reactions" or "emotional incontinence"—they respond to stimuli by excessive laughing, hostility, or weeping, or by suddenly becoming dazed, evasive, or immobile. Also common is *confabulation* (the fabrication of stories to conceal memory loss); so, too, are suspiciousness and paranoid ideation, especially when the patient has trouble hearing or seeing. Fear invades the memory vacuum: Forgetting where he left his wallet, the patient assumes it was stolen and may accuse others, including loved ones, of the crimes.

Whereas memory loss is an early symptom and the hallmark of Alzheimer's disease, it is often behavioral problems that precipitate referral to a physician. Difficult behaviors occur in up to 70% of patients with Alzheimer's disease, usually isolated to the middle stages of the chronic, deteriorating illness.

Delusional syndromes commonly present include delusions of theft, *Capgras syndrome* (misidentifying familiar people, often believing they are someone else or strangers), *Charles Bonnett's syndrome* (visual hallucations of little people often dressed in uniforms, coming and going), *one's house is not one's home* (belief they are in an unfamiliar place despite being at home), *phantom boarder syndrome* (a stranger is living in the house, often the one accused of leaving the oven on, etc.) and many more. Often delusions and behavior do not require medication, but rather environmental manipulations and an understanding on the part of the family.

The patient's deterioration may go unrecognized for months or even years because intellectual decline is usually insidious. Memory loss is dismissed as the natural result of normal aging or of not paying attention. The patient's impaired judgment and poor impulse control are explained by stereotyping (e.g., "Old folks naturally get crusty and cantankerous with age"). If Granddad starts making lewd gestures to teeny-boppers, he's a fun-loving "dirty old man." (Dirty old women don't exist?) Inappropriate jocularity, which arises from impairments of the brain's frontal lobe, is dismissed as "simply being in good spirits." The patient's loss of intellectual sharpness or wit may be too subtle or gradual to be noticed. It is important to have some knowledge of the patient's premorbid levels of intellectual and cognitive function, given the usually slow and frequently insidious onset and progression of symptoms, along with the usual self-denial and denial to others that occur. In most cases a person of high intellectual ability, significant education, and application of both is not going to demonstrate clearly recognizable signs or symptoms until the dementia has been present for a long time. On average, dementia is diagnosed at least 2 years into the disease process. Persons with lower levels of premorbid function will usually demonstrate these symptoms "sooner." Any form of memory loss, especially progressive loss, must be evaluated and should not be chalked up to "normal aging" or "senility."

When presenting clinically, patients with dementia may move slowly or fidget. They may look glum, bored, or tense. On a formal mental-status examination, they show recent memory loss and disorientation and usually have difficulties subtracting serial 1's or 7's and performing abstractions. However, it is possible they will present without any identified abnormality at all!

The Mini Mental State Examination (MMSE) is a widely used screening test for dementia (see Figure 10-1). It does not detect very early, mild dementias but is effective at detecting dementias that are mild to moderate or worse. (A score of 24 or below indicates probable dementia.) Although of value, the practitioner should remember the above-discussed issues and account for them. It is likely that an individual with a fourth-grade education and relatively low premorbid function will not score well on this test, even if no dementia is present. At the same time, a highly educated and highly functioning patient is likely to "ace" this test, even though serious deterioration has already happened. Patients should never be diagnosed with dementia or Alzheimer's disease while in the hospital where complicating medical (e.g., delirium) and environmental conditions are present. Unless history is very evident or the patient is in the moderate to severe stages of Alzheimer's disease, it may take several outpatient appointments and several MMSE scores before a diagnosis is comfortably made. The diagnosis of Alzheimer's disease can have a high probability, is never definite, and involves ruling out several other conditions.

Subtypes

There are four major subtypes of dementia: (1) *Alzheimer's disease* (in DSM-IV-TR, "dementia of the Alzheimer's type") is the most common type and accounts for over 60% of all dementias. (2) *Vascular dementia* (formerly called "multi-infarct dementia") accounts for 9–15% of dementias and is mainly caused by hypertension or emboli. (Emboli are small blood clots that break off from the heart or a carotid artery in the neck, flow to the brain, block part of the blood supply, and cause the death, or infarct, of those brain cells.) Contrary to popular belief, vascular dementia is not directly caused by arteriosclerosis ("hardening of the arteries"). Many experienced clinicians believe that vascular dementia is often overdiagnosed and is frequently comorbid with Alzheimer's disease (AD). (3) *Dementia due to other general medical conditions* accounts for 20% of the dementias. This category includes dementias that are primarily caused by neurological diseases or by systemic illnesses. Parkinson's disease is included because 20–30% of patients with this disease develop dementia. Two rare dementias, the rapidly progressive Creutzfeldt–Jakob disease (prion infections) and the slowly progressive Huntington's disease ("Woody Guthrie" disease), are also included here. Human immunodeficiency virus (HIV) dementia is more complicated because it can include dementia from HIV itself or treatable dementias from secondary infections. Toxoplasmosis, a protozoan infection, has been identified as a cause of dementia in HIV-positive patients. Pick's disease is the prototype of the frontotemporal dementias with

FIGURE 10-1
Mini Mental State Examination (MMSE)

Date _____

Patient's Name _____

Examiner's Name _____

Maximum Score	Score	
		ORIENTATION
5	( )	What is the (year) (season) (date) (day) (month)?
5	( )	Where are we: (state)(county)(town or city)(hospital)(floor)?
		REGISTRATION
3	( )	Name three common objects (e.g., "apple, table, penny"): Take 1 second to say each. Then ask the patient to repeat all three after you have said them. Give 1 point for each correct answer. Then repeat them until he/she learns all three. Count trials and record:
		ATTENTION AND CALCULATION
5	( )	Serial 7's backward. Give 1 point for each correct answer. Stop after five answers. Alternatively, spell WORLD backward. One point for each correct letter.
		RECALL
3	( )	Ask for the three objects repeated above. Give 1 point for each correct answer. (Note: Recall cannot be tested if all three objects were not remembered during registration.)
		LANGUAGE
2	( )	Name a "pencil" and "watch."
1	( )	Repeat the following: "No ifs, ands, or buts."
3	( )	Follow a three-stage command: "Take a paper in your right hand, fold it in half, and put it on the floor."
1	( )	Read and obey the following: Close your eyes.
1	( )	Write a sentence.
1	( )	Copy the following design:

Total Score _____

Adapted from Folstein et al. (1975).

other, less defined entities such as dementia associated with amyotrophic lateral sclerosis. Onsets of these dementias occur earlier than in other types and are believed to account for between 2.5 and 10% of all dementias. Interestingly but not unexpectedly, given the neuroanatomy involved, other cognitive domains than memory are generally more affected. The triad of cognitive impairment, Parkinson-type symptoms, and visual hallucinations classically defines this Lewy body dementia. The presence of histiologically distinct Lewy bodies in the brain, which are different from the classical plaques and neurofibrillary tangles associated with Alzheimer's disease, argue for a distinct etiology of DLBD. This issue remains controversial. (4) *Substance-induced persisting dementias* produce 7–9% of the dementias, with alcoholic dementia accounting for most. See Table 10-3 for a summary of incurable dementias.

Unlike AD and vascular dementia, many secondary dementias are treatable. Patients who present with dementias *must* receive thorough medical and neurological examinations to determine if they are among the roughly 20% of patients with dementia who can be treated and sometimes cured, either medically or surgically. Excluding depression, 1–3% or <5% of dementias are considered reversible, partially reversible, or able to be halted from further progression. Table 10-4 presents diagnostic modalities for the evaluation of dementia.

First a thorough history and corroboration are vital. Neuropsychological evaluation can be important, and the Halstead–Reitan and Nebraska-Luria are both sensitive

---

TABLE 10-3

Summary of Defined Incurable Dementias

A. Alzheimer's disease

B. Vascular dementia (multiinfarct, Lacunar, Binswanger's Disease)

C. Dementia due to other medical condition

    HIV (Human immunodeficiency virus)

    Parkinson's disease

    Creutzfeldt–Jakob disease

    Huntington's disease

    Pick's disease and other frontotemporal dementias

    Lewy body dementia

D. Substance-induced persisting dementias

    Alcohol (by far the most common)

TABLE 10-4

Useful Studies in the Clinical Evaluation of Patients with Dementia

Initial Studies Performed on All Patients

—Detailed history and physical examination (MOST IMPORTANT—including history of onset from collateral source).

—Chest x-ray

—Electrocardiogram (EKG)

—Complete blood count with red cell indices and erythrocyte sedimentation rate (ESR) and/or C-reactive protein

—Urinalysis

—Urine and serum drug levels, as indicated

—Electrolytes, blood urea nitrogen (BUN), calcium

—hepatic enzymes, bilirubin

—thyroid function tests

—serum B_{12} level

—Serum VDRL

—CAT or MRI (only as indicated by history, quick onset, review of systems, and physical exam)

Additional Studies Tailored to Individual Patients

If a metabolic cause is suspected

—Serum ammonia level

—Urine heavy metal screen – rarely needed

—Urine porphyrins

If an infectious cause is suspected

—Lumbar puncture with thorough cerebrospinal fluid (CSF) evaluation, including glucose, protein, cell count, India ink, VDRL, cultures (bacterial, TB, fungal, viral), protein electrophoresis

—Evaluation of possible systemic infection

If a structural or neoplastic cause is suspected

—CAT scan or MRI

—Vascular studies (cerebral arteriogram, carotid doppler ultrasound)

—CSF cytology

Other Helpful Studies in Some Patients

—Electroencephalogram (metabolic, degenerative, or structural processes)

—Intrathecal cisternogram (normal pressure hydrocephalus)

—Antinuclear factor (vasculitis)

—Serum copper and ceruloplasmin (Wilson's disease)

—Measurement of alpha, beta, peptide 42, and tau protein

—PET, fMRI, SPECT

tools. Positron emission tomography (PET) scanning with the necessary software can be diagnostic by measuing regional cerebral blood flow and neuroreceptor density. Single-photon emission computed tomography (SPECT) can also be valuable and has cost advantages over PET. Functional magnetic resonance imaging (fMRI) and magnetic resonance spectroscopy (MRS) scanning measure regional cerebral blood flow and brain chemistry. Some cerebrospinal fluid tests, such as a combined measurement of alpha, beta, peptide 42, and tau protein, may be of value. Coordination of the primary-care physician and other pertinent specialists is essential.

The "big four" treatable dementias—each accounting for about 6% of all dementias that are treatable—are *normal pressure hydrocephalus, chronic drug toxicity, respectable brain masses,* and *major depression.* About 50% of patients with normal pressure hydrocephalus improve with the help of a brain shunt that diverts cerebrospinal fluid. During the first year of abstinence, alcoholic dementia improves some but seldom completely. By preventing further strokes, low-dose aspirin therapy may arrest or slow the progress of vascular dementias. There are also many less common but treatable dementias (see Table 10-5). Other somewhat common reversible dementias or cognitive disorders that can be stabilized include hypothyroidism and anemia/B12 deficiencies.

On her 70th birthday, widowed, modest Mrs. Kass moved to Miami. Quite unlike her "normal self," she launched her first of many sexual flings "for the hell of it." As she informed relatives, "life is short." Hotly debated was whether Mrs. Kass belonged in a motel or a mental hospital. While the family was paralyzed by worry, Mrs. Kass was thrilled and active. She'd laugh at anything, so much so that one night a policeman noticed her on a fishing pier, lost, confused, and giggling. When he asked her where she was, she burst into "Swanee River," until she forgot a lyric and began weeping all the way to the hospital. Her dementia, initially attributed to Alzheimer's disease, was due to a benign (frontal lobe) brain tumor, which was surgically removed. After a full recovery, she regained her normal temperament and settled down with a retired businessman. This case illustrates a cluster of symptoms common to the frontal lobes (impulsivity, hypersexuality, personality change) and a reversible dementia.

Clinical Course

Although it usually appears after age 65, early-onset Alzheimer's disease (AD) can emerge during the 40s, rarely even younger, as it did in the case first

TABLE 10-5

The "Treatable" Dementias

CAUSE	TREATMENT
A. INFECTIONS	
1. Abscesses	Antibiotics
2. Encephalitis	Antibiotics, antiviral
3. Meningitis, chronic	Antibiotics
3. Syphilis of the brain	Penicillin
4. AIDS with secondary fungal, bacterial, viral, or protozoal infection	Antibiotics, antifungal, antiviral, antiprotozoal agents
B. AUTOIMMUNE DISEASES	
1. Lupus Erythematosis	Steroids, anti-inflammatories
2. Multiple sclerosis	
C. MECHANICAL DISORDERS	
1. Normal pressure hydrocephalus	Ventricular shunt
2. Chronic subdural hematoma	Surgery
3. Vascular (cerebral aneurysm, AV malformation, vasculitis)	Surgery
D. METABOLIC DISORDERS	
1. Porphyria	Hematin
2. Hypothyroidism (myxedema)	Thyroid replacement
3. Hyponatremia (low sodium)	Treat underlying disease (#3–9)
4. Hypo- or hypercalcemia (low or high calcium)	
5. Hyperadrenalism	
6. Wilson's disease	
7. Uremia (kidney failure with toxicity)	
8. Hepatic encephalopathy (liver failure with toxicity)	
9. Pulmonary failure	
E. NEOPLASMS	
Benign tumors	
1. Gliomas, meningitis	Surgery
2. Other brain tumors	Surgery
Primary and metastatic	Irradiation, chemotherapy, surgery

(*continued*)

TABLE 10-5
Continued

CAUSE	TREATMENT
F. CHRONIC INTOXICATION AND POISONS	Remove exposure and remove poison (#1–8)
1. Alcohol	
2. Barbiturates	
3. Anticholinergics	
4. Bromides	
5. Carbon monoxide	
6. Metals (e.g., mercury, lead, arsenic, manganese)	
7. Organic phosphates	
8. L-dopa	
G. COGNITIVE DISORDERS RESEMBLING DEMENTIA ("PSEUDODEMENTIAS")	
1. Major depressive disorder	Antidepressants, electroconvulsive therapy
2. Psychoses	Antipsychotics, electroconvulsive therapy
H. VITAMIN DEFICIENCIES	Replace vitamin (#1–4)
1. B_1 (Wernicke's encephalopathy)	
2. B_{12} (pernicious anemia)	
3. Folic acid	
4. Niacin (pellagra)	

described by the German neuropsychiatrist Alois Alzheimer in 1906. Its stealthy onset typically manifests with memory loss and intellectual decline. In about 15–20% of these cases, the initial complaints are personality change with "negative" symptoms—apathy or withdrawal—or "positive" symptoms—agitation, irritability, suspiciousness, or moodiness. Most accept the staging of AD as "mild," "moderate," or "severe." In general, patients with AD in the milder stages deteriorate gradually and do not have marked diurnal changes. Difficulties with speech (finding the right words) and getting lost in familiar places are early signs. Aphasia, apraxia, or agnosia typically appear after several years in the moderate stage. Hallucinations and delusions become more common as the disease progresses, again in the moderate stage. Patients with severe AD are often mute, bed-bound, and malnourished.

During the end stage of AD, memory is almost totally gone. Patients cannot recognize their closest relatives; everyone becomes a stranger. Speech is reduced to a phrase or two; they cannot dress or feed themselves; bladder and bowel control fail; muscles deteriorate and insomnia plagues. At the very end, full nursing care is required, as patients are bedridden, disoriented, oblivious, and incoherent. They may become mute, stop eating, and lose the ability to swallow. They frequently aspirate food into their lungs and get pneumonia. Patients with AD may survive up to 15 years, but they usually expire in 7–10 years, dying most often from malnutrition, dehydration, infections, pneumonia, or heart failure.

Vascular dementia usually occurs in patients with histories of strokes and cardiovascular disease, causing "patchy" focal neurological signs such as inarticulate speech, small stepped gait, abnormal reflexes, and specific weak muscles. These neurological signs are rarely seen in mild to moderate AD and are reliable clues for vascular dementia. In contrast to the slow, generalized deterioration of AD, vascular dementia may begin abruptly and progress in a stepwise, individual fashion. In people with many microinfarcts, this disease may appear to progress gradually, as in AD. For unknown reasons, this stepwise worsening is also occasionally seen in other dementias and is therefore not a completely reliable symptom in diagnosing vascular dementia. To further complicate the differential between vascular dementia and AD, recent evidence suggests that microvascular disease may be the second leading risk factor for AD (second to advancing age as the primary risk factor).

Although many dementias look alike in their early stages, several develop very specific symptoms that can be used to make a differential diagnosis. These include vascular dementia, Parkinson's disease, normal pressure hydrocephalus, Huntington's chorea, Wernicke–Korsakoff, and the very rare contagious (only if you eat or handle their brains or body fluids) Creutzfeldt–Jakob disease. Table 10-6 lists the causes and symptoms of these quite recognizable dementias.

In the late stages of dementia, reflexes last seen in infancy reappear. When touched on the mouth or cheek, the patient shows a *rooting reflex* in which the mouth, face, or head moves toward the touch. This is an adaptive reflex in breast- and bottle-feeding babies. When an object is put in the patient's mouth or on the lips, a *sucking reflex* is often seen. Passively moving the patient's limbs elicits a semipurposeful resistance called *paratonia* or *gegenhalten*. The very demented patient may show *perseveration*, the continued repetition of a verbal or motor response that is no longer required (e.g., "Good morning! Oh boy! Oh boy! Oh boy!"). The same answer may be given to a series of different questions. A variation is perseveratory groping, in which the patient constantly and aimlessly picks at bed sheets or clothing. The apparent

TABLE 10-6

Dementias with Specific Diagnostic Clues

DISEASE	CAUSE	DIAGNOSTIC CLUES
Normal pressure hydrocephalus	Increased fluid in lateral ventricles	Incontinence, gait disturbance
Huntington's chorea	Genetic	Writhing, choreiform movements
Wernicke-Korsakoff syndrome	Thiamine (B_1) deficiency from alcoholism and poor nutrition	Diplopia, ataxia
Creutzfeldt–Jakob disease	Prions (smaller than viruses, contagious)	Rigidity and myoclonic jerks, abnormal EEG, fatal in months
Vascular dementia	Multiple infarctions (strokes) from emboli, thrombosis, or rupture of small vessels; hypertension most common cause	Focal neurological signs, abnormal reflexes, specific weak muscles
Parkinson's disease	Destruction of dopamine-containing cells	Slow, shuffling gait, bradykinesia, "pill-rolling" hand tremor, lack of facial expression

opposite of this is *motor impersistence*, the inability to continue a simple action such as extending a hand; within seconds, the patient drops her hands into her lap.

Complications

Dementia is a life-shortening illness. Demented patients are susceptible to medical illness and delirium. Their work and social functioning gradually decline. As their condition worsens, they may evidence life-threatening behavior such as wandering away from home, falling off a ladder, or tripping on a curb.

> If a patient smashes his head and loses consciousness, he may suffer a potentially fatal subdural hematoma—a sudden or gradual bleeding under the outer lining (or dura) of the brain. The patient may lose consciousness immediately, yet more often there is a fluctuating course of drowsiness, headache, and confusion that persists for weeks to months, until the patient finally loses consciousness.

Although dementia often induces severe despair and depression, it rarely leads to suicide. Major depression occurs in 20–40% of patients with AD; it is more common in the early milder stages because insight about what is lost is still intact.

Epidemiology

Currently there are 35 million Americans over the age of 65 with dementia. The incidence of dementia increases with age, arising most often in people between the ages of 70 and 80 years. The prevalence of dementia is 15% for people over 65 years; 10% in all persons between 65 and 74 years; 25% in persons 75–84 years; 45% for those over 80 years old. Over half of all hospitalized elderly mental patients have dementia, and over half of those with dementia have AD—the fourth leading cause of death in the United States. With more people surviving to old age, the number of individuals with dementia is expected to at least triple in the next 20 years. The direct and indirect costs (both financial and emotional) associated with dementia are substantial and incalculable to families and society.

Etiology and Pathogenesis

In general, the biological factors that produce a dementia vary according to the subtype. For example, Huntington's chorea is caused by an autosomal (comes from either sex) dominant gene. In contrast, vascular dementia has numerous biological causes that are not so directly related genetically. Psychosocial influences depend more on the individual's personality and circumstances.

As noted, during the early stages of most dementias, patients respond with either exaggerations of their normal personality traits or their exact opposite. As discussed later, those close to the patient may also influence the patient's experience and quality of life. During the later stages, most dementias "take over" personalities, irrespective of psychosocial influences.

Genetic. First-degree relatives (e.g., brother, mother, daughter) of patients with AD demonstrate three to four times the prevalence of this disease as the general population. The incidence is even higher among relatives of those few who develop AD before age 60. Some researchers believe that an autosomal dominant gene is *a* (not *the*) culprit. In some families, if one parent has the gene, the child has a 50% chance of having AD; this likelihood increases to 75% if both parents have the gene. Children in these families tend to manifest the disease at the same age their parents did. In other cases, genetic vulnerability to AD is less clear. In some cases, a dominant gene may express itself late in life so that only some live long enough to show the disease. Estimates vary from 30 to 80% of the disease as being genetically induced. In many of these cases, a sporadic or polygenetic transmission is the cause. Most think AD represents a variety of diseases that will become clearer with future research. While there is a small subset of familial AD (usually clearly genetic or with early onset) the majority of cases appear to be sporadic and multi-factorial with less genetic and familial contributions the later the onset. Down's syndrome is also a predisposition, with most Down's patients developing a pattern of AD in their 20s. An autosomal dominant gene definitely causes Huntington's chorea ("Woody Guthrie's disease"). There are some racial differences, with those of African, Spanish, and Asian descent having increased to high risk. Although still unclear, studies have linked the allele APOE4 as a major risk factor for the development of late-onset of AD (> 65 y.o.) Gene expression patterns of the hippcampus show substantial risk in patients with APOE3/4 and APOE4/4 types. Demonstrated associations with APOE4 alleles include activation of multiple tumor suppressors, tumor inducers, negative regulators of cell growth or repressors possibly leading to cell arrest, senescence or apoptosia, reduction of neurotransmitter receptors and decreased expression of large gene clusters associated with synoptic plasticity, fusing, and axonal/neuronal outgrowth.

Medical. In addition to the etiologies of treatable dementias listed in Table 10-5, some untreatable dementias are probably due to "slow" viruses or prions (infectious particles that lack nucleic acid) and immunological deficiencies. Alcohol aggravates all dementias. High-risk factors for vascular dementia include hypertension, cigarette smoking, obesity, hyperlipidemia, family history of stroke, and heart disease.

Physiological. In normal aging, although the blood supply to the brain decreases, the brain extracts oxygen more efficiently. In AD, however, the brain's blood supply is also diminished, but the brain extracts both *less* oxygen and glucose. Additionally, AD patients show a distinctly different pattern of reduced cerebral blood flow with decreases bilaterally in the temporoparietal areas. Moreover, the enzymes that both synthesize and metabolize acetylcholine are deficient. Ultimately, most neurotransmitters are affected. On autopsy, inside the neurons of patients with AD are twisted clumps of tau protein called "neurofibrillary tangles," which are probably microtubules that normally maintain the shape of the cell (a cytoskeleton) and assist in the internal transport of molecules. Coating the outside of blood vessels are remnants of nerve-cell endings, called "neuritic plaques" (not neurotic!), around a core of beta-amyloid protein. These occur in the normal aging process, but in AD there are usually more than 10 times as many. There is a high correlation between the number of these plaques and tangles and the severity of the dementia. Beta-amyloid precursor protein (BAPP) is ubiquitous in the normal brain. Some think that in AD this amyloid protein is not broken down normally and leaves behind neurotoxic or nonsoluable amyloid fragments that interfere with the brain's functioning and cause dementia. Others believe that the hyperphosphorylation of tau, creating tangles, is the primary cause of AD.

Differential Diagnosis

As discussed earlier, dementia must be distinguished from *delirium*. Because delirium presents with disorientation and memory loss, dementia cannot be diagnosed until *after* a delirium clears. Agnosia, apraxia, and aphasia are much more common in Alzheimer's dementia than in delirium. In *normal aging* there is a 10–15% loss in neuropsychological functioning. This decline includes some memory loss (names and dates are forgotten and papers misplaced), new learning becomes harder, thinking becomes slower, and problem-solving is more difficult. Much of the loss in function is due to slowed performance speed. (Give the seniors enough time, and they come much closer to their abilities.) These changes do not substantially interfere with occupational or social functioning, whereas the changes from AD and other dementias do. In AD the decline in neuropsychological functioning is typically over 85%. Some intellectual deterioration may occur in *chronic schizophrenia* ("dementia praecox"), but it is milder than in dementia, specific neurological abnormalities are not usually found, and there usually is a clear history of schizophrenic symptoms.

The second most important fact about dementia is that it may be confused with "pseudodementia" or dementia syndrome of depression (DSD), a sign of *major depression* that is a true cognitive impairment but highly treatable.

> *Pseudodementia* is somewhat of a misnomer and has gone out of favor with most geriatricians. In fact, there is nothing "pseudo" about late-life depression that presents with quicker onset, multiple somatic and cognitive complaints, poor sleep, poor appetite and energy, and anxiety, while "tired all the time." It may take twice as long to complete an MMSE in a depressed patient, who discusses and highlights every question with correct or near-miss answers, than in a patient with dementia who quickly answers the question but gets it wrong. Asking whether one has memory difficulties can be very telling: Answers such as "Oh, I'm glad you asked—it's horrible" (depression); "It ain't what it used to be, but I get by" (normal), or "Oh, its great" (dementia) are generally accurate rules of thumb.

From 10 to 33% of older adults with major depressive disorder are misdiagnosed as having dementia, because both disorders may present initially with the same symptoms of memory loss, confusion, disorientation, apathy, and hypochondriasis. To further complicate matters, as indicated above, 20–40% of patients with dementia also have a major depressive disorder. For patients with pseudodementia (more appropriately termed *late-life depression*), antidepressants may completely improve the "dementia" and in depressed patients with dementia, antidepressants may improve the dementia.

Interestingly, patients with depression are more likely to complain about memory problems than patients with *real* memory problems. Patients with dementia are often brought in by their families. For example, Aunt Maude, who has AD, was brought in by her family after burning the pots on the stove three nights in a row. She wonders what the fuss is all about and doesn't complain about memory problems. In contrast, the patient with depression paces the floor, complaining that he can't remember all the stocks he owns and that he has forgotten his friend's phone number.

Another symptom, the *anhedonia* seen in depression, differs from the normal *narrowing of interest in activities* seen in dementia. When a patient with depression is asked what she enjoys doing, she might say, "Nothing." The patient with dementia might say, "I like picking up the mail, reading large-print books, and watching my TV shows." A typical interviewer who has a wide range of interests might mistakenly conclude that the dementia patient is depressed, because *she* (the interviewer) would feel depressed with so few activities. The patient with dementia can't do the more complex ones, such as cooking, gardening, or handicrafts, but still likes to do the few that she is still able to do. Patients with depression frequently respond to questions with silence or by saying, "I don't know"; patients with dementia answer with near misses. In depression, the cognitive problems develop relatively abruptly within days to 2 months. True dementia usually evolves much more slowly. Unlike dementia, pseudodementia does not have accompanying neurological symptoms such as aphasia, apraxia, or agnosia. Disorientation to time, getting lost easily, and difficulties with dressing are also much more common in dementia (Reynolds et al., 1988). In the patient who has both depression and dementia, dementia symptoms are present before depression symptoms. Pervasive sadness, feelings of guilt, and genuine suicidal ideation are primarily associated with depression.

Patients with cognitive decline associated with depression or dementia syndrome of depression (DSD) often have a prior, or family history of mood disorder. Although the CT or MRI scan is more likely to show cortical atrophy and enlarged ventricles in dementia than in depression, 20% of the time the CT or MRI scan may be misdiagnosed (Charatan, 1985). Up to 70–80% of older adults with depression have abnormal MRI scans; a significant number of normal older adults have abnormal imaging studies. The diagnosis is therefore clinical, not radiological, the key test being whether the patient improves with biological treatments such as antidepressants or ECT. (That electroconvulsive therapy *increases* instead of diminishes the memory of patients with

DSD suggests that it does not harm brain cells.) Van Gorp and Cummings (1996) highlighted the importance of multiple neuropsychiatric (test-retest) evaluations in differentiating DSD from dementia syndromes. However, many of these patients develop true dementia several years later (Emery & Oxman, 1992). Unfortunately, between one-third to one-half of people with first onset of major depressive disorder after age 65 years will go on to develop a diagnosable dementia. In these cases, major depressive disorder can be viewed as a physiological stressor that brings out a nascent dementia that later manifests on its own. Fortunately, many patients with DSD do not develop true dementia.

Subsyndromal or apathetic late-life depression is somewhat different from the typical late-life depression wherein patients present with multiple somatic/physical complaints. In apathetic depression, patients are less of a "squeaky wheel," don't complain, and are content not participating. Many feel this apathy is due to executive cognitive dysfunction. This type of memory involves sequencing and planning, and is impaired early in cognitive disorders and in these depressive states. With executive cognitive impairment, patients are not able to plan multistep activities such as gardening, social conversations, and grocery shopping so they quit doing these things. This presents as apathy and whether with depression or early cognitive loss, apathy is a "red flag" for further cognitive problems to come. These patients should be closely monitored and treated with stimulants, stimulating antidepressants, and memory enhancers. Fortunately, many patients with late-life depression, especially nonapathetic, although at risk, do not develop true dementia.

Management and Treatment

AD is a chronic, terminal illness. The goal of currently available treatments is palliative in nature. Treatment can improve cognitive function, self-care, behavior, and quality of life but not stop overall decline. Part of treatment, as with any terminal illness, is to support the family's educational and emotional needs to minimize caregiver burden and depression. Many patients qualify for hospice in the final stages of the illness.

Biomedical Interventions

After the treatable dementia is treated, there may be residual dementia. In AD there is a deficiency of acetylcholine along with other neurotransmitters. Cholinesterase inhibitors (e.g., tacrine, rivastigmine, donepezil) increase brain acetylcholine by preventing its breakdown and are sometimes used to help these patients. A few improve significantly, but most patients improve minimally or not at all with these drugs. Memantine is a NMDA antagonist that is sometimes beneficial by increasing glutamate. It is significantly more so when prescribed with one of the cholinesterase inhibitors. There is a widespread belief that these drugs can slow the deterioration caused by AD. This is very unlikely and unproven. It is more plausible that these drugs may enhance the function that remains as the disease progresses. The most likely future focus is the development of drugs that block the deposition of amyloid into the brain cells or normalize the phosphorylation of tau proteins so as to arrest or delay the terrible decline in AD. No successful agent has yet been developed.

Management with a palliative approach is the main goal. A majority of people with AD develop at least one psychotic symptom. Not infrequently, the psychosis does not cause the patient any discomfort, further loss of function, or disruptive behavior. If it does, treatment is indicated. Although not FDA approved for this purpose, very low doses of typical and atypical antipsychotics (e.g., haloperidol 0.5–3 mg or quetiapine 25–100 mg) are usually effective for this, as well as for the agitation that may accompany the psychosis. Cholinesterase inhibitors and SSRIs may be the only tolerated and effective medications in diffuse Lewy body dementia (DLBD). Antidepressants should also be used as a first-line intervention for anxiety, restlessness, lability of mood, and nonaggressive agitation. Common clinical mistakes include using higher doses, more anticholinergic antipsychotics, or using hypnoanxiolytics, all of which can worsen the dementia. Parkinson's-related dementia is also not really treatable, but adequate treatment of the disease itself can improve cognition.

Depression is a common complication developing in up to 40% of patients with dementia. Antidepressants must be used with caution because these patients are more prone to delirium. Those with strong anticholinergic side effects (e.g., TCAs) are not the first choice. Antidepressants that are low in cognitive side effects, such as SSRIs and SNRIs, are preferred. As with all medications in older patients, the adage "Start low and go slow" is good to keep in mind. However, older patients frequently require the same antidepressant doses as younger patients. The biggest treatment mistakes made by physicians with this population involve prescribing too low a dose of antidepressant and for too short a time.

For calming agitation and alleviating insomnia, psychoactive drugs should be used cautiously, because they can also aggravate the patient's confusion and generate intolerable side effects. The patient, and especially his family, should be questioned about other drugs used medically or surreptitiously that might compound (or produce) symptoms. Anticholinergic agents, including those sold over the counter or prescribed for glaucoma, are common culprits. Drugs that show some promise of calming agitation in dementia without increasing confusion include SSRIs, atypical antipsychotics, SNRIs, buspirone, and propranolol. Benzodiazepines must be used cautiously, if at all, as they can be disinhibiting. Shorter-acting agents should be used first to prevent the serious side effects often seen with long-acting drugs in older adults. The use of several anticonvulsants utilized in bipolar disorder, most commonly valproic acid, lamotrigine, and carbamazepine, can also be safe and effective.

If the patient has a vascular dementia, then removing the risk factors of hypertension (e.g., cigarette smoking) is the starting point. Low-dose aspirin may reduce the risk of new infarcts.

Psychosocial Interventions

Because the care of patients with dementia falls mainly to loved ones and custodians, they must become partners in the patient's treatment plan. For family members, being a caretaker is usually a novel but highly stressful experience; it is difficult and draining, demoralizing and devastating. Relatives need support and practical instruction, and a major task of the physician or therapist is to provide both.

Patient care. The primary goal is to make the patient with dementia as comfortable as possible. The environment should be kept simple and helpful. Clocks, calendars, labels, lists, familiar routines, short-term tasks, brief walks, and simple physical exercises (to prevent muscle atrophy) are the elements that improve the patient's quality of life and foster self-respect. In a majority of patients with AD, memory for facts is much worse than memory for how to do things; they may still enjoy activities such as golf as long as someone else keeps score.

Patients should be allowed and encouraged to do what they can, but *only* what they can. Pressing too hard—for example, trying to preserve memory by exercising it—only leads to frustration and resentment. Patients with dementia dislike abdicating familiar tasks such as handling money, driving, cooking, and later on, the self-care of bathing, dressing, using the toilet, and living alone. Attempts should be made to at least pretend to include the patient in these tasks. It is helpful to break tasks down into small steps and keep possessions simple and organized. Attempts to help may be greeted with insults, complaints, annoying questions, tears, or rage. Responding with hostility is pointless and harmful; distracting and calming patients works better. When these patients lose things and then blame others for stealing them, instead of refuting the accusation, which is pointless, offer to look for the lost items. Reassurance repeated several times each hour is never too much. Later, as words fail, touch may still reassure. Music, television, and other distractors may help calm the individual. Sleeping areas should be made safe, since patients are likely to become more confused at night, wander about, and hurt themselves.

Moving patients to a senior citizen's apartment, sheltered housing, or a nursing home is usually necessary when they become dangerous to themselves, hallucinate, lose bowel or bladder control, or otherwise make life impossible for their caretakers. The reasons for such a move should be calmly reiterated; patients will forget the content of the explanations, but the *repeated reassurance* is what counts. Caretakers often feel guilty for "putting Mom away." However, caretakers need to recognize that many facilities today provide very positive environments. After successful placement, most caretakers state, "I waited too long to do this. I now see I should have done this much sooner."

Family counseling. When dementia is first diagnosed, some relatives deny the patient's illness (e.g., "Everybody grows old"), others blame the patient for being "deliberately difficult" (e.g., "She remembers when she wants to!"), while others are relieved to have an explanation for the patient's difficult behavior. In time, the family members feel overwhelmed and helpless. They may become angry at professionals for "not doing enough"; they may vent their frustrations on each other, and latent family tensions may surface under the strain of caring for a relative with dementia. A son or daughter may feel guilty about resenting the ill mother or father; the children may be ashamed of the parent or think he or she would be better off dead. A spouse may regret the "loss" of the golden years. The professional must care for the caretakers, who must be told that caring for a loved one with dementia is an impossible, no-win, and thankless task, over which the family members must not destroy themselves. Thorough education about dementia and how to manage it is critical in order to prevent the many destructive approaches families may use. Loved ones often benefit from a self-help group and the kind of literature often provided through the national Alzheimer's Association or local chapters. The "caregiver bill of rights" should be given to families. Families should be told to lower expectations, understand why psychosis occurs with memory loss, try to live with it rather than react, and use humor whenever and wherever possible. Of course, to be a good caregiver, the caregiver must remain healthy, which requires trusting others to help and giving him- or herself clear and scheduled breaks, among other things. Caregivers should be encouraged to take advantage of private sitters, bath aides, day-care facilities, and respite beds, so that they can have several hours to a couple of days off from their responsibilities. Addressing legal issues as early after a diagnosis of dementia is made is an extremely important action. Having a legal, durable power of attorney, including medical decision-making, assigned to a person who is chosen and trusted by the patient, while he or she remains competent to do so, will greatly ease the stressful and extremely difficult course and problems that come with dementia. Matter-of-factly and calmly addressing legal issues, including monies and driving, will help the patient and family. Driving is often a volatile issue and one the physician should not avoid.

In summary, there are four treatable aspects of dementia: memory loss, depression, psychosis and agitation, and the caregiver/family. By diagnosing and treating depression and reversible dementias, by removing risk factors, by helping families help the patient, and by monitoring the treatment of the memory symptoms, today's clinicians can offer enormous assistance to these patients and their families. Treatment of AD and dementias can be very rewarding and is a great example of the virtues of palliative medicine, where all interventions are aimed at improving quality of life and slowing disease progression while not creating additional discomfort or symptoms.

AMNESTIC DISORDERS

Clinical Presentation

Amnesia, Latin for "forgetfulness," may occur by itself. The patient with an amnestic disorder may have profound difficulty remembering anything from yesterday or from 1 hour ago, but can converse sensibly with clear awareness and reasonable judgment. Only memory is affected. The *DSM-IV-TR* criteria for amnestic disorders are listed in Table 10-7.

Clinical Course and Complications

If the memory loss resulted from a single event, such as a stroke in the hippocampus, all events after that date will be vaguely or never remembered. Events prior to the stroke have been stored and still can be recalled. Toxins, including alcohol, can more insidiously cause pure memory loss. Social, intelligent patients may attempt to mask the problem with confabulation ("Didn't I see you at Harry's Bar last week?") or bunting questions back to the examiner ("What do you usually call this place?"). Those who have had no memory for years will be perplexed each day at how old people around them look, because they only remember how they looked many years ago. In some, remote memory

TABLE 10-7
DSM-IV-TR *Criteria for Amnestic Disorder*
Common Criteria for Amnestic Disorder

A. The development of memory impairment as manifested by the inability to learn new information or the inability to recall previously learned information.

B. The memory disturbance causes significant impairment in social or occupational functioning and represents a significant decline from a previous level of functioning.

C. The memory disturbance does not occur exclusively during the course of a delirium or dementia.

Additional Criterion for Amnestic Disorder Due to a General Medical Condition

D. There is evidence from the history, physical examination, or laboratory findings that the disturbance is the direct physiological consequence of a general medical condition (including physical trauma).

Additional Criterion for Substance-Induced Persisting Amnestic Disorder

D. There is evidence from the history, physical examination, or laboratory findings that the memory disturbance is etiologically related to the persisting effects of substance use (e.g., a drug of abuse, a medication).

Note. From *DSM-IV-TR,* pp. 172, 175, 177, 179.

may also deteriorate, but unlike in dementia, other areas of function remain intact.

Management and Treatment

Removal of risk conditions such as alcohol use, poor nutrition, exposure to toxins, and hypertension can prevent further deterioration. Patients should be kept in familiar environments as long as possible, because new ones may be difficult or impossible for them to learn. As in dementia, memory devices such as clocks, calendars, labels, lists, and familiar routines help. If patients have completely lost the ability to establish new memories, the deficit can be used to their advantage, as the following case illustrates.

> A 72-year-old woman with no recent memory had always liked her lifelong work as a cherry picker. She was brought into the hospital after hitting an attendant at a nursing home. When she had asked "When can I go back to cherry picking?", the attendant had told her "Never." The attendant later regretted this choice of words. The woman was not usually violent and, in the hospital, continued to ask when

she could work. She got increasingly agitated as staff stalled, trying to avoid confrontations. Then one day she sat by a window smiling; this continued for several
days. When her nurse was asked what had caused this pleasant transformation, the
nurse said she realized that the patient never remembered yesterday, so each day
she told the patient that she could go cherry picking tomorrow. From then on, she
happily anticipated the coming day.

OTHER COGNITIVE DISORDERS

As would be expected, there are patients who present with cognitive deficits
or frank impairment who do not "fit" into the categories previously discussed.
As new scientific evidence comes to light, our diagnostic categories may expand and become increasingly precise. For the present time, this category is
for those people with cognitive dysfunction that is not easily explained.

Two entities stand out: mild neurocognitive disorder and postconcussional
disorder. Mild neurocognitive disorder, per *DSM-IV-TR*, is defined as impairment in cognitive functioning as evidenced by neuropsychological testing or
quantified clinical assessment, accompanied by objective evidence of a systemic general medical condition or central nervous system dysfunction. This
disorder bears some relationship to what was called benign senescent forgetfulness, or now mild cognitive impairment (MCI). Since this condition can develop into a full dementia, there is considerable interest and controversy
concerning its diagnosis, etiology, and mechanisms.

Postconcussional disorder follows head trauma. Usually, specific areas of
the brain suffering injury correlate with the impairment seen, but not always.
This condition again represents our "edge of knowledge" and has various presentations that do not always make sense with our current understanding of
the brain and its function. Prevention of head trauma is the prudent course
of action—parents may want to look into headgear for their aspiring soccer
stars. Boxers, such as Mohammed Ali, provide testimonials to the dementing
effects of repeated head trauma (*dementia pugilistica*).

References

Advancing Excellence in America's Nursing Homes. (2008). Available at http://www.nhqualitycam
    paign.org.

Alzheimer's Association National Office, 225 N. Michigan Ave., Fl. 17, Chicago, IL 60601. 24/7
    Helpline: 1.800.272.3900 Online: http://www.alz.org.

Changing Aging in America. (2008). Available at http://www.almosthomedoc.org.

Charatan, F. (1985). Depression and the elderly: Diagnosis and treatment. *Psychiatric Annals, 15,* 313–316.

Emery, V.L., & Oxman, T.E. (1992). Update on the dementia spectrum of depression. *American Journal of Psychiatry, 149,* 305–317.

Folstein, M.F., Folstein, S.E., & McHugh, P.R. (1975). "Mini-Mental State": A practical method for grading the cognitive state of patients for the clinician. *Journal of Psychiatry Research, 12,* 196–198.

Goodwin, D.W. (1985). Alcoholism and genetics: The sins of the father. *Archives of General Psychiatry, 42,* 171–174.

Institute for Healthcare Improvement. (2008). Available at http://www.ihi.org.

Mayo-Smith, M.F. (1997). Pharmacological management of alcohol withdrawal: A meta-analysis and evidence-based practice guideline. *JAMA, 278,* 144–151.

Reynolds, C.F., Hoch, C.C., Kupfer, D.J., Buysse, D.J., Houck, P.R., Stack, J.A., et al. (1988). Bedside differentiation of depressive pseudodementia from dementia. *American Journal of Psychiatry, 145,* 1099–1103.

Stern, T. (1983). Continuous infusion of physostigmine in anticholinergic delirium: A case report. *Journal of Clinical Psychiatry, 44,* 463–464.

Tune, L., Carr, S., Hoag, E., & Cooper, T. (1992). Anticholinergic effects of drugs commonly prescribed for the elderly: Potential means for assessing risk of delirium. *American Journal of Psychiatry, 149,* 1393–1394.

van Gorp, W.G., & Cummings, J.L. (1996). Depression and reversible dementia in an HIV-1 seropositive individual: Implications for the dementia syndrome of depression. *Neurocase, 2,* 455–459.

Wells, C.E., & McEvoy, J.P. (1982). Organic mental disorders. In J.H. Greist, J.W. Jefferson, & R.L. Spitzer (Eds.), *Treatment of mental disorders* (pp. 3–43). New York: Oxford University Press.

Wengel, S.P., Roccaforte, W.H., & Burke, W.J. (1998). Donepezil improves symptoms of delirium in dementia: Implications for future research. *Journal of Geriatric Psychiatry and Neurology, 11,* 159–161.

11

Substance-Related Disorders

Substance abuse is as old as the substances abused. Rock carvings in caves from the fourth millennium B.C. display workmen making beer from barley. In 2285 B.C. a gentleman in China was allegedly banished for getting soused on a rice beverage. Individuals and religions of every era have sought to suspend reality and alter moods by the simplest and quickest way possible—"better living through chemistry."

> *Substance* is a general term encompassing alcohol, recreational drugs, and medications. *Substance*, *chemical*, and *drugs* are employed interchangeably. Nonpsychoactive drugs (e.g., insulin) are also abused, but like *DSM-IV-TR*, this book solely discusses *psychoactive* substances. Unless otherwise specified, *this* text uses *misuse* and *abuse* synonymously.

The current frequency of this "better living" is hard to assess epidemiologically: The drug scene constantly changes, users are reluctant to mention their drug-taking, antidrug/alcohol groups have vested interests in exaggerating dangers, definitions of drug misuse vary considerably, and it is unclear which substances are deemed problematic—tobacco? caffeine? alcohol? Having said this, seven facts are worth noting: (1) The National Epidemiologic Survey on Alcohol and Related Conditions (NESARC) by adult Americans revealed yearly prevalence rates of 8.5% for alcohol abuse and alcoholism and 9.4% for any other substance of abuse in 2001–2002. (2) These figures do not include the most frequent substance disorder among Americans, tobacco use disorder, which has a lifetime prevalence of 36%. (3) Substance abuse varies across the life cycle, with changes over time in the prevalence of various drug use. During middle age, alcoholism is more of a problem. As the perceived risk of using a drug increases, the actual use of that drug decreases (and vice versa). (4) After age 44, substance misuse declines for both sexes. (5) Substances are abused more by men than women, more by inner-city residents than country dwellers, more by nongraduates than college graduates. (6) European-Americans and African-Americans have the same overall rate of substance abuse. (7) people with psychiatric disorders, including anxiety, antisocial personality, and mood disorders, have greatly increased rates of substance abuse. The NESARC results show substantial comorbidity between substance use disorders and independent mood and anxiety disorders: About 20% of persons with a substance use disorder within the past year experience a mood or anxiety disorder within the same time period. Similarly, about 20% of persons with a current mood or anxiety disorder experience a current substance use disorder. Seventy-eight percent of people with drug and alcohol problems experience a psychiatric disorder in their lifetime, and 65% at a particular time. The most common disorders are antisocial personality disorder, anxiety disorders, psychosexual dysfunctions, major depression, and dysthymia. Alcohol and other substance abusers have a higher rate of mood and anxiety disorders than the general population (Conway et al., 2006).

DEFINITIONS

Intoxication and withdrawal are the most prevalent substance-related disorders. *Intoxication* is a reversible substance-specific syndrome that arises during or shortly after ingesting a substance and often disturbs perceptions, wakefulness, sleep, attention, judgment, emotionality, and movement. Intoxication becomes a disorder when clinically significant maladaptive behavioral changes (e.g., picking fights with everyone, driving into a ditch) or psychological changes (e.g., alternatively laughing and crying, inability to compute the restaurant bill) occur during or soon after ingestion. All drugs of abuse have an intoxication syndrome. *Withdrawal* is a substance-specific syndrome that follows when a chronic intake of a substance has been abruptly stopped or greatly diminished and usually manifests as restlessness, apprehension, anxiety, irritability, insomnia, and impaired concentration. It becomes a disorder when clinically significant distress or impaired function occur. Not all drugs have a withdrawal syndrome. Table 11-1 lists *DSM-IV-TR* criteria for substance intoxication and withdrawal.

Intoxication and withdrawal involve two pharmacological phenomena: *tolerance*, which is the need to markedly increase a drug's intake to attain its original effects, or experiencing a markedly diminished effect with continued use of the same amount of the drug; and *cross-tolerance*, which occurs when a drug exhibits tolerance to other drugs, usually in the same class. For exam-

TABLE 11-1

DSM-IV-TR *Criteria for Substance Intoxication and Withdrawal*

Substance Intoxication

A. The development of a reversible substance-specific syndrome due to recent ingestion of (or exposure to) a substance. **Note:** Different substances may produce similar or identical syndromes.

B. Clinically significant maladaptive behavioral or psychological changes that are due to the effect of the substance on the central nervous system (e.g., belligerence, mood lability, cognitive impairment, impaired judgment, impaired social or occupational functioning) and develop during or shortly after use of the substance.

C. The symptoms are not due to a general medical condition and not better accounted for by another mental disorder.

Substance Withdrawal

A. The development of a substance-specific syndrome due to the cessation of (or reduction in) substance use that has been heavy and prolonged.

B. The substance-specific syndrome causes clinically significant distress or impairment in social, occupational, or other important areas of functioning.

C. The symptoms are not due to a general medical condition and not better accounted for by another mental disorder.

Note. From *DSM-IV-TR,* pp. 201, 202.

ple, patients tolerant to diazepam are tolerant to barbiturates, but not to heroin. In general, the greater the tolerance to a drug, the worse the withdrawal and the greater the amount needed to become intoxicated.

DSM-IV-TR subdivides substance use disorders into substance *dependence* and substance *abuse.* The *consequences* of the substance use define these illnesses. Drug *dependence* is the repeated, nonmedical use of a substance that harms the user or incites behavior in the user that harms others, and involves psychological and/or physical dependence. *Addiction* is the common name for dependence. *Psychological dependence* is characterized by the compulsive misuse of a substance; taking it longer than planned, intense craving (urges and anticipation); unsuccessful efforts to cut down (loss of control); a preoccupation with obtaining it; the sacrifice of social, occupational, and recreational activities; and often physical or psychological consequences. *Physiological dependence* is the repeated use of a drug to avert physical withdrawal reactions or taking larger amounts to get the same effects (tolerance). Psychological and physical dependencies often coexist. Table 11-2 lists *DSM-IV-TR* criteria for substance dependence.

TABLE 11-2

DSM-IV-TR *Criteria for Substance Dependence*

A maladaptive pattern of substance use, leading to clinically significant impairment or distress, as manifested by three (or more) of the following, occurring at any time in the same 12-month period:

(1) tolerance, as defined by either of the following:

    (a) a need for markedly increased amounts of the substance to achieve intoxication or desired effect

    (b) markedly diminished effect with continued use of the same amount of the substance

(2) withdrawal, as manifested by either of the following:

    (a) the characteristic withdrawal syndrome for the substance (refer to Criteria A and B of the criteria sets for Withdrawal from the specific substances)

    (b) the same (or closely related) substance is taken to relieve or avoid withdrawal symptoms

(3) the substance is often taken in larger amounts or over a longer period than was intended

(4) there is a persistent desire or unsuccessful efforts to cut down or control substance use

(5) a great deal of time is spent in activities necessary to obtain the substance (e.g., visiting multiple doctors or driving long distances), use the substance (e.g., chain-smoking), or recover from its effects

(6) important social, occupational, or recreational activities are given up or reduced because of substance use

(7) the substance use is continued despite knowledge of having a persistent or recurrent physical or psychological problem that is likely to have been caused or exacerbated by the substance (e.g., current cocaine use despite recognition of cocaine-induced depression, or continued drinking despite recognition that an ulcer was made worse by alcohol consumption)

Specify if:

With Physiological Dependence: evidence of tolerance or withdrawal (i.e., either Item 1 or 2 is present)

Without Physiological Dependence: no evidence of tolerance or withdrawal (i.e., neither Item 1 nor 2 is present)

Note. From *DSM-IV-TR,* pp. 197–198.

Substance abuse involves the misuse of a substance resulting in significant impairment or distress *without actually developing substance dependence.* Table 11-3 lists *DSM-IV-TR* criteria for substance abuse. Problems caused by substances include car accidents, demotions or job terminations, divorce, loss of child custody, arrests, and loss of friends. This diagnosis applies to the person who minimizes: "Yeah, sure I've had a few DWIs (driving while intoxicated), paid a few visits to the emergency room for stitches after bar fights, and spent the night in jail once—but I'm no alcoholic. I can stop anytime I want. I always drink the same amount and I never have withdrawal."

TABLE 11-3
DSM-IV-TR *Criteria for Substance Abuse*

A. A maladaptive pattern of substance use leading to clinically significant impairment or distress, as manifested by one (or more) of the following, occurring within a 12-month period:

(1) recurrent substance use resulting in a failure to fulfill major role obligations at work, school, or home (e.g., repeated absences or poor work performance related to substance use; substance-related absences, suspensions or expulsions from school; neglect of children or household)

(2) recurrent substance use in situations in which it is physically hazardous (e.g., driving an automobile or operating a machine when impaired by substance use)

(3) recurrent substance-related legal problems (e.g., arrests for substance-related disorderly conduct)

(4) continued substance use despite having persistent or recurrent social or interpersonal problems caused or exacerbated by the effects of the substance (e.g., arguments with spouse about consequences of intoxication, physical fights)

B. The symptoms have never met the criteria for Substance Dependence for this class of substance.

Note. From *DSM-IV-TR,* p. 199.

ETIOLOGY AND COMORBIDITY

The underlying neurobiological mechanisms for substance intoxication are still being elucidated. Drugs of abuse seemed to have a final common reward pathway in the brain, leading from the ventral tegmental area and the nucleus accumbens to the frontal and prefrontal cortex, where dopaminergic pathways complete the reward process.

According to the "self-medication hypothesis," the original choice of an abused drug is not random, but is partly made to alleviate a specific distressing symptom or affect. At first, narcotics are used to mask pain, hypnotics to induce sleep, cocaine to eliminate depression, amphetamines to "get up," marijuana to join the crowd, or bourbon to rid boredom. No matter how substance abuse begins, however, once it becomes habitual and stopping it causes severe distress, drug dependence has occurred. At this juncture the habit is sustained less from original motives and more to quell a drug-induced biological imperative. Therefore, treating only the initial cause is less effective: Drug dependence must be directly treated, along with the original problems. An example: When hospitalized, a chronic alcoholic was very suspicious. After 3 weeks of "drying out," his "head cleared" and his suspiciousness disappeared. Only then did it become apparent that marital problems greatly affected his alcoholism.

Although the comorbidity between substance abuse and other psychiatric illnesses is high, use of many substances mimic psychiatric illnesses. Many problems, including conditions likely to prompt relapse, cannot be evaluated properly until the substance abuser has been drug-free for 10 days. (Some experts suggest 1–3 months.) Table 11-4 outlines the major pharmacological effects of psychoactive

TABLE 11-4
DSM-IV-TR *Major Substance Diagnoses*

SUBSTANCE (examples)	DEPENDENCE	ABUSE	INTOXICATION	WITHDRAWAL
Alcohol	X	X	X	X
Amphetamines	X	X	X	X
Stimulants including dextroamphetamine and methamphetamine				
Caffeine		X	X*	
Xanthine derivative, stimulant and performance enhancers, coffee, tea, soft drinks				
Cannabis	X	X	X	
Hashish from resin, marijuana from leaves stems and buds				
Cocaine	X	X	X	X
Hydrochloride powder, freebase (ether/ammonia extract), crack (sodium bicarbonate extract)				
Hallucinogens	X	X	X	
LSD, mescaline from cactus, psilocybin from mushrooms, myristicin from nutmeg				
Inhalants	X	X	X	
Organic solvents such as gasoline, toluene, ether; nitrous oxide, amyl nitrite				
Nicotine	X		X*	X
Stimulant in cigarettes and chewing tobacco				
Opioids	X	X	X	X
Pain-killers including fentanyl, morphine, heroin, oxycodone, methadone, codeine				
Phencyclidine		X	X	X
Animal tranquilizer, anesthetic				
Sedatives	X	X	X	X
Hypnotics and anxiolytics including barbiturates, chloral hydrate, and benzodiazepines				
Polysubstance		X		
Other:	X	X	X	X
MDMA (3,4-methylene-dioxy-methamphetamine)				
Anticholinergics including atropine, belladona, and diphenhydramine				
Steroids				

*Not classified in *DSM-IV-TR* but does exist.

substances. In general, the substances that have no withdrawal syndromes (e.g., marijuana) are likely to elicit only psychological dependence. Marijuana and hallucinogens can also induce "reverse tolerance" in the user: The *more* the drug is used, the less is needed to obtain the original effects. Alcohol, barbiturates, opiates, phencyclidine, solvents, and inhalants are most likely to kill in overdose.

ASSESSMENT OF SUBSTANCE MISUSE

Many factors complicate the diagnosis and treatment of substance abusers. For starters, many potential patients are unreliable informants. Unlike most patients, their objectives differ from their therapists': Many abusers *want* their habit—or as a heroin addict put it, "If I had to choose between heroin and food and sex, I'd take heroin." Denial and lying are often their norms; at times, even addicts don't know which they are doing. Outright lying is common to avoid detection and to hasten discharge. On admission, however, already-discovered addicts may exaggerate their intake to garner more of the drug during detoxification. For all these reasons, clinicians should favor objective signs and social behaviors over subjective reports, and corroborate and supplement this information by interviewing family and friends and obtaining a urine drug screen. Because these patients frequently lie, deny, manipulate, and relapse, they habitually frustrate and infuriate clinicians. Therefore, therapists should constantly monitor their own angry and moralistic feelings. Moreover, therapists should not take these patients' provocations and relapses personally: They are a "natural" part of the history of substance abuse.

There are many screening instruments for alcoholism. The CAGE questionnaire (Ewing, 1984) is so called because the name is an acronym for the four areas probed (Cut down, Annoyed, Guilty, and Eye Opener) and because one is prisoner to an addiction. The following questions are used:

Cut down	1. Have you ever felt you should cut down on your drinking?
Annoyed	2. Have other people annoyed you by criticizing your drinking?
Guilty	3. Have you ever felt guilty about drinking?
Eye Opener	4. Have you ever taken a drink in the morning to steady your nerves or get rid of a hang-over?

Two or more positive answers indicate alcohol dependence and predicts ≥8 drinks per day. This questionnaire accurately determines the presence or absence of alcoholism over 85% of the time (Beresford, Blow, Hill, Singer, &

Lucey, 1990); however, it misses more cases of alcohol dependence in women than it does in men, and is relatively insensitive on picking up alcoholism early in the illness. Substituting question 3 with "How many drinks does it take to make you high?" may improve sensitivity (more than two drinks suggests tolerance). Some clinicians use the CAGE questions with slight modification (substitute "drug use" for "drinking") to screen for other drugs of abuse. For adolescents and young adults who have not yet experienced negative consequences from their drug use, a positive response to "Have you used street drugs more than five times in your life?" suggests the need for further assessment.

A more sensitive instrument is the Alcohol Use Disorders Identification Test (AUDIT), a 10-item questionnaire. With a maximum score of 40, a score of 8 or above indicates problematic drinking. A very simple screening tool derived from the DSM-IV-TR criteria is to ask two questions: (1) "Has use of the substance caused behavioral or physical harm to the patient or other people?" (2) "If so, has the patient continued to use the substance?" After screening patients for substance misuse, Table 11-5 can be used to assess substance intoxication by applying its extensive evaluation guidelines to those who are suspected of having substance-related disorders.

As soon as clinicians identify and treat one drug problem, another typically pops up, resulting in a constant information lag about drug abuse. More serious is that *polydrug abuse* has increased sharply. In comparison to single-drug abusers, polydrug abusers have more severe and complicated withdrawals and bleaker prognoses. They are harder to diagnose and treat, especially in emergencies, since they present a more confounding mix of signs and symptoms than single-substance abusers. Not uncommonly, an inpatient being successfully treated for an opiate intoxication suddenly convulses from barbiturate withdrawal 4 days later. The lesson is that polydrug abuse must be evaluated for every substance abuser.

In general, withdrawal, intoxication, and dependence should be addressed in this sequence. The most dangerous acute problem is *hypnoanxiolytic* (including alcohol) withdrawal, since this can be lethal, whereas opiate or stimulant (cocaine, amphetamine) withdrawal is uncomfortable, at most. However, some patients with serious medical problems may die from opiate withdrawal, and opiate intoxication can certainly be lethal. When it is unclear whether patients are intoxicated or withdrawing from a hypnoanxiolytic, err by treating withdrawal, since that poses a greater threat than intoxication. Table 11-6 lists *DSM-IV-TR* criteria for intoxication and withdrawal from alcohol, sedatives, hypnotics, and anxiolytics.

TABLE 11-5

The Assessment of Substance Misuse in Suspected Abusers

Quick Recognition of Substance Intoxication

		Drugs Used	
Eyes	Pupils dilated	Stimulants	Cocaine
		Hallucinogens	Amphetamines
		Anticholinergics	
	Pupils constricted	Opioids	PCP
	Conjuctival injection (bloodshot eyes)	Cannabis, marijuana	
Psychomotor	Unsteady gait, ataxia	Alcohol	Hynoanxiolytics
	Nystagmus (rhythmic oscillation of the	Sedatives	PCP
	eyeballs)	Anesthetics	Inhalants

I. HISTORY

    A. Substance(s)

        1. Name(s) (e.g., diazepam, cocaine)

        2. Polydrug use: Indicates names and preferred combinations

        3. Special preparations (e.g., freebasing)

    B. Route (e.g., ingestion, inhalation, injection)

    C. Amount

        1. Typical dose, frequency, and duration of drug use

        2. Dose and duration of drug use during past 10 days

        3. The time and amount of the most recent drug use

    D. Patterns of use

        1. Self-medication: Is it for physical, psychiatric, or emotional problems or "just for fun"?

        2. Identifiable events or stressors that increase or decrease the use of a substance (e.g., drinking before sex, "chipping" heroin before job interviews, smoking after meals)

        3. History: How did substance abuse begin? Why does it continue? Are there conditioned relapses? What began and ended the patient's longest drug-free period?

        4. Timing: How early in the day does the patient first use the substance?

        5. Style (e.g., sneaking drugs, hiding bottles, boasting, running away, using substances with others or alone)

    E. Acquisition

        1. Sources: legal, illegal, prescription, theft, "mobsters," friends

        2. Time and money spent obtaining substances (e.g., illegal activities such as theft, prostitution, and drug dealing)

    F. Network

        1. Family and friends: Who exert beneficial and harmful influences on the patient?

        2. Family history of antisocial personality, substance misuse, or mood disorders?

(continued)

TABLE 11-5
Continued

G. Functioning

1. Interference with social, occupational, recreational, academic, and familial functioning

2. Adverse influence on physical health, appearance, finances, and self-image

3. Legal problems

4. How does the patient feel *without* the drug?

5. Impaired organic functioning such as forgetting location of "stash," poor concentration, impaired judgment

6. Does patient become suicidal or assaultive on the drug?

H. Medical and psychiatric history

1. Drug-related medical illnesses: hepatitis, infections, insomnia, allergies, cirrhosis, TB, AIDS, epilepsy

2. All recently taken prescribed and over-the-counter drugs. Does the patient use these medications differently from what they were prescribed or intended to treat? Does the patient take or sneak other family member's or people's medications? Does the patient use multiple doctors and pharmacies to avoid detection? (Have family bring all medications from the patient's home.)

3. History of psychiatric symptoms or mental illness prior to substance misuse

4. History of substance-related syndromes: flashbacks, delirium, idiosyncratic intoxication, hallucinosis

I. Prior treatment

1. Type, duration, degree of participation, including experiences with community agencies and self-help groups

2. Results as seen by (a) the patient, (b) his or her relatives, and (c) his or her therapist

J. Current motivations to change

1. Why is the patient seeking treatment *now?*

2. Current threat of jail, divorce, etc.

II. COMMON SYMPTOMS AND SIGNS

[With special signs of abuse by adolescents and teenagers in brackets]

A. Prodromal phase

1. Increased tolerance

2. Sneaking chemicals [frequently odd places during school, such as closets or storage rooms, to take drugs]

3. Temporary amnesia

4. Preoccupation with chemical use

5. Avoids talking about personal use

6. More frequent loss of memory

TABLE 11-5
Continued

B. Crucial or basic phase

1. Time lost from work [or changes in school attendance, grades, or discipline]

2. Loss of control (unusual or apparently unmotivated temper outbursts)

3. Alibis [especially about not doing homework]

4. Increased extravagance—time, money, advice; being a "know-it-all"

5. Aggressive or abusive behavior

6. Persistent remorse

7. Periodic abstinence

8. Losing or changing friends

9. Losing clients or position

10. Persistent resentments

11. Diminished self-care and unhealthy appearance

12. Slovenly dress, sunglasses at inappropriate times (to hide dilated or constricted pupils and to diminish glare) and long-sleeved shirts (to hide needle marks)

13. Borrowing money [and theft of small items from school] to buy drugs

14. Escape—geographical, psychological, social

15. Protecting supply [furtive looks to avoid stash being detected]

16. Morning use of chemical(s)

C. Chronic phase

1. More-or-less continuous use over 10-hour period

2. Ethical deterioration

3. Decreased tolerance

4. Sleeping at inappropriate times

5. Indefinable fears

6. Tangential or incoherent speech; inappropriate remarks

7. Tremors

III. PHYSICAL EXAMINATION

A. Rectal and pelvic examinations

1. Should be considered since substance abusers have a higher incidence of unprotected sexual activity with resulting increased risk of sexually transmitted diseases.

B. Physical signs

1. Marks: Scarring along a vein, tattooing over a vein, abscesses, ulcers, and needle tracks. The quantity and age of needle marks can serve as a rough check on the validity of the patient's history.

2. Nose: Is it dripping? Are nasal membranes infected, swollen, or septum eroded from snorting cocaine?

(*continued*)

TABLE 11-5

Continued

3. Pupils: Constricted (miosis) with opiates and PCP? Dilated (mydriasis) with amphetamines, anticholinergics, and hallucinogens?

4. Signs of intoxication or withdrawal

IV. LABORATORY EXAMINATIONS

A. Urine screens

1. Thin layer chemistry (TLC): Sometimes inaccurate; used only for screening

2. Enzyme immuno assay (EIA) and radio immuno assay (RIA): These two tests have relatively high degrees of sensitivity and specificity; the EIA is a qualitative test, the RIA, quantitative. Detects people who eat poppy seed cake as opiate positive.

3. Gas chromatography mass spectrometry (GC/MS): The most reliable and informative of tests; expensive but the "gold standard."

B. Serum levels

1. Abused substances (primarily to establish quantity when urine tests are positive or abused substances are already known)

2. Other psychotropic drugs (e.g., antidepressants)

C. Liver and renal function tests

1. GGT: This liver enzyme (gamma glutamyl transerase) is often the first to rise in alcoholism.

2. Carbohydrate deficient transferrin (CDT) is a liver enzyme that rises only in heavy drinking over a long period of time.

ALCOHOL

There are more English synonyms for *drunk* than for any other word. Benjamin Franklin was the first to publish them—228; recently Flexner listed 353 synonyms and said that he had just scratched the surface. *Alcohol* comes from the Arabic *alkuhl*, because Arabs distilled it in 600 A.D. The practice spread and so did the problems. Ghengis Khan counseled his troops, "A soldier must not get drunk oftener than once a week. It would, of course, be better if he did not get drunk at all, but one should not expect the impossible" (Goodwin & Guze, 1984, p. 148).

Annual per capita alcohol consumption in 2005 in the United States was estimated at 2.24 gallons of pure ethanol. Today, alcoholism, along with nicotine dependence, is America's most serious substance abuse problem, as it is for every other industrialized nation (it costs New York City alone over $1 billion a year). Alcoholism is an illness of "normal" people, not bums. The

TABLE 11-6

DSM-IV-TR Criteria for Alcohol, Sedative, Hypnotic, or Anxiolytic Intoxification and Withdrawal

Substance Intoxication

A. Recent ingestion of alcohol, sedative, hypnotic, or anxiolytic.

B. Clinically significant maladaptive behavioral or psychological changes (e.g., inappropriate sexual or aggressive behavior, mood lability, impaired judgment, impaired social or occupational functioning) that developed during, or shortly after, alcohol, sedative, hypnotic, or anxiolytic ingestion.

C. One (or more) of the following signs, developing during, or shortly after, alcohol, sedative, hypnotic, or anxiolytic use:

    (1) slurred speech

    (2) incoordination

    (3) unsteady gait

    (4) nystagmus

    (5) impairment in attention or memory

    (6) stupor or coma

D. The symptoms are not due to a general medical condition and are not better accounted for by another mental disorder.

Substance Withdrawal

A. Cessation of (or reduction in) alcohol, sedative, hypnotic, or anxiolytic use that has been heavy and prolonged.

B. Two or more of the following, developing within several hours to a few days after Criterion A:

    (1) autonomic hyperactivity (e.g., sweating or pulse rate greater than 100)

    (2) increased hand tremor

    (3) insomnia

    (4) nausea or vomiting

    (5) transient visual, tactile, or auditory hallucinations or illusions

    (6) psychomotor agitation

    (7) anxiety

    (8) grand mal seizures

C. The symptoms in Criterion B cause clinically significant distress or impairment in social, occupational, or other important areas of functioning.

D. The symptoms are not due to a general medical condition and are not better accounted for by another mental disorder.

Specify if:

With Perceptual Disturbances

Note. From DSM-IV-TR, pp. 201–202, 215–216, 287–289.

typical person with alcoholism is in his or her mid-30s and has a good job, home, and family; less than 5% of this population lives on Skid Row.

A practical definition of alcoholism would assign it diagnostically "when a person's alcohol consumption repeatedly interferes with occupational or social functioning, emotional state, or physical health," as does *DSM-IV-TR*. This definition stresses impairment of the individual rather than an arbitrary consumption figure, such as whether the person downs 1 or 5 or 50 drinks a week. People with a condition called "idiosyncratic intoxication" often become violent on a single drink; for them, one drink constitutes alcoholism. In the service of denial, patients and relatives will nitpick over the definition of alcoholism by stating that alcoholism exists whenever problems with alcohol arise repeatedly, the clinician circumvents semantic quibbling. Part of the clinician's job is to teach patients how the diagnosis is made so that they can make it for themselves. Many patients believe the term *alcoholic* only applies to Skid Row bums. For many, it is initially easier to agree to having "problems with alcohol."

Clinical Presentation

Although people with alcoholism vary considerably, in general they suffer from apprehension, agitation, dysphoria, guilt, remorse, despair, hopelessness, futility, self-deprecation, and insomnia. Their symptoms are usually worse in the morning, after not drinking for hours. *The Lost Weekend*—a "must-see" movie for every clinician—portrays with bone-chilling accuracy the "typical" life of a person with alcoholism: obsessed with drink, continually lying about it, hiding bottles, sneaking drinks, and disappearing repeatedly. After "going on the wagon," people with alcoholism typically reexperience anxiety or depression and start drinking again; a vicious spiral of abstinence–dysphoria–drinking escalates until the individual reaches "rock bottom."

DSM-IV-TR lists 13 mental disorders related to alcohol; Table 11-6 enumerates the diagnostic criteria for intoxication and withdrawal. Dependence and abuse are defined the same for alcohol as for any other drug (see Tables 11-2 and 11-3, respectively). The other mental disorders related to alcohol are delirium, persisting amnestic disorder, psychotic disorder (with delusions or hallucinations), mood disorder, anxiety disorder, sexual dysfunction, and sleep disorder.

Withdrawal is most critical, since 15% of alcoholics who develop delirium tremens ("DTs") die. The first and most common withdrawal symptom is tremulousness, which begins a few hours after stopping, or greatly reducing, alcohol intake. The others are the same for all hypnoanxiolytics (see Table 11-6).

Alcohol is one of the few drugs to cause *"blackouts,"* a temporary (anterograde) amnesia in which short-term (but not long-term) memory is lost, while other intellectual and motor functions remain intact. To illustrate: The day after a "bender" (remaining drunk for several days), a surgeon with alcoholism became angry at a nurse for allowing a tracheostomy to be done on one of his patients without notifying him. She reminded the surgeon that he himself had performed the procedure the day before. He apparently had a blackout, since he had no recollection of doing it. As in this case, people with alcoholism may appear to function normally and even perform complex tasks during a blackout. Research suggests that the forgotten material does not hold special psychological significance, but results from a neurological deficit in retrieving new information. Blackouts scare people with alcoholism, who are often terrified of having committed violence they can't remember; blackouts are also frightening because they appear to be dramatic proof that alcohol is destroying their brains. In truth, however, blackouts have little prognostic significance.

Clinical Course

A large number of males with alcoholism begin heavy drinking during their late teens or 20s, but only in their 30s, after a long and insidious course, do they fully acknowledge their problem. Jellinek's (1952) three phases of alcoholism—prodromal, crucial, and chronic—are still relevant today and are outlined in Table 11-7. In addition to recognized phases there are familiar patterns to problematic drinking. Several types of alcoholism have been described:

1. The *alcohol-dependent drinker* relies on alcohol for relief of stress. There is no loss of control or gross intoxication and little progression in the course of the illness. Gradually there is loss of physical health. These individuals are rarely recognized as having a problem.
2. The *wine drinker* is unable to abstain without withdrawal symptoms and is in a constant state of mild intoxication (especially prevalent in France and Italy).
3. The *compulsive person with alcoholism* exhibits extreme loss of control and will drink until unconscious (especially prevalent in the United States and Canada).
4. The person with *secondary alcoholism* drinks secondary to one or more psychiatric disorders (mood disorder, phobic or anxiety states, cognitive disorders, or psychoses).
5. The *person who drinks periodically* has long periods of sobriety interspersed with binges ("the weekend drunk").

TABLE 11-7

Jellinek's Three Phases of Alcoholism

PRODOMAL PHASE

Avid drinking (gulping)   Preoccupation with drinking

Avoiding reference to drinking   Surreptitious drinking

Guilt

Palimpsests (blackouts, amnesia not associated with loss
    of consciousness)

CRUCIAL PHASE

(Heralded by the onset of increased palimpsests)

Loss of control   Changes in interpersonal relationships

Rationalization   Geographic escape

Social pressures to quit drinking   Changed family habits

Grandiosity   Unreasonable resentments

Aggressiveness   Protecting the supply

Persistent remorse   Poor nutrition

Remaining abstinent for periods of time   Decreased libido

Setting rules as to when to drink   Morbid jealousy

Dropping friends   Regular morning drinking

First hospitalization for alcoholism   Quitting jobs

Alcohol-centered behavior   Loss of interests

CHRONIC PHASE

Benders (remaining drunk for several days)   Loss of tolerance for alcohol

Ethical deterioration   Undefinable fears

Impaired thinking   Tremors

Psychosis (10%)   Psychomotor inhibition

Decline in social level   Obsessive drinking

Drinking nonpotables   Religious desires

Rationalization fails and the patient becomes accessible
    to treatment

Note. Information from Jellinek, 1952.

6. The person with *chronic alcoholism* displays the final common path of many alcohol abusers. This type of alcoholism is associated with decreased tolerance, physical complications, and social deterioration.

Mortality rates of people with alcoholism are approximately twice normal in males, three times normal in females, and especially high in younger age groups. The predominant causes of death in this population are accidents, suicides, cancer of the upper digestive and respiratory organs, arteriosclerotic heart disease, pneumonia, cirrhosis, and ulcers. Selzer (1969) found that of 96 drivers responsible for fatal accidents, 88 were people with chronic alcoholism. In almost half of fatal auto accidents, the culpable drivers were drunk. In France, a 1999 law requires any driver involved in a fatal crash to undergo alcohol and possibly drug testing. In France the legal level is 0.05 g/mL, as opposed to the United States where the usual legal level is 0.08. 21% of drivers involved in severe accidents had a blood alcohol level above the French legal limit (Biecheler et al., 2008). Following liver transplantation for alcoholic liver disease, a surprising 15% of people resumed drinking within 6 months (De-Martini et al., 2006).

Because "spontaneous" improvement is more common than generally realized, if people with alcoholism can keep functioning when they reach midlife, their long-term prognosis improves considerably. In other words, alcoholism is *not* a hopeless condition!

Complications

Alcoholism is a major factor in 20% of divorces and 40% of problems brought to family court. Half of all police work, hospital admissions, homicides, and automobile fatalities are alcohol-related. One-fourth of all suicides involve alcohol, especially in men over 35 who have suffered a loss in the last 6 months. In addition, many people who are depressed and have suicidal thoughts do not act on them until they are intoxicated.

Alcoholism assaults every organ; it causes anemia, muscle weakness, gastritis, diarrhea, ulcers, pancreatitis, "fetal alcohol syndrome," and other birth defects. Pregnant women who drink put their unborn children at risk of low birth weight and fetal alcohol syndrome. Combined with poor nutrition, alcoholism may produce a fatty liver and cirrhosis. Three or four beers a day over 15 years results in cirrhosis in 18% of people (Sorensen et al., 1984). Poor nutrition and alcoholism also cause the rapidly erupting *Wernicke–Korsakoff syndrome* of eye movement disturbances (nystagmus and inability to look laterally in one or both eyes), ataxia, and mental disturbances (confusion, impaired recent memory). If this syndrome is not promptly treated with massive doses of thiamine, in several days the patient may develop *Korsakoff psychosis*—which is not really a psychosis but a potentially permanent dementia characterized by impaired recent memory with lowered ability to think, disorientation, and confabulation (confabulation is not necessary to make the diagnosis). In the less severe cases, complete recovery may occur slowly over a period of months. Severe cases may be left with serious memory deficits. Of patients who have both alcoholic and metabolic or nutritional problems, Wernicke's encephalopathy is seen in 65%, Korsakoff's psychosis in 53%, and alcoholic polyneuropathy in 70%.

Alcohol withdrawal can cause seizures (rum fits), *delirium tremens* (DTs or in *DSM-IV-TR* terms, "alcohol delirium with onset during withdrawal"), and alcoholic hallucinosis (*DSM-IV-TR* "alcohol psychotic disorder with hallucinations"). *Alcoholic grand mal seizures* usually occur within the first 3 days after stopping drinking. In about a third of the cases, they are associated with DTs, the seizures preceding the delirium. The best treatment is prophylaxis with phenytoin in patients who are known to be predisposed to seizures as well as aggressive use of benzodiazepines to ameliorate withdrawal. DTs usually occur within 1 week (3–4 days average) after stopping drinking and usually last 3 days or less, although more severe DTs may occur with more prolonged drinking. Symptoms of DTs include disorientation, visual hallucinations, wakefulness, tremulous picking motions, and frequently mild temperature elevations. People with long-term (5–20 years) alcoholism are most likely to get DTs. In the past, 6–15% of patients with DTs died, usually of head trauma, seizures, or pneumonia, but rapid diagnosis and treatment have lowered the death rate. Patients with DTs should be hospitalized and given oral fluids and sedation. Keeping someone with the patient and the lights on can help reduce terror and visual hallucinations.

Alcoholic hallucinosis (usually auditory) is a syndrome (somewhat rarer than DTs) in which patients complain of vivid, usually identifiable voices in a clear sensorium. The voices are frequently unpleasant, and patients' behavior is usually consistent with the content of the voices, including fearful attempts to escape and, occasionally, attempted suicide. This syndrome occurs as a withdrawal phenomenon, usually within the first 3 days after cessation of drinking in alcoholism of long standing. In some cases, hallucinations may persist for up to 6 months (Tsuang et al., 1994). Treatment should consist of supportive therapy, prevention of convulsions, and antipsychotics, when indicated.

Epidemiology

In the United States the National Institute on Drug Abuse (NIDA) approximately 8.5% of adults are alcoholic, for a total of perhaps 14 million people with alcoholism in the country. One-quarter of these individuals have an onset prior to the age of 20, and 85% have become alcoholic by the age of 40; onset is earlier for African-Americans and Native-Americans than for European-Americans. Many times (3:1 or greater) more men than women are alcoholic. Women develop alcoholism later but more rapidly than men; in women, an average of approximately 13 years elapses prior to treatment; in men, it is 21 years.

Etiology and Pathogenesis

About half of all hospitalized males with alcoholism have a family history of alcoholism. In contrast to people with nonfamilial alcoholism, these individuals develop alcoholism earlier in life, have greater dependency, bleaker prognoses, fewer nonalcoholic psychiatric problems, and are less able to maintain "controlled drinking" (Bohman et al., 1987). The best predictor of future alcoholism among adolescents is a family history of alcoholism (Goodwin, 1985).

Twin studies generally support this division by showing that heredity plays a major role in some, but not all, cases of alcoholism. Whether reared by biological parents with alcoholism or by nonalcoholic adopted parents, the sons of fathers with alcoholism have three to four times the normal rate of alcoholism, whereas daughters have only a slightly higher rate than the general population. Cloninger (Bohman et al., 1987) described "type 1 alcoholism" as milder, starts after age 25, hits men and women equally, needs environmental factors (e.g., social drinking in bars) as well as genetics, and is 20% heritable. "Type 2 alcoholism" is often severe, starts in the teens, hits men only, and is 90% heritable for male offspring of type 2 fathers. Twenty to 35% of sons of fathers with alcoholism develop alcoholism; 5–10% of daughters do so. Mood disorders may run in families with alcoholism, but this remains controversial. There may also be a relationship between anxiety disorders and alcohol problems: Alcohol problems are more likely to follow the onset of agoraphobia and social phobia; alcohol misuse is more likely to precede and perhaps cause panic disorder and generalized anxiety disorder (Kushner, Sher, & Bertman, 1990).

Treatment and Management

Thirty years ago, the primary measure and goal of treatment was complete abstinence and sobriety. Partial gains in treatment were at times glossed over. For example, an addict who had been injecting heroin went into treatment for this but later relapsed to swallowing opioid pain medication. Although this is a clearly less than optimal outcome, even temporarily, clinicians sometimes failed to reinforce the positive aspects of the change, in that oral abuse of opioids carries less risk than intravenous abuse.

Prochaska and DiClemente developed a model of change that applies very well to addiction (see Chapter 5). This model recognizes that simply warning people of the ill effects of their behavior will usually not result in a substantive change in that behavior. This model, sometimes called the transtheoretical model of change, characterizes six stages of change. First is *precontemplation*, wherein the individual is not even aware that there is a problem and is not considering change. Next is *contemplation*, in which the individual is ambivalent about change and is not considering change within the next month. This stage is followed by the *preparation* stage, wherein the individual has identified the wish to change and is experimenting with it and planning to act within the next month. Next comes the *action* stage, in which the individual is actively working on change and dealing with obstacles until the new behavior (e.g., sobriety) becomes habitual. This is followed by the *maintenance* stage, during which the change is sustained over a long period of time with less effort. The *relapse* stage exists when a trigger (often the dysphoric emotional state) precipitates resumption of the undesirable behavior. Approaching a patient in a hopeful manner to catalyze and effect change requires different techniques depending on which stage of change the individual occupies (e.g., motivational interviewing for precontemplation and Antabuse or Alcoholics Anonymous for the action stage).

The treatment of alcohol dependence is abstinence and Alcoholics Anonymous (or an equivalent recovery program). Since clinicians can't reliably predict the 5–15% of people with alcoholism who eventually will be able to drink moderately, abstinence should be urged, especially for the first 6–12 months after hospitalization, when 70–90% of patients relapse. The longer patients remain dry, the sharper their thinking and the better their occupational, social, and sexual functioning. Some patients are very tentative about their diagnosis and hence their treatment. It may be useful to elicit their agreement not to drink at all for 3–6 months, "just to see what abstinence feels like and how it affects them." In advance, patients are told that inability to follow through on this temporary abstinence is proof of alcoholism.

Supervised (but *not* unsupervised) Antabuse (disulfiram) treatment for alcoholism works better than placebo (Brewer, 1992). For the subgroup of people with alcoholism who sincerely believe in and desire this as an *adjunct* to treatment, Antabuse may be helpful. Cravings are mitigated by the knowledge that drinking within 3–5 days of taking the drug will produce severe nausea, flushing, tachycardia, and hypotension. The standard dose is 250 mg/day; higher doses offer no more deterrence and, if mixed with alcohol, are potentially lethal. Antabuse usually should not be the sole treatment. Lithium has been reported to help both depressed and nondepressed people with alcoholism stay abstinent (Fawcett et al., 1987). Acamprosate and naltrexone both show improvement in the sobriety rates of active alcoholics. Three months after an acute treatment episode, only about 15% of individuals are still sober. With these two agents, the sobriety rates doubled or tripled. There is some controversy about these drug approaches because the ability to stay *compliant* with any medication or placebo regime predicts abstinence.

Alcoholics Anonymous (AA) greatly benefits a majority of people with alcoholism. AA doesn't go into *why* people drink, just that they *do*, and shouldn't; it stresses a "one-day-at-a-time" philosophy, which allows people with alcoholism to deal with manageable units of time and end a "dry day" with a sense of accomplishment. On a trial basis at least, all people with alcoholism should attend AA meetings. Clinicians can help their patients by finding a socially appropriate AA chapter for them, by not giving into rationalizations for why they can't attend this or that AA meeting, and by getting patients linked up with an AA member who is on the same "wavelength." Finding sponsors can help patients begin the AA process and find the right meetings. Some meetings are open to drop-ins and beginners, whereas others are closed so that group members can focus on a certain aspect of their recovery. If there are several choices, patients should explore to see which location(s) is the best fit for them. If patients are on medication for a psychiatric problem such as depression, it is important to find AA groups that are supportive of pharmacological treatments. AA also welcomes people with other drug problems, especially hypnoanxiolytic, marijuana, and cocaine dependence. Polysubstance abusers can also go to more specialized meetings such as Narcotics Anonymous (NA). Some patients never feel comfortable with the AA philosophy of a "higher power" and do better with alternatives such as Rational or SMART Recovery groups that have a cognitive–behavioral emphasis. Women often feel more comfortable at "women only" groups.

The clinician must also attend to the needs of the family of the affected person. If one member drinks, the others needn't drown. Growing up with a parent with alcoholism can be devastating; so is living with a spouse who has alcoholism. The clinician should assure family members that they are not responsible for the individual's harmful drinking, nor do they have any ethical obligation to "reform" him or her. Whether or not the person with alcoholism goes to AA, the patient's relatives should attend Alanon, a support group for family members, or Alateen, which offers information and assistance to teenagers with alcoholism and their teenage relatives. For people with alcoholism who are resistant to diagnosis and treatment, the family can become an invaluable ally in penetrating the denial and rationalizations. In these cases, an "intervention" might be arranged: Significant people in the individual's life get together and, in a very firm, direct, and compassionate manner, confront the person regarding the alcoholism. Interventions are best done with the help of an experienced professional. Many people who have recovered from alcoholism look back on these dramatic confrontations as the turning points in their lives.

HYPNOANXIOLYTICS

Hypnoanxiolytics quell anxiety, induce sleep, or both. They are classified into three groups: barbiturates, barbiturate-like drugs, and benzodiazepines. *Barbiturates* are the prototypic hypnoanxiolytic. The first barbiturate, Veronal—named after the tranquil city of Verona in Italy—was introduced in 1902 as a "safe" replacement for alcohol. *Benzodiazepines* are now the most widely prescribed hypnoanxiolytics in the world.

When taken as an overdose, barbiturates are frequently lethal, but benzodiazepines only rarely. Relative to barbiturates, less tolerance develops to benzodiazepines, withdrawal is less frequent, and potentiation by alcohol is less (Goodwin & Guze, 1984). With benzodiazepines, tolerance tends to develop more often to the sedative than to the anxiolytic effects. Benzodiazepines, however, are not innocuous: Older adults are highly sensitive to them, and they are associated with birth defects (e.g., midline hypoplasia as in cleft palate). Longer-acting benzodiazepines may accumulate to toxic levels and insidiously retard cognition and movement. Psychological and physical dependence may arise from ongoing use; in one survey, 58% of long-term users admitted they would have "difficulty" without them (Salzman, 1985). Four to six years after being hospitalized for hypnoanxiolytic dependence, 84% of patients were using hypnoanxiolytics, 52% were abusing them, 42% had been rehospitalized for drug misuse, and 12% had withdrawal convulsions (Allgulander, Borg, & Vikander, 1984). Although benzodiazepine withdrawal is usually mild, it can be severe. Withdrawal symptoms are the same as with alcohol (see Table 11-6). Benzodiazepines that reach the brain the fastest and produce a "buzz" are most likely to be abused. For example, diazepam (Valium) and chlordiazepoxide (Librium) have similar characteristics, except that diazepam is a highly lipid soluble and quickly penetrates the blood–brain barrier, producing a rapid onset of action. Alprazolam (Xanax) is also lipophyllic but has a much shorter half-life than diazepam and reaches higher blood levels much faster. These medications, if crushed and injected or snorted, will have a faster onset of action because they bypass the gut.

In most clinic studies fewer than 5% of patients on benzodiazepines meet criteria for abuse or dependence. Many people are so worried about this happening that they underuse these drugs. People with a history of alcohol abuse or a family history of alcohol or hypnanxiolytic abuse are more likely to abuse benzodiazepines (Ciraulo et al., 1989). Several patterns in the development of dependence and abuse have been noted. One prototype—the "prescription pill popper"—is that of the middle-class, middle-aged woman who obtains a prescription because of anxiety or insomnia. Later she increases the dose and frequency of use on her own, using the drug to cope with even minor problems. Another pattern involves males in their teens or early 20s who obtain these drugs from illicit sources and use them for their euphorigenic effects. It is common for patients on methadone programs, who have discontinued opiate abuse, to continue to use benzodiazepines sporadically. Cognitive–behavioral approaches, SSRIs, or buspirone (a nonhabit-forming anxiolytic) are recommended as the first treatment in these high-risk groups.

When first prescribing any psychoactive agent, but especially a hypnoanxiolytic, physicians should warn patients that, for a week or so, their reflexes might be a tad slow and they should be extra careful around machines, crossing streets, and cooking. Daytime sedation might last a week. In older adult patients, when they must be used, the patients should be warned of unsteadiness and possible fall risk. As far as is known, the anxiolytic effect continues indefinitely in most patients. Patients without alcoholism can drink alcohol while taking hypnoanxiolytics (and other psychotropic drugs), but they should be told that one drink will probably feel like two to three drinks.

Benzodiazepines are classified as "short-acting," "intermediate-acting," or "long-acting," with half-lives of 2–6 hours, 8–12 hours, and over 24 hours, respectively. A drug's "half-life" is when 50% of it has become pharmacologically inactive. Complicating the picture is the fact that a parent drug may have a short-acting half life, but its major breakdown product may be long-acting (e.g., chlordiazepoxide's half-life is 4 hours, but its metabolite, nordiazepam, has a half-life of 96 hours). The chances of withdrawal increase with increased dosage and duration of use. More cases of benzodiazepine withdrawal have been reported with long-term, low-dose use than with short-term, high-dose use. For example, 15 mg of daily diazepam for 2 years apparently causes more physical dependence than 50 mg of daily diazepam for 6 weeks.

Longer-acting benzodiazepines are less likely to be abused than short-acting ones. The longer-acting benzodiazepines are eliminated more slowly and gradually, causing less and more delayed withdrawal than the shorter-acting ones. In a sense, they taper themselves. In some people, alprazolam may last only 6 hours. If their prescription specifies usage every 8 hours, this gap may result in three mini-withdrawals a day.

High-potency benzodiazepines may actually have higher withdrawal risks because they are often used in higher dosage equivalents than the older, low-potency benzodiazepines. For panic disorder, alprazolam is commonly used in doses over 3 mg a day, which would be equivalent to over 30 mg a day of diazepam, a dosage almost never used. A majority of patients with panic disorder who have taken alprazolam for over 1 year report withdrawal symptoms, even when gradually tapered off of it, that are worse than the original panic symptoms. Too often, physicians' decisions in treating patients can increase the chance of addiction. *Fast, frequent,* and *forceful* reinforcements are most likely to cause addiction. They often follow many of the principles of what we could title "How to Create an Addict":

1. Choose a fast and powerful reinforcer. Pick a substance that has a rapid onset of action and therefore gives a "buzz" or "rush."

2. Make sure the drug has to be used often to get the reinforcement and, better yet, use a drug that has nasty withdrawal symptoms. This will increase the craving to use the drug again to eradicate the withdrawal symptoms and to get the buzz. The wider the gulf between withdrawal symptoms and the buzz, the stronger the reinforcement provided. Short-acting drugs work best for this. Secobarbital meets all of these criteria.

3. Prescribe the drug prn (as needed) or schedule with a frequency that precipitates withdrawal before the next dose is taken. For example, if it is prn, tell the patient to take the drug "only when you feel very anxious"; and if it's scheduled, prescribe a drug to be taken every 6 hours that lasts only 4 hours.

Unfortunately, the steps that create addiction are too often used in pain and anxiety treatment. For patients who seek help for benzodiazepine dependence, a very gradual withdrawal extending over 2–3 months is often recommended. High-potency benzodiazepines probably should be replaced with low-potency benzodiazepines. For a gradual, gentler withdrawal, the longer-acting benzodiazepines such as chlordiazepoxide, clorazepate, and clonazepam can be substituted for the shorter-acting ones on which the patient has become dependent. For a comfortable withdrawal in under 7 days, divalproex sodium or carbamazepine (both anticonvulsants) can be used for dependent patients who have taken benzodiazepines in high doses or for a long period of time (Covington, 1998).

STIMULANTS

Cocaine

Sigmund Freud introduced cocaine into mainstream medicine as a safe, non-habit-forming treatment for opium addiction. He frequently used it himself. According to the National Survey on Drug Use and Health (NSDUH), the rate of past-year use for cocaine (powder and crack combined) among individuals age 12 and older (2.4%) has remained stable since 2002. Ten percent of Americans have taken "even one sniff" of cocaine, as Cole Porter's (1934) lyric goes. Chic in Porter's day, cocaine was snorted and was relatively expensive. Now cocaine powder for snorting has dropped in price and the availability of cheap "crack" cocaine has led to abuse in all social classes.

With growing use, there is a growing awareness of its hazards. Reflecting Porter's "Some get a kick from cocaine," its use has dropped in high school and among college students and professionals, but is unchanged among lower-class street users. In addition to abuse and dependence, *DSM-IV-TR* lists criteria for amphetamine and cocaine intoxication and withdrawal that are identical. For practical purposes, these are combined in Table 11-8. Six other disorders related to stimulant use are also listed: delirium, psychotic disorder (with delusions or hallucinations), mood disorder, anxiety disorder, sexual dysfunction, and sleep disorder.

A typical story of cocaine addiction in the 1980s started when the curious person payed $75–$150 a gram for a white powder, which is usually 30% cocaine and 70% adulterants (inactive sugars). After making a thin, 2-inch line of the powder, the user snorted it with a straw or rolled-up dollar bill. This launched a 30-minute high, which tapered off in 60–90 minutes. The user feels energetic, creative, talkative, attractive, excited, euphoric, motivated, grandiose, and "connected." Initial negative reactions include restlessness, agitation, anxiety, hyperexcitability, and hostility.

More recently, "crack" cocaine has been available, especially in inner-city areas, for $5–$15 a "rock." The rock is pure cocaine alkaloid extracted from the powder using heat with sodium bicarbonate. "Freebasing" is another method that has been used to separate the adulterants with ether (highly flammable solvent) or ammonia. The pure cocaine is vaporized and inhaled in a pipe (that may be home-

TABLE 11-8

DSM-IV-TR *Criteria for Amphetamine or Cocaine Intoxication and Withdrawal*

Substance Intoxication

A. Recent use of amphetamine or a related substance (e.g., methylphenidate) or cocaine.

B. Clinically significant maladaptive behavioral or psychological changes (e.g., euphoria or affective blunting; changes in sociability; hypervigilance; interpersonal sensitivity; anxiety, tension, or anger; stereotyped behaviors; impaired judgment; or impaired social or occupational functioning) that developed during, or shortly after, use of amphetamine or a related substance or cocaine.

C. Two (or more) of the following, developing during, or shortly after, use of amphetamine or a related substance or cocaine:

    (1) tachycardia or bradycardia

    (2) pupillary dilation

    (3) elevated or lowered blood pressure

    (4) perspiration or chills

    (5) nausea or vomiting

    (6) evidence of weight loss

    (7) psychomotor agitation or retardation

    (8) muscular weakness, respiratory depression, chest pain, or cardiac arrhythmias

    (9) confusion, seizures, dyskinesia, dystonias, or coma

D. The symptoms are not due to a general medical condition and are not better accounted for by another mental disorder.

Substance Withdrawal

A. Cessation (or reduction of) in amphetamine (or related substance) or cocaine use that has been heavy and prolonged.

B. Dysphoric mood and two (or more) of the following physiological changes, developing within a few hours to several days after Criterion A:

    (1) fatigue

    (2) vivid, unpleasant dreams

    (3) insomnia or hypersomnia

    (4) increased appetite

    (5) psychomotor retardation or agitation

C. The symptoms in Criterion B cause clinically significant distress or impairment in social, occupational, or other important areas of functioning.

D. The symptoms are not due to a general medical condition and are not better accounted for by another mental disorder.

Note. Adapted from *DSM-IV-TR,* pp. 227–228, 245–246.

made from a soda can), launching an intense high that peaks in 5 minutes and tapers off in 15, followed by extreme dysphoria, craving, and often by marathon "coke" binges of 24–96 hours, or until supplies run out. Because of its lower price, this form of cocaine is affordable even by middle- and high-school students.

Habitual cocaine abusers gradually become obsessed with the drug and securing its supply. Not uncommonly, the user blows over $3,000 a week on the drug. A week, and then a day, cannot pass without that "extra boost." When high, users are unable to sleep, and once asleep, cannot awaken. Among people snorting cocaine powder, an average of 2 years elapses before they seek help. Among crack users, this period is shortened to 6 months. Fifty to 70% of heavy cocaine users report paranoid episodes, which happen almost exclusively during the high (Satel & Edell, 1991). On crashing (withdrawing), users feel depressed, anergic, and unmotivated. Appetite disappears and weight drops, often to medically precarious levels. Snorters' noses drip and bleed continuously, exhausting endless supplies of gauze. Crack smokers cough up blood-tinged sputum with black flecks (carbonized cocaine and necrotic lung tissue). Work is missed, jobs are lost, friends lose patience, and marriages end.

Despite these serious consequences, of those who have called a cocaine hotline, most still preferred to continue their habit because it produced euphoria (82%), diminished boredom (57%), increased energy and self-confidence (48%), and stimulated sexuality (21%). Callers said that cocaine was more important than food (71%), sex (50%), family activities (72%), and friends (64%). Among all the callers, 61% snorted the drug, 21% smoked, and 18% injected it. Half used the drug daily. On average, users spent $637 a week on cocaine (Gold, 1984).

Although no definitive therapy for cocaine dependence yet exists, recent research into drugs acting on GABA, glutamate, or dopamine systems show promise (Karila et al., 2008). There has been some evidence suggesting that tricyclic antidepressants may help some cocaine-dependent patients (Gawin et al., 1989) and that bromocriptine (a dopamine agonist dosed at 0.625 mg four times daily) exerts an anticraving effect in 1–2 minutes. Early successes with these pharmacological treatments, used alone without other treatments, have been tempered by relapse rates 6 months later that are as high as when no treatment is received. However, by helping patients get off and stay off cocaine for some period of time, these drugs might enable abusers to participate more effectively in rehabilitative treatments such as Cocaine Anonymous or AA. As Sherlock Holmes's case illustrates (Chapter 9), cocaine's many "advantages" offer former abusers little incentive to remain drug-free. Therefore, therapy must help patients find or rediscover interests that will "replace" cocaine. One of the best things cocaine addicts can do is replace cocaine-using friends with abstinent friends (Kandel & Raveis, 1989). A multicomponent behavioral treatment—using money payments for negative urine specimens, significant others to reinforce abstinence, training in recognizing ante-cedents and consequences of cocaine, and help in developing new alternative activ-ities to cocaine use—has been shown to be superior to traditional drug counseling (Higgens et al., 1993). Less specific weekly psychosocial therapy does not improve abstinence (Kang et al., 1991).

Amphetamines

Intoxication and withdrawal from cocaine and amphetamine are similar. NIDA reports methamphetamine use has been stable in most regions in 2006. As overdoses, both are potentially fatal. Acute usage of amphetamines causes tachycardia, and with increased dosage, ventricular fibrillation and respiratory arrest may occur. Hyperpyrexia (increased body temperature) is frequent; sei-zures may occur, and deaths have resulted from status epilepticus (continuous seizures). The post-use depression may lead to suicide. After a high-dose binge, some users develop a transient psychosis with a mixture of paranoid and manic-like symptoms. Visual and tactile hallucinations may also be present. At other times, a confused toxic psychosis may develop. Anorexia and weight loss are common in regular users. Long-term use of amphetamines is associ-ated with increased morbidity, mortality, criminality, as well as ongoing, dif-fuse suspiciousness and a chronic delusional syndrome.

Noteworthy differences between cocaine and amphetamines exist. Because of cocaine's short half-life, tolerance may not develop as rapidly as it does to amphetamines: In just 3 days, "speed freaks" can go from ingesting 15 mg to 2,000 mg a day to obtain the original effects. Whereas the acute effects of a single amphetamine dose lasts 4–6 hours, those from cocaine rarely extend beyond 2 hours. Cocaine is typically used in binges, whereas amphetamines are used more continuously. More often than cocaine, amphetamines trigger a toxic psychosis resembling paranoid schizophrenia.

Seven days before taking the Medical College Admissions Test (MCAT), Darlene was frantic. Night and day she crammed, hourly popping a 5 mg "black beauty" (dextroamphetamine). Darlene was not only awake, she was flying. Never did she feel more alert and focused. After 2 days of nonstop studying, she began pacing "because I could concentrate better." By day 3, she repeatedly told her roommate that the MCATs were "dumb"—an insight that Darlene alone considered bril-liant—and by day 4, she began shouting this indictment out her apartment win-dow. By nightfall, she was convinced the MCAT people had hired mobsters to break her arms and legs. Already they were playing tricks on her eyes: One moment beetles were crawling in her hair, the next moment they disappeared. The telephone rang, wrong number, surely the MCAT mobsters. To protect herself, she bolted the door. Believing strangers in front of her apartment were also MCAT mobsters, she hurled darts and dishes at them. As typically occurs, Darlene became psychotic on 60 mg a day, remained psychotic for 2 weeks, and recovered fully. (Six months later she got high scores on the MCATs, but had trouble getting her driver's license renewed because she had been hospitalized for psychosis.)

The mainstay of acute treatment of stimulant abusers is observation, rest, and nutritious food. During the intoxication phase, benzodiazepines may be used to treat significant anxiety and agitation. Propranolol or clonidine are used for sympathetic overactivity. During an acute stimulant intoxication, safety should be ensured and patients should be observed continuously. Physical restraints may be needed. If paranoid, patients' environment should be simplified, as few people as possible should care for them, and anything they deem dangerous should be removed. An increasing body temperature indicates an increasingly dangerous toxicity. Antipsychotic drugs (e.g., haloperidol 2–5 mg orally or IM) are effective in treating intoxication.

Amphetamines have no safe role in dieting and a limited one in depression. They do have three legitimate medical indications: treating narcoleptic sleep attacks, childhood attention-deficit/hyperactivity disorder, and (occasionally) resistant depression. Even here they must be used cautiously—or, as rock star Frank Zappa warned, "Speed will turn you into your parents."

Nicotine

There are two "minor stimulants": caffeine and nicotine. Caffeine's intoxicating effects are presented in Chapter 11 on anxiety disorders. Caffeine withdrawal (not officially accepted as a disorder) is often accompanied by headache, lethargy, and dysphoria. It begins within 2 to 24 hours and lasts about 1 week (Hughes et al., 1992). This reaction occurs even when consumption is limited to two or three cups of coffee a day.

Nicotine has always been controversial. The Turkish and German governments once considered smoking in public an offense punishable by death; the Russians preferred castration. Americans, however, have subsidized its growth. DSM-IV-TR made nicotine dependence (see Table 11-4) and withdrawal a mental disorder. Table 11-9 presents DSM-IV-TR criteria for nicotine withdrawal.

Historically, men smoke more than women, but women have almost reached parity. Men have been more successful in stopping. The most effective treatment programs combine education, group support, and behavior

TABLE 11-9
DSM-IV-TR *Criteria for Nicotine Withdrawal*

A. Daily use of nicotine for at least several weeks.

B. Abrupt cessation of nicotine use, or reduction in the amount of nicotine used, followed within 24 hours by at least four (or more) of the following signs:

    (1) dysphoric or depressed mood

    (2) insomnia

    (3) irritability, frustration, or anger

    (4) anxiety

    (5) difficulty concentrating

    (6) restlessness

    (7) decreased heart rate

    (8) increased appetite or weight gain

C. The symptoms in Criterion B cause clinically significant distress or impairment in social, occupational, or other important areas of functioning.

D. The symptoms are not due to a general medical condition and are not better accounted for by another mental disorder.

Note. From *DSM-IV-TR,* p. 266.

---

modification, yet even here, within a year, 80% of patients relapse. People who have had a history of major depression are most likely to fail attempts at permanent abstinence. Hypnosis, nicotine gum, and gradual substitution with lower nicotine-containing cigarettes help only some smokers. Nicotine patches are more widely accepted and provide a continuous release of nicotine into the blood. The patch increases abstinence, decreases withdrawal symptoms and depressive symptoms associated with withdrawal, and reduces the rewarding effects of smoking (Levin et al., 1994). Bupropion in a sustained-release preparation (Zyban) is a proven aid to smoking cessation. Varenicline (Chantix), a nictotine receptor partial agonist, has recently be approved by the FDA for treatment of nicotine dependence. Behavioral treatment approaches have become increasing effective over time (LeFoll & George, 2007).

HALLUCINOGENS

In 1938, while investigating ergot preparations for a pharmaceutical firm in Basel, Switzerland, Albert Hofmann first synthesized LSD-25 (lysergic acid diethylamide). (The number 25 refers to nothing chemical, but to the date [May 2] when he first produced LSD.) Five years later, he unwittingly absorbed it through his fingers and experienced a "not unpleasant delirium." Several days later he swallowed 250 micrograms, and in 40 minutes he felt a "mild dizziness, restlessness, inability to concentrate, visual disturbance and uncontrollable laughter." His diary continues to describe "the bicycle trip heard round the world":

> . . . on the way home (a four-mile trip by bicycle), the symptoms developed with a much greater intensity than the first time. I had the greatest difficulty speaking coherently and my field of vision fluctuated and was distorted like the reflections in an amusement park mirror. I also had the impression that I was hardly moving, yet later my assistant told me that I was pedaling at a fast pace. So far as I can recollect, the height of the crisis was characterized by these symptoms; dizziness, visual distortions, the faces of those present appeared like grotesque colored masks, strong agitation alternating with paresis [partial paralysis], the head, body and extremities sometimes cold and numb; a metallic taste on the tongue; throat dry and shriveled; a feeling of suffocation; confusion alternating with a clear appreciation of the situation; at times standing outside myself as a neutral observer and hearing myself muttering jargon or screaming half madly.
>
> Six hours after taking the drug, my condition had improved. The perceptual distortions were still present. Everything seemed to undulate and their proportions were distorted like the reflections on a choppy water surface. Everything was changing with unpleasant, predominately poisonous green and blue color tones. With closed eyes multi-hued, metamorphizing fantastic images overwhelmed me. Especially noteworthy was the fact that sounds were transposed into visual sensations ["synesthesias"] so that from each tone or noise a comparable colored picture was evoked, changing in form and color kaleidoscopically. (Coles, Brenner, & Meagher, 1970, pp. 44–45)

Hofmann apparently slept well and the next day felt "completely well, but tired."

Despite some differences (see Table 11-10), most *pure* hallucinogens (or "psychedelics") produce experiences like Hofmann's. "Street acid," however, is rarely pure, usually consisting of anticholinergics (which are hallucinogens in toxic doses), quinine, sugar, and PCP (discussed later); it might even contain LSD. As a result, clinicians cannot assume that patients on a "bad trip" know what drug they've taken. Therefore, it is safest to "talk patients down" by reassuring them that the trip will end in a few hours, that they are safe, and that they are not going mad, shrinking, or becoming a zombie. Patients

TABLE 11-10

DSM-IV *Criteria for Hallucinogen Intoxication and Hallucinogen Persisting Perception Disorder*

Hallucinogen Intoxication

A. Recent use of a hallucinogen.

B. Clinically significant maladaptive behavioral or psychological changes (e.g., marked anxiety or depression, ideas of reference, fear of losing one's mind, paranoid ideation, impaired judgment, or impaired social or occupational functioning) that developed during, or shortly after, hallucinogen use.

C. Perceptual changes occurring in a state of full wakefulness and alertness (e.g., subjective intensification of perceptions, depersonalization, derealization, illusions, hallucinations, synesthesias) that developed during, or shortly after, hallucinogen use.

D. Two (or more) of the following signs, developing during, or shortly after, hallucinogen use:

    (1) pupillary dilation

    (2) tachycardia

    (3) sweating

    (4) palpitations

    (5) blurring of vision

    (6) tremors

    (7) incoordination

E. The symptoms are not due to a general medical condition and are not better accounted for by another mental disorder.

Hallucinogen Persisting Perception Disorder (Flashbacks)

A. The reexperiencing, following cessation of use of a hallucinogen, of one or more of the perceptual symptoms that were experienced while intoxicated with the hallucinogen (e.g., geometric hallucinations, false perceptions of movement in the peripheral visual fields, flashes of color, intensified colors, trails of images of moving objects, positive afterimages, halos around objects, macropsia, and micropsia).

B. The symptoms in Criterion A cause clinically significant distress or impairment in social, occupational, or other important areas of functioning.

C. The symptoms are not due to a general medical condition (e.g., anatomical lesions and infections of the brain, visual epilepsies) and are not better accounted for by another mental disorder (e.g., delirium, dementia, Schizophrenia) or hypnopompic hallucinations.

Note. From *DSM-IV-TR*, p. 253.

should not fight the experience, but "flow with it"; they should be encouraged to become curious about it, and if they wish, to talk about it. If clinicians do not have the time to offer this reassurance, or if patients remain terrified despite it, diazepam 5 mg or alprazolam 0.5 mg can be given orally every hour until patients are reasonably comfortable or asleep; either drug causes less hypotension and fewer bad drug interactions than antipsychotics. Because some antipsychotics increase anticholinergic activity, these drugs can worsen the condition of someone who already has anticholinergic toxicity. A person with an anticholinergic psychosis has been described as "dry as a bone, red as a beet and mad as a hatter." It's quite recognizable, if you know what to look for.

Less than 5% of Americans have ever tried a psychedelic, and if these drugs were legal, only 1% claimed they would take them. Traditionally, hallucinogens have been used more frequently by high school and college students, the affluent, artistic, and philosophically minded, rather than by the poor or antisocial. Chronic use is uncommon. Hallucinogens can trigger "flashbacks," in which a person off drugs reexperiences an LSD trip days to months and sometimes years after taking it. Hallucinogen abuse among teens and young adults increased from 1992 to 1995 but has remained stable since then.

What causes flashbacks is unknown. Psychedelics rarely, if ever, cause psychosis *de novo*, but they, as well as PCP and *high* doses of marijuana, can easily rekindle a preexisting psychosis. High-risk patients include those with borderline or schizotypal personality disorder, and those with a personal or family history of drug- or nondrug-induced psychoses. Clinicians should inform these patients about their increased risk. This is not moralizing; it is giving information.

CANNABIS

The hemp plant, *Cannabis sativa*, grows anywhere it doesn't freeze; marijuana comes from its stems and leaves, while hashish derives from the resin of female plants. (George Washington smoked hemp at a time when it was believed to be a treatment for "catarrh.") The main psychoactive substance in cannabis is THC (delta-9-tetrahydrocannabinol), which does not typically exceed 1%. However, through genetic selection, marijuana leaves have reached 24% THC in "prize" crops. Hashish can be in the 15–20% range, and hashish oil contains up to 70% THC. Smoking is the primary mode of use. With normal recreational use, marijuana intoxication peaks in 30 minutes, persists for 3 hours, and sometimes impairs driving for up to 6 hours. It stimulates appetite ("the munchies"), causes dry mouth, produces bloodshot eyes, elevates mood, intensifies experiences and perceptions, and heightens relaxation and apathy. Dronabinol (Marinol), a synthetic THC, is an FDA approved medication for anorexia and nausea. Table 11-11 presents *DSM-IV-TR* criteria for cannabis intoxication.

Over 60% of American adults and adolescents have smoked "grass" at least once, and relatively few have experienced severe reactions after 24 hours of using the drug. Panic attacks, which account for 75% of all severe *acute* side effects, can last 2–6 hours. Severe cases can be treated with benzodiazepines. Otherwise, heavier cannabis use can cause toxic delirium represented by the "4 D's": depersonalization, derealization, déjà vu, and dysphoria. Another effect is a cognitive disorder with impairment in goal-directed, memory-dependent behavior and in carrying out multiple-step tasks. The "short attention span theater" becomes a favored form of entertainment. Marijuana can also exacerbate a preexisting psychosis. Its effects are greatly influenced by "set and setting"—that is, by the user's "mind set" or attitudes toward the drug, and the degree of receptivity and safety in the environment. Adverse reactions occur more often among those who smoke because of peer pressure or who have negative expectations of the drug. In the 1980s less than 1% of university

---

TABLE 11-11
DSM-IV-TR *Criteria for Cannabis Intoxication*

A. Recent use of cannabis.

B. Clinically significant maladaptive behavioral or psychological changes (e.g., impaired motor coordination, euphoria, anxiety, sensation of slowed time, impaired judgment, social withdrawal) that developed during, or shortly after, cannabis use.

C. Two (or more) of the following signs, developing within 2 hours of cannabis use:

    (1) conjunctival injection

    (2) increased appetite

    (3) dry mouth

    (4) tachycardia

D. The symptoms are not due to a general medical condition and are not better accounted for by another mental disorder.

Specify if:

With Perceptual Disturbances

Note. From *DSM-IV-TR*, p. 238.

---

students at campuses with high marijuana use developed panic attacks, whereas 25% did so at rural Southern colleges where use of the drug is discouraged.

Longer-term psychological problems associated with marijuana use are fewer than with some other drugs. Only 9% of marijuana users meet *DSM-IV-TR* criteria for cannabis abuse. Marijuana hallucinosis, flashbacks, or transient delusional syndrome may occur. Although an "amotivational syndrome" of laziness, apathy, and a lack of ambition has been attributed to marijuana, this finding derived from biased samples of largely lower-class patients and has not been supported by more recent surveys in countries where marijuana use is extensive (Jamaica, Costa Rica, and Greece). Passive, unmotivated people may choose marijuana for chronic use. Medically, cannabis diminishes respiratory capacity, produces bronchial and pulmonary irritation (more than equal amounts of nicotine, and like tobacco, may result in constrictive pulmonary disease), causes tachycardia, temporarily impairs cognition and recent memory, reduces fertility, harms the fetus, reduces immune response, and impairs driving and school performance.

Two main types of marijuana dependence have been described. In the more severe type users smoke marijuana many times a day and finally seek treatment on their own. In the second type, users smoke it every day or two and end up in treatment only after involuntary drug testing (Tennant, 1986). Both types may produce a withdrawal syndrome days later and have high relapse rates (Tennant, 1986).

Ever since *Reefer Madness* obtained cult-film status, the dominant question has been whether marijuana leads to the abuse of "heavier" illegal substances. The answer is a qualified no. Repeated studies have strongly suggested that the best predictor of illegal drug use is *legal* drug use. In other words, the chief "gateway" drug is not marijuana but tobacco or alcohol (Rittenhouse, 1982). Nevertheless, patients are not statistics, and the hazards of marijuana use must be evaluated in the light of each person's history. Marijuana is the most used illicit drug in the United States with an average of 4% of Americans using marijuana each month, including 6% of 8th graders and 19% of 12th graders by recent NIDA statistics.

PHENCYCLIDINE

Originally an animal tranquilizer, "hog" or phencyclidine (PCP) became a battlefield anesthetic in Vietnam. It resurfaced as a recreational drug in California during the late 1960s, ironically rechristened as "angel dust." PCP produces a euphoric, floating, energized, invincible, other-worldly, and dream-like state in which time is slowed, thinking is quickened, fantasies are dramatic, life is intensified, and reality goes on holiday.

But PCP is *not* the dust of angels. Users may be immobilized and stare blankly. Myoclonic (leg) jerks and confusion are common. On large doses, patients may become stuporous, enter a coma, and convulse with their eyes wide open. If they recover from the coma, they exhibit an agitated delirium marked by persecutory delusions, hallucinations, illusions, disorientation, agitation, and episodic assaultiveness: Asleep or calm one moment, without warning they may become fanatically violent the next. For no apparent reason, users fight with police, wreck cars, commit suicide, kill strangers. This violence may stem from the extreme suspiciousness and persecutory delusions produced by PCP. Being a "dissociative" anesthetic, PCP makes users feel as if they are outside their bodies; users do not perceive pain and are unaware and amnestic for such experiences. This delirium can last a week. Some patients die, usually due to respiratory depression; others are killed in accidents—drowning, automobile crashes, falls, and fires. Medically, PCP intoxication causes ataxia, nystagmus, and muscle rigidity. Whereas hallucinogens produce dilated pupils, PCP produces normal or small pupils. Table 11-12 presents *DSM-IV-TR* criteria for PCP and related substances.

PCP is often sprinkled on top of marijuana or parsley. When smoked, its effects arise in 1–5 minutes, peak after 5–30 minutes, remain high for 4–6 hours, and dwindle over the next 18 hours. Snorting PCP hastens its effects. Intravenous use is uncommon.

NIDA reports that in 2006 187,000 Americans over age 11 had abused PCP at least once during the past year. Most users are polydrug abusers. They often drink alcohol while on PCP, even though the combination usually makes them dreadfully sick. Despite the drug's horrifying effects, PCP users typically say they take it because "it's the perfect escape." It is frequently—and misleadingly—sold as cannabinol, mescaline, LSD, amphetamine, or cocaine.

The treatment of acute PCP overdose includes cardiopulmonary resuscitation, treatment for seizures, acidification of the urine (to hasten the drug's elimination) with 500–1,000 mg ammonium chloride orally every 3–5 hours, until the urine pH is below 5. Since patients are unpredictably violent and frequently combative, a low sensory environment should be used; physical restraints may be needed until patients have been calm for several hours. Some clinicians recommend (as needed) hourly haloperidol 5 mg IM; others suggest diazepam 10–30 mg orally or IM. Response to aggressive treatment is generally slow. Most experts agree that phenothiazines should be avoided, since they may compound PCP's anticholinergic and hypotensive effects. After the acute psychosis, PCP users often do not remain in drug treatment programs.

TABLE 11-12

DSM-IV-TR *Criteria for Phencyclidine Intoxication or Phencyclidine-Related Disorders*

A. Recent use of phencyclidine (or a related substance).

B. Clinically significant maladaptive behavioral changes (e.g., belligerence, assaultiveness, impulsiveness, unpredictability, psychomotor agitation, impaired judgment, or impaired social or occupational functioning) that developed during, or shortly after, phencyclidine use.

C. Within an hour (less when smoked, "snorted," or used intravenously), two (or more) of the following signs:

   (1) vertical or horizontal nystagmus

   (2) hypertension or tachycardia

   (3) numbness or diminished responsiveness to pain

   (4) ataxia

   (5) dysarthria

   (6) muscle rigidity

   (7) seizures or coma

   (8) hyperacusis

D. The symptoms are not due to a general medical condition and not better accounted for by another mental disorder.

Specify if:

With Perceptual Disturbances

Note. From *DSM-IV-TR*, p. 281.

MDMA

Also known as "ecstasy" or "XTC," 3,4-methylene-dioxy-methamphetamine (MDMA) was synthesized in 1914, but it wasn't until the early 1970s that it quietly became a recreational and psychotherapeutic drug. In 1985 the popularity of this then legal drug was featured in *Time* and *Newsweek* magazines; by June of that year, the Drug Enforcement Agency had "temporarily" made it illegal. Many opposed this decision, claiming that MDMA had been confused with the psychedelic MDA, that harm allegedly due to MDMA was really from adulterants (e.g., Borax), and that research into a potentially therapeutic drug was being stymied. MDMA is the only drug discussed in this chapter that is not mentioned in *DSM-IV-TR*. Human recreational doses have been reported to be neurotoxic in primates (Barnes, 1988); memantine, a glutamate receptor modulator protects against this damage in rats (Chipara et al., 2008).

In recreational doses of 75–175 mg, MDMA produces a tranquil, floating, introspective, talkative, 2- to 4-hour "trip." Grinspoon and Bakalar (1985) claim that it "invites rather than compels intensification of feelings and self-exploration." Chemically related to amphetamines and mescaline (a psychedelic), ecstasy exerts some stimulant effects. It induces a sense of well-being without alterations of consciousness, perception, movement, or coordination. Unlike with psychedelics, information revealed during MDMA usage is more readily remembered and applied afterwards. The person does not feel "stoned."

The usage pattern of MDMA is unlike that of any other drug. Users tend to wait several weeks between doses, because taking it too soon increases negative effects and decreases positive effects. Because the positive effects seem to decrease over subsequent doses, MDMA probably is not addictive. The mean number of doses taken by users is only 5.4 (Peroutka, 1987, 1989). NIDA reports that in 2006 2.1 million Americans over the age of 11 used MDMA during the past year.

> Physical side effects, which are dose-related, include dry mouth, increased blood pressure and pulse rate, anorexia, nystagmus, urinary urgency, blurred vision, loss of balance, and jaw-clenching. Fatigue may persist for a day or two. Fatal overdoses have been reported. Bad trips, flashbacks, and psychotic reactions are rare; weekly use is also rare. At present, there have been no reports of MDMA-induced craving or withdrawal. However, animal studies have shown that relapse to MDMA use can be triggered by drug-related cues (Ball et al., 2007).

OPIOIDS

> Junk is the ideal product...the ultimate merchandise. No sales talk necessary. The client will crawl through a sewer and beg to buy....The junk merchant does not sell his product to the consumer, he sells the consumer to this product.
> —William S. Burroughs, *Evergreen Review*, Jan./Feb. 1960

Opioids (also called *opiates*) are compounds with morphine-like properties. *Opium* is derived from the Turkish word for juice—juice of the poppy—because opium, the original opioid, derives from the head of the opium poppy *Papaver somniferum*, cultivated mainly in the Middle East, Southeast Asia, China, India, and Mexico. Although growing it in the United States has always been illegal, throughout the 1840s it was the most popular sleep aid in Kansas. Heroin is the only illicit opioid, and morphine is the prototypic opioid.

Clinical Presentation

In therapeutic amounts, morphine produces analgesia, induces tranquility, constricts pupils, and elevates mood (although some get dysphoria). Anorexia, nausea, and vomiting may occur, as may reduction in sex, aggression, and hunger drives. As Taylor Mead once quipped, "Opium is very cheap considering you don't feel like eating for the next six days." Skin itches, constipation develops, and respiratory rate and other vital signs decline. Except for meperidine (whose metabolite normeperidine is a cerebral irritant), opioids do not cause seizures.

Most opioid intoxication comes from shooting morphine or heroin intravenously, which produces a "rush"—a strong, flushing sensation coupled with an orgastic feeling in the belly. However, the purity of street heroin seized by federal agents in the United States has risen from 3.8% in 1970 to 42% in 2005. As a result, snorting heroin has become much more addictive than it had been. Waves of pleasant, floating drowsiness ("the nod") and dreams follow. Tolerance to opioids develops quickly. Tables 11-13 and 11-14 list *DSM-IV-TR* criteria for opioid intoxication and withdrawal. Morphine withdrawal peaks up to 72 hours after the last dose and subsides slowly. Most opioid

---

TABLE 11-13
DSM-IV-TR *Criteria for Opioid Intoxication*

A. Recent use of an opioid.

B. Clinically significant maladaptive behavioral or psychological changes (e.g., initial euphoria followed by apathy, dysphoria, psychomotor agitation or retardation, impaired judgment, or impaired social or occupational functioning) that developed during, or shortly after, opioid use.

C. Pupillary constriction (or pupillary dilation due to anoxia from severe overdose) and one (or more) of the following signs, developing during, or shortly after, opioid use:

(1) drowsiness or coma

(2) slurred speech

(3) impairment in attention or memory

D. The symptoms are not due to a general medical condition and are not better accounted for by another mental disorder.

Specify if:

With Perceptual Disturbances

Note. From *DSM-IV-TR,* p. 272.

TABLE 11-14
DSM-IV-TR *Criteria for Opioid Withdrawal*

A. Either of the following:

   (1) cessation of (or reduction in) opioid use that has been heavy and prolonged (several weeks or longer)

   (2) administration of an opioid antagonist after a period of opioid use

B. Three (or more) of the following, developing within minutes to several days after Criterion A:

   (1) dysphoric mood

   (2) nausea or vomiting

   (3) muscle aches

   (4) lacrimation or rhinorrhea

   (5) pupillary dilation, piloerection, or sweating

   (6) diarrhea

   (7) yawning

   (8) fever

   (9) insomnia

C. The symptoms in Criterion B cause clinically significant distress or impairment in social, occupational, or other important areas of functioning.

D. The symptoms are not due to a general medical condition and are not better accounted for by another mental disorder.

Note. From *DSM-IV-TR,* p. 273.

withdrawal symptoms disappear within 7–10 days, although some craving, restlessness, weakness, and fitful sleep may persist. Serious medical consequences of withdrawal are rare. Insomnia and dysphoria usually occur throughout the withdrawal. Lacrimation, rhinorrhea, and sweating are early signs. Later, goosesflesh (piloerection, hence "cold turkey"), muscle twitches (hence "kick the habit"), and lack of appetite are experienced. Finally, muscle aches, severe nausea, vomiting, and diarrhea can develop. Opioid withdrawal is usually not dangerous unless dehydration from vomiting and diarrhea becomes severe. As can be seen in Table 11-15, the speed of the withdrawal syndrome depends on which opioid is being used.

Clinical Course

Although infrequently seen by professionals, many "chippers" use heroin in a controlled fashion. Otherwise, about half of all opioid abusers become opioid

TABLE 11-15

Opioid Onset and Withdrawal

DRUG	MG DOSE EQUIV TO 10 MG MORPHINE (IM/Oral)	ONSET/PEAK (minutes)	HALF-LIFE (hours)	WITHDRAWAL ONSET/DURATION (days)
Codeine	130/200	10-30/30-90	3	1-5
Fentanyl	0.1/NA	7-15/30-120	0.5-2	1-5
Heroin	5/30-60	2-15/10-90	2	1-5
Hydrocodone	20/25-30	10-30/30-60	4	1-5
Meperidine	75/100	15/60-90	3-5	1-5
Methadone	10/20	10-60/60-450	24	2-30
Morphine	10-30/60	10-20/20-90	2	1-5
Oxycodone	60-80/150-250	15/80	3	1-5

dependent. Whether this opioid dependency becomes chronic depends on the setting. For example, statistics on relapse and survival rates of heroin addicts were studied at the Washington University in St. Louis on two cohorts of individuals from 1972 through 1996. The first cohort were civilians; the second were individuals who had become addicted to heroin while serving in the military in the Vietnam War. This war, more than any other except possibly Afghanistan, was characterized by easy availability of heroin.

While 20% of veterans returned from Vietnam with heroin dependence, within a year only 0.7% continued to use and these were most likely veterans who had abused drugs prior to Vietnam (Price et al., 2001). This compares with a relapse rate of nearly 98% in non-veteran heroin addicts (Vaillant, 1966). The differences were attributed partly to baseline psychological stability of the veterans, but more so to the change in setting. One principle of addiction treatment is that the recovering addict must change "people, places, and things" that were associated with his or her active addiction. One non-Vietnam patient completing addiction treatment returned to opioid use within one year of discharge. Danny returned to his old New York neighborhood after 6 months of abstinence. As soon as he passed a street corner where he once had shot heroin, he immediately developed goose bumps, diarrhea, and hot flashes. As with Danny, such *conditioned withdrawal symptoms* often trigger a relapse. A month later, when Danny was asked why he used heroin, he explained, "If I had to be castrated to keep getting heroin, have me castrated."

The annual death rate of heroin addicts under age 30 is 1.6%; for those over age 30, 3%. Addicts usually die from accidental or intentional overdoses, allergic and acute toxic reactions (including pulmonary edema), infections and foreign material from shared unclean needles (hepatitis; AIDS; abscesses in liver, lung, and brain; tetanus; septic pulmonary emboli), a lowered immunological resistance, and from murder. Many addicts, if asked if they "share" needles, will say no, but if asked, "Do you ever *use* other people's needles?", will say yes.

Epidemiology

Although accurate epidemiological data on opioid misuse are especially elusive, household surveys during the 1970s revealed that under 1% of adults over age 25 had used an opioid at least once for nonmedical reasons. It is now much higher with extensive abuse of prescription pain medications. Among high school seniors in 2007, the lifetime prevalence of heroin is 1.5% and other opioids over 13% (Johnston, 2007).

The "demographic" heroin addict is male (four males to one female), from the inner cities of both coasts, nonwhite, and with a teenage history of truancy, poor school performance, and delinquency. Immediate availability of opioids greatly increases the number of *new* cases of heroin misuse, whereas *chronic* misuse depends less on neighborhood access. All the sorrows of social blight and community disorganization—poor housing, lack of sanitation, malnutrition, unemployment, low educational levels, lack of family cohesiveness, and low cultural morale—correlate with opioid misuse. However, over the past several years there has been rapid growth of a population of nonheroin opioid abusers. These people use prescription opioids obtained from diversion or theft. The incidence has been high in poor rural areas, especially of oxycontin, a slow release form of oxycodone that is extremely potent (and often lethal) when crushed and then snorted or injected.

In addition to personality disorders (particularly antisocial), depression and anxiety disorders commonly accompany opioid dependence. Many opioid addicts are polydrug abusers, especially with "downers" such as alcohol and hypnoanxiolytics. Polydrug abuse is a bad prognostic indicator for heroin addicts.

Treatment and Management

No single program works for a majority of opiate abusers, and considerable controversy remains over the preferred approach. In general, there are two schools of thought: The "soft" pro-methadone school and the "tough" antimethadone school. Methadone can be used for withdrawal and later for maintenance.

Methadone is an opioid with a long (12-hour) half-life that exerts pleasant effects when ingested. Because methadone is cross-tolerant with other opioids, once signs of opioid withdrawal begin, clinicians can initiate *methadone substitution* by giving patients roughly 10 mg three times daily, and then withdrawing them by gradually diminishing the dose by no more than 20% each day. However, federal law prohibits titrating outpatients (except in methadone clinics) with tapering doses of *any* opioid, or of detoxing an addict in an inpatient setting using an opioid for more than 72 hours. An exception is made for doctors who have been trained to use *buprenorphine* (a partial opioid antagonist) for maintenance or withdrawal of opioid addicts.

In addition, the alpha-2 adrenergic agonist clonidine has also been used for detoxification. Both drugs appear to be equally efficacious, if the level of tolerance is not greater than the equivalent of 30 mg of methadone per day. At higher levels methadone appears to more effectively suppress the abstinence syndrome. For those patients who have achieved considerable rehabilitation with methadone maintenance treatment, detoxification on an outpatient basis over a period of 2–6 months is reasonably effective. In any given year, less than 10% of chronic opioid abusers participate in community-based treatment programs. Giving up opioid use is a very slow process, and most users who have not achieved abstinence by their late 30s probably never will (Hser et al., 1993).

During opiate withdrawal, patients should be encouraged to participate in therapy. Small doses of a benzodiazepine may be given temporarily for insomnia. If patients convulse, they are probably also withdrawing from alcohol or hypnoanxiolytics and should be started on benzodiazepine withdrawal.

The loudest argument against methadone substitution is that using it makes withdrawal too easy and therefore fails to "teach the patient a lesson." No scientific evidence indicates that having this "lesson" prevents relapse. As one patient stated, "I've learned to never let myself run out of heroin again."

The rationale for *methadone maintenance* (MM), which begins following opiate withdrawal, is that ingested methadone usually blocks the euphoria of injected opiates. A high enough dose of heroin can override methadone blockade and, therefore, to achieve the objective, high doses of methadone may be required. Because methadone is taken orally and daily, it diminishes addicts' daily search for heroin and their commission of crimes to pay for it; the users become better workers and family members. Without needles, there are far fewer medical complications and deaths.

Although studies repeatedly support these findings and show that MM produces the best overall results, critics charge that one narcotic is merely being re-

TABLE 11-16
Treatment of Addictions in Relation to Stages of Change Model

STAGE OF ADDICTION	CHARACTERISTICS	TREATMENT GOAL	INTERVENTION	PHARMACOTHERAPY
Precontemplation Pretreatment	• Denial of problem/diagnosis • Disinterest in behavioral change	• Make accurate diagnosis • Engage the patient	• Pretreatment education (premotivational engagement groups)	**Acute treatment and stabilization** Detoxification • Alcohol (clonazepam) • Benzodiazepines (valproate) • Stimulants • Opioids (clonidine) • Nicotine (buproprion)
Contemplation Transition	• Considering change • Recognition of problem	• Interrupt denial and resistance	• Motivational counseling	
Determination Stabilization, preparation, decision-making	• Decision to change behavior	• Reduce or discontinue drug use	• Symptom management • Encouragement/advice • Structured living	**Maintenance and rehabilitation** • Aversive therapy (disulfiram) • Reduce craving (naltrexone, acamprosate) • Block reinforcing effects of opiates (naltrexone) • Treat underlying or drug-induced psychopathology (various psychotropics) • Opioid maintenance (methadone, LAAM, buprenorphine)
Action Early recovery	• Positive change in drug use	• Identify irrational thoughts, resulting negative emotions, and self-destructive behaviors	• Recovery groups (e.g., AA/NA, Double Trouble, Steps 1–3) • Sponsor–support, structure, accountability • Cognitive–behavioral therapy • Support system (e.g., church groups, volunteer organizations)	
Maintenance Sustained recovery	• Greater than 1 year of no drug use	• Maintain ongoing support for sobriety • Identify and manage relapse warning signs • Maintain relationship and lifestyle changes	• Psychotherapy groups • Relapse prevention groups • AA/NA Steps 4–12	
Relapse	• Return to drug use	• Return to recovery as soon as possible		

TABLE 11-17
Detoxification Protocols for Various Addictions

ALCOHOL	BENZODIAZEPINES	COCAINE/STIMULANTS	OPIOIDS	NICOTINE
Clonazepam 0.5 mg po tid for 2 days, bid for 2 days, then DC (adjust according to severity of withdrawal symptoms, liver functions, repeat blood alcohol level)	Switch to equivalent dose of long-acting BZDP (e.g. clonazepam)	Support	Grade 1: Yawning, sweating, lacrimation, rhinorrhea	Assess for history of seizures, eating disorders, cardiac disease
	Slowly taper to the lowest tolerated dose	Rest	Grade 2: Mydriasis, muscle twitching, piloerection, anorexia	Begin bupropion 150 mg SR po q am for 7 days, then increase to bid (breakfast and supper)
Thiamine 100 mg po or IM for 30 days	Begin valproate 250 mg po bid and increase as tolerated to 1000 mg po qd	Food	Grade 3: Insomnia, increased pulse, increased respirations, hypertension, abdominal cramps, vomiting	Patient instructed to reduce smoking by one half each week for 2 weeks
Multivitamin/mineral qd for 90 days	Discontinue BZDP	Psychotherapy	Taper down opioid if possible	Begin nicotine patch when patient is down to < ½ pack per day
Insomnia:	Continue valproate for at least 30 days, then gradually DC	Pharmacological treatment for depression	Increase clonidine: Begin with 0.1 mg test dose then 0.1–0.2 mg po q 4–6 hours as tolerated	Patient has not had cigarette for 12 hours prior to first nicotine patch
Trazodone 100 mg i-iii po qhs prn sleep	**Maintenance Medications:**		Various prn medications:	Begin transdermal nicotine patch at 21 mg qd for 4 weeks, then 14 mg for 2 weeks, then DC (with significant cardiac disease reduce to 14 mg qd x 4 weeks, then 7 mg qd x 2 weeks)
Seizures:	Disulfiram 250–500 mg po qhs	Naltrexone 50 mg ½ tab po q am with meal for 7 days, then increase to 1 tab (50 mg) po q am with meal	• loperamide or kaolin/pectin	
Phenytoin 100 mg iii po qhs for 7 days, ii po qhs for 3 days, i po qhs for 3 days, DC	• Careful education and consent	• No opiates for 2 weeks	• trazodone or amitriptyline	
	• Significant other involved	Buprenorphine	• antihistamines (hydroxyzine or diphenhydramine)	
Psychosis/delirium:	• No alcohol within 7 days		• promethazine	
Olanzapine 10 mg po qhs	• Exam q 4 months with liver enzymes		• NSAIDs	

DC = discontinue; BZDP = benzodiazepine; NSAIDs = nonsteroid anti-inflammatory drugs.

placed for another, that many addicts sell methadone illicitly, that many studies favorable to MM included only patients with initially good prognoses, that some addicts get a high from shooting up on methadone, and that many patients on methadone can overcome the blockade by taking high doses of heroin. These objections are significant, yet studies have indicated that after 4 years of MM, a majority of ex-addicts live productively, with 94% no longer committing crimes to obtain "smack."

Whereas buprenorphine maintenance seems to be a better approach, MM continues to be a reasonable treatment for some opioid addicts. The FDA has set very stringent criteria for admission and continued treatment in these programs. Most programs include group and individual counseling as well as vocational rehabilitation and educational guidance.

With or without buprenorphine or MM maintenance, the usefulness of psychosocial treatments—including self-help groups, therapeutic communities, and drug treatment centers—remains unknown. More people quit restrictive "tough love" programs; less than 10% of addicts are suitable for these programs. Those who do best are highly motivated, have good ego strength, and are legally committed to the programs. The effectiveness of any therapy for opioid dependence varies largely in relation to the characteristics of various subgroups.

Sometimes *antagonist therapy* is used as an adjunct to opioid treatments. It is based on the idea that if a person continues to use opioids without pleasurable effects, the opioid craving will subside over time. The most commonly used opioid antagonist, naltrexone, has been most effective for recently detoxified methadone patients who have made substantial recovery, professional people, and addicts who are court-referred.

Tables 11.16 and 11.17 provide treatment and detoxification summaries for various addictions.

References

Allgulander, C., Borg, S., & Vikander, B. (1984). A 4–6 year follow-up of 50 patients with primary dependence on sedative and hypnotic drugs. *American Journal of Psychiatry, 141*, 1580–1582.

Ball, K.T., Walsh, K.M., & Rebec, C.-V. (2007). Reinstatement of MDMA (ecstasy) seeking by exposure to discrete drug-conditioned cues. *Pharmacol Biochem Behav, 87*(4), 420–425.

Barnes, D.M. (1988). New data intensify the agony over ecstasy. *Science, 239*, 864–866.

Beresford, T.P., Blow, F.C., Hill, E., Singer, K., & Lucey, M.R. (1990). Clinical practice: Comparison of CAGE questionnaire and computer-assisted laboratory profiles in screening for covert alcoholism. *Lancet, 336*, 482–485.

Biecheler, M.D., Peytavin, J.F., SAM Group, Facy, F., & Martineau, H. (2008). SAM survey on "drugs and fatal accidents": Search of substances consumed and comparison between drivers involved under the influence of alcohol or cannabis. *Traffic Inj Prev*, 9(1), 11–21.

Bohman, M., Cloninger, R., Sigvaardson, S., & von Knorring, A.L. (1987). The genetics of alcoholisms and related disorders *J. Psychiatr Res.*, 21(4): 447–452.

Brewer, C. (1992). Controlled trials of Antabuse in alcoholism: The importance of supervision and adequate dosage. *Acta Psychiatr Scand Suppl.*, 369, 51–58.

Chipana, C., Torres, I., Camarasa, J., Pubill, D., & Escubedoe, E. (2008). Memantine protects against amphetamine derivatives induced neurotoxic damage in rats. *Neuropharmacology*, 54(8), 1254–1263.

Ciraulo, D.A., Barnhill, J.G., Ciraulo, A.M., Greenblatt, D.J., & Shader, R.I. (1989). Parental alcoholism as a risk factor in benzodiazepine abuse: A pilot study. *American Journal of Psychiatry*, 146(10), 1333–1335.

Coles, R., Brenner, J.H., & Meagher, D. (1970). *Drugs and youth: Medical, psychiatric, and legal facts*. New York: Liveright.

Comsay, K.P., Compton, W., Stinson, F.S., & Grant, B.F. (2006). Lifetime co-morbidity of DSM-IV mood and anxiety disorders: Results from the National Epidemiologic Survey on Alcohol and Related Conditions. *Journal of Clinical Psychiatry*, 67(2), 247–257.

Covington, E.C. (1998). Anticonvulsants for neuropathic pain and detoxification. *Cleveland Clin J Med*, 65, Suppl 1, 5121–5129.

DiMartini, A., Day, N., Deco, M., Javid, L., Fitzgerald, M.G., Jain, A., et al. (2006). Alcohol consumption patterns and predictors of use following liver transplantation for alcoholic liver disease. *Liver Transpl*, 12(5), 813–820.

Ewing, J.A. (1984). Detecting alcoholism: The CAGE questionnaire. *Journal of the American Medical Association*, 252, 1905–1907.

Fawcett, J., Clark, D.C., Aagesen, C.A., Pisani, V.D., Tilkin, J.M., Sellers, D., et al. (1987). A double-blind, placebo-controlled trial of lithium carbonate therapy for alcoholism. *Archives of General Psychiatry*, 44, 248–256.

Gawin, F.H., Kleber, H.D., Byck, R., Rounsaville, B.J., Kosten, T.R., Jatlow, P.I., et al. (1989). Desipramine facilitation of initial cocaine abstinence. *Archives of General Psychiatry*, 46, 117–121.

Gold, M.S. (1984). *800-Cocaine*. New York: Bantam.

Goodwin, D.W. (1985). Alcoholism and genetics: The sins of the father. *Archives of General Psychiatry*, 42, 171–174.

Goodwin, D.W., & Guze, S.B. (1984). *Psychiatric diagnosis* (3rd ed.). New York: Oxford University Press.

Grinspoon, L., & Bakalar, J. (1985). What is MDMA? *Harvard Medical School Mental Health Letter*, 2(2), 8.

Higgens, S.T., Budney, A.J., Bickel, W.K., Hughes, J.R., Foerg, F., & Badger, G. (1993). Achieving cocaine abstinence with a behavioral approach. *American Journal of Psychiatry*, 150(5), 763–769.

Hser, Y.I., Anglin, M.D., & Powers, K. (1993). A 24-year follow-up of California narcotics addicts. *Archives of General Psychiatry*, 50, 577–584.

Hughes, J.R., Oliveto, A.H., Helzer, J.E., Higgens, S.T., & Bickel, W.K. (1992). Should caffeine abuse, dependence, or withdrawal be added to *DSM-IV* and ICD-10? *American Journal of Psychiatry, 149,* 33–40.

Jellinek, E.M. (1952). Phases of alcohol addiction. *Quarterly Journal on Alcohol, 13,* 673–684.

Johnston, L.D., O'Malley, P.M., Bachman, J.G. & Schulenberg, J.E. (2007). Overall, illicit drug use by American teens continues gradual decline in 2007. University of Michigan News Service: Ann Arbor, MI.

Kandel, D.B., & Raveis, V.H. (1989). Cessation of illicit drug use in young adulthood. *Archives of General Psychiatry, 46,* 109–116.

Kang, S.Y., Kleinman, P.H., Woody, G.E., Millman, R.B., Todd, T.C., Kemp, J., et al. (1991). Outcomes for cocaine abusers after once-a-week psychosocial therapy. *American Journal of Psychiatry, 148*(5), 630–635.

Karila, L., Weinstein, A., Benjaminn, A., Coscass, L.C., Noble, F., Lowenstein, W., et al. (2008). Current pharmacotherapies and immunotherapy in cocaine addiction. *Presse Med, 37*(4), 689–698.

Kushner, M.G., Sher, K.J., & Bertman, B.D. (1990). The relation between alcohol problems and the anxiety disorders. *American Journal of Psychiatry, 147*(6), 685–695.

LeFoll, B., & George, T.P. (2007). Treatment of tobacco dependence: Integrating recent progress into practice. *CMAJ, 177*(11), 1373–1380.

Levin, E.D., Westman, E.R., Stein, R.M., Carnahan, E., Sanchez, M., Herman, S., et al. (1994). Nicotine skin patch treatment increases abstinence, decreases withdrawal symptoms, and attenuates rewarding effects of smoking. *Journal of Clinical Psychopharmacology, 14,* 41–49.

Peroutka, S.J. (1987). Incidence of recreational use of 3,4-methylenedioxymethamphetamine (MDMA, "Ecstasy") on an undergraduate campus. *New England Journal of Medicine, 817,* 1542–1543.

Price, R.K., Risk, N.K., Murray, K.S., Virgo, K.S., & Spitznagel, E.L. (2001). Twenty-five year mortality of US servicemen deployed in Vietnam: Predictive utility of early drug use. *Drug Alcohol Depend, 64*(3), 309–318.

Prochaska, J.O., DiClemente, C.C., & Norcross, J.C.. (1992). In search of how people change: Applications to addictive behaviors. *American Psychologist, 47,* 1102–1114.

Rankin, J.G., Winkenson, P., & Santamaria, J.N. (1970). Factors influencing the prognosis of the alcoholic patient. *Australian Annals of Medicine, 19,* 232–239.

Rittenhouse, J.D. (1982). Drugs in the school: The shape of drug abuse among American youth in the seventies. In G.G. Nahas & H.C. Frick (Eds.), *Drug abuse in the modern world: A perspective for the eighties* (pp. 99–105). New York: Pergamon Press.

Salzman, C. (1985). Benzodiazepine dependence. *Harvard Medical School Mental Health Letter, 1*(10), 8.

Satel, S.L., & Edell, W.S. (1991). Cocaine-induced paranoia and psychosis proneness. *American Journal of Psychiatry, 148,* 1708–1711.

Selzer, M.L. (1969). Alcoholics at fault in fatal accidents and hospitalized alcoholics: A comparison. *Quarterly Journal of Studies on Alcohol, 30*(4), 883–887.

Sorensen, T.I.A., Bentsen, K.D., Eghoje, K., Orholm, M., Haybye, G., & Christoffersen, P. (1984). Prospective evaluation of alcohol abuse and alcoholic liver injury in men as predictors of development of cirrhosis. *Lancet*, 2(8397), 241–244.

Tennant, F.S., Jr. (1986). The clinical syndrome of marijuana dependence. *Psychiatric Annals*, 16(4), 225–234.

Treatment Improvement Protocols (TIPS). Printed copies of these useful publications and materials are available from SAMHSA's National Clearinghouse for Alcohol and Drug Information NCADI. Publications may be ordered online, http://ncadistore.samhsa.gov/catalog/or by phone, at (800) 729–6686.

Tsuang, J.W., Iruin, M.R., Smith, T.L., & Schuckit, M.A. (1994). Characteristics of men with alcoholic hallucinations. *Addiction*, 90(2), 289–290.

Vaillant, G.E. (1966). A 12-year follow-up of New York narcotic addicts. *Archives of General Psychiatry*, 15, 599.

Victor, M., & Hope, J.M. (1958). The phenomenon of auditory hallucinations in chronic alcoholism. *Journal of Nervous and Mental Disorders*, 126, 451.

12

Schizophrenia and Related Disorders

Of all the psychiatric disorders, schizophrenia arguably devastates as no other, for no other disorder causes more pervasive or profound an impact—socially, economically, and personally. Patients with schizophrenia occupy about one-quarter of all American hospital beds and, excluding geriatric patients with cognitive disorders, two-thirds of all psychiatric beds. On any given day, there are over 2 million patients with schizophrenia needing care in the United States, and over 2 million new cases arising each year worldwide. The overall U.S. 2002 cost of schizophrenia was estimated to be $62.7 billion: $7.0 billion for direct outpatient services, $5.0 billion for pharmaceuticals, $2.8 billion for hospitalization, $8.0 billion for long-term care, $7.6 billion for total direct non-health care costs, including living cost offsets, and $32.4 billion for total indirect costs.

Parents and siblings of individuals with schizophrenia may endure years of uncertainty, guilt, dashed hopes, rage (at, and from, the patient), financial burdens, self-doubt, and futility. Siblings may resent their ill brother or sister getting "all" the attention, may berate themselves for feeling resentful, and may worry they too will develop an uncontrollable psychotic illness.

Yet it is not difficult to imagine that nobody suffers more than the individual who has schizophrenia. When Bleuler (see Chapter 1) invented the term *schizophrenia*, he did not mean a "split personality" (i.e., multiple personality), but rather a *shattered* or fragmented personality. Whereas patients with other severe mental disorders may share certain symptoms of schizophrenia, the curse of the person with schizophrenia is to be plagued by so many of them. While reading the following typical case vignette, try to imagine being that person and having to negotiate your most challenging everyday activities.

SCHIZOPHRENIA

David Sebastian, a 24-year-old single, Roman Catholic, ex-divinity student, was hospitalized for "episodes of inappropriate behavior and being out of touch with reality." For 16 hours nonstop, his inappropriate behavior consisted of masturbatory movements accompanied by groans, prayers, flailing limbs, and head-banging. During these episodes, he was totally self-absorbed: If asked questions, he wouldn't respond; all attempts to restrain him (for his own physical safety) were fiercely resisted. Eventually, he slept.

On awakening, he stared and smiled at a nurse, who described him as "Rasputin imitating the Mona Lisa." He accused the pope of "fornicating nuns," "spreading diarrhea and gonorrhea," and "plotting to assassinate me [David]." He was convinced that St. Christopher, the Roman Catholic patron saint of travel, was removed from the Catholic Chruch calendar because he [David] was having sexual thoughts while traveling. His thoughts seemed disorganized as he jumped incoherently from topic to topic. When asked if he feared anything, he replied with a flat affect: "Nothing, but the pope wants slivers up his ass or my ass or he's an ass; you know, this is not me talking but a taped recording of how you are today that couldn't communicate at any level as a dialectical incongruence of spiritual sexuality."

About a year ago, David began to exhibit changes in his behavior. He had previously been an outstanding biology student, a jogger, a bit of a loner prone to lengthy philosophical and religious discourses, and as his neighbors would remark, "such a sweet boy to live with his parents." At age 23, however, David's grades began to slip and he became more reclusive. Seven or so months later, and several weeks before his sister's wedding, he spent days and nights making his sister's wedding gift: a stained-glass penis. Two days before the wedding, his father accidentally knocked the gift off a table, and as it smashed into a million pieces, David did too. For the next month he attacked his family for destroying him, turning him into a robot, and sapping his vital fluids.

God's voice accused him of being too preoccupied with sex and proclaimed that becoming a priest was his only salvation. This instruction gave renewed purpose to his life while permitting a rapprochement with his family. He enrolled in divinity school, but a month later he could no longer concentrate. New and unfamiliar voices began discussing his plight, with one saying that "David's prick doesn't work," and the other saying, "If you were a *real* man, you'd go out and use your prick." He met a co-ed, went to her apartment, they went to bed, but when David was about to enter her, he began praying out loud and banging his head.

Horrified, she fled from the room, called the police, and David was taken to a hospital for evaluation.

Repeated neurological exams and tests revealed no physical disorder. He was placed on antipsychotic medication and over the next 10 days, his episodes (catatonic excitement alternating with negativism), delusions, hallucinations, incoherence, paranoia, and self-referential ideas gradually disappeared. Three days after admission he joined group therapy, but within minutes he pointed to the nine people in the room and exclaimed, "Eighteen eyes haunting my head, changing its size, televising my mind, eating it, bleeding it, feeding it. You gyrating Judases, how dare. . . . " Suddenly silent, he left the room. Days later he said he had felt besieged by the other members and that he left the room to escape this bombardment and to stop "embarrassing myself further." Once his psychotic symptoms abated, David actively participated in group and supportive individual psychotherapy. In meetings with the entire family, his parents vented their frustration, were told "the facts" about catatonic schizophrenia (David's diagnosis), and discussed how they could all live more peaceably together. After 3 weeks of inpatient care, he was discharged on medication and was to receive weekly psychotherapy.

For 3 months David worked at his father's grocery store, visited daily with a neighborhood priest, lived at home, read theology, painted a little, and saw friends. Then, when his father suggested that maybe he should live away from home, David stormed out of the house, wandered the streets, and stopped his medication because "it was digesting my sex organ." Within weeks he looked like a rag picker. He kept to himself. Voices (hallucinations) were mocking his "scrawny figure and sexual inadequacies" and insisted he "go out with prostitutes." With considerable guilt he succumbed, but upon entering the prostitute's room he quickly extricated himself, praying loudly and striking himself in the head. The prostitute called the police, and David's second hospital admission ensued. Later he told a therapist that he was in a "no-win" situation: If he did have intercourse, he was committing a sin; if he didn't, his voices were right and he wasn't a man.

David passed through the proverbial "revolving door" for three more hospitalizations; each occurred after a fight at home or a sexual confrontation. When his parents visited, at first he'd accuse them of "warping" his penis; these meetings, however, would eventually calm him down. Whenever the staff tried to separate David from his parents, he would vegetate in a corner, stop talking, and starve himself; one time, he had to be physically restrained from jumping out the window. After 6 tumultuous months, David returned home: He worked regularly in a bookstore, remained on moderate doses of antipsychotic drugs, and participated in weekly group therapy. He began a theology class, where he befriended a shy young woman who felt nobody would ever like her. David did. Three years later they are still seeing each other ("We'll marry when *he* can afford me!" she laughs). He works at the bookstore and lives at home. He remains on medication ("I go bonkers without it"), and although he stopped the group ("I outgrew it"), he continues to receive individual psychotherapy ("so my crazy ideas don't overwhelm me").

Students of psychopathology will appreciate the writings of Emil Kraepelin, which include rich and comprehensive descriptions of schizophrenia in its many forms, depressive disorders, and manic-depressive disorders in vivid clinical detail from an era decades before modern mood stabilizers, antidepressants, and antipsychotics were available.

Clinical Presentation

In *DSM-IV-TR* the essential features of schizophrenia are (1) a history of acute psychosis with delusions, hallucinations, disorganized speech, catatonia, grossly disorganized behavior, or flat affect; (2) chronic deterioration of functioning; (3) duration that exceeds 6 months, and (4) the absence of a concurrent mood disorder, substance abuse, or a general medical condition that would explain the clinical presentation.

The prognosis for a person who meets *DSM-IV-TR* criteria for schizophrenia generally is such that he or she will have great difficulty achieving full developmental potential. The usual course of the illness is chronic and episodically downhill. However, with timely and adequate treatment and support, this person may nevertheless become moderately independent and productive, and in some instances achieve extraordinary successes in their lives. Nobel laureate John Nash (economics) is an example of one who has succeeded in spite of schizophrenia. Table 12-1 lists *DSM-IV-TR* criteria for schizophrenia.

Criterion A indicates that two symptoms of schizophrenia, one of which must be an active or "positive symptom" (numbers 1–4), must be present for a significant portion of time during a 1-month period. Commonly observed

---

TABLE 12-1

DSM-IV-TR *Criteria for Schizophrenia*

A. *Characteristic symptoms.* Two (or more) of the following, each present for a significant portion of time during a 1-month period (or less if successfully treated):

(1) delusions

(2) hallucinations

(3) disorganized speech (e.g., frequent derailment or incoherence)

(*continued*)

TABLE 12-1
Continued

(4) grossly disorganized or catatonic behavior

(5) negative symptoms, i.e., affective flattening, alogia, or avolition

Note: Only one Criterion A symptom is required if delusions are bizarre or hallucinations consist of a voice keeping up a running commentary on the person's behavior or thoughts, or two or more voices conversing with each other.*

B. *Social/occupational dysfunction:* For a significant portion of the time since the onset of the disturbance, one or more major areas of functioning such as work, interpersonal relations, or self-care are markedly below the level achieved prior to the onset (or when the onset is in childhood or adolescence, failure to achieve expected level of interpersonal, academic, or occupational achievement).

C. *Duration:* Continuous signs of the disturbance persist for at least 6 months. This 6-month period must include at least 1 continuous month of symptoms (or shorter in duration if successfully treated in that time period) that met Criterion A (i.e., active-phase symptoms) and may include periods of prodromal or residual symptoms. During these prodromal or residual periods, the signs of the disturbance may be manifested by only negative symptoms or two or more symptoms listed in Criterion A present in an attenuated form (e.g., odd beliefs, unusual perceptual experiences).

D. *Schizoaffective and Mood Disorder exclusion:* Schizoaffective Disorder and Mood Disorder With Psychotic Features have been ruled out because either (1) no Major Depressive, Manic, or Mixed State Episodes have occurred concurrently with the active-phase symptoms; or (2) if mood episodes have occurred during active-phase symptoms, their total duration has been brief relative to the duration of the active and residual periods.**

E. *Substance/general medical condition exclusion:* The disturbance is not due to the direct physiological effects of a substance (e.g., a drug of abuse, a medication) or a general medical condition.

F. *Relationship to a Pervasive Developmental Disorder:* If there is a history of Autistic Disorder or another Pervasive Developmental Disorder, the additional diagnosis of Schizophrenia is made only if prominent delusions or hallucinations are also present for at least a month (or less if successfully treated).

Note. From *DSM-IV-TR,* p. 312.

*The added weight given to these symptoms is due to the widely accepted notion that they are indicative of the most serious and most reproducible of presentations of schizophrenia(Schneiderian "first-rank" symptoms, named after psychiatrist Kurt Schneider). In fact, they are seen not only in schizophrenia but also in bipolar disorder and other psychotic disorders, so be careful not to make your diagnosis based on these Criterion A components alone).

**Since mood disorders, substance-induced disorders, brain-injured states, dementias, and delirium states are so often accompanied by severe hallucinations, delusions, and thought disorder, you must be very careful to assess mood and general medical signs and symptoms and their detailed time courses in your History of Present Illness). Remember "All that hallucinates is not schizophrenia."

acute symptoms are delusions of persecution, delusions of control (bodily control or thought control), delusional perceptions, and particular forms of auditory hallucinations (especially voices commenting about the patient's actions or arguing back and forth). Less frequent, but no less important to note, are incoherence of speech (and thoughts), disturbed (or incongruent) affect, and catatonia (with decreased motor activity or excited motor activity).

Schizophrenic *delusions* are often bizarre and mood-incongruent. One can readily empathize with the delusions of the person with depression, but not those of the person with schizophrenia. His or hers are weird, from a different world or dimension. They may be of Schneiderian first-rank form (see Chapter 2 and glossary), such as delusions of bodily control in which the person with schizophrenia announces, "Martians have taken over my body," or thought control delusions (thought insertion, thought withdrawal, and thought broadcasting). In thought insertion, one's thoughts are not his own but have been somehow put there; in thought withdrawal one's thoughts have somehow been removed; in thought broadcasting one's thoughts have somehow been made known to all. Persecutory delusions are also common, but unlike when they appear in organic or mood disorders, in schizophrenia the source of the menace is often an ill-defined and remote source—a vague "they."

Hallucinations are reported by roughly 75% of newly admitted patients with schizophrenia; they are usually in one sensory modality, with about 90% being auditory but cases with all five are not uncommon. Fifteen percent of hallucinations are of the Schneiderian first-rank type (Ludwig, 1985) namely, in the third person, conversing or arguing about the patient, or commenting on his or her actions, or hearing his or her thoughts out loud. Voices may whisper or shout, comment on the patient's actions, or demand morally offensive acts ("command hallucinations"). The voices may be from known people (e.g., a dead grandmother) or strangers; they may be verbose or just one or two words repeated constantly. Because some people refer to their own thoughts as "voices," be sure to ask, "Do the voices come from inside or outside your head?" and "Is it your own voice or someone else's?" Visual hallucinations are often bizarre, frightening, and/or threatening (snakes crawling out of skulls, blood dripping from dead relatives) and when present usually occur in conjunction with the auditory hallucinations. Olfactory hallucinations are rare and should prompt an investigation into a seizure disorder; frequently cited are disgusting smells from the patient's body, smoke from burning substances, and toxic drugs or chemicals. Tactile (haptic) hallucinations are not as uncommon; the patient may report, for example, electric sensations along the spine, a needle puncturing the ear drum, or bones being broken; they may be in conjunction with delusions that so and so is beating me, hitting me, stabbing me, or causing the pain. Delusional perceptions were also among Kurt Schneider's first rank phenomena. These occur when a patient falsely attributes a bizarre meaning to a common perception, such as hearing a bird chirping and suddenly believing the patient will now be the savior of the world.

> Initially, many of those with schizophrenia present with an unshakable belief in their delusions and hallucinations. After months of consternation, patients may suddenly come up with another delusion that "explains" everything to their way of understanding; this "insight" may have enormous personal meaning to patients, while it mystifies everyone else. In normal recovery occurring over several weeks, patients typically gain increasing distance from their psychosis. They will go from assertions that "The telephone company is poisoning my food," to *"It seems like* the telephone company is poisoning my food." As the psychosis resolves further, the statement may become, "I'm not so sure about that telephone-company stuff." And later, "Every so often I think the phone company is poisoning my food. Isn't that crazy!" This process may be referred to as "softening" of the delusions. Frequently, however, delusions only partially soften, such as "I've learned not to pay attention to those ideas about the telephone company. They just get me in trouble."

Speech abnormalities in schizophrenia are caused by defects in cognitive processes and are the best evidence of a *thought disorder*. *Disorganized speech* is the third possible symptom of group A criteria and manifests as incoherence, frequent derailment, loose associations, tangentiality, circumstantiality, and/or illogical thinking. Poverty of content, perplexity, or severe thought blocking may occur, but more often, patients seem flooded with ideas and are unable to separate or filter the relevant from the immaterial. Such an example unexpectedly occurred when the author (Dr. Maxmen) received a telephone call from a total stranger speaking in a monotonously pert voice (the author's responses are in brackets):

> "Hello. I'm paranoid schizophrenic from Tampa. Are you the Dr. Maxim [*sic*] who wrote *The New Psychiatry?* [Yes.] Well, I'm 75 years old, but I grew up in the home of the very famous Dr. Zuckerman who graduated from P&S, your school. He was the Dr. Obsessive–Compulsive Neurosis psychiatrist, who was a brilliant cardiologist, and I was his only psychiatric patient, and he never said he was my father, but my mother was a borderline butch-lesbian personality, and Dr. Zuckerman was the first to take me to the Metropolitan Museum of Art because I have a tooth on the right side that's too big, just as in that Picasso painting, and I have a malformed skull, and a right leg also much longer than my left, and my daughter Infanta

Marguarita Pequina lives in Chicago, but Dr. Zuckerman didn't rescue me from a terrible marriage from 1948, to 1966 in which a man beat and raped me in the Jewish community—are you Jewish? [Yes] Dr. Zuckerman didn't end the marriage, but I got out of it in 1962 and have been on Mellaril every since. [What happens if you stop the Mellaril?] My brain waves flash too fast, just as you said in your book, which I'm taking to my clinical psychologist, where I go three times a week, although Dr. Zuckerman studied with A. A. Brill and Dr. Freud and belonged in psychoanalysis, but that couldn't help my skull, which was genetically deformed and made worse by my sadist husband in the Jewish community. Do you see patients?"

When incoherence is milder or first appears, many listeners will "read into" the patient's speech. Consider this example from a term paper written by an acutely disturbed college student with schizophrenia:

"we see the stately dimension of godly bliss that marlowe's *dOctOr fAUstUs* dies and lives. lucifer—oh lucy, luck, lackluster, lazy lucifer—devilishly adorns all sanctifarious, all beauty, all evil. Our world dissolves into *SACRED* nihilism."

Individually, the sentences might make sense, but collectively, they're nonsense. Punning without intentional humor, as around "lucifer," is typical of schizophrenic speech; so too is the neologism "sanctifarious." The strange punctuation would seem to have a private meaning, a hunch later confirmed by the patient, who explained, "It's all about Christ. Don't you see? Marlowe's first name is Christopher. Christ. Get it?"

With *catatonia*, patients have impaired interaction with, or responsiveness to, the environment. Characterized by disorganized motor and speech behavior, catatonia presents alternatively in a retarded or stuporous form or as an excited, activated form, like the case of David Sebastian, above. Signs include echolalia, echopraxia, posturing, catalepsy, mutism, negativism, akinesia, waxy flexibility, and automatic obedience.

Negative symptoms are the final criterion in group A; they are distinguished more by what is missing than what is present. A certain group of people with schizophrenia become *avolitional* and *unmotivated*. In the hospital, our nurses call it "bed flopping." The untrained mistake this behavior for laziness, but it's not. Many behaviors are diminished, including verbal behavior, resulting in fewer or no words spoken ("alogia" or "mutism"). These symptoms may be the consequence of giving all attention to internal stimuli, or they may be experienced as the complete absence of stimuli. One patient with schizophrenia described it as, "The light's not on and nobody's home."

Affects, flat and/or inappropriate, typically develop insidiously and persist chronically. At times they arise acutely. However, the pathological affects discussed below are not diagnostically specific: Depressed mood, drug-induced states, and akinesia (a frequent side effect of antipsychotic drugs) can appear as flat affect; brain-injury syndromes also may produce inappropriate affects. Flat affect is one of the common negative symptoms of schizophrenia. Inappropriate affect is a manifestation of disorganized behavior. A reasonable inference is that inappropriate affects emerge because patients are attending and responding to internal more than to external stimuli. They may cry when talking about the weather or laugh when hearing about a massive airplane crash. When a person with schizophrenia giggles for no obvious reason, the listener's skin crawls due to the bizarre nature of such behavior. The "humor" is not funny; it is, in fact, tragically pathetic.

Clinical Course

In most cases, schizophrenia first manifests during adolescence or early adulthood. Schizophrenia in childhood is extremely rare. It may present either abruptly or slowly. One-fourth of patients have an abrupt (acute) onset with active, positive, or *DSM-IV-TR* group A symptoms (numbers 1–4). The majority have an acute episode only after a slow, insidious onset of chronic or negative symptoms—social withdrawal, markedly impaired functioning, poor hygiene, flat or inappropriate affect, and the beginnings of positive symptoms—vague, rambling speech, odd or magical thinking, ideas of reference, overvalued ideas, persecutory thoughts, social isolation, and unusual perceptions such as illusions, derealization, or depersonalization. When these chronic symptoms occur before the initial full-blown flare-up, which we call an *acute phase*, they constitute schizophrenia's *prodromal phase*; when they occur following an acute phase, they constitute its *residual phase*, manifested by chronic signs and symptoms, including psychosocial and cognitive deficits. During these prodromal and residual phases, patients often seem unmotivated and burned out; in society at large, they are often labeled as "oddballs," "eccentrics," and "weirdos."

In order to support a diagnosis of schizophrenia the patient's social or occupational functioning must also be impaired (criterion B), and active and/or chronic symptoms must be present for at least 6 *months* (criterion C). Criterion C rules out shorter and potentially better prognosis psychoses, such as schizophreniform disorder and brief reactive psychotic disorders.

For most patients schizophrenia is a chronic illness characterized by exacerbations (relapses) and remissions. Women tend to have fewer rehospitalizations and shorter stays then men (Goldstein, 1988). Whereas the first several years of the disease are dominated by active symptoms and frequent hospitalizations, the condition eventually evolves into a nonpsychotic state with chronic symptoms of apathy, low energy levels, social withdrawal, and increased vulnerability to stress. At the worst end of the spectrum are patients who end up isolated completely from families, chronically symptomatic even on antipsychotic medications, socially unable to function or care for themselves, perhaps requiring a guardian or power of attorney to give substituted consent for important medical care and other life decisions. Most people with schizophrenia, however, function to some degree in the community. They can marry and work, usually at jobs involving moderate to low levels of stress. As with patients who have other chronic disorders, such as diabetes or congestive heart failure, these patients generally require many hospitalizations over the course of their lifetime. Figure 12-1 graphs the four patterns of clinical course in schizophrenia.

Roughly half of all patients with schizophrenia report depressive symptoms at some point during their illness. They'll complain of feeling depressed or of an affectless state in which they don't feel anything ("I'm empty, numb"). These depressive episodes, which occur most often after an acute psychotic episode ("postpsychotic depression"), are associated with an increased risk of suicide and relapse, poor social functioning, longer hospitalizations, and bleaker outcomes. This is a particularly dangerous period in the life of a person with schizophrenia, for she's apt to feel hopeless, abandon treatment, and

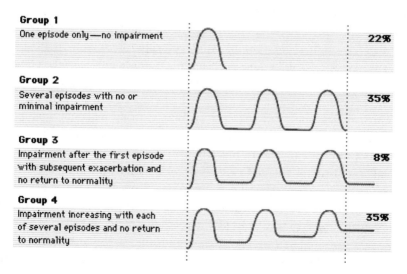

FIGURE 12-1
Patterns of Clinical Course in Schizophrenia

kill herself. The first indications of a pending psychotic relapse are often mood disorder symptoms such as decreased sleep, energy, and mood. Whether these depressive symptoms are inherent to schizophrenia or a reaction to it is unclear. In either case, criterion D points out that to qualify as schizophrenia, symptoms of depression (or mania) must not occur concurrently with the active-phase symptoms or, if they do, they are very brief.

How completely patients recover from an acute episode is not necessarily related to the severity of the psychosis. Instead, better prognoses are associated with (1) an abrupt acute onset, (2) a clear precipitant, (3) prominent confusion and disorganization that later completely resolve, (4) highly systematized and focused delusions whose symbolism is clear and often related to the precipitating event, (5) being married, (6) good premorbid functioning, (7) a family history of depression or mania, (8) no family history of schizophrenia, (9) a cohesive, supportive family, and (10) minimal negative symptoms.

Complications

As if the symptoms of schizophrenia weren't already bad enough, its timing in life couldn't be worse: It strikes at a stage of development when individuals are trying to establish themselves in the world as stable, self-sufficient, independent identities. Schizophrenia interferes with a person's ability to navigate the tasks of breaking away from home, stepping up performance and responsibility levels at school or in the workplace, planning and launching a career, and participating in ever more complex and demanding relationships. Patients with schizophrenia will have, on average, fewer children, will marry less often (the men far less than the women), will divorce and separate more frequently, and will have greater difficulties with intimacy and higher rates of celibacy.

The most life-threatening complication of schizophrenia is *suicide*. At least 1 of 10 will die by suicide; about 20% will attempt it, and some of these will attempt it many times. Fifty percent of those who do make an attempt will eventually succeed. In general, the most vulnerable time for completed suicide is not during a psychosis, but rather in its immediate aftermath. Thirty percent of outpatient suicides occur within 3 months of hospital discharge, and 50% occur within 6 months of discharge. Typically, suicides occur after a patient acquires a certain degree of insight into his or her illness, becomes discouraged, and may suddenly feel depressed and hopeless. In contrast to those with schizophrenia who do not commit suicide, the ones most likely to complete a suicide attempt tend to be those with better premorbid functioning and higher levels of education. These patients may have greater expectations of themselves, view schizophrenia as a greater obstacle to achieving their goals, and be less tolerant of a marginal existence. Patients on relatively low doses of medication, those who have abruptly stopped their medication, and those from relatively nonsupportive families are also at greater risk of completed suicide. Roughly 75% of these patients are male and usually unemployed, unmarried, isolated, and paranoid (Drake, Gates, Whitaker, & Cotton, 1985).

> Most people with schizophrenia do not commit violent crimes. When they are arrested, it's most often related to vagrancy, disturbing the peace, urinating in public, or other misdemeanors. However, individuals with schizophrenia, when compared to those with no psychiatric history, more often report using a weapon in a fight (4.2 times more). Unlike virtually any other group, women with schizophrenia commit violent crimes as often as the men. The meaning of these data in relation to the disease is complicated by the fact that one-third of people with schizophrenia also have alcohol or drug abuse or dependence—which greatly increases the risk of violence and homelessness. Despite sensational headlines, the insanity defense is used in only 1% of violent crimes that go to court, and most of these are not upheld. As *victims* of crime this population suffers a higher rate than the general populace.
>
> *Homelessness* is another frequent complication of schizophrenia. Compared to the general populace, schizophrenics have a 15–20 times higher risk of becoming "street people." However, they comprise a minority of the total number of homeless today. Socioeconomically there is a "downward drift" of those with chronic and persistent mental illness. Nationally, about 30% of the homeless have a severe psychiatric disturbance and at least 40% have substance abuse especially if mentally ill (Mowbray, 1985; Gonzalez & Rosenheck, 2002).

Subtypes

DSM-IV-TR lists five subtypes of schizophrenia, each based on the patient's most prominent presenting features. The *disorganized* type is characterized by marked incoherence along with a flat, silly, perplexed, or inappropriate affect. Formerly called "hebephrenic," these patients have an early and insidious onset, poor premorbid functioning, severe social impairment, and a chronic course.

The *catatonic* type primarily displays psychomotor disturbances. Patients with catatonia tend to have a more sudden onset, a better prognosis, a greater prevalence of mood disorders among first-degree relatives, and respond to electroconvulsive therapy—four features commonly associated with mood disorders. Pointing out that catatonic excitement and stupor may be due to severe psychomotor agitation and retardation, respectively, Ries (1985) and others claim that *catatonia occurs more often in bipolar disorders than in schizophre-nia*. Other studies have suggested that in some patients who present with cata-tonia, a mood disorder will be the most common diagnosis, and both *catatonia due to a general medical condition* (a *DSM-IV-TR* diagnosis that is in its own category because nobody could agree where else to put it) and *schizophrenia* will tie for second place.

The *paranoid* type of schizophrenia is characterized by prominent persecu-tory or grandiose delusions or hallucinations with similar content. These pa-tients are often unfocused, angry, argumentative, violent, and anxious. Stiff and mistrustful, they assume people can't be trusted and that anybody who likes them must be up to no good. Unsure of their own gender identity, they may project these fears onto others and be terrified of homosexuals. These patients live a "contained," highly structured existence. Relative to the other schizophrenic types, the paranoid type manifests later, interferes less with so-cial functioning, and has a stabler course. The lucky ones have highly encap-sulated delusions. For example, a patient might believe that everybody at a certain shopping center is a satanic murderer, but all other locations are safe. This person can live a relatively happy life simply by avoiding that shopping center.

Patients with schizophrenia who do not fit one of the above three types are diagnosed as *undifferentiated type* if they are actively psychotic, and as *re-sidual type* if, after an active phase, chronic symptoms predominate. The spe-cific *DSM-IV* criteria for the schizophrenic subtypes are listed in Table 12-2.

Epidemiology

The prevalence and incidence of schizophrenia tend to be the same regardless of political system, nationality, or historical time period. The lifetime preva-lence of schizophrenia varies between 0.8% and 1%. With an incidence of 0.3 to 0.6 per thousand, about 100,000 new cases of schizophrenia arise annually in the United States. For perspective, the prevalence of schizophrenia is about twice that of Alzheimer's disease and about six times that of insulin-dependent diabetes. The disorder afflicts men slightly more frequently than women (Hofner & Meiden, 1997; Lewine, Burbach, & Meltzer, 1984), European-Americans and African-Americans about the same, and urbanites more than rural folk. Less stressful rural settings may result in fewer and less severe epi-sodes, while affording a low-stress environment for the patient with chronic schizophrenia to function at maximum, but still likely diminished, potential. For example, a Wisconsin dairy farmer brought in one of his bachelor hired hands for evaluation because the man had stopped milking the cows. When

TABLE 12-2

DSM-IV-TR *Criteria for Schizophrenia Subtypes*

Paranoid Type

A type of Schizophrenia in which the following criteria are met:

A. Preoccupation with one or more delusions or frequent auditory hallucinations.

B. None of the following is prominent: disorganized speech, disorganized or catatonic behavior, flat or inappropriate affect.

Disorganized Type

A type of Schizophrenia in which the following criteria are met:

A. All of the following are prominent:

(1) disorganized speech

(2) disorganized behavior

(3) flat or inappropriate affect

B. The criteria are not met for Catatonic Type.

Catatonic Type

A type of Schizophrenia in which the clinical picture is dominated by at least two of the following:

(1) motoric immobility as evidenced by catalepsy (including waxy flexibility) or stupor

(2) excessive motor activity (that is apparently purposeless and not influenced by external stimuli)

(3) extreme negativism (an apparently motiveless resistance to all instructions or maintenance of a rigid posture against attempts to be moved) or mutism

(4) peculiarities of voluntary movement as evidenced by posturing (voluntary assumption of inappropriate or bizarre postures), stereotyped movements, prominent mannerisms, or prominent grimacing

(5) echolalia or echopraxia

Undifferentiated Type

A type of Schizophrenia in which symptoms meeting Criterion A are present, but the criteria are not met for the Paranoid, Disorganized, or Catatonic type.

Residual Type

A type of Schizophrenia in which the following criteria are met:

A. Absence of prominent delusions, hallucinations, disorganized speech, and grossly disorganized or catatonic behavior.

B. There is continuing evidence of the disturbance, as indicated by the presence of negative symptoms or two or more symptoms listed in Criterion A for Schizophrenia, present in an attenuated form (e.g., odd beliefs, unusual perceptual experiences).

Note. From *DSM-IV-TR,* pp. 314–317.

the farmer was asked if this man heard voices, the farmer said, "Yes, for 20 years, but we didn't mind until he stopped milking the cows."

Lower socioeconomic classes have a disproportionate number of people with schizophrenia. To explain why, two theories are usually advanced: "social causation" and "drift." The former asserts that poverty causes stress, which in turn causes schizophrenia. The drift theory holds that because schizophrenia devastates social and occupational functioning, people with schizophrenia migrate to society's lower echelons. Most evidence points to the drift theory. For example, studies in four nations revealed that, whereas the fathers of sons with schizophrenia were equally distributed among social classes, their sons had drifted downward (Goodwin & Guze, 1989; Hafner & Heiden, 1997).

Etiology and Pathogenesis

The causes of schizophrenia and the mechanisms of symptom production are not yet known, but evidence is strong for both genetic as well as environmental influences on its etiology and pathophysiology. Cases of schizophrenia involve abnormalities of the brain's anatomical structure and function, which in turn are associated with perceptual, cognitive, physiological, and behavioral abnormalities.

Biological Theories

Genetic. It is clear that schizophrenia is sometimes familial, conferring additional risk to relatives of those afflicted (see Table 12-3). First-degree relatives (parent or sibling) of individuals with schizophrenia have a 10% risk, whereas second-degree relatives (e.g., cousin, aunt, grandson) run a 3% chance of acquiring schizophrenia. Monozygotic twins have several times the concordance rate of dizygotic twins (Torrey, 1992). Adopted-away studies (Chapter 4) provide strong evidence for a genetic transmission of schizophrenia and "schizophrenia spectrum disorders" (SSD), variably inclusive of schizophrenia, schizotypal personality disorder, and sometimes borderline and paranoid personality disorders. These studies reveal that SSD is five to six times more common among biological, than among adoptive, parents of adults with schizophrenia. Furthermore, if an adoptive parent with schizophrenia rears an adoptee from biologically "normal" parents, the adoptee's risk of becoming schizophrenic is four times *less* than if the adoptee had a biological parent with schizophrenia and was reared by "normal" adoptive parents. The more severe the schizophrenia, the greater its likelihood of inheritability. Genetic studies have yielded many potential "candidate genes" for further study, in-

TABLE 12-3

Risk for Relatives of a Patient with Schizophrenia

PATIENT WITH SCHIZOPHRENIA	PERSON AT RISK	RISK (%)
General population	Everybody	0.8–1.0
Father	Each Child	10–18
Mother	Each Child	10–16
Both Parents	Each Child	25–46
Child	Each Parent	5
One sibling	Each Sibling	8–10
Second-degree relative	Another second-degree relative	2–3
Monozygotic twin	Other MZ twin	40–50
Dizygotic twin	Other DZ twin	12–15
Adoptive parents with schizophrenia	Adoptee with "normal" biological parents	4.8
Biological parents with schizophrenia	Adoptee reared by "normal" parents	19.7

cluding BDNF, COMT, uregulin (NRGI), Reelin, and DISC1 (OMIM, 2008; Ross et al., 2006). Still, about 7 of every 10 cases of schizophrenia arise spontaneously without a family history.

Biochemical. The longest-standing and most widely regarded theory, the *dopamine hypothesis*, states that the symptoms of schizophrenia arise from a relative excess of dopamine (DA) in the brain and an overstimulation of DA receptors. This theory does not necessarily contend that excessive DA is the "cause" of schizophrenia, but merely that it plays a role in producing the signs and symptoms of schizophrenia. Snyder (1981) demonstrated a positive correlation between how much an antipsychotic drug blocks DA receptors (in a receptor-binding assay) and how much it reduces schizophrenic symptoms. Amphetamines, which can produce a paranoid, psychotic state, stimulate the release of DA into synaptic clefts; they also inhibit the uptake of DA. L-dopa, a direct precursor of DA useful in the treatment of Parkinson's disease, can also trigger paranoid, psychotic symptoms. Both high levels of dopamine and its metabolite, HVA, as well as high levels of dopamine receptors have been found in subcortical regions of schizophrenic brains. However, the negative symptom cluster in schizophrenia may be associated with *low* dopamine activity in the prefrontal cortex (Davis et al., 1991). High activation of the dopamine system may be a nonspecific marker of psychosis. It also occurs in mania and psychotic depression.

Anatomic and physiological. The recent advances in biomedical technology (see Chapter 4) have uncovered changes in schizophrenia that were previously undetectable. For example, computed tomography (CT) scans reveal that a subgroup of patients with chronic schizophrenia, predominantly male, have enlarged lateral, and perhaps third, ventricles. These have been seen in patients undergoing their first episode of schizophrenia and are therefore unlikely to be a consequence of the illness or its treatment. What is clear is that cerebral atrophy produces these enlarged ventricles, a finding confirmed by magnetic resonance imaging (MRI). Positron emission tomography (PET) scan studies have indicated that the frontal lobes of patients with schizophrenia metabolize more slowly, and neuropsychological tests show that these individuals have impaired frontal-lobe performance. The frontal lobes are necessary for planning, organizing, and executing plans. Frontal-lobe dysfunction is thought to be responsible for the cognitive and psychosocial impairments associated with schizophrenia.

Psychosocial Theories

With an unusual consistency for scientific investigations of psychosocial influences, one finding stands out: *The amount of tension to which patients are exposed within their families is the most critical psychosocial variable affecting the course of schizophrenia.* American and British studies compared families with "high-expressed emotion" (HEE) to those with "low-expressed emotion" (LEE). The high emotion expressed is not positive; HEE families are more openly critical of the patient, display greater hostility and dissatisfaction, convey little warmth or encouragement, and form overprotective and symbiotic relationships. Typical comments from HEE relatives toward the patient are: "You do nothing but bitch"; "I wish you'd just get out of my hair!"; "I worry so much about you, I don't think you should go out tonight."

Nine months after their initial discharge, patients with schizophrenia living with HEE and LEE families relapsed at rates averaging 56% and 21%, respectively (Caton, 1984; Hogarty et al., 1974). Similar results occurred 2 years following discharge. Those in HEE families who took, or didn't take, their medication had relapse rates of 66% and 46%, respectively. Patients exposed to HEE families for more or less than 35 hours a week had relapse rates of 69% and 28%, respectively. In LEE families, relapse rates were uniformly low and unaffected by use of medication and duration of contact. Vaughn and Leff (1976) report that patients with the highest 9-month relapse rate (92%) had high exposure to HEE families and did not take their medications, whereas patients with the lowest relapse rate (12%) took their meds and lived with LEE families. Hogarty et al. (2004) successfully used cognitive restructuring to lower the impact of EE, which in turn correlated with clinical improvements.

Differential Diagnosis

Schizophrenia needs to be differentiated from other psychotic disorders such as schizophreniform disorder, schizoaffective disorder, bipolar disorder, delusional disorder, brief psychotic disorder, shared psychotic disorder (*folie à deux*), substance-induced psychotic disorder, and psychotic disorder due to a general medical condition such as a traumatic lesion, neoplasm, or epilepsy. Details on differential diagnosis are presented later in this chapter, when each disorder is examined individually. In general, patients with these potential imitators of schizophrenia do not display all the symptoms needed for a schizophrenia diagnosis or they have not had them long enough. The most important clue in distinguishing schizophrenia from a *mood disorder* or a *psychotic state* that is caused by substances or a medical condition is this: *Between psychotic episodes, people with schizophrenia most often do not completely resolve their symptoms or maintain completely normal behavior, whereas with these other conditions, patients usually do return to normal function with proper clinical management and treatment adherence.*

Patients appearing to have schizophrenia, *catatonic type,* are more likely to have a *mood disorder*, but may also have *catatonia due to a general medical condition*. Those with a mood disorder usually have normal baseline function, report previous episodes of depression or mania, and often have relatives with mood disorder, typically bipolar disorder. A sodium amytal interview or a brief trial of benzodiazepine can sometimes be of help to temporarily "unfreeze" a catatonic stupor and help clinicians elicit more information about the actual diagnosis of these patients. Profoundly elevated or depressed mood states are suggestive of mood disorder and may be accompanied by mood-congruent delusions without a formal thought disorder (e.g., disorganized speech, loose associations) and prominent psychomotor retardation or agitation. Patients with mania may temporarily have all the positive symptoms of schizophrenia, but also have very expansive moods. Remember well the clinical rule-of-thumb triad seen with mood disorders: prominent mood abnormality, altered sense of self and self worth, and altered vital sense (or sense of well-being). Disorientation and a worsening with amytal may be clues to a medically caused catatonia. Medical causes of catatonia to consider include neurological conditions (e.g., cerebrovascular disease, encephalitis) and metabolic conditions (e.g., hypercalcemia, hepatic encephalopathy, homocystinuria, diabetic ketoacidosis). A careful history, physical exam, and laboratory investigation are essential in assessing catatonia. Occasionally, neuroleptic medication can cause dystonias: acute spasms of particular muscle groups that may closely resemble the posturing of catatonia. This side effect is usually seen in proximity to antipsychotic medication dosing and administration schedules.

Anxiety and somatoform disorders may resemble schizophrenia intermittently, but not for long. Patients with obsessive–compulsive disorder or hypochondriasis may become preoccupied with their concerns to a near-delusional intensity. Yet, unlike patients with schizophrenia, the patients with obsessive–compulsive disorder know that their obsessions are "silly," and patients with hypochondriasis know, to some degree, that their fears are unfounded or excessive.

Schizotypal, schizoid, paranoid, and borderline personality disorders may intermittently present with psychotic symptoms and resemble the prodromal or acute phase of schizophrenia. But unlike schizophrenia, the unstable phase, perhaps including "mini"-psychotic symptoms, remits in hours or days and does not leave lasting changes of any profound nature. Severe *schizoid personality disorder* may produce a schizophrenic-like social withdrawal with odd affect and behavior; these patients, however, rarely become psychotic. When schizophrenia and a personality disorder coexist, they are coded on separate axes, on Axes I and II, respectively.

Management and Treatment

The goal of treatment for schizophrenia is usually not to *cure* but to improve *quality of life* by minimizing symptoms, preventing suicide, averting relapses, enhancing self-esteem, improving social and occupational functioning, and generally supporting the patients and their families and caregivers. These are similar to the goals of treating patients with heart disease, diabetes, arthritis, and other chronic nonpsychiatric ailments that affect the quality of everyday life.

Treatments vary in type and intensity depending on the stage of the disorder and the target symptoms under consideration. This section focuses primarily on *acute care*, which involves management of risks to the safety of the patient and others, stabilization of behaviors, and treatment of florid psychotic symptoms; *transition care*, which is focused on maintaining stability of the patient as he or she moves from one level of care to another; and *chronic care*, which is generally the posthospitalization, community-based outpatient treatment of relatively stable, albeit impaired, patients.

Biological Treatments

With each of these three stages of treatment, overwhelming evidence demonstrates that the vast majority of patients with schizophrenia benefit from antipsychotic medications. Traditional antipsychotics are most effective in eliminating the active positive symptoms, but they also diminish the negative symptoms. Newer antipsychotics, such as clozapine and risperidone, which block both dopamine and serotonin-2 receptors more effectively, treat negative symptoms and are also effective in about one-third of patients who exhibit resistance to traditional antipsychotics. When first prescribed, antipsychotics may take days or weeks to produce significant effects. *Some* neuroleptics also have a *sedative* effect, which manifests in 15–45 minutes following an oral dose, peaks around 2 hours, and subsides by 6 hours. Antipsychotic actions generally continue as long as patients are on the drug; sedative effects tend to diminish in 7–10 days as tolerance improves.

Acute care. Clinicians' first priority is to prevent patients from harming themselves or others. If this danger is imminent, observation, medication, and sometimes physical restraints are needed temporarily. Symptoms of aggression and agitation can be reduced most quickly by "rapid tranquilization," during which patients receive a small dose of an antipsychotic (e.g., 20 mg IM ziprasidone, 5 mg haloperidol, po or IM), every 30–90 minutes until symptoms subside. Caution must be observed in order to prevent or treat immediately any serious side effect such as dystonia, orthostatic hypotension, or neuroleptic malignant syndrome. As an initial safeguard, a reasonable target dose (such as 15 mg haloperidol) is established in advance. Benzodiazepines are often used to control aggression and agitation in patients who remain severely agitated or aggressive after receiving their target neuroleptic dose. To avert a hypotensive crisis or a fall, (1) blood pressure should be taken lying and standing before each dose, and (2) antipsychotics should be withheld if patients are ataxic, dizzy, or lightheaded on standing.

When immediate safety is not at issue, antipsychotic medication should not be given until diagnoses other than schizophrenia have been ruled out. Since all antipsychotic drugs have D-2 blockade in common as their primary mechanism of efficacy against hallucinations and delusions, the clinician's choice of antipsychotic agent and its dose will depend greatly on the side effect profile, the patient's history of treatment responses, and the clinician's experience with particular medications (see Chapter 6). In general, there is an inverse relation between parkinsonian side effects and anticholinergic (e.g., dry mouth) and sedative side effects. For example, the highly sedating thioridazine is among the most anticholinergic and sedating and yet the least parkinsonian of antipsychotics. Thus, if sedation is desired or if patients are at high risk for parkinsonian side effects, thioridazine could be used. On the other hand, the anticholinergic effect might be prohibitive in an elderly patient prone to delirium. Benzodiazepines also provide an alternative for sedating patients without anticholinergic side effects. Then when the psychotic symptoms that are driving the agitated and aggressive behaviors decrease, patients may no longer need sedation, and the benzodiazepines can be stopped while the less sedating antipsychotic is continued. Patients should receive only as much sedation as required to ensure their safety and to reduce their anguish. If patients are catatonic, a modest dose of a benzodiazepine can sometimes temporarily mobilize them enough to allow a better assessment of the underlying psychopathology—which may prove to be a mood disorder or some other disorder. Dosage is always tailored to the specific needs of an individual patient, taking into consideration age, hepatic and renal functions, medical comorbidities, allergies, history of treatment response, and concurrent medications, whether prescription or nonprescription.

Transition care. The general consensus in psychiatric practice is that patients should be discharged on the same regimen (i.e., dose and type of medication) on which they became stable when they were inpatients; prematurely decreasing medication opens up a grave risk of resurgence of acute-phase symptoms and behaviors and often leads to rehospitalization. After living in the relative security of a hospital, discharged patients may suddenly have to contend with all the environmental stressors that prompted their admission. To face these stressors, patients need a great deal of assistance, which means psychosocial support as well as medication. Since transition involves so many psychosocial changes, if medications are also changing, it is harder to pinpoint which changes account for any behavior problems or symptoms that might arise. Our patients often inquire about, or request, discontinuation of medications and do so for many understandable reasons, including weight gain, drowsiness, stigma of mental illness, they "feel fine," it is costly. Educating the patient and family members about early signs of relapse, advising them to develop plans for action should these signs appear, and encouraging the patient to attend outpatient visits on a regular basis are warranted and necessary in every case to ensure against relapse. Second-generation antipsychotics (SGAs) may help to reduce severe complications, such as tardive dyskinesia, while careful selection from among SGAs is necessary to avoid pathological weight gains.

At no time should caregivers or providers imply that taking medication is a crutch. That would be akin to telling a diabetic that using insulin is a crutch. In reviewing all well-controlled studies, Davis (1975) found that of 3,609 patients sampled over 4–6 months, 20% relapsed on drug and 53% relapsed on placebo. Davis determined that the probability of this difference being due to chance is quite low. Thus, every effort should be made to ensure that patients receive their medication, which includes educating patients and their families about the medication and ways to acquire the needed supply. There may be transportation issues, communication gaps, financial constraints, physical inabilities involved that were not foreseen or were not planned for, lack of oversight and supervision, and incompetent or impaired caregivers—all requiring psychosocial interventions.

When patients do not improve sufficiently on antipsychotic medication, the first consideration is whether the drug is being taken and properly absorbed. These questions can be answered by obtaining serum levels. If noncompliance (likely in two-thirds of patients with schizophrenia) is an issue, the physician may consider using injectable fluphenazine or haloperidol in the decanoate form (which persists for 2–4 weeks) as an alternative to oral doses, having parents or guardians monitor the daily/nightly intake of antipsychotic in liquid form, or having patients receive their once-a-day dose in front of a nurse or other responsible party. Of the SGAs, only risperidone is available in a long-acting (2 weeks) form (Consta®). Also, patients may not be improving because of misdiagnosis or because they have developed affective symptoms that might be better treated with antidepressants or lithium.

Chronic care. How long patients should remain on antipsychotic medications following *subsequent* hospitalizations depends on the duration and severity of the illness. Although the beneficial effects of antipsychotic drugs are greatest during the acute stage, they control symptoms for at least a year and decrease relapses for many years. Indefinite maintenance on antipsychotic medication is recommended for patients who have had multiple prior episodes or two episodes within 5 years. In patients for whom antipsychotic medications have been prescribed, monitoring for signs and symptoms of impending or actual relapse is recommended.

Unfortunately, this long-term use of antipsychotics creates one of the most difficult problems in psychopharmacology: *tardive dyskinesia* (TD). From 10–40% of patients who take antipsychotic medication for over 2 continuous years (though it can be as little as 6 months) develop involuntary, bizarre (choreoathetoid) movements of the mouth, limbs, and hips. Although 80–90% of cases are mild, severe impairment occurs in 3–5% of all patients. Most often TD appears as "tobacco-chewing," lip-smacking, and "fly-catching" movements of the mouth and tongue; less often, as hip jerks or slow, undulating motions of the hands or feet. When TD is present, these grotesque movements typically erupt within a few days of decreasing or stopping antipsychotics; they subside only when patients sleep or are put back on D2 blocking medication.

The precise causes and mechanisms of TD remain unknown. One prevalent theory, the dopamine supersensitivity hypothesis, maintains that when dopamine (DA) receptors are blocked for long periods of time, they develop what has been called "supersensitivity" to DA. Thus, when the antipsychotic medication is stopped or decreased, the now "supersensitive" receptors allow the uncontrolled jerking and writhing (choreoathetoid) movements of TD to occur. This hypothesis, however, does not explain why the receptors do not return to their normal functional level after the antipsychotic medications are stopped. There appears to be enduring pathological change of the synaptic function in the dopamine neuron system. This apparent change poses quite an intriguing problem for neuropathologists, who are also aware that pathology such as TD *was also observed in some patients with schizophrenia prior to the age of the so-called neuroleptic* (i.e., literally nerve paralyzing) drugs, which points to the possibility of additional causative factors or to the possibility that TD is another manifestation of the same disease process.

TD may be most successfully avoided by treating schizophrenia with clozapine. Since this is not always an option because of adverse reactions (may dangerously lower white blood cell count) or intolerance, the next best alternative appears to be another SGA medication. SGAs currently (2008) approved for use in the United States are aripiprazole, olanzapine, quetiapine, paliperidone, risperidone, and ziprasidone. These seem to have a much lower risk of TD and are better tolerated in general. Curiously the widespread use of these agents has not improved compliance (adherence), despite equal efficacy to traditional antipsychotics in treating positive symptoms (Lieberman et al., 2005).

In some cases TD can be reversed if it is detected early enough and is not too severe by removing gradually the offending medications (generally first-generation antipsychotic drugs). Worsening of the condition may also be averted by changing to clozapine, if possible. Although other drugs may occasionally counteract it, once TD occurs, there is usually *no* easy way to eliminate it. The risk and severity of TD may be reduced by maintaining patients on the lowest possible dose and by periodically testing if the drug might feasibly be discontinued. The only way to avoid TD is to avoid the use of, or minimize exposure to, first-generation antipsychotics. For unknown reasons, when TD appears, it reaches a plateau in most patients, beyond which there is no further worsening, and in some cases, there may be spontaneous improvement. Doctor and patient (or responsible substituted consent giver) must decide, as with any medication, if the side effects of treatment are worse than the disease.

Psychosocial Treatments

Acute care. When hospitalized, most actively psychotic patients with schizophrenia have a short attention span, are overwhelmed by stimuli, and cannot easily discern reality; they often feel lost, alone, and frightened. Therefore, contacts with these patients should be no longer than they can tolerate; in one day most acute patients will benefit more from several 5-minute contacts than

from one 40-minute contact. These frequent contacts should stress reality testing and reassurance, while avoiding psychologically sensitive material. Patients
with schizophrenia may not think they need help for their hallucinations or
delusions, but they may have problems upon which both they and staff can
agree. Treating poor sleep, "worrying" too much (paranoia), or disorganized
thinking can become the cornerstones of a treatment alliance. Arguing with
patients about their delusions not only won't work but may worsen their condition and the treatment alliance. Contacts should be performed by as few staff
as possible. As the patient's psychosis diminishes, the role of psychosocial treatments increases. At some point, individual supportive therapy should identify
the stressors (e.g., as high-expressed emotion) that led to hospitalization and
prepare patients to contend with similar stressors following discharge, for example, cognitive restructuring (Hogarty et al., 2004).

> Hospitalization is also a major crisis for the patient's family. Prior to hospitalization,
> most relatives deny or "explain away" the person's symptoms (e.g., "It's normal for
> teenagers to lock themselves in a room"; "Kids often fly off the handle"). When
> the patient is psychotic and finally admitted, the family is shell-shocked: Members
> might insist "nothing is wrong," telephone the ward 15 times a day, not leave the
> unit, etc. These are typical responses to an acute and severe stress (see Figure 4-5);
> they are not indicative of the "craziest family on earth." Only *after* the immediate
> crisis is it possible to assess the family's normal behavior.
>
> Because schizophrenia is a chronic disorder, the family's long-term involvement
> as an extension of the treatment team is essential. On admission, most families
> already feel guilty about "creating a schizophrenic"; this guilt is only compounded
> if therapists blame them, either directly or euphemistically (e.g., "The family has
> problems communicating"). Not only do attempts to rectify a family's "communi-
> cation problems" and "pathological relations" reinforce the family's guilt, but they
> don't work—at least not during short-term hospitalizations. Similarly, separating
> patients with schizophrenia from their families is usually not necessary or advisable.
>
> Near the outset of hospitalization, several members of the staff should begin
> forming a *collaborative* relationship with the family. Nurses should monitor visits
> to gather information. A new family should be introduced to relatives of other
> patients with schizophrenia so that the family members feel less alone, embar-
> rassed, and guilty. Since research demonstrates that most acutely psychotic patients
> with schizophrenia do as well, if not better, during 3 weeks, rather than 3 months,
> of hospitalization, discharge planning that *includes* the family should begin the day
> the patient is admitted. This is even more critical now in this era of "managed
> care." In many cases, even 3 weeks has become a luxury; 7 days has become a
> more typical length of stay. The goal is to begin treatment and stabilize patients

enough to allow treatment to continue in less restrictive settings such as (partial) hospital intensive outpatient, or outpatient care.

Transitional care. Chance of relapse and suicide is greatest within the first 6 months, and especially within the first 14 weeks, following discharge. In general, the patients who fare best during these 14 weeks are those who have the most stability in their lives. This transitional phase is *not* the time to introduce major alterations in the patient's living arrangements, social life, medications, therapists, and so on. Some changes may be necessary but should be kept to a minimum. Considerable research and experience show that discharge planning should focus on preventing the conditions most likely to produce relapse:

1. *The failure to take medication* is the most frequent cause of readmission— and a common prelude to suicide. Because two-thirds of outpatients with schizophrenia discontinue or take less than the prescribed dose, *all* patients and their families should be educated regarding the purpose and importance of medication (Lieberman et al., 2005).
2. *The failure to continue aftercare* stems less from a lack of resources than from patients' refusal to participate in available programs. Dropout rates from aftercare programs are as high as 75%. Effective discharge planning ensures that patients have visited the aftercare facility, know how to travel there, understand the nature and purpose of aftercare treatment, feel comfortable with the outpatient staff, and know the time of their first aftercare appointment.
3. *Inadequate life support*, especially in housing and income, but also in money-management skills, hygiene, and medical care, should be addressed in occupational therapy.
4. *Inadequate socialization and recreation* often prompt rehospitalization. If a bowler stops bowling, the bowling skills atrophy; so too with the leisure-time and social skills of the patient with schizophrenia. Recreational and group therapy should prevent further deterioration of these skills.
5. *The effects of HEE families* can be reduced by using a "psychoeducational approach," whose effectiveness has been repeatedly demonstrated (Anderson, Hogarty, & Reiss, 1980; Cozolino et al., 1988). This approach aims to reduce the guilt, overresponsibility, confusion, and helplessness of families, and although its implementation varies in different settings, it generally involves five steps: (1) The patient and family are given "the facts" about schizophrenia, including information about its symptoms, natural course, genetics, etc. (2) The family and patient are encouraged to express pent-up concerns about

the illness and each other, preferably with other families. (3) The family is taught about the psychonoxious effects of HEE environments. (4) Next, family members are trained to contain emotional outbursts, to avoid (or at least delay and mute) criticisms, to praise positive activities, to reduce unrealistic guilt and overresponsibility, and to be less judgmental. (5) If the family is, for whatever reason, an immutably HEE family, than the patient's amount of contact with the family should be reduced. Community-based self-help groups for the families of schizophrenics often provide a kind of psychoeducational approach over the long haul. (6) The patient can benefit from cognitive enhancement therapy to learn better stress management.

The greatest danger during the transitional period is suicide, which mostly occurs when patients (1) have a postpsychotic depression, (2) are discouraged about their treatment, (3) believe their future is hopeless, (4) misconstrue a drug-induced akinesia for depression and futility, or (5) stop taking medication. Therapists should be alert to these specific warning signs, tell family members also to be aware of them, and meet frequently with patients to check on them.

Inpatient treatment plans should include the following goals for discharge planning to ensure continued stabilization and momentum toward recovery:

1. Arrangements made for psychiatrist follow-up appointment(s); or,

2. Alternative to outpatient care for the more vulnerable or symptomatic hospitalized patients include day hospital or intensive outpatient services to more gradually transition to the level of outpatient care; or, referring to physicians who can provide the patient with weekly or twice-weekly appointments until more stability is observed;

3. Prescription amounts necessary to assure continuity until the next opportunity for the physician to identify tolerability, adherence, side effects, and, of course, efficacy and continued indications for prescribing, and renew or make necessary adjustments to the regimen;

4. Involve family and orchestrate ancillary support network to enable a supportive, LEE recovery-promoting environment that minimizes stressors and other contributors to relapse as presented above.

Chronic care. Contrary to many long-held assumptions, more therapy is not always better therapy. Hogarty, Goldberg, Schooler, and Ulrich (1974) found that supportive psychotherapy is more beneficial with patients who take medication, more likely to hasten relapse in nonmedicated patients, and more effective the longer the patients have not been actively psychotic. However, even at the best facilities, long-term intensive psychotherapy is ineffective in treating schizophrenia. A 15-year follow-up at Chestnut Lodge showed that only 14% of these patients were functioning "good" or better (McGlashan, 1984). More recently, it is being discovered that certain programmatic applications of cognitive therapy, called *cognitive remediation*, can be significantly beneficial to patients with schizophrenia (Lindenmeyer et al., 2008; Hogarty et al., 2004). Chronically hospitalized patients function better in the community when they are *gradually* released from the hospital, often to day hospital care, halfway houses, or to group settings with patients they knew in the hospital. Assertive community treatment (ACT) teams provide more intensive outpatient services, such as weekly home visits with medication delivery. Clubhouses and compensated work–therapy programs offer opportunities for social integration and gainful activity that promote self-worth and full recovery.

Despite the severity and chronicity of schizophrenia, modern treatments can enable patients to live more satisfying lives. We know many patients who, after 5–15 years of institutionalization, went on to become independent and productive with persistent, appropriate forms of treatment. These cases are not rare; patients and families should be made aware of these successes, if for no other reason than to combat demoralization with a vision of hope.

SCHIZOPHRENIFORM DISORDER

The *DSM-IV-TR* criteria for schizophreniform disorder and schizophrenia (Table 12–1) are identical, except that schizophreniform disorder has (1) shorter duration (between 1 and 6 months) and (2) social or occupational function need not be impaired. This 6-month cutoff point and absence of poor functioning were chosen because they appear (for now) to be the best predictors of which patients recover (schizophreniform) and which become chronic (schizophrenia).

Schizophreniform disorder is further classified in *DSM-IV-TR* as having *good prognostic features* if the patient has two of the following four indicators: (1) onset of prominent psychotic symptoms within 4 weeks of first noticeable unusual behavior or functioning; (2) confusion or perplexity at the height of the psychotic episode; (3) absence of blunted or flat affect; and (4) good premorbid social and occupational functioning.

Roughly half of patients *initially* diagnosed as having schizophreniform disorder will improve or recover substantially; in general, the longer the disorder persists, the worse the prognosis. Although findings conflict, most suggest that there is no increased prevalence of schizophrenia among relatives. The ECA survey (Chapter 1) found a lifetime prevalence of 0.1% for schizophreni-form disorder in the general population. The disorder's etiology is unknown. All the factors for differentiating *medical- and substance-induced syndromes* and *mood disorders* from schizophrenia also apply to schizophreniform disorder. Schizophreniform disorder is treated symptomatically, with observation, anti-psychotic medication, supportive psychotherapy, suicide precautions, family involvement, and close follow-up.

Schizophreniform disorder differs from *brief psychotic disorder*, which re-solves in under 1 month and does not include negative symptoms as part of the criteria. Brief psychotic disorder often occurs after a major stressor (brief reactive psychosis), and the content of the psychoses often involves the stressor. For example, an intern, after 3 weeks of substantial sleep deprivation and feeling overwhelmed by his duties, began complaining that the nurses were persecuting him by paging him all the time. The nurses told him that they hadn't paged him in hours. Then he knew there was a plot.

Mood disorders with psychotic features involve delusions and hallucina-tions, but they are most often mood-congruent. Delusions of poverty, sin, and disease are common in psychotic depression; those of overconfidence and grandiosity are common with mania; patently bizarre, Schneiderian, and mood-incongruent delusions are more typically schizophrenic. When asked why he is being persecuted, the person with mood disorder is likely to say "because I deserve it," whereas the patient with paranoid schizophrenia might say, "I am angry and will seek revenge." Persecutory delusions may occur in both mood and schizophrenic disorders. Indeed, distinguishing these two disorders is a frequent and difficult problem, since at some point over half of all patients with schizophrenia have depressive symptoms, and patients with mood disorders may show deterioration, isolation, thought disorder, catatonia, cognitive disturbance, and a wide variety of hallucinations and delusions. When patients exhibit symptoms of both disorders, the timing and duration of symptoms are critical to determine the best *DSM-IV-TR* formulation consis-tent with available history and examination findings. Schizophrenia should be diagnosed only if (1) no major depressive or manic episodes have occurred along with the active psychosis, and (2) the schizophrenic symptoms have persisted for 6 months. In the prodromal or residual phase, these may be only negative symptoms or attenuated positive symptoms. When mood disorders with psychotic features and schizophrenia-related disorders cannot be distin-guished from each other and truly occur simultaneously, *schizoaffective disor-der* would be diagnosed.

SCHIZOAFFECTIVE DISORDER

In 1933 the term "schizoaffective disorder" was introduced to describe a psychosis with prominent schizophrenic *and* affective symptoms; since then, the term's use has been equally "schizophrenic" and "affective." Experts disagree whether schizoaffective disorder is an actual disorder: Some claim it is nothing more than a mere label, a fudge-factor, a provisional diagnosis to be used until the patient's *real* diagnosis—schizophrenia or affective disorder—becomes apparent. Others contend that schizoaffective disorder is a genuine entity that includes features of both disorders. *DSM-IV-TR* has included the diagnosis, suggesting that, at least in some patients, schizoaffective disorder is a genuine entity (see Table 12-4).

By these criteria, Fred, a 24-year-old librarian, would seem to have a schizoaffective disorder. At first, over a period of 7 months, he developed typical signs of schizophrenia: He believed a nearby hospital was zapping his brain with x-rays, thereby controlling his actions. By stringing together the first letter of each book title returned to the library, Fred uncovered a secret code, which auditory hallucinations later informed him was part of a plot to destroy Dartmouth College. After a 3-week period of hospitalization, including treatment with antipsychotics, Fred recovered,

---

TABLE 12-4
DSM-IV *Criteria for Schizoaffective Disorder*

A. An uninterrupted period of illness during which, at some time, there is either a Major Depressive Episode, a Manic Episode, or a Mixed Episode concurrent with symptoms that meet Criterion A for Schizophrenia.

Note: The Major Depressive Episode must include Criterion A1: depressed mood.

B. During the same period of illness, there have been delusions or hallucinations for at least 2 weeks in the absence of prominent mood symptoms.

C. Symptoms that meet criteria for a mood episode are present for a substantial portion of the total duration of the active and residual periods of the illness.

D. The disturbance is not due to the direct physiological effects of a substance (e.g., a drug of abuse, a medication) or a general medical condition.

Bipolar Type: if the disturbance includes a Manic or a Mixed Episode (or a Manic or a Mixed Episode and Major Depressive Episodes)

Depressive Type: if the disturbance only includes Major Depressive Episodes

Note. From *DSM-IV-TR,* p. 323.

---

returned to work, and then secretly stopped his medication. Within a week his delusions reappeared, but this time accompanied by symptoms of major depression: insomnia, anorexia, anhedonia, psychomotor retardation, and severe dysthymia. The delusions and syndrome of major depression continued for 6 more weeks. Did Fred have a postpsychotic depression? Probably not, because in postpsychotic depression the patient feels hopeless, or anergic, or depressed—in other words, a *symptom*, instead of a *syndrome*, of depression. Fred had the syndrome and met criteria for a schizoaffective disorder.

When schizoaffective disorder is used as a temporary diagnosis awaiting further clarification, appending the term *provisional* clarifies the clinician's intention. In Fred's case, however, schizoaffective disorder was diagnosed as a disorder. Little is known about this "true" disorder. It may be a heterogeneous entity with numerous etiologies. Some genetic studies have shown that these patients have an increased family history of alcoholism, affective, and schizophrenic disorders. It appears to occur more often in women. Age of onset, degree of recovery, natural history, and prognosis fall roughly between those for schizophrenia and affective disorders. Treatment is focused on both the mood disorder component as well as the schizophrenia component, such that schizophrenia symptoms would be treated with antipsychotics, manic symptoms with mood stabilizers (e.g., lithium), and depressive symptoms with antidepressants. Psychosocial rehabilitation should include all of the elements and considerations as for schizophrenia, including a low-stress, LEE environment, to the greatest degree possible.

A history of normal baseline functioning between each psychotic episode and a mood disorder with every psychosis indicate the possibility of an atypical psychotic mood disorder, which has a better prognosis.

DELUSIONAL DISORDER

Delusions, such as delusional jealousy, lasting over a month are the chief features of delusional disorder (Table 12-5), in which the delusions are enduring, systematized, interrelated, and internally consistent. Their themes can be single or multiple, simple or complex. Delusional disorder does not manifest the prominent hallucinations, incoherence, disorganized or catatonic behavior, or negative symptoms seen in schizophrenia. The delusions are not bizarre or Schneiderian, such as thought broadcasting or delusions of control. Delusional disorder, which is rare, is characterized by delusions involving nonbi-

TABLE 12-5

DSM-IV-TR *Criteria for Delusional Disorder*

A. Nonbizarre delusions (i.e., involving situations that occur in real life, such as being followed, poisoned, infected, loved at a distance, being deceived by spouse or lover, or having a disease) of at least 1 month's duration.

B. Criterion A for Schizophrenia has never been met. **Note:** Tactile and olfactory hallucinations may be present in Delusional Disorder if they are related to the delusional theme.

C. Apart from the impact of the delusion(s) or its ramifications, functioning is not markedly impaired and behavior is not obviously odd or bizarre.

D. If mood episodes have occurred concurrently with delusions, their total duration has been brief relative to the duration of the delusional periods.

E. The disturbance is not due to the direct physiological effects of a substance (e.g., a drug of abuse, a medication) or a general medical condition.

Specify type (the following types are assigned based on the predominant delusional theme):

Erotomanic Type: delusions that another person, usually of higher status, is in love with the individual

Grandiose Type: delusions of inflated worth, power, knowledge, identity, or special relationship to a deity or famous person

Jealous Type: delusions that the individual's sexual partner is unfaithful

Persecutory Type: delusions that the person (or someone to whom the person is close) is being malevolently treated in some way

Somatic Type: delusions that the person has some physical defect or general medical condition

Mixed Type: delusions characteristic of more than one of the above types but no one theme predominates

Unspecified Type

Note. From *DSM-IV-TR,* p. 329.

---

zarre real-life situations in otherwise well-functioning people. There are five types of this disorder.

In the *grandiose type*, patients may believe that they have created a wonderful secret invention, discovered a cure for AIDS, or are confidantes of the president.

With *delusional jealousy*, a spouse's "unfaithfulness" is fabricated on issues of "evidence"—a misplaced stocking, a misconstrued remark.

A patient with the *erotomanic type* may believe that she is secretly Robert Redford's lover and badgers him with phone calls or angry letters of feeling rejected, and perhaps even stalks him. About 80% with erotomanic type are women. The typical erotomanic patient leads a socially empty life, is unmarried, unattractive, and from a lower socioeconomic stratum. The object of their attention is believed to be, and usually is, of superior status, looks, intelligence, and/or has authority (Segal, 1989). Movie and entertainment stars are commonly targets of people with erotomanic delusions.

A patient with the *somatic type* of delusional disorder may believe that he has cancer and is giving it to other people, or that his head is so small that most people can't see it. *Somatic type delusional disorder* is to be distinguished from *body dysmorphic disorder*, which is classified as a somatoform disorder and is a morbid preoccupation with an imagined defect in appearance ("My nose is too big"; "My eyes are too close together"). Somatic delusions are more extreme, far exceeding the magnifications of imperfections normal to adolescence.

In the *persecutory type*, patients may think that they are being drugged, poisoned, followed, conspired against, or maligned. It may begin with a plausible suspicion or grievance against an individual, government agency, or business. As the patient becomes increasingly frustrated in trying to rectify her complaint, she may develop psychotic fantasies as she presses for justice. She may bring legal action, recruit supporters, make public appeals, or send petitions. With growing self-importance and messianic zeal, she may sometimes display a pressured form of speech similar to what is observed, to a much greater degree, in mania. Yet unlike mania or schizophrenia, *the psychopathology does not affect other areas of functioning.*

Most cases of persecutory delusions arise gradually during middle or late adult life, have chronic and stable courses with few remissions and exacerbations, and disproportionately affect those who are female, married, immigrants, and in lower socioeconomic groups. Paranoia constitutes 1–4% of all psychiatric hospital admissions, with an incidence of first admissions between 1 and 3/100,000 population per year. Its etiology is unknown. Paranoia does not run in families; social isolation and stress may foster paranoia in older adults. Projection is its chief defense mechanism.

Because the delusions are usually ego-syntonic, patients with delusional disorder seldom seek treatment. If they do—and it's usually under coercion—a trial of antipsychotic medication is indicated, even though they are unlikely to take it, as prescribed or as needed to be effective. The somatic type may respond to pimozide, an atypical-like first-generation antipsychotic if other antipsychotics fail. If the somatic or jealousy delusions are mild and it is a preoccupation that dominates, treatments for obsessive–compulsive disorder (e.g., SSRIs) can be tried. The erotomanic type of delusional disorder may lead to behaviors that require a restraining order to keep the patient from abusing the love object.

BRIEF PSYCHOTIC DISORDER

Occasionally, a real psychotic break looks just like it does in the movies. "Brief psychotic disorder" is just what the director ordered. Typically the victim is a relatively normal person in whom psychosis develops rapidly (the person "snaps") after a very stressful event. This is accompanied by emotional turmoil with rapid shifts of mood, perplexity, or confusion. Negative symptoms are not a usual feature. Most recover entirely. In a few cases this is an unusual, abrupt beginning of a schizophrenic disorder. A clinical rule of thumb is that the faster the onset of the disorder, the faster the offset. Table 12-6 presents *DSM-IV-TR* criteria for brief psychotic disorder.

Marc, a 30-year-old hotel executive, was at work when a "moderate" earthquake toppled the hotel, killing four occupants and injuring many others. Dazed but physically unharmed, Marc wandered away from the rubble, arrived home hours later, and kept mumbling that he was responsible for the hotel's collapse. Staring into space as if listening to someone, Marc would mumble, "The devil is saying, 'You're to blame, you're to blame. You'll fry in hell.'" At times Marc would sit and sulk, rigid and mute, while at other times he would pace the floor, apparently arguing loudly with "the devil." Marc had had no previous psychiatric difficulties, and his mental state was stable prior to the earthquake.

Marc's wife took him to the emergency room for treatment. His drug screen was negative and his brief reactive psychosis was treated with 5 mg of haloperidol stat and 2 mg tid for the next 2 days. Marc's psychotic symptoms began to recede the day after the earthquake, and 3 days later, they resolved and he was able to return to work and regular activities. His treatment plan included scheduled visits to an outpatient therapist to provide additional support for him to work through the effects of the tragic experience and a psychiatrist to taper carefully the antipsychotic medication.

Differential Diagnosis

If Marc's symptoms had lasted under 2–3 hours, his diagnosis would have been *psychotic disorder* NOS; if they had persisted for 1 month, his diagnosis would have been *schizophreniform disorder*. Gradually increasing psychopathology before the florid psychosis characterizes schizophrenic and schizophren-

TABLE 12-6

DSM-IV-TR *Criteria for Brief Psychotic Disorder*

A. Presence of one (or more) of the following symptoms:

(1) delusions

(2) hallucinations

(3) disorganized speech (e.g., frequent derailment or incoherence)

(4) grossly disorganized or catatonic behavior

Note: Do not include a symptom if it is a culturally sanctioned response pattern.

B. Duration of an episode of the disturbance is at least 1 day but less than 1 month, with eventual full return to premorbid level of functioning.

C. The disturbance is not better accounted for by a Mood Disorder With Psychotic Features, Schizoaffective Disorder, or Schizophrenia and is not due to the direct physiological effects of a substance (e.g., a drug of abuse, a medication) or a general medical condition.

Specify if:

With Marked Stressor(s) (brief reactive psychosis): if symptoms occur shortly after and apparently in response to events that, singly or together, would be markedly stressful to almost anyone in similar circumstances in the person's culture

Without Marked Stressor(s): if psychotic symptoms do not occur shortly after, or are not apparently in response to events that, singly or together, would be markedly stressful to almost anyone in similar circumstances in the person's culture

With Postpartum Onset: if onset within 4 weeks postpartum

Note. From *DSM-IV-TR,* p. 332.

---

iform disorders, but not brief psychotic disorder. In contrast to *schizophrenia,* brief psychotic disorder usually has an acute precipitant, a rapid onset, delusions and hallucinations that pertain to the stressor, and a relatively quick recovery with eventual complete resolution without recurrence. However, not all cases have acute precipitants, making them look more like other disorders. If the patient meets the full *DSM-IV-TR* criteria for *mood disorders,* brief psychotic disorder should not be diagnosed. At their worst, *adjustment disorders* and *uncomplicated bereavement* do not usually produce florid psychosis. Auditory and visual hallucinations of the deceased are commonly experienced in an otherwise normal bereavement and require only supportive therapy. *Malingering* and *factitious disorder with psychological symptoms* must be considered, as should organic conditions, especially *delirium* and *psychomotor* or *partial complex seizures* that suddenly produce delusions, hallucinations, anxiety, and repeated automatisms with fluctuating levels of consciousness; a third of these cases occur without significant confusion (McKenna, Kane, & Parrish, 1985). EEG abnormalities are found in approximately 50% of patients with partial complex seizures. *Petit mal seizures*, which present as absence attacks, may resemble catatonia, but no other psychotic symptoms are present. Finally, *substance abuse*, intoxication, or withdrawal are prime suspects and very important to diagnose and treat promptly to avoid life-threatening complications.

Management and Treatment

The priorities in treating brief psychotic disorder are the following: First, prevent suicide attempts, dangerous and destructive behaviors, or even assaultiveness. Second, hasten recovery by prescribing antipsychotics or mood-stabilizing agents or sedatives as indicated. If the patient is imminently suicidal or dangerous, rapid sedation with benzodiazepines as well as antipsychotics may be indicated. Tapering medication should begin only after the patient is clearly recovering. Third, initiate psychotherapy that emphasizes reality orientation and repeated assurances of safety and improvement to the patient. At this point, relatives and therapists should refrain from "psychologizing" the meaning of the psychosis with the patient. (For instance, probing Marc's guilt over the earthquake might have further disorganized him.) Fourth, *after* the psychosis resolves, some patients benefit from several sessions of psychotherapy that address (1) the stressor and its personal meaning, or (2) incompletely resolved issues related to the psychosis. For example, on returning to his wife's grave a year after she died, a well-functioning man developed an acute psychosis that disappeared in a week. Recognizing that his psychotic episode indicated that he was more distressed by his wife's death than he had realized, he entered brief psychotherapy to examine this concern.

The genetics and prognosis of brief psychotic disorder are not clear. Some patients have more than one brief psychotic episode. A family history of mood disorder is frequently found in those who experience stress-induced brief psychotic episodes. These patients may have a higher risk of developing a mood disorder at a later time in their life.

SHARED PSYCHOTIC DISORDER (*FOLIE À DEUX*)

This very rare, strange disorder looks like psychosis by contagion, in which one person "catches" another's "delusion virus." However, no virus or other

TABLE 12-7

DSM-IV-TR *Criteria for Shared Psychotic Disorder (folie à deux)*

A. A delusion develops in an individual in the context of a close relationship with another person(s), who has an already-established delusion.

B. The delusion is similar in content to that of the person who already has the established delusion.

C. The disturbance is not better accounted for by another Psychotic Disorder (e.g., Schizophrenia) or a Mood Disorder With Psychotic Features and is not due to the direct physiological effects of a substance (e.g., a drug of abuse, a medication) or a general medical condition.

Note. From *DSM-IV-TR*, p. 334.

---

detectable means of transmission is actually involved. The person who "gives" the delusions (the primary case) already has a psychotic disorder with delusions and usually dominates in a very close, long-term relationship with a socially isolated, more passive, initially healthy person who "gets" the delusions too. This person acquires the same or very similar delusions as the delusion "donor." That is, they "share" the same delusions. Table 12-7 presents *DSM-IV-TR* criteria for shared psychotic disorder.

The delusions in shared psychotic disorder are usually within the realm of possibility and may stem from common past experiences of the two people. Although most commonly involving two people (*folie à deux*), cases have been reported involving up to 12 family members. The disorder tends to be chronic, with the recipient typically less impaired because only part of the primary person's delusional system is adopted. Treatment involves either successful antipsychotic medication of the primary person or interrupting the relationship with the primary person.

PSYCHOTIC DISORDER DUE TO A GENERAL MEDICAL CONDITION

This psychotic disorder presents with delusions or hallucinations often accompanied by incoherence and inappropriate or labile affects. In *DSM-IV-TR*, dementia and delirium are not considered general medical conditions. Therefore, psychotic symptoms with profound confusion, memory loss, fluctuating levels of consciousness, and disorientation would be diagnosed as dementia or delirium "with delusions" or "with hallucinations." Schizophrenic hallucinations are most often auditory and frequently visual. On the other hand, hallucinations seen in cases involving a primary medical condition may involve any

TABLE 12-8

DSM-IV-TR *Criteria for Psychotic Disorder Due to a General Medical Condition*

A. Prominent hallucinations or delusions.

B. There is evidence from the history, physical examination, or laboratory findings that the disturbance is a direct physiological consequence of a general medical condition.

C. The disturbance is not better accounted for by another mental disorder.

D. The disturbance does not occur exclusively during the course of a delirium.

With Delusions: if delusions are the predominant symptom

With Hallucinations: if hallucinations are the predominant symptom

Note. From *DSM-IV-TR,* p. 338.

of the senses, including olfactory, tactile, and gustatory. Patients with schizophrenia generally defend their hallucinations as reasonable and valid—i.e., these patients are delusional and lack insight into these phenomena—whereas patients with general medical causes of hallucinations more often recognize them as inexplicable, crazy, and foreign—not their "real selves." However, in either situation, patients may become terrified and act on the delusions or hallucinations, causing danger to self or others unless treated. Table 12-8 lists *DSM-IV-TR* criteria for psychotic disorder secondary to a general medical condition. It is crucial for clinicians to rule out general medical conditions causing psychotic symptoms before giving a patient a primary diagnosis of schizophrenia, bipolar disorder, etc.

If there is no family history of *schizophrenia,* or if schizophrenic-like symptoms first arise in a person over 40, the diagnosis is less likely to be schizophrenia. *Complex partial seizure disorder* can simulate schizophrenia, but is usually associated with complete or nearly complete remissions and abrupt recurrences (unless the seizures are nearly constant). Many other medical conditions, including *hormone abnormalities* (hypothyroidism, hyperthyroidism), *Cushing's disease* (too much cortisol), *head injury* (traumatic brain injury), and *brain tumor* can be the culprits in causing this form of psychosis.

SUBSTANCE-INDUCED PSYCHOTIC DISORDER

Substance-induced psychotic disorder, especially intoxication from amphetamines, cocaine, hallucinogens, PCP, cannabis, and alcohol, may be indistinguishable from the active phase of schizophrenia, schizophreniform disorder, or acute psychosis. Symptoms are usually temporary and can be confirmed by urine screening. Although *alcoholic hallucinosis* typically stops within 48 hours of withdrawal, it may persist for weeks and resemble the early stages of schizophrenia. However, in alcoholic hallucinosis, the hallucinations are most commonly auditory, not visual, and the patient's response to them is appropriate

---

TABLE 12-9

DSM-IV *Criteria for Substance-Induced Psychotic Disorder*

A. Prominent hallucinations or delusions. **Note:** Do not include hallucinations if the person has insight that they are substance-induced.

B. There is evidence from the history, physical examination, or laboratory findings of either (1) or (2):

    (1) the symptoms in Criterion A developed during, or within a month of, Substance Intoxication or Withdrawal

    (2) medication use is etiologically related to the disturbance

C. The disturbance is not better accounted for by a Psychotic Disorder that is not substance-induced. Evidence that the symptoms are better accounted for by a Psychotic Disorder that is not substance-induced might include the following: the symptoms precede the onset of the substance use or medication use; the symptoms persist for a substantial period of time (e.g., about a month) after the cessation of acute withdrawal or severe intoxication, or are substantially in excess of what would be expected given the type or amount of the substance used or the duration of use; or there is other evidence that suggests the existence of an independent non-substance-induced Psychotic Disorder (e.g., a history of recurrent non-substance-related episodes).

D. The disturbance does not occur exclusively during the course of a delirium.

Note: This diagnosis should be made instead of a diagnosis of Substance Intoxication or Substance Withdrawal only when the symptoms are in excess of those usually associated with the intoxication or withdrawal syndrome and when the symptoms are sufficiently sure to warrant independent clinical attention.

Specify if:

With Onset During Intoxication: if criteria are met for Intoxication with the substance and the symptoms develop during the intoxication syndrome

With Onset During Withdrawal: if criteria are met for Withdrawal from the substance and the symptoms develop during, or shortly after, a withdrawal syndrome

Note. From *DSM-IV-TR,* pp. 000.

---

to their content, e.g., anxiety in response to threatening voices. Of course, patients with schizophrenia can also have a superimposed drug-induced psychosis. Amphetamine psychosis can blend into a prolonged and sometimes chronic paranoid delusional and hallucinated state. People who already have risk factors for schizophrenia are more likely to experience this prolonged result; the amphetamines may push the vulnerable person "over the brink." Table 12-9 presents *DSM-IV-TR* criteria for substance-induced psychotic disorder.

Psychosis can also be induced by drug withdrawal. Here lab tests are useless in making the diagnosis, but a history of recent, usually prolonged, drug use may help. Changes in vital signs (e.g., increased blood pressure, heart rate, and temperature), sweating, and tremulousness frequently accompany serious withdrawal from alcohol or hypnoanxiolytics. Prescribed drugs can also cause psychotic symptoms: Corticosteroids, thyroid hormone, and anticholinergics are common culprits. Sleuthing through these numerous and varied substance-induced and medically induced syndromes makes most psychiatrists glad that they went to medical school!

References

Anderson, C.M., Hogarty, G., & Reiss, D.J. (1980). Family treatment of adult schizophrenic patients: A psycho-educational approach. *Schizophrenia Bulletin, 6,* 490–505.

Caton, C.L.M. (1984). *Management of chronic schizophrenia.* New York: Oxford University Press.

Cozolino, L.J., Goldstein, M.J., Nuechterlein, K.H., West, K.L., & Snyder, K.S. (1988). The impact of education about schizophrenia on relatives varying in expressed emotion. *Schizophrenia Bulletin, 14,* 675–687.

Davis, J.M. (1975). Overview: Maintenance therapy in psychiatry: I. Schizophrenia. *American Journal of Psychiatry, 132,* 1237–1245.

Davis, K.L., Kahn, R.S., Ko, G., & Davidson, M. (1991). Dopamine in schizophrenia: A review and reconceptualization. *American Journal of Psychiatry, 148*(11), 1474–1486.

Drake, R.E., Gates, C., Whitaker, A., & Cotton, P.G. (1985). Suicide among schizophrenics: A review. *Comprehensive Psychiatry, 26,* 90–100.

Goldstein, J.M. (1988). Gender differences in the course of schizophrenia. *American Journal of Psychiatry, 145,* 684–689.

Gonzalez, G., & Rosenheck, R.A. (2002). Outcomes and service use among homeless persons with serious mental illness and substance abuse. *Psychiatric Services, 53*(4), 437–446.

Goodwin, D.W., & Guze, S.B. (1989). *Psychiatric diagnosis* (4th ed.). New York: Oxford University Press.

Hafner, H., & ander Heiden, W. (1997). Epidemiology of schizophrenia. *Canadian Journal of Psychiatry,* 139–151.

Hogarty, G.E. Flasher, S., Ulrich, R., Carter, M., Greenwald, D., Pogue-Gelle, M., et al. (2004).

Cognitive enhancement therapy for schizophrenia: Effects of a 2-year randomized trial on cognition and behavior. *Archives of General Psychiatry, 61*(9), 866–876.

Hogarty, G.E., Goldberg, S.C., Schooler, N.R., & Ulrich, R.P. (1974). Drugs and sociotherapy in the aftercare of schizophrenic patients: II. Two-year relapse rates. *Archives of General Psychiatry, 31,* 603–608.

Lewine, R., Burbach, D., & Meltzer, H.Y. (1984). Effect of diagnostic criteria on the ratio of male to female schizophrenic patients. *American Journal of Psychiatry, 141,* 84–87.

Lieberman, J.A., Stroup, T.S., McEvoy, J.P., Swartz, M.S., Rosenheck, R.A., Perkins, D.O., et al. (2005). Effectiveness of antipsychotic drugs in patients with chronic schizophrenia. *New England Journal of Medicine, 353*(12), 1209–1223.

Lindenmeyer, J.P., McGurk, S.R., Mueser, K.T., Khan, A., Wance, D., Hoffman, L., et al. (2008). A randomized controlled trial of cognitive remediation among inpatients with persistent mental illness. *Psychiatric Services, 59,* 241–247.

Ludwig, A.M. (1985). *Principles of clinical psychiatry* (2nd ed.). New York: Free Press.

McGlashan, T.H. (1984). The Chestnut Lodge follow-up study, II. *Archives of General Psychiatry, 41,* 586–601.

McKenna, P.J., Kane, J.M., & Parrish, K. (1985). Psychotic syndrome of epilepsy. *American Journal of Psychiatry, 142,* 895–904.

Mowbray, C.T. (1985). Homelessness in America: Myths and realities. *American Journal of Orthopsychiatry, 55,* 4–8.

Noga, J.T. (1999). Schizophrenia as a brain disease: What have we learned from neuroimaging studies of twins? *Medscape General Medicine, 1*(3). Available at http://www.medscape.com/view article/ 430605.

OMIM, On-line Mendelian Inheritance in Man. (2008). Available at http://www.ncbi.nlm.nih.gov/ sites/entrez?db=omim

Ries, R.K. (1985). DSM-III implications of the diagnosis of catatonia and bipolar disorder. *American Journal of Psychiatry, 142*(12), 1471–1474.

Ross, C.A., Margolis, R.L., Reading, S.A.J., Pletnikov, M., & Coye, J.T. (2006). Neurobiology of schizophrenia. *Neuron, 52,* 139–153.

Segal, J.H. (1989). Erotomania revisited: From Kraepelin to *DSM-III-R. American Journal of Psychiatry, 146*(10), 1261–1266.

Snyder, S. (1981). Dopamine receptors, neuroleptics, and schizophrenia. *American Journal of Psychiatry, 138,* 460–464.

Sorensen, J. (2006). Relapse prevention in schizophrenia and other psychoses. Manual with workbooks. ISBN-10-902806-60-3.

Torrey, E.F. (1992). Are we overestimating the genetic contribution to schizophrenia? *Schizophrenia Bulletin, 18,* 159–170.

Vaughn, C.E., & Leff, J.P. (1976). The influence of family and social factors on the course of psychiatric illness: A comparison of schizophrenic with depressed neurotic patients. *British Journal of Psychiatry, 129,* 125–137.

Weinberger, D.R., Berman, K., Suddath, R., & Torrey, E. (1992). Evidence of dysfunction of the prefrontal-limbic network in schizophrenia: A magnetic resonance imaging and regional cerebral blood flow study of discordant monozygotic twins. *American Journal of Psychiatry, 149,* 890–897.

Wu, E.Q., Birnbaum, H.G., Shi, L., Ball, D.E., Kessler, R.C., Moulis, M., et al. (2005). The economic burden of schizophrenia in the United States in 2002. *Journal of Clinical Psychiatry, 66*(9), 1122–1129.

http://www.ncl.ac.uk/nnp/teaching/video/case.html. Newcastle University Medical Student Teaching Resource Videos simulating various psychiatric diagnoses and signs/symptoms. Includes models of treatment of Alzheimer's disease and ECT. Authors: Faculty of Newcastle University, Director, Professor Chris Day.

13

Mood Disorders

Some people experiencing depression say they would rather have cancer. Depression is an example of a mood disorder with increasing prevalence, and suicide as its most serious complication. Morbidity from mood disorders extends to body, soul, and spirit, profoundly impacting all spheres of a person's life. Its cost to society is enormous, but its ravages are often preventable. When most people speak of depression, they usually mean dysthymia—i.e., the *emotion* of feeling sad, "blue," down in the dumps, unhappy, or demoralized. When clinicians speak of depression, they are usually referring to a *syndrome* or mental disorder consisting of many symptoms and signs, including appetite loss, anhedonia, hopelessness, insomnia, and dysthymia. Whereas the emotion of depression affects everyone to some degree, the syndrome afflicts only some—a "mere" 17% of Americans during their lives and well over a 100 million earthlings every day. So in this text *dysthymia* refers to the emotion or symptom of depression, whereas *depression* refers to the syndromes and disorders of depression. *Dysphoria* refers to any unpleasant mood, including dysthymia.

Mood disorder is the overall category for entities whose predominant symptom is usually a pathological mood: dysphoria, euphoria, or both. In *DSM-IV-TR*, mood disorders that consist solely of "lows" are called "major depression" and its milder version, "dysthymic disorder"; those that combine "highs" and "lows" are called "bipolar disorder" and its milder form, "cyclothymic disorder."

Mood disorders have also been classified according to at least four different conceptual models. First, the *endogenous versus reactive model* considers endogenous depression to be a strictly biological event unrelated to any environmental forces, whereas reactive depression must be psychosocially triggered and devoid of any biological factors. This distinction unjustifiably assumes that the etiology of depression is (1) known and (2) either biological *or* psychosocial. Indeed, many "endogenous" depressions follow environmental stressors, and many "reactive" depressions emerge without any obvious precipitant. Second, in the *primary and secondary model depressions*, secondary depressions are preceded by another physical or mental disorder (e.g., alcoholism, hypothyroidism, anxiety disorder), whereas primary depressions are not. Third, in the *unipolar versus bipolar model*, a bipolar disorder exists whenever a manic episode has occurred. Patients with bipolar depression must have a history of mania or hypomania, whereas those with unipolar depressions don't. Fourth, historically *psychotic* and *neurotic depressions* were distinguished, with psychotic depressions referring to any severe depression, even when the patients were not psychotic. In *DSM-IV-TR*, however, a "psychotic depression" must display psychosis. Neurotic depressions are roughly equivalent to dysthymic disorder.

Clinical Presentation

Major Depression

The first essential feature of major depression is either a depressed mood or anhedonia—that is, a pervasive loss of interest or ability to experience pleasure in normally enjoyable activities. The mood is usually sad, but it can also be irritable or apprehensive. Patients describe this mood as "living in a black hole or in a deep pit," "feeling dead," "overwhelmed by doom," or "physically drained." However, many patients with major depression do *not* feel depressed or even dysphoric, but anhedonic. A baseball fan suddenly doesn't care about the World Series; a loving father loses interest in his child; a devoted nurse cares little for her patients. Just because individuals don't look unhappy or complain about "being in the dumps," if anhedonic, they might still have a major depression. A majority of persons with major depression look lifeless, boring, or dull, rather than sad and crying. Persons suspected of having a major depression should be asked not only if they feel depressed (or sad, blue, down, etc.), but also if they no longer enjoy things anymore. In medically ill patients, questions about enjoyment should be restricted to things they can still do. For example, a person with back pain may still enjoy reading, watching TV, or even taking walks, but it would be clinically unproductive to ask "Do you still like bowling?"

The second essential feature of major depression is the presence of at least five other symptoms. The *biological (also called vegetative) signs and symptoms of depression* generally include appetite loss, unintentional weight loss or gain, insomnia or hypersomnia, psychomotor retardation or agitation, a lack of energy or fatigue, and diminished libido. With another common biological sign, "diurnal mood variation," persons feel worse in the morning and slightly better by night; this pattern continues through weekends and is not just a result of facing work or school. These individuals typically awake in the middle of the night (middle insomnia) or in the early morning (terminal insomnia), and find it hard or impossible to return to sleep. Individuals who have improved slightly may say that their sleep and appetite are okay when both are still abnormal. Continue to probe by asking, "How does that compare to normal?" The psychological signs and symptoms of depression include a diminished ability to think or make decisions, negative thinking about the past (e.g., guilt), present (e.g., low self-esteem), and future (e.g., hopelessness), and thoughts about death and suicide.

As presented in Table 13-1, *DSM-IV-TR* criteria for major depression require a mood change *or* anhedonia *and* several biological signs of depression, which must exist nearly every day for at least 2 weeks. The acronym **DEPRESSING** can be used to help remember the criteria for depression. The letters represent **D**epression (sadness), **E**nergy (loss of), **P**leasure (diminished interest), **R**etardation (psychomotor slowing or agitation), **E**ating (changes in weight or appetite), **S**uicide (recurrent thoughts of death), **S**leep (insomnia or hypersomnia), **I**ndecisive (poor concentration), **N**egative thinking (worthlessness, hopelessness, or inappropriate **G**uilt). The diagnosis of depression is based on *symptoms*, not on whether the disorder is produced by stressors in the environment.

Everything about people with psychomotor retardation is slow—walking, talking, thinking, eating, reacting. Frame-by-frame analysis of movies shows that, in walking, depressed people lift their thighs with their lower legs lagging behind, whereas most people propel their lower legs and feet forward. If asked their spouse's name or their own occupation, it may take 20–30 seconds to answer. For unknown reasons, this latency of response also occurs with psychomotor agitation. Concentration can be so impaired that they may be unable to sit through a sitcom or to read a simple paragraph. Their slowed thinking, impaired concentration, and negative worldview paralyze their decision-making abilities. Readily overwhelmed by easy tasks, depressed individuals no longer try to do anything. In contrast, those with psychomotor agitation may fidget, pace, wring their hands, and exhibit frenzied preoccupation with somatic concerns. In milder forms, it is important to find out if the psychomotor behavior is a change from normal. Sometimes family members can more accurately determine this than the depressed person.

Individuals with depression view the world through gray-tinted glasses. To them, everything is bleak—their life, their world, their future, and their treat-

TABLE 13-1

DSM-IV-TR *Criteria for Major Depressive Episode and Disorder*

Major Depressive Episode

A. Five (or more) of the following symptoms have been present during the same 2-week period and represent a change from previous functioning; at least one of the symptoms is either (1) depressed mood or (2) loss of interest or pleasure.

Note: Do not include symptoms that are clearly due to a general medical condition, or mood-incongruent delusions or hallucinations.

(1) depressed mood most of the day, nearly every day, as indicated by either subjective report (e.g., feels sad or empty) or observation made by others (e.g., appears tearful). **Note:** In children and adolescents, can be irritable mood.

(2) markedly diminished interest or pleasure in all, or almost all, activities most of the day, nearly every day (as indicated either by subjective account or observation made by others)

(3) significant weight loss or weight gain when not dieting (e.g., a change of more than 5% of body weight in a month), or decrease or increase in appetite nearly every day. **Note:** In children, consider failure to make expected weight gains.

(4) insomnia or hypersomnia nearly every day

(5) psychomotor agitation or retardation nearly every day (observable by others, not merely subjective feelings of restlessness or being slowed down)

(6) fatigue or loss of energy nearly every day

(7) feelings of worthlessness or excessive or inappropriate guilt (which may be delusional) nearly every day (not merely self-reproach or guilt about being sick)

(8) diminished ability to think or concentrate, or indecisiveness, nearly every day (either by subjective account or as observed by others)

(9) recurrent thoughts of death (not just fear of dying), recurrent suicidal ideation without a specific plan, or a suicide attempt or a specific plan for committing suicide

B. The symptoms do not meet criteria for a Mixed Episode.

C. The symptoms cause clinically significant distress or impairment in social, occupational, or other important areas of functioning.

D. The symptoms are not due to the direct physiological effects of a substance (e.g., a drug of abuse, a medication) or a general medical condition (e.g., hypothyroidism).

E. The symptoms are not better accounted for by Bereavement, i.e., after the loss of a loved one, the symptoms persist for longer than 2 months or are characterized by marked functional impairment, morbid preoccupation with worthlessness, suicidal ideation, psychotic symptoms, or psychomotor retardation.

TABLE 13-1

Continued

Major Depressive Disorder—Single or Recurrent Episode

Presence of a single Major Depressive Episode. (two or more if recurrent)

Note: To be considered separate episodes, there must be an interval of at least two consecutive months in which criteria are not met for a Major Depressive Episode.

B. The Major Depressive Episode is not better accounted for by Schizoaffective Disorder and is not superimposed on Schizophrenia, Schizophreniform Disorder, Delusional Disorder, or Psychotic Disorder Not Otherwise Specified.

C. There has never been a Manic Episode, a Mixed Episode, or a Hypomanic Episode. **Note:** This exclusion does not apply if all of the manic-like, mixed-like, or hypomanic-like episodes are substance- or treatment-induced or are due to the direct physiological effects of a general medical condition.

Specify (for current or most recent episode):

Mild, Moderate, Severe without Psychotic Features/Severe with Psychotic Features
Chronic
With Catatonic Features
With Melancholic Features
With Atypical Features
With Postpartum Onset
In Partial Remission, In Full Remission (if full criteria are not currently met)

Note. From *DSM-IV-TR,* pp. 356, 375, 376.

---

ment. "I beg you to shoot me," a depressed woman pleaded, "if they'll put a sick horse out of its misery, why not a person?" They ruminate over personal failures, real or imagined, often making mountains out of molehills. With a nearly delusional conviction, they may feel utterly hopeless, helpless, worthless, or guilty. A self-made millionaire declared that he was a "financial flop" who had "forced his family into the poorhouse." Whereas the unhappiness of everyday life comes and goes, the dysphoria of major depression never leaves. With everyday unhappiness, one can go to a movie and temporarily enjoy it, but with major depression, individuals cannot be distracted by a movie. The suicidal preoccupations of depressed patients often arise more from a wish to escape unrelenting dysphoria than to actually die. These patients frequently revise their history so that what was good, average, or at least bearable now becomes terrible and deserving of infinite guilt. In revising their life events, they can be so convincing that the interviewing clinician also feels dysphoric and becomes convinced that the person's depression was inevitable.

Virtually diagnostic of major depression is that relatives or others have devoted hours to reassuring the depressed person, but to no avail; no matter how effective or frequent their pleas, nothing they say "sticks" for more than a minute or two. People with depression view all decisions as a choice between something awful and something terrible. Loved ones may become impatient or even furious at the person: They realize she is ill, but feel that she has spurned their advice and does nothing to help herself. Depression is also "contagious" in that the person's futility may become the family's futility. People avoid depressed people—they are depressing! Although the withdrawal of others may aggravate the depression, at other times it doesn't really matter, since the depressed person is too self-absorbed to care. For these people, it feels like No Exit: They can't escape depression; they can't talk about it, and they can't *not* talk about it.

Bipolar Disorder

Perhaps 15% of those with major depression eventually exhibit mania or its attenuated version, hypomania. By definition, a person with bipolar disorder displays mania with or without a period of depression. Most patients, however, have both manic and depressive episodes in various sequences and frequencies.

An elevated, euphoric, expansive, or irritable mood is the cardinal feature of mania. People with mania may be hyperactive, highly distractible, and grandiose. They may experience flight of ideas, pressured speech, tangentiality, and a diminished need for sleep. They may be prickly and quick to anger. As their disorganization worsens, they may develop persecutory and grandiose ideas of reference that often become delusions. Sherlock Holmes's obsession that Professor Moriarty was interfering with his attempt to rid the world of evil was a typical manic persecutory delusion. About a quarter of people with mania develop hallucinations that are usually auditory or visual and of shorter duration than those in schizophrenia; disorganization may also occur, but more briefly than in schizophrenia. Table 13-2 lists *DSM-IV-TR* criteria for a manic episode. The mnemonic "**DIGFAST**," referring to the increased activity in mania, may assist in committing the cardinal symptoms of mania to memory. The letters represent **D**istractibility, **I**mpulsiveness (pleasure seeking), **G**randiosity (elevated self-esteem), **F**light of ideas (or racing thoughts), **A**ctivity (increase in goal-directed activities), **S**leep (decreased need for), and **T**alkativeness (pressured speech).

TABLE 13-2

DSM-IV-TR *Criteria for Manic and Hypomanic Episodes*

Manic Episode

A. A distinct period of abnormally and persistently elevated, expansive, or irritable mood, lasting at least 1 week (or any duration if hospitalization is necessary)

B. During the period of mood disturbance, three (or more) of the following symptoms have persisted (four if the mood is only irritable) and have been present to a significant degree:

(1) inflated self-esteem or grandiosity

(2) decreased need for sleep (e.g., feels rested after only 3 hours of sleep)

(3) more talkative than usual or pressure to keep talking

(4) flight of ideas or subjective experience that thoughts are racing

(5) distractibility (i.e., attention too easily drawn to unimportant or irrelevant external stimuli)

(6) increase in goal-directed activity (either socially, at work or school, or sexually) or psychomotor agitation

(7) excessive involvement in pleasurable activities that have a high potential for painful consequences (e.g., engaging in unrestrained buying sprees, sexual indiscretions, or foolish business investments)

C. The symptoms do not meet criteria for a Mixed Episode.

D. The mood disturbance is sufficiently severe to cause marked impairment in occupational functioning or in usual social activities or relationships with others, or to necessitate hospitalization to prevent harm to self or others, or there are psychotic features.

E. The symptoms are not due to the direct physiological effects of a substance (e.g., a drug of abuse, a medication, or other treatment) or a general medical condition (e.g., hyperthyroidism).

Note: Manic-like episodes that are clearly caused by somatic antidepressant treatment (e.g., medication, electroconvulsive therapy, light therapy) should not count toward a diagnosis of Bipolar I Disorder.

Hypomanic Episode

A. A distinct period of persistently elevated, expansive, or irritable mood, lasting throughout at least 4 days, that is clearly different from the usual nondepressed mood.

B. During the period of mood disturbance, three (or more) of the following symptoms have persisted (four if the mood is only irritable) and have been present to a significant degree:

(1) inflated self-esteem or grandiosity

(2) decreased need for sleep (e.g., feels rested after only 3 hours of sleep)

(3) more talkative than usual or pressure to keep talking

(4) flight of ideas or subjective experience that thoughts are racing

(*continued*)

TABLE 13-2
Continued

(5) distractibility (i.e., attention too easily drawn to unimportant or irrelevant external stimuli)

(6) increase in goal-directed activity (either socially, at work or school, or sexually) or psychomotor agitation

(7) excessive involvement in pleasurable activities that have a high potential for painful consequences (e.g., the person engages in unrestrained buying sprees, sexual indiscretions, or foolish business investments)

C. The episode is associated with an unequivocal change in functioning that is uncharacteristic of the person when not symptomatic.

D. The disturbance in mood and the change in functioning are observable by others.

E. The episode is not severe enough to cause marked impairment in social or occupational functioning, or to necessitate hospitalization, and there are no psychotic features.

F. The symptoms are not due to the direct physiological effects of a substance (e.g., a drug of abuse, a medication, or other treatment) or a general medical condition (e.g., hyperthyroidism).

Note: Hypomanic-like episodes that are clearly caused by somatic antidepressant treatment (e. g., medication, electroconvulsive therapy, light therapy) should not count toward a diagnosis of Bipolar II Disorder.

Note. From *DSM-IV-TR,* pp. 362, 368.

People with mania may talk incessantly, do "20 things at once," and launch outrageous projects. These individuals often resemble fast-talking comics of the Robin Williams and Jim Carey genre. People laugh with, not at, people with mania. They have pressured speech, and it's hard to get a word in edgewise. People with mania can be supersalespeople. Caught unaware, a clinician was visited by a salesman with mania who almost sold him a set of encyclopedias for his children—the problem was that he didn't have any children.

A person, when manic, spent $100,000 hiring city planners, attorneys, architects, and a guru to construct a 90-story building on 1 square foot of land. Another, a UCLA undergraduate, telephoned the Russian president to invite him to the Rose Bowl, and although the president didn't get the message, the student did reach a high Kremlin official (who declined).

On the spur of the moment, a Dartmouth graduate who resided in California jumped on a plane and admitted himself to "the hospital of my alma mater." He arrived with four tennis rackets, three suitcases, a fishing rod, dozens of lollipops, and a swimsuit; it was winter. Five minutes after his grand entrance, he coaxed all the patients and staff into singing, "The Yellow Rose of Texas." Further demonstrating tangential thinking, he declared that everybody should wear a yellow ribbon and surrender peacefully.

Many females with mania dress in bright multicolored clothing. Women may present with excessive makeup, provocative clothing, and high heels. They may become angry if asked about their clothing or flirtatious behaviors, providing further evidence of their lack of insight and judgment. Their sexual disinhibitions make it prudent to have a chaperone in the room.

But eventually, things get out of control in mania. When crossed, or when people don't go along with them, people with mania become irritable, nasty, and sometimes cruel. They may play the "manic game," in which they are constantly testing everybody's limits; they manipulate others' self-esteem, perceive and exploit people's vulnerabilities, and project responsibility. After wreaking havoc and infuriating everybody, they blame everyone but themselves. On the slightest whim, people with mania will call total strangers and amass enormous phone bills. These individuals may have no inhibitions. A well-respected "Southern gentleman" was brought into the hospital by neighbors when he was found dancing naked on a pizza in his backyard. He told the staff, "I wanted to raise my spiritual awareness and that was the best way to do it."

Patients with mania develop reputations as normally being a Dr. Jekyll— upstanding, likeable, and productive—yet sometimes becoming a Mr. Hyde— outrageously excitable, intrusive, and demanding. *Unpredictable* is what some people call them: fine one month, profoundly depressed the next month. Because periods of high energy, creativity, and achievement are not recognized as hypomania, bipolar disorder may go undiagnosed. Clinicians find that an excellent barometer of these hypomanic periods is the patient's diminished need for sleep. The adaptiveness of moderate hypomanic behavior allows many individuals with bipolar disorder to stand with society's most accomplished members.

Bipolar disorder is more severe than major depression. Patients with bipolar depressions stay depressed longer, relapse more frequently, display more depressive symptoms, show more severe symptoms, have more delusions and hallucinations, commit more suicides, require more hospitalizations, and experience more incapacitation. Bipolar I disorder most often starts with a depression; only 10–20% experience exclusively manic episodes. Manic spells may evolve rapidly or slowly. Yet when a person first presents with a severe depression, it's usually hard to tell if it is bipolar or major (unipolar) depression. However, because prognoses and treatments differ substantially, it's desirable to distinguish these two depressions as soon as possible.

Patients with bipolar depression are more likely than patients with unipolar depression to have extremely low energy, psychomotor retardation and the reverse vegetative symptoms: hypersomnia, hyperphagia, and mood worsening in the evening. In general, people with bipolar depression prefer to remain in bed and have what are termed "laying-down depressions." They are also more likely to have psychotic depressions and many lack insight into past manic episodes. They minimize or deny having poor judgment and acting grossly different from normal. However, they can describe episodes lasting many days or weeks in which they did not need much sleep and still had a lot of energy. Close friends, roommates, or family members are often helpful allies in making the right diagnosis of bipolar disorder. Table 13-3 lists the characteristics that tend to distinguish unipolar from bipolar depressions.

TABLE 13-3

Characteristics That Tend to Distinguish Unipolar from Bipolar Depressions

UNIPOLAR DEPRESSION	BIPOLAR DEPRESSION
PRESENTING SYMPTOMS	
Psychomotor agitation or retardation	Psychomotor retardation
Anxiety	Lethargy
Insomnia	Hypersomnia
Anorexia	Hyperphagia
Underweight	Overweight
Feel worse in the A.M. and better in the P.M. ("diurnal mood variation")	Feel worse in the P.M. and better in the A.M. ("reverse diurnal mood variation")
Psychosis less likely	Psychosis more likely
LONGITUDINAL FEATURES	
Less family history of mood disorders	More family history of depression and mania
Premorbidly obsessional, shy, moralistic, insecure	Premorbidly outgoing, active, uninhibited, successful
No prior mania or hypomania	Prior mania or hypomania
No prior hospitalizations	Prior hospitalizations

Dysthymic Disorder

Formerly called "depressive neurosis," dysthymic disorder presents with a chronic dysphoria or anhedonia that is not severe enough to meet all the criteria for major depression. *DSM-IV-TR* requires that symptoms exist for at least 2 years. This dysphoria or anhedonia may be continual or episodic; euthymia may exist for several days to weeks, but no longer than several weeks. The diagnosis should not be made if an interval of normal mood lasts for more than a few months. Whereas many patients with major depression are unable to work or to socialize, those with dysthymic disorders function, though not at their peak. By definition, dysthymic disorders never present with delusions or hallucinations. When a major depression is superimposed on a dysthymic disorder, it's dubbed a "double depression." Table 13-4 lists *DSM-IV-TR* criteria for dysthymic disorder.

In contrast to major depression, dysthymic disorder is more relenting and less consuming. Patients may laugh and tell a joke and on occasion, they even enjoy themselves. Although loved ones find dysthymic disorders less infuriating and frustrating than major depressions, others become bored with the person's habitual moaning and complaining. Patients with dysthymia often become upset over matters that others take in stride. A woman whose brother had dysthymic disorder described him as having a "garlic depression—he makes everyone around him feel a little worse." Patients with dysthymic disorder have been shown to have slightly more impairment than those with major depression alone. Only about half fully recover from dysthymic disorder alone and, if major depression occurs with dysthymia, only about one-third recover (Klein et al., 1988).

A 40-year-old married woman from a traditional Italian family sought treatment because "I'm anxious and shaky most of the time, especially at work. I can't be that way at home, ever since my mother-in-law moved in for good and I have to be on my best behavior when I'm around her." The patient said she'd been unhappy most of her life, but had felt much worse since her mother-in-law camped in 5 months ago. "She comes from the old country. She expects me to wait on her, but nothing I do ever satisfies her. She complains; otherwise she does nothing. I return exhausted from work and immediately prepare dinner; so what does she say? 'You made the carrots wrong; you should cut them at angles, not up-and-down.' When I ask my husband to do something about *his* mother, all he says is, 'You're overreacting.' I feel unappreciated and drained. I cry all the time, but only in private: I don't want anybody to see I'm weak."

TABLE 13-4
DSM-IV-TR *Criteria for Dysthymic Disorder*

A. Depressed mood for most of the day, for more days than not, as indicated either by subjective account or observation by others, for at least 2 years. **Note:** In children and adolescents, mood can be irritable and duration must be at least 1 year.

B. Presence, while depressed, of two (or more) of the following:

   (1) poor appetite or overeating

   (2) insomnia or hypersomnia

   (3) low energy or fatigue

   (4) low self-esteem

   (5) poor concentration or difficulty making decisions

   (6) feelings of hopelessness

C. During the 2-year period (1 year for children or adolescents) of the disturbance, the person has never been without the symptoms in Criteria A and B for more than two 2 months at a time.

D. No Major Depressive Episode has been present during the first 2 years of the disturbance (1 year for children and adolescents); i.e., the disturbance is not better accounted for by chronic Major Depressive Disorder, or Major Depressive Disorder, In Partial Remission.

Note: There may have been a previous Major Depressive Episode provided there was a full remission (no significant signs or symptoms for 2 months) before development of the Dysthymic Disorder. In addition, after the initial 2 years (1 year in children or adolescents) of Dysthymic Disorder, there may be superimposed episodes of Major Depressive Disorder, in which case both diagnoses may be given when the criteria are met for Major Depressive Episode.

E. There has never been a Manic Episode, a Mixed Episode, or a Hypomanic Episode, and criteria have never been met for Cyclothymic Disorder.

F. The disturbance does not occur exclusively during the course of a chronic Psychotic Disorder, such as Schizophrenia or Delusional Disorder.

G. The symptoms are not due to the direct physiological effects of a substance (e.g., a drug of abuse, a medication) or a general medical condition (e.g., hypothyroidism).

H. The symptoms cause clinically significant distress or impairment in social, occupational, or other important areas of functioning.

Specify if:

Early Onset: if onset is before age 21

Late Onset: if onset is age 21 or older

Specify (for most recent 2 years of Dysthymic Disorder):

With Atypical Features

Note. From *DSM-IV-TR,* pp. 380, 381.

For the first time, somebody did. Tears and words gushed out, as this woman revealed her darkest fear: "I'm terrified I'm turning into my mother. Our family lived near Rome, which is where my mother was hospitalized for shock treatment, but she was depressed most of her life. She would sit in the corner for hours and say nothing. At other times, she'd act crazy and speak nonsense; she'd talk to the dead and accuse the milkman of stealing. My mother wasn't mean to me; it was more like she was mentally absent. That's when I learned you can't rely on anybody to solve your problems but yourself. . . . When I was 16, my mother began to improve. Suddenly, I had the mother I always wanted. I loved it. Two years later, though, she died of cancer. I still miss her, and I know I can't expect my mother-in-law to replace her, yet sometimes I do, and *that's* nuts. Far worse is that I'm acting like my mother—snapping at people, never laughing, overly serious, avoiding people, not talking, and always hopeless. I'm frightened I'll be crazy like her."

The patient's marriage ("my ticket to America") was sexless and passionless ("all he does is eat"). Because of financial limitations, she quit premed and became a secretary. Over the years, she's been promoted to administrator, but far slower than "other women with less skill." She claimed to have "always" had initial insomnia and poor appetite. During the past year she has shed 25 pounds, felt increasingly sluggish and restless during the day, preferred being alone, and seemed immune to praise. She had no history of hypomania or mania, nor did she ever contemplate suicide.

Her dysthymic disorder was treated with an antidepressant, and after 2 weeks, her sleep and appetite normalized and her dysthymia lifted. She could laugh and enjoy people. Although she still felt just as unappreciated at home and at work, she stopped fretting about it. After a month of treatment, her symptoms abated completely, but she refused to have any of her family meet with the therapist, saying simply, "I will handle things myself." (Note: Another example of how Axis I problems resolve much easier than Axis II problems.) Two months after her first visit, she observed, "I must have been depressed my entire life. Until now, I didn't know what it was like *not* to be depressed. . . . I feel like a new person, and yet I still worry that someday I'll go crazy like my mother." It was only after 8 months of psychotherapy that this fear disappeared.

Cyclothymic Disorder

Patients with cyclothymic disorder have hypomanic *and* dysphoric periods that are not severe enough to qualify as a bipolar disorder. Moreover, whereas bipolar disorder is episodic, cyclothymic disorder is continual; it, like dysthymic disorder, must exist for at least 2 years without the patient being euthymic

TABLE 13-5
DSM-IV-TR *Criteria for Cyclothymic Disorder*

A. For at least 2 years, the presence of numerous periods with hypomanic symptoms and numerous periods with depressive symptoms that do not meet criteria for a Major Depressive Episode. **Note:** In children and adolescents, the duration must be at least 1 year.

B. During the above 2-year period (1 year in children and adolescents), the person has not been without the symptoms in Criterion A for more than 2 months at a time.

C. No Major Depressive Episode, Manic Episode, or Mixed Episode has been present during the first 2 years of the disturbance.

Note: After the initial 2 years (1 year in children and adolescents) of Cyclothymic Disorder, there may be superimposed Manic or Mixed Episodes (in which case both Bipolar I Disorder and Cyclothymic Disorder may be diagnosed) or Major Depressive Episodes (in which case both Bipolar II Disorder and Cyclothymic Disorder may be diagnosed).

D. The symptoms in Criterion A are not better accounted for by Schizoaffective Disorder and are not superimposed on Schizophrenia, Schizophreniform Disorder, Delusional Disorder, or Psychotic Disorder Not Otherwise Specified.

E. The symptoms are not due to the direct physiological effects of a substance (e.g., a drug of abuse, a medication) or a general medical condition (e.g., hyperthyroidism).

F. The symptoms cause clinically significant distress or impairment in social, occupational, or other important areas of functioning.

Note. From *DSM-IV-TR,* p. 400.

for more than 3 months. *DSM-IV-TR* criteria for cyclothymic disorder are listed in Table 13-5.

Clinical Course

Major Depression

The age of onset is equally distributed throughout the adult life cycle; age 40 is the mean, and it can arise during childhood and infancy. Major depression usually appears over days or weeks, but it may erupt in a day or evolve over months or years. Anxiety, phobia, panic, or dysthymia may predate a major depression. The sequence of events leading to a depression should be precisely determined, since it is a mistake to assume that, for example, a person's termination from his job caused his depression, whereas it was actually his depression (and poor functioning) that caused the termination. Some depressions arise out of the blue, some after a precipitant. If untreated, major depression usually persists 6–13 months. By 1 year, 85% of major depressions have remitted. Most episodes of treated depression last about 3 months. As the course progresses, episodes tend to be more frequent and last longer. Recurrences are common and typically there will be six episodes over a 20-year period. Single and recurrent episodes of major depression may be slightly different species. Roughly half of all people with a major depression never have another episode. Of those having a second episode, 50% have a third one, and so on. People with recurrent major depressions continue to have about a 10% risk of their next episode being manic, no matter how many depressive episodes they have had. They also have more difficulties between depressive episodes. Recurrence rates are greatest during the first 4–6 months after recovery; thereafter, the further away from the episode, the lower the chance of a recurrence. For individuals with major (or bipolar) depression, the risk of future episodes increases if they have a history of dysthymic disorder, a persistent dysthymia after a major or bipolar depression, a substance abuse or anxiety disorder, an older age of onset, or a greater number of previous episodes. Roughly 20% of patients with major depression become chronically depressed. For the vast majority, major depression is an episodic condition where outside of distinct periods of illness, patients may be productive with few if any residual symptoms.

Bipolar Disorder

On average, bipolar disorder arises by age 30, although on rare occasions it may begin in octogenarians. First-onset mania in older adults is almost always associated with medical conditions, particularly neurological disease or medications. Mania more often precedes depression. Whereas most bipolar depressions emerge over days or weeks, mania can erupt suddenly. The most common prodromal symptoms of mania are increased activity, elevated mood, and a decreased need for sleep. On the average, these develop about 3 weeks prior to the manic episode (Molnar, Feeney, & Fava, 1988). If biologically untreated, bipolar depressions typically persist 6–9 months, manic episodes, 2–6 weeks. As with major depression, almost half of those with bipolar disorder experience more than one episode. One-third of all patients have chronic symptoms and evidence of social decline. However, good prognostic indicators are short duration of manic episodes, advanced age of onset, few suicidal thoughts, and few coexisting psychiatric or medical problems.

The sequence and frequency of manic and depressive episodes vary: Some patients have three or four depressive periods before exhibiting mania; others alternate between highs and lows. Some have an episode every 10 years, whereas others, known as "rapid cyclers," have four episodes of either mania or depression in a single year. The episodes of bipolar disorder tend to become more frequent and longer over time.

> The term *bipolar* is misleading because it implies that mania and depression are opposites and that euthymia occurs between them. Yet careful observation reveals that mania and depression are closer to each other than to normality. For instance, it's common to see a depressive affect intrude on mania; a patient will be talking a mile a minute, when for no apparent reason he cries a eulogy to a long-departed mother, and then just as suddenly, starts imitating Tina Turner. It is also common to see mania and depression alternate, with no intervening period of normalcy. There is also an increasingly recognized species of mania called "dysphoric mania" or mixed manic–depression, in which people have manic and depressive symptoms at the same time (or ultra-rapid cycling). Sometimes mixed episodes are misdiagnosed as treatment-resistant depression. Patients who experience mixed episodes have higher rates of suicidality or substance abuse.

Dysthymic Disorder

This disorder typically emerges during early adult life, although it occurs in children and adolescents. Its onset is gradual and often hard to pinpoint. Its course is chronic, its symptoms fluctuating.

Cyclothymic Disorder

The age of onset for cyclothymic disorder is most often in early adulthood. It begins gradually and persists chronically. Intermixing or alternating hypomanic and dysphoric symptoms may fluctuate within hours, days, weeks, or months. Intermittent euthymic periods may exist for up to 2 months.

Complications

Suicide is one of the leading causes of death worldwide, resulting in about 1 million deaths annually, and within the top 12 leading causes of death in the United States. Suicide is committed eventually by 15% of patients with severe depression, i.e. major or bipolar depression. It rarely occurs with dysthymic and cyclothymic disorders. Men commit suicide nearly three times as often as women, whereas women make suicide attempts much more often than men. Some of these differences can be explained by the fact that men are more likely to choose violent, highly lethal methods (e.g., shooting, hanging, jumping, crashing), whereas women more often overdose. More than 90% of those who commit suicide have a diagnosable psychiatric disorder, with major and bipolar depressions accounting for 50–70%, making depression the chief cause of suicide. Alcoholism and schizophrenia are the second and third leading causes, respectively. Although the evaluation of suicide is discussed in Chapter 2, it's worth repeating that, contrary to myth, those who talk about suicide *are* more likely to commit suicide.

The pathophysiology of suicide (and depression) is likely to be related to serotonin depletion and reduction in the 5-HT receptors in the brain's limbic system and frontal cortex. Because of the favorable safety profile of these medications and effectiveness in treating depression, SSRI antidepressants have been increasingly prescribed and credited with the reduction in suicide rates over the last few years. After the recent advisories by the FDA that SSRIs may increase the risk of suicidal thoughts in youth and young adults, there has been a reduction in the use of these medications. This reduction in antidepressant prescriptions has coincided with an 8% increase in suicide in 10- to 24-year-olds for 2003–2004 after a 13-year decline. A causal relationship is suspected.

Substance abuse, particularly from alcoholism, is a frequent complication in all mood disorders. Patients "medicate" their dysphorias with alcohol, cocaine, amphetamines, and less often with marijuana and hypnoanxiolytics. Convinced they're immune from danger and oblivious to their own limitations, patients with hypomania or mania take drugs to remain "up." *Death* from physical illness is four times more prevalent among patients with major depression. In adults, this prevalency is not accounted for by the increased suicide rate, but rather by a large increase in the usual "natural" deaths from illnesses such as cancer and cardiovascular disease (Murphy et al., 1987). The reasons for this increase are unknown, but it is known that impairments in the immune system and disturbances in heart rhythms are more likely to occur during depressive episodes.

Impaired judgment and *lousy decisions* are common. If a depressed patient thinks she's a terrible person or, because of anhedonia, feels "no love," she may try to divorce a loving spouse; if he's sure he's incompetent, he may quit a perfectly good job. People with bipolar disorder may also initiate divorce and quit work, thinking they are too good for their spouse or job. Clinicians should inform patients that their pathological moods are distorting their judgment and that they should postpone major decisions until they've recovered. *Occupational and academic failures* result from poor judgment, and more: Depressed patients function slowly, work inefficiently, and display little effort. Neuropsychiatric tests show that their abstract thinking abilities, attention spans, and short-term (but not long-term) memories are impaired. Patients with depression and/or mania often trap colleagues into covering for them.

Familial consequences, including an increased rate of marital difficulties, separation, and divorce, occur in major depression. Although the mechanisms are unclear, roughly 40% of children with a depressed parent develop major, longstanding impairments, especially mood, anxiety, and conduct disorders. Because of the the increased risk of inheritance and the long-term burdens of serious mood disorders, some afflicted individuals consider not getting married or not having children.

In summary, mood disorders have an enormous impact on a person's life. When compared with 10 major medical disorders, including heart disease, diabetes, and back pain, depression and cardiac disease were tied for having the worst impact on social, occupational, familial, and physical function.

Subtypes

Types and subtypes of mood disorders are important to identify for several reasons: Some require different treatments; some often escape detection (and treatment) because they resemble other disorders; some suggest different etiologies; some of these have research implications. Some have already been mentioned: endogenous/reactive, primary/secondary, unipolar/bipolar, psychotic/neurotic. (Reader beware! The classifications presented above and below are commonly used but not fixed in stone.)

DSM-IV-TR's most important subtypes of major depression are those with "psychotic," "melancholic," or "atypical features." *Major depressive episode with psychotic features* displays either delusions or hallucinations. The delusions and hallucinations may be either *mood-congruent* ("the devil is taking me to hell") or *mood-incongruent* ("the FBI is trying to program my brain to become an informant"). Patients with depression rarely hallucinate without also having delusions. During the first 6 months, psychotic depressions are more severe than nonpsychotic depressions. The chief reason for distinguishing psychotic from nonpsychotic depressions is that they benefit from different treatments.

Major depressive episode with melancholic features is dominated by symptoms seen in endogenous depressions, but no attempt is made to include cause or lack of cause as a feature. These patients are both lucky and unlucky; they are *unlucky* because they feel awful, but *lucky* because they have a depression that has an especially good chance of responding to biological treatments (e.g., antidepressants and electroconvulsant therapy); better than to psychotherapy or placebo (Peselow et al., 1992). Table 13-6 lists *DSM-IV-TR* criteria for melancholic features.

TABLE 13-6

DSM-IV-TR *Criteria for Mood Disorder with Melancholic or Atypical Features*

Specify if:

With Melancholic Features (can be applied to the current or most recent Major Depressive Episode in Major Depressive Disorder, and to a Major Depressive Episode in Bipolar I or Bipolar II Disorder only if it is the most recent type of mood episode)

A. Either of the following, occurring during the most severe period of the current episode:

    (1) loss of pleasure in all, or almost all, activities

    (2) lack of reactivity to usually pleasurable stimuli (does not feel much better, even temporarily, when something good happens)

B. Three (or more) of the following:

    (1) distinct quality of depressed mood (i.e., the depressed mood is experienced as distinctly different from the kind of feeling experienced after the death of a loved one)

    (2) depression regularly worse in the morning

    (3) early morning awakening (at least 2 hours before usual time of awakening)

    (4) marked psychomotor retardation or agitation

    (5) significant anorexia or weight loss

    (6) excessive or inappropriate guilt

Specify if:

With Atypical Features (can be applied when these features predominate during the most recent weeks of a Major Depressive Episode in Major Depressive Disorder or in Bipolar I or Bipolar II Disorder when the Major Depressive Episode is the most recent type of mood episode, or when these features predominate during the most recent 2 years of Dysthymic Disorder)

A. Mood reactivity (i.e., mood brightens in response to actual or potential positive events)

B. Two (or more) of the following features:

    (1) significant weight gain or increase in appetite

    (2) hypersomnia

    (3) leaden paralysis (i.e., heavy, leaden feelings in arms or legs)

    (4) long-standing pattern of interpersonal rejection sensitivity (not limited to episodes of mood disturbance) that result in significant social or occupational impairment

C. Criteria are not met for With Melancholic Features or With Catatonic Features during the same episode.

Note. From *DSM-IV-TR,* pp. 420, 422.

Major depressive episode with atypical features is almost the opposite of melancholic depressions. Atypical episodes display reverse biological signs and an extreme reactivity to environmental events, which often manifest as "rejection sensitivity." The slightest rejection plunges these patients into dark despair, whereas the slightest good news induces ecstasy.

> An example of rejection sensitivity occurred when Mary Rae's fiancé met her at the airport. He casually remarked to Mary Rae that a passerby was "attractive." Mary Rae became incensed, opened her suitcase, threw clothes all over the place, spent 30 minutes screaming at him, and then left the airport by herself. By evening she had calmed down, yet for weeks she pouted that, "The cluck doesn't realize I'm sensitive about my looks. Why couldn't he say something nice about *my* body?"

Patients with atypical features don't respond very well to tricyclic antidepressants or electroconvulsive therapy, but do better on MAOIs and SSRIs.

Bipolar disorder is divided into "bipolar I," which meets the full diagnostic criteria for a manic episode, and "bipolar II," in which there is a major depressive episode and hypomania, not mania; the patient's "highs" do not merit hospitalization. Although bipolar II disorder is generally considered to be a milder version of bipolar I, it may be an intermediate entity between bipolar I and major depression, or a completely distinct entity. Many clinicians find it useful to conceptualize bipolar disorder as a spectrum illness ranging from the narrow bipolar I definition to broader phenotypes that do not meet the strict *DSM-IV-TR* criteria for number of symptoms, episodic presentation, severity, or duration.

In *rapid cycling bipolar disorder*, patients have four or more episodes per year of mania, hypomania, or major depression. Each episode is followed by either remission or a switch into an episode of opposite polarity. This subtype represents a particularly severe form of bipolar disorder in which lithium is less effective than anticonvulsants.

Mood disorder with seasonal pattern, formerly called seasonal affective disorders (SAD) (or "the winter blues," as patients call it), refers to those depressions that invariably occur in the fall and winter; they improve within days of moving from cold to warm climates or from areas with short to long exposures to daylight. When depressed, these patients tend to eat more and sleep longer or later in the morning. SAD seems to be alleviated by artificial bright (2500 LUX) light, particularly if given in the early morning. If these patients develop hypomania or mania, it's usually in the summer. Clinicians should inquire about seasonal patterns of mood with every patient who presents with any type of mood disorder.

Epidemiology

Mood disorders are the most common mental disorders in outpatients treated by mental health professionals and comprise roughly one-quarter of a typical practice. However, in the general population mood disorders rank third behind anxiety and impulse control disorders. The 1-year prevalence rate for mood disorders using *DSM-IV* is 9.5%, with the rate for major depression at 6.7%, for dysthymic disorder at 1.5%, and for bipolar disorder at 2.6%. When looking at the broader expressions of bipolar disorder (including cyclothymia and not otherwise specified), lifetime prevalence may be as high as 5%. Just one-third of those with bona fide bipolar illness have been diagnosed and fewer treated.

In general, mood disorders strike twice as many women as men; however, this ratio varies depending on the disorder. Ninety percent of "atypical depressions" occur in women. Major depression and dysthymic disorder afflict two to three times more women than men. Bipolar disorder is closer to one and one-half times more common in women. During a lifetime, roughly 20% of women and 10% of men will suffer a major depressive episode; about a third of these patients will be hospitalized. Patients with recurrent depression have high rates of avoidant (30%), obsessive–compulsive (19%), and dependant (16%) personality disorders (Pilkonis & Frank, 1988). Contrary to popular belief, older adults do not have an increased risk for major depression. One high risk group for depression is young women who have children and minimal support in child rearing (Ensel, 1982). It may be more common in divorced, separated, or single people.

It appears that each successive generation since World War II has had an increased rate of depression and an earlier age of onset. Simultaneously, the rate of suicide, especially among youth, has also escalated with each generation. For instance, since the 1950s, the suicide rate for 15- to 24-year-olds has tripled, replacing homicide as the second leading cause of death among youth. These increased rates of depression and suicide are distressingly genuine; they are not methodological artifacts. Why depression and suicide have increased is unknown. Nevertheless, despite suicide still being most prevalent among older adults, more than ever, today's clinician must be alert to teenage suicide. The prevalence of mood disorders varies widely from culture to culture.

Etiology and Pathogenesis

Some mood disorders arise for no apparent reason; others are triggered by a precipitant. Unless the precipitant is blatantly obvious, clinicians should be cautious about attributing a depression to it. If clinicians look hard enough, they can always find a stressor to "explain" a depression. (Review your past month and you will surely discover some stressor to "account" for why you should be depressed.) Stress is the way of the world; therefore, the path toward depression must involve more than stress.

With or without environmental stressors as a triggering event ("situational" versus "nonsituational" or "reactive" versus "endogenous"), major depressions present with similar symptoms, overall clinical pictures, types and amounts of stress, premorbid social supports, and family psychopathology. The reason they present the same is because no matter how a depression begins, at some point a *final common pathway* of biological dysfunction is reached. In this way depression may be more like fever, for which there are many causes but a final common pathway and presentation. This commonality may explain why particular biological abnormalities are seen only in subgroups of mood disorders and usually in less than 60% of people with depression. The final common pathway may arise from many biological or psychosocial causes, a genetic vulnerability, a "depressogenic" medication, an early loss, a lack of positive reinforcement, and so on.

Biomedical Factors

Genetics. Because concordance rates for mood disorders in MZ and DZ twins are about 60% and 15%, respectively, genetic transmission is suspected. Severe endogenous depression and bipolar illness carry a higher genetic loading than milder forms. Families with predominantly unipolar depression are most likely to have relatives with unipolar depression, but they also have increased rates of bipolar disorders compared to the general population (and vice versa, in families with predominantly bipolar illness). The fact that bipolar and unipolar mood disorders do not breed absolutely true supports the notion that these conditions are not precisely distinct from each other. Genetic linkage studies have identified different sites of transmission in different families, so there is no one depression gene. Because genetic penetrance is incomplete, not all carriers of "depression" genes may get depressed.

Biochemistry. Many studies suggest that during depression, there is decreased serotonergic function and/or dysregulated noradrenergic function in the brain. The dysregulation involves a high basal (tonic) rate of firing but, when stimulated, a low response rate. In the noradrenergic system the result is like a TV with poor reception. There is a lot of "snow" in the picture (high basal rate of firing), and images come in weakly and poorly (low response). Most antidepressants normalize both the decreased serotonergic and dysregulated nonadrenergic function. It is thought that these abnormalities occur only during the depressive episode. Increased cholinergic sensitivity is found during and after many depressions (Dilsaver, 1986). Many of the relatives of depressed patients have this increased cholinergic sensitivity, including those who have never had depression. This cholinergic sensitivity may create a vulnerability to depression and underlie a trait abnormality in many people with depression.

Abnormalities in endocrine challenge tests (such as the dexamethasone suppression test and the TRH–TSH stimulation test) in patients with major depression occur 40–60% of the time. With a variety of endocrine challenges, a lack of the normal response occurs. If suppression normally occurs, nonsuppression or "escape" is seen, and if stimulation usually occurs, blunting of the stimulation manifests in depression. These probably are state abnormalities that normalize with recovery. One explanation for how stressful events may precipitate depression is through release of the hormone, cortisol. A persistent surge of cortisol may trigger or worsen depression in a person who is predisposed because of genetic or psychosocial factors.

Psychosocial Factors

The *loss of either the mother or father* during the first 5 years of life, or the loss of the father between the ages of 10 and 14, is associated with increased risk of adult depression. Losses during these time periods are also later associated with increased doctor visits (help-seeking behavior), whether or not the patient is depressed. In adulthood, although many different kinds of stressful events can contribute to depression, losses are most directly associated with increased risk for depression.

Little or no support system leads to a much higher risk for depression. Social support has been shown to mitigate the effects of negative stressors such as losses.

Sexual, physical, and/or emotional abuse leads to a much higher adult rate of major depression as well as to a variety of other psychiatric disorders. Children in environments in which their self-esteem is constantly threatened, or in which a very negative view of life is communicated, are more likely to become depressed as adults.

A *biopsychosocial continuum of response vulnerabilities* is always present. One person might carry a very high genetic biological risk for depression and need little environmental stress to precipitate the disorder, whereas another person may have a high psychological risk for depression and need little genetic predisposition. Most individuals are likely to fall between these two poles on the continuum.

Psychosocial Theories

Despite the variety of psychosocial theories of depression, their differences often rest more in language than content. Most of these theories involve the factors of *loss* and *self-esteem*. Many types of losses can trigger depression. Besides the obvious—deaths, separations—depression may occur after the removal of a bodily organ or on the anniversary of a personally significant loss. A manifestly good development may bring on a depression. For example, after winning a Pulitzer prize, a once-obscure writer is suddenly inundated with admirers—groupies, money-management types, the cocktail set, publishers—all wanting a "piece" of him. Unable to meet everyone's expectations, dissatisfied with his own inability to write another masterpiece, and missing his old friends, he becomes depressed. Loss can also trigger mania.

Psychoanalytic theories. Freud proposed that an *early severe loss* or trauma during childhood causes a vulnerability to depression. Although subsequent research has tended to support this hypothesis, the research has also raised doubts about how much and how frequently early loss contributes *specifically* to depression. Brown (1961) showed that the loss of a parent during childhood occurred in 51% of adults with depression and in 16% of controls. In contrast, Roy (1985) demonstrated that early parental separation and loss accounted for relatively few additional cases, that ages 5–11 were most crucial, and curiously, that loss of a father was slightly more psychonoxious than losing a mother.

In *Mourning and Melancholia* (1917), Freud observed that the normal mourner accepts both positive and negative feelings about the deceased, whereas the melancholic mourner cannot tolerate or consciously acknowledge any negative feelings toward the deceased; this *"ambivalence toward the lost object"* induces guilt and depression. Mourning is a reaction to a realistic loss, but melancholia may be a reaction to an imagined, or an unconsciously exaggerated, loss.

A controversial yet widely touted hypothesis is that depression results from "retroflexed anger"—that is, patients turn their rage against a lost object onto themselves. Today, hundreds of therapists hear a similar story: A patient's fiancé suddenly breaks their engagement, but rather than getting angry at the fiancé, the patient becomes depressed and says things like "This proves I'm unworthy." The concept of retroflexed anger neatly dovetails with the inverse relationship between suicide and homicide; it may also account for the low self-esteem of the depressed, for why some believe that they deserve punishment, and for why many are terrified of expressing and experiencing anger. The Catch-22 is, the more patients with depression express their fury, the more depressed they become—it's "proof" they're terrible people—and the more likely they are to commit suicide. Retroflexed anger may be germane to some depressions as either a contributor or a consequence; it may be more prominent in people who normally blame themselves for everything.

Ego psychologists initially claimed that many patients with depression were "mourning" more for their *loss of self-esteem* than for the loss of the object itself. Whether the object is a job or a lover, when patients believe their self-esteem is an extension of that lost object, then depression becomes increasingly likely. Later, ego psychologists stressed that depression arose from a discrepancy between the patient's actual and idealized self-esteem.

Many *behaviorists* view depression as a product of *"learned helplessness"*—that is, patients experience themselves as continually trying and failing. Repeated loss of positive reinforcement and concomitant increase of negative reinforcement results in discouragement, giving up (which further reduces rewards), and depression (Abramson, Seligman, & Teasdale, 1978; Beck, Rush, Shaw, & Emery, 1979).

The *cognitive theory* of depression emphasizes the patient's conscious thoughts. Patients with depression display the "cognitive triad": a negative view of self, the world, and their future. They think of themselves as inadequate, their world as unrewarding, their future as hopeless. Cognitive theory claims that these attitudes distort patients' perceptions of reality and cause depression; however, other studies suggest that the cognitive triad is a consequence of depression.

Differential Diagnosis

Substance-Induced Mood Disorder

When mood disorders exist, clinicians should consider that medications, exposure to neurotoxic chemicals, or recreational drugs may have caused a mood disturbance. Before it can be assumed that a drug causes depression, it should be demonstrated that the drug increases the rate for a major depression over the prevalence in the general population. In most reports on drugs "causing" depression, there was no screening for depression when the drug was started. However, it is important to realize that any medication may have any side effect, including the side effect of depression. Retinoids for acne and interferon for hepatitis C are just two examples of nonpsychotropic medications recently suspected to cause depression.

Mania can be precipitated by stimulants such as *cocaine* and *dextroamphetamine*. Sometimes patients report frequent manic episodes that are really 2- to 4-day cocaine binges. When people abruptly stop using stimulants, they may appear depressed: They sleep a lot, are apathetic, and show extreme psychomotor retardation, but they might not actually *say* they are depressed. This phase of stimulant withdrawal usually passes in a few days. Antidepressants can induce mania; TCAs, about 2% of the time and SSRIs about 1%. This rate is much higher in patients with a known bipolar disorder. A variety of other drugs (e.g., hallucinogens, corticosteroids) occasionally are associated with manic episodes. Agents frequently implicated in mood disturbance are listed below.

Oral contraceptives. Women on oral contraceptives (containing 50 mcg. estrogen) in the 1970s appeared to have an increased rate of depression, with features such as hypersomnia, hyperphagia, and retardation. Half of the depressed women on oral contraceptives had an absolute pyridoxine (vitamin B_6) deficiency, secondary to estrogen's competitive effects with pyridoxine coenzyme systems. When they were treated with pyridoxine 50 mg bid, there was a 90% recovery rate. Women without a deficiency responded to pyridoxine about 30% of the time (placebo response rate). It seems that the new lower estrogen oral contraceptives are safer in this regard. On the other hand, estrogens have been used to help treat depression in peri- and postmenopausal women.

Antihypertensives. Reserpine induces depression in about 15% of cases, probably through its ability to deplete biogenic amines. The beta-blocker propranolol increases the risk of depression two-fold or at least creates a depression-like syndrome (insomnia, low energy, apathy). Less lipophilic beta-blockers such as atenolol have a lower depression risk because they don't reach the brain. Methyldopa has also been reported to induce depressions. In some instances, calcium channel blockers and ACE inhibitors have been reported to cause mild improvement in depressive symptoms and may be preferred treatments in people at risk for mood disorders.

Steroids. High doses of corticosteroids (> 80 mg equivalent of prednisone) result in major psychiatric sequelae in about 20% of the cases; depression and mania are frequent among these.

Opiates. Produced naturally in the brain as endorphins but included in many pain preparations, opioids impact mood directly and profoundly through specific brain receptors. The opiates include morphine, oxycodone, fentanyl, methadone, and codeine. Initially mood improves, sometimes too much to the point of euphoria, but after a few weeks tolerance develops and symptoms of withdrawal emerge. It is extremely difficult to successfully treat someone who is depressed and on opiate pain medications.

Hypnoanxiolytics. Although diazepam and chlordiazepoxide have often been touted to induce depression, there is little convincing evidence of this. Many patients with depression present with anxiety, which treatment with a benzodiazepine may relieve while unmasking the remaining depressive symptoms. In higher doses

(> 30 mg equivalent of diazepam) benzodiazepines, barbiturates, and alcohol all probably exacerbate or cause depression. A 25% depression rate has been reported in patients who were started on alprazolam 4 mg a day for panic disorder without depression. Diazepam 30 mg is equivalent to alprazolam 3 mg, clonazepam 1.5 mg, lorazepam 4–6 mg, or beer 5–6 bottles.

Stimulants. These include cocaine, amphetamines, methylphenidate, and xanthine derivatives (caffeine). All can transiently improve mood through outpouring of monoamine neurotransmitters, even to the point of mania. However, tolerance and withdrawal symptoms emerge within a couple of weeks causing rebound dysphoria and even severe depression.

Mood Disorder Due to a Medical Condition

Generally, medical illnesses (e.g., TB, hepatitis, mononucleosis, anemia, hypothyroidism) differ from depression in that fatigue tends to be associated with hypersomnia (rather than the insomnia of depression), and depressed mood increases as the day progresses, rather than peaking in the morning, as is typical in depression. In medical conditions that produce several "vegetative symptoms," such as cancer, psychological symptoms such as dysphoric mood, hopelessness, guilt, worthlessness, and suicidal ideation are the best indicators of a major depression. For unknown reasons, pancreatic cancer seems to be associated with higher depression rates than other cancers. Depression may be the first indication of an occult pancreatic carcinoma before any metabolic disturbance. Certain medical illnesses have higher depression rates than others. These include:

Neurological conditions such as multiple sclerosis, Parkinson's disease, and strokes (particularly in the frontal left hemisphere). Mania is also more frequent in multiple sclerosis.

Endocrine diseases such as hypothyroidism and Cushing's disease are associated with higher depression rates. Cushing's disease and hyperthyroidism have higher mania rates. Women with treatment-resistant depression have higher thyroiditis rates, but may have no other obvious thyroid abnormality.

Autoimmune disorders such as rheumatoid arthritis and systemic lupus all carry higher depression rates than nonautoimmune disorders that have the same degree of disability. For example, rheumatoid arthritis has a higher depression rate than osteoarthritis.

Other Conditions Related to Mood Disorders

• Uncomplicated bereavement may present with the biological signs and symptoms of depression. In normal grief reactions, self-esteem tends to be preserved and anhedonia fluctuates considerably. Severe motor retardation, diurnal variation of mood, suicidal ideation, and significant disturbance of functioning are more often characteristics of depression. During normal bereavement, mourners episodically fantasize about their own death, berate themselves for not visiting or saving the deceased, or feel guilty that the wrong person died (survivor guilt). But when bereavement evolves into major depression, people can think of nothing but their loss, themselves, and their depression. Normal mourners acknowledge the deceased's unfavorable traits; those with depression idealize the departed and repress their faults. Bereavement with symptoms of depression may be delayed, but it usually emerges within 2 or 3 months of the loved one's death. After 3 months, normal mourners have moments of grief, but gradually return to their usual activities and can sustain thoughts about matters unrelated to the death. In contrast, when bereavement is complicated by depression, the depression often persists for more than 3 months, may get more (instead of less) severe over time, presents with numerous biological signs, and prevents the person from getting back into the "swing of things." In about 10% of individuals, bereavement becomes major depression. Those at highest risk have no, or minimal, support systems.

- *Secondary anorgasmia* or *secondary impotence* can occur with depression or as a result of a medical problem such as diabetes. In patients with depression these two symptoms are a result of the decrease in libido. In men, nocturnal erections can be lost in diabetes, whereas in depression, nocturnal erections usually occur. In diabetes, normal libido is initially present despite the impotence. Women who have had normal sexual desire and orgasms may become anorgasmic with depression.

- *Somatization* can be the result of depression or a disorder in its own right. Patients with a somatization disorder have had it, by definition, since at least the age of 30. In contrast, people with depression often start somatizing only when they get depressed; while depressed, they will double their doctor visits with an average of five to six visits a year. Before the depression and after treatment, somatic complaints and doctor visits return to normal levels. These patients may acknowledge anhedonia but deny depressed mood or blame depressive symptoms on their somatic complaint. For these reasons, they are often called "masked depressions."

- *Alcoholism or hypnoanxiolytic dependence* can cause depression or be a result of attempts to self-medicate depression. The diagnosis of depression should not be made until at least a 4- to 6-week trial of abstinence has been completed.

- *Pain* occurs in many depressed patients, with headache, back pain, or abdominal pain the most common. About a quarter of patients presenting with chronic pain have a diagnosis of major depressive disorder. Antidepressants have been effective in treating chronic pain with or without depression, particularly if a "pain lifestyle" has not yet been established.

- *Juvenile delinquents* have major depression about 25% of the time. These are the youngsters who are treatable and much less likely to have antisocial personalities. They manifest classic vegetative signs of depression and, while possibly denying depression, will acknowledge persistent boredom (anhedonia). Another reason for boredom in this population is that many of these kids are high stimulus seekers (low basal dopamine in the frontal lobes, present in ADHD) who get into trouble as they impulsively chase excitement (unfortunately, incarceration can be boring). The girls may be promiscuous, but driven by a need for warmth and affection and not by increased libido. The boys frequently abuse drugs to escape their situation rather than for strictly recreational purposes. Sometimes these were the good kids in grade school who "went bad." Kids with depression commit antisocial acts in an effort to be accepted by other kids, whereas antisocial kids behave in this way no matter what the consequences to others.

- *Anxiety* is a presenting complaint for many patients, more than half of whom really have a major depression. All symptoms of depression are present, but patients attribute them to anxiety. Antidepressants are more effective than anxiolytics in treating this combination. Nearly 60% of patients with Major Depression have a comorbid anxiety disorder. Accumulating evidence indicates that in patients with comorbid depression and anxiety, there is a tendency toward greater illness severity and a lower treatment response than those with either illness alone. Also, social functioning and quality of life are more greatly impaired.

- Since *schizophrenia* and mood disorders can display psychotic, catatonic, and dysphoric features, the most likely diagnosis is the one that presents first, occurs in first-degree relatives, shows the characteristic natural history, and meets *DSM-IV-TR* criteria. If catatonia is present and the patient is mute, an amytal interview or brief treatment with benzodiazepines may help with the diagnosis by allowing the patient to talk. Psychosis in depression and mania is usually briefer and less bizarre than in schizophrenia. If criteria for schizophrenia are met and there is an additional major depressive or manic episode, than the patient has a schizoaffective disorder (see Chapter 9).

Management and Treatment

The management and treatment of mood disorders employ one or more of the following interventions: (1) suicide prevention, (2) biotherapies, (3) psychotherapies, and (4) family involvement. These interventions tend to be used in this sequence; for example, preventing suicide precedes psychotherapy. However, these interventions are also interrelated such that, for example, suicide prevention often entails family involvement. Each of these interventions serves a different purpose: Biotherapies rectify symptoms by correcting biochemical abnormalities, psychotherapies address issues arising from and contributing to the disorder, and family involvement can be used to support patients or to remedy pathogenic family systems.

Regardless of the intervention, working with affectively disturbed patients is ultimately rewarding, since most patients recover—though in the short run, treatment may frustrate the most experienced of therapists and evoke considerable countertransference. Patients with depression frequently present with marked dependency, which they themselves disdain, expect others to meet, yet when this occurs, they get furious. Relatives may respond with pity, which patients will overtly reject yet feel they deserve. This dynamic of dependency strivings, anger over deprivation, anticipated rejection, and "entitled pity" leads clinicians to feel guilty, helpless, angry, and drained—feelings therapists should keep in check. Clinicians, often feeling that nothing they do for these patients is ever enough, should be careful not to try to run patients' lives. Therapists should avoid overpromising; they should dispense hope, not saccharine. Especially during the more impaired or serious periods of the disorder, therapists should be warm, "real," and accepting. To quote Sederer (1983):

> The therapist must be able to bear the patient's pain with him; extra time may be needed for this affect to emerge, especially in view of the depressed patient's psychomotor retardation. . . . The depressed patient feels unworthy of and unable to reciprocate excessive warmth and tends to withdraw and feel worse when this is offered. Excessive humor on the part of the therapist denies the patient his grief and is devaluing. (p. 22)

If therapists identify with patients who have depression, they will begin to feel depressed and trapped by the nihilistic view of the world. Instead, empathy is needed, allowing appreciation and acceptance of patients' feelings, but in the larger context of a more objective viewpoint.

Suicide Evaluation, Management, and Prevention

As indicated above, 15% of patients with severe depression will eventually die by suicide. This accounts for about 60% of all suicides. Approximately 80% of people who kill themselves have seen their physicians in the previous 6 months, often for symptoms of major depressive disorder (e.g., insomnia, decreased energy) or exaggerations of ongoing medical complaints. Therefore, all patients with depression should be asked about suicidal ideation. This can be done by approximations. One recommended questioning sequence follows:

1. "Do you sometimes have a feeling that life isn't worth living, or do you think about death much?"
2. "Do you sometimes think that if you died tomorrow from an accident or illness, that it just wouldn't matter?" (This is *passive* suicidal ideation.)
3. "Have you had thoughts of killing yourself?" (This is *active* suicidal ideation.)
4. "Have you thought of a way or plan to kill yourself?" (Is there a detailed plan, with the means to carry it out, and without the possibility of rescue?)

If patients answer yes to passive but not to active suicidal ideation, for now they are probably low risk, unless they are engaging in high-risk behavior (e.g., auto racing). If patients answer yes to the third question, further risk assessment is in order. Many patients who acknowledge ideation are at minimal risk if they have strong reasons for not committing suicide. Ask patients, "What has kept you from acting on your suicidal ideas?" Patients who respond that they could not actually do it because of their religious beliefs or because of their families are usually at lower risk. Similarly, patients who experience suicidal ideation as ego alien and frightening are at lower risk. The higher demographic risks are male, white, increasing age over 45 years, alone, socially alienated, with chronic disease, obsessive–compulsive or perfectionist tendencies, and/or substance abuse issues. People who have already made a suicide attempt are at higher risk, and, perhaps the best predictor of suicide is a prior attempt. The presence of a major psychiatric illness and family history of suicide are important risk factors.

How can actively suicidal patients be managed? Suicidal impulses, like alcoholic impulses, can be managed better 1 day or 1 week at a time. Many suicidal patients can agree to go for 1 or 2 weeks or a month without killing themselves, but cannot agree to *never* kill themselves. This "no suicide decision," which they make for themselves (and not as a promise to the clinician or anyone else), can help to buy time while treatment is started (Drye, Goulding, & Goulding, 1973). It should also include a "no-escape clause": that is, "no matter what happens." This allows for crisis situations (e.g., a cocaine-using boyfriend leaving the relationship). Suicidal ideation should be reassessed at least weekly and at the end of the agreed-upon time period, and if patients are still suicidal, a new "no suicide decision" should be made. Patients who are unreliable because of substance abuse, personality disorders, or indicate that a week is too long to defer suicide, require expert evaluation and possible hospitalization.

The clinician's next priority is to prevent suicide, which in most cases entails breaking the patient's "inertia cycle." When they finally seek professional help, most suicidal patients have been mired in painful, unproductive ruminations that have intensified their helplessness. One way to avert suicide and to stop this inertia is to hospitalize the patient. This key decision may depend less on the patient's actual suicide potential and more on his or her network of support. It's crucial to immediately involve the patient's family or close friends, not only to determine how well they can care for the patient, but also to teach them how to be extensions of the treatment team—how to mobilize the patient, what warning signs to look for, what to do with medications, what to discuss (and not discuss) with the patient, and so on.

Interrupting the inertia cycle is the start to treatment, not its end, and a good place to start is to assign patients household chores. No matter how mundane this sounds, patients feel that "at last" something is happening, that they are a part of it, and that they are finally "giving" instead of just "getting." Outpatients should have follow-up appointments within days, not weeks. Until the first appointment, the therapist can have the patient telephone, if only for 3 minutes a day. Since a 10-day supply of tricyclic antidepressants ingested all at once can be lethal, only a few days worth of pills should be prescribed, or low-lethality antidepressants such as SSRIs should be substituted. Two medications are reported in the literature to be antisuicidal. Clozapine carries an FDA-approved indication for preventing suicide in patients with schizophrenia or schizoaffective disorder. Lithium has been reported to reduce risk of suicide as well as suicide attempts by as much as 80% in patients with bipolar disorder.

Potentially suicidal patients might also be reminded that "suicide is a permanent solution to a temporary problem," and that patients with depression, after they are successfully treated, invariably stop feeling suicidal.

Biological Treatments

The biological treatment of mood disorders includes selective serotonin reuptake inhibitors (SSRIs), serotonin and norepinephrine reuptake inhibitors (SNRIs), heterocyclic antidepressants (mainly tricyclic antidepressants, TCAs), atypical antidepressants (bupropion, trazodone, mirtazapine), monoamine-oxidase inhibitors (MAOIs), mood stabilizers (lithium and anticonvulsants), atypical or traditional antipsychotics, augmentation agents (e.g., triiodothyronine), electroconvulsive therapy (ECT), and vagal nerve stimulation (VNS). The therapeutic categories and side effects of medication are outlined in Chapter 6, and their applications are discussed below. Patients need to be told that none of these medications causes physical or psychological dependency. In regard to tolerance, over time these medications may "poop out" or stop working (tachyphylaxis) even though they are faithfully taken (adherence) and properly dosed.

Major depression. Considering patients with *all* types of major depression, 78% improve with ECT, 60–70% improve with antidepressants (heterocyclic, atypical, MAOIs, SNRIs, SSRIs), and 23% improve with placebo alone. Of the seven well-controlled studies comparing ECT and TCAs, four showed no difference and three favored ECT. Nonetheless, because ECT is more inconvenient to administer and ominous to laypeople, antidepressant medications are usually the first biological treatment for major depression. In general, patients who benefit from antidepressants have *biological signs* of depression, whereas those without biological signs do not.

• *TCAs.* The predictors of response to TCA antidepressants include insomnia, anorexia, psychomotor retardation, anhedonia, insidious onset, and one puzzling nonbiological predictor: guilt (Jewish, Catholic, or Protestant guilt — it doesn't matter). It also doesn't matter whether or not the depression has been environmentally triggered, or whether it is "understandable." If a patient lost her job and then developed major depression with its accompanying biological symptoms, antidepressants still work. One or more atypical and reverse biological signs, including hypersomnia, hyperphagia, profound anergy, mood reactivity, rejection sensitivity, and nocturnal worsening of mood, appear to reduce effectiveness of TCAs to 50%, whereas SSRIs and MAOIs may retain their 70% effectiveness.

• *SSRIs.* When choosing an antidepressants, it makes sense to begin with an SSRI because of lower side effects (tolerability), easy dosing, and safety even in overdose (high therapeutic index). The SSRIs (fluoxetine, sertraline, citalopram, paroxetine, fluvoxamine) usually don't have any of the tricyclic or heterocyclic side effects. Furthermore, the starting dose is often sufficient to treat a depression. The SSRIs may perform better than the tricyclics in patients with reverse vegetative symptoms and atypical depressions. When looking at the grouped data in clinical trials, no SSRI has demonstrated clear efficacy over another; however, individuals may respond much better to one antidepressant over another even in the same category. Often the initial choice of antidepressant is based on side effect profile or previous response by the person or a family member to the particular medication. Despite relative safety in overdose, SSRIs have been reported to increase suicidal thinking and impulsiveness, especially early in the treatment course, for a small (2%) but statistically significant number of adolescents and young adults. This observation may particularly apply to younger people whose depression may be of the bipolar variety but not yet accurately diagnosed, not fully developed, or otherwise undetected.

• *Monoamine-oxidase inhibitors.* MAOIs have the same efficacy as other antidepressants in treating typical depressions, but they do not lose efficacy in depressions with one or more atypical symptoms (hypersomnia, hyperphagia, mood worse at night, severe anergy, rejection sensitivity, mood reactivity, or in depression with panic attacks). But MAOIs are rarely chosen first because of dietary concerns: Patients on MAOIs who ingest tyramine-containing foods (e.g., herring, aged cheese, salami) or sympathomimetic drugs (e.g., cocaine, amphetamines, decongestants) can develop a "hypertensive crisis"—soaring blood pressure—that can be life-threatening. MAOIs should be stopped for 2 weeks before the initiation of another type of antidepressant.

In order for any antidepressant to work, patients must be on the *proper dose* for the *proper duration.* Therapeutically effective dosages of SSRIs and TCAs vary from one patient to another. For example, the typical adult dose for a TCA such as imipramine is usually 150–300 mg/day (a third to half this amount for older adults). Moreover, the patient's mood may not begin to lift until she's been on an adequate dose for at least a few weeks. Patients (and relatives) should be told, "Don't give up because you don't feel better in a day or so. Valium acts right away, but antidepressants don't; they usually take 4–6 weeks." Most patients on antidepressants show some improvement before 4 weeks but an adequate trial should last from 4 to 8 weeks.

Despite their overall effectiveness, antidepressants do not completely eliminate symptoms in 25% of patients with major depressions. If patients have not begun to improve after 4 weeks, the options include (1) increasing the dose of the currently prescribed antidepressant; (2) adding lithium or triiodothyronine (T3, a thyroid compound); (3) adding another antidepressant, particularly one that works on a different neurotransmitter system; (4) changing to another category of antidepressant; (5) adding an antipsychotic, especially when psychotic symptoms are present; (6) considering ECT.

• *Antipsychotics.* Patients with psychotic depression respond only about one-third of the time to antidepressants alone and just under half the time to antipsychotics alone. Combining the two treatments results in 65–75% response rates. Failing this combination or if a faster response is necessary, ECT is the preferred treatment.

• *Benzodiazepines.* Supplemental low-dose benzodiazepines may initially alleviate prominent anxiety and insomnia, but typically should be discontinued after a couple of weeks because of tolerance to their beneficial effects and the risk for dependency.

Patients should remain on antidepressants until they have been symptom-free for at least 16–20 weeks and until stressors in their lives are down to manageable levels. Discontinuing medication at the time of a child-custody battle would be a bad idea. To encourage staying on medication, patients should be informed that there is a 50% chance of relapse if they stop sooner than 6 months after complete symptom resolution. Mild symptoms are just as predictive of relapse as major symptoms, so that even when major symptoms have disappeared, the presence of minor symptoms indicates that the disorder has not run its full course (Prien & Kupfer, 1986). This is all about homeostasis—the brain tends to maintain itself where it's at. If not given enough time to reset its neurotransmitters and receptors, it tends to revert to the previous settings. Antidepressants should be prescribed for longer periods in patients with more frequent depressive episodes, longer depressive cycles, and an older age of onset. If depression is severe and frequent enough (more than two episodes), prophylactic, long-term antidepressant therapy may be indicated.

TCAs should always be discontinued slowly—no faster than 25 mg/day; they should never be stopped abruptly. If they are, in two to four days patients may experience insomnia, nightmares, or nausea and a flu-like syndrome without a fever. Fluoxetine probably can be stopped all at once, because it stays in the blood for weeks. But when the shorter-acting SSRIs such as paroxetine are abruptly withdrawn, nausea and headache may ensue.

• *Electroconvulsive therapy.* ECT, as it is now administered, is the most effective of all the antidepressant treatments, with nearly 80% responding. Historically, ECT was frightening: Patients would receive over 20 treatments for just about any condition; they'd convulse wildly, fracture spines, lose memories, and be dazed silly. Those days are gone. Today ECT is a safe and effective treatment for severe depressions (and sometimes for life-threatening mania). Usually six to twelve treatments, one every other day, are given. Fractures and wild convulsions no longer occur; memory loss and confusion are either nonexistent or minimal and short-lived. ECT may work by massively discharging or releasing neurotransmitters throughout the cortex and subcortex. (It does not scare patients into getting better—sham ECT doesn't work.) Perhaps more importantly, the seizure stimulates the hypothalamus to discharge its hormones, which stimulate the anterior pituitary and inhibits the discharge of cortisol.

Now patients are given a short-acting anesthetic (about 10 minutes), oxygen, and a temporary muscle paralyzer to prevent fractures. The seizure is monitored with an EEG because the motor seizure is masked. The convulsion usually lasts from 25 to 60 seconds. Convulsions less than 25 seconds have less therapeutic effect. Several minutes later patients awaken from the anesthesia with no memory of the shock.

First-time observers of ECT invariably describe it as "underwhelming." Patients, too, are surprised they don't feel anything, and why should they?—brain tissue is free of pain fibers. A survey of patients who received ECT revealed that two-thirds found going to the dentist more upsetting than getting ECT. The mortality rate from ECT is lower than for tonsillectomy, the former ranging from 0.008 to 0.05%. Indeed, the most dangerous aspect of ECT is not ECT *per se*, but the anesthesia. The main side effects of ECT are short-term memory loss and confusion; these may not occur or they may be so bad that the patient urinates in public or can't name his or her spouse. These problems, which are greatly minimized by unilateral ECT, significantly decrease within 2 weeks of the final treatment. When compared to bilateral, unilateral ECT is less effective when using the same amount of electrical energy. ECT does not cause any permanent brain damage or memory loss. Six months later, patients who have had ECT do as well on memory and other neuropsychological tests as do people who have never had ECT. It is considered a safe and effective treatment for major depression, mania, and schizophrenia. Relative contraindicators to the use of ECT include space-occupying lesions, increased intracerebral pressure, or recent myocardial infarction. Transcranial magnetic stimulation is still being studied as a possible alternative to ECT but is not consistently effective and lacks FDA approval.

• *Vagal nerve stimulation* (VNS). An electric device is surgically implanted and the left vagus nerve is electrically stimulated at the cervical level. This expensive FDA-approved procedure is reserved for patients with chronic or recurrent depression who are not responsive to all other treatments.

Bipolar disorder. Whether the patient presents manic or depressed, treatment should begin with a bone fide mood stabilizer, either lithium or an anticonvulsant. The use of antidepressants in bipolar disorder is controversial because they may be ineffective for depression and may actually increase cycling of moods, thereby worsening the long-term prognosis of this illness. If an antidepressant is prescribed during a depressive phase, it is generally recommended that it be tapered and discontinued once the depression is controlled. Lithium is effective in bipolar depression but has a more robust impact on mania. Lamotrigine may have more antidepressant activity than other anticonvulsants and is effective in both preventing and treating depressive episodes. Some of the newer antipsychotics seem to have some mood-stabilizing and antidepressant effects and may be used in combination with mood stabilizers.

Quetiapine is currently the only second-generation (atypical) antipsychotic approved for depression.

For the manic phase, the effectiveness of lithium has been documented for about 50 years. Divalproex and carbamazepine have also been supported by about 20 years of clinical study (lamotrigine is the new kid on the block). The atypical antipsychotics (aripiprazole, olanzapine, quetiapine, risperidone, and ziprasidone) are FDA approved for acute mania. As in bipolar depression, lithium or divalproex sodium may be used in combination with an antipsychotic for severe mania, rapid cycling, or mixed states. Patients with mixed episodes respond more slowly to, and experience less improvement with, lithium, and divalproex sodium may be more effective in these instances. Benzodiazepines may be added temporarily for resting, sleep, or reducing anxiety. Once the acute episodes (mania, depressions, or mixed) are under control, the same medications are often continued to prevent return episodes (maintenance pharmacotherapy).

Lithium is a salt, much like table salt, except that lithium replaces sodium. The immediate predecessor to the beverage 7-Up contained lithium and was marketed as a lithium soda that took the "ouch out of the grouch." Trace amounts of lithium are in the water supply, a tidbit that encourages some patients to reason, "It's okay to take lithium because it is a natural substance and not a drug."

Lithium is best for preventing mania and usually effective for preventing bipolar depression. Acute bipolar depression is often treated with lithium and antidepressants, whereas acute mania responds best to lithium with the addition of benzodiazepines for agitation or antipsychotics for psychosis. Although lithium usually takes 10 days to take effect, the benzodiazepines and antipsychotics can calm people with mania within hours for up to a few days. One to three treatments of ECT can be effective in treating mania that does not respond quickly to medication. Following the first manic or depressive episode, lithium is sometimes stopped if there is no other episode for 6 months. However, there is evidence that with each new episode, the bipolar disorder worsens both in frequency and severity. Some recommend that most patients should stay on lithium for life to prevent this deteriorating course.

Overall, a majority of patients with bipolar disorder substantially improve on lithium. A common problem, especially with "rapid cyclers," is the occurrence of mania or depression in lithium-treated patients. When this happens, first serum lithium levels are checked to see if patients are actually taking the drug and have a high enough lithium level to treat an acute episode. Bipolar patients often stop lithium because they miss their highs—can you blame them? Second, patients' thyroid functioning is checked, since hypothyroidism mimics the symptoms of depression and may result from prolonged lithium therapy. Third, if patients become depressed, an antidepressant may be added. Although usually helpful, giving antidepressants to patients with bipolar depression may increase the rapidity of cyclic mood changes or "switch" patients to mania. (Bupropion may have a lower risk of switching patients.) Fourth, if none of the above works, or if patients cannot tolerate lithium's side effects, anticonvulsants divalproex sodium, lamotrigine, or carbamazepine are prescribed. Divalproex sodium can significantly decrease mania in 5 days.

Psychotherapies

The psychotherapy of mood disorders can help patients to (1) learn the "facts" about their disorder, (2) feel less alone, (3) cope better with their disorder, (4) identify and avert situations likely to rekindle another episode, (5) abort episodes that have just begun by early symptom recognition, (6) view themselves and their world more rationally and constructively, (7) improve interpersonal relations, and (8) address the problems plaguing them.

Which of these goals are pursued depend primarily on patients' current mental state. If they are in an acute manic or depressive episode, psychotherapy should stress support more than insight, since they lack the attention span, abstract thinking abilities, and emotional perspective to use insight appropriately. For example, a man with major depression who "suddenly discovers" his sexual feelings toward his daughter will not apply this realization to understand his marital problem but to "prove his depravity." Patients with melancholia or psychotic depression are especially unable to profit from insight, and if anything, will use it for self-flagellation. Cognitive–behavioral or interpersonal psychotherapies benefit about 70% of patients with mild to moderate depression. These psychotherapies work as well but more slowly than antidepressants. Typically, 12–16 weeks are needed. Psychotherapy is indicated if patients with mild to moderate depression prefer this treatment. Patients with severe and/ or psychotic depressions or with personality disorders don't do as well with psychotherapy and should be treated with antidepressants first. Among the more commonly used therapies are the following:

Interpersonal psychotherapy (ITP). This therapy is based on the theory that almost all people who become depressed have a major interpersonal problem—conflicts with a significant other, a boss, difficult role transitions, or deficient social skills and the consequent social isolation. These problem areas are identified and addressed. Instead of concentrating on intrapsychic material with a goal of personality change, ITP focuses on interpersonal matters, both inside and outside of therapy. Some studies have shown that combining ITP and medications yields superior results and lower dropout rates than either treatment alone especially in more seriously depressed patients (Schramm et al., 2007). By teaching patients how to cope with problems, ITP may reduce the risk of relapse. The conduct of ITP has been detailed in a manual (Klerman et al., 1984).

Behavior therapies. These approaches assume that depressed patients lack positive reinforcement and would benefit from being taught to identify the relation between events and feelings, to maximize praise from self and others, to avoid self-punishment, to set realistic goals, and to improve social skills. Behavior therapy for depression is detailed in a manual (Lewinsohn et al., 1984).

Cognitive therapy (CT). Because CT focuses on more accessible conscious and preconscious material, it can be used by many more patients with depression than can traditional psychoanalytic treatments. The actual technique of CT is summarized in Chapter 5, and its use for depression is best detailed by Beck et al. (1979). It is usually combined with behavioral therapy.

Group therapy. Group behavioral, cognitive, and psychodynamic therapy may be only slightly less effective than their individual versions.

Brief psychodynamic psychotherapy. The goal of this therapy is to resolve core conflicts based on personality and situational variables. Compared to the other therapies, it may be somewhat less effective for depression. Treatment manuals are available (Luborsky, 1984; Malan, 1979; Sifneos, 1979; Strupp & Binder, 1984).

Marital therapy. Marital therapy may treat both the depression and the marital and family problems by modifying negative interaction patterns and increasing mutually supportive aspects of the relationship (Barbato & D'Avanzo, 2007). Marital discord or separation often precedes depression, persists after depression, and frequently precedes relapses. In more than half of distressed couples who are considering, or are in the process of, separation and divorce, one spouse will be clinically depressed. This form of therapy might be considered as the main psychotherapy or as an adjunct with a patient who has both depression and marital discord.

Family Involvement

The importance of involving family members cannot be overemphasized. Like therapists, family members often feel that their advice and support are ignored, but unlike therapists, family members *live* with the relative who has depression, and doing so can drain the most caring and resilient of loved ones. Perhaps this accounts for higher divorce rates and higher rates of psychopathology in spouses of depressed patients.

There are three general therapeutic reasons for involving relatives: (1) to support the patient, (2) to support the family, and (3) to treat the family. During acute affective episodes, therapists should employ family members as extensions of the treatment. Relatives should be told the "facts" about mood disorders—their symptoms, natural history, genetic risks, prognosis, and treatment. They should be counseled on how to respond to the patient's disorder. They should be cautioned about getting sucked into the patient's pessimistic views, as well as to understand the limits of what they can do to alleviate their loved one's misery. By helping the family help the patient, the therapist helps support the family.

Citing confidentiality, some patients with depression seek to prevent any family involvement. Although confidentiality is usually respected, when a patient's *judgment is impaired*, maintaining confidentiality may be senseless and harmful. Some patients exclude relatives so that the relatives "won't be contaminated by me"; others "use" confidentiality to deny that they are ill and need help; still others invoke confidentiality as a way of avoiding intimacy. In each case, the therapist must assess what information should be shared with the family and what should remain private. That a patient has sexual fantasies about aardvarks is nobody's business; that he's contemplating suicide or selling the family business is!

After a severe episode has passed, there are times when it is best to examine the family's or couple's role in causing or aggravating the patient's depression. This possibility is especially important to consider with female patients, since they tend to assume full responsibility for the problem, which is actually the entire family's. As a result, these patients seek individual treatment when couple or family therapy would be more appropriate.

Family treatment is also of special use for teenagers with depression, because they often come from families with a low tolerance for individuation and anger. The kid will rebel but succumb in despair. One parent might frequently abuse substances while the other is chronically depressed. A common pattern is for the parents to be furious with each other, yet bait their child by being "injustice collectors" and "grave-diggers"—that is, resurrecting past misdeeds and using them as accusations. Therapists should help these adolescents distinguish their problems from their parents', while also addressing the depression and substance abuse that usually afflict other family members. Adolescents with depression can be very convincing about the utter malevolence of their parents. They often tell their own version of the Cinderella story, with them as the victims and the parents as the evil persecutors. This may be an example of the negative thinking of depression, and a face-to-face meeting with the family is needed to see where truth lies.

Finally, in the ultimate tragedy—suicide—clinicians should talk with the family to afford comfort, to prevent others from committing impulsive suicides, to minimize the self-blame of relatives (which might require pointing out to them that suicide is a hostile act because it hurts everyone), and finally, to learn from any therapy mistakes that might have been made. Sometimes lawyers recommend against this approach, but the chances of lawsuit are much higher if the family sees the clinician as cold, distant, or uncaring.

References

Abramson, L.Y., Seligman, M.E., & Teasdale, J. (1978). Learned helplessness in humans: Critique and reformulation. *Journal of Abnormal Psychology, 87,* 49–79.

Barbato, A., & D'Avanzo, B. (2007). Efficacy of couple therapy as a treatment for depression. *Journal of Rehabil. Res. Dev., 44*(6), 775–784.

Beck, A.T., Brown, G., Berchick, R.J., Stewart, B.L., & Steer, R.A. (1990). Relationship between hopelessness and ultimate suicide: A replication with psychiatric outpatients. *American Journal of Psychiatry, 147,* 190–195.

Beck, A.T., Rush, A.J., Shaw, B.F., & Emery, G. (1979). *Cognitive therapy of depression: A treatment manual.* New York: Guilford Press.

Brown, F. (1961). Depression and childhood bereavement. *Journal of Mental Science, 107,* 754–777.

Dilsaver, S.C. (1986). Cholinergic mechanisms in affective disorders: Future directions for investigation. *Acta Psychiatrica Scandinavica, 74,* 312–334.

Drye, R.C., Goulding, R.L., & Goulding, M.E. (1973). No-suicide decisions: Patient monitoring of suicidal risk. *American Journal of Psychiatry, 130*(2), 171–174.

Ensel, W.M. (1982). The role of age in the relationship of gender and marital status to depression. *Journal of Nervous and Mental Diseases, 170,* 536–543.

Freud, S. (1917). Mourning and melancholia. In E. Jones (Ed.), *Collected papers.* New York: Basic Books.

Keller, M.B., Lavori, P.W., Rice, J., Coryell, W., & Hirschfeld, R.M.A. (1986). The persistent risk of chronicity in recurrent episodes of nonbipolar major depressive disorder: A prospective follow-up. *American Journal of Psychiatry, 143,* 24–28.

Klein, D.N., Taylor, E.B., Harding, K., & Dickstein, S. (1988). Double depression and episodic major depression: Demographic, clinical, familial, personality, and socioenvironmental characteristics and short-term outcome. *American Journal of Psychiatry, 145,* 1226–1231.

Klerman, G.L., Weissman, M.M., Rounsaville, B.J., & Chevron, R.S. (1984). *Interpersonal psychotherapy of depression.* New York: Basic Books.

Lewinsohn, P.M., Antonuccio, D.A., Steinmetz, J., & Teri, L. (1984). *The coping with depression course: A psychoeducational intervention for unipolar depression.* Eugene, OR: Castalia.

Lieberman, P.B., & Strauss, J.S. (1984). The recurrence of mania: Environmental factors and medical treatment. *American Journal of Psychiatry, 141*, 77–80.

Luborsky, L. (1984). *Principles of psychoanalytic psychotherapy.* New York: Basic Books.

Malan, D.H. (1979). *Individual psychotherapy and the science of psychodynamics.* Boston: Butterworth.

Merikangas, K.R. (1984). Divorce and assortative mating among depressed patients. *American Journal of Psychiatry, 141*, 74–76.

Molnar, G., Feeney, M.G., & Fava, G.A. (1988). Duration and symptoms of bipolar prodomes. *American Journal of Psychiatry, 145*, 1576–1578.

Murphy, J.M., Monson, R.R., Olivier, D.C., Sobol, A.M., & Leighton, A.H. (1987). Affective disorders and mortality. *American Journal of Psychiatry, 44*, 473–480.

Peselow, E.D., Sanfilipo, M.P., DiFiglia, C., & Fieve, R.R. (1992). Melancholic/endogenous depression and response to somatic treatment and placebo. *American Journal of Psychiatry, 149*(10), 1324–1334.

Pilkonis, P.A., & Frank, E. (1988). Personality pathology in relationship to treatment response. *American Journal of Psychiatry, 145*, 435–441.

Prien, R.F., & Kupfer, D.J. (1986). Continuation drug therapy for major depressive episodes: How long should it be maintained? *American Journal of Psychiatry, 143*, 18–23.

Roy, A. (1985). Early parental separation and adult depression. *Archives of General Psychiatry, 42*, 987–991.

Schramm, E., vanCalker, D., Dykierek, P., Lieb, K., Kech, S., Zobel, I., et al. (2007). An intensive treatment program of interpersonal psychotherapy plus pharmacotherapy for depressed inpatients: Acute and long-term results. *American Journal of Psychiatry, 164*, 768–777.

Sederer, L.I. (1983). Depression. In L.I. Sederer (Ed.), *Inpatient psychiatry: Diagnosis and treatment* (pp. 2–27). Baltimore: Williams & Wilkins.

Sifneos, P. (1979). *Short-term dynamic psychotherapy, evaluation, and technique.* New York: Plenum Press.

Strupp, H.H., & Binder, J.L. (1984). *Psychotherapy in a new key: A guide to time-limited dynamic psychotherapy.* New York: Basic Books.

Ward, N.G. (1990). Pain and depression. In J.J. Bonica (Ed.), *The management of pain* (pp. 310–319). Malvern, PA: Lea & Febiger.

14

Anxiety Disorders

A nationwide study of mental disorders in the United States revealed the surprising fact that anxiety disorders, not depression, were the most prevalent psychiatric diagnoses. Anxiety disorders are seen in 18% of the population in a given 12-month period, and about 29% will meet criteria for an anxiety disorder over the course of their lifetime. In general, females seem to have increased prevalence for all anxiety disorders. Table 14-1 summarizes the epidemiology of the most frequent anxiety disorders and points to the fact that individuals who have one anxiety disorder are likely to meet *DSM-IV-TR* criteria for another. This may represent diagnostic overlap as opposed to real co-occurring illness and suggests that the categories are not entirely valid discriminations (a discussion for the DSM-V committee).

The majority of these individuals is not seen by mental-health professionals, but present instead to medical-care settings with anxiety-related physical complaints or to substance abuse treatment settings. In medical settings, anxiety and anxiety-induced insomnia are the most common psychological complaints. People with anxiety-related problems represent approximately 30% of patients seeking help from primary-care physicians. Frequently, these patients complain about somatic symptoms related to anxiety—for example, heart racing, diarrhea, upset stomach, dizziness, chest tightness—rather than about the anxiety itself. When both the patient and physician maintain a strictly somatic orientation, the underlying anxiety frequently goes unrecognized. In the following discussions, it is assumed that anxiety is not a unitary phenomenon, but rather a complex and variable response that frequently co-occurs with other psychiatric disorders and by itself may define one of five distinct anxiety disorders (panic, phobic, obsessive–compulsive, stress, and generalized anxiety).

NORMAL VERSUS PATHOLOGICAL ANXIETY

Although everybody experiences anxiety, only some are impaired by it. Anxiety in moderation can be highly adaptive, since optimal learning and adaptation to a variety of problems occur at moderate rather than high or low levels of anxiety/arousal. In addition to arousal, information about what to expect and how to cope with the situation increases adaptiveness. Thus it may be counterproductive for clinicians to provide blanket reassurance or to implore patients "not to worry."

While moderate levels of anxiety may be normal and adaptive, the ability to vary anxiety levels in response to different situations is also desirable. Most people have a characteristic range of anxiety responses that is relatively fixed and can be viewed as a personality trait. This is called "trait anxiety." In clinical settings, when trait anxiety is uniformly high and maladaptive, it is called "chronic anxiety." In contrast to trait anxiety, the anxiety response at a particular time and situation is called "state anxiety"; it is not fixed and is time-limited. In clinical settings, when state anxiety is high and maladaptive, it is referred to as "acute anxiety," which may continue beyond the particular stressful situation and become chronic anxiety.

How is pathological anxiety diagnosed? In diagnosing an anxiety syndrome, the presence of both psychological and physiological symptoms should be ascertained. Psychological symptoms include a subjective sense of apprehension, worry, tension, and uneasiness without a known object or event, or out of proportion to known specific events. Hypervigilance, in which the person becomes excessively attentive to the point of distractibility, irritability, or insomnia, is also frequently seen. Physiological symptoms include motor tension (tremors, twitches, muscle aches, jitters) and autonomic hyperactivity (sweating, heart racing, frequent urination, diarrhea, dizziness, hot or cold spells). For example, these autonomic symptoms are easily set off in most "normal" people without anxiety disorders by the appearance of flashing police car lights in the rearview mirror, combined with the sound of a siren. Making the diagnosis of anxiety can be difficult when patients present only with physiological symptoms, since each of these symptoms may stem from a host of other medical disorders. For example, if patients complain only of headache or diarrhea, direct but supportive questioning may reveal additional symptoms of an anxiety syndrome that they have been reluctant to reveal.

It is important to recognize anxiety in patients who are not complaining of it. High levels of anxiety can exacerbate a wide variety of medical conditions, including gastric and duodenal ulcers, ulcerative colitis, asthma, hypertension, hives, hypoglycemia, and some seizure disorders. It may also be an important component in the aggressive, pressured, "type A" cardiac personality, who is at increased risk for myocardial infarction.

Just eliciting reports of anxiety-related symptoms is not enough, however. Many of these symptoms may exist with normal anxiety. Normal and pathological anxieties are quantitatively and qualitatively different. In anxiety syndromes the anxiety is high and maladaptive; there is decreased functioning because of the anxiety; the physiological symptoms are distressing and disturb normal functioning, and/or the psychological symptoms interfere with the individual's ability to cope. Even when complete information is available, diagnosing anxiety is not a simple task. There are no concrete or cardinal signs; rather, clinicians have to exercise considerable judgment, for example, when concluding that the patient's emotional reactions are out of proportion to the situation.

That relatively few people with anxiety disorders seek treatment is unfortunate, since treatment is usually effective, and without it, less than a quarter of these patients fully recover. In general, the earlier in life patients receive treatment, the better their long-term outcome. Thus, early detection matters.

THE CAUSES OF ANXIETY

Psychodynamic Theory

At first, Freud postulated that pathological anxiety resulted from a failure to repress painful memories, impulses, or thoughts. When the psychic energy used for this repression is particularly intense, the repressed material breaks into consciousness in a disguised form. For instance, after "discovering" that she was sexually molested as a child, a woman was flooded not with sexual thoughts but with anxiety, difficulty breathing, hyperventilation, and other symptoms of a panic attack. Later, Freud introduced the concept of "signal anxiety," the experience of which enables the person to avoid dangerous thoughts, impulses, etc., through repression, phobic avoidance, compulsions, etc.

Behavioral Theories

In Pavlov's classic experiment, a dog salivated on repeated simultaneous exposure to food and the sound of a bell. When Pavlov removed the food, the dog had become conditioned to salivate on hearing the bell alone. When students walk into a classroom and hear the instructor say "Surprise exam!", immediately the effects of years of associating exams with anxiety trigger anxiety before the content of the exam is even glimpsed. Most behaviorists view conditioning as essential in perpetuating and intensifying anxiety. In the 1970s and 1980s, Kandel (1983) photographed the actual changes in nerve cells produced by behavioral conditioning.

Although many assume that psychic anxiety causes and conditions somatic anxiety, William James (1893) proposed the opposite: That is, subjectively experienced anxiety is a conditioned response to the physical signals of anxiety such as tachycardia and rapid breathing. When injected with norepinephrine (noradrenaline), people report feeling angry if they are watching a fight and more anxiety if they are watching a chase. Here there was no difference in the somatic symptoms but in how they were labeled. Under stress and at rest, anxious subjects have a higher rate of these bodily signals than do controls. Some evidence suggests that patients who report higher levels of psychic anxiety do so, not because they have greater physiological arousal, but because they are more sensitive to perceiving physiological arousal and are more likely to label it *anxiety* instead of *excitement* or *anger*.

Biological Theories

Whereas James, in what came to be known as the James–Lange theory, claimed that peripheral symptoms provoked central anxiety, Cannon (1932) argued that anxiety originates in the brain, which in turn produces peripheral symptoms. In Cannon's view, anxiety and panic are not consequences but causes of tachycardia, sweating, rapid respiration, etc. Yet if anxiety and panic tend to go from the brain to the body (and not vice versa), where and how do these reactions originate in the brain?

During the late 1970s, two major discoveries began to address this question. The first advance (Redmond, 1979) involved the locus coeruleus (LC), a dense cluster of neurons that produces 70% of the brain's norepinephrine. When the LC is stimulated electrically or by the drug yohimbine, anxiety increases; when the LC is inhibited by drugs called "adrenergic blockers" (e.g., clonidine, propranolol), anxiety diminishes. In addition, benzodiazepines and tricyclic antidepressants slow the LC's firing and reduce anxiety.

The second major advance (Skolnick & Paul, 1983) was the discovery of benzodiazepine (BZ) receptors in the brain. BZs (e.g., diazepam) appear to work by augmenting the antianxiety action of the GABA inhibitory system in different parts of the brain, including the limbic system (LS). There is evidence of neuronal connection between the LC and the LS. Many investigators suspect that the LC and BZ receptors pertain to different clinical syndromes—

the very ones that Freud and *DSM-IV-TR* have characterized!—the LC to panic disorder and the BZ receptors to generalized anxiety disorders (GAD). When stimulated, the LC produces the symptoms and intense somatic signs characteristic of panic anxiety. In contrast, the BZ receptors may play more of a role in GAD.

The third major advance was the discovery that several drugs that primarily affect the serotonin system also affect anxiety disorders (Murphy & Pigott, 1990). Buspirone is mainly used for GAD, whereas the SSRIs are effective in panic, obsessive–compulsive disorder, and GAD. The cell bodies of the nucleus raphe (the brain's main group of serotonin neurons) send projections to the LC, LS, and prefrontal cortex. There are complex interactions among serotonergic, noradrenergic, and GABA-ergic neuronal systems within these brain areas that regulate anxiety.

ANXIETY DISORDER DUE TO A GENERAL MEDICAL CONDITION AND SUBSTANCE-INDUCED ANXIETY DISORDER

One of the first steps in the diagnosis of an anxiety disorder is to determine if it has a known specific cause. If it is caused by a medical condition or is substance-induced, treatment can then be directed at the underlying problem.

The *DSM-IV-TR* criteria for anxiety disorders due to a general medical condition and substance-induced anxiety disorder are listed in Table 14-1.

Several medical conditions can mimic *panic disorder*. These include:

Cardiopulmonary Disorders

(1) Recurrent pulmonary emboli (blood clots in the lungs) produce repeated episodes of acute anxiety with hyperventilation or dyspnea (shortness of breath) in conjunction with decreased oxygen concentration in the blood. Functional anxiety is associated with slightly increased oxygen concentrations. (2) Paroxysmal atrial tachycardia starts with a sudden increase in heart rate and then, unlike panic disorder, suddenly decreases. (3) Chronic obstructive pulmonary disease (COPD) can lead to symptoms of anxiety, which may then be exacerbated by bronchodilators. (4) Silent myocardial infarction, which more often occurs in people with diabetes, produces palpitations, sweating, and dyspnea in the absence of chest pains. (5) In mitral valve prolapse (MVP), diagnosed by auscultation and echocardiogram, the mitral valve doesn't close properly and produces a murmur or "systolic click." It is associated with panic disorder but is *not* a definite cause of panic. Because patients with panic attacks often

TABLE 14-1

DSM-IV-TR *Criteria for Anxiety Disorder Due to a General Medical Condition and Substance-Induced Anxiety Disorder*

Common Criteria for Both Disorders

A. Prominent anxiety, Panic Attacks, or obsessions or compulsions predominate in the clinical picture.

B. The disturbance does not occur exclusively during the course of delirium.

C. The disturbance causes clinically significant distress or impairment in social, occupational, or other important areas of functioning.

Additional Criteria for Anxiety Disorder Due to a General Medical Condition

D. There is evidence from the history, physical examination, or laboratory findings that the disturbance is the direct physiological consequence of a general medical condition.

E. The disturbance is not better accounted for by another mental disorder (e.g., Adjustment Disorder With Anxiety in which the stressor is a serious medical condition).

Specify if:

With Generalized Anxiety
With Panic Attacks
With Obsessive–Compulsive Symptoms

Additional Criteria for Substance-Induced Anxiety Disorder

D. There is evidence from the history, physical examination, or laboratory findings of either (1) or (2):

(1) the symptoms in Criterion A developed during, or within 1 month of, Substance Intoxication or Withdrawal

(2) medication use is etiologically related to the disturbance

E. The disturbance is not better accounted for by an Anxiety Disorder that is not substance induced. Evidence that the symptoms are better accounted for by an Anxiety Disorder that is not substance induced might include the following: the symptoms precede the onset of the substance use (or medication use); the symptoms persist for a substantial period of time (e.g., about a month) after the cessation of acute withdrawal or severe intoxication or are substantially in excess of what would be expected given the type or amount of the substance used or the duration of use; or there is other evidence suggesting the existence of an independent non-substance-induced Anxiety Disorder (e.g., a history of recurrent non-substance-related episodes).

Specify if:

With Generalized Anxiety
With Panic Attacks
With Obsessive–Compulsive Symptoms
With Phobic Symptoms

Note. From *DSM-IV-TR,* pp. 479, 483.

think that something is wrong with their heart, they go see cardiologists, who on finding MVP, decide that this caused the panic. The evidence does not support this conclusion. MVP sometimes improves after the panic is satisfactorily treated, suggesting that panic disorder may actually cause some forms of MVP. In others, the MVP remains unchanged, but the panic attacks remain successfully treated. Because the MVP does not need to be corrected in order for the panic attacks to get better, it is unlikely that MVP is the cause of the attacks.

"Temporal Lobe" Epilepsy

Sudden, paroxysmal episodes of fear accompanied by derealization, depersonalization, and epigastric discomfort often constitute the prodrome of a complex partial seizure in which chewing, lip smacking, or other automatisms occur without the patient remembering. When there is no grand mal seizure component in the patient's history, this can be a difficult differential diagnosis. Information from people living with the patient can be the key to diagnosis.

Pheochromocytoma

This is a rare (less than 1 in 10,000) catecholamine-secreting tumor that produces marked episodic elevations of blood pressure and vasomotor lability in conjunction with a wide array of anxiety symptoms. However, patients with this tumor do not usually complain of the psychological symptoms of anxiety. Blood pressure rises in panic disorder are modest by comparison.

Other medical conditions can mimic *generalized anxiety disorder* (GAD). These include:

Hyperthyroidism

In this syndrome, unlike in GAD, a fine tremor, heat intolerance, and weight loss—despite normal or increased appetite—usually accompany symptoms of anxiety.

Hypoglycemia

A constellation of symptoms occur together, including hunger, weakness, headache, sweating, palpitations, and anxiety. The syndrome, including anxiety, is episodic, predictably occurring several hours after meals. It can be reversed by glucose ingestion (e.g., eating a candy bar). Differentiating anxiety from hypoglycemia is somewhat complicated by the fact that anxiety can worsen glucose tolerance. Generalized anxiety does not have predictable waves of anxiety associated with hunger, and panic attacks come on much faster and stronger. *Hypoglycemia is a very rare cause of anxiety* and is probably grossly overdiagnosed in patients actually suffering from anxiety disorders.

Postconcussion Syndrome

Anxiety frequently accompanies this medical condition for several months after the head trauma. This is not just a psychological phenomena. It is seen in people with no memory of the accident (secondary to the concussion), and usually the anxiety is not related to the traumatic event. Anticonvulsants sometimes are effective.

Delirium

Anxiety sometimes is the prominent feature in delirium, but unlike in anxiety disorder, fluctuations in alertness, interrupted attention, and problems in cognitive functioning are also always present.

Several drugs often cause symptoms that mimic GAD and can worsen all other anxiety disorders. These include:

Alcohol or Hypnoanxiolytic Withdrawal

Frequently, patients do not recognize alcohol as a cause of anxiety but, rather, see it only as a treatment for anxiety. Direct questioning about alcohol and hypnoanxiolytic use is necessary, as many patients may try to conceal this information. If patients have been using long-lasting medications such as diazepam or clonazepam, withdrawal symptoms might not appear for 4–7 days following drug discontinuation. In some anxiety disorders, even the ingestion of small amounts of alcohol can produce severe anxiety several hours later, as blood levels of alcohol fall (a "rebound" from the brief calming effect of alcohol). Thus, "social drinking," not just alcoholism, may cause anxiety.

Caffeine Overuse

This is frequently not recognized by patients as the cause of their anxiety symptoms. For example, increased sensitivity to caffeine can precipitate a new anxiety-like syndrome in an older adult who has maintained a constant intake over the years. Only a reduction in caffeine intake will relieve the symptoms.

It has also been shown that patients suffering from certain anxiety disorders are more sensitive to caffeine. Some have discontinued use of caffeinated beverages on their own in an attempt to reduce their symptoms; others, however, remain unaware of the link between caffeine and anxiety. Symptoms of caffeine intoxication—nervousness, irritability, agitation, headache, rapid heart rate, tremulousness, and occasional muscle twitches—can result from ingesting over 250 mg of caffeine a day (about 2 cups of coffee). These effects can last 7 hours. There are many other sources of caffeine, including tea, most soft drinks, pain relievers, and cold preparations.

Other Stimulants

Both legal and illegal stimulants can cause significant anxiety. Common legal sources are decongestants, over-the-counter diet pills, and antiasthmatic medications that rely on beta-adrenergic stimulation. Common illegal sources are methamphetamine and cocaine.

Other Drugs

Yohimbine, marijuana, phencyclidine, and organic solvents have all been reported to increase anxiety and induce panic attacks.

PANIC DISORDER

Suddenly and without reason, panic attacks engulf the victim with a sense of imminent doom, death, or destruction. Since most victims have never heard of panic attacks, they fear that they're going mad and won't tell loved ones or physicians about them. Panic attacks are terrifying—"worse than Auschwitz," according to one concentration camp survivor.

Clinical Presentation

The essential feature of panic disorder is a history of *panic attacks*. These attacks affect women more often than men and strike outside the victim's home—most often in a store, sometimes on the street. The person feels she's in a life-threatening situation from which she must escape—immediately. She might fear an imminent stroke, heart attack, or nuclear explosion. Very often she can't pinpoint what she fears, but knows it's horrendous. Her imagination takes over: She might die right on the spot, go berserk, or be killed, butchered, or maimed. Her heart pounds so, it could bust or burst through her chest. She may scream or look blank, even though she's frozen in fear and unable to move. The woman from Auschwitz, now quite elderly, says she's terrified of falling and clutching onto strangers. Another woman described her arm turning to stone and people appearing miles away. Most patients gasp for air, hyperventilate, develop parethesias, or feel dizzy and lightheaded. They may race outside and only then will their breathing slow and their attack subside. Most attacks last 3–10 minutes, and rarely more than 30 minutes.

Many patients shrug off the first attack, but in several days, unprovoked attacks recur; these may be less intense but still frightening. Patients begin to dread future attacks. Although the timing of panic attacks is unpredictable, the locations may follow a pattern. A patient may panic in the same bank on three occasions, but not on the fourth nor in any other bank. A patient's attacks usually have their own symptom cluster: Some patients have primarily respiratory distress, some worry about going crazy, some fear death. *DSM-IV-TR* criteria for panic attack and disorder are listed in Table 14-2. Some patients have serious dysfunction from *limited-symptom anxiety* in which they experience fewer than four of the defining symptoms of panic attacks.

Panic attacks can occur in a variety of anxiety disorders (e.g., panic disorder, social phobia, simple phobia, generalized anxiety disorder, and posttraumatic stress disorder). In determining the differential diagnostic significance of a panic attack, it is important to consider the context in which the panic attack occurs. There are two prototypical relationships between the onset of a panic attack and situational triggers: (1) *unexpected* (uncued) panic attacks, in which the onset of the panic attack is not associated with a situational trigger (i.e., occurring "out of the blue"); and (2) situationally *bound* (cued) panic attacks, in which an attack almost invariably occurs immediately upon exposure to, or in anticipation of, the situational trigger (cue). The occurrence of unexpected panic attacks is required for a diagnosis of panic disorder, whereas situationally bound panic attacks are most characteristic of social and specific phobias.

Moreover, there are panic attack presentations that do not conform to either of these prototypical relationships. These *situationally predisposed* panic attacks are more likely to occur upon exposure to the situational trigger (cue) but are not invariably associated with the cue. In addition, these panic attacks may not necessarily occur immediately after the exposure. There is some evidence that situationally predisposed panic attacks are especially frequent in panic disorder, but may at times occur in specific phobia or social phobia.

In time, instead of returning to their baseline state, most patients develop *anticipatory anxiety* in between panic attacks. This anxiety resembles that seen

TABLE 14-2

DSM-IV-TR *Criteria for Panic Attack and Panic Disorder*

Common Criteria for Panic Attack

A discrete period of intense fear or discomfort, in which four (or more) of the following symptoms developed abruptly and reached a peak within 10 minutes:

(1) palpitations, pounding heart, or accelerated heart rate

(2) sweating

(3) trembling or shaking

(4) sensations of shortness of breath or smothering

(5) feeling of choking

(6) chest pain or discomfort

(7) nausea or abdominal distress

(8) feeling dizzy, unsteady, lightheaded, or faint

(9) derealization (feelings of unreality) or depersonalization (being detached from oneself)

(10) fear of losing control or going crazy

(11) fear of dying

(12) paresthesias (numbness or tingling sensations)

(13) chills or hot flushes

DSM-IV-TR Criteria for Panic Disorder

A. Both (1) and (2):

(1) recurrent unexpected Panic Attacks

(2) at least one of the attacks has been followed by 1 month (or more) of one (or more) of the following:

(a) persistent concern about having additional attacks

(b) worry about the implications of the attack or its consequences (e.g., losing control, having a heart attack, "going crazy")

(c) a significant change in behavior related to the attacks

B. Specify "with agoraphobia" or "without agoraphobia"

C. The Panic Attacks are not due to the direct physiological effects of a substance (e.g., a drug of abuse, a medication) or a general medical condition (e.g., hyperthyroidism).

D. The Panic Attacks are not better accounted for by another mental disorder, such as Social Phobia (e.g., occurring on exposure to feared social situation), Specific Phobia (e.g., on exposure to a specific phobic situation), Obsessive–Compulsive Disorder (e.g., on exposure to dirt in someone with an obsession about contamination), Posttraumatic Stress Disorder (e.g., in response to stimuli associated with a severe stressor), or Separation Anxiety Disorder (e.g., in response to being away from home or close relatives).

Note. From *DSM-IV-TR*, pp. 432, 440, 441.

in GAD and includes continued motor tension, autonomic hyperactivity, apprehension, hypervigilance, and initial insomnia. Patients say this anxiety stems from a terror of having future attacks. This anxiety can be mild or severe; it may be the most dominant symptom, thereby misleading clinicians into diagnosing GAD.

Over time, a majority of patients with panic disorder will also develop situationally bound panic attacks. In some cases, these become the main form of panic attack. Subsequently, some patients—and there's no way of knowing which ones—develop *phobic avoidance*. They may be phobic for situations associated with the panic attacks. This avoidance may be based on the mistaken belief that the situation caused the attack or on the reality that many of the panic attacks have become situationally bound. For example, a patient may avoid driving because she thinks driving caused her to panic. More often, patients avoid situations in which they fear being trapped or unable to get help (e.g., buses, elevators, bridges, department stores). In lectures or movies they may take an aisle seat near the door to assure the possibility of escape. When restrictions on travel away from home significantly impair functioning, the diagnosis of *agoraphobia* is merited. The number of blocks a patient ventures away from home is a simple and reliable measure of impairment.

Clinical Course

Panic disorder usually begins during the late teens and 20s (usually in the 20s) and rarely after age 35. There is usually an initial discrete attack, although chronic anxiety, fatigue, or dizziness may precede it. Most patients originally consult a physician for difficulty breathing or chest discomfort, and less often, for abdominal distress or "irritable colon." In one survey, 70% of the patients had visited more than 10 physicians, 95% had had prior psychiatric treatment, and 98% had long and frequent use of hypnoanxiolytics.

Over time, the intensity of panic attacks, anticipatory anxiety, and phobic avoidance varies. Spontaneous remissions occur for months and sometimes for years. A patient may go 5–10 years without an attack, suddenly have three attacks in a month, and then not have another attack for a decade. In general, 5–20 years after the initial attack, 50–60% of patients will recover substantially, whereas 20% will remain moderately impaired. Some studies suggest bleaker prognoses with substantial rates of suicide.

The earlier patients get treatment, the better the outcome. If panic attacks can be squelched relatively early, anticipatory anxiety and phobia may be averted or minimized. Even if the latter stages occur, early treatment can reduce their incapacitations and complications.

Complications

Substance abuse is a frequent complication because patients discover that alcohol and benzodiazepines will temporarily calm their anticipatory anxiety. Unfortunately, tolerance develops resulting in overuse and chemical dependency. Occupational, social, and marital impairments are common, often compounded by the patient's concealment of the attacks and by others not knowing that panic disorder exists.

Depression may affect up to 50% of all patients with panic disorder. These depressions are usually mild, two-thirds last under 3 months, and most are associated with a precipitating stress, such as a divorce. Yet a third of patients with panic disorder have had a major depression years *before* having their first panic attack. This suggests that for some patients, depression is not a complication of panic disorder, but a second disorder.

Epidemiology

The 1-year prevalence of panic disorder is 2.7% and lifetime prevalence is 4.7%. Two to three times more women than men get it, and it is most prevalent between the ages of 16 and 40. During pregnancy, the frequency of panic attacks appears to decline sharply. Severe separation anxiety or sudden object loss during childhood may predispose to panic disorder.

Etiology

Panic disorder runs in families. About 20% of these patients' first-degree relatives have panic disorder, in comparison to about 4% of normals' first-degree relatives. Given an MZ to DZ ratio of 5:1 for panic disorder, genetics seem to play a major role in this familial transmission. (Knowing this, parents with panic disorder can spare their children considerable grief by ensuring that their kids know about the disorder and obtain early treatment.)

The initial panic attack, though not triggered by a specific stressor, usually occurs during an unusually stressful period. Relocation to new places commonly precede the onset of panic attacks (Roy-Byrne, Geraci, & Uhde, 1986). When repressed, unacceptable thoughts invade one's consciousness, panicky anxiety may ensue. For example, over the last 2 years, Sally provided round-the-clock care for her seriously injured son. She experienced anxiety attacks each time her unacceptable wish for her son's death threatened to break through into consciousness.

First attacks frequently happen in patients with thyroid disorders, during the immediate postpartum period, and after using marijuana, cocaine, or amphetamines. Caffeine produces panic attacks in up to 70% of patients with panic disorder, and stopping caffeine reduces the frequency and intensity of the attacks.

Lactic acid, which builds up in muscles during exercise and causes soreness and stiffness, plays a role in panic disorder. Intravenous infusions of sodium lactate trigger panic attacks in those with panic disorder but not in controls. Vigorous physical exercise, which produces lactic acid, can trigger panic attacks in some patients (Pitts & McClure, 1967). Yet if patients with panic disorder receive a tricyclic antidepressant (TCA) prior to being infused with lactate, they do not develop an attack. This finding is noteworthy, given that TCAs block panic attacks. Carbon dioxide may increase during vigorous exercise as well, and brainstem hypersensitivity to changes in CO_2 has been postulated as a trigger for panic. This is related to the panic people experience with air hunger and suffocation. In fact, lactate can create a sense of breathlessness. Donald Klein proposed two theories based on the idea that panic attacks are "normal" in little children who have been abandoned and in people of all ages who feel suffocated. The abnormalities that then predispose an adult to panic attacks would be fear of separation or an abnormally low "suffocation" alarm threshold.

Differential Diagnosis

As discussed earlier, several medical conditions can mimic panic disorder. Differentiating *generalized anxiety disorder* from panic disorder may be complicated because anticipatory anxiety may be the dominant symptom of panic disorder, even when the patient has long forgotten that he or she ever had panic attacks. A history of repeated discrete attacks points to panic disorder. Several anxiety disorders, including *obsessive–compulsive, posttraumatic stress, separation anxiety,* and *social phobia,* have very specific fears that, in severe form, may look like a panic attack. Unlike panic attacks, however, these fears are *only* precipitated by very specific cues related to these disorders.

Panic attacks may occur during sleep. It is easy to confuse these with *nightmare disorder* and *sleep terror disorder,* but there are a few important differences. People with sleep panic attacks usually also have panic attacks during the day. Unlike nightmare disorder, there is no nightmare remembered and, unlike sleep terror disorder, the person with a panic attack remembers it well (does not have amnesia) and is quite responsive.

Management and Treatment

From the start, clinicians should help patients and their families develop reasonable expectations of treatment. It should be pointed out that panic disorder is not a figment of the patient's imagination, but a genuine illness with biological components that often cause severe impairments. They should be told that panic disorder has a fluctuating course, and that patients should not feel that they, or the treatment, has failed if some symptoms persist or recur. They should know that improving the patient's ability to function and to travel are key goals of treatment.

Treatment of Mild Panic Disorder

Patients who have had only a few panic attacks or get them very intermittently but do not have much anxiety between episodes should be given an explanation of how the attacks occur, emphasizing that they are not life-threatening, dangerous to health, or a symptom of impending insanity. Cognitive–behavioral therapies aimed at changing patients' catastrophic thinking about attacks are highly effective in patients with infrequent attacks, especially if there is high anticipatory anxiety between attacks. These therapies have been systematized and are available in manual form.

Treatment of Moderate and Severe Panic Disorder

If attacks are occurring frequently (five to seven times a week) or there is significant anxiety between attacks and some disability, in addition to the cognitive–behavioral approach there are three classes of medications that can be considered. Imipramine at doses of 150 mg or higher has been show to be effective about 70% of the time. Most other TCAs are probably equally effective, but there are fewer well-controlled studies on them. Imipramine, desipramine, or nortriptyline had been the first choice for treating panic disorder pre-SSRIs. Selective serotonin reuptake inhibitors (SSRI) such as fluoxetine, sertraline, citalopram, and paroxetine have become the treatment of choice, as they appear to be equally effective and better tolerated. Full response can take six to twelve weeks. Early overstimulation with exacerbation of panic may occur unless the initial doses are small (10 mg imipramine/5 mg fluoxetine), and titration proceeds slowly.

Monoamine oxidase inhibitors (MAOIs) such as phenelzine appear to be effective in panic disorders about 75–80% of the time and are particularly effective in treatment-refractory cases. Because of the need to stay on a low-tyramine diet to avoid hypertensive crisis, these drugs are probably underutilized by most physicians.

Benzodiazepines in doses two to three times higher than usually used for simple anxiety have been reported to be effective in about 70–90% of panic disorder cases. There are many controlled studies supporting alprazolam's effectiveness, and a few for clonazepam, lorazepam, and diazepam. High doses of benzodiazepines present a risk of physical dependence, but nonetheless should be considered in patients who have not responded to, or cannot tolerate, antidepressants or who may be fearful of taking MAOIs because of the danger of dietary interactions. Response to benzodiazepines (days) is much faster than to antidepressants (weeks). Short-term use for a few weeks during administration of antidepressant treatment may be indicated to prevent early overstimulation and to provide more rapid relief of panic, especially in patients with occupational or familial dysfunction. Unfortunately, when attempts to withdraw the benzodiazepines are made, patients may not only experience a return of the original symptoms but also rebound withdrawal symptoms. During this withdrawal period, patients can have worse symptoms than when they started treatment ("rebound anxiety"). Beta-blockers have *not* been shown to effectively block panic attacks.

Long-term Management of Panic Attacks

When the *anticipatory anxiety* of having panic attacks continues for months or years, the anxiety that develops in anticipation of these attacks becomes entrenched and resistant to treatment. Although it may seem redundant to the therapist, repeatedly telling the patient that she will experience fewer and less severe panic attacks while on her medication goes a long way to quelling anticipatory anxiety. Cognitive–behavioral approaches for mild to moderate panic disorder can help to prevent further symptoms. Because medications have become the patient's "security blanket," stopping them is usually difficult. Extremely slow decreases are recommended. In the case of benzodiazepines, a slowly titrated decrease is also necessary to minimize withdrawal symptoms. Sometimes patients will get stuck on the last tiny dose which, though they know it is pharmacologically inactive, remains psychologically quite active for them.

The *agoraphobia* that frequently accompanies panic disorder is discussed below. In general, any treatment that eventually exposes patients to the phobic stimulus is likely to work, whereas any treatment that never exposes them to the stimulus is likely to fail.

PHOBIC DISORDERS

A phobia is an irrational dread of, and compelling desire to avoid, a specific object, situation, or activity. People with phobias know that their phobias are "crazy," unreasonable, or excessive. Unlike panic attacks, phobias are always anticipated and never happen spontaneously. Patients with both unpredictable panic attacks and phobias may be diagnosed as having both disorders.

The *original phobia* is usually followed by mild to severe *anticipatory anxiety*, although if the phobic stimulus is avoided, some patients will remain anxiety-free. Patients' degree of anticipatory anxiety depends primarily on their confidence in being able to avoid the phobic situation. Patients who are phobic to unusual things, such as snakes, are generally calm in other circumstances; those who dread common things that might suddenly appear, such as pigeons, tend to be chronically anxious unless they're in a safe haven (e.g., home).

A set of *avoidant behaviors* often occurs. A person with a fish phobia is so uncomfortable around fish that before visiting new friends, he or she may phone ahead to make sure they won't serve herring and don't have goldfish. If the fish can't be hidden or trashed, the person with the fish phobia won't visit.

On occasion, virtually everyone, especially children, are bugged by some phobia—mice, snakes, insects, etc. Phobic *symptoms* become phobic *disorders* when they cause undue distress and impair functioning. Roughly 20% of patients with phobic symptoms develop phobic disorders.

Many phobias remit quickly without therapy, but if they endure for over a year, they're unlikely to remit spontaneously. Many childhood phobias vanish within a year; treatment hastens their disappearance. The prognosis is worse in adults: In a 5-year span, 50% of patients will improve, but only 5% will be symptom-free.

One medical dictionary lists 275 types of phobia; *DSM-IV-TR* lists three: agoraphobia (Table 14-3), social phobia (Table 14-4), and specific phobia (Table 14-5). *Agoraphobia* literally translates to "fear of the marketplace," but now refers to fear of being in places or situations where escape might be difficult or, in cases involving panic attacks, of being where help is not available (e.g., shops, theaters, streets). The most severe of phobic disorders, agoraphobia accounts for about 60% of phobic disorders in clinical practice. *Social phobia* refers to the fear of being scrutinized and judged, as in "stage fright"; social phobias comprise 10% of all phobic disorders. *Specific phobia* encompasses irrational fear and avoidance of specific objects or situations not covered by

TABLE 14-3
DSM-IV-TR *Criteria for Agoraphobia*
Common Criteria for Agoraphobia

A. Anxiety about being in places or situations from which escape might be difficult (or embarrassing) or in which help may not be available in the event of having an unexpected or situationally predisposed Panic Attack or panic-like symptoms. Agoraphobic fears typically involve characteristic clusters of situations that include being outside the home alone; being in a crowd or standing in a line; being on a bridge; and traveling in a bus, train, or automobile.

Note: Consider the diagnosis of Specific Phobia if the avoidance is limited to one or only a few specific situations, or Social Phobia if the avoidance is limited to social situations.

B. Agoraphobic situations are avoided (e.g., travel is restricted) or else endured with marked distress or with anxiety about having a Panic Attack or panic-like symptoms, or require the presence of a companion.

C. The anxiety or phobic avoidance is not better accounted for by another mental disorder, such as Social Phobia (e.g., avoidance limited to social situations because of fear of embarrassment), Specific Phobia (e.g., avoidance limited to a single situation like elevators), Obsessive–Compulsive Disorder (e.g., avoidance of dirt in someone with an obsession about contamination), Posttraumatic Stress Disorder (e.g., avoidance of stimuli associated with a severe stressor), or Separation Anxiety Disorder (e.g., avoidance of leaving home or relatives).

DSM-IV-TR Criteria for Agoraphobia Without a history of Panic Disorder

A. The presence of Agoraphobia related to fear of developing panic-like symptoms (e.g., dizziness or diarrhea)

B. Criteria have never been met for Panic Disorder.

C. The disturbance is not due to the direct physiological effects of a substance (e.g., a drug of abuse, a medication) or a general medical condition.

D. If an associated general medical condition is present, the fear in Criterion A is clearly in excess of that usually associated with the condition.

Note. From *DSM-IV-TR,* p. 443.

---

agoraphobia or social phobia. Simple phobias usually involve animals or insects (e.g., dogs, spiders), things (e.g., hypodermic needles), or places (e.g., heights, closed spaces). Whereas social phobias are normally confined to a few stimuli, simple phobias usually involve only one object. In comparison to social phobias, simple phobias begin earlier in life, rarely incapacitate, and have better prognoses. Among the phobias, simple phobias are most common in the population, but agoraphobias are most common in the office.

TABLE 14-4

DSM-IV-TR *Criteria for Social Phobia (formerly Social Anxiety Disorder)*

A. A marked and persistent fear of one or more social or performance situations in which the person is exposed to unfamiliar people or to possible scrutiny by others. The individual fears that he or she will act in a way (or show anxiety symptoms) that will be humiliating or embarrassing. **Note:** In children, there must be evidence of capacity for social relationships with familiar people and the anxiety must occur in peer settings, not just in interactions with adults.

B. Exposure to the feared social situation almost invariably provokes anxiety, which may take the form of a situationally bound or situationally predisposed Panic Attack.
Note: In children, the anxiety may be expressed by crying, tantrums, freezing, or shrinking from social situations with unfamiliar people.

C. The person recognizes that the fear is excessive or unreasonable. **Note:** In children, this feature may be absent.

D. The feared social or performance situations are avoided or else endured with intense anxiety or distress.

E. The avoidance, anxious anticipation, or distress in the feared social or performance situation(s) interferes significantly with the person's normal routine, occupational (academic) functioning, or with social activities or relationships with others, or there is marked distress about having the phobia.

F. In individuals under 18 years, the duration is at least 6 months.

G. The fear or avoidance is not due to the direct effects of a substance (e.g., a drug of abuse, a medication) or a general medical condition, and is not better accounted for by another mental disorder (e.g., Panic Disorder With or Without Agoraphobia, Separation Anxiety Disorder, Body Dysmorphic Disorder, a Pervasive Developmental Disorder, or Schizoid Personality Disorder).

H. If a general medical condition or other mental disorder is present, the fear in Criterion A is unrelated to it, e.g., the fear is not of Stuttering, trembling in Parkinson's disease, or exhibiting abnormal eating behavior in Anorexia Nervosa or Bulimia Nervosa.

Specify if:

Generalized: if the fears include most social situations (also consider the additional diagnosis of Avoidant Personality Disorder)

Note. From *DSM-IV-TR,* p. 456.

Clinical Presentation

Agoraphobia

The public places or open spaces typically feared by these patients include driving a car, riding a bus, crossing bridges, standing in lines, passing through

TABLE 14-5

DSM-IV-TR *Criteria for Specific Phobia (Formerly Simple Phobia)*

A. Marked and persistent fear that is excessive or unreasonable, cued by the presence or anticipation of a specific object or situation (e.g., flying, heights, animals, receiving an injection, seeing blood).

B. Exposure to the phobic stimulus almost invariably provokes an immediate anxiety response, which may take the form of a situationally bound or situationally predisposed panic attack. **Note:** In children, the anxiety may be expressed by crying, tantrums, freezing, or clinging.

C. The person recognizes that the fear is excessive or unreasonable. **Note:** In children, this feature may be absent.

D. The phobic situation(s) is avoided or else endured with intense anxiety or distress.

E. The avoidance, anxious anticipation, or distress in the feared situation(s) interferes significantly with the person's normal routine, occupational (academic) functioning, or with social activities or relationships with others, or there is marked distress about having the phobia.

F. In individuals under 18 years, the duration is at least 6 months.

G. The anxiety, Panic Attacks, or phobic avoidance associated with the specific object or situation are not better accounted for by another mental disorder, such as Obsessive–Compulsive Disorder (e.g., fear of dirt in someone with an obsession about contamination), Posttraumatic Stress Disorder (e.g., avoidance of stimuli associated with a severe stressor), Separation Anxiety Disorder (e.g., avoidance of school), Social Phobia (e.g., avoidance of social situations because of fear of embarrassment), Panic Disorder with Agoraphobia, or Agoraphobia Without History of Panic Disorder.

Specify if:

Animal Type

Natural Environment Type (e.g., heights, storms, water)

Blood-Injection-Injury-Type

Situational Type (e.g., planes, elevators, enclosed places)

Other Type (e.g., phobic avoidance of situations that may lead to choking, vomiting, or contracting an illness; in children, avoidance of loud sounds or costumed characters)

Note. From *DSM-IV-TR,* pp. 449, 450.

---

tunnels, walking through crowds, or shopping. Exposure to the phobic stimulus often triggers intense somatic anxiety. Some patients with phobias fear going berserk in public—screaming without reason, propositioning strangers, guffawing nonstop, disrobing, or masturbating. Agoraphobia mushrooms: Fears of taking a bus may escalate to fears of going anywhere by any means. Because people with agoraphobia often become terrified of leaving safe places (e.g., home), of being without a familiar object (e.g., a cane), or of traveling alone, they become highly dependent on others. Unless treated early, patients may increasingly restrict their activities and venture outside only with a trusted companion.

When agoraphobia is not a sequela of panic attacks, it usually arises during the early 20s, even though it may begin at any age. Many patients delay getting treatment for a decade or more. Over time, symptoms typically fluctuate from mild to severe. Spontaneous remissions occur, but uncommonly. Without early treatment or a spontaneous remission, patients tend to get worse.

Complications are frequent. If the patient is housebound, depression is common. Alcohol and hypnoanxiolytic abuse may result from patients medicating their anticipatory anxiety or from physicians incorrectly treating patients' depressions or anxieties. Many people with agoraphobia develop compulsions: They cannot leave home, for example, without repeatedly checking if the oven is turned off or the back door is locked. Marital and sexual problems may precede or follow agoraphobia.

Social Phobia

These patients have an irrational fear of being scrutinized, judged, or humiliated in public. It may be a dread of embarrassing oneself while speaking in public, eating in restaurants, or using public lavatories. People with social phobia tend to blush and twitch, whereas people with agoraphobia become dizzy, faint, short of breath, weak in the limbs, and have ringing or buzzing in their ears (Liebowitz et al., 1985). Social phobia is diagnosed if the fear or avoidant behavior interferes with occupational or social activities or relationships. The phobia may be discrete (public speaking) or extend to more widespread social situations. In the latter case, it is easily confused with panic disorder, unless patients are asked if they've ever panicked when *not* in social situations.

With a mean age of onset of 19, social phobias usually begin before agoraphobia. Without early therapy, social phobia has an unremitting, chronic course. At some point, a third to a half will have depressive symptoms, a majority will stop work or school, 60% will abuse alcohol or drugs, and about half will avoid all social interaction outside the immediate family (and then may qualify for the diagnosis of avoidant personality disorder).

Specific Phobia

The most common, benign, and circumscribed of the phobias, these usually start in childhood or early adolescence and cease within 5 years in 50% of patients. Specific phobia is the elevation of a particular fear to phobic proportions. Animals and "creepy-crawlies" are the most common phobias for which treatment is sought. The more ubiquitous the phobic object, the more incapacitating the phobia. For example, phobias for common household pets are socially inconvenient, and discomfort may be excessive and frequent. Animal phobias almost always begin in childhood. Before puberty, specific phobias occur equally in males and females. It is not known why the animal phobias tend to persist in women and not men. Acrophobia (fear of heights) and claustrophobia (fear of closed spaces) are examples of other common specific phobias. Blood/injury/illness phobias are distinguished by their unique physiology (bradycardia, hypotension, and fainting, as opposed to tachycardia and hypertension) and may be encountered more often in medical settings. In the wild, this response would protect humans from profuse bleeding.

Epidemiology

Epidemiological surveys of phobias can yield very different results because what qualifies as a phobia can vary considerably. Is somebody phobic if she's queasy around snakes? Does one count phobias that appear with other disorders? In the general population, the lifetime prevalence for phobic *symptoms* is near 40%, whereas for phobic *disorders*, around 15%.

Although women have two to three times more agoraphobia and simple phobia than men, social phobias affect the sexes more equally. Adults who are phobic and nonphobic had the same rates (4%) of phobias during their childhoods. Separation anxiety during childhood and sudden loss of a loved one predispose to agoraphobia. Social phobia is a more common psychiatric precursor to schizophrenia than any other psychiatric disorder. Social phobia is also common in some alcoholic populations ("Have a few drinks to help your confidence").

Etiology and Pathogenesis

As a general proposition, it can be said that unknown biological or psychosocial mechanisms cause patients with phobias to acquire an ingrained and unconscious stimulus–response association, which generates fear on subsequent exposure to the phobic stimulus. However, why some objects and not others are feared, and why some phobias vanish whereas others intensify, are unknown. The standard (tautological) explanations are: The phobic object is "chosen" because it carries enormous symbolic importance, of which patients are unaware; and repression and displacement are the chief defense mechanisms that cause phobias.

For example, a woman who was usually punished as a child by being locked in her bedroom may become claustrophobic when fired by her boss. If she has forgotten (or repressed) these childhood banishments, she will be unaware of having been conditioned to associate punishment with being locked in a room, and she will be puzzled by her current claustrophobia. As in any phobia, conditioning of the "sick role" through secondary gain may extend her claustrophobia into anticipatory anxiety and avoidant behaviors (e.g., not seeking jobs).

Agoraphobia runs in families; most social and simple phobias do not. Nevertheless, some studies show that children specifically phobic to insects and animals are likely to have mothers with similar phobias. This suggests that imitation, indoctrination, or identification may transmit phobias in some cases. Genetic factors may also play a role in the pathogenesis of phobia. Identical twins raised apart have a significantly increased chance of having a phobia and, not only that, but the *same* phobia.

Differential Diagnosis

A phobic disorder should not be diagnosed when another mental or personality disorder better accounts for the phobia. For example, fear of contamination results from *obsessive–compulsive disorder*, and fear of a specific past stressor occurs with *posttraumatic stress disorder*. Yet whereas the feared object leads the person with an obsession to perform rituals or to block out intrusive thoughts, it primarily induces anxiety in the patient with the phobia. *Schizophrenia* may produce social withdrawal resembling agoraphobia and social phobia, but people with schizophrenia have many more symptoms and may avoid situations because of delusions, whereas people with phobias know that their phobia is absurd. *Paranoid disorders* can lead to avoidant behavior, but unlike the person with the phobia, the person with paranoia sees nothing irrational about his or her behavior. Because many patients with *depressive disorders* feel worthless, gradually restrict their activities, and become reclusive, they may appear agoraphobic. However, pervasive symptoms, biological signs of depression, and excessive guilt and shame point to depression rather than to an anxiety disorder. Patients with *dementia* may withdraw to "think clearly," but this phobic-like avoidance is not associated with a specific feared stimulus; MSE testing will eliminate any remaining diagnostic confusion. Phobias commonly occur in patients with *borderline, paranoid,* and *avoidant personality disorders.*

Normal fears of public speaking should be distinguished from social phobia, as should "normal fears" of bugs or snakes from specific phobia. In these cases, the border between "normal" and pathological depends on the degree of distress and disability the phobia generates.

Management and Treatment

> One can hardly master a phobia if one waits till the patient lets the analysis influence him to give it up…one succeeds only when one can induce them by the influence of the analysis to…go [about alone]…and to struggle with their anxiety while they make the attempt.
>
> —Sigmund Freud (1919)

Essential in the treatment of phobias is exposing patients to the feared object or situation for an uninterrupted period of time. This principle applies to all treatment approaches, including psychoanalytic psychotherapy, behavior therapy, hypnosis, and medication. Historically, the preferred treatment for phobias was primarily behavior therapy involving relaxation training, mental rehearsal and exposure, supplemented by supportive individual, family, and group therapy, whenever appropriate. More recently, however, evidence suggests that supportive psychotherapy may be just as effective as behavior therapy, as long as patients encounter the feared situation. Freud believed that because phobias were based on underlying conflicts, just removing the symptom (the phobia), but not the underlying conflict, would result only in "symptom substitution"—another symptom popping up. On the contrary, eliminating phobias by "superficial" behavioral or pharmacological means rarely, if ever, leads to this substitution.

Biotherapies

Most studies show little use for TCAs and MAOIs in patients with phobias but without panic attacks or social phobia. Social phobias appear to respond well to MAOIs and more modestly to SSRIs and TCAs. In many cases in which the social phobia was so severe that the person developed avoidant personality disorder, a year on MAOIs produced such dramatic improvement that the avoidant personality disorder diagnosis no longer existed. Because beta-adrenergic blockers (e.g., propranolol) diminish somatic (but not psychic) anxiety, they may be useful for some social phobias, such as stage fright, in which somatic anxiety is paramount. Hypnoanxiolytics can be used temporarily to reduce anticipatory anxiety, but their long-term use risks habituation.

Behavior Therapies

Live exposure to the phobic stimulus—the essential therapeutic intervention—can be performed in three ways. First is *flooding*, in which patients are
directly confronted with the phobic stimulus for sessions lasting from 30 minutes to 8 hours. Flooding may also involve bombarding the patient with the
feared stimulus. One man was cured of his pillow phobia by sitting for two
45-minute sessions in a hospital room stuffed with 127 pillows. Second is a
graduated exposure, in which patients initially confront the phobic object for
a brief time, and then gradually in subsequent sessions escalate the duration
of exposure. Therapist-aided graduated exposure seems to have nominal benefit and may actually "prolong the agony" for some patients. The third approach
is *systematic desensitization*, usually involving progressive *muscle relaxation*, as
described in Chapter 5. To be effective, this technique must be followed (at
some point) by direct exposure to the phobic object.

> *Assertiveness training.* Modeling, role-playing, behavioral rehearsal, and *in vivo*
> homework assignments may also be helpful for those with social phobias and those
> with chronic phobias who also have marked dependence needs.
>
> *Psychotherapies.* Individual psychotherapy can supplement behavior therapy by
> encouraging patients to enter the phobic situation, by addressing any secondary
> gain that might perpetuate their avoidant behaviors, and by exploring the symbolic
> meaning of the phobic object. Group psychotherapy may help patients redevelop
> social skills, foster assertiveness, reduce or distribute dependency, and decrease
> loneliness. For some patients and their families, self-help groups for people with
> phobias are invaluable.
>
> *Virtual reality.* By simulating exposure to the phobic object in a controlled and
> safe environment, the patient may be desensitized and learn to tolerate exposure
> to the phobic object. Some researchers have similarly applied virtual reality tech-
> nology to trauma therapy by exposure to previous trauma in order to promote emo-
> tional processing of trauma-related memories.

OBSESSIVE-COMPULSIVE DISORDER

Being "obsessive" or "compulsive" is not the same as having *obsessions* or
performing *compulsions*. The distinction between "obsessive" and "obsession"
is the difference between a personality *style* with some adaptive features and
a mental *disorder* that's often incapacitating.

Obsessions are persistent, disturbing, intrusive thoughts or impulses that the patient finds illogical but irresistible. Unlike delusions, patients consider obsessions absurd and actively resist them. Most of us have experienced these in a mild form when we have had an advertising jingle or catchy little song like "It's a Small World" take over our minds for a few hours or days. *Compulsions* are obsessions expressed in action. Obsessions and compulsions are methods for reducing anxiety. True obsessions and compulsions are the essential traits of obsessive–compulsive disorder (OCD), a surprisingly common disorder occurring in almost 3% of the population.

Clinical Presentation

The first and most important point to remember is that people with OCD rarely reveal their symptoms; they are too embarrassed and keep them a big secret. Clinicians usually must ask gently about the most common obsessions and compulsions and not wait for patients to offer the information on their own. *DSM-IV-TR* diagnostic criteria for OCD (Table 14-6) illustrate the many ways obsessions and compulsions can present. Obsessions may appear as *ideas*—words, rhymes, or melodies that annoyingly interrupt normal thought and are often considered nonsensical, obscene, or blasphemous by the patient; and they may appear as *images* that are usually violent or disgusting (e.g., children burning, rape).

Underlying most cases of OCD is some form of pathological doubting— "Something bad will happen unless I do this." If there is any possibility of something bad happening, these patients can rapidly elevate the possibility to a probability and, in many cases, to a near certainty. We all have some fears about contracting disease and even occasionally feel compelled to wash our hands, but a person with OCD is plagued by this dreaded possibility and may wash all day long. All patients with OCD have obsessions and a majority have compulsive rituals based on those obsessions. The compulsive rituals are either directly linked to the obsession (e.g., washing hands to prevent disease) or linked by magical thinking (e.g., "My parents might die if I don't wash my hands").

Most forms of OCD fall into the following five categories (most people with OCD have symptoms in more than one category):

1. *Washers* fear contamination and usually have cleaning compulsions (e.g., "If I don't clean this, something bad will happen").
2. *Checkers* repeatedly check things such as ovens ("Are they turned off?") and doors ("Are they locked?"), etc. Each time the pathological doubt recurs ("If

TABLE 14-6

DSM-IV-TR Criteria for Obsessive–Compulsive Disorder

A. Either obsessions or compulsions:

Obsessions as defined by (1), (2), (3), and (4):

(1) recurrent and persistent thoughts, impulses, or images that are experienced, at some time during the disturbance, as intrusive and inappropriate and cause marked anxiety or distress

(2) the thoughts, impulses, or images are not simply excessive worries about real-life problems

(3) the person attempts to ignore or suppress such thoughts or impulses or to neutralize them with some other thought or action

(4) the person recognizes that the obsessional thoughts, impulses, or images are a product of his or her own mind (not imposed from without as in thought insertion)

Compulsions as defined by (1) and (2):

(1) repetitive behaviors (e.g., hand washing, ordering, checking) or mental acts (e.g., praying, counting, repeating words silently) that the person feels driven to perform in response to an obsession, or according to rules that must be applied rigidly

(2) the behaviors or mental acts are aimed at preventing or reducing distress or preventing some dreaded event or situation; however, these behaviors or mental acts either are not connected in a realistic way with what they are designed to neutralize or prevent, or are clearly excessive

B. At some point during the course of the disorder, the person has recognized that the obsessions or compulsions are excessive or unreasonable. **Note:** This does not apply to children.

C. The obsessions or compulsions cause marked distress, are time consuming (take more than 1 hour a day), or significantly interfere with the person's normal routine, occupational functioning, or usual social activities or relationships.

D. If another Axis I disorder is present, the content of the obsessions or compulsions is not restricted to it (e.g., preoccupation with food in the presence of an Eating Disorder; hair pulling in the presence of Trichotillomania; concern with appearance in the presence of Body Dysmorphic Disorder; preoccupation with drugs in the presence of a Substance Use Disorder; preoccupation with having a serious illness in the presence of Hypochondriasis; preoccupation with sexual urges or fantasies in the presence of Para-philia; or guilty ruminations in the presence of Major Depressive Disorder).

E. The disturbance is not due to the direct physiological effects of a substance (e.g., a drug of abuse, a medication) or a general medical condition.

Specify if:

With Poor Insight: if, for most of the time during the current episode, the person does not recognize that the obsessions and compulsions are excessive or unreasonable

Note. From *DSM-IV-TR,* pp. 462, 463.

I left the oven on, the house will burn down"), the person checks it again, up to 20 times a day or more.

3. *Doubters and sinners* fear that terrible things will happen if everything is not perfect ("Am I a good Catholic?"; "Did I do this job right?"). They are more likely to be paralyzed into inaction than to have compulsions.

4. *Counters and arrangers* are ruled by magical thinking and superstitions. Obsessions about order, symmetry, and number fuel the counting and arranging. Certain numbers or colors may be "bad," and asymmetry may lead to imagined catastrophes. Pencils all must face north or no work proceeds.

5. *Hoarders* cannot throw anything away because if they do, terrible things might happen. Not all hoarding is based on OCD, however. Some people are poorly organized and never get around to throwing things out; others intend to sort those piles but don't find the time. The important question to ask a hoarder is, "What would happen if all that stuff were thrown out?" A catastrophic answer suggests OCD. A more banal one—"Oh, well, I needed to get rid of stuff anyway"—suggests procrastination or poor organization.

Clinical Course

Two-thirds of patients with OCD have substantial symptoms before the age of 15 and almost all have some symptoms in childhood. On the average, men develop OCD 5 years earlier than women. It is rare to develop OCD after the age of 35 years. The first psychiatric contact is in the 20s and the first hospitalization (if any), during the 30s. Although it tends to begin gradually, OCD may erupt suddenly after a severe psychosocial stressor. In the average patient it is a chronic life-long illness with waxing and waning of symptoms. Outcome is not related to the content of the obsessions; patients with milder symptoms, no compulsions, briefer duration of symptoms, and higher premorbid functioning have better prognoses.

Complications and Comorbidity

Attempts to resist an obsession or compulsion may produce anxiety of panic proportions; hence the inclusion of this disorder with the anxiety disorders. Depression is the most frequent (80% of patients) comorbidity for these patients. It may be difficult to sustain interpersonal relationships. Although going insane, being totally incapacitated, or permanently incarcerated are all common fears of people with obsessions, these fears rarely materialize. Despite much suicidal thinking, less than 1% of these patients commit suicide.

Several uncommon disorders may coexist with OCD about 10–15% of the time, but are not necessarily a result of it. These include anorexia and bulimia nervosa, trichotillomania, and Tourette's disorder. Body dysmorphic disorder (e.g., "My nose is too big, my lips too small")—sometimes called the "Michael Jackson syndrome"—often occurs with OCD. Underlying many of these conditions is pathological doubting (e.g., "I'm too fat" in the anorectic).

Epidemiology

The lifetime prevalence of OCD in the general population is 2.6% (see Table 14-1). The sexes are more equally affected. OCD is more common among the higher educated, higher socioeconomic groups, and those with higher IQ scores—three interrelated factors. Obsessive–compulsive personality disorder is not particularly more common in OCD, but avoidant and dependent personality disorders are. More recent data suggest that believing the thoughts or behaviors are real or reasonable does not indicate a poor prognosis.

Etiology and Pathogenesis

Freudian psychodynamic theory states that obsessions and compulsions develop in three phases: (1) an internally perceived dangerous impulse, (2) the threat of what would occur if this impulse were acted upon, and (3) the defenses to avert the threat. The most commonly used defenses are repression, reaction formation, isolation, and undoing.

Individuals with neurological disorders and brain insults due to trauma or infection are more prone to develop OCD. Research indicates that there are abnormalities in the frontal lobes, basal ganglia, and cingulus areas of patients with this disorder. Cingulotomy in extreme cases can substantially relieve or cure OCD. The basal ganglia is involved in overlearned routine behaviors such as grooming, and the prefrontal areas mediate planning and organizing behaviors. Because drugs that treat OCD all markedly affect serotonin transmission, the serotonin system is probably involved.

Psychopathology in general and obsessions in particular run in the families of people with obsessions. Given that concordance rates for OCD are 70% and 50% among MZ and DZ twins, respectively, genetic transmission is involved. A patient with OCD has a 25% chance of having a first-degree relative with this disorder.

Differential Diagnosis

Normal obsessive thoughts and compulsive behaviors are not resisted or considered ridiculous by the person having them. Avoiding sidewalk cracks and other compulsive actions are common during childhood, but kids don't mind them; they do mind OCD. Kids have a lot of magical thinking and don't see the senselessness of their acts. Adults may feel that their obsessive brooding, ruminations, and preoccupations are annoying and excessive, yet they usually think they're meaningful; not being fully ego-dystonic, these are not the true obsessions of OCD. This disorder was once believed to be intimately related to *obsessive–compulsive personality disorder*, but more recent evidence suggests no real relationship between the two. The obsessive and compulsive traits in obsessive–compulsive personality disorder are ego-syntonic, whereas they are usually ego-dystonic in OCD; moreover, patients with obsessive–compulsive personality disorder do not have true obsessions or compulsions. Neither are so-called *"compulsive" gambling, eating, and sexual behaviors* true compulsions; the person usually enjoys doing them, does not imagine any disaster occurring if they are not done, and at least is temporarily distracted from unpleasant feelings.

OCD should not be diagnosed when specific obsessions and compulsions arise directly from other disorders. *Schizophrenic delusions* may resemble obsessions, but they are usually ego-syntonic and occur without patients' insight. Obsessions are overvalued ideas, not delusions; patients with OCD usually accept the fact that their obsessions are not realistic. Because *major depression* is often accompanied by ruminative, guilt-ridden, and self-critical obsessions, and since major depression and OCD both have episodic courses, differentiating the two can be difficult. In general, the diagnosis of OCD should be reserved when OCD clearly precedes major depression, or when the obsessions are not directly related to the depression. If the obsession or preoccupation is confined to body parts, somatic symptoms, or having an illness then somatoform disorders are diagnosed. Similarly, in disorders in which preoccupations normally occur, OCD is diagnosed only if the obsessions include other areas of concern.

Management and Treatment

Medication

The only proven effective drug treatment for this disorder are the SSRIs (fluoxetine, sertraline, paroxetine, citalopram, escitalopram, fluvoxamine) and the highly serotonergic TCA clomipramine. As the chlorinated derivative of imipramine (itself ineffective), clomipramine must be given in an eventual dose of 150–250 mg after gradual titration. High doses of SSRIs (fluoxetine 60–80 mg, sertraline 150–200 mg, paroxetine 40–50 mg) may be required, although one recent study showed that doses traditionally effective for depression do work.

Response can take 10–12 weeks, so premature termination of medication trials should be avoided. Although 70% of patients respond to some degree, most are left with residual symptoms. Only about 10–15% of patients have full remissions. The average partial responder has a 40% reduction in symptoms. In OCD, however, that may mean 3–5 more hours of good functioning each day—a big improvement. Most patients stay on medication chronically; about 85% relapse in a month or two after stopping medication.

Behavior Therapy

A combination of behavior therapy and antidepressants is generally recommended for OCD patients. Behavior-based approaches have been moderately successful, particularly with patients who have compulsions. Graded exposure and response prevention are usually used for the compulsions. For example, a hand-washer might be taken into a "contaminated" place and prevented from washing his hands for two minutes. Catastrophic thoughts are identified as the patient watches his anxiety peak and then subside. In another case, a woman who fears contamination if she touches anything without wearing gloves is directed to not wear gloves for half an hour and to touch a variety of feared objects (e.g., food, newspapers, silverware, old sweat socks). Eventually, she becomes desensitized to touching these objects.

Surgery

Stereotactic cingulotomy has been used occasionally for very severe, very treatment-resistant cases. About 25–30% of these patients substantially benefit from this procedure (Jenike et al., 1991). The non-invasive repetitive Transcranial Magnetic Stimulation (rTMS), by targeting magnetic waves to the caudate nucleus or prefrontal cortex, shows some promise in treating OCD.

POSTTRAUMATIC STRESS DISORDER

Posttraumatic stress disorder (PTSD) occurs after a severe and extraordinary stressor: a massive fire, hurricane, holocaust, rape, mugging, military combat, or terrorist bombing. The stressful events are usually more than "normal" bereavement, chronic illness, business losses, divorce, etc.

Hours or months following the stressor, patients waver between two main features of PTSD: reexperiencing (also called intrusion) and avoidance of the event. Often, *avoidance* or *denial* comes first, with "psychic numbing" dominating. These individuals minimize the significance of the stress, forget it happened, feel detached from others, lose interest in life, display constricted affect, daydream, and abuse drugs or alcohol. In reexperiencing the trauma, patients are flooded by intrusive recollections while awake (flashbacks), while asleep (nightmares), or while waking up (hypnopompic hallucinations). They then manifest the third cardinal feature of PTSD, which is autonomic arousal (e.g., being hypervigilant and "on edge"). They cannot sleep or concentrate; they ruminate about the stressor, cry "without reason," show emotional lability, are startled or upset by the slightest reminders of the trauma, and develop somatic anxiety. Patients compulsively relive the stressful event, are often unable to think about anything else, and fear "going crazy." In *DSM-IV-TR*'s criteria for PTSD (Table 14-7), the reexperiencing phase is generally covered under criterion B, the avoidance phase under criterion C, and hyperarousal under D.

Normal and pathological responses to traumatic events are usually, but not always, easy to distinguish (see Figure 4-5). Normal responders react with sadness or anxiety and find it harder to acknowledge guilt, rage, or shame. They may undergo periods of denial and intrusion. They often go through stages similar to those associated with grief, but without resolution. Indeed, this is one of the few times that producing symptoms is healthy.

There is a very brief (less than 4 weeks) variation of PTSD called Acute Stress Disorder that emphasizes dissociative symptoms (see Table 14-8). Dissociation as an early symptom may predict the development of PTSD. PTSD has three subtypes: the *acute* form lasts less than 3 months; the *chronic*, 3 months or more; and the *delayed-onset* form emerges at least 6 months past the trauma.

The delayed subtype has the worst prognosis with frequent development of mood and substance use disorders. These comorbid disorders may be different manifestations of the same underlying illness of PTSD. Perhaps two-thirds of these individuals had family members with a psychiatric disorder, usually substance abuse or an anxiety disorder, suggesting an underlying predisposition.

After spending 16 months on active duty in Iraq, a 29-year-old soldier returned to his home in the rural mid-West. He found a job at a close-by factory. He was doing reasonably well adjusting to civilian life, when fireworks on the 4th of July unleashed memories of being fired at, explosions from rocket propelled grenades, and helping transport dead bodies. This was accompanied by withdrawal from family, easy irritability, episodes of crying, nightmares of seeing people die, and being easily startled. Cognitive–behavioral therapy (described in Chapter 5) aimed at normalizing his reactions, relaxation techniques, and the use of an SSRI, helped de-

TABLE 14-7

DSM-IV-TR *Criteria for Posttraumatic Stress Disorder*

A. The person has been exposed to a traumatic event in which both of the following were present:

   (1) the person experienced, witnessed, or was confronted with an event or events that involved actual or threatened death or serious injury, or a threat to the physical integrity of self or others

   (2) the person's response involved intense fear, helplessness, or horror. **Note:** In children, this may be expressed instead by disorganized or agitated behavior.

B. The traumatic event is persistently reexperienced in one (or more) of the following ways:

   (1) recurrent and intrusive distressing recollections of the event, including images, thoughts, or perceptions. **Note:** In young children, repetitive play may occur in which themes or aspects of the trauma are expressed.

   (2) recurrent distressing dreams of the event. **Note:** In children, there may be frightening dreams without recognizable content.

   (3) acting or feeling as if the traumatic event were recurring (includes a sense of reliving the experience, illusions, hallucinations, and dissociative flashback episodes, including those that occur upon awakening or when intoxicated). **Note:** In young children, trauma-specific reenactment may occur.

   (4) intense psychological distress at exposure to internal or external cues that symbolize or resemble an aspect of the traumatic event

   (5) physiologic reactivity upon exposure to internal or external cues that symbolize or resemble an aspect of the traumatic event

C. Persistent avoidance of stimuli associated with the trauma and numbing of general responsiveness (not present before the trauma), as indicated by three (or more) of the following:

   (1) efforts to avoid thoughts, feelings, or conversations associated with the trauma

   (2) efforts to avoid activities, places, or people that arouse recollections of the trauma

   (3) inability to recall an important aspect of the trauma

   (4) markedly diminished interest or participation in significant activities

   (5) feeling of detachment or estrangement from others

   (6) restricted range of affect (e.g., unable to have loving feelings)

   (7) sense of a foreshortened future (e.g., does not expect to have a career, marriage, children, or a normal life span)

D. Persistent symptoms of increased arousal (not present before the trauma), as indicated by two (or more) of the following:

   (1) difficulty falling or staying asleep

   (2) irritability or outbursts of anger

   (3) difficulty concentrating

(continued)

TABLE 14-7

Continued

(4) hypervigilance

(5) exaggerated startle response

E. Duration of the disturbance (symptoms in Criteria B, C, and D) is more than 1 month.

F. The disturbance causes clinically significant distress or impairment in social, occupational, or other impor-
    tant areas of functioning.

Specify if:

Acute: if duration of symptoms is less than 3 months

Chronic: if duration of symptoms is 3 months or more

Specify if:

With Delayed Onset: if onset of symptoms is at least 6 months after the stressor

Note. From *DSM-IV-TR,* pp. 467, 468.

crease the severity and frequency of his symptoms, enabling him to return to work
in 6 weeks.

In both acute and chronic subtypes, encountering a circumstance similar
to the original stressor often aggravates or rekindles symptoms. Many persons
with PTSD continue to experience intermittent and residual symptoms
throughout life. The intensity and duration of symptoms are usually less severe
if the trauma is caused by nature (e.g., hurricane) than people (e.g., rape,
torture). *Single-event traumas* are less likely to cause PTSD than *complex traumas* that repeat and persist. However, many single-event traumas (e.g., hurri-
canes) are associated with secondary adversities, such as loss of home, school,
friends, and income, which transform them into complex traumas with indistinguishable clinical results.

Epidemiology

The lifetime prevalence of PTSD in the general population is approximately
7% with females being twice as likely to meet the diagnostic criteria. This
disorder can occur at any age, but children and older adults generally have a
more difficult time coping with traumatic events. Studies conducted after the
San Fernando earthquake of 1971 and the Chowchilla bus kidnapping in

TABLE 14-8

DSM-IV-TR *Criteria for Acute Stress Disorder*

A. The person has been exposed to a traumatic event in which both of the following were present:

   (1) the person experienced, witnessed, or was confronted with an event or events that involved actual or threatened death or serious injury, or a threat to the physical integrity of self or others

   (2) the person's response involved intense fear, helplessness, or horror

B. Either while experiencing or immediately after experiencing the distressing event, the individual has three (or more) of the following dissociative symptoms:

   (1) a subjective sense of numbing, detachment, or absence of emotional responsiveness

   (2) a reduction in awareness of his or her surroundings (e.g., "being in a daze")

   (3) derealization

   (4) depersonalization

   (5) dissociative amnesia (i.e., inability to recall an important aspect of the trauma)

C. The traumatic event is persistently reexperienced in at least one of the following ways: recurrent images, thoughts, dreams, illusions, flashback episodes, or a sense of reliving the experience; or distress on exposure to reminders of the traumatic event.

D. Marked avoidance of stimuli that arouse recollections of the trauma (e.g., thoughts, feelings, conversations, activities, places, people).

E. Marked symptoms of anxiety or increased arousal (e.g., difficulty sleeping, irritability, poor concentration, hypervigilance, exaggerated startle response, motor restlessness).

F. The disturbance causes clinically significant distress or impairment in social, occupational, or other important areas of functioning or impairs the individual's ability to pursue some necessary task, such as obtaining necessary assistance or mobilizing personal resources by telling family members about the traumatic experience.

G. The disturbance lasts for a minimum of 2 days and a maximum of 4 weeks and occurs within 4 weeks of the traumatic event.

H. The disturbance is not due to the direct physiological effects of a substance (e.g., a drug of abuse, a medication) or a general medical condition, is not better accounted for by Brief Psychotic Disorder, and is not merely an exacerbation of a preexisting Axis I or Axis II disorder.

Note. From *DSM-IV-TR*, pp. 471, 472.

1976 demonstrated the effects of significant trauma on children. In the latter instance, all 25 kidnapping victims who had been held for 27 hours (16 of those hours, they were buried in their school bus) demonstrated pessimism, shame, increased fearfulness, repeated nightmares, and related symptoms 4 years after the trauma. Frequently, traumatized children stop thinking about the future, feeling that they have none. Childhood trauma more often results in dissociative experiences, self-injurious behavior, difficulties with impulse control, traumatic reenactments, "repetition compulsions," social isolation, and profound restrictions in emotional responsiveness (Terr, 1991).

Etiology

To qualify for diagnosis of PTSD, the etiology must include a sufficiently traumatizing event.

> In men, military trauma is the most common cause of PTSD; and in women rape and/or physical abuse are the most common causes. Men entering the military who are most likely to get PTSD are younger, have had less military training, were previously emotionally or physically abused, or already have had some psychiatric symptoms. Particularly severe traumas involving witnessing the death or dismemberment of buddies, witnessing or participating in atrocities, and physical injury with permanent disability are more likely to cause chronic and severe PTSD (Kulk et al., 1990). Soldiers who had been deployed to Iraq more than once were 1.6 times more likely to have PTSD than those deployed only once. Soldiers deployed for more than six months were also 1.5 times more likely to have PTSD than those deployed for less than 6 months.
>
> Women who have been raped are more likely to develop PTSD if physical force, display of a weapon, or injury to the victim occurred (Bownes et al., 1991). They also tend to have more acute guilt, shame, and suicidal ideation (Dahl, 1989). A woman who was sexually abused in childhood by a male is less likely to develop PTSD if she had a supportive mother who intervened and an overall positive family environment. Later, a gentle, caring boyfriend can help a woman desensitize to her trauma and to men in general. Women with PTSD from childhood sexual abuse may display less obvious but highly related symptoms, such as going to bed fully clothed with a night light on, having insomnia until dawn comes, and then sleeping well. These are all understandable responses to being regularly sexually abused at bedtime or during the night. A dissociative disorder more often accompanies PTSD induced by childhood versus adult trauma.

Perhaps 20% of those exposed to such an event develop PTSD, which means that the vast majority do not. Risk factors include proximity to the trauma, prolonged exposure, complex trauma, previous psychiatric history, minimal support network, and early dissociative symptom response. Sustained hyperarousal seems to elevate cortisol levels and thereby alter the hypothalamic–pituitary–adrenal axis. Chronically high cortisol may damage the hippocampus (reducing its volume), which, along with the anterior cingulate, are involved with cognitive memory. The amygdala (a major member of the limbic system), which controls emotional memory, is overactived in PTSD. The essence of treatment is to help the person suffering from PTSD to move from pure emotional to cognitive memory of the event and essentially reverse these neurophysiological concomitants. The noradrenergic and serotonergic neurotransmitter systems have been implicated in this disorder.

Differential Diagnosis

On one hand, PTSD may go undiagnosed because (1) patients don't report the initial trauma or the subsequent symptoms, (2) substance abuse masks the symptoms, or (3) their traumatic visual imagery is misattributed to schizophrenia, LSD intoxication or flashbacks, temporal lobe epilepsy, or a dissociative disorder. On the other hand, when PTSD is used to justify financial compensation, malingering might be the diagnosis. Differentiating PTSD from *malingering* can be difficult, partly because the patient may no longer be able to distinguish reality from fabrication. People who deliberately malinger may not present with the specific diagnostic criteria in *DSM-IV-TR*, but rather display their own version of what they (or television) consider madness. Careful coaching by an attorney or others may later help them get the symptoms "right." The differential diagnosis includes the other *anxiety disorders, major depression,* and *adjustment disorder. Adjustment disorder with anxiety* should not be confused with PTSD. Adjustment disorders are triggered by more ordinary stressors (e.g., exams to graduate from college, a court hearing, or divorce). Over 95% of patients with PTSD have a past psychiatric disorder of some kind and over 50% have an additional current diagnosis.

Management and Treatment

Debriefing immediately after the trauma may actually worsen outcome by unwittingly reinforcing overwhelming feelings through forced disclosure of events and exploration of feelings. There is general agreement that immediate interventions should include ensuring safety while addressing concerns of the moment and practical needs, encouraging use of the existing natural supports (family and friends), expressing hope while tolerating the person's expressions of emotion, expecting recovery and providing reassurance for successful coping, educating on common and maladaptive responses to trauma, and evaluating mental status, especially for dissociative symptoms and other risk factors. Often the trauma victim will accept support only from a person who has experienced a similar trauma. This is based on the mistaken belief that a person who has had the same experience will automatically understand and empathize with the victim. A well-functioning support group can be especially helpful for those temporarily overwhelmed by the trauma by providing practical support that reinforces the victim's reactions as "normal"; addressing common fears, concerns, and traumatic memories; increasing the capacity to tolerate disturbing emotions; and sharing strategies for coping. Unfortunately, some support groups may encourage endless catharsis and a posttraumatic group identity without treatment progress or improvement in adaptive functioning.

Acute PTSD may remit spontaneously, and mild and acute cases may respond to supportive psychotherapy. Most chronic (more than 5 months) and severe cases do not remit spontaneously or with supportive approaches alone and require more intensive and specialized psychotherapy. Individual or group therapy for chronic and severe cases involves active confrontation of feared topics and memories, examining misinterpretation of the events, and developing better methods of coping with the trauma. However, treatment occurs in carefully orchestrated phases, and its ultimate success is measured by restored relationships and community integration. Although eventually returning to the trauma is considered necessary, former adaptive defenses are restored and a safe therapeutic environment is established before traumatic memories are gradually and gently explored. Typically one works through the trauma by creating a narrative account with an understanding of its personal meaning and its proper context.

In cognitive–behavioral therapy, exposure approaches are used to reduce fear responses to both the original trauma and present reminders. Cognitive restructuring methods focus on distorted views of the original trauma and the subsequent changes in basic assumptions regarding self-invulnerability, self-esteem, and life meaningfulness. Even with successful treatment, symptoms of PTSD may resurface in response to stress from life events and developmental stages and require intermittent psychotherapy (preferably with the same therapist). If untreated, the syndrome continues for decades or a lifetime and spawns associated substance abuse; mood, panic, or phobic disorders; and occupational and interpersonal impairments. These must also be a focus of therapy. Medications are often indicated, since phobic and anxiety symptoms and major depressive disorder are typically dominant features that interfere with psychotherapy.

Medications for PTSD can be used adjunctively for some symptoms. There is some evidence to suggest that early treatment of hyperarousal with adrenergic blockers may reduce the risk of developing the full syndrome. In addition to reducing the physiological arousal (e.g., excessive hypervigilance and startle response), the adrenergic blockers such as propanol and clonidine can decrease anger. SSRIs, TCAs, and MAOIs are useful in treating PTSD. These drugs can reduce symptoms such as nightmares, flashbacks, and intrusive recollections. An 8-week trial might be needed to show full effect. Anticonvulsants increase behavioral control, particularly for irritability and aggression. Prazosin has been shown to decrease flashbacks, and cyproheptadine to improve nightmares in war veterans. Benzodiazepines have not been shown to work and may disinhibit. MAOIs should not be used in substance abusers, because of the risk of hypertensive crisis from a drug–MAOI interaction. Trazodone can be used safely for insomnia in this population.

GENERALIZED ANXIETY DISORDER

Persons with generalized anxiety disorder (GAD) tend to worry excessively, out of proportion to what the situation warrants. These patients are chronic "worrywarts." During a majority of their days, they are tense, highly distractible, irritable, restless, and so "on edge" that they're often fatigued and mildly depressed. Unrelenting anxiety is, by itself, very exhausting. The anxiety is diffuse, unfocused, free-floating, and ongoing; it may or may not be accompanied by prominent physical complaints such as sweating, dizziness, clammy hands, and tachycardia. When somatic symptoms dominate, patients tend to consult numerous medical specialists, chiropractors, physiotherapists, or nutritionists, which may lead them to fad diets and substance abuse. GAD also impairs social and occupational functioning. The *DSM-IV-TR* criteria are listed in Table 14-9. GAD occurs in persons of all ages and is believed to be twice as common in women than in men. Lifetime prevalence is estimated at over 5% and 12-month prevalence at over 3%. In practice, persons are frequently assigned to this diagnosis when they have some of the features of the other disorders, but do not meet diagnostic criteria.

Differential Diagnosis

As discussed earlier, drugs and medical conditions commonly mimic GAD. Patients with early *schizophrenia* and extensive anxiety also manifest disorganized thinking, will be suspicious and distrustful, and may appear to be emotionally remote, with very constricted affect. A *mood disorder* is the most common diagnosis (more than 50%) in patients presenting with anxiety. Dif-

TABLE 14-9

DSM-IV-TR *Criteria for Generalized Anxiety Disorder*

A. Excessive anxiety and worry (apprehensive expectation), occurring more days than not for at least 6 months, about a number of events or activities (such as work or school performance).

B. The person finds it difficult to control the worry.

C. The anxiety and worry are associated with three (or more) of the following six symptoms (with at least some symptoms present for more days than not for the past 6 months). **Note:** Only one item is required in children.

   (1) restlessness or feeling keyed up or on edge

   (2) being easily fatigued

   (3) difficulty concentrating or mind going blank

   (4) irritability

   (5) muscle tension

   (6) sleep disturbance (difficulty falling or staying asleep, or restless unsatisfying sleep)

D. The focus of the anxiety and worry is not confined to features of an Axis I disorder, e.g., the anxiety or worry is not about having a Panic Attack (as in Panic Disorder), being embarrassed in public (as in Social Phobia), being contaminated (as in Obsessive–Compulsive Disorder), being away from home or close relatives (as in Separation Anxiety Disorder), gaining weight (as in Anorexia Nervosa), having multiple physical complaints (as in Somatization Disorder), or having a serious illness (as in Hypochondriasis), and the anxiety and worry do not occur exclusively during Posttraumatic Stress Disorder.

E. The anxiety, worry, or physical symptoms cause clinically significant distress or impairment in social, occupational, or other important areas of functioning.

F. The disturbance is not due to the direct physiological effects of a substance (e.g., a drug of abuse, a medication) or a general medical condition (e.g., hyperthyroidism) and does not occur exclusively during a Mood Disorder, a Psychotic Disorder, or a Pervasive Developmental Disorder.

Note. From *DSM-IV-TR,* p. 476.

---

ferentiating anxiety from *depression* is somewhat difficult. Since the frequency of mixed anxiety and depression is perhaps as high as 50%, patients complaining mainly of anxiety who have definite symptoms of the depressive syndrome should be treated as having depression. Antidepressants have been shown to be more effective than antianxiety agents in this group. Although these anxious people with depression may not complain of depression, they usually do experience anhedonia, a distinct loss of pleasure in situations that were formerly enjoyable, along with other classic depressive symptoms such as insomnia, anorexia, and fatigue.

Panic disorder is the second most common diagnosis in patients presenting with anxiety. It may be confused with GAD, since chronic anxiety often occurs between panic attacks; yet unlike GAD, panic disorder has distinct episodes of intense anxiety. In *phobic disorder* the patient's anxiety is specific for the phobic stimulus, whereas in GAD it is unfocused and ongoing. The somatic complaints of GAD may resemble *hypochondriasis*, but the person with hypochondriasis more gravely exaggerates the danger of his or her symptoms and is a "specialist" in the fear of disease.

Management and Treatment

Psychotherapies

Several studies show that psychotherapy of various kinds is as effective as medication for all but a minority of individuals. All psychotherapies seek to identify the stressors producing the anxiety, offer better means of handling stress, and eliminate dietary or physical sources of anxiety. Insight-oriented psychotherapies will explore the *unconscious* and symbolic meanings of the patient's anxiety and clarify its defensive and "signal" functions. In cognitive therapy, patients identify the precise events or circumstances that trigger *conscious* dysphoric "automatic thoughts" and then develop more rational ways of thinking and feeling in response to the same stressors.

Behavior Therapy

Muscle relaxation, meditation, biofeedback, and autogenic training are frequently employed either by themselves or as supplements to the previously mentioned therapies.

Pharmacotherapy

SSRIs, SNRIs, TCAs, and buspirone, an anxiolytic with no sedative or amnestic properties and no risk of dependence, are probably all reasonable and safe choices with which to treat chronic anxiety. Benzodiazepines can be used to treat acute, paralyzing exacerbations of anxiety. Generally, these should be prescribed for limited durations, such as 2–4 weeks, to avoid long-term physical and psychological dependence. Patients who are primarily distressed by the physiological symptoms of anxiety, such as increased heart rate or "butterflies," may respond well to beta-blockers. Several studies have reported that both sedating and nonsedating antidepressants are effective for GAD without depression.

An example of a treatment manual for GAD is *Mastery of Your Anxiety and Worry*, developed by Craske, Barlow, and O'Leary (1992).

References

Bourne, E.J. (1995). *The anxiety and phobia workbook.* Oakland, CA: New Harbinger Workbooks.

Bownes, I.T., O'Gorman, E.C., & Sayers, A. (1991). Assault characteristics in post-traumatic stress disorder in rape victims. *Acta Psychiatrica Scandinavica, 83,* 27–30.

Cannon, W.B. (1932). *The wisdom of the body.* New York: Norton.

Craske, M.G., Barlow, D.H., & O'Leary, T.O. (1992). *Mastery of your anxiety and worry.* Albany, NY: Graywind.

Dahl, S. (1989). Acute responses to rape: A PTSD variant. *Acta Psychiatrica Scandinavica, 80*(Supp), 355.

Freud, S. (1919). Lines of advance in psychoanalytic therapy. In J. Strachey (Ed. and Trans.), *The complete psychological works, the standard edition* (Vol. 17, pp. 157–168). New York: Norton.

Gil, E. (2006). *Helping abused and traumatized children, integrating directive and nondirective approaches.* New York: Guilford Press.

James, W. (1893). *The principles of psychology.* New York: Hold & Co.

Jenike, M.A. (1993). Augmentation strategies for treatment-resistant obsessive–compulsive disorder. *Harvard Review Psychiatry, 1,* 17–26.

Jenike, M.A., Baer, L., Ballantine, T., Martuza, R.L., Tynes, S., Giriunas, I., et al. (1991). Cingulotomy for refractory obsessive–compulsive disorder. *Archives of General Psychiatry, 48,* 548–554.

Kandel, E.R. (1983). From metapsychology to molecular biology: Explorations into the nature of anxiety. *American Journal of Psychiatry, 140,* 1277–1293.

Klein, D.F. (1993). False suffocation alarms, spontaneous panics, and related conditions: An integrative hypothesis. *Archives of General Psychiatry, 50,* 306–317.

Kulk, R.A., Schlenger, W.E., Fairbank, J.A., Hough, R.L., Jordan, B.K., Marmon, C.R., et al. (1990). *Trauma and the Vietnam war generation.* New York: Brunner/Mazel.

Liebowitz, M.R., Gorman, J.M., Fyer, A.J., & Klein, D.F. (1985). Social phobia: Review of a neglected anxiety disorder. *Archives of General Psychiatry, 42,* 729–736.

Maxmen, J. S. (1986). *A good night's sleep: A step-by-step program for overcoming insomnia and other sleep problems.* New York: Warner.

Mental Health Advisory Team (MHAT) IV Operation Iraqi Freedom 05-07 Final Report: 23–24. Available at: http://www.armymedicine.army.mil/news/mhat/mhat_iv/MHAT_IV_Report_17Nov06.pdf.

Murphy, D.L., & Pigott, T.A. (1990). A comparative examination of a role for serotonin in obsessive–compulsive disorder, panic disorder, and anxiety. *Journal of Clinical Psychiatry, 51*(4, Supp.), 53–60.

Pitts, F.N., & McClure, J.N. (1967). Lactate metabolism and anxiety neurosis. *New England Journal of Medicine, 277,* 1329–1336.

Redmond, D.E., Jr. (1979). New and old evidence for the involvement of a brain norepinephrine system in anxiety. In W.E. Fann, I. Karacan, A.D. Porkorney, & R.L. Williams (Eds.), *Phenomenology and treatment of anxiety* (pp. 153–203). New York: Spectrum.

Roy-Byrne, P., Geraci, M., & Uhde, T.W. (1986). Life events and the onset of panic disorder. *American Journal of Psychiatry, 143,* 1424–1427.

Skolnick, P., & Paul, S.M. (1983). New concepts in the neurobiology of anxiety. *Journal of Clinical Psychiatry, 44,* 12–19.

Solomon, S.D., Gerrity, E.T., & Muff, A.M. (1992). Efficacy of treatment for posttraumatic stress disorder. *Journal of the American Medical Association, 268,* 633–638.

Terr, L. (1991). Childhood traumas: An outline and overview. *American Journal of Psychiatry, 148,* 10–20.

http://www.psych.org. Web site of the American Psychiatric Association.

15

Somatoform Disorders

DOCTOR: It's all in your head.
PATIENT: But it's *not* in my head; it's in my stomach.

What the doctor considers reassurance, the patient may consider an accusation. The doctor says that nothing is *physically* wrong with the patient, but the patient hears that *nothing* is wrong. Yet there *is* something wrong: The patient's stomach hurts. Even when psychological factors produce the pain, for the patient that pain is just as real and just as miserable. When the physician ignores this central fact, the patient feels accused of being a fake or crazy.

Patients with psychogenic physical symptoms frustrate professionals because they don't have "real" illnesses, don't respond to conventional medical treatments, shop around for doctors, are stubbornly unpsychological, and dwell on their physical complaints. The professional claims that the patient's physical problems are psychogenic, and because the patient disagrees, he or she is, in essence, rejecting the professional's expertise.

Consequently, these patients receive poor care. Not knowing what else to do and succumbing to these patients' demands for medication, physicians often prescribe drugs, expecting them not to work. These medications are frequently hypnoanxiolytics, and patients become addicted. (At least now they have a "real" problem!) These patients undergo countless tests, procedures, and operations. In comparison to controls, patients with somatoform disorders have three times the weight of body organs removed surgically (Cohen et al., 1953). Sensing, often correctly, that doctors consider them "crocks" and "gomers," these patients distrust doctors and don't follow their advice. Yet they also feel helplessly dependent on doctors and glom onto them, causing further alienation. In a "no-win situation," these patients distrust the very doctors on whom they must rely.

In *DSM-IV-TR*, somatoform disorders are those in which patients have physical symptoms that cannot be fully explained by medical findings or known physiological mechanisms; if there are medical findings, these patients' complaints or impairment exceed what would be expected. There must also be positive evidence, or at least a strong presumption, that psychological factors play an important role in the onset, severity, exacerbation, or maintenance of symptoms. These symptoms are not under voluntary control.

Somatoform disorders differ from three other psychiatric conditions that generate symptoms resembling physical illness. In *malingering* and *factitious disorders*, patients deliberately make and fake symptoms, whereas in somatoform disorders, symptoms are produced involuntarily. In *psychological factors affecting physical conditions*, often called "psychosomatic disorders," emotional factors trigger, aggravate, or exacerbate a clearly existing medical condition, such as ulcers or hypertension, through a known pathophysiological mechanism. In many somatoform disorders, however, there is no identifiable medical disease or any known pathophysiological mechanism to account for the patient's symptoms.

DSM-IV-TR describes six major somatoform disorders: (1) somatization disorder, (2) conversion disorder, (3) hypochondriasis, (4) body dysmorphic disorder, (5) psychogenic pain disorder, and (6) undifferentiated somatoform disorder.

SOMATIZATION DISORDER

Clinical Presentation

Somatization disorder—also named "Briquet's syndrome" after the French physician who first described it in 1859—is a chronic condition featuring multiple, unexplained somatic symptoms in numerous organ systems. Vomiting, aphonia (inability to produce sounds), painful limbs, muscle weakness, dizziness, painful menstruation, burning sensations in sex organs, paralyses, and conversion symptoms are common. Table 15-1 presents *DSM-IV-TR* criteria for somatization disorder.

As "few" as eight unexplained or excessive symptoms distributed in the right way can qualify a person for somatization disorder. This is a little simpler than *DSM-III*, which listed 37 symptoms; women with 14 and men with 12 symptoms qualified for the diagnosis. Still it is not easy to remember all the possible symptoms. For clinical convenience, Othmer and DeSouza (1985) found that the presence of any two out of seven specific symptoms predicted the correct diagnosis of *DSM-III* somatization disorder in 80–90% of cases; they incorporated this finding into the screening test outlined in Table 15-2.

TABLE 15-1

DSM-IV-TR *Criteria for Somatization Disorder*

A. A history of many physical complaints beginning before age 30 years, that occur over a period of several years and result in treatment being sought or significant impairment in social, occupational, or other important areas of functioning.

B. Each of the following criteria must have been met, with individual symptoms occurring at any time during the course of the disturbance:

   (1) *four pain symptoms:* a history of pain related to at least four different sites or functions (e.g., head, abdomen, back, joints, extremities, chest, rectum, during menstruation, during sexual intercourse, or during urination)

   (2) *two gastrointestinal symptoms:* a history of at least two gastrointestinal symptoms other than pain (such as nausea, bloating, vomiting other than during pregnancy, diarrhea, or intolerance of several different foods)

   (3) *one sexual symptom:* a history of at least one sexual or reproductive symptom other than pain (e.g., sexual indifference, erectile or ejaculatory dysfunction, irregular menses, excessive menstrual bleeding, vomiting throughout pregnancy)

   (4) *one pseudoneurological symptom:* a history of at least one symptom or deficit suggesting a neurological condition not limited to pain (conversion symptoms such as impaired coordination or balance, paralysis or localized weakness, difficulty swallowing or lump in throat, aphonia, urinary retention, hallucinations, loss of touch or pain sensation, double vision, blindness, deafness, seizures; dissociative symptoms such as amnesia; or loss of consciousness other than fainting)

C. Either (1) or (2):

   (1) after appropriate investigation, each of the symptoms in Criterion B cannot be fully explained by a known general medical condition or the direct effects of a substance (e.g., a drug of abuse, a medication)

   (2) when there is a related general medical condition, the physical complaints or resulting social or occupational impairment are in excess of what would be expected from the history, physical examination, or laboratory findings

D. The symptoms are not intentionally produced or feigned (as in Factitious Disorder or Malingering).

Note. From *DSM-IV-TR,* p. 490.

Everyone has physical symptoms, but they mostly ignore them. Not so for patients with somatization disorder. For every ache and pain they will see a doctor, want a complete workup, and expect a prescription. (Any patient who enters a doctor's office with three dozen medications has a somatization disorder till proven otherwise.) These patients don't just present symptoms, they dramatize them: "I'm puking like a volcano." "I almost fainted in front of a

TABLE 15-2

Screening Test for Somatization Disorder

MNEMONIC	SYMPTOM	ORGAN SYSTEM
S omatization	Shortness of breath	Respiratory
D isorder	Dysmenorrhea	Female reproductive
B esets	Burning in sex organs	Psychosexual
L adies	Lump in throat	Pseudoneurological
A nd	Amnesia	Pseudoneurological
V exes	Vomiting	Gastrointestinal
P hysicians	Painful extremities	Skeletal muscle

Questions used to assess the presence of the seven symptoms of the screening test for somatization disorder.

S. Have you ever had trouble breathing?

D. Have you ever had frequent trouble with menstrual cramps?

B. Have you ever had burning sensations in your sexual organs, mouth, or rectum?

L. Have you ever had difficulties swallowing or had an uncomfortable lump in your throat that stayed with you for at least an hour?

A. Have you ever found that you could not remember what you had been doing for hours or days at a time? If yes, did this happen even though you had not been drinking or taking drugs?

V. Have you ever had trouble from frequent vomiting?

P. Have you ever had frequent pain in your fingers or toes?

If any two of the above seven questions are answered affirmatively, this *screening* test is positive; a positive test simply means that the patient *might* have a somatization disorder. To confirm the diagnosis, the patient should meet *DSM-IV-TR* criteria for somatization disorder (Table 15-1).

Note. This table is adapted from Othmer & DeSouza (1985).

bus." "I'm breathing so hard, I'm going to suffocate." Hyperbole is their norm: Headaches aren't headaches, they're "the worst headaches ever." Their histories are vague; it's never clear when their symptoms began, why they seek help now, and what they want. On repeated tellings, symptoms "change": One day a backache is dull, the next day it's sharp; one day it began 12 months ago, on the next visit it started a month ago. Symptoms never end; as soon as the clinician thinks he's heard them all, another pops up. However, these histrionics should not mislead clinicians into underestimating these patients' genuine discomfort.

Somatization disorder usually arises during adolescence, but always before age 30. Its course is fluctuating, lifelong, and exacerbated by environmental stressors—a fact deemed irrelevant or accusatory by the patient. Hardly a year passes without intense discomfort and medical treatment. Frequent complications are substance abuse, excessive laboratory tests and surgery (and its complications), work and social impairment, chronic demoralization, dysthymia, anxiety, marital problems, and divorce. The disorder is important to diagnose, if only to reduce these complications. These patients commonly attempt suicide, but rarely commit it.

Epidemiology

Somatization disorder is rarely diagnosed in men. Reported lifetime prevalence rates range widely from 0.1% to 2.0% (Mai, 2004). Its frequency among general psychiatric patients is reported to range from 1.1% to 6.0%, whereas among medical/surgical patients referred for psychiatric consultation, it may be as high as 14%. In outpatient primary-care settings, 5–10% may meet the diagnostic criteria for somatization disorder. In the United States it tends to be more common among African-Americans, lower socioeconomic groups, and less formally educated people.

Etiology and Pathogenesis

About 20% of first-degree female relatives of these patients will have a somatization disorder—that's roughly 20 times the normal frequency for women in the general population. Somatization disorder appears to be genetically and environmentally linked to antisocial personality disorder and alcoholism. Adopted children have a higher risk for alcoholism, antisocial personality disorder, and somatization disorder if they have a biological parent or an adoptive parent with any of these disorders.

Family studies reveal a high prevalence of antisocial personality disorder and alcoholism among the *male* relatives of patients with somatization disorder. Conversely, there's an increased prevalence of somatization disorder among the *female* relatives of convicted male felons. Many delinquent girls develop somatization disorder as adults, and adult female felons have an increased prevalence of medical contacts (Goodwin & Guze, 1989).

Somatization is often considered a defense mechanism in which the patient unconsciously avoids painful affects by experiencing physical discomfort. Supposedly, the central defense mechanism is somatization and the painful affect, depressive. Indeed, alexithymia, the inability to recognize and express feelings, has been especially associated with somatization disorder. Other studies reveal that patients with somatization disorder are more troubled by confused and negative self-identities (Oxman et al., 1985) and have higher rates of childhood sexual abuse. For some, somatization may be learned from a parent with somatization. In others, physical symptoms may have been the only or best way to get attention or escape abuse.

Differential Diagnosis

Hypochondriasis and somatization disorder share many features, including an early and gradual onset. However, in somatization disorder patients focus on *symptoms* of disease, whereas hypochondriacs are preoccupied with a *fear* of disease. Hypochondriasis may appear in somatization disorder, but not as the dominant symptom.

A patient with *schizophenia* or a *psychotic depression* with multiple somatic delusions—e.g., "Insects are eating my liver"—may appear to have a somatization disorder, but patients who truly have a somatization disorder specialize only in nondelusional complaints. Patients with *dysthymia, generalized anxiety, major depression,* and *panic disorder* all complain about physical symptoms more than normal, but they rarely meet full criteria for somatization disorder; most do not have a pseudoneurological symptom. However, somatization disorder can be diagnosed concurrently with any of these psychiatric disorders and it is commonly comorbid with anxiety and depressive disorders. In *factitious disorder* and *malingering*, symptoms are intentionally produced. Certain *medical conditions* mimic somatization disorder and need to be ruled out. For example, multiple sclerosis, systemic lupus erythematosus, porphyria, hemochromatoses, and hyperparathyroidism can all cause vague, multiple, and confusing somatic symptoms. Patients may have a variety of syndromes, including atypical chest pain, fibromyalgia, chronic fatigue syndrome, premenstrual syndrome, temporomandibular joint dysfunction, and "syndrome that incorporates many unexplained symptoms." (Having a name to describe a nebulous constellation of symptoms may help the patient to feel better but may not improve functioning.) Features useful in discriminating between somatization disorder and general medical conditions include (1) involvement of multiple organ systems, (2) early onset and chronic course without the development of physical signs or structural abnormalities, and (3) absence of characteristic laboratory abnormalities for the suggested physical disorder.

Management and Treatment

Since most of these patients are leery of psychiatry, they rely on nonpsychiatric, especially primary-care, physicians. Doctors can greatly help these patients if they remember to do the following: (1) Repeatedly check their own annoyance. Somatization disorders are chronic, lifelong conditions, and being angry at these patients for complaining about symptoms is akin to being angry at diabetics for having uncooperative blood sugars. (2) The primary goal of treatment is not to eliminate patients' physical complaints but to improve their functioning. (3) Avoid raising false hopes or promises, such as, "You're going to feel completely better." (4) Protect patients from needless laboratory tests, medical treatments, and surgical interventions. (5) Relate to patients "as they are": Try changing their personality and the only change will be one less patient. (6) Offer positive reinforcement for "noncomplaining behaviors," ignore complaining behaviors, and teach the families to do likewise.

> More specifically: On her first visit to the doctor, a patient with somatization disorder should receive a thorough history and physical. Assuming this examination is "negative," the doctor should tell her, "I'm pleased there is nothing *seriously* wrong with you, but I know you're experiencing considerable discomfort. So I want to follow you carefully and see you in a (week, 2 weeks, or a month—doctor's choice)." An appointment is made, whether or not the patient has symptoms; therefore, the patient doesn't *have* to get sick to see the doctor. The scheduled interval between visits should coincide with doctor-going frequency, but as-needed visits should be discouraged. At the next appointment, the doctor conducts a briefer exam, repeats the same message, and schedules another appointment. Each week, the doctor devotes full attention to the patient for 15 minutes, telling her how marvelously she's doing despite her symptoms, lauds her planned trip to Arizona, restates that she doesn't have cancer and that nothing else is seriously wrong. Eventually, the patient not only *complains* less about symptoms, but actually *experiences* fewer symptoms.
>
> Typically these patients are avoided by all because of their incessant complaining. They then become socially isolated, more miserable, and complain more. One approach may be to have a family meeting to establish a very specific goal: From then on, the patient should not talk to family members or friends about her symptoms but only to an expert, her doctor. For a while she will not know what to talk about, but over time, normal social conversation gradually replaces the medical litany. After a good physician–patient alliance has been established, some instructions about symptoms and explanations may help; for example, informing the patient that the average person has 1.7 weird-but-temporary symptoms a week.

In addition to improving the patient–physician relationship, especially by recognizing and controlling the negative reactions (countertransference), other elements of treatment include addressing the underlying or co-occurring mood and anxiety disorders. SSRIs, SNRIs, and TCAs are prescribed for that purpose; polypharmacy (multiple medications) should be minimized, and addictive drugs avoided. Social reintegration, relaxation therapy, meditation, physical reactivation, and therapy using graded exercise and biofeedback are some examples of the specific therapies that can be provided when appropriate. Individual psychotherapy that includes psychoeducation, cognitive and behavioral approaches, and support appears to improve functioning. Group psychotherapy may be useful to reduce dependency upon, and confrontation with, the therapist.

HYPOCHONDRIASIS

Clinical Presentation

Hypochondriasis is an overwhelming, persistent preoccupation with physical symptoms based on unrealistically ominous interpretations of physical signs or sensations. (The Greeks believed that the seat of these troubles was the *hypochondrion*, the area between the rib cage and the navel.) Hypochondriacs may have a physical disease, but what distinguishes them is their unrealistic and dire interpretation of it. As noted in the previous section, patients with somatization disorder worry about *symptoms*, whereas hypochondriacs *fear* a serious disease—the symptoms being only harbingers. The somatizing patient who coughs complains that it hurts; the patient with hypochondriasis who coughs concludes he has lung cancer. To this person, a skipped heart beat is a heart attack, a headache, a brain tumor. People with hypochondriasis may present with many symptoms in many organ systems, or they may have a single preoccupation, as does the "cardiac neurotic." *DSM-IV-TR* criteria for hypochondriasis are listed in Table 15-3.

Hypochondriasis affects the sexes equally and usually begins between ages 20 and 30. One recent study reported a 6-month prevalence of 4–6% in the general medical clinic population but it could be as high as 15%. At least two-thirds of these patients meet the criteria for mood and anxiety disorders, which suggests that, in many cases, it may be a variant of those diagnoses. The severity of hypochondriasis fluctuates over time but rarely stops completely or permanently. It may or may not impair occupational and social functioning, but almost always strains patients because needless operations and tests occur.

Etiology and Pathogenesis

Little is known about the etiology of hypochondriasis, but it probably arises for a number of reasons: For some patients, secondary gain is crucial (e.g.,

TABLE 15-3

DSM-IV-TR *Criteria for Hypochondriasis*

A. Preoccupation with fears of having, or the idea that one has, a serious disease based on the person's misinterpretation of bodily symptoms.

B. The preoccupation persists despite appropriate medical evaluation and reassurance.

C. The belief in Criterion A is not of delusional intensity (as in Delusional Disorder, Somatic Type) and is not restricted to a circumscribed concern about appearance (as in Body Dysmorphic Disorder).

D. The preoccupation causes clinically significant distress or impairment in social, occupational, or other important areas of functioning.

E. The duration of the disturbance is at least 6 months.

F. The preoccupation is not better accounted for by Generalized Anxiety Disorder, Obsessive–Compulsive Disorder, Panic Disorder, a Major Depressive Episode, Separation Anxiety, or another Somatoform Disorder.

Specify if:

With Poor Insight: if, for most of the time during the current episode, the person does not recognize that the concern about having a serious illness is excessive or unreasonable.

Note. From *DSM-IV-TR,* p. 507.

---

repressed desire to escape insurmountable stressors through assuming the sick role); for others the disorder may be a defense against low self-esteem or a fear of being defective; for still others, introjection may be paramount purpose — these patients "prefer" punishing themselves over being angry at others. Given the higher incidence of painful injuries and diseases among close relatives of people with hypochondriasis, identification may be a key influence on some patients. A previous legitimate medical illness also predisposes to hypochondriasis. The prevalence of this disorder does not appear to be elevated in relatives of patients with hypochondriasis.

Differential Diagnosis

The differential diagnosis for hypochondriasis is the same as for somatization disorder. Unlike the delusions of *schizophrenia* or *psychotic depression*, in hypochondriasis the patient will entertain the possibility that another interpretation of the symptoms is valid. This individual has an overvalued idea but not a delusion. In *mood* and *anxiety disorders*, dread or misinterpretation of disease is not a central feature, nor is it usually a longstanding preoccupation.

Management and Treatment

Investigations of treatment for hypochondriasis are few and rarely controlled. Although hypnoanxiolytics diminish somatic symptoms in anxious patients, and TCAs diminish somatic complaints in patients with depression, most clinicians find that neither class of drugs lessens hypochondriasis. Most of the treatment principles outlined above for somatization disorder apply.

Some researchers (Fallon et al., 1993) have redefined hypochondriasis as a variant of obsessive–compulsive disorder: The patient has a symptom, then obsessively thinks about it with catastrophic expectations (obsession), and then goes to the doctor (the compulsion) to receive temporary reassurance. As with OCD, the relief is fleeting. Armed with this theory, patients with hypochondriasis have been successfully treated with high doses of fluoxetine (40–80 mg) given over 8–12 weeks. As with most cases involving OCD, response speed is slow, but in the end, more than 70% improve with serotoninergic antidepressants in higher doses. They still thought about their bodies excessively, but they were no longer driven by obsessive fears and the need to see a doctor. Cognitive–behavioral therapy may reduce symptoms by up to 80% (Abramowitz, 2005).

In Kellner's (1982, 1987) literature review, the beneficial interventions for hypochondriasis included *repeatedly* (1) giving patients the facts about their difficulties, (2) clarifying the difference between pain and the *experience* of pain, (3) describing how emotions affect the *perception* of physical sensations (e.g., "real" pain is experienced as more painful when one is anxious than when one is calm), (4) demonstrating how selective attention and suggestion contribute to overestimating a symptom's seriousness, (5) stressing that "life can go on" despite physical symptoms, (6) conveying acceptance and empathy for the hypochondriasis, and (7) applying the approach described for treating somatization disorder. Several studies indicate that these strategies yield complete or vast improvement in roughly 75% of people with hypochondriasis for 1–3 years, and for over 3 years in a third of the patients. In view of the generally unfavorable prognosis of this condition, these results are striking, even if they reflect nothing more than a more invested physician.

CONVERSION DISORDER

Clinical Presentation

The cardinal feature of a conversion disorder is an involuntary loss or alteration of a function, which, although resembling a physical disorder, appears to arise from psychological mechanisms. Conversion disorders usually consist of a single motor or neurological symptom (e.g., blindness, paralysis). Also common are tunnel vision, seizures, coordination disturbances, akinesia, dyskinesia, anosmia (no smell), anesthesia, and paresthesias. A single non-neurological symptom may arise, such as pseudocyesis (false pregnancy). By *DSM-IV-TR* criteria (Table 15-4), if pain is the only symptom, the diagnosis is psychogenic pain disorder; if the only disturbance is psychosexual, a psychosexual disorder is diagnosed.

The strong psychological evidence required for the diagnosis can assume various forms. The conversion symptom may have symbolic meaning to the patient: For example, pseudocyesis may represent a fear of, and wish for, pregnancy. Psychogenic vomiting may symbolize revulsion or disgust. Conversion symptoms may arise from unconscious mechanisms. (Freud was right some of the time.) For instance, a man developed paralysis of his right arm after discovering his wife in bed with his best friend. The arm had normal nerve conduction and muscle tone. During a sodium amytal interview, the patient

---

TABLE 15-4
DSM-IV-TR *Criteria for Conversion Disorder*

A. One or more symptoms or deficits affecting voluntary motor or sensory function that suggest a neurological or general medical condition.

B. Psychological factors are judged to be associated with the symptom or deficit because the initiation or exacerbation of the symptom or deficit is preceded by conflicts or other stressors.

C. The symptom or deficit is not intentionally produced or feigned (as in Factitious Disorder or Malingering).

D. The symptoms or deficit cannot, after appropriate investigation, be fully explained by a general medical condition, or by the direct effects of a substance, or as a culturally sanctioned behavior or experience.

E. The symptom or deficit causes clinically significant distress or impairment in social, occupational, or other important areas of functioning or warrants medical evaluation.

F. The symptom or deficit is not limited to pain or sexual dysfunction, does not occur exclusively during the course of Somatization Disorder, and is not better accounted for by another mental disorder.

Specify type of symptom or deficit:
With Motor Symptom or Deficit
With Sensory Symptom or Deficit
With Seizures or Convulsions
With Mixed Presentation

Note. From *DSM-IV-TR*, p. 498.

---

revealed that he used to be a fighter but quit after badly injuring a man in a bar fight. When asked what would happen if his arm still worked, he thrust his "paralyzed" arm out and said, "I'd kill the bastard, but then I could never live with myself."

Often the conversion is a medical impossibility. "Glove anesthesia," in which sensation is felt to stop evenly at the wrist, is neurologically impossible (unless one's wrist is slashed!), but it conforms to the patient's conception of the nervous system. (Remember Frankenstein?) Soon after the swine-flu vaccine was found to produce Guillain-Barré syndrome, an ascending paralysis *arising* from the feet, cases of "Guillain-Barré" presented in the emergency room: These patients had a "paralysis," but they misread the newspapers: Their "paralysis" spread *downward*!

Although patients with conversion disorder are often said to have histrionic personalities, many do not. Typically patients are interested in their symptoms, but they also may display *la belle indifference*—a nonchalance to their impairment—which has the paradoxical effect of making the impairment more noticeable. This trait is of little diagnostic value, because it is also found in seriously ill medical patients who are stoic about their situation.

Conversion symptoms may begin at any age, but usually surface during adolescence and early adulthood. An acute psychosocial stressor generally triggers the symptom, which will arise suddenly, last for several days or weeks, and then stop abruptly. Conversion symptoms can persist for months or years. When this occurs, organic pathology must be reevaluated, since many of these patients turn out to have neurological disease. Long-term conversion symptoms may cause disuse atrophy and muscle contractures. "Psychological contractures" also occur: Patients become so mired in the sick role that after a conversion symptom disappears, work and social functioning may remain impaired.

Epidemiology

Conversion disorder presents far less today than during Freud's time; back then, it mainly afflicted women. Today, it appears more around battlefronts and in military hospitals; its sex distribution is now equal, although globus hystericus (a discomfort in swallowing) is more common in females. Conversion symptoms are reported to be twice as prevalent among African-Americans than European Americans; they are also more common in lower socioeconomic classes, and they occur more commonly in those less psychologically sophisticated or in subcultures that consider these symptoms expectable, not crazy. Perhaps 1–3% of psychiatric outpatients and 5–15% of psychiatric hospital consults have conversion disorder.

Etiology and Pathogenesis

A conversion symptom affords patients either *primary gain*—that is, it *protects* them from experiencing a painful underlying feeling—or *secondary gain*—that is, it *gratifies* them by enabling them to receive concern and support from others. For example, a nurse who cared for her dying father became "blind" immediately after his death. The psychological evidence for a conversion disorder was the temporal relation between the death and the symptom's onset. The primary gain from this "blindness" was that it prevented her from seeing her father dead; the secondary gain was the added sympathy she would receive. Moreover, because she interpreted her father's death as a profoundly personal/professional failure, her "blindness" unconsciously relieved her of guilt (primary gain) and protected her from others' blame (secondary gain). In the military, a "paralyzed" hand usually serves a secondary gain—to circumvent any demand to fire a gun.

Clinicians should be careful in deciding what constitutes psychological evidence. Because environmental stressors occur all the time, only those of obviously substantial impact on the patient should qualify. Furthermore, if clinicians want to find something, almost anything can have unconscious significance. Consider psychogenic vomiting: If the reader tries, he or she surely can find something in his or her psyche to explain psychogenic vomiting.

Differential Diagnosis

Conversion disorder typically involves one symptom, whereas other *somatoform disorders* present with many symptoms in numerous organ systems (except for "undifferentiated somatoform disorder"). Patients with conversion disorders tend to minimize their problems; those with other somatoform disorders dramatize them. Conversion disorders arise suddenly, whereas *somatization disorder* and *hypochondriasis* emerge gradually. Unlike conversion disorders, there is no loss of function in hypochondriasis. Unlike *undifferentiated somatoform disorder*, symptoms tend to be dramatic and discrete, not vague and/or subjective (e.g., fatigue, loss of appetite).

Physical disorders, especially those with vague, episodic, and hard-to-document symptoms, must be considered, such as *multiple sclerosis* and *systemic lupus erythematosus*. Because it is common for a neurological disorder to be uncovered a full decade after symptoms first present, *all* patients with a longstanding conversion symptom should be evaluated *repeatedly* for underlying medical conditions.

Management and Treatment

Because many conversion symptoms spontaneously disappear within a few weeks to months of their onset, very early treatment may be unnecessary. Therapy aims to temporarily remove patients from the situation that has overwhelmed their usual coping mechanisms, to reassure them that they will soon recover, to minimize any secondary gain that may prolong recovery, and to reinforce alternative coping strategies. Occasionally hypnosis, with posthypnotic suggestions of recovery, is helpful. Sometimes suggestions without hypnosis can be helpful, such as, "How much better are you today?" or "Let's see how quickly you get better."

BODY DYSMORPHIC DISORDER

Clinical Presentation

Body dysmorphic disorder (BDD), originally called "dysmorphophobia," is the preoccupation in a normal-appearing person with an imagined defect in appearance or a markedly excessive concern with a slight physical anomaly. People with this disorder complain, "My nose is too big," "My mouth is too small," or "My face is crawling with wrinkles." The preoccupation must also be very upsetting or impair some important areas of functioning, such as a job, marriage, or social situations. People with BDD run to their dermatologist or plastic surgeon, but almost never to a psychiatrist. Table 15-5 lists the *DSM-IV-TR* criteria for body dysmorphic disorder.

The focus of concern can be virtually any area of the body or anything on the face. Frequent mirror checking, sometimes consuming hours each day, is common. Others *avoid* mirrors with equal passion and consequent distress. Because of embarrassment, it's usually a secret problem, shared only with doctors. Camouflage tactics are common and may include makeup, hats, or the use of hands or hair to cover the imagined defect, or countermeasures such as jutting forward a receding jaw.

Clinical Course and Complications

Body dysmorphic disorder affects women slightly more often than men, often begins in adolescence, can wax and wane for years, and if untreated, can go

TABLE 15-5

DSM-IV-TR *Criteria for Body Dysmorphic Disorder*

A. Preoccupation with an imagined defect in appearance. If a slight physical anomaly is present, the person's concern is markedly excessive.

B. The preoccupation causes clinically significant distress or impairment in social, occupational, or other important areas of functioning.

C. The preoccupation is not better accounted for by another mental disorder (e.g., dissatisfaction with body shape and size in Anorexia Nervosa).

Note. From *DSM-IV-TR,* p. 510.

on for decades. Major depression and dysthymia are associated with this disorder, but probably as complications rather than causes. Usually the depression comes *after,* not *before,* the onset of BDD. Another complication is unnecessary plastic surgery. Obsessive–compulsive disorder has also been reported to travel with BDD. Nobody really knows what causes it. Sometimes it is acutely triggered by a chance remark such as "My, you have a small head," or "You're very handsome considering how big your nose is." Sometimes it comes after a threat to, or breakup of, a relationship.

Differential Diagnosis

Body dysmorphic disorder shouldn't be diagnosed in people who are concerned about minor defects if their concern is not excessive (e.g., typical adolescents). "Bad hair" days don't count! One study found that 70% of college students had at least some dissatisfaction with their appearance, and 46% were somewhat preoccupied with one particular aspect of their appearance (Fitts et al., 1989). If the preoccupation is about weight, the distorted body image is part of an *eating disorder,* not BDD. In BDD the belief is not delusional in intensity, as it is in a *delusional disorder, somatic type.* Patients recognize the possibility that they have exaggerated the extent of the defect or that there isn't a defect at all. Exaggerated concerns about appearance are common in *major depressive disorder, avoidant personality disorder, social phobia,* and *narcissistic personality disorder,* but unlike in BDD, they aren't the predominant feature.

Management and Treatment

The literature is full of reported successes and failures, often with the same purported treatment. Plastic surgery usually leads to new problems—the surgery wasn't quite right or there are other parts of the body that aren't right. Some people with BDD undergo as many plastic surgeries as Michael Jackson. *Behavior therapies,* using progressive exposure techniques, audiovisual self-confrontation, and systematic desensitization have all been successful. Psychodynamic approaches seek to uncover unconscious conflicts regarding patients' feelings of inadequacy.

A successful result is more often a response along the lines of "Who cares about my big nose?" rather than an all-out assertion, "My nose is normal." The *serotonergic antidepressants* clomipramine and fluoxetine work at least 50% of the time in depressed and nondepressed patients with BDD and occasionally even in the patient who has crossed the line into delusion. Responses with less selective antidepressants have been mixed. This pattern of treatment response parallels those for OCD, leading some to suggest that BDD is a variant of OCD.

PAIN DISORDER

Eighty percent of all patients who consult physicians do so for pain-related problems. Low back pain alone disables 7 million Americans and prompts more than 8 million doctor visits a year. In 1986, estimated health care and indirect (loss of work days, compensation litigation, and quackery) costs for chronic pain were $79 billion. What percent of these patients have a psychogenic pain disorder is unknown.

Not all patients with psychogenic pain have a pain *disorder.* For instance, among patients hospitalized in a 3-week program for chronic pain, 32% had a major depression, and over half had had a psychiatric disorder before their chronic pain developed (Katon et al., 1985). In fact, chronic pain may be a symptom of major depression. In *DSM-IV-TR,* pain disorder is not diagnosed if the pain is due to a mood, anxiety, or psychotic disorder.

Clinical Presentation

Pain disorder is characterized by a predominant complaint of significantly distressing or impairing pain in which psychological factors play an important role. The pain can have a medical cause but is not totally explainable on a medical basis. Table 15-6 lists *DSM-IV-TR* criteria for pain disorder. The following case is typical.

Carol, a 45-year-old high school teacher, was standing outside her classroom when three students began taunting her with lewd remarks. When she objected, one

TABLE 15-6
DSM-IV-TR *Criteria for Pain Disorder*

A. Pain in one or more anatomical sites is the predominant focus of the clinical presentation and is of sufficient severity to warrant clinical attention.

B. The pain causes clinically significant distress or impairment in social, occupational, or other important areas of functioning.

C. Psychological factors are judged to have an important role in the onset, severity, exacerbation, or maintenance of the pain.

D. The symptom or deficit is not intentionally produced or feigned (as in Factitious Disorder or Malingering).

E. The pain is not better accounted for by a Mood, Anxiety, or Psychotic Disorder and does not meet criteria for Dyspareunia.

Subtypes:

Pain Disorder Associated with Psychological Factors: psychological factors are judged to have a major role in the onset, severity, exacerbation, or maintenance of the pain. (If a general medical condition is present, it does not have a major role in the onset, severity, exacerbation, or maintenance of the pain.) This type of Pain Disorder is not diagnosed if criteria are also met for Somatization Disorder.

Pain Disorder Associated with Both Psychological Factors and a General Medical Condition: both psychological factors and a general medical condition are judged to have important roles in the onset, severity, exacerbation, or maintenance of the pain.

Note. From *DSM-IV-TR,* p. 503.

---

picked her up, wheeled her around, and threw her to the ground, breaking her left arm and causing numerous facial contusions. The next day Carol developed sharp pains radiating up her neck and both arms, across her chest, and toward her pelvis. After a month, her arm and face had mended, but her radiating pains continued, even though no medical explanation could account for this pain. Although Carol was medically approved to return to work and was eager to do so—she needed the money—her pain kept her home. She then sued the school for not protecting its teachers. Carol frequently expressed her rage about these students, not just for hurting her, but especially because of their sexual innuendos.

On psychiatric examination, Carol wore a neck brace and made sure one noticed how slowly she sat down. While her flitting forefinger pointed to every radiating pain in her body, she said, "The pain just zaps you like shock waves. It attacks your entire body. If I touch anything, it triggers another shooting pain." Initially she denied any psychiatric problems, but later admitted that for months before her injury, her boyfriend had been "trying real hard to get me into the sack, and when I refused he'd always call me a prude." However, since her pains developed, "he's been a prince—he's stopped pushing me sexually and has been very considerate."

Carol's case raises three questions: First, is there sufficient physical evidence to explain her pain? No. Second, is she faking the pain? Probably not. As with many pain patients, possible compensation suggests malingering, but the apparent genuineness of Carol's pain and her eagerness to return to work suggest otherwise. Third, is there psychological evidence to account for her pain? Yes. Her pain affords the secondary gain of cooling her boyfriend's sexual advances while eliciting his support and affection. There is also temporal and psychodynamic evidence: When she was having sexual conflicts with her boyfriend, the students' sexual insults especially hit "below the belt," just where her pains were shooting. Therefore, the most likely diagnosis was pain disorder. With the treatment described below, her pain gradually disappeared in 3 months and she returned to school.

Although pain disorder may arise any time in life, it especially surfaces during young to middle adulthood. Symptoms are usually initiated by an acute stressor, erupt suddenly, intensify over the next several days or weeks, and subside when the acute stressor is gone. Less often, presumably because of secondary gain, the pain persists long after the acute stressor, waxes and wanes for months or years, worsens under stress, and may continue indefinitely. These patients "doctor-shop," become demoralized, abuse analgesics, undergo unnecessary surgery and tests, get stuck in the sick role, restrict social and occupational functioning (some are bedridden for years), and develop secondary muscle spasms and pins-and-needles sensations around painful areas.

Epidemiology

In the absence of proper epidemiological study, it appears that pain disorder more often afflicts women and is common in clinical practice. However, surveys might find that after disorders associated with psychogenic pain (e.g., major depression) are eliminated, pain disorders may be less frequent.

Etiology and Pathogenesis

In Katon et al.'s (1985) study of hospitalized patients with all types of chronic pain, about 60% had a first-degree relative with chronic pain, 38% with alcohol misuse, and 30% with a mood disorder. These figures may be high, but many believe that they suggest a link—psychological or biological—between chronic pain, alcoholism, and depression. Given that pain runs in families, identification with a family member may also play an etiological role for some patients. That roughly 50% of patients with chronic pain improve with antidepressants fuels the old speculation that chronic pain is a "depressive equivalent." However, antidepressants also help chronic arthritis pain and work in a variety of nondepressive disorders such as panic (Ward, 1990).

Pain patients may repress intense affects and conflicts, or their cognition or perception of internal feeling states may be greatly distorted. Pain disorder may allow some patients to escape an unpleasant situation such as work (secondary gain). People without physical abnormalities who work in dangerous, exhausting jobs (e.g., coal mining) more often stop working because of a pain disorder then those in less physically taxing jobs.

Differential Diagnosis

The dramatic presentation of organic pain may appear excessive, but this alone does not qualify as a pain disorder. Dramatic presentations may reflect a person's normal or cultural style of communicating. To qualify as a pain disorder, pain must be severe, and psychological factors must play an important role. Patients with pain disorder may or may not have a medical condition. If a patient's pain is produced by another mental disorder, pain disorder is not diagnosed.

Management and Treatment

Acute Pain Management

It is important that hospitalized medical or surgical patients in acute pain receive adequate doses of analgesics to maximize their comfort. The main reasons (rationalizations) doctors and nurses give for underusing narcotics is a fear of "addicting" and "overdosing" patients, even though both are highly unlikely and rarely occur with such patients. Another common excuse is that "patients don't really hurt *that* much." Since nobody can know how much pain another person feels, it's never clear how patients are supposed to *prove* the extent of their pain. Professionals may point to the fact that patients *demand* narcotics as evidence of their being "manipulative." This is a false premise because many patients in severe pain just want narcotics because they're in pain!

It is best to dispense pain medications on a regular schedule (e.g., every 4–6 hours) as opposed to "as needed." When given as needed (or prn), the drug may arrive late and the patient may become conditioned to associate complaining of pain with getting a drug-induced euphoria. Thus, for hospitalized medical/surgical patients in acute pain, narcotics should be given freely and on a regular schedule, without patients having to ask (or beg) for them.

Chronic Pain Management

There are few studies of pain disorder per se, but many of chronic pain in general. Research demonstrates that patients with all kinds of chronic pain clearly benefit from antidepressants, behavior and activity therapy, couple therapy, and supportive group therapy. Individual psychotherapy seems less useful. These treatments are effective (or ineffective) whether or not the patient's pain has a physical basis. Group therapy for inpatients hasn't been studied systematically, but with outpatients it reduces their perception of pain and their use of medication; dysthymia is alleviated and employment increases. These groups provide support, ventilation, education about pain mechanisms, relaxation techniques to reduce the experience of pain, and reinforcement of nonpain behaviors.

A wide variety of antidepressants is effective in chronic pain for patients with and without depression. For most types of pain the results are modest, with about 50–55% of patients getting 50% (or more) pain reduction (Ward, 1990). For migraine and neuropathy, 60–70% response rates are seen. Benzodiazepines afford little benefit, and opioids should be avoided on a long-term basis because of tolerance to their therapeutic effects and rebound pain. Opioids may adversely impact mood and anxiety when used chronically. ECT helps patients with severe depression and chronic pain. Most patients with chronic pain deserve a trial on antidepressants, usually an SSRI, SNRI, or TCA. Some antiepileptic drugs (e.g., gabapentin, pregabalin) are beneficial.

Pain clinics employ a multidisciplinary team to provide antidepressants, behavior therapy, and group psychotherapy. In a typical program, Fordyce et al. (1973) treated 36 patients whose pain had lasted an average of 7 years and who did not improve from conventional medical treatments. Patients were hospitalized 1–3 months and continued as outpatients for another 3 weeks. The program's aims and methods were: (1) To decrease the patient's use of medication, drugs were given at regular intervals and not "on demand"; over time, drugs were tapered. Frequently, chronic pain improved when hypnoanxiolytics and opiates were stopped. (2) To diminish pain behavior, the staff praised patients for conducting non-pain-related activities; when patients exhibited pain-related behavior (e.g., not going to movies on account of pain), the staff ignored them. (3) To increase functioning, patients were rewarded for participating in a tailored program of gradually increasing physical activity. Rest was contingent on performing the activity, not on complaining of pain. (4) To maintain the patient's gains after discharge, the staff trained relatives to reinforce nonpain, instead of pain, behaviors.

At discharge, there was a 50% increase in time spent sitting, standing, walking, and exercising; most patients were taking little or no medication. At other pain centers, 60–80% of patients have shown similar gains in functional activity, decreased medication, and improved quality of life for at least 3–5 years. These improvements occurred regardless of whether patients were still in pain. What's more, most patients not only *talked* less about pain, they *experienced* less pain (Ochitill, 1982).

References

Abramowitz, J.S. (2005). Hypochondriasis: Conceptualization, treatment, and relationship to obsessive–compulsive disorder. *Annals of Clinical Psychiatry, 17*(4), 211–217.

Barsky, A. (2001). The patient with hypochondriasis. *New England Journal of Medicine, 345,* 1395.

Barsky, A.J., & Ahern, D.K. (2004). Cognitive–behavior therapy for hypochondriasis: A randomized controlled trial. *JAMA, 291*(12), 1464–1470.

Barsky, A.J., Orav, E.J., & Bates, D.W. (2005). Somatization increases medical utilization and costs independent of psychiatric and medical comorbidity. *Archives of General Psychiatry, 62,* 903–910.

Bleichhardt, G., Timmer, B., & Rief, W. (2004). Cognitive–behavioural therapy for patients with multiple somatoform symptoms—a randomised controlled trial in tertiary care. *Journal of Psychosomatic Research, 56*(4), 449–454.

Cohen, M.E., Robins, E., Purtell, J.J., Altmann, M.W., & Reid, D.W. (1953). Excessive surgery in hysteria. *Journal of the American Medical Association, 151,* 977–986.

Fallon, B.A., Liebowitz, M.R., Salman, E., Schneier F., Jusino, C., Hollander, E., et al. (1993). Fluoxetine for hypochondriacal patients without major depression. *Journal of Clinical Psychopharmacology, 13,* 438–441.

Fitts, S.N., Gibson, P., Redding, C.A., & Deiter, P.J. (1989). Body dysmorphic disorder: Implications for its validity as a *DMS-III–R* clinical syndrome. *Psychological Reports, 64,* 655–658.

Fordyce, W.E., Fowler, R.S., Lehmann, J.F., DeLateur, B.J., Sand, P.L., & Trieschmann, R.B. (1973). Operant conditioning in the treatment of chronic pain. *Archives of Physical Medicine and Rehabilitation, 54,* 399–408.

Goodwin, D.W., & Guze, S.B. (1989). *Psychiatric diagnosis* (4th ed.). New York: Oxford University Press.

Katon, W., Egan, K., & Miller, D. (1985). Chronic pain: Lifetime psychiatric diagnoses and family history. *American Journal of Psychiatry, 142,* 1156–1160.

Kellner, R. (1982). Hypochondriasis and atypical somatoform disorder. In J.H. Greist, J.W. Jefferson, & R.L. Spitzer (Eds.), *Treatment of mental disorders* (pp. 286–303). New York: Oxford University Press.

Kellner, R. (1987). Hypochondriasis and somatization. *Journal of the American Medical Association, 258,* 433–437.

Mai, F. (2004). Somatization disorder: A practical review. *Canadian Journal of Psychiatry, 49*(10), 652–662.

Ochitill, H. (1982). Somatoform disorders. In J.H. Greist, J.W. Jefferson, & R.L. Spitzer (Eds.), *Treatment of mental disorders* (pp. 266–286). New York: Oxford University Press.

Othmer, E., & DeSouza, C. (1985). A screening test for somatization disorder (hysteria). *American Journal of Psychiatry, 142*, 1146–1149.

Oxman, T.E., Rosenberg, S.D., Schnurr, P., & Tucker, G.J. (1985). Linguistic dimensions of affect and thought in somatization disorder. *American Journal of Psychiatry, 142*, 1150–1155.

Phillips, K.A., Albertini, R.S., & Rasmussen, S.A. (2002). A randomized placebo-controlled trial of fluoxetine in body dysmorphic disorder. *Archives of General Psychiatry, 59*(4), 381–388.

Smith, G.R., Jr., Rost, K., & Kashner, T.M. (1995). A trial of the effect of a standardized psychiatric consultation on health outcomes and costs in somatizing patients. *Archives of General Psychiatry, 52*(3), 238.

Smith, R.C., Gardiner, J.C., Lyles, J.S., et al. (2005). Exploration of *DSM-IV* criteria in primary care patients with medically unexplained symptoms. *Psychosomatic Medicine, 67*(1), 123–129.

Ward, N.G. (1990). Pain and depression. In J.J. Bonica (Ed.), *The management of pain* (pp. 310–319). Malvern, PA: Lea & Febiger.

16

Factitious Disorders

Factitious disorders are rare conditions in which patients feign physical or psychological symptoms with the sole intent of being a patient. Their "symptoms" so closely resemble known illnesses that they trick doctors into hospitalizing them, conducting numerous tests, and performing unnecessary surgeries. Little is known about these patients, because when they're finally detected, they flee the hospital and are lost to follow-up. They will repeat their charade at many hospitals.

These patients create symptoms *intentionally*, in the sense of feeling that they control their production. Clinicians infer this intentional quality from the adeptness at simulating illnesses. However, although these patients intentionally generate symptoms, they are also driven to do so. Their fakery is compulsive; they can't refrain from subjecting themselves to procedures they know are dangerous and needless. Their illness-feigning behavior is deliberate and purposeful, but their motivations are not; for reasons beyond their control, they are impelled to be a patient.

Factitious disorders lie in the middle of a continuum between the outright fakery of physical symptoms (malingering) and their unconscious production (somatoform disorders). Unlike patients with factitious disorders, *malingerers* fabricate symptoms for reasons other than being a patient, such as draft evasion, drugs, disability payments, or missing classes. The malingerer's behavior *and* motivations are conscious, deliberate, and easily understandable. Unlike patients with factitious disorders, those with somatoform disorders are not consciously faking illness.

DSM-IV-TR divides factitious disorders into those with *psychological signs and symptoms* and those with *physical signs and symptoms*. In both, symptoms can't be explained by another mental disorder, but are often superimposed on one. In the latter, the patient's physical "symptoms" result in multiple hospitalizations. Table 16-1 lists *DSM-IV-TR* criteria for these two factitious disorders.

TABLE 16-1

DSM-IV-TR *Criteria for Factitious Disorder*

A. Intentional production or feigning of physical or psychological signs or symptoms.

B. The motivation for the behavior is to assume the sick role.

C. External incentives for the behavior (such as economic gain, avoiding legal responsibility, or improving physical well-being, as in Malingering) are absent.

Subtypes

With Predominantly Psychological Signs and Symptoms: if psychological signs and symptoms predominate in the clinical presentation

With Predominantly Physical Signs and Symptoms: if physical signs and symptoms predominate in the clinical presentation

With Combined Psychological and Physical Signs and Symptoms: if both psychological and physical signs and symptoms are present but neither predominates in the clinical presentation

Note. From *DSM-IV-TR,* p. 517.

Clinical Presentation

With Predominantly Physical Signs and Symptoms

Asher (1951) coined the name "Munchausen syndrome" to designate patients who travel from hospital to hospital, dramatically presenting plausible histories and receiving surgery. Their stories are so elaborate that Asher named their condition after Baron Karl Friedrich Hieronymus Freiherr von Munchausen (1720–1797), a German cavalry officer and world-class liar. *DSM-IV-TR* equates Munchausen syndrome with chronic factitious disorder with physical symptoms.

These patients' "symptoms" are limited only by their creativity and medical knowledge; many work in hospitals as nurses or technicians; some study medical texts and speak "medicaleze." Most will dramatically enter an emergency room with a classical description of a disease (e.g., crushing chest pain, sudden loss of breath, convulsions). Once hospitalized, they may insist on narcotics or tell staff which lab tests and procedures to perform.

Their *pièce de résistance* is feigning objective physical signs and abnormal laboratory findings. One patient "raised" his rectal temperature by relaxing and contracting his anal sphincter. Another swallowed blood, strolled into the ER, and puked. Patients will spit saliva into urine samples to elevate urinary amylase, or they may prick a finger and squeeze a little blood into their urine to "develop" hematuria. Self-injecting insulin will produce hypoglycemia. Fecal bacteria will somehow find their way into urine. Patients have swallowed nails, fish hooks, and paint. By self-inducing disease, some of these patients become genuinely sick, although death is rare.

Factitious patients often spin intriguing yarns ("pseudologia fantastica")— false accounts of famous parents, financial wizardry, or show-biz exploits; they might be still another bastard descendant of Aaron Burr or claim a surgical scar came from battlefield heroics. For all their "accomplishments" or "notoriety," the staff begin to wonder why they have so few visitors, phone calls, or friends. Further clues to this diagnosis are extensive travel, self-mutilation, *la belle indifference* to pain and painful procedures, drug abuse (in 50% of cases), ever-changing medical complaints, and substantial evidence of prior treatment (e.g., venous cutdown scars), signs of recent cardioversion, or a "gridiron abdomen" from multiple operations (Sussman & Hyler, 1985).

When the staff becomes suspicious, these patients become increasingly strident and may present new evidence of illness. Any suggestions of a psychiatric consult are angrily rejected. If confronted with their contradictory stories or inconsistent findings, instead of recanting or displaying embarrassment, factitious patients will question the staff's competence or threaten litigation. Once these ploys fail, patients will sign out of the hospital against medical advice or leave surreptitiously. A few days later they may pop up at another hospital, recycling the same saga.

Factitious disorder usually begins during early adulthood, but can start during childhood. Although initially these patients may receive medical care for a real illness, they then develop a pattern of repeated ambulatory treatments and hospitalizations. The prognosis worsens as patients escalate from (1) giving a fictitious history, to (2) simulating signs of illness, to (3) inducing pathological states.

With Predominantly Psychological Signs and Symptoms

These factitious patients will fake several, often psychotic-like symptoms, which laypeople would take as a mental illness, but professionals would realize are inconsistent with any known psychiatric disorder. Patients may complain of hallucinations, erratic memory loss, itchy feet, facial twitches, and episodic blindness—a symptom cluster that, although inventive, doesn't exist. They're also highly suggestible: If told that hallucinating patients don't sleep, these patients don't sleep. When observed, their symptoms get worse. Some are negativistic and refuse to answer questions. Many have a (genuine) borderline personality disorder.

Some present with overwhelming grief instead of psychosis (Phillips, Ward, & Ries, 1983). Invariably, many family members have been killed, usually by dramatic means (train wrecks, murders). Authenticity of the story is rarely questioned because these patients are already enduring enough suffering and need support rather than suspicions. They differ from those really grieving in not having any family members ("they all died") or friends who can be contacted to verify the story. The best way to confirm suspected factitious mourning is to ask for the place and date of the alleged death(s) and call the appropriate coroner.

Others, especially prisoners, may have Ganser syndrome, whose chief symptom is *vorbeireden*—that is, giving approximate answers, near misses, or talking past the point. They appear to understand questions, but to deliberately give false answers: Ask when Santa comes, and they'll say Halloween; ask them to subtract 7 from 100 and they'll respond, "92, 84, 76," etc. *Vorbeireden*, however, is also found in other disorders and malingering.

Epidemiology

Factitious disorder is rare, but its true prevalence is unknown: The rate may be underestimated, because patients don't stay around to be detected or counted; or overestimated, since patients move from hospital to hospital and the same patient may be reported many times. One patient had over 420 documented hospitalizations. Epidemiological figures from university populations may be inflated, since these patients are drawn to these facilities. Perhaps 1% of inpatients referred for psychiatric consultation have factitious disorders. Males seem to have more factitious disorders than females.

Etiology and Pathogenesis

What causes factitious disorders is unknown, but they probably develop from a confluence of factors, which vary depending on the patient. People with factitious disorder with physical symptoms are more likely to have had physical disorders (often requiring extensive treatment) while growing up; a close relationship with a doctor in the past, such as having a doctor in the family or having been sexually abused by a doctor; or a grudge against the medical profession, sometimes based on bad past medical care. For all types of factitious disorders, a severe personality disorder—often borderline, dependent, or antisocial—is a predisposing factor.

All patients with factitious disorders engage in "inappropriate care-getting behavior." They probably want care and attention but can't or don't know how to get it in usual, healthy ways. Given their self-destructiveness, *masochistic impulses* may feed on a *love–hate relationship* with health-care professionals. If they could say it, their underlying message might be, "Help me, you bastard." These patients often suffer from *childhood deprivation, neglect, and abuse*, which may steer them into dependent roles even as they expect health professionals to make up for lost parenting. This need also might account for factitious disorder *"by proxy,"* a rare phenomenon in which a parent induces symptoms in his or her child in order to live vicariously through the child as he or she receives the parental affection of doctors and nurses. Some Munchausen patients *identify* with health-care professionals, while enjoying a *sense of mastery and control* from learning about illness, coping with pain, and outwitting physicians.

Differential Diagnosis

The main reason for identifying factitious disorder is to spare patients from unnecessary hospitalizations and potentially harmful medical procedures and operations. The chief diagnostic problem is to distinguish factitious disorder from *true medical illness*. Factitious disorders should be considered when patients stage their history as high drama, exhibit pseudologia fantastica, disrupt a ward and break hospital rules, argue continuously with staff, show off medical jargon and knowledge, demand narcotics, "advertise" signs of numerous prior medical treatments and surgeries, give contradictory histories, develop frequent or inexplicable medical complications, present new symptoms after every negative workup, or become hostile when questioned about their medical history or personal background.

As discussed previously, factitious disorder should be distinguished from *somatoform disorder* and *malingering. Antisocial personality disorder* may be misdiagnosed on account of these patients' pseudologia fantastica, impostership, lying, drug abuse, and lack of close relations. Sociopaths, however, usually avoid painful tests and hospitals, unless these might get them out of a jail sentence; Munchausen patients "attract" them. Some people with *schizophrenia* self-induce physical symptoms, but secondarily to a specific delusion or command hallucination.

Diagnosing factitious disorder with psychological symptoms is especially difficult, because most psychological symptoms can't be objectively verified.

Whenever symptoms don't fit the pattern of a *known mental disorder*, factitious disorder merits consideration. Factitious disorder with psychological symptoms *and* another mental disorder can both be diagnosed, as long as the factitious symptoms are produced without an ulterior motive (as in malingering). For a malingerer whose motive is as simple as "three hots and a cot" (three meals and a bed), a psychiatric hospitalization with its "painless patienthood" may seem like a good alternative for the patient (but not for anyone else).

Management and Treatment

Wilhelm Kaiser claimed the only requirement for successful therapy is that two people be in a room. And since patients with factitious disorders don't stay in the room, the only thing that's clear about treating them is that nothing is known to work. Failed treatments include hypnosis, medications (of all kinds), ECT, insulin coma, and lobotomy. Several authors advocate psychotherapy, but have too few treatment cases to establish its efficacy. Even when physicians gently confront these patients with their true diagnoses, patients usually react with hostility and reject any offer of help.

Despite the absence of any clearly effective treatment, experts generally recommend that, once the diagnosis of factitious disorder is established, clinicians should (1) be careful not to overlook genuine medical disease; (2) keep patients in the hospital—for once out, always out—to begin to involve them in extended psychiatric treatment; (3) if necessary to ensure safety, commit children with factitious disorders by proxy to hospitals, and report the caregiver to child protective services; (4) carefully check annoyance with these patients, avoid power struggles and public humiliations, and be ever alert to the behaviors and dynamics (including splitting) commonly associated with borderline personality disorder; (5) if outsmarted by these patients, do not get bent out of shape; and (6) track these patients through electronic health records and funding databases to effectively coordinate care.

References

Asher, R. (1951). Muchausen's syndrome. *Lancet, 1,* 339–341.

Phillips, M.R., Ward, N.G., & Ries, R.K. (1983). Factitious mourning: Painless patienthood. *American Journal of Psychiatry, 140,* 420–425.

Pope, H., Jonas, J.M., & Jones, B. (1982). Factitious psychosis: Phenomenology, family history, and long-term outcome of nine patients. *American Journal of Psychiatry 139,* 1480–1483.

Wang, D., Nadiga, D.N., & Jenson, J.J. (2005). Factitious disorders. In B.J. Sadock & V.A. Sadock (Eds.), *Comprehensive textbook of psychiatry* (8th ed., pp. 1829–1843). Philadelphia: Lippincott, Williams & Wilkins.

17

Dissociative Disorders

How come dissociative disorders, although relatively uncommon, are of such uncommon interest? *Sybil*, *The Three Faces of Eve*, *The Boston Strangler*, and (if brainwashed) Patty Hearst fascinate many because they are very ordinary individuals who have made an extraordinary transformation. And if these people can become completely different people, then couldn't we? If such strangeness can lurk within them, why not within us?

Dissociative states refer to the "splitting off" from conscious awareness of some ordinarily familiar information, emotion, or mental function. In other words, selected mental contents are removed or dissociated from conscious experience but continue to produce motor or sensory effects. These are the *elsewhere* disorders: Part of the person (e.g., memory, identity) is elsewhere and not available at the present time. In dissociative states, people can appear unconscious and focus selectively on the environment (e.g., sleepwalking, trance), act bizarrely (e.g., running "amok," going "berserk"), lose their identity and wander away from home (e.g., fugue), lose memory without wandering away from home (e.g., amnesia), assume an alien identity (e.g., multiple personality, witchcraft, possession), or be brainwashed.

Some dissociative states are not pathological, and to some extent, some are highly adaptive. We all forget things. We all switch states of consciousness, from meditating to sleeping to working to daydreaming, and to do so, sets of memory and attitudes must also switch. Dissociation also may occur in crystal gazing, intense prayer, "mass hysteria," religious revivals, healing ceremonies (e.g., Holy Spirit possession, glossolalia ["speaking in tongues"]), and hypnosis. Amazingly enough, it can even occur during lectures or while reading textbooks (not this one)—"I blanked out on what he said" or "I spaced out on that page—I'll have to read it again."

Most dissociative states are activated by a psychosocial trigger, arise suddenly, and end abruptly. During normal intervals, people are partly or totally amnestic for their dissociative episodes. For example, using *posthypnotic sug-*

gestion, a hypnotist may instruct a hypnotized subject, "After you awaken, you'll sing 'God Save the Queen' when I scratch my head but not remember that I told you to." Ten minutes after the subject awakens, the hypnotist scratches and the subject wails "God Save the Queen." Ask why she's singing, she may confess she doesn't know or confabulate, "I thought people would like the music."

Dissociative experiences are common. On the Dissociative Experience Scale, 29% of the general population agreed that the following happened to them in almost one-third of their conversations: "Some people find that sometimes they are listening to someone talk and they suddenly realize that they did not hear part or all of what was said" (Ross, Joshi, & Currie, 1990). In the same study, 5% scored over 30, a score highly associated with having a dissociative disorder. There were no differences in scores based on gender, income, occupation, education, or religion. However, dissociative experiences (e.g., hypnotizability, a phenomenon highly correlated with dissociation) decrease with age (Frischholz et al., 1992). Men and women differed only on two items. Men more often endorsed the statement, "Some people find that they have no memory for important events in their lives, for example, a wedding or graduation" (until now, something women had suspected was happening but couldn't prove), while women more often endorsed the statement, "Some people sometimes find that when they are alone, they talk out loud to themselves."

DSM-IV-TR defines dissociative disorders as conditions whose predominant feature is a disturbance or alteration in the normal integrative functions of consciousness, identity, or memory. The type of alteration dictates the type of dissociative disorder: In *dissociative amnesia*, consciousness is altered and significant personal events forgotten. In *dissociative fugue*, identity and motor behavior are altered; patients unexpectedly travel far from home, assume a new identity, forgetting their old one. In *dissociative identity disorder* (multiple personality disorder), numerous identities arise. In *depersonalization disorder*, patients feel as if they are outside of their mind or body, as an observer. Table 17-1 presents *DSM-IV-TR* criteria for these disorders. There's also a residual category, *dissociative disorder not otherwise specified*, which covers *brainwashing*, dissociative trance disorder, and derealization without depersonalization.

Clinical Presentations

Dissociative Amnesia

These patients are suddenly unable to remember significant personal information, which is far in excess of ordinary forgetfulness. Patients know they've forgotten something, but don't know what. Often they don't seem to care.

TABLE 17-1

DSM-IV-TR *Criteria for Dissociative Disorders: Dissociative Amnesia, Fugue, Identity, and Depersonalization Disorders*

Common Criteria

A. The symptoms or experiences cause clinically significant distress or impairment in social, occupational, or other important areas of functioning (not criterion for Dissociative Identity Disorder).

B. The disturbance is not due to the direct physiological effects of a substance (e.g., a drug of abuse, alcohol intoxication, a medication) or a general medical condition (e.g., partial complex seizures, head trauma).

Dissociative Amnesia—Specific Criteria

C. The predominant disturbance is one or more episodes of inability to recall important personal information, usually of a traumatic or stressful nature, that is too extensive to be explained by ordinary forgetfulness.

D. The disturbance does not occur exclusively during the course of Dissociative Identity Disorder, Dissociative Fugue, Posttraumatic Stress Disorder, Acute Stress Disorder, or Somatization Disorder.

Dissociative Fugue—Specific Criteria

C. The predominant disturbance is sudden, unexpected travel away from home or one's customary place of work, with inability to recall one's past.

D. Confusion about personal identity or assumption of new identity (partial or complete).

E. The disturbance does not occur exclusively during the course of Dissociative Identity Disorder.

Dissociative Identity Disorder (Multiple Personality Disorder)—Specific Criteria

C. The presence of two or more distinct identities or personality states (each with its own relatively enduring pattern of perceiving, relating to, and thinking about the environment and self).

D. At least two of these identities or personality states recurrently take control of the person's behavior.

E. Inability to recall important personal information that is too extensive to be explained by ordinary forgetfulness. **Note:** In children, the symptoms are not attributable to imaginary playmates or other fantasy play.

Depersonalization Disorder—Specific Criteria

C. Persistent or recurrent experiences of feeling detached from, and as if one is an outside observer of, one's mental processes or body (e.g., feeling like one is in a dream).

D. During the depersonalization experience, reality testing remains intact.

E. The depersonalization experience does not occur exclusively during the course of another mental disorder, such as Schizophrenia, Panic Disorder, Acute Stress Disorder or another Dissociative Disorder.

Note. From *DSM-IV-TR,* pp. 519–533.

Feeling perplexed, disoriented, and purposeless, they're often picked up by the police as lost or for wandering aimlessly. During their amnesia, patients are able to perform relatively simple tasks (e.g., taking a bus) and, less often, more complicated ones (e.g., shopping, cooking).

Most often, patients' amnesias are *localized* to several hours or days during and after a highly disturbing event and are only rarely *generalized* for an entire life. They may be *selective* for only some events, usually the most traumatic. An uninjured person may remember driving and talking to staff at a hospital, but not the car accident itself. Rare is *continuous* amnesia, wherein patients forget everything from the time of the stress until the present. (Some politicians have been accused of selective amnesia because they seem unable to remember any promises they made from before the election to the present.)

> An example of localized amnesia is the case of a photojournalist in Vietnam who, confused and bewildered, strolled into the office of Army Intelligence. He had no recollection of the past 3 days, but his camera did. It showed photographs of a Buddhist monk immolating himself. Like most dissociative amnesias, his completely cleared within 24 hours of being discovered.

Dissociative Fugue

These patients flee from home or their customary locale, forget (or are confused about) their previous identity, and adopt a partial one. During a fugue, patients usually behave with sufficient skill to go unnoticed by most casual observers. Fugues typically are precipitated by an acute stressor and consist of a several-day excursion with minimal social contact. Perplexity and disorientation may occur in some fugues, but if they dominate, the condition is diagnosed as dissociative amnesia and not fugue. Other fugues are more elaborate, lasting weeks to months: Previously quiet and very ordinary people may establish a new residence, fashion a completely new, more gregarious identity, have a full social calendar, and appear no different than any other colorful new arrival in town. Patients have traveled thousands of miles and passed numerous customs officials without detection. A rare few are violent. Afterward, patients can't remember what transpired during the fugue. In contrast to amnesia patients, who are aware of their memory loss, fugue victims are usually not aware. Most patients with dissociative fugue recover rapidly.

Dissociative Identity Disorder

This new name for "multiple personality disorder" is used because the most common and fundamental alteration in this disorder is the presence of more than one discrete identity, i.e., what the person calls herself and believes herself to be. The quiet, careful guy at the lab who is a "wild man" at parties may look to others like a multiple personality, but he sees these ways of being as different aspects of his identity and does not suffer from dissociative identity disorder.

These patients have two or more distinct identities or personality states, each dominant at a particular moment. Each identity is a complex, integrated being with its own name, memories, behavioral traits, emotional characteristics, social relations, employment histories, mental and physical disorders, and psychological test responses. Even rates of cerebral blood flow and evoked electrical potentials differ between the identities. Needing to eat for three identities, one patient ate nine meals a day! The average number of identities is 8–13, but more than 50 have been reported. Sybil had 16 personalities, and Eve, 22 faces.

Transitions from one identity to another are usually sudden, follow a stressor, and catch most observers off-guard. They're spooky to watch, since the "new" person seems to have taken over the patient's body and soul. Dress, speech, gait, and facial expressions may change so much the person goes unrecognized. The original (or primary) personality is usually unaware of the other (or secondary) personalities, but most secondary personalities are aware of the primary personality. The secondary personalities generally have some inkling of the others; they converse with each other, protect each other, or one may act while others watch. Secondary personalities are often extreme caricatures of the original personality. A shy, conventional primary personality may have secondary personalities as a whore, drag queen, devil, and social worker. Secondary personalities may have a different sex, race, or age from the original personality.

Clinicians are frequently unaware that they're treating a multiple identity, since these patients are tough to detect. One psychiatrist reported that 7 years had passed before he realized his patient had this disorder. Few enter treatment complaining of a multiple personality, and if they come at all, it's usually for depression. These patients may reveal themselves through memory lapses, time distortions ("lost weekends"), using "we" rather than "I" in conversations, being charged for items they don't remember buying (imagine the Visa bills!), and encountering friends who act like strangers and strangers who act like friends. If asked to write their thoughts freely for a half-hour, another personality may emerge. Another personality breaks through half the time in psychotherapy (Harvard, 1985).

Multiple identity, and the proliferation of new identities, often continues for life, making this condition the worst of the dissociative disorders. These patients are frequently depressed, abuse substances, mutilate themselves, attempt suicide, and have psychotic episodes, tension headaches, phobias, conversion symptoms, and hypochondriasis. "Hallucinated" voices in "psychotic" episodes are often one or more other personalities talking.

Depersonalization Disorder

Depersonalization is a common perceptual distortion in which the person experiences his body, or mental processes, as if he were a detached, outside observer. The person may feel anesthetized or wooden; a sense of unreality or self-estrangement may confound him. The size and shape of objects may seem altered. Although the person feels, and indeed fears, that he's not in full control, gross reality testing is *not* impaired.

Because temporary depersonalization frequently occurs during normal, psychopathological, or physiologically altered states, depersonalization *disorder* is only diagnosed in the absence of another mental disorder, a general medical condition, or a direct effect of a substance, and when it's so persistent or recurrent that it significantly interferes with social or occupational functioning. Depersonalization episodes can last for seconds, minutes, days, or years. The course is chronic, but its severity fluctuates over time.

Dissociative Disorder NOS

This category of disorders that doesn't fit anyplace else includes brainwashing.

> Three myths about brainwashing abound: (1) that it doesn't exist; (2) that it's no different from education, advertising, and psychotherapy; and (3) that it's an irresistible method that robs people of their beliefs and personalities. Instead, brainwashing can be defined as a "comprehensive, systematic, and total program using psychological techniques, to stress *confession* and then *reeducation* in order to change fundamental beliefs. During confession, the subject admits to past errors and renounces past affiliations; during reeducation, the subject is refashioned to conform to the idealized image of the brainwasher" (Lifton, 1963, p. 000).

This category also includes derealization without depersonalization and dissociative trance disorder, in which the person feels she has been taken over by a new identity attributed to the influence of a spirit, power, deity, or other person. Running "amok" in Malaysia is an example. To be called a disorder, the patient's symptoms can't be part of a broadly accepted culture or religious practice. Therefore, "speaking in tongues" when "possessed" by the Holy Spirit would not be classified as a disorder if the person is a "Holy Roller"—but might be if the person is a Unitarian!

Epidemiology

Dissociative disorders were once thought to be rare but recently there have been reports of increased incidence and prevalence. Few studies have investigated the epidemiology of dissociative amnesia. The recent increase in the case reports of dissociative amnesia can be due to increased awareness of the diagnosis among physicians or overdiagnosis in individuals who are highly suggestible.

Dissociative fugue has been reported in 0.2% of the general population. Although there are no conclusive studies on the epidemiology of Dissociative Identity Disorder (DID), the estimate on prevalence can range from rare to 1 in 100. The prevalence of depersonalization disorder is not known. Half of all individuals can experience depersonalization at some time in their lives at a time of increased stress.

Psychogenic amnesia and fugue are common during war and natural disasters. In battle, young males are at highest risk. Away from battle, adolescent and young adult women have slightly more dissociative disorders. In psychiatric populations, DID is reputed to affect four times as many women as men, but if prison populations were included, the sex differential would narrow. Except for the variable age of onset of psychogenic fugue, dissociative disorders rarely begin after the age of 40 and almost never originate in older adults. Prevalence studies of dissociative disorders in the past 15 years are summarized in Table 17-2.

Etiology and Pathogenesis

Because dissociative states induced by substances or medical conditions are excluded by definition, dissociative disorders are produced psychosocially. Most often, the immediate precipitating factor is an imminent threat of injury or death, the performance of a guilt-provoking act (e.g., an affair), or a serious auto accident.

Psychoanalytic theory suggests that dissociative states protect the individual from experiencing painful sexual or aggressive impulses. With amnesia, one forgets what's painful; with fugue, one runs away from it; with multiple personality, one displaces it onto a new identity; with depersonalization, one abandons it.

TABLE 17-2

Studies of the Prevalence of Dissociative Disorders Among Psychiatric Inpatients

STUDY	YEAR	LOCATION	NUMBER OF PATIENTS COMPLETING THE DISSOCIATIVE EXPERIENCES SCALE	NUMBER OF PATIENTS COMPLETING A STRUCTURED INTERVIEW	PATIENTS WITH A DISSOCIATIVE DISORDER (%)	PATIENTS WITH DISSOCIATIVE IDENTITY DISORDER (%)
Ross et al.	1991	Canada	299	80	21	3-5
Saxe et al.	1993	Massachusetts	110	20	13	4
Horen et al.	1995	Canada	48	11	17	6
Latz et al.	1995	North Carolina	176[a]	176[a]	15	4
Knudsen et al.	1995	Norway	85	23	8	5
Lussier et al.	1997	Connecticut	—	70[b]	9	7
Tutkun et al.	1998	Turkey	116	40	10	5
Rifkin et al.	1998	New York	—	100	?	1
Friedl and Draijer	2000	Netherlands	122	56	8	2
Gast et al.	2001	Germany	115	15	4-8	1-2

[a]Female patients only.

[b]Acute day hospital patients.

Adapted from Foote et al., 2006.

Almost all patients with DID report being physically or sexually abused as children (Ross, Miller, et al., 1990). (However, most abused children do not appear to develop dissociative disorders). Sybil's mother tortured her as a child; Billy Milligan's father frequently raped him from the ages of 9–16 and threatened to kill him if he told anybody. These children have been cannon fodder in custody fights, raised as the opposite sex, had their genitals squeezed in a vice, and kidnapped by parents. Dissociation into different identities defends against these trauma by isolating the horror, sectioning off the child's negative self-images, and permitting a modicum of self-control. By compartmentalizing emotions, the child says, in effect, "I can't deny that this is happening, but I can deny that it's happening to me" (Harvard, 1985).

Several studies suggest an association between attachment difficulties and dissociation. Ogawa et.al (1997) demonstrated in a longitudinal study that avoidant and disorganized patterns of attachment were predictors for dissociation. There has been little research in the neurobiological mechanisms of dissociation, but several studies report impairment in thalamic–limbic–cortical feedback networks. Inability of the prefrontal cortex to integrate perceptual, cognitive, and emotional process results in dissociation. One recent study found that patients with DID had smaller hippocampal and amydalar volumes.

Differential Diagnosis

Neurological disorders (NDs) can simulate dissociative amnesia, except that in NDs, memory loss is more recent than remote and usually unrelated to a specific stressor. Most NDs arise slowly, rarely improve, and are accompanied by other signs, such as confusion, disorientation, attention deficits, and clouding of consciousness. Delirium may arise quickly but will also have all of these other signs and symptoms. Unlike those with dissociative fugue, most patients with neurological disorders who wander off are unable to perform complex, purposeful tasks.

Substance-induced intoxications can produce *hypnoanxiolytic* and *alcoholic* "black-outs," an amnesia for events occurring while intoxicated. In blackouts, the history of drinking and the lack of a complete recovery exclude psychogenic amnesia. In *alcohol amnestic disorder*, 5-minute (not immediate) memory is lost. *"Dissociative"* anesthetics, primarily phencyclidine (PCP), frequently cause depersonalization, but a drug history and urine screen are sufficiently diagnostic.

Acute stress disorder emphasizes dissociative symptoms in response to a traumatic event. It differs from a dissociative disorder in occurring within 4 weeks of the traumatic event and being time-limited to 4 weeks of symptoms. *Posttraumatic stress disorder* may have some persistent dissociative symptoms (e.g., flashbacks, amnesia for the trauma, feelings of detachment) but also requires others such as increased arousal for the diagnosis.

In *postconcussion amnesia*, patients generally have a retrograde memory loss for the period before the head trauma, whereas in psychogenic amnesia there's generally an anterograde memory loss for the period since the precipitating stress. Hypnosis and amytal interview can usually retrieve lost memories in psychogenic amnesia, but not in concussion. In dissociative amnesias, memory loss tends to be global and total; after concussion, it tends to be spotty and patchy. Patients with concussive amnesia do not form new identities. In psychogenic amnesia patients retain prior skills, have little difficulty conducting current tasks, and apparently benefit from secondary gain; patients with postconcussion amnesia lose some prior skills, have problems coping with present tasks, and do not appear to acquire secondary gain (Ludwig, 1985).

Partial complex seizures (PCSs) may cause sudden memory loss and flight, but unlike psychogenic fugue, patients can't perform complex tasks or form a new identity; they often have stereotyped movements, such as lip smacking, and about half the time there's an abnormal EEG. Sometimes PCS is hard to distinguish from dissociative amnesia. Because people with severe dissociative disorders often were physically abused as children, including being knocked unconscious many times, they may have both PCS and dissociative amnesia. A trial of anticonvulsants may be useful. Many who exhibit PCSs but have a normal EEG during the seizures (called a pseudoseizure) are found to have dissociative symptoms often precipitated by guilt-laden grief (Ramchandani & Schindler, 1993).

Malingering must always be considered, especially if there's obvious secondary gain. Attorneys are seeing many more claims of multiple identity by criminals. "Hey, judge, it's not *me* who slaughtered the guy, it's that *other* personality." Kiersch (1962) found that in 32 cases of suspects with alleged amnesia who were standing trial, 21 subsequently confessed to lying about their memory loss. Patients with dissociative conditions usually recover during hypnosis and amytal interviews, but malingerers do not. Remember, amytal is not truth serum. Liars can keep on lying under amytal.

Descriptively and psychodynamically, multiple identity often resembles *borderline personality disorder.* Emotional lability, low self-esteem, impulsivity, substance abuse, chronic boredom, identity confusion, temper tantrums, manipulative interpersonal relations, and suicide attempts characterize both disorders. In fact, in one investigation (Horevitz & Braun, 1984), 70% of patients with multiple personality were also diagnosed as borderline. Observing the patient's abrupt personality changes settles the diagnosis.

Distinguishing among dissociative disorders is usually easy. When a person forgets *and* travels to another locale, the diagnosis is psychogenic fugue; when the person "merely" forgets, it's psychogenic amnesia. Patients with dissociative amnesia look more befuddled, rarely conduct complex tasks, and are more readily spotted by lay observers. Awareness of one's original identity is absent in psychogenic amnesia and fugue, but present in multiple personality.

Management and Treatment

The treatment of dissociative disorders is still mainly anecdotal. Patients with these disorders present with challenging symptomatology that can overwhelm experienced clinicians. A summary of treatment follows:

Dissociative amnesia and fugue. Because of the relatively acute onset, brief duration, and high rate of spontaneous recovery of these states, this sequence of interventions is recommended: (1) *Evaluate* patients, allowing a few days for a spontaneous remission. Suggest that they might find their memory returning slowly day by day. If patients do not fully recover, (2) provide *discussion, support,* and *persuasion.* Encourage them to talk freely of recent events, periodically suggest avenues for exploration, and gently persuade them to keep looking for lost memories. If these methods are not sufficient, (3) employ an *associative anamnesis* by having patients free-associate to events surrounding the amnesia. (4) Use *hypnosis;* amnestic patients, as most patients with dissociative disorders, are extremely good subjects. Instruct them to give a running commentary of known past incidents, which usually leads to abreaction. Once these emotions calm, patients are told to keep talking and then to wake up. When awake, patients are surprised to find themselves recounting past events and their amnesia ends. If it doesn't, (5) administer an *amytal interview* and then gently prod them to review events around the forgotten period. The closer in time to the onset of the amnesia, the more effective the interview. (6) If memory still hasn't returned, reconsider *neurological causes,* and if none is found, (7) gather a more exhaustive *psychological history* with attennae attuned to possible secondary gain (Coombs & Ludwig, 1982).

Dissociative Identity Disorder

Only very experienced therapists should treat this disorder. Initially these patients fascinate, but then soon overwhelm and exasperate therapists. As soon as psychotherapy with the primary identity is underway, a secondary identity (often referred to as an "alter") takes over, and then another, and another, and another. Many are hostile, seductive, and manipulative; some will bait the primary identity, try blocking alliances with the therapist, or act out by drug-taking and wrist-slashing. All resist recalling traumatic events. These patients sense the therapist's fascination with the drama and may try to please him or her by exaggerating past horrors, which were already bad enough. Because these patients are very suggestible, leading questions must be avoided, such as, "Don't you think your parents may have been involved in a Satanic cult?" (something the FBI and police have seldom been able to prove), or "Aren't there many more personalities in there?" Too often, leading questions are experienced as new suggestions which are dutifully followed.

Hypnosis may engage certain personalities, but it should not be introduced too early, since the patient may experience it as an emotional assault. *Group therapy* often backfires (unless all participants share the same diagnosis), because they consider the patient a fraud. An intriguing approach is "internal group therapy" in which the therapist "moderates" a discussion between the patient's personalities and facilitates the quiescent ones to speak via hypnosis. *Videotaping* early in treatment may help personalities get acquainted. *Family counseling* should also be considered. Medications (SSRIs, clonidine, and benzodiazepines) can be helpful in reducing anxiety and arousal symptoms. SSRIs are the antidepressants most often used to treat co-occurring depression. Often it is tempting to use neuroleptics for "the voices," but those are other personalities and not usual hallucinations.

References

Coombs, G., & Ludwig, A.M. (1982). Dissociative disorders. In J.H. Greist, J.W. Jefferson, & R.L. Spitzer (Eds.), *Treatment of mental disorders* (pp. 309–319). New York: Oxford University Press.

Foote, B., Smolin, Y., Kaplan, M., Legatt, M.E., & Lipschitz, D. (2006). Prevalence of dissociative disorders in psychiatric outpatients. *American Journal of Psychiatry, 163*, 623–629.

Frischholz, E.J., Lipman, L.S., Braun, B.G., & Sachs, R.G. (1992). Psychopathology, hypnotizability, and dissociation. *American Journal of Psychiatry, 149*, 1521–1525.

Harvard Medical School Mental Health Letter. (1985). Multiple personality. *1*(10), 1–6.

Horevitz, R.P., & Braun, B.G. (1984). Are multiple personalities borderline? *Psychiatric Clinics of North America, 7*, 69–87.

Kiersch, T.A. (1962). Amnesia: A clinical study of ninety-eight cases. *American Journal of Psychiatry, 119*, 57–60.

Lifton, R.J. (1963). Thought reform and the psychology of totalism: A study of "brainwashing" in China. New York: Norton.

Ludwig, A.M. (1985). *Principles of clinical psychiatry* (2nd ed.). New York: Free Press.

Ogawa, J.R., Sroufe, L.A., Weinfield, N.S., Carlson, E.A., & Egeland, B. (1997). Development and the fragmented self: Longitudinal study of dissociative symptomatology in a nonclinical sample. Development and Psychopathology, 9, 855–879.

Ramchandani, D., & Schindler, B. (1993). Evaluation of pseudoseizures: A psychiatric perspective. *Psychosomatics, 34*, 70–79.

Ross, C.A., Anderson, G., Fleisher, W.P., & Norton, G.R. (1991). The frequency of multiple personality disorder among psychiatric inpatients. *American Journal of Psychiatry, 148*, 1717–1720.

Ross, C.A., Joshi, S., & Currie R. (1990). Dissociative experiences in the general population. *American Journal of Psychiatry, 147*, 1547–1552.

Ross, C.A., Miller, S.D., Reagor, P., Bjornson, L., Fraser, G.A., & Anderson G. (1990). Structured interview data on 102 cases of multiple personality disorder from four centers. *American Journal of Psychiatry, 147*, 596–601.

18

Sexual and Gender Identity Disorders

Sex plays a uniquely pervasive role in people's lives; it influences how we think, feel, dress, flirt, play, mate, and love. Thus, when individuals experience a psychosexual disorder, it can produce a pervasive sense of discomfort, conflict, and distress for that person and/or for others around them. The *DSM-IV-TR* lists diagnostic codes under the subheadings of *sexual dysfunctions, paraphilias, gender identity disorders,* and *sexual disorders not otherwise specified.* At the outset, some basic terms and concepts need clarification.

DEFINITION OF TERMS

A person's *anatomical sex* is his or her biological sex as determined by whether he has XY, or she has XX, chromosomes. *Intersex conditions* occur when one or more of the physical variables of biological sex—including chromosomal status, external genitals, internal sexual anatomical structures, sex hormonal status, and/or secondary sex characteristics—are discordant (e.g., partial androgen insensitivity syndrome or congenital adrenal hyperplasia). The medical conditions of intersex variations, by themselves, are not considered sexual or gender identity disorders by the *DSM-IV-TR,* but can be a contributing factor in the development of a sexual or gender identity disorder.

Gender identity is the individual's *internal* feelings or self-perception as to whether he or she is a male or a female.

Gender role refers to whether a person wishes to be seen by others (or by oneself) as a male or as a female; or it refers to role behaviors empirically associated predominantly by most individuals to one biological sex while observed in only a small minority of the other sex. Gender role involves the person's *external* appearance and behavior, including sexual behavior.

Sexual orientation describes a person's erotic attraction and preference for partners of the same (homosexual) or opposite (heterosexual) sex or for both (bisexual). Only about 1% of adult females and 2–3% of adult males report homosexual orientation expressed in enduring homosexual or bisexual behavior.

DIAGNOSTIC CATEGORIES

DSM-IV-TR lists seven categories of sexual and gender disorders that fall into the three major groupings of sexual dysfunctions (common), paraphilias (less common), and gender identity disorder (rare).

The general category of *sexual dysfunctions* includes disturbances in the human sexual response cycle or disturbances involving pain associated with sexual intercourse. The phases of the sexual response cycle are as follows: (1) desire; (2) excitement or arousal; (3) orgasm; and (4) resolution. *Sexual desire disorders* refer to excessive interest in, or aversion to, sexual activity. *Sexual arousal disorders* refer to the inability to attain or maintain gender-normal psychophysiological changes during sexual activity. *Orgasmic disorders* involve either delays or absence of orgasm in men and women after normal sexual excitement, or in men, the opposite: premature ejaculation. *Sexual pain disorders* are characterized by the chronic presence of genital pain or spasms during sexual activity. *Sexual dysfunctions due to a general medical condition* or *substance-induced sexual dysfunction* include the preceding four disorders if they are caused by a medical problem (e.g., diabetes or hypothyroidism) or substance use.

Paraphilias are persistent patterns of sexual arousal in response to atypical or bizarre stimuli and include the following subtypes classified by the stimulus (noted in parentheses): *exhibitionism* (exposing one's genitals), *fetishism* (material object), *frotteurism* (touching and rubbing against a nonconsenting individual), *pedophilia* (a prepubescent child), *sexual masochism* (being humiliated, beaten, bound, or other suffering), *sexual sadism* (causing physical or psychological suffering of a victim), *transvestic fetishism* (cross-dressing), *voyeurism* (observing unsuspecting naked or sexually involved individuals), and related conditions that are diagnosed as *paraphilia not otherwise specified.*

Gender identity disorders are characterized by discomfort with one's anatomical sex to such an extent that one adopts the behavioral patterns and identity associated with the other sex. Although well-publicized political activist groups advocate the removal of "transgendered" conditions from diagnostic nomenclature, gender identity disorders are recognized diagnostically because they invariably cause significant distress, or as one patient said, "How would you like to go through life as a woman trapped in a man's body?" Although variations in gender role are not listed as disorders, "transient, stress-related cross-dressing behavior" is diagnosed as "gender identity disorder not otherwise specified."

SEXUAL DYSFUNCTIONS

Sexual dysfunctions are disturbances in a phase of the human sexual response cycle. Table 18-1 defines the four phases of this cycle.

The nine specific sexual dysfunctions defined in *DSM-IV-TR* are outlined in Table 18-2. In each of these the problem (1) is persistent or recurrent; (2) is not better explained as exclusively occurring during the course of another Axis 1 disorder (other than another sexual dysfunction) such as major depressive disorder and is not due to the direct physiological effects of a substance (e.g., a drug of abuse, a medication) or a general medical condition; and (3) causes marked distress or interpersonal difficulty. In describing a sexual dysfunction, clinicians also should indicate if it's *acquired* or *lifelong* (with or

---

TABLE 18-1
The Human Sexual Response Cycle

PHASE	KEY FEATURES
I. DESIRE	Fantasies about sexual activity and the desire (i.e., libido) to have it.
II. EXCITEMENT	Subjective sense of sexual pleasure with accompanying physiological changes in the male leading to erection, and in the female leading to vaginal lubrication and expansion, vasocongestion in the pelvis, and swelling of the external genitals. Associated with "foreplay" and mediated by the parasympathetic nervous system, this phase includes the "excitement" and "plateau" stages described by Masters and Johnson (1970) and the "vascular" stage described by Kaplan (1974).
III. ORGASM	The peaking of sexual pleasure and the release of sexual tension. This phase is mediated by the sympathetic nervous system and called the "muscular" stage by Kaplan. During it, males sense an inevitable ejaculation, which is followed by intense muscular contractions that emit semen. In a more variable response, females contract the outer third of their vagina.
IV. RESOLUTION	There is a generalized and muscular relaxation, during which males are physiologically refractory to further erection or orgasm, whereas females may be able to respond immediately to additional sexual stimulation for multiple orgasms.

TABLE 18-2

DSM-IV-TR *Sexual Dysfunctions*

SEXUAL DESIRE DISORDERS (Occurring in Phase I of the sexual response cycle)

Hypoactive sexual desire disorder is a deficiency (or absence) of sexual fantasies and desires for sexual activity. It is the most common sexual dysfunction in women and is often accompanied by other sexual dysfunctions.

Sexual aversion disorder is an extreme aversion to and avoidance of all (or almost all) genital sexual contact with a partner. This may occur in those sexually victimized as part of a posttraumatic stress disorder.

SEXUAL AROUSAL DISORDERS (Occurring in Phase II of the sexual response cycle)

Female sexual arousal disorder and *male erectile disorder* are persistent conditions in which there is a partial or complete failure in women to attain or maintain the lubrication-swelling response, or in men to attain or maintain an erection (impotence) prior to the sexual act being completed.

ORGASMIC DISORDERS (Occurring in Phase III of the sexual response cycle)

Female and male orgasmic disorders are persistent or recurrent conditions in which there is a delay in or absence of orgasm following a normal sexual excitement phase.

Premature ejaculation is a persistent or recurrent condition in males in which ejaculation occurs with minimal sexual stimulation before, on, or shortly after penetration and before the person wishes it. The clinician must take into account factors such as the person's age and the frequency and duration of coitus.

SEXUAL PAIN DISORDERS

Dyspareunia (Not Due to a General Medical Condition) is recurrent or persistent genital pain (usually in women, but sometimes in men) that occurs before, during, or after sexual intercourse.

Vaginismus (Not Due to a General Medical Condition) is recurrent or persistent involuntary muscular spasm of the outer third of the vagina that interferes with sexual intercourse by making penetration difficult, painful, or impossible. Vaginismus may be secondary to pain or vice versa.

Note. From *DSM-IV-TR,* pp. 535–558.

---

without previously normal functioning); if it's *generalized* or *situational* (only under certain conditions or with a particular partner); or if it's due to *psychological* or *combined* (psychological and medical or substance) factors. Clinicians should also note its frequency, setting, duration, degree of sexual impairment, level of subjective distress, and effects on other areas of functioning (e.g., social, occupational).

Most sexual dysfunctions arise during young adulthood or with first sexual encounters. The overall clinical course is highly varied; a disorder may be brief, recurrent, smoldering, or permanent. Patients usually delay seeking treatment for 3–12 years and then do so only after several years of a prolonged problematic sexual relationship. Dysfunctions also may arise later in life; for males, inhibited sexual desire and excitement is more common in middle adulthood. Women tend to have increasing sexual responsiveness until their 30s and often maintain their responsiveness into old age. Men often retrospectively report that their peak sexual responsiveness was in their teens or early 20s.

Some sexual dysfunctions tend to be associated with specific psychiatric traits. For example, women with histrionic personalities are more likely to have inhibited sexual desire and inhibited orgasm. Men with obsessive–compulsive personalities are prone to inhibited sexual desire and excitement. Anxiety predisposes one to premature ejaculation and also impotence.

A patient's dysfunction will involve one or more etiological factors. These may be (1) *intrapsychic*, such as "performance anxiety," guilt, low self-esteem, denial, undue self-monitoring, or prior learning and conditioning effects; (2) *interpersonal*, such as fear of abandonment, power struggles, lack of trust, failure to explicitly inform partners about one's particular sexual needs and specific pleasures, a "sex manual mentality," displaced anger, or past experience of sexual victimization; (3) *cultural*, such as sexual myths, insufficient or incorrect information, and negative attitudes about sex learned from parents or others; (4) *medical*, such as drugs, alcohol, or illness; or (5) *psychiatric*, such as depressive and obsessive–compulsive disorders.

A 38-year-old man sought psychotherapy for his inability to obtain an erection during sexual activity with his wife without viewing a new pornographic video. Reviewing a recently viewed pornographic video would not suffice, but using a video that he had not seen for a couple of years would work. As a result, he had an entire double garage full of pornographic videos that he would "recycle" to view before sex in order to be able to attain an erection. The only other way he could become sexually aroused would be to bring another man or woman to join him and his wife in a "threesome." He reported that his wife enthusiastically went along with the "threesomes." However, later in marital therapy, his wife made it clear that it repulsed her; she had complied only because she knew her husband would be impotent without another person or yet another pornographic video. In this case, the man's self-described "liberal" sexual practices eventually contributed to a sexual dysfunction through a conditioning process in which the man consciously disassociated sex from love through years of pairing sexual arousal with pornographic stimuli.

The most common failure in treating sexual dysfunctions is overlooking the presence of a medical illness, another mental disorder, or a drug effect. No matter how obviously emotional problems are affecting the patient, no sexual dysfunction should be treated until *after* the patient has had a complete medical workup, preferably by a physician well versed in the medical causes of sexual dysfunction. A common example is a 55-year-old man with impotence. Diabetes is the most likely cause and loss of nocturnal erections is the best clue. In addition, almost all psychiatric and many nonpsychiatric drugs can cause sexual side effects (over 30% of those taking SSRIs). When a sexual dysfunction is clinically determined to be the direct effect of a medical condition, it is diagnosed as one of the "sexual dysfunctions due to a general medical condition," in which the type of dysfunction and specific medical condition are identified. If the sexual dysfunction is clinically attributed exclusively to the direct effects of a substance (whether a medication, toxin exposure, or abused substance), then the condition is specifically diagnosed as one of the "substance-induced sexual dysfunctions," in which the type of dysfunction and specific substance are identified.

Modern sex therapies are short-term and experiential, aim for behavioral improvement, focus on the here-and-now sexual interactions of a couple, and combine treatments such as education, couple therapy, cognitive–behavioral therapy, directed masturbation exercises, Kegel exercises, homework assignments, desensitization, the squeeze technique, stop–start (actually, start–stop) technique, and sensate focus exercises. The squeeze and stop–start techniques are used mainly to treat premature ejaculation, which is the most common male sexual dysfunction (30% of men). Clients concentrate on arousal while the penis is stimulated, and then stop stimulation just before ejaculatory inevitability. With the stop–start ("pause") technique, control quietly returns. With the squeeze technique, the partner squeezes the penis below the corona until the erection slumps, after which stimulation is resumed. Sensate focusing teaches partners to enjoy sexual activity that is not intended to lead to intercourse. Instead of emphasizing performance, sexual pleasure is separated from intercourse. Pharmaceutical interventions that may delay ejaculation include applying anesthetic to the coronal ridge or prescribing paroxetine 20 mg each day.

Forty years ago using what were the latest sex therapies, Masters and Johnson (1970) reported an 80% overall success rate, with 5% of patients having a recurrence of symptoms within a 5-year period. In general, male dysfunctions respond best, with success rates highest for (in declining efficacy) premature ejaculation, retarded ejaculation, secondary impotence, and primary impotence. Treatment is reputed to reverse vaginismus virtually 100% of the time, with less success for generalized unresponsiveness and inhibited orgasm among women. Anal stimulation may improve anorgasmia. Medications that have been reported to enhance responsiveness include testosterone (in men), yohimbine (α-2-presynaptic antagonist), L-arginine (nitrous oxide precursor), and cyproheptadine (serotonin antagonist).

Primary erectile dysfunction (primary impotence) affects less than 1% of men under 35 years. *Primary* refers to the fact that these men have never been able to attain or maintain an erection. On the other hand, secondary erectile dysfunction (i.e., having lost the ability) is common and occurs in about 40% of males over 60 years old. A physical cause for impotency is present 75% of the time. If the patient is able to have erections in sleep or with masturbation, then the cause is psychological. The medical workup for this condition may include the measurement of nocturnal penile tumescence, penile blood pressure with penile plethysmography or Doppler flow meter, pudendal nerve latency time, dorsal nerve somatosensory evoked potentials, and blood parameters (glucose, thyroid, liver function, prolactin, testosterone, luteinizing and follicle stimulating hormones). Correcting hormonal deficiencies and other medical conditions is the first treatment step. A vacuum pump with ring, penile implants (inflatable or bendable rods) are mechanical interventions. Prostaglandins(PGE1), particularly alprostadil, relax smooth muscle and can be delivered by intercavernosal injections (Caverject) or more comfortably by gel (Topiglan) or urethral suppository (MUSE). Phosphodiesterase (PDE5) inhibitors amplify the natural effects of nitrous oxide in relaxing smooth muscle and increasing penile blood flow. These medications include sildenafil (Viagra), vardenafil (Levitra), and tadalafil (Cialis), which are taken orally and have half-lives ranging from a couple hours to about 3 days, respectively. Because they potentiate nitrates, these medication may cause severe hypotension in those already taking nitroglycerin or related medications.

PARAPHILIAS

Derived from the Greek meaning "along side of" and "love," a paraphilia is the involuntary and repeated need for unusual or bizarre imagery, acts, or objects to induce sexual excitement. Paraphilias involve either (1) inanimate objects, (2) suffering or humiliation, or (3) sexual activity with nonconsenting partners. To qualify as a disorder, the patient's sexually arousing imagery, sexual urges, or actions must be intense and recurrent over a period of at least 6 months. Individuals with paraphilias are rarely self-referred and paraphiliac disorders are rarely diagnosed, but judging from the sales of pornographic magazines, movies, and paraphernalia, they may be more common in the community than we know. They almost always occur in men. Although some people enjoy their paraphilias, others feel guilty, develop psychosexual dysfunctions, or end up behind bars. The common paraphilias are described in Table 18-3.

The diagnoses of pedophilia, exhibitionism, voyeurism, and frotteurism are made if the individual has *either* acted on these urges *or* experiences marked distress or interpersonal difficulties associated with the urges. The diagnosis of sexual sadism is made if the individual has acted on the urge with a nonconsenting person *or* experiences marked distress or interpersonal difficulties associated with the sadistic urges. The diagnoses of fetishism, transvestic fetishism, and sexual masochism are made only if the sexual fantasies, urges, or behavior result in clinically significant distress or impairment in social, occupational, or other important areas of living.

Persons with transvestic fetishism are generally heterosexual men (or less commonly, bisexual men) who derive erotic pleasure from dressing as women. Usually beginning during childhood or adolescence, these individuals first experiment with cross-dressing in private (typically becoming paired with masturbation at some point) and then increase the frequency and number of worn items. They may join a transvestite subculture wherein they experience acceptance and encouragement for public cross-dressing. In time, cross-dressing may no longer provide erotic stimulation, but they continue it because it relieves anxiety and/or depression. When not cross-dressing, transvestites look like regular guys. Although heterosexual, their sexual experiences are typically limited, involving few heterosexual encounters and may include occasional homosexual activity. Some people with transvestic fetishism claim that during childhood, they were punished and humiliated by mothers or sisters who forced them to put on female attire. Others begin with masturbating to images or fantasies of the scantily clad female body to finding the female garments themselves becoming sexually arousing.

In pedophilia, the erotic stimulus is a prepubescent child (generally age 13 or younger), either of the same or opposite sex. The offender must be at least 16 years old and at least 5 years older than the child. A late adolescent involved in an ongoing sexual relationship with a 12- or 13-year-old does not count. Pedophiles are almost always male. Heterosexual pedophilia is twice as common as homosexual pedophilia, even though heterosexual men outnumber homosexual men approximately 35:1 in the general population. Thus, on a percentage basis, disproportionately higher rates of pedophiliac behavior occur in homosexual men compared to heterosexual men. Certain subtypes of pedophilia should be noted: (1) Is the *sexual attraction to males, females, or*

TABLE 18-3

The Paraphilias

Any one of these must occur over a period of at least 6 months and involve recurrent, intense sexual urges and sexually arousing fantasies or behaviors regarding the paraphilia.

Exhibitionism involves achieving sexual excitement by compulsively and repetitively exposing one's genitals to an unsuspecting stranger. Masturbation may occur, but more often erections can't be obtained. Usually, this behavior is not just a sexual experience but an aggressive act to shock and disgust females. Without the shock value, many exhibitionists get little pleasure. Exhibitionism, which typically begins in the mid-20s, tends to occur in shy, married, heterosexual males.

Fetishism involves the use of nonliving objects (fetishes) for sexual arousal and usually focuses on clothes, such as women's undergarments. This diagnosis is not applied to the use of devices solely designed for sexual stimulation (e.g., vibrators).

Transvestic fetishism occurs when female clothes are used exclusively in cross-dressing (transvestism), by a heterosexual or bisexual male who finds women's garments sexually arousing as symbols of femininity, without manifesting a gender identity disorder (although gender dysphoria can be a component of the condition).

Pedophilia involves fantasizing about or engaging in sexual activity with a prepubescent child or children (generally age 13 or younger). The pedophile must be at least 16 years old and at least 5 years older than the child or children molested. Often sexually abused as children, these patients usually turn (on) to pedophilia in midlife during a setback in marriage or in another close relationship. Most people with pedophilia are males with low self-esteem, who enjoy a sense of mastery and safety when fondling children. Pedophilia is usually a chronic disorder with frequent relapses and **is** resistant to therapy.

Sexual masochism involves real, not simulated, acts of being humiliated, bound, whipped, beaten, or made to suffer in some other way. Masochistic fantasies often arise during childhood, but are not acted on until early adulthood. Some men engage in sexual masochism, but the ratio is 20 females to each male. Unintentional deaths have resulted from sexual masochism.

Sexual sadism involves real, not simulated, acts in which the psychological or physical suffering (including humiliation) of the victim is sexually exciting to the perpetrator. The sexual activity may involve a consenting or nonconsenting partner. Although sexual sadism may lead to murder and rape, few rapists are sexual sadists.

Voyeurism involves the act of observing an unsuspecting person who is naked, in the process of disrobing, or engaging in sexual activity. Most "Peeping Toms" are more erotically stimulated by watching than by other sexual acts. They typically don't wish to have sex with the observed and would be frightened if it were offered. They prefer to masturbate while observing or to fantasize about the observed woman feeling helpless, mortified, or terrorized if she knew Tom was observing her.

TABLE 18-3

Continued

Frotteurism involves touching and rubbing against a nonconsenting person. It is the touching, not the coercive nature of the act, that is sexually exciting.

Paraphilia not otherwise specified is a residual category for paraphilias not meeting criteria for any of the specific paraphilias. Examples include *coprophilia* (feces); *klismaphilia* (enemas); *mysophilia* (lying in filth); *partialism* (exclusive focus on part of the body, such as the feet); *zoophilia (sexual activity with animals)*; *necrophilia* (sexual activity with a corpse); *telephone scatologia (making lewd phone calls)*; *urophilia* (urinating on others or observing someone urinating), and *asphyxiophilia* (inducing oxygen deprivation through temporary strangulation by a rope around the neck or a plastic bag over the head in order to induce sexual arousal or to enhance sexual excitement and orgasm).

---

both? (2) Is the pedophilia *limited to incest?* (3) Is the person *exclusively* or *nonexclusively* attracted to children?

For the most part, the person with pedophilia engages in genital petting or oral–genital contact. Physical aggression against children in such situations is relatively rare, although because of the publicity when this happens, the public has come to associate pedophilia with murderous violence. Probably between a quarter and a third of the sexual offenses committed by adults against children are committed by true pedophiles. Most sexual offenses against children are committed by individuals with mental retardation, psychosis, neurological disease, sociopathy, or (occasionally) males who impulsively approach children while under the influence of drugs or alcohol.

In sharp contrast with common belief, most men with pedophilia are mild-mannered and innocuous appearing, with profound feelings of masculine inadequacy. They are often adults who are unable to relate comfortably to the opposite sex and have turned to children instead. Many were sexually abused as children; as teenagers, they were frequently shy and awkward. In their relations with mature women, they typically suffer from inadequate sexual performance or impotence, all of which reinforces their profound sense of masculine inadequacy and impaired self-esteem.

Individuals with pedophilia are notorious rationalizers, using excuses such as "It has educational value for the child," "The child gets rewarded with sexual pleasure," or "The child was sexually provocative and wanted it." Methods of preventing the child's disclosure range from direct threats to being very generous and attentive to the child's needs.

Not all paraphilias are impulsive. Exhibitionism usually is, but pedophilia is often planned. Arrest for paraphilia typically occurs after the average pedophile has committed 30 or more molestations and after the exhibitionist has committed hundreds of exposures.

Paraphilic-related problems can cause much distress, break up marriages, and end jobs. Though sometimes referred to as "sexual addictions," they are classified in *DSM-IV-TR* as "sexual disorders not otherwise specified." Like "real" addictions, these behaviors have a compulsive, repetitious, and ultimately unsatisfying quality.

Men with paraphilia in stable relationships often experience paraphiliac fantasies that intrude during sexual activity with their partners, and paraphilic behaviors typically replace most normal sexual behaviors. They usually do not specialize in one paraphilia, but rather have two or more during a lifetime. If they have another Axis I diagnosis, it is usually dysthymic disorder (but with more libido, not less) or substance abuse (most commonly, the typical disinhibitor—alcohol).

> A 63-year-old man initially sought treatment, referred by his physician, for coping with the impact of a medical condition on his physical activity level. In addition, he had been treated for years with medication for a bipolar mood disorder. Within a few sessions, he began talking about dissatisfaction in his relationship with his wife. Tearfully, he described his loneliness, stating that his wife had not kissed him on the lips in years. She had reportedly started rejecting him sexually long ago, no longer willing to wear the lingerie he bought for her. Early in the relationship, she had complied, to his delight. The client explained his desire for his wife to dress "ultrafem" like the women and men he frequently views on Internet sites. He was especially aroused sexually by seeing men dressed as women in "ultrafem." Without this visual stimulation, he is impotent. More recently, even hugs and hand-holding have ceased. The client stated that he longs and "begs" for physical affection from his wife. His wife was invited to counseling, but refused. The couple had attended marital counseling once previously, but did not find it to be helpful. Currently, the client masturbates to completion while on the Internet. He hides this almost nightly behavior from his wife, who has been sleeping in a separate bedroom for years. Again, this case illustrates the multidimensional impact that a paraphilia can have on the individual, on their marital relationship, and on their sexual behavior pattern.

Management and Treatment

A good way to assess sexual functioning is to ask (without apologies or embarrassment), "*What is the total number of behaviors in a week that culminate in orgasm?*" Kinsey referred to this number as the "total sexual outlet." Only 5%

of men have an outlet of seven or greater, whereas a majority of men with paraphilic disorder have persistent hypersexual desire and tie or exceed this number. A good way to find out what abnormal and normal sexual behaviors are occurring is to ask, "*What are the different ways that you become aroused to the point of orgasm?*" Honest answers to this question will reveal paraphilias and paraphilic-related behavior problems such as promiscuity, dependence on pornography, and compulsive masturbation.

Few individuals with paraphilia seek treatment, and if they do, it's usually to extricate themselves from secondary legal or marital difficulties. Many males with paraphilic disorder are shy or immature and have difficulty establishing mature heterosexual relations. For them, the paraphilia becomes the main sexual outlet. Therapy attempts to (1) diminish sexual arousal in response to the paraphilia, (2) increase normal heterosexual arousal, (3) teach appropriate assertiveness and social skills (since many of these patients have trouble simply talking to the opposite sex), (4) provide sex education, (5) treat psychosexual dysfunctions, (6) modify distorted thinking and rationalizations with cognitive therapies, and (7) prevent relapse. Also, 12-step programs (modeled on Alcoholics Anonymous), which combine group support, cognitive restructuring, and spiritual resources, are offered for persons with paraphilias.

Older behavior therapy methods such as shock or noxious odors paired with pictures or fantasies of the arousing stimuli, or more recent imaginal covert sensitization techniques, coupled with deliberate fantasizing only about heterosexual activity during masturbation, can help reduce the power of the paraphilia. Cognitive–behavioral treatments focus on relapse prevention by identifying high-risk thoughts, feelings, and situations. If possible, the patient tries to avoid these. When avoidance isn't possible, cognitive restructuring strategies are implemented to address the faulty thinking used to justify the problematic behaviors.

Pharmacological approaches include drugs that reduce libido, such as medroxyprogesterone acetate at 100–400 mg each day (long-acting Depo-Provera at 200–400 mg is injected into muscle every 7–10 days) or luprolide (a luteinizing hormone releasing hormone agonist) at 7.5 mg intramuscular every month. Triptorelin, another gonadotropin releasing hormone analog, is not available in the United States. These medications are usually reserved for men who have exhibited violent or illegal paraphilic behaviors and are essentially forms of "chemical castration" by lowering testosterone levels. Naltrexone, an opiate receptor blocker, has been prescribed by some clinicians in an attempt to interfere with the biological reinforcement (reward) of the paraphilia. High doses of SSRIs (e.g., 40–80 mg fluoxetine) have been reported to decrease paraphilic fantasies, aberrant sexual urges, and compulsions while sparing conventional sexual behaviors (Kafka, 1993). The total number of sexual outlets also decreases from hypersexual to normal levels.

Although homosexuality (homosexual orientation or homosexual behavior patterns) by itself is no longer listed as a mental disorder, individuals with "persistent and marked distress about sexual orientation" (whether homosexual or bisexual) are diagnosed with "sexual disorder not otherwise specified" using the DSM-IV-TR, and diagnosed as "Egodystonic Sexual Orientation" in the International Classification of Diseases (ICD) published by the American Medical Association and World Health Organization (American Medical Association, 2005; World Health Organization, 2007). Egodystonic sexual orientation is used in the ICD when the individual desires that his or her orientation "were different because of associated psychological and behavioral disorders, and may seek treatment in order to change it" (World Health Organization, 2007, p. F66.1). While many mental health care providers and professional associations have expressed considerable skepticism that sexual orientation could be changed with psychotherapy and also assumed that therapeutic attempts at reorientation would produce harm, recent empirical evidence demonstrates that homosexual orientation can indeed be therapeutically changed in motivated clients, and that reorientation therapies do not produce emotional harm when attempted (e.g., Byrd & Nicolosi, 2002; Byrd et al., 2008; Shaeffer et al., 1999; Spitzer, 2003).

GENDER IDENTITY DISORDERS

These disorders involve a profound disturbance in a person's sense of being a male or a female in concordance with his or her sexual anatomy—i.e., a conflict between a person's anatomical sex and his or her gender identity. A person with a gender identity disorder has both (1) a strong and persistent desire to be, or insistence that one is, a member of the opposite sex to one's actual sexual anatomy, and (2) a persistent discomfort with one's sexual anatomy or a pervasive aversion to participate in the gender role associated with one's anatomical sex. This class of disorders can be diagnosed in childhood, adolescence, or adulthood. Formerly called "transsexualism" in adult cases, gender identity disorder is such a persistent feeling of severe discomfort with one's own anatomical sex, strong wish to be rid of one's genitals, and wish to live as the opposite sex, that anatomical males with the condition often say, "I'm a woman trapped in a man's body," and anatomical females with the condition similarly complain, "I'm a man trapped in a woman's body." Table 18-4 presents DSM-IV-TR criteria for gender disorder.

TABLE 18-4

DSM-IV-TR *Criteria for Gender Identity Disorder*

A. A strong and persistent cross-gender identification (not merely a desire for any perceived cultural advantages of being the other sex).

In children, the disturbance is manifested by four (or more) of the following:

(1) repeatedly stated desire to be, or insistence that he or she is, the other sex

(2) in boys, preference for cross-dressing or simulating female attire; in girls, insistence on wearing only stereotypical masculine clothing

(3) strong and persistent preferences for cross-sex roles in make-believe play or persistent fantasies of being the other sex

(4) intense desire to participate in the stereotypical games and pastimes of the other sex

(5) strong preference for playmates of the other sex

In adolescents and adults, the disturbance is manifested by symptoms such as a stated desire to be the other sex, frequent passing as the other sex, desire to live or be treated as the other sex, or the conviction that one has the typical feelings and reactions of the other sex.

B. Persistent discomfort with his or her sex or sense of inappropriateness in the gender role of that sex.

In children, the disturbance is manifested by any of the following: in boys, assertion that his penis or testes are disgusting or will disappear or assertion that it would be better not to have a penis, or aversion toward rough-and-tumble play and rejection of male stereotypical toys, games, and activities; in girls, rejection of urinating in a sitting position, assertion that she has or will grow a penis, assertion that she does not want to grow breasts or menstruate, or marked aversion towards normative feminine clothing.

In adolescents and adults, the disturbance is manifested by symptoms such as preoccupation with getting rid of primary and secondary sex characteristics (e.g., request for hormones, surgery, or other procedures to physically alter sexual characteristics to simulate the other sex) or belief that he or she was born the wrong sex.

C. The disturbance is not concurrent with a physical intersex condition.

D. The disturbance causes clinically significant distress or impairment in social, occupational, or other important areas of functioning.

Note. From *DSM-IV-TR,* p. 581.

By definition, this intrapsychic gender conflict must not be the product of psychosis or of congenital sexual anomalies, such as occurs in a hermaphrodite who has both testicular and ovarian tissues (but ambiguous genitalia) and develops an accompanying gender dysphoria. (This latter problem, usually caused by congenital adrenal hyperplasia or 5-alpha-reductase deficiency, would be diagnosed "gender identity disorder not otherwise specified.") With a psychotic delusion, an individual may truly *believe* he or she is a member of the other sex, but an individual with a gender identity disorder strongly *feels* like a member of the other sex rather than believing it is factually true. Gender identity disorder is rare, with an estimated prevalence among men of 1 in 30,000; among women, 1 in 100,000.

Those with gender identity disorder usually, but not always, cross-dress to be in accord with their own gender identity. The patient's family members typically recollect that as a child *he* wanted to be a *she,* or vice versa, even as early as 3 years old. This cross-gender identification perplexes and frustrates the child as well as his or her family and peers. While growing up, these children often experience correction, criticism, ostracism, and/or marginalization by peers and some relatives. These interpersonal difficulties, combined with the person's own strong and disturbing intrapsychic cross-gender conflicts, result in high rates of oppositional and antisocial behavior, self-mutilation (frequently of the genitals), attempted suicide, and completed suicide. For example, a 24-year-old anatomical male with gender identity disorder was referred for psychotherapy after he had medically recovered from a self-inflicted injury in which he had deliberately sliced off his unwanted penis with a kitchen knife and flushed it down the toilet.

Males with *gender identity disorder* differ from males with *transvestic fetishism* in that the former have female gender identities and don't experience sexual excitement by wearing women's clothes, and the latter have male gender identities and do not wish to get rid of their genitals. (Don't confuse "transvestism" with "transsexualism": The former changes his vest, the latter, his sex.) Interfering with cross-dressing frustrates males with transvestic fetishes and is a useful diagnostic clue for this differential diagnosis. However, if a man with transvestic fetishism develops a persistent discomfort with the male gender role or identity, the diagnosis is transvestic fetishism with gender dysphoria. When transvestic fetishism occurs in conjunction with the full criteria for gender identity disorder, both diagnoses are given. When *male homosexuals* dress as "drag queens"—for a goof, for masquerade, or for attracting another man—there's typically no erotic sensation in conjunction with the cross-dressing. And *female impersonators* are not typically sexually aroused by cross-dressing.

A quiet evening for unsuspecting parents was suddenly interrupted by shrieks from their 6-year-old son. They raced to the bedroom to find the walls splattered with blood and their child writhing in pain. Next to their son was a thin rope—one end was attached to a doorknob, the other to his penis and testicles. Having tied the rope thusly, the child slammed the door shut in a deliberate act of auto-castration.

This tragedy is extreme, but the intensity of the distress and unhappiness is unfortunately typical for cross-gender identified individuals.

Health care and mental-health care clinicians too often incorrectly reassure concerned parents that their child's cross-dressing and/or cross-gender identity statements are "just a passing phase." But to the contrary, the best therapeutic intervention for gender identity disorder and its developmental precursors—in order to alleviate the profound suffering associated with the condition—is early detection and early intervention with effective, specifically developed child behavior therapy together with family counseling (Rekers, 1995a, 1995b; Rekers & Kilgus, 1995).

Eight-year-old Carl talked with a pronounced high feminine voice inflection, with his conversation dominated by topics such as cosmetics, female roles, dresses, female undergarments, and delivering babies—a pattern that began at the age of 4. His gestures were exaggerations of an effeminate swishy gait and arm movements. He preferred playing with girls and assumed a female role frequently. He preferred girls' toys, particularly dolls, avoiding boys' toys and games. Other boys teased him and called him "sissy" and "queer." Fearing getting hurt, he repeatedly feigned illnesses and injuries to avoid playing with other boys. He repeatedly referred to himself with a girl's name, and even called himself a "sissy" and "fag." On the school playground, the other boys fought over who "had to take Carl" on their team.

Fortunately, Carl's mother sought psychological treatment for him. Carl was behaviorally treated in the clinic, at home, and at school (Rekers et al., 1974). His mother was trained to administer a token economy program in the home, and his schoolteacher was taught to apply a response–cost procedure in the classroom. As a result of treatment, Carl's gender role behaviors became normal compared to other boys, and he developed a normal male identity. But he still retained his negative reputation among his peers. So his mother and therapist arranged for him to be transferred to a different school; at the new school, Carl was elected captain of the sports team with the opportunity to pick other boys for his team. This was a defining moment for Carl, solidly confirming his new male identity. On follow-up in his adolescence, Carl thanked the psychologist for treating him and told him, "You saved me from the fire" (Rekers et al., 1990).

As adults, those with gender identity disorder try to live as if they belong to the opposite sex. Many successfully hide their sex from coworkers and friends. Sexual intimacy is restricted; a majority of transsexuals don't marry, and when they do, the marriages usually fail. Because they experience themselves as members of the opposite sex, they prefer normal heterosexual partners of the same biological sex, but they do not view themselves as "homosexual" because of their cross-gender identity. Drugs and talk therapies alone do not alter the transsexual's cross-gender identification. (However, psychotherapy can alleviate emotional problems arising from the transsexualism.) A combination of behavior therapy, cognitive therapy, and group therapy has been demonstrated to successfully reverse cross-gender identification in adolescents and young adults (e.g., Barlow et al., 1973).

Once the older adult with cross-gender identity clearly decides to switch sexes, some professionals support the patient in seeking hormonal and surgical sex reassignment. Other clinicians have moral qualms about supporting the individual's desire for surgical sex reassignment, and if the person declines the therapeutic goal of changing his identity to match his anatomy, they remove themselves from the case and refer the person to another clinician.

A majority of adults with cross-gender identity express the strong desire to change their sex permanently. In the United States, two to eight times more men than women seek surgical sex reassignment. To qualify for a surgical sex transformation, psychiatrically sophisticated surgeons require that patients live as the opposite sex for at least 2 years, during which time they should demonstrate minimally adequate social and occupational functioning, be able to sustain enduring friendships, and be free of major psychopathology. However, some surgeons in private practice perform sex reassignment surgery without any psychiatric evaluation. And some individuals with gender identity disorder seek surgery in foreign countries at a lower cost, where psychiatric evaluations are rare. Surgical procedures are accompanied by prescriptions for estrogen or testosterone to induce the secondary sex characteristics of the other sex. The surgical transformation is more successful for males than females. The man's genitals are amputated, an artificial vagina is constructed from existing fascial planes, and the urethra is moved to feminine location. Bladder infections are the most common postoperative physical complication. Most individuals with cross-gender identities do not regret having the surgery although many sexual, personal, and occupational problems persist after sex reassignment.

Research has found that the psychological, relational, and vocational adjustment of individuals with gender identity disorder is not significantly different for those who obtain sex reassignment surgery and those who do not. For this reason, university medical schools that offered sex reassignment surgery in the past closed down those programs. In terms of a cost–benefit analysis, surgical sex reassignment cannot be justified. However, many adults with gender identity disorder continue to work for years to save up money to pay for this surgery from surgeons in private practice (i.e., it is not typically covered by health insurance) for the gender satisfactions they anticipate. Informed consent to any clinical procedure requires full disclosure of the available clinical knowledge regarding the risks and potential benefits, if any, of a procedure. Adults with gender identity disorder should be fully informed that outcome studies find no significant improvement in psychological, social, or vocational adjustment after surgical sex reassignment, and that some individuals regret the irreversible surgery.

> A 26-year-old anatomical male with gender identity disorder obtained surgical sex reassignment to become a woman. But within a year after the last surgical procedure, he came to the conclusion that he was better off as a male and that he had sinned against God who had created him to be a man. He resumed male clothing and a male role, but feeling that the surgeons had made him only a mutilated man, not a real woman. Now preoccupied with his incomplete male body, he developed severe depression and attempted suicide. Fortunately, his sister sought psychotherapeutic help for him, but achieving a normal psychological adjustment would require years of intensive psychotherapy.

This chapter began with the observation that sex plays a uniquely profound role in people's lives, influencing their thoughts, their emotions, their social relationships, and their ability to express love. Because sexual maladjustment can have such a pervasive, troublesome impact on people's lives, patients can be especially appreciative of mental health care professionals who can accurately diagnose their sexual disorder, explain the disorder to them in lay terms, answer their pressing questions, and then either skillfully provide empirically validated treatment or refer them to another professional who has the specialized clinical skills to provide this care.

References

American Medical Association. (2005). *International statistical classification of diseases* (9th ed.). Chicago: American Medical Association.

American Psychiatric Association. (2000). *Diagnostic and statistical manual of mental disorders* (4th ed., text rev.). Washington, DC: American Psychiatric Association.

Barlow, D.H., Reynolds, E.J., & Agras, W.S. (1973). Gender identity change in a transsexual. *Archives of General Psychiatry, 28,* 569–576.

Byrd, A.D. & Nicolosi, J. (2002). A meta-analytic review of treatment of homosexuality. *Psychological Reports, 90,* 139–152.

Byrd, A.D., Nicolosi, J., & Potts, R.W. (2008). Clients' perceptions of how reorientation therapy and self-help can promote changes in sexual orientation. *Psychological Reports, 102,* 3–28.

Kafka, M.P. (1993). Update on paraphilias and paraphilia-related disorders. *Currents in Affective Illness,* 12, 5–13.

Kaplan, H.S. (1974). *The new sex therapy.* New York: Brunner/Mazel.

Kinsey, A., Pomeroy, W., & Martin, C. (1948). *Sexual behavior in the human male.* Philadelphia: Saunders.

Kinsey, A., Pomeroy, W., Martin, C., & Gebhard, P. (1953). *Sexual behavior in the human female.* Philadelphia: Saunders.

Masters, W.H., & Johnson, V.E. (1970). *Human sexual inadequacy.* Boston: Little, Brown.

Rekers, G.A., Kilgus, M.D., & Rosen, A.C. (1990). Long-term effects of treatment for childhood gender disturbance. *Journal of Psychology and Human Sexuality,* 3(2), 121–153.

Rekers, G.A. (1995a). Early detection and treatment of sexual problems. In G.A. Rekers (Ed.), *Handbook of child and adolescent sexual problems* (pp. 3–13). New York: Lexington Books.

Rekers, G. A. (1995b). Assessment and treatment methods for gender identity disorder and transvestism. In G.A. Rekers (Ed.), *Handbook of child and adolescent sexual problems* (pp. 272–289). New York: Lexington Books.

Rekers, G.A., & Kilgus, M.D. (1995). Differential diagnosis and rationale for treatment of gender identity disorders and transvestism. In G.A. Rekers (Ed.), *Handbook of child and adolescent sexual problems* (pp. 255–271). New York: Lexington Books.

Shaeffer, K.W., Nottebaum, L., Smith, P., Dech, K., & Krawczyk, J. (1999). Religiously-motivated sexual orientation change: A follow-up study. *Journal of Psychology and Theology,* 27, 329–337.

Spitzer, R.L. (2003). Can some gay men and lesbians change their sexual orientation? 200 participants reporting a change from homosexual to heterosexual orientation. *Archives of Sexual Behavior,* 32, 403–417.

World Health Organization. (2007). International statistical classification of diseases and related health problems (10th ed.). Available at http://www.who.int/classifications/apps/icd/icd10online/.

19

Eating Disorders

In 1689, Dr. Richard Morton described a self-starving 18-year-old female who looked like a "skeleton only clad with skin." He called her condition "nervous consumption"; in 1874, Sir William Gull called it *"anorexia nervosa."* This disorder is characterized by an irrational dread of becoming fat, a zealous pursuit of thinness, massive weight loss, a disturbed body image, and an almost delusional belief of being too fat. *Bulimia*, which wasn't recognized until the 1950s, is characterized by binge-eating and self-induced vomiting. Unlike anorexia nervosa, bulimia usually afflicts individuals with normal, or slightly excessive, weight. Preoccupation with weight and the use of pathological approaches to losing weight are shared by the two disorders.

The frequency of eating disorders has leveled off in Western nations after rapidly escalating. For example, in Rochester, Minnesota, the incidence of anorexia nervosa among women ages 10–19 jumped a walloping 375% between 1950 and 1954 and 1980 and 1984 (Lucas et al., 1991); similar increases have been reported in Zurich and London. These dramatic increases, which initially mainly occurred in the most vulnerable group (teenage girls) were genuine and not merely the result of greater awareness. More recently, anorexia nervosa has also been increasing in young and middle-aged women, many of whom suffer from chronic anorexia nervosa (Strober et al., 1997). Anorexia nervosa is also *lethal*, with its mortality rate ranging from 5 to 10%. The combined prevalence of anorexia nervosa and bulimia in the highest risk group, adolescent and young adult women—mainly upper- and middle-class students—has ranged between 1 and 4% over the past 10 to 20 years and has become more evenly distributed world-wide (Yager et al., 2006).

This chapter discusses only anorexia nervosa and bulimia, but *DSM-IV-TR* describes two other eating disorders that occur during infancy and childhood: *pica*, in which children persistently ingest nonnutritive substances (e.g., lead paint chips, hair, dirt; *pica* is the Latin word for "magpie," a renowned avian scavenger); and *rumination disorder of infancy*, or merycism, a rare and sometimes fatal disorder of repeated regurgitation. *Obesity* isn't a *DSM-IV-TR* mental disorder because it lacks a consistent psychological pattern. *DSM-IV-TR* suggests that when psychological forces promote obesity, they should be indicated as "psychological factors affecting physical condition" in the section entitled, Other Conditions That May Be a Focus of Clinical Attention. *Binge-eating disorder*, in which the individual engages in binge eating but without compensatory purging, may accompany obesity. The prevalence of binge eating disorders is estimated to be 2% in community samples and accounts for 1.3 to 30.1% of patients seeking medical treatment for obesity (Fairburn, Marcus et al., 1993; Dingemans et al., 2002).

ANOREXIA NERVOSA

Clinical Presentation

The essential features of anorexia nervosa are a dread of being fat and a compulsion to be thin, substantial weight loss, refusal to maintain a healthy weight despite being very thin or even emaciated, distorted internal and external perceptions of one's body as fat despite being underweight, and in women, amenorrhea. Table 19-1 lists *DSM-IV-TR* criteria for anorexia nervosa.

In the typical individual with anorexia nervosa—a teenager or woman in her early 20s, formerly a "model child"—starts dieting due to mild overweight; this weight gain may occur after a stressor (e.g., puberty, a broken romance, a family divorce) or for no apparent reason. After shedding a few pounds, she decides that's not enough. This cycle repeats itself until she virtually stops eating. Only in the most severe stages (near emaciation) does she lose her appetite (hence the term *anorexia* nervosa is a misnomer). Most of the time she has a raging appetite and constantly thinks about food. Unfortunately, her food choices are very restricted ("Romaine versus iceberg lettuce? With or without lemon juice?"). She may memorize the calorie content of foods and prepare meals for everyone but herself. She may hide food, steal it, or play with it, but avoids eating in public and often consumes what little she eats in secrecy. To lose weight, she exercises frenetically, goes on fad diets, abstains from carbohydrates and fats, takes laxatives and diuretics, and gorges food and induces vomiting (i.e., bulimic episodes).

At first, she's energetic, enthusiastic, and pert, but then depressive symptoms set in, especially dysthymia, insomnia (or hypersomnia), social withdrawal, and decreased

TABLE 19-1
DSM-IV-TR *Criteria for Anorexia Nervosa*

A. Refusal to maintain body weight at or above a minimally normal weight for age and height (e.g., weight loss leading to maintenance of body weight less than 85% of that expected; or failure to make expected weight gain during period of growth, leading to body weight less than 85% of that expected).

B. Intense fear of gaining weight or becoming fat, even though underweight.

C. Disturbance in the way in which one's body weight or shape is experienced, undue influence of body weight or shape on self-evaluation, or denial of the seriousness of the current low body weight.

D. In post-menarcheal females, amenorrhea, i.e., the absence of at least three consecutive menstrual cycles. (A woman is considered to have amenorrhea if her periods occur only following hormone, e.g., estrogen, administration.)

Specify type:

Restricting Type: during the current episode of Anorexia Nervosa, the person does not regularly engage in binge-eating or purging behavior (i.e., self-induced vomiting or the misuse of laxatives, diuretics, or enemas)

Binge-Eating/Purging Type: during the current episode of Anorexia Nervosa, the person regularly engages in binge-eating or purging behavior (i.e., self-induced vomiting or the misuse of laxatives, diuretics, or enemas)

Note. From *DSM-IV-TR,* pp. 589.

libido. She's usually perfectionistic and introverted. She'll have stomach pains, nausea, constipation, cold intolerance, headaches, frequent urination, low blood pressure, and diminished secondary sex characteristics. Vomiting that started intentionally may become automatic. As teenagers, female anorectics may shy away from boys and sex. Normal overt anger is curiously lacking in many anorectics (i.e., in those with the "restricting type" not the "binge-eating/purging type").

The anorectic's family members are usually described as being "as nice as you could find." However, they frequently speak for the patient and avoid any sort of disagreement or conflict to an extreme degree ("No, you [to the patient] don't get angry, do you?"). They proudly tell you that "before this all started, we never fought." Efforts to get her to eat have backfired—she just starves herself more.

Clinical Course and Complications

Although milder anorexia nervosa may stop within 12 months, it usually persists for years, punctuated by remissions and exacerbations. About half of these patients have intermittent bulimic symptoms of binge-eating and purging. Nutritionally, patients usually recover in 2–3 years, but even then about half continue to have menstrual problems, sexual and social maladjustment, massive weight fluctuations, or disturbed appetite, and two-thirds continue to fret over their weight and body image. In terms of their overall prognosis, on average 44% recover completely (weight 85% or more of recommended weight), 28% improve considerably, 24% remain unimproved or severely impaired (weight never approaches 85% of recommended weight), and 5% die prematurely. About half die from medical complications (such as cardiac arrest secondary to electrolyte imbalance from vomiting or purging), but the other half die from suicide (Hsu, 1986, 1990; Norman, 1984). In the past, death rates reached 20% among patients followed for 20 years (Theander, 1985). Because many patients with chronic anorexia nervosa develop osteoporosis leading to pathological fractures, complaints of bone or back pain should be investigated. The bone calcium loss may never be regained. Brain mass decreases in 50% of patients, a loss that also may be permanent. An increasing number of people with chronic anorexia nervosa is chronically incapacitated by the disorder and end up in a state of disability. Table 19-2 summarizes the medical complications of anorexia.

Predictors of a favorable outcome include onset in the early teen years, good premorbid functioning, more education, being single, less weight loss, less denial of illness, overactivity, greater psychosexual maturity, and feeling hunger when hospitalized. Indicators of a poor prognosis are the opposite of above, plus premorbidly disturbed family relationships, perinatal complications, bingeing, self-induced vomiting and purging, longer duration of illness, longer delay in initially obtaining treatment, failure to respond to previous treatment, severe dysthymia and obsessions, severe personality disorder, and greater exaggeration of body size.

Epidemiology

The typical female with anorexia is a white, teenage girl from the middle or upper classes, who will attend college. However, there is an increasing prevalence of anorexia nervosa in females in minority populations in the United States (Latina and Asian-American teens and adults, and African-American adult women). There also is a major worldwide increase in this disorder among residents of Third World nations and Third World immigrants in Europe. This increased prevalence of anorexia nervosa is associated with the increased adoption of European/Western body image ideals of thinness as required for attractiveness in women, either in the nations of origin or by acculturating immigrant groups (Pumariega, 1986; Pumariega et al., 1994;

TABLE 19-2
Medical Complications of Anorexia

Condition in bold

Endocrine/Metabolic:

Amenorrhea*	Decreased somatomedin C
Constipation*	Elevated growth hormone
Osteoporosis*	Decreased or erratic vasopressin secretion
Lanugo hair*	Hypercarotenemia
Abnormal temperature regulation (hypothermia)*	Elevated cortisol and abnormal dexamethasone tolerance test
Euthyroid sick syndrome	Hair Loss
Decreased norepinephrine secretion	Abnormal glucose tolerance test

Cardiovascular:

Bradycardia*	Arrhythmias
Hypotension*	Impaired cardiac function with normal EKG (with increased sudden death)

Renal:

Increased BUN	Renal calculi
Decreased glomerular filtration rate	Pedal edema (also caused by decreased albumin)

Hematologic:

Anemia*	Leukopenia
	Thrombocytopenia

*Most common complications.

Miller & Pumariega, 2001). Given that 90–95% of anorectics are female, the diagnosis should be made extra cautiously in males, where it is frequently associated with homosexual orientation, serious personality disorders, or psychosis (Andersen & Holman, 1997). Dancers, modeling students, and athletes (e.g., gymnasts, marathon runners) have a higher incidence of anorexia nervosa, but only *after* they began these activities. Individuals with chronic illnesses where food or nutrition is affected (e.g., cystic fibrosis or diabetes) are at higher risk (Pumariega et al., 1986). Eating disorders have also been found in male athletes, especially wrestlers and racehorse jockeys, who learned to starve and vomit "to get down to weight." Males with anorexia often don't say that they started dieting because they were too fat but rather to get "better muscle definition." All in all, the prevalence of anorexia nervosa is between 0.2 and 0.3% for females and 0.02% for males. Rates for teenage girls are around 0.5–0.8%.

Etiology and Pathogenesis

Psychologically, individuals with anorexia share three cardinal features: perfectionism, dread of losing control, and the distorted perception of their own bodies. Before becoming ill, the typical patient is a "model child"; afterward, everything's a power struggle. Superficially strong and defiant, she's devoid of self-confidence, paralyzed by helplessness, and terrified by her lack of self-control. This individual reacts to gaining a pound with the same distress that the reader might have if she gained 50 pounds overnight. When frantic parents fight with her about eating, they merely feed the patient's stubbornness, since to her, the issue isn't health or even love, but control.

Struggles over control are inflamed by the patient's internal and external misperceptions of her own body. She minimizes internal stimuli: In comparison to normals, she says she feels less hunger after not eating and feels less exhaustion after exercising. Externally, she sees her body differently from the way others see it. Precise measuring shows that anorectics greatly overestimate their front profile width (often twofold), yet correctly estimate their height, the height and width of female models, and the size of physical objects. However, such body misperception (and extreme "black–white" perfectionism) has been seen in experimentally starved individuals, so the cognitive effects of starvation may also fuel these characteristics.

Psychosocial Theories

Biopsychosocial. Our culture has an absurd thinness ideal for females but not for males. This thinness ideal is a historical and cultural aberration, largely confined to Western civilization of the mid- to late-20th century. Prior to this, more rounded and filled-out women were the ideal. Examples include the women in Ruben's paintings in the 1800s and movie stars such as Marilyn Monroe in the 1950s. By today's standards these women would be labeled "too fat." In countries where food is not plentiful, such as China, India, and parts of Africa, being thin means not getting enough food. Anorexia and bulimia had been very rare in these settings, but as these world regions have overcome food shortages, there has been increasing adoption of Western body image ideals. The proportions of representatives of feminine beauty—Miss America contestants (and winners), *Playboy* centerfolds, movie stars, models, and even department store mannequins—have been getting progressively thinner and are now typically below ideal body weight. In modern Western civilization, a woman's appearance tends to be scrutinized and evaluated more than a man's, with a high premium placed on youthfulness and attractiveness. All this is happening during a time when young American women are actually becoming heavier in relation to their height, apparently owing to improved nutrition, creating a progressively greater discrepancy between the real situation and the so-called ideal. The increasing pressure to conform to the ideal drives many to diet. In one study of normal-weight adolescents, 80% of the girls "felt fat," compared to 20% of the boys. The women's popular press responds to this pressure by publishing increasing numbers of articles featuring reducing diets (more than 100 per year). Two theoretical perspectives address this phenomenon: (1) The feminist perspective proposes that as women become more socially autonomous, there is added pressure to conform to ideals imposed by male-dominated society (explaining the increased prevalence in women); and (2) the ethological perspective proposes that dieting in the face of plenty serves to rein in fertility and excessive population growth (Gustavson et al., 1991; Miller & Pumariega, 2001).

In spite of strong societal influences on the development of eating disorders in women, only a minority of women actually develop eating disorders. Therefore, individual factors in those women must play a role. Adolescents have several daunting developmental tasks to perform, including developing and solidifying their own identities, individuating from their families, coming to terms with their sexuality, and feeling accepted by peers. Adolescents who have greater difficulty accomplishing these goals are vulnerable to developing anorexia. At highest risk are those with low self-esteem (individuals with anorexia have high rates of depression), rigid approaches in dealing with problems (25% also have obsessive–compulsive personality disorder), overcontrolling (or, in some cases, undercontrolling) families in which problems don't get worked out, and those with serious conflicts about sexuality. In some, the initial massive weight loss may alter their biological homeostatic mechanisms in such a way as to maintain the anorexia.

Psychodynamic. Analysts blame "domineering" parents for preventing the young person with anorexia from the two chief psychosocial tasks of adolescence: separating and individuating. Adolescents with anorexia demand independence even as they cling to their parents. Yet with these, as with most etiological theories of anorexia nervosa, what's purported to be a cause of the disorder may be both a cause and consequence of it.

Family. Many papers describe the father of the affected youngster as ineffective, her mother as overbearing, and both parents as intrusive. The family system is dysfunctional—but, once again, is this cause or effect? Though some family theorists proposed that this was causative (Minuchin et al., 1978), others

(Amdur et al., 1969) proposed that once the disorder has arisen, family psychopathology was more a reaction to the patient's difficulties than a cause for them. Such reactions surely aggravate and perpetuate matters and merit addressing in treatment.

Biological Theories

A major debate in recent biological research has been whether or not eating disorders share common biological pathways with depression. The affirmative side points to the high frequency of depression in people with anorexia (40–75%), and the higher prevalence of mood disorders in close relatives of those with anorexia and especially those with bulimia. The negative side points out that eating and depressive disorders are more different than alike. Although the question remains open, anorexia nervosa might be a heterogeneous disorder, with some cases having, and other cases not having, a biological link to depression.

    Genetic. Family and twin studies suggest a high heritability of anorexia and bulimia, and researchers are searching for genes that confer susceptibility to these disorders. Scientists suspect that multiple genes and gene combinations may interact with environmental and other factors to increase the risk of developing these illnesses. Identification of susceptibility genes will permit the development of improved treatments for eating disorders (Ramoz, Versini, & Gorwood, 2007).

    Neurobiological and anatomical. Biochemical and Studies are investigating the neurobiology of emotional and social behavior relevant to eating disorders and the neuroscience of feeding behavior. Scientists have learned that both appetite and energy expenditure are regulated by a highly complex network of nerve cells and molecular messengers called neuropeptides. These discoveries and follow-up research will provide potential targets for the development of new pharmacologic treatments for eating disorders (Torsello et al., 2007; Baranowska et al., 2008). Other studies are investigating the role of gonadal steroids. Their relevance to eating disorders is suggested by the clear gender effect in the risk for these disorders, their emergence at puberty or soon after, and the increased risk for eating disorders among girls with early onset of menstruation (Lawson & Klibanski, 2008). Gustavson et al. (1991) also found a major increase in diagnosed anorexia nervosa or unexplained weight loss in the offspring of women who took diethylstilbestrol (DES), with a higher risk than the reproductive cancer risk associated with DES exposure. They suggested that androgenic exposure in utero might explain increased risk for women, who may develop conditioned aversions to their own estrogen after puberty (thus starve to reduce it). More recently, a study suggested that the rate of anorexia was higher in males born from opposite sex fraternal twin pairs than in monozygotic same-gender twin pairs, suggesting hormonal exposure in utero as a factor (Procopio & Marriott, 2007). Perinatal complications have also been associated with higher prevalence of anorexia nervosa and bulimia, suggesting that impairments in neurodevelopment could be factors in their development (Favaro, Tenconi, & Santonastaso, 2006).

Differential Diagnosis

Anorexia nervosa is easy to distinguish from other disorders, primarily *schizophrenia* and *depression*, in which significant weight loss is also found. Besides lacking the common symptoms seen in these disorders, those with anorexia of either type (restricted, binge-eating/purging) misjudge their body image, misperceive internal body cues, may binge and purge, and display hyperactivity, inordinate cheerfulness, a zealous preoccupation with food, and a dread of obesity. These distinctions also apply for *malnutrition* and *starvation* (e.g., as may occur in *tuberculosis, Crohn's disease, ulcerative colitis, extreme poverty*), as well as various *neurological diseases* (e.g., *epilepsy, brain tumors*). One question can usually distinguish a very thin person from a person with anorexia: "What is your ideal body weight?" Almost all people with anorexia will say something less than their current weight, whereas all others will say, "I need to gain weight, I'm too thin."

Management and Treatment

The legacy of Karen Carpenter, the young pop singer who died from anorexia nervosa (most likely from complications of rapid refeeding), should remind clinicians that the first goal in treatment is always to (1) keep the patient alive. Beyond this, the goals are (in order of priority and treatment focus) (2) establish adequate nutrition, (3) treat physical complications, (4) correct abnormal eating habits, (5) supplant family overinvolvement with more appropriate intrafamilial relationships, (6) enhance self-control, identity, and autonomy, (7) identify and begin correcting dysfunctional thoughts, attitudes, and beliefs, and (8) correct defects in affect and behavioral regulation.

Hospitalization and Behavior Therapy

If the patient's weight is *medically precarious*, hospitalization is mandatory. If matters have so deteriorated that the patient is in danger of losing her life, professionals must take charge. Once hospitalized, treatment follows the same principles set down in 1874 by Sir William Gull, who named the disorder. Patients should be fed at regular intervals and surrounded by persons who would have "moral control" over them; relatives and friends generally are the worst attendants.

Behavior therapy is used first to prevent starvation, restore nutritional balance, and increase weight. Programs can vary as to whether a prescribed minimum weight goal or a minimum caloric goal (using a prescribed diet) must be met to gain privileges or reinforcers. Dietician consultation can be useful, though individuals with anorexia are usually experts on caloric content and daily requirements, albeit distorting these as applying to all except them. The patient may request liquid nutritional supplements because she has difficulty with solid foods. She's weighed every morning in the nude or in a hospital gown, a half hour after voiding, since these patients are pros at adding extra weight in the heels of shoes, hems of night-gowns, by water loading, etc. Bed rest can be a natural consequence of not taking in sufficient calories to burn in daily activities. Tube feeding is used only when the patient goes blow a critical weight associated with medical complications (usually 30% below ideal body weight). All efforts are made to help the patient begin to regain weight naturally, since extended tube feeding not only has medical compli-cations but reinforces feelings of loss of control. Consequences are sometimes built in for bingeing weight gains, e.g., more than 1 pound a day. This program is con-tinued until the patient reaches medically safe weight, usually within 10–15% of the norm. Discharging only at an acceptable weight (below 15% of norm) is risky. After discharge medical personnel, *not the family*, should follow her weight, typi-cally at weekly intervals. Nursing and therapy staff members can offer reassurance to patients by helping them resist the urge to binge and even by assuring them that they (the staff) will not allow the patients to gain excessive weight. Staff members show that they understand her dread of becoming fat and are allies *with* her, not *against* her. This approach undercuts the rebellious aspect of the disorder and circumvents power struggles and fears of loss of control.

Family Therapy

Early on, parents should not have any responsibility for the patient's care. This approach diffuses family tension, permits autonomy for the patient, and gracefully lets the parents "off the hook." In some programs, either a week after admission or once the patient begins to gain weight, informal lunches with the entire family are held to evaluate family interactions at mealtime, to reduce intrafamilial power struggles, and to promote more helpful behavior around the table. These family therapy lunches are continued after discharge to establish more balanced family relationships. Most programs just use traditional family therapy.

Psychotherapy

Psychotherapies are no substitute for proper nutrition and weight gain, and nutrition must be established for the patient to have sufficient cognitive function to be able to utilize psychotherapy. Individual psychotherapy focuses on helping the patient learn to abandon her self-destructive approach to establishing autonomy and find more enduring sources of self-worth and self-control. Variations on assertiveness training are helpful so that patients can learn to say "no" in family conflicts without undercutting or capitulation. *Group therapy* helps patients reestablish lost social skills and view themselves in a more normative manner. Many locales offer self-help groups for patients with eating disorders; these groups are helpful adjuncts, especially when they include consulting professionals.

Medication

Many patients with anorexia have comorbid depression, which sometimes improves with weight restoration. Between 40 and 60% of patients benefit from antidepressants. Malnourished patients are especially sensitive to drugs, so lower doses may be indicated. Orthostatic hypotension and arrhythmias are the biggest risk with the tricyclic antidepressants in malnourished or dehydrated patients. The SSRIs are recommended as a first choice because they don't cause orthostatic hypotension and have minimal effects on heart rhythms. Cyproheptadine (Periactin), a serotonin agonist and antihistamine, is a useful adjunct for weight restoration, primarily if the patient has lost her appetite and can view appetite as a cue to eat and not exercise or play with her food or feel that she is losing control.

BULIMIA NERVOSA AND BINGE-EATING DISORDER

The word *bulimia* means "the hunger of an ox" from the Greek: *bous* = ox, *limos* = hunger. Binge-eating is the central feature of *bulimia*. People with bulimia view their bingeing as pathological, dread their inability to control their eating, and become unhappy and self-deprecating after bingeing. Because they're ashamed, a majority try to hide their problem from those close to them and even clinicians. Although self-induced vomiting occurs in 88%

of patients, it is not a diagnostic requirement. In contrast to anorexia nervosa, severe weight loss is uncommon, and amenorrhea is less common (40%). DSM-IV-TR criteria for bulimia are listed in Table 19-3.

Eating binges last a few minutes to 2 hours. People with bulimia may binge twice a week or over 10 times a day, but between binge episodes they typically engage in food restriction or dieting. Dysphoria usually precedes a binge and is relieved by it. Patients typically give more than one reason for bingeing: feeling anxious or tense (83%), craving certain foods (70%), feeling unhappy (67%), "can't control appetite" (59%), hunger (31)%, and/or insomnia (22%)(Mitchell et al., 1985). Those with bulimia are more likely to binge as the day goes on. While gorging themselves, most patients aren't aware of hunger and don't stop even when satiated. They don't chew, they gobble,

---

TABLE 19-3
DSM-IV-TR *Criteria for Bulimia Nervosa*

A. Recurrent episodes of binge eating. An episode of binge eating is characterized by both of the following:

(1) eating, in a discrete period of time (e.g., within any 2-hour period), an amount of food that is definitely larger than most people would eat during a similar period of time and under similar circumstances

(2) a sense of lack of control over eating during the episode (e.g., a feeling that one cannot stop eating or control what or how much one is eating)

B. Recurrent inappropriate compensatory behavior in order to prevent weight gain, such as self-induced vomiting; misuse of laxatives, diuretics, enemas, or other medications; fasting; or excessive exercise.

C. The binge eating and inappropriate compensatory behaviors both occur, on average, at least twice a week for 3 months.

D. Self-evaluation is unduly influenced by body shape and weight.

E. The disturbance does not occur exclusively during episodes of Anorexia Nervosa.

Specify type:

Purging Type: during the current episode of Bulimia Nervosa, the person has regularly engaged in self-induced vomiting or the misuse of laxatives, diuretics, or enemas

Nonpurging Type: during the current episode of Bulimia Nervosa, the person has used other inappropriate compensatory behaviors, such as fasting or excessive exercise, but has not regularly engaged in self-induced vomiting or the misuse of laxatives, diuretics, or enemas

Note. From *DSM-IV-TR,* p. 594.

preferably foods high in calories and carbohydrates, and easy to devour. Three thousand calories is an average binge, but calorie consumption ranges from 1,200 to 11,500 calories (not a normal portion of food or "three carrots," as a person with anorexia might report). These individuals might binge on 3 pounds of chocolate, popcorn for an army, and 4 pints of ice cream; they might spend well over $100 a day on food; some steal food. To avoid detection, most binge in secrecy, with windows covered and the telephone disconnected.

Bingeing typically stops when the patient is discovered, falls asleep, develops stomach pain, or induces vomiting. By diminishing abdominal cramps and distention, this self-induced vomiting permits further binges. People with bulimia continue to binge in order to delay the inevitable postbinge dysphoria. This dysphoria is described as guilt (87%), feeling too full (64%), worrying (53%), still feeling hungry (22%). (This dysphoria is also associated with a drop in blood sugar associated with the rush of insulin stimulated by carbohydrate bingeing.) A minority feels relaxed (23%) or satisfied (15%). In therapy, patients with bulimia describe their bingeing as "disgusting" but irresistible. When having a normal meal, they fear bingeing again or gaining weight.

These patients are preoccupied with their appearance, body image, and sexual attractiveness, as well as how others, men especially, perceive and respond to them. By using various techniques—binge eating (100%), fasting (92%), exercise (91%), vomiting (88%), spitting out food (65%), laxatives (61%), diet pills (50%), diuretics (34%), saunas (12%)—patients with bulimia can readily add or shed 10 pounds a day. These patients are rarely underweight, and 5% are overweight. Prior to their bulimia, 14% were underweight, and 56% were overweight. They frequently have problems controlling their impulses in other areas. About a third has abused drugs and alcohol and about a fifth has received treatment for it. A minority will steal, engage in self-mutilation, or attempt suicide. To look thin and sexually attractive—a redundancy to bulimics—and to alleviate sadness, they'll go on clothes-buying sprees ("retail therapy"). Unlike those with anorexia, people with bulimia are usually sexually active, and some are promiscuous.

Individuals with *binge-eating disorder* (usually classified in *DSM-IV-TR* under eating disorder NOS) have similar characteristics as those with bulimia but also some differences. They engage in binge eating to a similar extent (though less intensely), but do not engage in compensatory purging behaviors. They have some tendencies toward impulsive behaviors, but not as extreme, with lower association with substance abuse, stealing, and self-mutilation. They are almost always overweight, are less preoccupied with their bodies, and have somewhat of a "hopeless" attitude about their appearance and weight, often shunning sexual activity. They may engage in dieting over a period of weeks or months, only to fall back into binge-eating behaviors (Fairburn, et al., 1993).

Clinical Course and Complications

Bulimia and binge-eating disorder both usually arise later than anorexia, during the late teens or 20s, and rarely after 30. The first episode commonly follows a traumatic event or a period of stringent dieting. Bulimia and binge-eating disorder are chronic disorders, with fluctuating intensity and alternating periods of normal and binge eating. Less often, normal eating doesn't occur; the patient cycles between periods of bingeing and fasting. Anecdotally, patients with bulimia generally improve or completely recover. Death, usually from hypokalemia (low potassium) in people with bulimia, is rare.

> During periods of rapid weight gain, the hands, feet, and ankles of people with bulimia often swell from a "refeeding edema." These patients endure weakness (84%), abdominal bloating (75%), stomach pain (63%), headaches, and dizziness. They get sore throats from the vomiting (54%), painful swellings of salivary and parotid glands (called "chipmunk" or "puffy" cheeks) (50%), dental caries from loss of enamel (37%), and finger calluses (on their gagging fingers). Menstrual irregularities are common, and 40% have intermittent or sustained amenorrhea. If they use Ipecac to make them vomit, they are at risk of death from cardiomyopathy. Individuals with binge-eating disorder suffer more from the complications of obesity, often morbid obesity.
>
> Dehydration is common in underweight patients with bulimia who use diuretics or vomit after bingeing. Electrolyte imbalance, most often hypokalemic alkalosis, occurs in about half of these patients. It can result from vomiting as well as diuretic and laxative abuse. The hypokalemia can cause patients to feel lethargic and cognitively dulled and may even lead to serious or life-threatening cardiac conduction abnormalities. Because of the problems in thinking, hypokalemia should be corrected before psychotherapy is attempted. Patients report problems with intimate or interpersonal relations (70%), family (61%), finances (because of food purchasing) (53%), and work (50%).

Epidemiology

Like the young woman with anorexia, the prototypic youngster with bulimia is a white, adolescent girl from the middle or upper class, who attends a university. However, bulimia has been increasing among Latinas and African-

Americans of college age and young adulthood, and in people of lower socioeconomic status, as they increasingly adopt Western and upwardly mobile body image ideals. Ninety to 95% of people with bulimia are female. The prevalence of bulimia varies enormously depending on the particular subpopulation. Although the prevalence is less than 0.5% in the general population, in a survey of 500 college students, 4.4% reported eating disorders; 86% of these had bulimia using the less restrictive *DSM-III* criteria, whereas only 14% had anorexia nervosa (Strangler & Printz, 1980).

Binge eating disorder has a higher male representation, approximately 30% though it too is seen predominantly in women. It is seen in greater frequency in people of lower socioeconomic status. It may also have an overall greater prevalence in the general population (2%) and is common (about 30%) in patients seeking treatment for obesity at university affiliated weight programs (Dingemans, Bruna, & van Furth, 2002). One characteristic in common between individuals with bulimia and binge eating disorders is a personal history of sexual abuse, which may explain both their impulsivity and ambivalence about their bodies and sexuality.

Etiology and Pathogenesis

Very little is known about the causes of bulimia. Descriptive and biological psychiatrists have noted a relationship between bulimia and other psychiatric disorders. About 75% of individuals with bulimia develop major depression; 43% have anxiety disorders; 49% have substance disorders; and 50–75% has personality disorders or trait disturbances (usually in cluster B). First-degree relatives of people with bulimia have a higher frequency of mood disorder, substance abuse, and obesity (Yager, Devlin, et al., 2006). A similar association exists between binge eating disorders and mood, anxiety, and personality disorders or traits—clusters B and C (Dingemans, Bruna, & van Furth, 2002).

Families in which a member has bulimia appear enmeshed but disengaged. In comparing 105 bulimic with 86 control families, Johnson and Flach (1985) found that the former set high expectations, but placed small emphasis on their daughter's intellectual, cultural, or recreational activities. Despite the fact that the overall structure and rules of families with a bulimic member resembled those in normal families, the "bulimic families" were more disorganized, showing lack of ability to solve problems, manage crises, or get things done. A high prevalence of domestic violence and abuse is found in these families. Although high expectations were also seen in the control families, the disorganization and lack of concern for patients' activities in the affected families best correlated with the severity of the patients' symptoms. The families of individuals with binge eating disorder have been found to be disorganized, but more neglectful than abusive.

Differential Diagnosis

Distinguishing between anorexia nervosa and bulimia is the only common diagnostic difficulty. Few people make a habit of bingeing and vomiting, except for those with bulimia and 40–50% of those with anorexia. There is a continuum between the two disorders, with pure "restricting type" of patients with anorexia at one end and "pure bulimics" at the other. Those with anorexia who binge and purge are in the middle of that spectrum. Those with anorexia who binge (the bulimic subtype) are more akin to normal-weight individuals with bulimia than to those with anorexia who don't binge (the restrictive subtype). In comparison to those with restrictive anorexia, normal-weight individuals with bulimia and those with bulimia anorexia perceive more family conflict and are more impulsive, outgoing, sexually active, and emotionally disturbed; they may be more prone to depression and have twice as many relatives with mood disorders.

Management and Treatment

Medical Complications

The medical complications associated with bulimia are related to the individual aspects of the illness. These must always be addressed first in evaluation and treatment because several are life-threatening and disabling.

Electrolyte imbalance, resulting from vomiting as well as diuretic and laxative abuse, occurs in about half of patients with bulimia. Hypokalemic alkalosis is particularly common. The hypokalemia (low potassium) can lead to serious, even life-threatening cardiac conduction abnormalities. This condition can cause patients to feel lethargic, weak, and cognitively dulled.

Patients with bulimia who use diuretics may experience dehydration and rebound edema as well as the electrolyte disturbances mentioned earlier. Some patients use syrup of Ipecac to induce vomiting. Its active ingredient, emetine, can produce myopathies, both generalized and cardiomyopathy. This is a particularly insidious complication because the effect of the emetine is cumulative. Patients with bulimia who misuse laxatives are at risk for laxative dependency, steatorrhea, protein-losing gastroenteropathy, and gastrointestinal bleeding. Laxatives will cause the person with bulimia to lose only 3% of calories consumed. Many individuals with bulimia, when informed of this fact, quit this dangerous method. To avoid an atonic bowel, excessive laxatives should be slowly tapered, not stopped abruptly.

Parotid gland enlargement (chipmunk cheeks) is common among patients with bulimia, but the mechanism for this is unknown. As many as a third of these patients may have elevated serum amylase levels; however, this does not appear to be correlated with the presence of parotid gland enlargement, and both salivary and pancreatic isoenzyme may be involved. Dental erosion and numerous cavities are common with vomiting. Menstrual irregularities are also common in these patients, even those of normal weight. Gastric or esophageal rupture (which can be fatal) is a rare complication of binge eating, whereas acute gastric dilation is a common and a painful result of it.

Hospitalization

Most patients with bulimia are best treated as outpatients, but four conditions warrant the intervention of hospitalization: (1) to manage a medical emergency (electrolyte imbalances, severe orthostatic hypertension, or precipitous weight loss); (2) to break a severe, recalcitrant binge–starve cycle; (3) to evaluate diagnostically or deal with a family crisis; or (4) to respond to a suicidal crisis.

Medication

Bulimia, or at least bingeing, is moderately responsive to antidepressants (TCAs, SSRIs, and MAOIs) over 6–8 weeks (Yager, Devlin, et al., 2006). On average, antidepressants decrease binge frequencies of patients with bulimia by 50%, with 20% achieving complete recovery. Both depressed and nondepressed patients with bulimia show equally effective responses. Higher doses (approximately 60 mg) of fluoxetine, work better than the usual antidepressant dose (20 mg). When patients with bulimia are treated with antidepressants alone for 6 months or more, there are many dropouts, and by 12 months, antidepressants do no better than placebo (Walsh, 1991). When antidepressants are combined with cognitive–behavioral therapy, there are fewer dropouts and possibly an additive effect of the therapy (Abbot & Mitchell, 1993). Patients who don't respond to the usual antidepressants still may respond to MAOIs. Antidepressants may be most useful in "jumpstarting" a person's recovery while awaiting the delayed positive effects of psychotherapy. Those who are excellent responders could elect to stay on their medication, but antidepressants could also be reserved for patients who aren't progressing with psychotherapy alone. Similar results are reported with binge eating disorder in terms of antidepressant responsiveness and the benefits of combined pharmacological and psychotherapeutic approaches.

Psychotherapy

Individual and group therapy using either cognitive–behavioral or psychodynamic (particularly, interpersonal) approaches are quite effective in treating bulimia and binge eating disorders. Generally there are two phases to the treatment. Phase 1 focuses on breaking the binge–purge cycle in the case of bulimia (for binge eating disorders the focus is on the binge eating triggers) — a behavioral approach can quickly reduce bingeing and purging. The patient keeps a careful record of food intake, vomiting, purgative abuse, and the context of bingeing (time, place, mood, etc.). The abnormal pattern of eating is then shaped into a more normal pattern by avoiding precipitants of binges and substituting alternative pleasurable activities (e.g., showers, baths, walks, talk to a friend on the phone). Patients are also instructed to practice delaying (but not necessarily stopping) vomiting, especially if it happens after normal meals. For example, they may try to wait 30 minutes before vomiting, having succeeded at waiting 25 minutes the day before.

Phase 2 focuses on broad areas of behavior and attitudes — cognitive–behavioral therapy (CBT) appears to be best. CBT is as effective as behavioral and interpersonal therapy at reducing bingeing and depression and more effective in modifying disturbed attitudes toward shape, weight, dieting, and the use of vomiting to control shape and weight (Agras, 1991; Yager, Devlin, et al., 2006). Patients who participate in CBT show greater overall improvement. Dietary management helps further. One goal is eating for weight maintenance to break the binge–fast roller coaster. Group therapy works at least as well as individual therapy in this phase. Behavioral therapy is particularly effective in reducing binge eating in individuals with binge eating disorder, but interpersonal psychotherapy may be equally effective after binge control is established, given its focus on reducing interpersonal isolation (Dingemans, Bruna, van Furth, 2002).

Mortality for bulimia is 1% within 10 years of diagnosis (Sullivan, 1995) and is largely associated with suicide over medical complications. The overall short-term prognosis is about 70% reduction in bingeing and purging, with reasonably good maintenance of gains over 6 years. The mortality for binge eating disorder is not known.

References

Abbott, D.W., & Mitchell, J.E. (1993). Antidepressants vs. psychotherapy in the treatment of bulimia nervosa. *Psychopharmacology Bulletin, 29,* 115–119.

Agras, W.S. (1991). Nonpharmacologic treatments of bulimia nervosa. *Journal of Clinical Psychiatry, 52,* 29–33.

Amdur, M.J., Tucker, G.J., Detre, T.D., & Markhus, K. (1969). Anorexia nervosa: An interactional study. *Journal of Nervous and Mental Diseases, 148,* 559–566.

Andersen, A.E., & Holman, J.E. (1997). Males with eating disorders: Challenges for treatment and research. *Psychopharmacology Bulletin, 33*(3), 391–397.

Baranowska, B., Baranowska-Bik, A., Bik, W., & Martynska, L. (2008). The role of leptin and orexins in the dysfunction of hypothalamo-pituitary-gonadal regulation and in the mechanism of hyperactivity in patients with anorexia nervosa. *Neuro Endocrinol Lett., 29,* 37–40.

Dingemans, A., Bruna, M., & van Furth, E. (2002). Binge eating disorder: A review. *International Journal of Obesity and Related Metabolic Disorders, 26,* 299–307.

Fairburn, C.G., Jones, R., Peveler, R.C., Hope, R.A., & O'Connor, M. (1993). Psychotherapy and bulimia nervosa. *Archives of General Psychiatry, 50,* 419–428.

Fairburn, C.G., Marcus, M., & Wilson, G. (1993). Cognitive–behavioral therapy for binge eating and bulimia nervosa: A comprehensive treatment manual. In C. Fairburn & G. Wilson (Eds.), *Binge eating: Nature, assessment, and treatment* (pp. 361–404). New York: Guillford Press.

Favaro, A., Tenconi, E., & Santonastaso, P. (2006). Perinatal factors and the risk of developing anorexia nervosa and bulimia nervosa. *Archives of General Psychiatry, 63,* 82–88.

Gustavson, C., Gustavson, J., Noller, K., O'Brien, P., Melton, L., Pumariega, A., et al. (1991). Increased risk of profound weight loss among women exposed to diethylstilbestrol in utero. *Behavioral Neural Biology, 55,* 307–312.

Hart, K.J., & Ollendick, T.H. (1985). Prevalence of bulimia in working and university women. *American Journal of Psychiatry, 142,* 851–854.

Hsu, L.K.G. (1986). The treatment of anorexia nervosa. *American Journal of Psychiatry, 143,* 573–581.

Hsu, L.K.G. (1990). *Eating disorders.* New York: Guilford Press.

Johnson, C., & Flach, A. (1985). Family characteristics of 105 patients with bulimia. *American Journal of Psychiatry, 142,* 1321–1324.

Lawson, E.A., & Klibanski, A. (2008). Endocrine abnormalities in anorexia nervosa. *Nat Clin Pract Endocrinol Metab., 4,* 407–414.

Lucas, A.R., Beard, C., O'Fallon, W., & Kurland, L. (1991). Fifty-year trends in the incidence of anorexia nervosa in Rochester, Minn.: A population-based study. *American Journal of Psychiatry, 148,* 917–922.

Miller, M., & Pumariega, A.J. (2001). Eating disorders: A historical and cross-cultural review. *Psychiatry: Interpersonal and Biological Processes, 64*(2), 93–110.

Mitchell, J.E., Hatsukami, D., Eckert, E.D., & Pyle, R.L. (1985). Characteristics of 275 patients with bulimia. *American Journal of Psychiatry, 142,* 482–488.

Minuchin, S., Rosman, B.L., & Baker, L. (1978). *Psychosomatic Families*. Boston: Harvard University Press.

Norman, K. (1984). Eating disorders. In H.H. Goldman (Ed.), *Review of general psychiatry* (pp. 464–480). Los Altos, CA: Lange.

Procopio, M., & Marriott, P. (2007). Intrauterine hormonal environment and risk of developing anorexia nervosa. *Archives of General Psychiatry, 64*, 1402–1408.

Pumariega, A.J. (1986). Acculturation and eating attitudes in adolescent girls: A comparative and correlational study. *Journal of the American Academy of Child Psychiatry, 25*(2), 276–279.

Pumariega, A.J., Gustavson, C.R., Gustavson, J.C., Motes, P., & Ayers, S. (1994). Eating attitudes in African American women: The *Essence* Eating Disorders Survey. *Eating Disorders: The Journal of Treatment and Prevention, 2*(1), 5–16.

Pumariega, A.J., Pursell, J., Spock, A., & Jones, J.D. (1986). Eating disorders in adolescents with cystic fibrosis. *Journal of the American Academy of Child Psychiatry, 25*(2), 269–275.

Ramoz, N., Versini, A., & Gorwood, P. (2007). Eating disorders: An overview of treatment responses and the potential impact of vulnerability genes and endophenotypes. *Expert Opin Pharmacother., 8*, 2029–2044.

Strangler, R.S., & Printz, A.M. (1980). DSM-III: Psychiatric diagnosis in a university population. *American Journal of Psychiatry, 137*, 937–940.

Strober, M., Freeman, R., & Morrell, W. (1997). The long-term course of severe anorexia nervosa in adolescents: Survival analysis of recovery, relapse, and outcome predictors over 10–15 years in a prospective study. *International Journal of Eating Disorders, 22*, 339–360.

Sullivan, P.F. (1995). Mortality in anorexia nervosa. *American Journal of Psychiatry, 152*, 1073–1074.

Theander, S. (1985). Outcome and prognosis in anorexia nervosa and bulimia. *Journal of Psychiatric Research, 19*, 493–508.

Torsello, A., Brambilla, F., Tamiazzo, L., Bulgarelli, I., Rapetti, D., Bresciani, E., & Locatelli, V. (2007). Central dysregulations in the control of energy homeostasis and endocrine alterations in anorexia and bulimia nervosa. *J Endocrinol Invest., 30*, 962–976.

Walsh, B.T. (1991). Psychopharmacologic treatment of bulimia nervosa. *Journal of Clinical Psychiatry, 52*, 34–38.

Walsh, B.T., Hadigan, C.M., Devlin, M.J., Gladis, M., & Roose, S.P. (1991). Long-term outcome of antidepressant treatment for bulima nervosa. *American Journal of Psychiatry, 148*, 1206–1212.

Yager, J., Devlin, M., Halmi, K., Herzog, D., Mitchell, J., Powers, P., & Zerbe, K. (2006). *Practice guidelines for the treatment of patients with eating disorders* (3rd ed.). Washington, DC: American Psychiatric Association. http://www.psychiatryonline.com/praGuide/praGuideHouse.ASPX (Accessed on August 10, 2008).

20

Sleep Disorders

After centuries of studying disorders in patients in the awake state, more emphasis is now being focused on the abnormalities that may occur in patients while asleep. The results of the National Sleep Foundation's 2008 Sleep in America Poll emphasize the current adverse effects of American sleep patterns. Nearly a third of those surveyed said they only get a good night's sleep a few nights per month. Twenty-nine percent said they became sleepy or fell asleep at work in the past month, and 36% of drivers admitted to having nodded off in the past year. Twenty percent said they have lost interest in sex because of sleepiness. The negative responses correlate with increased work hours.

The study of sleep disorders did not occur until the development of the electroencephalograph in the late 1920s. Before the development of EEG, sleep was assumed to be a uniform state of cortical suppression, and sleep stages were unknown. In 1937, Dr. Robert Schab opened the first clinical department for EEG services in the United States at Massachusetts General Hospital.

Sleep disorders medicine encompasses several disciplines, including neurology, psychiatry, pulmonary, otolaryngology, urology, and primary care. The first issue of *Sleep*, the major journal, was published in 1979. There has been a steady rise of sleep medicine practitioners, sleep disorders clinics, and public awareness of the importance of sleep.

An important discovery in the field of sleep occurred in 1951. Rapid eye movement (REM) and nonrapid eye movement (NREM) were identified as differing in significant ways in sleeping infants. The eyes moved slowly after sleep onset but then began moving more rapidly in vertical and horizontal directions for several minutes. The movement ceased for a while but then restarted in a similar pattern. The same ocular movements were noted in sleeping adults, but the timing was different. In infants, rapid eye movements appeared earlier; in adults there was a latency after sleep onset of 60–90 minutes before the eye movements began. The slow tracings were called nonrapid eye movements (NREM), and the fast tracings rapid eye movements (REM). Later, other discoveries about REM sleep were made. It was found that dreams were recalled if the subject was awakened during REM sleep but were seldom recalled in NREM sleep. Inserting an electromyogram needle into voluntary muscles showed near silence when subjects were in REM sleep. Erections were noted in REM sleep, and they disappeared in NREM sleep. The longer that patients were in NREM sleep, the harder they became to arouse. This depth of sleep coincided with the appearance on EEG tracings of large-amplitude slow waves, which were called delta waves. In NREM sleep, cardiac rate, blood pressure, respirations, and cortical blood flow decrease, whereas in REM these functions are more variable. In infants, NREM is termed "quiet sleep" and REM "active sleep" because of the eye movements and variability in pulse and respiration. Dreaming is no longer seen as a REM-only activity; in fact, some dreaming may occur in NREM sleep, but these dreams are of shorter duration and less exciting, whereas REM-related dreams are more vivid, action-filled, and exotic (Dement & Kleitman, 1957; Dement, 1990).

NREM sleep consumes about three-quarters of all sleep time in adults. At bedtime, older children and adults doze off into NREM sleep, descending from light stages (N1) to intermediate (N2), which comprises about 50% of our total sleep time, and then into deep, or delta, stage (N3). With each stage, the brain waves become slower and of higher amplitude as sleep deepens, and the patient becomes harder to arouse. The greatest percentage of delta, or deep, sleep is in the first third of the sleep-period time, and most REM sleep is in the last third. About 70–90 minutes after sleep onset, the first REM sleep appears. As the night proceeds, the duration of REM sleep increases so that the initial REM period lasts a few minutes whereas the final REM episode may last about 20–30 minutes. If a sleeping individual awakens during or immediately after a dream, he or she is more likely to recall the dream. Four to five NREM–REM sleep cycles complete the night. When not fully awake but drowsy, people are in the N1 stage, and some awareness of the environment is often present; hence, patients may deny that they were sleeping when actually they were. Any awakening from deeper sleep lasting less than 2–3 minutes may be forgotten the next morning, for example, a phone call or a storm at night.

Sleep patterns fluctuate throughout the lifespan. Newborns sleep from 14 to 18 hours each day and spend 50% of total sleep time in REM sleep. By 6 months, the total sleep time declines to about 14 hours, and REM sleep time declines to about one-third of the sleep time. NREM sleep time increases to two-thirds and reaches adult percentages by adolescence. Between ages 20 and 60, the average total sleep time dips from 8 or 9 to about 7 hours, but delta sleep declines from 23 to 8% of the total sleep time. So, when older adults complain about insomnia, they need to understand the natural change in the length of their sleep and the sleep architecture.

How much sleep do people need? Only as much as to feel refreshed the following day. Sleep requirements vary with age and individuals (Table 20-1), and all agree that one main function of sleep is to eliminate sleepiness the following day. There is nothing magical or sacred about 8 hours of sleep. Short sleepers are often more efficient at sleeping and have higher percentages of deep and REM sleep. What is more, total sleep time can vary from night to night as long as the general sleep pattern is restorative and refreshing over time.

Three sources are available to diagnose sleep disorders: patients, bed partners, and sleep clinics. Each has their own limits and strong points. For example, people with insomnia typically overestimate the time it takes them to fall asleep and underestimate their total sleep time. Therefore, self-reports may reflect sleep-state misperceptions, which are common in patients who are dissatisfied with their sleep. For some disorders, bed partners can provide key facts that the patients cannot, such as snoring, sleep apnea, and periodic leg movements, which can be part of restless legs syndrome. Sleep clinics, whose numbers have increased dramatically across the country, have provided much-needed help for patients. These clinics are a source of diagnostic and therapeutic assistance for a variety of sleep disorders, which now number 85, according to the latest classification (International Classification of Sleep Dis-

TABLE 20-1

Average Amount of Sleep per Day

AGE	SLEEP IN HOURS
Newborn	Up to 18
1–12 months	14–18
1–3 years	12–15
3–5 years	11–13
5–12 years	9–11
Adolescents	9–10
Adults, including elderly	7–8
Pregnant women	variable

orders, 2005). Clinics accredited by the American Academy of Sleep Medicine offer four forms of tests: a polysomnogram, multiple sleep latency test, maintenance of wakefulness test, and portable screening studies for home use, which offer an advantage of convenience for patients unable to come to the sleep center or who simply need a follow-up screening study rather than a complete polysomnogram.

The polysomnogram (PSG) records brain-wave activity (electroencephalogram or EEG), an electromyogram (EMG) that transcribes minute electrical currents from muscle fibers to detect muscle relaxation, and an electrooculogram (EOG) that charts slow and rapid-eye movements. The EMG and EOG are important in detecting REM sleep. A finger pulse oximeter measures moment-by-moment oxygen saturations, an EKG monitor for heart rhythm and rate, and surface electrodes to detect periodic leg movements. The PSG is performed overnight unless the patient is a night worker and then the study is performed in daytime.

The multiple sleep latency test (MSLT) is an objective way to measure daytime sleepiness. The patient is given five nap opportunities throughout the day, and the number of naps and speed of sleep onset are noted. In addition, the presence and number of REM sleep periods are noted. Since REM sleep normally does not occur until 70–90 minutes after sleep onset, the appearance of REM sleep in a 20-minute nap is important and suggests narcolepsy, a hypersomnolent condition, or prior REM sleep deprivation. Among the medications causing REM suppression are tricyclic antidepressants (TCAs) and selective serotonin reuptake inhibitors (SSRIs).

The maintenance of wakefulness test (MWT) is the third type of sleep procedure performed. This test measures a patient's ability to stay awake and is important in occupations where vigilance determines safety, such as truck drivers, railroad engineers, and pilots. This test is similar to the MSLT except that the subject is instructed to stay awake rather than try to sleep. An inability to stay awake may disqualify the person from his or her occupation until sleepiness is corrected. Several illustrative sleep tracings are included at the end of this chapter.

Understanding sleep disorders requires a familiarity with, but not a mastery of, their classifications. The original classification consisted of four categories:

1. Disorders of initiating and maintaining sleep (insomnias)
2. Disorders of excessive somnolence (e.g., obstructive sleep apnea syndrome, narcolepsy)
3. Disorders of the sleep–wake schedule (circadian rhythm disturbance)

TABLE 20-2

International Classification of Sleep Disorders-2 (ICSD-2) 2005

I.   Insomnias

II.   Sleep-related breathing disorders

III. Hypersomnias, of central origin, not due to a circadian rhythm sleep disorder, sleep-related breathing disorder, or other cause of disturbed nocturnal sleep

IV.   Circadian rhythm sleep disorders

V.   Parasomnias

VI.   Sleep-related movement disorders

VII. Isolated symptoms, apparently normal variants, and unresolved issues

VIII. Other sleep disorders

---

4. Dysfunctions associated with sleep, sleep stages, or partial arousals (parasomnias)

This initial classification has been revised and expanded to eight categories but remains basic to the understanding of sleep disorders and still serves as an important introductory model (Table 20-2).

The categories apply to adults and children. Some sleep disorders may overlap categories or be multifactorial; hence the reason for categories VII and VIII. Some entities are grouped more on the basis of symptoms, and some more on presumed etiologies.

This classification is quite compatible with the International Classification of Diseases (ICD-10) and the *DSM-IV-TR*. Codes for various disorders are revised and listed annually on the National Center for Health Care Statistics website (http://www.cdc.gov/nchs/icd9.htm). The secondary sleep disorders, i.e., those due to mental, neurological, or other medical disorders, are not included in the ICSD-2. Following ICD rules, as soon as the underlying mental, neurological, or other medical disorder is diagnosed, it becomes the primary diagnosis, and the previous sleep-related diagnosis is usually dropped as it is seen as a symptom of the underlying disorder. This chapter discusses the more common sleep conditions and the ones most likely to be encountered in clinical settings.

INSOMNIA

Insomnia is characterized by reports of some, or all, of the following three complaints: trouble getting to sleep, trouble staying asleep, and daytime symptoms resulting from the first two symptoms. There must be a report of sleep dissatisfaction affecting daytime functioning for a diagnosis of insomnia. It may be expressed as feelings of fatigue, altered mood, frustration, or all of these, but seldom do people with insomnia report excessive daytime sleepiness to the extent reported by normal individuals with sleep apnea, narcolepsy, or temporary sleep deprivation. People with chronic insomnia are seldom able to nap, although they report feeling very fatigued. Another way to express the impact of insomnia, which patients should understand, is that it is a 24-hour problem, not just a nocturnal one. It is a disorder of hyperarousal, both nocturnal and daytime. Support for hyperarousal is found in the EEG pattern. Less deep sleep (delta) and frequent awake rhythm (alpha) intrusions into the sleep rhythms are commonly seen in insomniac tracings.

Taking a history from individuals with insomnia frequently elicits some precipitating factor (or factors) that predated the onset of insomnia. Such causes may be found in the psychiatric realm, such as depression or anxiety disorders, whereas other causes may include circadian factors (e.g., shift work), a variety of medical conditions, or substance dependence. Once insomnia begins, it may be propagated unintentionally by the person's excessive concern about sleeplessness and the negative conditioning it elicits. The fear and apprehension of another bad night become a self-fulfilling prophecy. If awakened from sleep, the person's first thoughts may be about whether he or she will be able to return to sleep. These individuals often become anxious as bedtime approaches, and they begin their nightly rituals. Excessive clock watching reinforces their negativity about getting a good night's sleep. Such situations may lead to self-prescribing alcohol, over-the-counter sleep aids, or seeking a prescription from their health-care provider. The longer this hyperarousal state persists at night, the more difficult it becomes to treat.

> No discussion of insomnia would be complete without mention of the contribution of Arthur Spielman and colleagues (1987). His model of insomnia is widely quoted and known as the "three P's"—predisposition, precipitation, and propagation. The first is that some individuals have a predisposition to insomnia. Spielman's explanation focuses on personality traits that make one vulnerable to insomnia in the face of certain stressors. Some stressors may precipitate insomnia, which, if it resolves, would fit the category of transient, or situational, insomnia. But maladaptive reactions to the insomnia may perpetuate poor sleep, which becomes chronic insomnia. These reactions may come in the form of napping, self-medication, or excessive preoccupation about poor sleep—all of which cause hyperarousal at bedtime. Not all people with insomnia fit this model, but many do.

TABLE 20-3
DSM-IV-TR *Criteria for Primary Insomnia*

A. The predominant complaint is difficulty in initiating or maintaining sleep, or nonrestorative sleep, for at least 1 month.

B. The sleep disturbance (or associated daytime fatigue) causes clinically significant distress or impairment in social, occupational, or other important areas of functioning.

C. The sleep disturbance does not occur exclusively during the course of Narcolepsy, Sleep-Related Breathing Disorders, Circadian Rhythm Disorders, or a Parasomnia.

D. The disturbance does not occur exclusively during the course of another mental disorder (e.g., Major Depressive Disorder, Generalized Anxiety Disorder, Delirium).

E. The disturbance is not due to the direct physiological effects of a substance (e.g., a drug of abuse, medication) or general medical condition (*DSM-IV-TR,* p. 604).

Transient, or short-term, insomnia is the most common type and familiar to most adults. Precipitating causes are numerous and range from events such as anticipation of an important activity to relationship problems to illnesses, ad infinitum. Short-term insomnia usually lasts a month or less. Once the problem has resolved, the person regains his or her normal sleep pattern. Trouble arises when excessive concern about sleep loss leads to negative conditioning, and the process becomes chronic. Preventing the evolution of a transient, or situational insomnia into a chronic one can often be achieved by short-term use of hypnotics or antianxiety medications, under close supervision and tapering the medication quickly when indicated. A few office visits and counseling can be helpful as well. Patients who do not come to their health care providers for situational insomnias may begin to self-medicate; if their condition evolves into chronic insomnia with medication dependency, it can be much more difficult to treat.

Primary insomnia is a disorder that persists for more than a month and is not caused by a mental disorder, medical condition, or substance abuse. Although stress often initiates this insomnia, sleeplessness by itself may persist long after the stress is resolved. Before primary insomnia is diagnosed, all other specific causes of insomnia must first be considered and eliminated. The *DSM-IV-TR* criteria for primary insomnia give a succinct description of the disorder (Table 20-3).

EPIDEMIOLOGY

The overall prevalence of insomnia in the United States varies from 8 to 18% and may be higher in people over 60 years old. It is not known how many of these have primary insomnia. Insomnia occurs more often in women, unemployed, and unmarried individuals. People with primary insomnia tend to have higher depression, hypochondriasis, and hysteria scales on the Minnesota Multiphasic Personality Inventory (MMPI). It is well known among sleep medicine physicians that people with insomnia often underestimate their time asleep. They adopt the notion that everyone needs 8 hours of sleep and worry that they do not get it. Ideally, one should obtain the amount of sleep that leaves one feeling refreshed in the mornings and eliminates excessive sleepiness and fatigue the next day. Catastrophizing about not meeting a certain goal of 8 hours of sleep, especially in the middle of the night, is very counterproductive. Dysfunctional thinking that one will not be able to function without more sleep is negative thinking to be avoided.

Management and Treatment

In many cases, eliminating obvious causes of insomnia may be enough. Adding activities that help promote sleep may help even more. Vigorous daytime exercise often improves sleep, but exercise in the hours just before bedtime may actually delay sleep. Pleasurable and satisfying sexual intercourse can help people get to sleep, but unsatisfying sex will delay it. Relaxation and stretching exercises may be helpful (Ohayon, 2002), but the exercises need to be practiced regularly so that they can be condensed to under 15 minutes. Doing 45 minutes of relaxation exercises to treat a 35-minute-sleep-onset latency problem doesn't make much sense. Ear plugs or reading may help to decrease stimulation and create a soothing environment.

How to Become an Insomniac

1. Keep an unrealistic goal of the number of hours of sleep you should have. If you really only need 6 or 7 hours, make 8 or 9 the goal. If you are age 65 or over and once needed 8 hours but now need only 7 hours, ignore that and shoot for 8 hours.
2. Catastrophize about not meeting this goal, especially in the middle of the night. For example, think, "I will never be able to function tomorrow unless I get more sleep. I probably will [fail, flunk, get fired—nonsleeper's choice] if I don't sleep enough."
3. Remember, hours of insomnia expand proportionally to the number of hours spent in bed. If you need 7 hours of sleep in every 24 hours and spend 9 hours in bed, you can guarantee at least 2 hours of insomnia. Taking a 1-hour nap during the day can help increase this to 3 hours of insomnia.

Because you now have had 3 hours of insomnia, spend 10 hours in bed the next night trying to get enough sleep.

4. Spend all of the desperate hours fighting to get to sleep in bed. In Pavlovian fashion, this will make the bed a stimulus for profound upset.

5. Make the bed a center for many other daily activities—reading, writing, TV, etc. The bed then becomes a cue for many more things than sleep.

6. If you have the opportunity, start taking sleeping medications. Over-the-counter antihistaminic ones are best because they are relatively ineffectual, tolerance develops within days, and they suppress REM sleep. Consequently, if you try to stop taking them, you will have vicious REM rebound with many nightmares. Continue to increase the dosage to get enough sleep. The benzodiazepines aren't quite as effective at creating insomnia, but over weeks and months tolerance can develop, REM rebound can occur, and variations on benzodiazepine withdrawal might also occur, worsening the insomnia.

Cognitive–Behavioral Therapy

Cognitive–behavioral therapy is often applied to the treatment of insomnia. It includes the application of good sleep hygiene, sleep restriction, and stimulus control to the person's behavior. One tries to counter the dysfunctional beliefs and attitudes as well as cognitive distortions to which the person with insomnia adheres. But replacing these thoughts with positive ones pertaining to sleep is not easy. When encountering a person with chronic insomnia, the clinician begins with a discussion of what is known about sleep and how it evolves over an adult's lifetime. The variations in individual sleep patterns and the reality that everyone has a bad night now and then are emphasized. The patient is reassured that she can regain better sleep but may have to be content with less than perfection every night. The patient is made aware of the fact that long-term insomnia seldom leads to any predictable, serious deteriorations in health, although it does have a negative effect on mood and can lead to depression. Use of sleep hygiene is always a cornerstone of treatment of any sleep disorder (see Table 20-4). Stimulus control, which is directed at reducing undesirable time awake in bed, is important, as is sleep restriction, which is a paradoxical intention of changing the patient's focus from trying to sleep to trying to stay awake. Natural, nonpharmacological methods effective in promoting sleep are sleep deprivation, regular exercise, and muscle relaxation—preferably all three together. Reading often decreases stimulation at night and changes one's mental imagery into more interesting areas than the ruminating, worrisome thoughts that preoccupy the person with insomnia. If the patient is on chronic medication for sleep, a slow tapering plan may be introduced, but

TABLE 20-4
Sleep Hygiene

1. Keep a fairly regular sleep onset and awakening schedule.
2. Avoid excessive napping, especially in the evening.
3. Make your sleep environment as noise- and light-free as possible. Pets and children sleep in another room. Cooler room temperatures may help.
4. Avoid watching television in bed. If some activity is preferred before lights out, read or listen to music. Sexual activity usually promotes sleep.
5. Regular exercise is helpful if not too close to bedtime. Otherwise, it may be stimulating.
6. Avoid caffeine, nicotine, and alcohol 4 hours before bedtime.
7. Do not watch the clock if you awaken at night. Setting the alarm eliminates worry about oversleeping.
8. Winding down 1 to 2 hours before bedtime with a warm shower or bath as well as stretching exercises is encouraged. Cooling off promotes sleep.
9. Avoid upsetting discussions just before bedtime.

---

some patients can never seem to completely desist from intermittent use at stressful or anxious times, and infrequent doses are allowed to be used as a rescue therapy if they have experienced two or three bad nights. Tapering hypnotic medication involves two steps. First, the nightly dose is reduced. Next, an attempt is made to omit one dose per night per week. The actual number of hours these patients are sleeping is determined.

Pharmacological Treatment

When given the choice between the above cognitive–behavioral approach— which involves several sessions, an uncomfortable separation from a sleeping aid, and the time and expense of the program—or medication, some patients may choose the route of taking a sleeping pill at bedtime. A novel group of nonbenzodiazepine hypnotic agents—benzodiazepine receptor agonists—are now available and offer advantages over older hypnotic drugs. Because of their specific agonist effects on certain gamma-aminobutyric acid (GABA) receptors, they promote sleep but do not have myorelaxant and anticonvulsive properties, as do older benzodiazepines. These newer drugs have less effect on the sleep stages, and produce much less rebound insomnia. Three are available in the United States and differ mainly in their durations of action. Zaleplon (Sonata) is rapidly absorbed and has a half-life of about 1 hour, making it useful for patients with sleep-onset insomnia or for the troublesome older-age problem of awakening too early in the morning. In either situation, lingering side effects are not very prevalent in the morning. Zolpidem (Ambien, Ambien CR) is also rapidly absorbed and has a half-life of 2–3 hours, so it should be taken at sleep-onset only. A longer-acting preparation with both fast-release and delayed-release properties is available as Ambien CR. The last is eszopiclone (Lunesta), which has a longer half-life, is also suited for sleep-onset and sleep-maintenance insomnias, and should definitely be given only at sleep onset. Eszopiclone received approval for a longer-term use, which was a change from the short-term usage previously recommended for earlier drugs. The newest hypnotic to be approved, ramelteon (Rozerem), differs from others by being a melatonin agonist and targeting the circadian sleep–wake cycle.

An understanding of ramelteon's action requires a review of the circadian physiology. Light, especially from outdoors, stimulates the retinohypothalamic pathway and activates a group of neurons called the "suprachiasmatic nucleus" (SCN), which in turn connects to the pineal gland and shuts off melatonin production, setting in motion the awake portion of the sleep cycle. Darkness favors melatonin production, inhibition of the SCN, and the onset of sleep. Exogenous melatonin given in the evening phase-advances the sleep cycle by inhibiting the SCN and allowing sleep-promoting areas of the brain to dominate. Ramelteon is a potent melatonin agonist, which shuts off the waking stimulation of the SCN in the hypothalamus. Ramelteon is given as a single dose before bedtime and has very little immediate hypnotic effect itself, acting to promote sleep by affecting the circadian sleep–wake cycle. Several nights' usage is usually required before sleep improves.

Benzodiazepines and other drugs used as hypnotic agents are numerous and include both prescription and over-the-counter preparations. A partial list of these agents is shown in Table 20-5. Benzodiazepines have been on the

TABLE 20-5
Commonly Used Medications for Insomnia

Alprazolam	Quetiapine
Amitriptyline	Ramelteon
Clonazepam	Temazepam
Eszopiclone	Trazodone
Hydroxyzine	Zaleplon
Mirtazepine	Zolpidem

market for many years and are now available in less costly generic forms. They differ mainly from the newer benzodiazepine receptor agonists in their effect on sleep architecture. With chronic usage they reduce delta or slow-wave sleep (N3) at the expense of increasing intermediate stage sleep (N2). Some REM suppression also occurs with chronic usage. These changes in sleep architecture often result in morning reports of nonrefreshing sleep. However, the discomfort of tapering the drugs is often worse than continuing them, and so dependence develops.

Trazodone, an older and inexpensive sedating antidepressant, is the most prescribed prescription agent for sleep and is not FDA-approved as a hypnotic agent. It is given in lower doses for hypnotic effects than for antidepressant usage. Some studies report favorable effects on sleep architecture and patient satisfaction. Undesirable side effects are infrequent but should be noted and include arrhythmias and priapism. Other sedating antidepressants, such as amitriptyline and mirtazepine, are also frequently used for sleep. None of the sedating antidepressants have FDA approval as hypnotic agents. Antihistamines, melatonin, and valerian are popular nonprescription drugs widely marketed to the public. They have not been approved by the FDA, but their low side effect profile, low expense, and availability have made them frequent first choices of patients having a variety of sleep problems. The three agents have different proposed mechanisms of action. Histamine is a naturally occurring cerebral neurotransmitter with strong wake-promoting properties; older antihistamines enter the CNS and therefore promote sleepiness.

HYPERSOMNIAS

The hypersomnias (excessive sleepiness) are predominantly those related to sleep-associated breathing disorders, such as *obstructive sleep apnea* and a non-obstructive sleep-associated breathing disorder (*central sleep apnea*). Examples of the nonobstructive forms of sleep-related breathing disorders include chronic obstructive pulmonary disease, emphysema, and congestive heart failure with Cheyne–Stokes respiration ("periodic breathing"). Obstructive sleep apnea, with its sleep fragmentation from repeated apnea-related arousals, causes the greatest degree of daytime sleepiness. That obstructive sleep apnea was not better known until the 1970s is hard to understand. Most estimates place the current prevalence of the condition at 4% for males and 2% for females in the United States. In the 40- to 60-year-old male group, estimates are higher, at 8%. Females approach the incidence in males after menopause. Charles Dickens's 1836 *Pickwick Papers* contains a reference to a "fat boy,

Joe" who was noted to be inappropriately sleepy. The association between obesity and hypersomnolence became known as the *Pickwickian syndrome,* a term that now describes obesity with hypoventillation. *Obstructive sleep apnea* refers to recurrent upper airway obstructions occurring during sleep causing arterial oxygen desaturation. The two entities, sleep apnea and obesity hypoventilation, have some dissimilar features, but their common ones include excessive weight, nocturnal breathing disturbance, and hypersomnolence during the daytime (Young et al., 1993).

Snoring may call attention to obstructive sleep apnea and is a result of airflow causing vibration of soft tissues in the throat. Snoring represents a partial obstruction to airflow and can be a forerunner of obstructive sleep apnea. The OSA patient has recurrent apneas where breathing stops for longer than 10 seconds and results in declines in oxygen saturations of 3–4% or more. Without realizing it, the patient might not breathe for 30–120 seconds, 100–200 times a night. A hypopnea is a partial airway obstruction lasting at least 10 seconds and resulting in oxygen desaturation of 3–4%. Both apneas and hypopneas result in EEG arousals, which fragment sleep continuity and lead to excessive daytime sleepiness. Even patients who are primary snorers with few apneas may have arousals and sleep fragmentation due to increased effort of breathing. A newer term, *upper airway resistance syndrome,* describes the condition of these patients. To date, commercial insurance carriers and Medicare only cover expenses for continuous positive airway pressure units and bilevel units for apneas and hypopneas, but not pure snoring and upper airway resistance, even though symptoms may be similar. The end result of sleep-related breathing disorders is excessive daytime sleepiness, which at times is so profound as to be pathological.

The predisposing factors for development of obstructive sleep apnea (OSA) are, most importantly, obesity, increased neck circumference, age, male gender, anatomical structures of nasal and oral passages, family history, and associated medical conditions. Among the latter are hypothyroidism, neuromuscular disorders, chronic lung disease, and Down syndrome. The obese, hypoventilating patient without apnea may show more tendency to elevations in carbon dioxide levels during sleep and wakefulness—a chemical marker of hypoventilation. OSA is suspected when there is a history of snoring, witnessed apnea, and daytime sleepiness. The body habitus may show obesity (BMI > 30), increased neck circumference of more than 17 inches in males and 15 inches in females, and reduction in space between the soft palate and base of tongue. The "Mallampati classification" (Mallampati et al., 1985) describes the tongue–soft palate relationship and is helpful for determining a patient's likelihood of having obstructive sleep apnea. Class III and IV patients have reductions in the area between the base of the tongue and soft palate (see Figure 20-1).

In the central form of sleep apnea (CSA), the respiratory drive center in the medulla is diminished. These patients may not snore, have more insomnia than hypersomnia, and are less apt to be obese. The most common causes of central sleep apnea are congestive heart failure, central nervous system disorders, and an increasing incidence of central apnea due to suppression of the medullary respiratory center by chronic narcotic usage. The basic difference between obstructive and central sleep apnea is that the upper airway is obstructed in OSA and open in CSA. The diaphragm and intercostal muscles contract against a closed upper airway in OSA but are noncontractile in CSA, with a patent upper airway.

> The diagnosis of sleep apnea is accomplished by performing a polysomnogram (PSG) in a sleep center where patients are monitored by trained technologists. Respiratory pauses of 10 seconds or longer may be accompanied by desaturation and cardiac arrhythmias. Because of muscle atonia, apneas and hypoxemia may be worse in REM sleep. Recently, Medicare (March 2008) approved less-expensive screening tests that can be performed outside of a sleep facility. The devices usually measure airflow, respiratory effort, and oxygen saturation. They are not as informative as full PSG studies, but are useful when patients are unable to undergo full PSG testing. A positive PSG study for obstructive sleep apnea has an apnea/hypopnea index of five or more events per hour of sleep. There is usually accompanying oxygen desaturation, snoring, and multiple arousals.

Treatment of sleep apnea depends on the severity and type of apnea. Weight loss, sleeping on one's side, and avoiding hypnotics and alcohol near bedtime have improved nighttime breathing in patients with milder apnea. Wedge-shaped pillows and tennis balls sewn into one's nightshirt on the back side may help the patient spend most of the sleep time on his or her sides. In more abnormal cases, with high numbers of apneas and hypopneas per hour of sleep (the apnea–hypopnea index, or AHI), continuous positive airway pressure is the proven, preferred treatment.

Surgery for OSA was performed in past decades more frequently than now. The earliest surgical procedure, tracheostomy, is very successful because it completely bypasses the pharyngeal obstruction. The procedure is performed infrequently since the development of continuous positive airway pressure (CPAP) units. Several surgical techniques aimed at remodeling oral and nasal

The Mallampati classification relates tongue size to pharyngeal size. This test is performed with the patient in the sitting position, the head held in a neutral position, the mouth wide open, and the tongue protruding to the maximum. The subsequent classification is assigned based upon the pharyngeal structures that are visible.

Class I = visualization of the soft palate, fauces, uvula, anterior and posterior pillars
Class II = visualization of the soft palate, fauces, and uvula
Class III = visualization of the soft palate and the base of the uvula
Class IV = soft palate is not visible at all

The classification assigned by the clinician may vary if the patient is in the supine position (instead of sitting). If the patient phonates, this falsely improves the view. If the patient arches his or her tongue, the uvula is falsely obscured. A class I view suggests ease of intubation and correlates with a laryngoscopic view grade I 99 – 100% of the time. Class IV view suggests a poor laryngoscopic view, grade III or IV 100% of the time. Beware of the intermediate classes, which may result in all degrees of difficulty in laryngoscopic visualization.

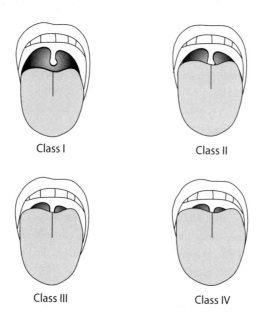

Class I   Class II

Class III   Class IV

FIGURE 20-1
Mallampati Classification

Although originally presented as predicting difficulty with intubation, the classification is also used in the examination of patients to predict the likelihood of obstructive sleep apnea. From Mallampati et al. (1985), 429–432.

airways have evolved to treat obstructive sleep apnea but have been found less effective than CPAP for eliminating the abnormality. These surgical procedures are now performed for milder apnea cases and snoring when CPAP is not tolerated by the patient. One condition that is responsive to surgery is that of large tonsils. Adenotonsillectomy is very effective in relieving snoring and apnea in children and young adults whose tonsils have not regressed with age. However, if weight becomes excessive, symptoms of apnea may reappear later in life. Children and young adults may not complain of excessive sleepiness as prominently as older adults and are more likely to have behavioral problems resulting from their sleep apnea.

Examination of the upper airway makes it easy to understand why CPAP and its variations are more effective than surgery for obstructive sleep apnea. The portion of the airway between the nasopharynx and epiglottis has little rigid or bony support, making it susceptible to collapse. As the chest expands on inspiration, negative pressure develops in the upper airway, resulting in collapse and obstruction to airflow. Simply removing the uvula and palate may not prevent closure of the airway below the palate. Positive air pressure opposes collapse of the airway and prevents an apnea or hypopnea from developing. The benefits of positive airway pressure devices include:

1. Eliminates snoring.
2. Reduces sleep fragmentation from arousals.
3. Prevents nocturnal hypoxia and hypercarbia.
4. Helps reduce hypertension, cardiac arrhythmia, myocardial infarction, stroke, congestive heart failure.
5. May positively affect blood sugar control and weight.
6. Reduces chance of accidents by eliminating excessive sleepiness.
7. Improve job performance, depression, family discord, and quality of life.

Central sleep apnea is more variable in its response to positive airway pressure. Some patients respond to CPAP, whereas others require bilevel pressure settings with automatic backup rates to deliver breaths during long apneic periods. If the central sleep apnea is related to respiratory center depression, removal of the offending agent is, of course, the treatment of choice when possible. Sometimes patients with obstructive sleep apnea syndrome develop transient central sleep apneas after being placed on positive airway pressure, but these are seldom clinically significant and usually disappear with time. Successful treatment of congestive heart failure may often eliminate central apneas of the Cheyne–Stokes type.

NARCOLEPSY

Of the non-sleep-related breathing disorders causing daytime sleepiness, narcolepsy is best known. Narcolepsy was the first, and for years the only, sleep disorder known to cause hypersomnolence. In its full expression, it may be accompanied by cataplexy (sudden loss of voluntary muscle control provoked by emotion), hypnagogic hallucinations, and sleep paralysis in addition to disturbed sleep at night. *DSM-IV-TR* criteria are included in Table 20-6. A paradoxical situation exists in that people with narcolepsy are sleepy throughout the day but fail to sleep at nighttime. Of greatest concern is that they have attacks at the wrong time, as when flying a plane or driving a car. Understanding narcolepsy and associated symptoms had to await the discovery of REM sleep in 1951 by a physiology graduate student, Eugene Aserinsky, working in Chicago. He, along with Dr. William Dement, were studying sleep in infants and noted the periodic bursts of REMs and the appearance of low-amplitude faster cortical waveforms. Variations in autonomic functions, such as respiration, temperature, heart rate, blood pressure, and skeletal muscle tone, were also observed. Later, reports of dreaming in REM-stage sleep, along with penile and clitoral erections in adults, was documented. These REM-related changes contrasted with non-REM sleep patterns of slower cortical rhythms and eye movements, and a more stable autonomic state.

Further investigation showed that cataplexy, sleep paralysis, and hypnagogic hallucinations coincide with an intrusion of REM sleep into the waking

---

TABLE 20-6
DSM-IV-TR *Criteria for Narcolepsy*

A. Irresistible attacks of refreshing sleep that occur daily over at least 3 months.

B. The presence of one or both of the following:

   (1) cataplexy (i.e., brief episodes of sudden bilateral loss of muscle tone, most often in association with intense emotion)

   (2) recurrent intrusions of elements of rapid eye movement (REM) sleep into the transition between sleep and wakefulness, as manifested by either hypnopompic or hypnogogic hallucinations or sleep paralysis at the beginning or end of sleep episodes

C. The disturbance is not due to the direct physiological effects of a substance (e.g., a drug of abuse, a medication) or another general medical condition.

Note. From *DSM-IV-TR,* p. 615.

---

or near-wakeful state ("REM on a rampage"), thereby accounting for skeletal muscle hypotonia (cataplexy) and visual imagery (dreaming or hallucinations). Some people with narcolepsy have only hypersomnolence without the other features. It is essential to have two or more sleep-onset REM periods, plus a short mean sleep latency of 8 minutes or less, for five daytime nap opportunities on the MSLT to make a diagnosis of narcolepsy.

> An important step in unraveling the cause of narcolepsy has been the discovery of a reduction in cells of the lateral hypothalamus, which produce the peptide hypocretin, also know as orexin. This substance can be assayed in the spinal fluid, and low to absent levels exist in people who have narcolepsy with cataplexy. Intermediate levels are present in narcolepsy without cataplexy. Hypocretin, or orexin, is thought to be an alerting neuropeptide that serves to regulate the transitions from wake to REM sleep. On a practical or clinical basis, assays of hypocretin are not available. They are only available in research settings in a few university centers (Mignot et al., 2002).

The incidence of narcolepsy is 1 in 2,500 in the United States but occurs more frequently in Japan. A weak familial incidence exists, as does the link to human leukocyte antigens, especially in patients who have narcolepsy with cataplexy. Over 90% of patients with narcolepsy and cataplexy are HLADQB1*0602 positive, reaching nearly 100% in African-Americans. Human leukocyte antigens cannot be used as an independent diagnostic test because about 20% of normals without narcolepsy are also HLADQB1*0602 positive.

Differential Diagnosis

Because narcolepsy and sleep apnea both generate fatigue or prolonged sleep, ask patients these two questions: (1) "Do you snore a lot?" (If so, sleep apnea, probably obstructive, is more likely.) (2) "Do you lose control of your muscles or posture when stimulated?" (If true, cataplexy suggests narcolepsy.) To pin down narcolepsy, the PSG must display immediate and repeated outbursts of REM sleep during the transition between wakefulness and sleep.

Bipolar depression and *atypical depression* frequently show hypersomnia, but rarely as a chief complaint. Although *physically ill* patients sleep excessively, they often deem it a relief. Narcoleptic attacks resemble epileptic *psychomotor seizures*, but seizures usually have perserverative motor movements, such as repeated swallowing, hand rubbing, head turning, or eye deviation.

Management and Treatment

The treatment of narcolepsy involves three areas of emphasis. The first is the importance of sleep and realization that a short nap can be as restorative as a pill. Scheduling a morning and/or afternoon nap may obviate the need for a higher dose of an alerting medication. Second, there are several choices of FDA-approved medications for hypersomnolence. Amphetamine preparations (Dexedrine) were the first compounds to be used and remain important. They are well absorbed in the GI tract and have a favorable peak onset of action of 2 hours. They activate the dopaminergic system to enhance wakefulness. Methylphenidate (Ritalin) has a similar action. Several long-acting, once-daily preparations of amphetamines and methylphenidate are available. They are all Schedule Class II drugs, indicating a tendency to possible dependency. They can only be prescribed for a month at a time and then must be refilled by a written prescription.

Modafinil (Provigil) is a newer agent and a Class IV drug, allowing the clinician to write a larger supply with refills. The mode of action is not a dopamine reuptake inhibitor, as occurs with amphetamines, and the exact mechanism is controversial. It is a long-acting, well-absorbed medication with few side effects: The main ones are initial headache, which subsides with time and lowering the dose, and reducing the potency of oral contraceptives, sometimes necessitating an increase in the birth control pill dosage. Modafinil has become the preferred drug of choice for treating hypersomnolence due to narcolepsy.

The third area emphasizes the treatment of cataplexy. Most medications that control hypersomnolence in patients with narcolepsy do not work for cataplexy. In some patients, cataplexy may be so mild and infrequent that additional medications are not required.

Cataplexy is characterized by muscle weakness provoked by emotion. Of the emotional triggers, laughter is more likely to cause cataplexy than anger or fear. Among the other symptoms accompanying narcolepsy, cataplexy is more common than sleep paralysis or hypnagogic hallucinations. REM-suppressant medications have been the mainstay of treatment for cataplexy in the past. TCAs are effective, but anticholinergic and sedating side effects limit their tolerance. Recently, fluoxetine and venlafaxine have gained in popularity and are effective in tolerable doses. The latter medication inhibits reuptake of both noradrenalin and serotonin and is effective in reducing cataplexy. None of the SSRI drugs are FDA approved for treatment of cataplexy. Sodium oxybate (Xyrem) is the only medication that is FDA-approved for the treatment of cataplexy. Sodium oxybate is the sodium salt of gamma-hydroxybutyrate (GHB), which became infamous as the date-rape drug. It is effective in controlling daytime sleepiness as well as cataplexy. The drug requires in-depth knowledge of its prescribing method and potential side effects. It is certainly an option for patients with cataplexy and excessive sleepiness who fail to respond to other medications (U.S. Xyrem Multicenter Study Group, 2003).

Hypnopompic hallucinations are experienced upon awakening, whereas *hypnagogic hallucinations* appear when dropping off. When either hallucination emerges *without* narcolepsy, it is a benign curiosity that still scares patients into thinking they are crazy. Professionals should tell them that these images are a normal variation of "premature dreaming" or "dreaming while awake." Approximately 10% of the U.S. population has experienced these pre- and post-sleep hallucinations. Even when the person feels alert, narcoleptic hallucinations can be alarming—such as sensing something sinister is close and threatening.

Idiopathic hypersomnia is a term reserved for patients who have no demonstrable cause for their sleepiness. The histories are of long duration and consist of inappropriate sleepiness in spite of long periods of nocturnal sleep. The patients seem never to satisfy their sleepiness, even for short periods. People with narcolepsy, by contrast, may awaken quite refreshed after a nap but show signs of sleepiness in a few hours. The idiopathic group will show a short-mean sleep latency but no sleep-onset REM periods on multiple sleep latency testing (MSLT), even after a full night's sleep. Treatment is much like that for narcolepsy except the idiopathic group does not have associated features of cataplexy, hypnagogic hallucinations, or sleep paralysis. Alerting medications are used for these patients.

For far too long, society has ignored serious accidents that result from inadequate sleep or poor-quality sleep. There are numerous examples of accidents and large catastrophes that have occurred during periods of sleep deprivation, most notably, early-morning automobile accidents. Sleep-related accidents involving transportation and industry have caused labor, management, and government to pay more attention to the problems associated with altered sleep schedules. One state, New Jersey, has passed a law making it a felony to injure another person in an accident that was caused by sleep deprivation. In recent years, the notion of scheduling naps on the job has seemed closer to reality, as information on vigilance, reaction times, and accuracy have been shown to deteriorate from sleepiness (Findley et al., 1989; George et al., 1996).

CIRCADIAN RHYTHM DISORDER

Circadian rhythm sleep disorders exist when there is a misalignment between the patient's sleep–wake pattern, or biological clock, and the actual time. This misalignment may be transient, as in jet lag, or persistent, as in shift-work sleep disorder. The patient may complain of sleepiness at work or inability to sleep when off work. The sleep–wake cycle is just one of the body's circadian rhythms, and it is strongly entrained in most individuals to the light–dark cycle. Markers of the circadian rhythm include core body temperature, which fluctuates from higher in day to lower at night; cortisol secretory patterns, which are characteristically lower at sleep onset and increase by early morning; and growth hormone secretion, which is higher in slow-wave sleep. These three markers are among the strongest of the 24-hour body rhythms. External stimuli, which synchronize our circadian rhythms, are called "zeitgebers." Sunlight is the strongest one exerting its effect through an anatomical pathway from the retina to the suprachiasmatic nucleus in the hypothalamus. This nucleus is important in alerting our brains and maintaining wakefulness. The duration and quality of sleep are unaffected, but sleep is out of phase with the environmental time in circadian sleep disorders.

One example of a circadian rhythm disorder is the delayed sleep phase syndrome (DSPS). This well-known entity is prevalent in childhood and adolescence, and defined by staying up late and desiring to sleep late into the mornings. DSPS is not solely due to nocturnal activities such as telephone, TV watching, or computers, but an actual delay in the timing of sleep onset, which is supported by the core body temperature and cortisol secretory patterns. An individual with a normal sleep–wake pattern can develop DSPS because of late-night activities, such as those that occur in a college setting. Once DSPS is established, it may be difficult to phase-advance the person so that he or she goes to bed at a reasonable hour. Many college students do not take morning classes because of this tendency. Establishing a rigid wakeup time followed by exposure to early-morning light or use of a light box (sitting 3 feet away from intense light 2,500–10,000 lux; ordinary room light is 150–200 lux and does not suffice) for 30–60 minutes in the morning may correct the phase delay, but requires determination on the part of the young individual. Melatonin works opposite from light therapy. Melatonin administered in the morning causes a phase delay, and in the evening, a phase advance of sleep-onset time. A more rapid way to correct this delayed sleep phase tendency is to have the individual remain awake the entire night and the following day, and then go to sleep at a more reasonable hour, i.e., 11:00–12:00 midnight. With more difficult cases, the individual is rotated around the clock as follows: Sleep onset is delayed for 3 hours each night until, after several days, the time of sleep onset is chosen to be around 11:00 P.M., and the patient goes to bed at that time hoping that his or her circadian clock has been reset. A fixed wakeup time is essential for maintaining the normal pattern.

With advancing age, our sleep phase tends to advance and can be likened to farmers who go to bed shortly after sundown and awaken at or before sunrise. One can imagine that our nocturnal sleep time has declined a few hours since the invention of the electric light bulb in 1879, and widespread lighting after sunset was available. Illuminating the workplace for 24 hours has resulted in shift-work sleep disorder, a fairly recent addition to the sleep disorders classification and a very important one, since an estimated 20 million Americans are involved in shift work. There are numerous variations in shift-work schedules. Some workers have fixed nighttime hours whereas others rotate shifts, which is a more difficult situation in which to adapt. Common to night or rotating shift workers is changing sleep times whenever the individual is off work and trying to blend in to his or her home schedule. Some night-shift workers continue to maintain their work-shift schedule as best they can, especially for the 24-hour period before they return to work. Complaints of insomnia are common during the hours the patients try to sleep, and sleepiness during work periods may interfere with productivity as well as endanger individuals on the job. Shift work is less well tolerated by older workers; alerting and/or hypnotic medications can be helpful if needed. Time-zone changes, or *jet lag*, have some features in common with shift work, but are usually of shorter duration. Jet lag is also better tolerated by younger individuals. The body's circadian system is out of synchrony with the environmental time and may take several days to adjust; approximately 1 hour of adjustment per day, per time zone crossed, seems to fit most travelers.

Irregular sleep–wake pattern is not a rarity in psychiatric practice. The usual patient with this problem has a cognitive dysfunction and is often a resident of a nursing home. Sleep disturbances are very common in nursing home patients and constitute a most troublesome problem. Sedating the patient may not be easy, and often paradoxical agitation and further confused behavior make the patient more difficult to control. Because of a breakdown in the sleep–wake cycle, daytime napping is common and hard to prevent, and interferes with nocturnal sleep. Adverse drug effects may occur with increased frequency due to potential hepatic interactions of multiple drugs, decreased renal clearance with age, increased volume of distribution of fat-soluble drugs due to increased body fat with age, and reduction of total body water, causing higher concentrations.

PARASOMNIAS

Parasomnia is a term designating the occurrence of undesirable events during sleep. The sleep architecture itself is usually not affected, except by an arousal. Parasomnias may occur during entry into sleep, within sleep, or during arousals from sleep. Some parasomnias are among the best-known sleep disorders because they are so prevalent and attract attention of bed partners and other family members. They may be more prevalent in certain age groups; for example, confusional arousals, sleepwalking, and sleep terrors are normal events in childhood but unusual in adults. Among the REM sleep-related parasomnias, nightmares are present in childhood and adults.

A distinction should be made between night terrors and nightmares. Children with *night terrors* suddenly awaken from slow-wave or delta sleep in the first third of the sleep period with a cry or scream, and when parents arrive, the child shows increased autonomic activities such as tachypnea, tachycardia, diaphoresis, and dilated pupils. The child is hard to awaken because he or she is in deep sleep, and when awakened, there is no dream recall. Night terrors occur from ages 4 to 12 and are not usually associated with any behavioral or physical abnormality. Like sleepwalking, there can be an autosomal dominant inheritance. By noting the usual time when these phenomena occur during the early part of the night and awakening the child just prior to that time, these parasomnias are averted. Medications that reduce N3 delta-wave sleep, such as benzodiazepines, will reduce or eliminate the behavior. Night terrors and sleepwalking are not associated with psychopathology, and they typically remit spontaneously with increasing age. Sleep-talking (somniloquy) is a common benign related NREM sleep phenomenon which may occur alone or accompany sleepwalking.

Sleepwalkers are often confused, bump into objects, and are not well-coordinated. Rarely, somnambulists can be dangerous and leap from windows. A typical episode starts with the patient sitting up and repeating acts, such as picking at pajamas or bedsheets. What follows, aside from walking, are more complicated behaviors, including dressing, eating, and urinating. With blank and staring faces, these patients are rarely affected by those who attempt to contact them. Episodes typically persist for several minutes to half an hour. Sometimes patients don't walk but just fret in bed. When they do walk, they may return to bed without recalling their sleepwalking, or they may be surprised to arise from a different bed. Hostility is uncommon among sleepwalkers; if they sleep-talk, they're usually inarticulate. Sleepwalkers may need to sleep on the ground floor, have the outside doors securely locked, and have the car keys unavailable.

For patients the scariest of delta-sleep attacks are sleep terrors. Children increase their breathing, heart rate, sweating, and movement. Eyes are open and screams may erupt. Despite this panic, which typically strikes in the early evening, these children remember nothing on waking up or in the morning, although concerned family members certainly do. In contrast to nightmares, sleep terrors do not respond to psychotherapy. Low doses of benzodiazepines before bedtime often reduce sleep terrors as does briefly waking the child prior to the typical time when the terrors occur. It is best to limit the medication's dose and time—for instance, prescribing the drug only for the summer during camp.

Nightmares are REM-associated parasomnias that occur universally, but when in excess, constitute a sleep disorder. Commonly present in preschool children, nightmares may overlap with night terrors but are very different from them. Nightmares are more common in the last third of the night. They are associated with visual imagery, which can be recalled, especially if the individual awakens close to the time the dream is occurring. Nightmares in the young are more colorful, action-packed, and contain more sexual content than in older individuals. The content of dreams in nightmares is mostly random, although usually threatening, such as being chased. The recurrent nightmares that follow a traumatic event may contain related content, whereas in nondepressed persons nightmare content is random. Occurring frequently after stress, nightmares cause a sleep-onset insomnia condition in patients due to fear of experiencing another bad dream. Medications such as thioridazine, TCAs, SSRIs, and benzodiazepines may trigger nightmares by reducing NREM deep sleep. Suddenly withdrawing REM-suppressant medications and drugs such as alcohol, TCAs, and MAOIs causes REM rebound, which can likewise result in nightmares.

One of the most dramatic sleep disorders is that of *REM behavior sleep disorder* (RBSD). This condition is listed as a REM sleep-related parasomnia. The clinical presentation is similar from case to case, but the long-term course may be quite different, depending on whether it remains idiopathic or is a forerunner of a neurodegenerative disorder. Usually, an older male and less often, older female, begins to report an increase in dream frequency and content after many years of less-frequent, bland dreams. The dreams are often action-filled and contain imagery of fighting, being chased, or threatened by another person or animal. The bed partner is suddenly awakened by vocal and motor activity, and may flee from the bed to avoid violent arm flailing and kicking. One woman was awakened by her husband choking her; fortunately, she was able to awaken him before injury occurred. When awakened, patients will recount vivid dreams of violent encounters that are completely out of character, and they are embarrassed by their actions. The activity usually occurs in the latter half of the sleep period when REM sleep and dreaming are most common. After several years of this activity, nearly half of the affected patients may develop a neurodegenerative disorder such as Parkinson's disease, multisystem atrophy, or Lewy body dementia.

The theory behind this disorder concerns a proposed disconnection between REM-generating cells in the pons and descending inhibiting fibers to the skeletal muscles, thereby freeing the skeletal muscles from atonia. The subject is then able to act out his or her dreams. Why the dreams become more frequent and vivid in the first place is not completely understood. Fortunately, both dreams and motor activity respond to low doses of clonazepam (Klonopin, 0.5 mg) better than any other treatment. Polysomnograms during these episodes fail to show any epileptiform activity, but there is increased motor activity in REM sleep, which is a paradox. RSBD may be caused by antidepressants and chronic alcohol abuse. Among the antidepressant agents are TCAs and SSRIs. Brainstem tumors have caused nocturnal behavior similar to RSBD. These diverse situations all have in common interference with REM sleep generation in the brainstem (Mason & Pack, 2007).

SLEEP-RELATED MOVEMENT DISORDERS

Restless legs syndrome (RLS) is classified under sleep-related movement disorders. RLS presents as an uncomfortable, usually painless sensation in the legs, extending occasionally into the thighs but less often in the arms. The clinical description most appropriate to describe RLS in patients is that they relate to note an urge to move the limbs. The feet may fidget by day, but the symptoms are always worse later at night. In fact, morning may be the only time of relief. The symptoms are relieved by activity and worsened with inactivity. Symptoms differ from the restlessness of neuroleptic drugs, termed akathisia, which remains throughout the day and are not as well relieved by activity. The circadian activity of RLS is very notable and helps to distinguish it from other movement disorders.

Periodic limb movement disorder (PLMD) was initially called *nocturnal myoclonus*. This term was given to patients because they kicked and moved their legs rhythmically during sleep every 20–40 seconds without realizing it. The motor activity may last for several minutes, then subside, only to recur in one or both legs. Movements resemble the sudden extension of the toes and feet, as seen with a positive Babinski sign. Most often complaints come from the bed partner, although some patients are aware of disturbed sleep, do not feel refreshed in the morning, and suffer daytime fatigue. About 50–80% of patients with RLS also have PLMD, but PLMD may occur without the awake discomfort of restless legs. Patients with PLMD usually complain more of fatigue, whereas those with RLS alone complain of insomnia. RLS may affect 10% of people with chronic insomnia who consult sleep clinics. PLMD afflicts both sexes and increases with age.

RLS may be familial, secondary to other causes, or sporadic. When familial, the onset occurs earlier in life and behaves like a autosomal dominant. Secondary RLS is seen in three settings: iron deficiency, pregnancy, and chronic renal failure on dialysis. Isolated or sporadic cases usually appear beyond middle age, and no family history or identifiable cause is apparent.

The pharmacology of RLS is most interesting. By accident, dopaminergic agents were found to be of great benefit for daytime and night symptoms of RLS. Carbidopa-levodopa (Sinemet) is the mainstay of Parkinson's treatment and also beneficial for restless legs symptoms, both the urge to move the extremities and the periodic limb movements at night when asleep. The dopaminergic agonists ropinirole and pramipexole are the current treatment of choice and less likely to cause rebound symptoms in the night or *augmentation*, a term used to describe the appearance of restless legs earlier in the daytime. If iron deficiency is present, replacement is therapeutic, relying on serum ferritin as a guide to therapy. The theory behind the effectiveness of iron therapy is that iron is a cofactor in the synthesis of dopamine. Regular exercise and stretching the limbs offer some benefit, although transient. Substances making RLS worse are caffeine, tricyclic and newer antidepressants, and agents with strong dopamine antagonistic properties such as metoclopramide (Reglan). See Table 20-7.

Seldom is a polysomnogram necessary for the diagnosis of RLS. The diagnosis is clinical and should be accompanied by an examination of the limbs, noting the presence or absence of reflexes or sensory deficits. If the latter are present, nerve conduction and EMG testing may be indicated to discover an underlying polyneuropathy, which can mimic RLS in some ways. A serum ferritin level is most helpful to determine the presence of iron deficiency anemia; and oral or parenteral iron is often very helpful in eliminating the symptoms of RLS if related to diminished iron stores. A serum ferritin less than 50 micrograms per liter has been associated with diminished sleep in patients with RLS (Mason & Pack, 2007).

TABLE 20-7

Agents and Conditions Affecting RLS and PLMD

IMPROVES	WORSENS
Dopamine agonists:	Iron deficiency
Pramipexole (Mirapex)	Dopamine antagonists
Ropinirole (Requip)	Antipsychotics (e.g., haloperidol)
Carbidopa-levodopa	Antidepressants (e.g., TCAs)
Narcotics:	Antiemetics (e.g., metoclopramide)
Codeine	Pregnancy
Hydrocodone	Renal failure on dialysis
Tramadol	
Propoxyphene	
Benzodiazepines, less effective	
Sleep hygiene measures, with avoidance of caffeine, alcohol, and tobacco	

Other interesting sleep-related movement disorders include nocturnal leg cramps, bruxism, and rhythmic movement disorder. *Nocturnal leg cramps* are sudden, painful muscle spasms that occur during the night, usually in the calves and/or small muscles of the feet, which are acutely relieved by stretching or massaging the affected areas. They may be followed by a vague, uncomfortable sensation and can be very disruptive to sleep, especially in adults and

* The more recent classification of deep sleep combines stages 3 and 4 into one stagae N3.

FIGURE 20-2

Stages of Sleep

*The more recent classification of deep sleep combines stages 3 and 4 into one stage N3.

elderly persons who have more sleep problems. Etiology of leg cramps is not always apparent, and treatments are imprecise.

Bruxism consists of clenching and grinding motions of the jaw, and disturbs sleep of the bed partner more than the patient. More commonly occurring in children, the condition usually subsides with age. However, bruxism may occur in some highly stressed adults and require oral appliances to lessen the grinding noise and wear on permanent teeth. There is a familial incidence to bruxism, but it is not pronounced.

Rhythmic movement disorders in sleep are mainly confined to infants and children. Other descriptive terms are *head banging, body rocking,* and *jactatio*

FIGURE 20-3
NREM Stage Sleep Polysomnography (PSG)

This PSG tracing shows a transition from wake to Stage 1 sleep. The first six channels record frontal, central, and occipital cortical regions. Low-amplitude (alpha 8–13 cps) waves are admixed with slower theta (4–7 cps) waves. The chin EMG is low amplitude, reflecting quiet inactivity. Slow-roving eye movements (E_1, E_2) are present in Stage 1 sleep and differ from rapid eye movements (REM) of REM sleep. The EKG shows normal sinus rhythm and no leg movements are present. Nasal pressure and airflow channels show quiet, regular breathing pattern. Thoracic effort waveforms rise and fall with respirations. The abdominal tracing shows little movement. Oxygen saturations are in the lower 90s and pulse in the 60s. The snore channel suggests audible heavy breathing and light snoring. If awakened, the patient may deny having been asleep.

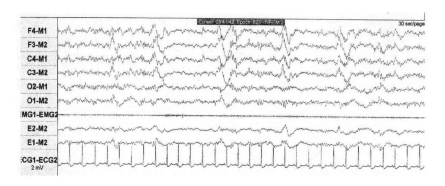

FIGURE 20-4
NREM Stage 2 Sleep

This stage is identified by high-amplitude biphasic waveforms linked to faster rhythms and termed *K complexes*. This stage comprises at least 50% of adult sleep activity. Sometimes K complexes are reflected in the eye leads, as in this patient (E_1, E_2). Sleep spindles are the other forms that identify Stage 2. Spindles are groups of waveforms with a frequency of 7–14 cycles per second, often appearing early in stage N2 sleep. They originate in the thalamus and project to cortical surfaces. Spindles are often adjacent to K complexes but may be apart from them. Patients awakened from Stage 2 will realize that they have been asleep. People with insomnia stay predominantly in this intermediate stage. Benzodiazepines, barbiturates, alcohol, and other drugs may increase sleep spindle density.

FIGURE 20-5
NREM Stage 3

High-voltage, low-frequency waves are dominant in this stage. These waveforms are termed *delta waves* and comprise a large portion of children's sleep but less in adults. Delta sleep may occupy only a small part of sleep in older adults. Patients who report their sleep as refreshing or restorative are likely to have more delta than those who are not satisfied with their sleep. Patients with insomnia and fibromyalgia often have faster-frequency alpha waves superimposed on the sparse, slower delta waves, which is termed *alpha–delta pattern*. This finding cannot be used to make an absolute diagnosis by PSG of a particular sleep disorder but often accompanies the tests of patients with insomnia and fibromyalgia.

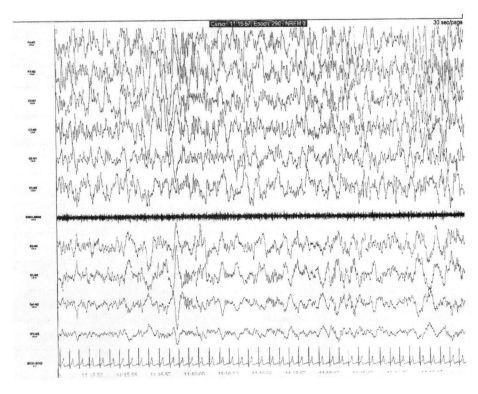

FIGURE 20-6
Slow-Wave N3 Sleep in Children

A 9-year-old boy shows high-amplitude slow waves typical of Stage N3 delta. Delta activity is present in large amounts in children and gradually diminishes with age. It is best seen in recordings from frontal cortical areas. Although a normal finding in young sleeping individuals, delta is abnormal in the awake state and indicates cortical dysfunction. Delta activity predominates in the first third of the night and is the time during which there is a spurt in growth hormone secretion.

capitis nocturna. These are large, rhythmic muscle movements that begin at sleep onset and persist into Stage 2 sleep for about 15 minutes, then subside. Polysomnograms show only the rhythmic muscle artifact; most cases cease by the time the child enters first grade. Rarely does head banging/body rocking cause injury or important sleep disturbance other than worry for the parents.

Our appreciation for the impact of normal and abnormal sleep upon the individual's psychological and physical health is still evolving. For example, chronic insomnia, once considered to be a result of depression, is now recognized as a cause of depression. Long-term studies of patients with apnea show tendencies toward hypertension, cardiac arrhythmias, myocardial infarction,

FIGURE 20-7
REM Sleep

This important and interesting state of sleep has low-amplitude, fast-frequency cortical rhythms, suppressed EMG activity, and high-amplitude out-of-phase waveforms indicating rapid eye movements. Two examples are present in this 30-second epoch. Many classes of compounds may suppress REM sleep. These include TCAs, SSRIs, some anticonvulsants, drugs, and alcohol. When chronic REM suppressants are withdrawn, a REM rebound with increased density of rapid eye movements occurs, which can result in increased disturbing dreams. This aspect of withdrawal can be unsettling to patients and reported as nightmares and restless sleep.

congestive heart failure, and stroke (Shahar et al., 2001). Sleep deprivation may predispose to obesity and diabetes by promoting insulin resistance and lower leptin levels. An understanding of circadian rhythms has resulted in later school-starting times in some districts because of children's delayed sleep-phase tendency. Revising shift-work schedules to rotate *with* the clock instead of against it is now recognized as beneficial. And finally, allowing brief naps in the workplace will increase safety for workers and productivity for employers.

FIGURE 20-8
Obstructive Sleep Apnea

A middle-aged female with history of loud snoring, witnessed apneas, and daytime sleepiness in Stage N2 of sleep. The tracings show a prominent snore artifact, which coincides with deep recovery breaths between apneas. During the breaths, there is a movement artifact shown on the EMG channel and arousals in the upper six EEG channels. Continuous oxygen saturation values (S_aO_2) range from 90 to 81%.

FIGURE 20-9
Periodic Limb Movements

A middle-aged female in Stage N2 sleep shows a prominent snore artifact (bottom of figure) without accompanying sleep apnea or oxygen desaturation. In the leg channel, EMG activity occurs every 20–30 seconds, consistent with a diagnosis of periodic limb movement in sleep (PLMS). Such limb movements frequently accompany patients who have restless legs syndrome but may occur as an isolated finding. The leg movements are not causing arousals in the EEG of this patient. Frequent PLMS with arousals can produce an insomnia complaint, although in most patients PLMS are an incidental finding. The incidence of PLMS increases with age and may be related to low iron (ferritin) stores.

FIGURE 20-10

Obstructive Sleep Apnea on Positive Airway Pressure

A middle-aged female with obstructive sleep apnea has been placed on continuous positive airway pressure (CPAP) and is in REM sleep. Note the regular waveforms on the CPAP flow channel indicating an absence of sleep apneas. Channels E_2–M_1 are recording rapid eye movements. Electrodes placed above and below the eyes pick up horizontal and vertical eye movements of REM sleep. Since the cornea is electropositive with respect to the retina, eye movements create differences in electropotential, which can be measured by the recording electrodes and produce deflections of the recording pens.

FIGURE 20-11

Tachycardia in a Patient Without Cardiac History

A nine-beat episode of wide-complex tachycardia is present during deep sleep in the absence of apneas or hypoxia. Unexpected cardiac findings may be detected in patients undergoing polysomnogram testing and initiates a cardiac evaluation hoping to avoid unexplained deaths in sleep. A Holter monitor study showing only cardiac arrhythmias during nighttime hours should raise suspicion for sleep-related breathing disorders being a cause of the arrhythmia.

Maintenance of Wakefulness Test

Name:	Medical Record #
Study Date: 3/17/2008	DOB. 1969

Protocol

The MWT is used to assess a patient's ability to maintain wakefulness under conditions of low stimulation. The study is performed after completion of a preceding full PSG study.

The patient sits comfortably in a room that is quiet, secure, at a comfortable temperature and has a low constant level of light that allows the patient to see, but is not overly stimulating.

The montage includes central and occipital electroencephalogram, chin muscle activity, and eye movements. A total of four trial periods are recorded at 2-hour intervals beginning 1.5 – 3 hours after awakening.

Each trial is terminated after three epochs of sleep if the patient falls asleep, or after 40 minutes if no sleep occurs. A sleep latency of 40 minutes indicates that no sleep occurred during the trial(s). Normal sleep latency value is 32.6 minutes ± 9.9 minutes.

Parametric Analysis

Total Number of Trials	4

Trial #	Time of Trial	Sleep Latency (mins)	REM Latency (mins)
1	08:32:35	25.0	—
2	10:44:05	39.5	—
3	12:42:35	38.0	—
4	14:42:05	40.0	—

Mean Values for All Trials	
Mean sleep latency	35.6
Mean REM latency	—
Number of REM episodes	0
Number of naps with REM episodes	0

The patient was cooperative although not happy that he had to do this test. He was able to maintain wakefulness between trials, watching television. This is a normal study.

FIGURE 20-12
Maintenance of Wakefulness Test (MWT)

A mean latency during four trials of nearly 36 minutes indicates the patient's ability to maintain wakefulness. This would be considered an acceptable test result for transportation work. Adapted from Doghramji et al. (1997).

Multiple Sleep Latency Report

Name:	Medical Record #:
Study Date: 4/8/2008	DOB:

Protocol

This polysomnographic procedure is designed to evaluate (1) the complaint of excessive daytime sleepiness by quantifying the time required to fall asleep and (2) the possibility of narcolepsy by checking for abnormally short latencies to REM sleep. Electrographic variables include EEG, EMG, and EOG. Patients are monitored throughout four or five 20-minute opportunities to sleep (naps) at 2-hour intervals. For each nap, the patient is allowed 20 minutes to fall asleep. Once asleep, the patient is awakened after 15 minutes. Between naps, the patient is kept as alert as possible. *A sleep latency of 20 minutes indicates that no sleep occurred.*

Parametric Analysis

Total Number of Naps	4

Nap #	Time of Nap	Sleep Latency (mins)	REM Latency (mins)	Sleep Time Percent	Awake Time Percent
1	09:03:07	3.0	—	70.3	29.7
2	10:48:07	1.5	6.5	80.0	20.0
3	12:54:07	2.0	—	82.9	17.1
4	14:47:37	6.5	10.5	63.2	36.8
5	—	—	—	—	—

Mean Values for All Naps	
Mean sleep latency	3.3
Mean REM latency	8.5
Number of REM episodes	6
Number of naps with REM episodes	2

Results from Preceding PSG Study			
Sleep onset time	22:35:59	Sleep Efficiency (%)	92.6
Rise time	06:27:28	Sleep Latency (min)	6.5
Total sleep time	446.0	REM Latency (min)	74.0

The patient was pleasant and cooperative. She seemed sleepy but was able to maintain wakefulness between naps watching television and working on a computer. A fifth nap was not required, with two naps showing REM sleep. She was given an educational brochure on narcolepsy and was reminded to keep her follow-up appointment. This study strongly suggests a diagnosis of narcolepsy.

FIGURE 20-13
Multiple Sleep Latency Report (MSLT)

This MSLT study on a 32-year-old female with a complaint of excessive sleepiness shows a mean sleep latency for 4 daytime naps of less than 4 minutes. In addition, she had two sleep-onset REM periods and admitted to dreaming. The study indicates pathological daytime sleepiness and strongly suggests a diagnosis of narcolepsy. The MSLT is an excellent method for identifying both latent and manifest sleepiness. Some individuals can mask their sleepiness with stimulating activity, but if placed in a quiet, soporific setting, the latent sleepiness will become manifest. Too often that will occur while driving.

References

American Academy of Sleep Medicine. (2005). *International classification of sleep disorders* (2nd ed.): *Diagnostic and coding manual*. Westchester, IL.

American Thoracic Society. (1994). Sleep apnea, sleepiness and driving risk. *American Journal of Respiratory Critical Care Medicine, 150,* 1463–1473.

Carney, P.R., Berry, R.B., & Geyer J.D. (Eds.). (2005). *Clinical sleep disorders*. Philadelphia: Lippincott, Williams & Wilkins.

Compton-McBride, S., Schweitzer P. K., & Walsh, J. K. (2004). Most commonly used drugs to treat insomnia in 2002. *Sleep, 27*(Suppl.), A255.

Dement, W. (1990). A personal history of sleep disorders medicine. *Journal of Clinical Neurophysiology, 1,* 17–47.

Dement, N., & Kleitman, N. (1957). Cyclic variations in EEG during sleep and their relation to eye movements, body motility and dreaming. *Electroencephalography Clinical Neurophysiology, 9,* 673–690.

Earley, C. (2003). Restless legs syndrome. *New England Journal of Medicine, 348*(21), 2103–2109.

Findley, L., Fabrizo, M., & Suratt, P. M. (1989). Severity of sleep apnea and automobile crashes. *New England Journal of Medicine, 320*(13), 868–869.

George, C.F.P., Boudreau, A.C., & Smiley, A. (1996). Simulated driving performance in patients with obstructive sleep apnea. *American Journal of Respiratory Critical Care Medicine, 154,* 175–181.

Kryger, M.H., Roth, T., & Dement W.C. (Eds.). (2005). *Principles and practice of sleep medicine*. Philadelphia: Saunders.

Mallampati, S. R., Gugino, L.D., Ga, S. P., et al. (1985). A clinical sign to predict difficult tracheal intubation: A prospective study. *Canadian Anesthetists Society Journal, 32,* 429–432.

Mason, T., & Pack, A. (2007). Pediatric parasomnias. *Sleep, 2,* 141–151.

Maxmen, J.S. (1986). *A good night's sleep*. New York: Norton.

Mignot, E., Lammers, G. J., Ripley, M.S., et al. (2002). The role of cerebrospinal fluid hypocretin measurements in the diagnosis of narcolepsy and other hypersomnias. *Archives of Neurology, 59,* 1553–1562.

Mindell, J.A., & Owens, J.A. (Eds.). (2003). *A clinical guide to pediatric sleep diagnosis and management of sleep problems*. Philadelphia: Lippincott, Williams & Wilkins.

National Sleep Foundation. 2008 Sleep in America Poll. Available at http://www.sleepfoundation.org.

Ohayon, M.M. (2002). Epidemiology of insomnia: What we know and what we still need to learn. *Sleep Medicine Review, 6*, 97–111.

Peppard, P. E., Young, T., & Skatrud, J. (2000). Prospective study of the association between sleep-disordered breathing and hypertension. *New England Journal of Medicine, 342*(19), 1376–1384.

Shahar, E., Whitney, C. W., Redline, S., Lee, E. T., et al. (2001). Sleep-disordered breathing and cardiovascular disease: Sleep heart health study. *American Journal of Critical Care Medicine, 163*(1), 19–25.

Shepard, J.W., Jr. (1992). Hypertension, cardiac arrhythmias, myocardial infarction, and stroke in relation to obstructive sleep apnea. *Clinics in Chest Medicine, 13*(3), 437–458.

Spielman, A., Caruso, L., & Glovinsky, P. (1987). A behavioral perspective on insomnia treatment. *Psychiatric Clinics of North America, 10*, 541–553.

U.S. Xyrem Multicenter Study Group. (2003). A randomized double-blind, placebo-controlled multicenter trial comparing the effects of three doses of orally administered sodium oxybate with placebo for the treatment of narcolepsy (cataplexy). *Sleep, 25*, 42–49.

Walsh, J., Roehrs, T., & Roth, T. (2005). Pharmacologic treatment of primary insomnia. In M.H. Kryger, T. Roth, & W.C. Dement (Eds.), *Principles and practice of sleep medicine* (4th ed., chapter 63). Philadelphia: Saunders.

Young, T., Palta M., Dempsey, J., Skatrud J., Weber, S., & Badr, S. (1993). The occurrence of sleep-disordered breathing among middle-aged adults. *New England Journal of Medicine, 328*(17), 1230–1235.

Wise, M., Arand, D.L., et al. (2007). Treatment of narcolepsy and other hypersomnias of central origin. *Sleep, 30*, 1712–1727.

21

Impulse Control Disorders Not Classified Elsewhere

On occasion, everyone is impulsive, many like to gamble, and some may follow fire engines to a fire. Almost everyone has impulsively eaten a sweet at some time. Unlike these normal behaviors, however, people with impulse control disorders experience three essential features: (1) They *can't resist* an impulse or drive to do something that they know will be harmful to themselves or others. (2) They experience increasing *tension* before performing (or while attempting to resist performing) the act. (Patients often describe this tension as "pressure," "restlessness," "anxiety," or "discomfort.") (3) They feel *relief*, gratification, or satisfaction when committing the act. As a result, whereas acting on the impulse is momentarily ego-syntonic, later these individuals might feel guilt, self-reproach, or regret. They may act in haste and repent at leisure. However, repenting is not a necessary part of these diagnoses. Patients may or may not be aware of their impulses, and their deeds may or may not be premeditated. Patients with impulse control disorders may portray themselves as weak souls who readily cave into temptation or are easily overwhelmed by external forces. In a way, they're right, in that pathological impulsivity stems less from deliberate intent and more from an irresistible urge to discharge tension. People with impulse control disorders share two historical features: (1) onset in childhood, adolescence, or early adulthood (except for gambling, which doesn't start as early as childhood), and (2) associated psychopathology and family history—mood disorders and substance-use disorders are frequent (McElroy et al., 1992).

DSM-IV-TR groups impulse control disorders in a residual category called, "Impulse Control Disorders Not Classified Elsewhere." Impulse-related disturbances also occur in other mental illnesses such as attention-defitcit/hyperactivity disorder, bulimia, mania, substance abuse, paraphilias, and also in borderline and antisocial personality disorders. However, this category contains five specific impulse control disorders: pathological gambling, kleptomania, pyromania, intermittent explosive disorder, and trichotillomania. This chapter highlights pathological gambling as a prototypic impulse disorder; the other impulse disorders are briefly described.

PATHOLOGICAL GAMBLING

Distinguishing "social" from pathological gambling is akin to differentiating the social drinker from the alcoholic. Social gambling, like social drinking, is done for pleasure, with friends, and feels optional. Pathological gambling, like alcoholism, is done because the person can't stop, excludes friends, and feels obligatory. In most respects, pathological gambling, like alcoholism, is an *addiction*.

Clinical Presentation

People with gambling addictions feel unable to resist gambling, despite knowing that they'll lose and can't afford it. As one patient explained, "I've placed hundreds of bets, not caring whether I win or lose. Why? Because, I love the action. I'm drawn to the excitement. When I bet, I feel good and important."

Like other addictions, pathological gambling begets further gambling, which goes on to disrupt and damage every aspect of a person's life. Gambling debts take precedence over grocery bills. Forgery, fraud, arrests, tax evasion, excessive borrowing, stealing from friends, defaulting on loans, juggling financial obligations, lying, and forgetting who's owed what—it's all part of the disorder. Obligations to family and friends are supplanted by obligations to loan sharks and pawnbrokers. Even when these patients are not gambling, they're preoccupied with gambling. Everything they do is a result of gambling. They may sneak away from home to borrow money or to place a bet. Some people who gamble compulsively develop a perverse thrill or pride in the creativity of their reasons for why their debts aren't being paid and why their "big winnings" aren't paying off. Short of violence, anything will be done for money. As a "big game" approaches, these individuals reach an intolerable level of tension, which only the game relieves. Winning or losing has no effect on their gambling; they gamble as long as people will let them. Table 21-1 presents *DSM-IV-TR* criteria for pathological gambling; the problems listed under criterion A highlight the disorder's chief problems.

The person who gambles compulsively turns every nongambling situation into a gamble. Explains such a person, "When a normal person is driving with a quarter

TABLE 21-1

DSM-IV-TR *Criteria for Pathological Gambling*

A. Persistent and recurrent maladaptive gambling behavior as indicated by five (or more) of the following:

(1) is preoccupied with gambling (e.g., preoccupied with reliving past gambling experiences, handicapping or planning the next venture, or thinking of ways to get money with which to gamble)

(2) needs to gamble with increasing amounts of money in order to achieve the desired excitement

(3) has repeated unsuccessful efforts to control, cut back, or stop gambling

(4) is restless or irritable when attempting to cut down or stop gambling

(5) gambles as a way of escaping from problems or of relieving a dysphoric mood (e.g., feelings of helplessness, guilt, anxiety, depression)

(6) after losing money gambling, often returns another day to get even ("chasing" one's losses)

(7) lies to family members, therapist, or others to conceal the extent of involvement with gambling

(8) has committed illegal acts such as forgery, fraud, theft, or embezzlement to finance gambling

(9) has jeopardized or lost a significant relationship, job, or educational or career opportunity because of gambling

(10) relies on others to provide money to relieve a desperate financial situation caused by gambling

B. The gambling behavior is not better accounted for by a Manic Episode.

Note. From *DSM-IV-TR,* p. 674.

---

tank of gas on a highway and spots a sign saying that the next gas station is 50 miles away, she'll stop for gas. The gambler won't. He'll make a bet with himself that he can reach the next station without stopping for gas. This is a typical "mind bet," and when I'm not making a real bet, I'm making a mind bet."

Gambling, or talk of gambling, tends to dominate conversation; it's as if every social skill has atrophied, except for gambling or talking about gambling. Damon Runyon's characters might be fiction, but his descriptions of the gambler's mentality are not. For instance, a Runyon character says that whenever Feet Samuels—so-named because his feet are always at 90° angles—stands at a corner, gamblers will bet on which way Feet Samuels will go. In *Guys and Dolls,* Nathan Detroit calls Sky Masterson "the highest player of them all. . . . Another time he was sick and would not take penicillin because he bet his fever would go to 104°."

Generalizations surely, but people who gamble impulsively tend to be "big talkers" and "big spenders." Normally overconfident, self-centered, abrasive, energetic, and jovial, their moods reflect their earnings: On winning, they're temporarily elated; on losing, they're moody and anxious.

Clinical Course and Complications

While still teenagers, future pathological gamblers bet socially. Their gambling usually becomes serious by early adulthood, often after some modest winnings and during some stressful period.

Gamblers Anonymous (discussed later) describes four phases in the deterioration of people who gamble pathologically. First is the *winning phase*, in which they gamble occasionally, fantasize about winning, escalate their bets, and win big. Next comes the *losing phase*, in which they gamble alone, skip work, lie, borrow heavily, don't pay debts, and return the next day to win back losses ("chasing"). Third is the *desperation phase*, during which they are filled with remorse and their reputation suffers: They become separated from family and friends, get fired, blame others, panic, and steal. Last is the *hopeless phase*, in which they feel utterly futile, may get arrested and divorced, may drink heavily and abuse drugs, and typically become depressed. On hitting "rock bottom," up to 20% contemplate or attempt suicide.

Pathological gambling impairs most aspects of the person's life: Lost jobs, broken marriages, imprisonment, financial ruin, and attempted suicide are common.

While stressing the many similarities between pathological gambling and alcoholism, a "reformed" gambler aptly pointed out a big difference: "If you're an alcoholic with $1,000, you'll drink $50 worth of booze and fall asleep; when you awake, you've still got $950. If you're a druggie and shoot up $400 worth, you'll drift off and still awake with $600. But if you're a gambler, you'll blow all $1,000 and end up with *nothing!*"

Epidemiology

With the growth of legalized gambling in the United States, the number of people who gamble pathologically has climbed from 4 million in 1976 to 12 million in 1990—which is about 2% of the population. A 2000 study of gambling in U.S. adolescents and young adults found a similar prevalence of 2.1%. A parallel pattern has occurred in Great Britain, suggesting that legalized gambling may promote pathological gambling. Nearly two-thirds of Americans patronize legalized gambling: casinos, horse racing, dog racing, church bingo, state-run lotteries, etc. Their promoters don't call it "gambling" but run ads imploring listeners to "Get where the action is!"—a most telling phrase, given the gambler's thirst for excitement.

In a New York state study (Volberg & Steadman, 1988), 1.4% of the population was classified as pathological gamblers. Men outnumbered the women at least 2:1. A 2005 review of pathological gambling noted that the prevalence of pathological gambling in the United States is between 1 and 2%, but the prevalence is twice as high in areas located within a 50-mile radius of a casino. Gambling affects all social classes, though it is more common in those making under $25,000 a year than in those earning more. However, this yearly income figure may be a *result* of gambling and not a cause of it.

Etiology and Pathogenesis

Little is known about the etiology of pathological gambling; a combination of psychological and psychosocial factors is generally cited. The typical person who gambles impulsively comes from a family in which social gambling was at least condoned, or in which a parent of the same sex was a compulsive gambler or an alcoholic.

Several studies report that physiological arousal reinforces and maintains pathological gambling. High-sensation seekers and extraverts may be particularly vulnerable. The trait "sensation seeking" is correlated with bigger bet size and higher heart rate in casino gamblers and also with how extensive their gambling is, in general. People who gamble pathologically have higher levels of norepinephrine and dopamine than normals do during gambling, suggesting they experience greater "reward" than do nonproblem gamblers who show more modest increases in these neurotransmitters when gambling (Meyer, 2004). In the past decade, newer, dopamine enhancing treatments for Parkinson's disease have been associated with the untoward side effect of inducing problem gambling, lending further support to the idea that the behavior is mediated through specific neurotransmitter systems.

Other lines of research suggest that pathological gambling may belong to the depressive spectrum disorders. People who gamble pathologically have more first-degree relatives with mood and substance-use disorders (McElroy et al., 1992).

Differential Diagnosis

When a patient's chief complaint is *depression*, pathological gambling can be overlooked. If seeking treatment during the desperation or hopeless phases, the gambler may be so ashamed of his "moral weakness" that he avoids the topic, complaining instead of hopelessness, helplessness, suicidal thoughts, insomnia, and other depressive symptoms. Since clinicians rarely ask patients with depression if they gamble excessively, the disorder can elude diagnosis. Unlike people with *antisocial personality disorder*, most people who gamble pathologically have good work records prior to their serious gambling, and they steal solely to pay debts or to have money for gambling.

> Pathological gambling may be confused with *manic* or *hypomanic episodes*, since (a) mania often leads to outrageous betting, (b) both conditions involve poor judgment and little foresight, and (c) euphoria usually follows a gambler's winning streak. The presence of other manic behaviors, however, easily rules out pathological gambling. Pathological gambling is distinguished from *social gambling*, which occurs between friends, limits potential losses, and does not cause substantial harm.

Management and Treatment

Many people with gambling problems enter treatment simply to get relatives off their back; once things cool down, gambling resumes. If they remain in treatment, four attitudes frequently undermine their progress: (1) Lack of money is seen as *the* problem; (2) an instant or miraculous cure is expected; (3) life without gambling is inconceivable; and (4) repaying debts is desirable but impossible (Custer, 1979). Denying these attitudes during treatment, especially near the beginning, may raise doubts about the authenticity of the patient's commitment to change. Since these patients are often bright and have a gift of gab, place little stock in what they *say* and far more in what they *do*. Treatment should be judged on the duration of gambling-free intervals, on debts being paid, and on developing interests other than gambling.

The last goal, often overlooked, is crucial, since substitute excitements and pleasures must eventually replace gambling; hence, vocational counseling and recreational therapy may be an invaluable adjunct to therapy. Meeting periodically with relatives is also important, as much for the relatives as for the person with the gambling problem. Clinicians should remind themselves and the patient's loved ones that pathological gambling is a *chronic* disorder in which lapses are expected and do not necessarily mean that therapy is a bust.

> If the patient is on trial for problems secondary to his or her gambling, such as tax evasion, the best sentence might involve an extended probation *contingent* on the patient's participating fully in therapy, repaying all debts on schedule, not gambling, being employed regularly, and periodically showing financial accountability. Imprisonment is only useful when the person doesn't fulfill this program.

Founded in 1957, Gamblers Anonymous (GA) is modeled after Alcoholics Anonymous (AA), claims 12,000 members, and affiliates with Gam-Anon, which is similar to Alanon in that it is for relatives of gamblers. (Contact: GA's National Service Office, P. O. Box 17173, Los Angeles, CA 90017, 213/386–8789. www. gamblersanonymous.org). Only 5–8% of people who gamble and join GA stop gambling, but if GA is combined with comprehensive care, half who complete the program refrain from gambling for a year, and a third do so for several years (Kellner, 1982). Given the similarities between gambling and alcoholism and between GA and AA, if a GA chapter isn't available, attending AA may be a good substitute.

KLEPTOMANIA

Kleptomania is the recurrent failure to resist impulses to steal objects that are not for immediate use or for economic gain. People with kleptomania typically have enough money to buy the objects, and once possessing them, they have no use for them; they are likely to give the objects away, return them, or forget them. Unlike other thieves or shoplifters, people with kleptomania experience mounting tension before stealing and a gratifying relief of tension afterward; they steal by themselves, spontaneously, and without compatriots. Because they steal to alleviate tension, when that tension becomes unbearable, they're more concerned with discharging anxiety than with taking precautions. Hence, people with kleptomania make lousy thieves: Their bounty isn't worth much, and they're frequently caught. Contrary to myth, people with kleptomania do *not* want to be caught: What they *do* want is the thrill of discharging that tension. Table 21-2 presents *DSM-IV-TR* criteria for kleptomania.

Kleptomania is more common among women, seems to wax and wane over time, and often decreases with age. Four percent of apprehended shoplifters are people with kleptomania. Because most patients aren't people with kleptomania, the best question to ask to make the diagnosis is "Why did you do it?" People with kleptomania will give their own version of the tension and relief cycle. People with *psychosis* will tell you things like "The CIA made me do it." People with *antisocial and conduct disorders* will say "I wanted it," unless they are *also malingerers* and have learned to give the "right" answers for kleptomania. Then you have to see what was being stolen—pencils, lipstick?—or what really counts—jewelry, money, or valuable electronics items! (*antisocial*). People with *mania* will say it was the fun thing to do and have all the other symptoms of mania. Other people without kleptomania may admit doing it out of anger or for revenge.

TABLE 21-2

DSM-IV-TR *Criteria for Kleptomania*

A. Recurrent failure to resist impulses to steal objects that are not needed for personal use or for their monetary value.

B. Increasing sense of tension immediately before committing the theft.

C. Pleasure, gratification, or relief at the time of committing the theft.

D. The stealing is not committed to express anger or vengeance and is not in response to a delusion or a hallucination.

E. The stealing is not better accounted for by Conduct Disorder, a Manic Episode, or Antisocial Personality Disorder.

Note. From *DSM-IV-TR*, p. 669.

Kleptomania is associated with extraordinarily high rates of other psychiatric disorders. In one study using *DSM-III-R lifetime diagnosis* (McElroy, 1992), 100% had a mood disorder, 80% had at least one anxiety disorder, 60% had an eating disorder (most often bulimia), 50% had a substance disorder, 45% had obsessive–compulsive disorder, and 40% had some other impulse control disorder. Similarly high rates of these disorders were found in the patients' families. In a majority of cases, one of the other psychiatric disorders came first.

Almost nothing is known about the specific treatment of kleptomania. However, treating the other disorders associated with it is essential. Bulimia and obsessive–compulsive disorders, and to some extent substance abuse, also share the tension–relief cycle, so approaches to this cycle, such as response prevention, alternative forms of tension release, and antidepressants (particularly the SSRIs) may be helpful.

PYROMANIA

Pyromania is the recurrent failure to resist setting fires, along with an intense fascination with igniting and watching them. Setting fires is gratifying because it discharges mounting tension. People with pyromania thrill at seeing flames leap up and destroy things; by definition, these individuals do not set fires for any other reason (e.g., greed, revenge, politics). They rarely feel remorse or regret, despite knowing that they've destroyed property, maimed victims, or even murdered. Even planning arson, which they do far in advance, brings pleasure. This planning feature makes pyromania different from the other impulse disorders. Table 21-3 lists *DSM-IV-TR* criteria for pyromania.

Case studies show that as children, most future pyromaniacs are fascinated by fires, fire engines, firefighters, and any firefighting equipment. They have pulled many a false alarm and relished the sight of firefighters rushing to the scene; orchestrating this whole to-do may afford children an enormous sense of power, control, and mastery, which they probably lack in other areas of life.

People with pyromania are drawn to any huge fire (which is the first place police look to nab a firesetter). Since most people with pyromania come to psychiatrists via the courts, the literature about them is skewed. They are often diagnosed with alcohol abuse (91%), mood disorder (95%, usually dysthymia), and intermittent explosive disorder (68%). Also associated with pyromania is a higher rate of borderline personality disorder, attention-deficit/hyperactivity disorder, and learning disabilities. In one study, impulsive firesetters were found to be low in serotonin metabolites (Virkkunen et al., 1989). Low serotonin has been correlated with increased aggression and impulsivity.

Pyromania is a rare disorder. Firesetters are men 90% of the time; females tend to set fires in their own homes and to experience marital discord and depression. Pyromania in children differs from *normal childhood fascination with fires*, in that the latter is less frequent, pernicious, and all-consuming. Although patients with *antisocial personality disorders* sometimes set fires, their reasons are not limited to

---

TABLE 21-3
DSM-IV-TR *Criteria for Pyromania*

A. Deliberate and purposeful fire setting on more than one occasion.

B. Tension or affective arousal before the act.

C. Fascination with, interest in, curiosity about, or attraction to fire and its situational contexts (e.g., paraphernalia, uses, consequences).

D. Pleasure, gratification, or relief when setting fires, or when witnessing or participating in their aftermath.

E. The fire setting is not done for monetary gain, as an expression of sociopolitical ideology, to conceal criminal activity, to express anger or vengeance, to improve one's living circumstances, in response to a delusion or hallucination, or as a result of impaired judgment (e.g., in dementia, Mental Retardation, Substance Intoxication).

F. The fire setting is not better accounted for by Conduct Disorder, a Manic Episode, or Antisocial Personality Disorder.

Note. From *DSM-IV-TR,* p. 671.

being gratified by the fire. Deliberate sabotage, as "paid torches," political terrorism, and good old-fashioned revenge must be ruled out. Individuals with psychotic symptoms may set fires, but they do so in response to delusions or hallucinations. Unlike people with pyromania, patients with dementia may accidentally set fires, always without planning and without realizing the consequences of the act.

There are no controlled studies assessing treatment. Anecdotal reports indicate that most child pyromaniacs recover fully, whereas adults do not. With the majority having mildly low intelligence and ingrained impulsiveness, few people with pyromania benefit from insight-oriented psychotherapy. Behavior therapies might be more useful by substituting healthy gratifications, by improving social skills, or by applying aversive techniques. Perhaps the most useful intervention is to ensure that these individuals don't drink or use other substances that might further impair judgment and enhance impulsivity.

INTERMITTENT EXPLOSIVE DISORDER

This very rare disorder is characterized by discrete episodes of violence based on little or no provocation. The outbursts, which start and stop abruptly, usually last several minutes but may last for several hours. The person suddenly breaks windows, throws chairs, and so on. The "seizures" or "spells" may be immediately preceded by a rapid mood change, flushing, tachycardia, or altered sensorium (e.g., confusion, amnesia). Patients then describe an "irresistible impulse that comes over" them to smash everything in sight. Afterward, most assume responsibility for the act and express genuine remorse. Table 21-4 lists *DSM-IV-TR* criteria for intermittent explosive disorder.

This disorder primarily affects men; age of onset may be in childhood to the early 20s. Individuals with intermittent explosive disorder may have childhood histories of attention-deficit/hyperactivity disorder, and may also have some mild neurological abnormalities.

In the past, people with this disorder have been labeled "explosive characters" and "epileptoid personalities" because their explosive rages may resemble seizures. Despite this, their EEGs are usually normal or have only nonspecific changes that cannot be attributed to a known medical disorder. At times there may be historical evidence of delayed development (e.g., speech delay, coordination delay) in people who suffer from intermittent explosive disorder.

The "mean drunk" may seem explosive, but shows "intermittent" violence only when intoxicated. Intoxication with any psychoactive substance and any neurological condition (e.g., head trauma) must be ruled out as the cause of the violent

TABLE 21-4

DSM-IV-TR *Criteria for Intermittent Explosive Disorder*

A. Several discrete episodes of failure to resist aggressive impulses that result in serious assaultive acts or destruction of property.

B. The degree of aggressiveness expressed during the episodes is grossly out of proportion to any precipitating psychosocial stressors.

C. The aggressive episodes are not better accounted for by another mental disorder (e.g., Antisocial Personality Disorder, Borderline Personality Disorder, a Psychotic Disorder, a Manic Episode, Conduct Disorder, or Attention-Deficit/Hyperactivity Disorder) and are not due to the direct physiological effects of a substance (e.g., a drug of abuse, a medication) or a general medical condition (e.g., head trauma, Alzheimer's disease).

Note. From *DSM-IV-TR*, p. 667.

episodes, before a diagnosis of intermittent explosive disorder is given. *All the DSM-IV-TR disorders associated with increased violence and outbursts must be excluded to make sure they aren't the main source of the destructive behavior.* Keep in mind that many people with intermittent explosive disorder also have a personality disorder; separating out the two diagnoses is not an easy task. As with pyromania, people with intermittent explosive disorder have been found in some studies to have signs of altered serotonin metabolism.

There is no clearly effective treatment, although some patients have been helped by anticonvulsant medications (e.g., carbamazepine), beta-blockers (e.g., propranolol, metoprolol), lithium, antipsychotics, and antidepressants. Benzodiazepines (e.g., diazepam, lorazepam, clonazepam) may worsen the condition by disinhibiting the individual. Group therapy is claimed to be more useful than individual therapy.

TRICHOTILLOMANIA

Trichotillomania is the recurrent failure to resist pulling out one's own hair. Unlike the other four impulse control disorders listed, it usually causes harm only to the individual affected. Trichotillomania is commonly associated with depressive and anxiety disorders, and may run in families. There has been some controversy surrounding the grouping of trichotillomania with the other impulse control disorders not elsewhere classified, and some authors have suggested that it may be a variant of obsessive–compulsive disorder.

The disorder causes distress because hair loss can be extensive, and the obvious hair loss can attract social scrutiny. Children with the disorder are often teased or ostracized. For many (but not all) individuals with trichotillomania, tension mounts before the moment of plucking and is reduced during or after the act. The majority pull out one hair at a time, concentrate on scalp hair, and report that pulling the hair out doesn't hurt. Some pull out clumps of hair, often by first twirling a group of hairs together and then pulling them out as a group.

Hair loss varies from barely noticeable thinning to total loss. This loss usually occurs in patches, as individuals often have a preferred pulling spot, often the crown area or at the temples. Eyelashes (22%) and eyebrows (8%) are other favored sites. Multiple sites (two on average) are eventually used, and because it's easily concealed, even pubic hair (17%) is included. After pulling out the hair, many people with trichotillomania will manipulate or examine the hair in some way. They may put the hair in or around their mouths (25%), lick it (8%), and/or eat it (10%) (Christenson et al., 1991).

Most patients with trichotillomania are females with some studies reporting the female to male ratio to be as high as 10:1. This difference may reflect some bias in seeking treatment, but there does seem to be a greater occurrence of the disorder in females. Estimates from university surveys suggest that 1.5% of males and 3.4% of females endorse significant hair pulling, and 0.6% of these university students met all diagnostic criteria for trichotillomania (Dell'Osso, 2006). Table 21-5 lists *DSM-IV-TR* criteria for trichotillomania.

TABLE 21-5
DSM-IV-TR *Criteria for Trichotillomania*

A. Recurrent pulling out of one's hair resulting in noticeable hair loss.

B. An increasing sense of tension immediately before pulling out the hair or when attempting to resist the behavior.

C. Pleasure, gratification, or relief when pulling out the hair.

D. The disturbance is not better accounted for by another mental disorder and is not due to a general medical condition (e.g., a dermatological condition).

E. The disturbance causes clinically significant distress or impairment in social, occupational, or other important areas of functioning.

Note. From *DSM-IV-TR,* p. 677.

Many people with trichotillomania don't come in for treatment. A third of the women who came to a clinic for treatment said that they had the problem less than a year. A broader, nonclinic study (Christenson et al., 1991) found that most had started the behavior within 5 years before or after puberty and had had the problem for two decades. Only 18% did *not* have another Axis I disorder. The rest had a lifetime diagnosis of mood disorders (65%), anxiety disorder (57%), eating disorders (20%), and/or substance use disorder (22%). Within the anxiety disorders, 18% had panic disorder, 10% had obsessive–compulsive disorder, and another 18% had obsessions or compulsions but did not meet the full criteria for obsessive–compulsive disorder.

Because people with trichotillomania are, at times, secretive about their pulling, a medical cause for their hair loss may be considered. With a biopsy, a dermatologist can easily distinguish between the medical condition of *alopecia areata* and hair loss from trichotillomania. If the patient insists to the clinician that she never pulls out her hair, and the dermatologist can verify that this is a lie; then the person really has a *factitious disorder* with physical symptoms. One important question is "What makes you pull out your hair, and how do you feel once you've done it?" People with *obsessive–compulsive disorder* will say that they are doing it to prevent or produce some future situation. Kids and adults with *stereotypic movement disorder* will say that they don't know why they do it, they just do, and it doesn't bother them. Fiddling with the hair and occasionally pulling out a hair is normal; no tension–relief cycle is noted. Normals might say "I barely thought about it—I was spaced out." In contrast, individuals with trichotillomania will often describe urges to pull, and relief after, or pleasure during, pulling. The behavior often occurs during passive activities such as reading or TV viewing. Usually the individuals pull when they are alone, suggesting some degree of voluntary control. Sessions of pulling may last many minutes and result in the loss of significant (noticeable) amounts of hair. Other impulsive behaviors seen in individuals with trichotillomania include nail biting and excessive picking at skin.

Along with behavioral approaches, treatment with antidepressants may be helpful. As in obsessive–compulsive disorder, serotonin agents such as clomipramine and fluoxetine have shown efficacy. There are established cognitive–behavioral treatment models for the disorder, and these have also shown efficacy. There have also been reports of benefits from hypnosis.

References

Christenson, G.A., Mackenzie, T.B., & Mitchell, J.E. (1991). Characteristics of 60 adult chronic hair pullers. *American Journal of Psychiatry, 148,* 365–370.

Custer, R.L. (1979). *An overview of compulsive gambling.* Paper presented at South Oaks Hospital, Amityville, New York.

Dell'Osso, B., Altamura, A.C., Allen, A., Marazziti, D., & Hollander, E. (2006). Epidemiologic and clinical updates on impulse-control disorders: A critical review. *European Archives of Psychiatry and Clinical Neuroscience, 256*(8), 464–475.

Kellner, R. (1982). Disorders of impulse control. In J.H. Greist, J.W. Jefferson, & R.L. Spitzer (Eds.), *Treatment of mental disorders* (pp. 398–418). New York: Oxford University Press.

McElroy, S.L., Hudson, J.I., Pope, H.G., & Keck, P.E. (1991). Kleptomania and associated psychopathology. *Psychological Medicine, 21*(1), 93–108.

McElroy, S.L., Hudson, J.L., Harrison, G.P., Jr., Keck, P.E., Jr., & Aizley, H.G. (1992). The *DSM-III-R* impulse control disorders not elsewhere classified: Clinical characteristics and relationship to other psychiatric disorders. *American Journal of Psychiatry, 149,* 318–327.

Meyer, G., et al. (2004). Neuroendocrine response to casino gambling in problem gamblers. *Psychoneuroendocrinology, 29*(10), 1272–1280.

Petry, N.M. (2007). Gambling and substance use disorders: Current status and future directions. *American Journal of Addictions, 16*(1), 1–9.

Roy, A., Adinoff, B., Roehrich, L., Lamparski, D., Custer, R., Lorenz, V., et al. (1988). Pathological gambling. *Archives of General Psychiatry, 45,* 369–373.

Roy, A., DeJong, J., & Linnoila, M. (1989). Extraversion in pathological gamblers. *Archives of General Psychiatry, 46,* 679–681.

Stein, D.J., Christenson, G., & Hollander, H. (Eds.). (1999). *Trichotillomania.* Washington, DC: American Psychiatric Association.

Sumitra, L.M., & Miller, S.C. (2005). Pathologic gambling disorder: How to help patients curb risky behavior when the future is at stake. *Postgraduate Medicine, 118*(1), 31–37.

Virkkunen, M., DeJong, J., Bartko, J., & Linnoila, M. (1989). Psychobiological concommitants of history of suicide attempts among violent offenders and impulsive fire setters. *Archives of General Psychiatry, 148,* 652–657.

Volberg, A., & Steadman, H.J. (1988). Refining prevalence estimates of pathological gambling. *American Journal of Psychiatry, 145,* 502–505.

Voon, V., & Fox, S.H. (2007). Medication-related impulse control and repetitive behaviors in Parkinson disease. *Archives of Neurology, 64*(8), 1089–1096.

Welte, J.W., Barnes, G.M., Tidwell, M.C., & Hoffman, J.H. (2008). The prevalence of problem gambling among U.S. adolescents and young adults: Results from a national survey. *J. Gambling Sudies, 24*(2), 119–133.

22

Personality Disorders

"Personality" or "character" *traits* are ingrained, enduring patterns of behaving, feeling, perceiving, and thinking that are prominent in a wide range of personal and social contexts. Personality is the psychological equivalent of physical appearance: We grow up with both, and although we can adjust each, they remain essentially the same and affect the rest of our lives. As Heraclitus observed, "A man's fate is his character." An individual's personality has been compared with the body's immune system. Just as the immune cells protect us against viruses and bacteria, so does the individual's personality enable him or her to cope with life challenges (Millon, 2004). Personality may be understood as composed of *character*, which is the component of the personality evolving from upbringing, and *temperament*, which is comprised of those features of the personality that have biological bases and are often inherited.

Personality features may or may not be adaptive. Compulsiveness in a student is adaptive when it promotes orderly study habits, but it's maladaptive when the student spends hours sharpening pencils instead of studying. Personality traits turn into personality *disorders* when they (1) become inflexible and maladaptive, and (2) significantly impair social and occupational functioning or cause substantial subjective distress. People with personality disorders are not always in significant emotional distress. Often, the people they are living or working with are more distressed. Freud once defined a successful mature adult as someone "who is able to love and to work." People with personality disorders frequently fail at both.

This chapter summarizes the 10 personality disorders listed in *DSM-IV-TR*. In general, personality disorders first become apparent during adolescence or earlier, persist through life, and become less obvious by middle or old age. The diagnosis is not made until adulthood, since behavioral disorders of childhood and adolescence are frequently transient. Personality disorders are more pronounced during periods of high energy (as in adolescence) and under stressful conditions; they should be diagnosed only when they cause lifelong problems, not just discrete periods of dysfunction. Except for schizotypal, borderline, and antisocial personalities, hospitalizations are rare.

In *DSM-IV-TR*, personality traits and disorders are listed on Axis II, whereas mental disorders are indicated on Axis I. This separation distinguishes patients' current and more florid mental disorders from their ongoing, baseline personalities; this distinction should result in more *realistic* treatment goals. Since Axis I mental disorders are more responsive to treatment than Axis II personality disorders, a realistic treatment goal may be to remedy the former but not the latter. For instance, it may be unrealistic to expect a dependent personality who develops a major depression to be rid of both after a brief hospitalization. The symptoms of a chronic Axis I disorder, undiagnosed or incompletely treated, may negatively influence personality so that over time the individual develops a more pervasive manner of interacting with the environment that is characteristic of a personality disorder. For example, someone with social phobia develops an avoidant personality or someone with rapidly cycling bipolar disorder develops a borderline personality.

Kahana and Bibring (1964) show how identifying medical patients' personality types may alter how clinicians relate to patients. For example, when a doctor pats Mr. Moscowitz on the shoulder and says, "Don't worry, everything will be fine," a dependent patient will be greatly relieved; do the same with a paranoid patient and he'll draw away and think, "How does he know I'll be okay? Why's he being so chummy? How dare he touch me?" Paranoid patients feel safer with clinicians who keep their distance. Thus in many settings, clinicians should not attempt to change the patient's personality, but rather should adjust their own behavior to fit the patient's. When treatment for a personality disorder is attempted, the goal is not to reverse a constitutional defect but to help the person live more comfortably and efficiently within his or her limitations; treatment can help modify and reduce the defect. The task of therapists who treat individuals with personality disorders is to help them (and others around them) recognize and accept their defects, and having done so, to organize their lives in such a way that their defects are minimized and their remaining talents and strengths maximized.

Understanding a patient's personality traits can guide psychotherapy, medication use, family involvement, nurses' monitoring, etc. To illustrate: During group therapy, Mrs. Grant suddenly asked to see her hospital chart. If Mrs. Grant had a paranoid personality, the group therapist could be fairly sure she wanted to uncover malicious information that the staff were writing about her. However, Mrs. Grant is not paranoid; she has an avoidant personality, and as such, the therapist can reasonably guess that she wanted to know whether the therapist liked her—a proposition he raised for the group's consideration. Another illustration: If during a highly stressful period, a patient asked for a 3-day supply of sleeping pills, all things being equal, a patient with a borderline personality would be far more likely to abuse the pills than would a patient with a schizoid personality. Or, if a psychiatric nurse has to leave patients in the care of another patient, she would much prefer an obsessive–compulsive to an antisocial personality.

Physicians must be aware that patients with personality disorders may be less compliant with their medicines (Colum et al., 2000; Herbeck, 2005) and thus require more attention to their medical management. Patients with personality disorders have more troubled lives, as evidenced by more contact with police (Gandhi et al., 2001), increased use of medical services (Reich et al., 1989), and more suicide attempts (Pirkis et al., 1999). Substance-abuse disorders were the most common Axis I diagnosis found among those with personality disorders (Koeningsberg et al., 1985).

Personality disorders are not uncommon. Lenzenweger et al. (1997) report that about 11% of the general population suffers from a personality disorder. In a retrospective chart review, 36% of 2,462 psychiatric patients had personality disorders. Borderline personality disorder was diagnosed most frequently (12% of total); next (at 10%) was *DSM-III*'s residual category of "mixed, atypical, or other personality disorder." The other personality disorders were diagnosed in under 3% of the patients.

The etiology of personality disorder is probably multifactorial. Analytic theory strongly implicates environmental factors such as how the individual is raised. Others such as Torgersen et al. (2000), suggest more biological factors. The answer is most likely a combination of environmental and genetic components.

Differential Diagnosis

In general, never diagnose a personality disorder in the midst of an episode of a major psychiatric illness without having information about the person's behavior before this episode. Too often, mole hills in a personality become mountains during an acute psychiatric episode. Minor traits such as dependency may look like full-blown personality disorders during the acute stress. Consider the following:

1. *Neurosis* (i.e., nonpsychotic mood and anxiety disorders) *versus personality disorder*. Patients who develop a nonpsychotic mood or anxiety disorder regard their anxious behavior as uncharacteristic of their

usual self, as different for them. In contrast, the pathological behavior exhibited by patients with personality disorders is in character— i.e., usual for them. Anxiety disorders may develop at any time; personality disorders are longstanding. Anxious individuals are usually uncomfortable with their symptoms, whereas individuals with personality disorders often justify and rationalize their behavior.

2. *Personality trait versus disorder.* Some people have only one or two characteristics of a disorder, which do not significantly impair functioning as does the full-blown disorder.

3. *Major mood disorders and schizophrenia versus personality disorders.* Impairment in functioning is seldom as profound in personality disorders as in major mood disorders and schizophrenia. Individuals with personality disorders seldom require hospitalization; they are not psychotic.

4. *Late-onset mental disorder.* Late-onset (adulthood) personality changes suggest the presence of a major mental or medical disorder.

DSM-IV-TR divides personality disorders into three clusters: The first (Cluster A) consists of paranoid, schizoid, and schizotypal personality disorders, characterized by odd or eccentric behavior. The second (Cluster B) includes histrionic, narcissistic, antisocial, and borderline personality disorders, characterized by dramatic, overemotional, and erratic behavior. The third (Cluster C) consists of avoidant, dependent, and obsessive–compulsive personality disorders, characterized by highly anxious and fearful affects.

PARANOID PERSONALITY DISORDER

"I only trust me and thee and I'm not so sure of thee."

—Anonymous

The essential features of a paranoid personality disorder (PPD) include: (1) pervasive and unwarranted suspiciousness and mistrust of people, (2) hypersensitivity, and (3) emotional detachment. None of these features should stem from another mental disorder, such as schizophrenia or paranoid disorder. Table 22-1 lists the *DSM-IV-TR* criteria for PPD.

"Paranoids have enemies" mainly because they're paranoid. Paranoid people are very unpleasant, always blaming and suspicious of others. In general, suspicions may be justified and adaptive from time to time, but when contradictory evidence is presented, most people abandon them. People with PPD do not, but rather view the evidence as further proof that the person intends

Table 22-1

DSM-IV-TR *Criteria for Paranoid Personality Disorder*

A. A pervasive distrust and suspiciousness of others such that their motives are interpreted as malevolent, beginning by early adulthood and present in a variety of contexts, as indicated by four (or more) of the following:

(1) Suspects, without sufficient basis, that others are exploiting, harming, or deceiving him or her

(2) Is preoccupied with unjustified doubts about the loyalty or trustworthiness of friends or associates

(3) Is reluctant to confide in others because of unwarranted fear that the information will be used maliciously against him or her

(4) Reads hidden, demeaning, or threatening meanings into benign remarks or events

(5) Persistently bears grudges, i.e., is unforgiving of insults, injuries, or slights

(6) Perceives attacks on his or her character or reputation that are not apparent to others and is quick to react angrily or to counterattack

(7) Has recurrent suspicions, without justification, regarding fidelity of spouse or sexual partner

B. Does not occur exclusively during the course of Schizophrenia, a Mood Disorder with Psychotic Features, or another Psychotic Disorder and is not due to the direct physiological effects of a general medical condition.

Note. From *DSM-IV-TR*, p. 694.

to harm them. The world of the person with PPD is hostile, devious, and dark, filled with persecutory forces for which he must be eternally vigilant. On entering a restaurant, the person will scan the room to ensure that no enemies are present and then sit with his back to the wall so that nobody can sneak behind him. Highly secretive, he may hide behind dark glasses. People with PPD bristle at the slightest contradiction or criticism, distrust other's loyalty, and misconstrue what is said to them. When a coworker congratulated a man with paranoia on plans to buy a home, he snapped, "It's mine! You can't have it!" These individuals may be ambitious and bright, yet they are also stubborn and defensive. They're quick to argue and find fault. They'll seize an alleged injustice, blowup its significance, and distort the facts to fit their suspiciousness.

An English professor with PPD discovered that a classroom he had reserved was occupied by another faculty member. The professor became enraged, citing it as "this draconian administration's efforts to drive me from the university." The next day, after learning that the university press would not publish his definitive study of Iago, he launched a $3 million lawsuit against the university. Four months later, the university threatened not to renew his contract. He dropped the suit but then instigated student protests against the university for "stifling academic freedom."

People keep their distance from people with PPD, which merely confirms the validity of these individuals' general distrust. People with PPD are pathologically jealous, tense, rigid, unwilling to compromise, moralistic, always detecting ill intent and special messages, litigious, humorless, coldly objective, overly rational, haughty, and distant. That's why "paranoids have enemies," have few friends, and fewer, if any, intimate relationships. They have contempt for weakness in others and disdain the sickly, defective, and imperfect—that is, everybody, but themselves. They think in hierarchical terms: Who's superior to whom? Who controls whom? With their egocentricity and exaggerated self-importance, they make a great show of self-sufficiency. They're drawn to politics, history, science, and technology; to them, the arts are for sissies. As unpleasant as these individuals can be, it's possible to muster compassion by remembering that it's a terribly uncomfortable existence for them.

PPD is more common in men than women. The prevalence of PPD is estimated at 2% of the general population, 20% among those in inpatient psychiatric settings, and 5% among those in outpatient psychiatric clinics. Social relations and job advancement are often severely impaired. Unlike paranoid disorders and paranoid schizophrenia, paranoid personalities are *not* psychotic. When a person with paranoid disorder is challenged about the certainty of his allegations, he will say, "I'm quite sure," or "It's highly probable." If pushed further about alternative explanations, he might say, "Yes, those alternatives are possible but highly unlikely." The psychotic will say, "It is fact and there are no alternative explanations." People with PPD can become psychotic when highly stressed. A person with PPD has overvalued ideas, not delusions.

These patients seldom come for psychiatric treatment since they do not perceive weaknesses or faults in themselves. They may be sent by bosses or wives under threat of the loss of a job or marriage, but the relationship they form with a therapist tends to be adversarial rather than collaborative and thus is often doomed to failure. They do, of course, need medical treatment from time to time, and when this happens, they interact with their physicians in the same manner as they interact with others. They tend to be guarded in giving information about themselves, suspicious of the intent behind the questions asked, and distrustful of examinations, procedures, and treatments. They often question the training and qualifications of those who treat them. They are particularly apt to bring suit. It is therefore important that clinicians who deal with this group of people do so in an honest and comprehensive fashion. They should be thoroughly informed and their consent obtained for whatever is done. Further, careful documentation of both the information given and the informed consent is advised.

In psychological treatment, the therapist's main task is to minimize the patient's distrust of the therapist and of therapy. It often takes months before the patient feels at all relaxed in treatment. Clinicians should be respectful and business-like, avoiding intimacy and too much warmth, which people with PPD experience as invasive. Deep psychological interpretations are verboten, since people with PPD are already leery of "shrinks who read people's minds and trick them." What is insight to a therapist is "messing with my mind" to a person with PPD. In the office, clinicians should *not* sit between the patient and the door; the person feels far less threatened if nobody "blocks" her exit way. What's an office to a therapist is an observation chamber to a person with PPD. When clinicians err, they should admit the mistake, apologize, and get on with it; overapologizing fosters distrust. Nor should clinicians ask these individuals to trust them, since to them, that's like a Nazi guard asking a Dachau inmate to trust him. Being straightforward and "professional" is the most reassuring approach. When starting medications, these patients should be given detailed and accurate side-effect information. They already expect the worst but feel better knowing about it.

SCHIZOID PERSONALITY DISORDER

The central features of a schizoid personality disorder (SDPD) include: (1) minimal or no social relations, (2) restricted expression of emotion, (3) a striking lack of warmth and tenderness, and (4) an apparent indifference to others' praise, criticism, feelings, and concerns. Unlike schizotypal personalities (see below), patients with SDPD do *not* exhibit eccentricities of speech, behavior, or thinking. Table 22-2 lists *DSM-IV-TR* criteria for SDPD.

Patients with SDPD are often "in a fog," absentminded, loners, detached from others, self-involved, "not connected." What appears as aloofness is actually profound shyness. Often dull and humorless, they will disavow feelings of anger or interest in sex; they prefer solitary activities and daydreaming to friendships. Dating is painful, marriage rare. Although SDPD greatly impedes social relationships and professional advancement, these patients can excel if permitted minimal interpersonal contact. The prevalence of SDPD is unknown, though these individuals may be common on skid row. SDPD is diagnosed slightly more often in males, who seem to suffer more impairment from the disorder than their female counterparts.

TABLE 22-2
DSM-IV-TR *Criteria for Schizoid Personality Disorder*

A. A pervasive pattern of detachment from social relationships and a restricted range of expression of emotions in interpersonal settings, beginning by early adulthood and present in a variety of contexts, as indicated by four (or more) of the following:

    (1) Neither desires nor enjoys close relationships, including being part of a family

    (2) Almost always chooses solitary activities

    (3) Has little, if any, interest in having sexual experiences with another person

    (4) Takes pleasure in few, if any, activities

    (5) Lacks close friends or confidants other than first-degree relatives

    (6) Appears indifferent to the praise or criticism of others

    (7) Shows emotional coldness, detachment, or flattened affectivity

B. Does not occur exclusively during the course of Schizophrenia, a Mood Disorder with Psychotic Features, another Psychotic Disorder, or a Pervasive Developmental Disorder and is not due to the direct physiological effects of a general medical condition.

Note: If criteria are met prior to the onset of Schizophrenia, add "Premorbid," e.g., "Schizoid Personality Disorder (Premorbid)."

Note. From *DSM-IV-TR,* p. 697.

SDPD resembles *avoidant personality disorder,* since both display prominent social isolation. Whereas the avoidant personalities want friends, people with SDPD don't; whereas those who are avoidant are alone because they're afraid people won't like them, people with SDPD have no interest in personal involvement. Once considered a prodromal phase of *schizophrenia,* SDPD and schizophrenia are now considered to be unrelated (see below). Few patients with SDPD become psychotic.

Little is known about the treatment of this disorder; most persons with this condition probably do not seek professional help or do so only when seeking help for depression, substance abuse, or other problems. Most undoubtedly these people lack the insight or motivation for individual psychotherapy and probably would find the intimacy of typical group therapy too threatening. If the patient is motivated, behavioral techniques may be helpful, such as graded exposure to a variety of social tasks. For example, the clinician might encourage the patient to attend a concert, then join a bridge club, and eventually enter a dance class. Long-term group psychotherapy with other patients who have SDPD has also been reported to be successful (Yalom, 2005). Some clinicians have postulated that schizoid personality may be a variant of high-functioning autism.

SCHIZOTYPAL PERSONALITY DISORDER

In *DSM-IV-TR* the essential feature of a schizotypal personality disorder (STPD) "is a pervasive pattern of social and interpersonal deficits marked by acute discomfort with, and reduced capacity for, close relationships as well as by cognitive or perceptual distortions and eccentricities of behavior" (p. 701). These patients have few friends because they are very strange and eccentric. They live in "The Twilight Zone," filled with weird thoughts, ideas of reference, paranoid ideation, illusions of telepathy, and "magical thinking"—e.g., "If I think hard enough, I can make the wind blow"; or "My teeth itch." Their speech may be hard to follow, although without loose associations or incoherence. Their affect is flat or inappropriate. Sloppy, unkempt, giggling for no reason, and often talking to themselves, they are hypersensitive to criticism and dreadfully anxious around people, especially if more than three are together. Table 22-3 lists the *DSM-IV-TR* criteria for STPD.

Unlike *schizoid* personalities, *schizotypal* personalities are more likely to (1) display bizarre and peculiar traits, (2) develop fanatic, eccentric, or racist beliefs, (3) become dysthymic and anxious, (4) have an accompanying borderline personality disorder, (5) become transiently psychotic under stress, (6) evolve into schizophrenia, (7) run in families (Baron, Guren, Asnis, & Lord, 1985), and (8) have a relative with schizophrenia. Unlike STPD, patients with *schizophrenia, residual type* would have previously displayed a florid schizophrenic psychosis. If schizophrenia develops in a patient with STPD, the schizotypal diagnosis is dropped. Indeed, schizophrenia should always be suspected in these patients if they are under 35.

Treatment of patients with STPD often centers on issues that led them to seek treatment. These issues may include feelings of alienation due to paranoid ideation or ideas of reference. A supportive approach has been recommended, whereas exploratory and group psychotherapies are felt to be overly threatening. Social skills training may be useful in helping eccentric, odd persons to feel more comfortable with others. Lower doses of antipsychotics have been recommended to alleviate some of the intense anxiety and cognitive symptoms, such as odd speech and unusual perceptual experience; this approach has some empirical support. However, enthusiasm for using these medications must be tempered by their tendency to induce troublesome and potentially irreversible side effects.

TABLE 22-3
DSM-IV-TR *Criteria for Schizotypal Personality Disorder*

A. A pervasive pattern of social and interpersonal deficits marked by acute discomfort with, and reduced capacity for, close relationships as well as by cognitive or perceptual distortions and eccentricities of behavior, beginning by early adulthood and present in a variety of contexts, as indicated by five (or more) of the following:

    (1) Ideas of reference (excluding delusions of reference)

    (2) Odd beliefs or magical thinking that influence behavior and are inconsistent with subcultural norms (e.g., superstitiousness, belief in clairvoyance, telepathy, or "sixth sense"; in children and adolescents, bizarre fantasies or preoccupations)

    (3) Unusual perceptual experiences, including bodily illusions

    (4) Odd thinking and speech (e.g., vague, circumstantial, metaphorical, over elaborate, or stereotyped)

    (5) Suspiciousness or paranoid ideation

    (6) Inappropriate or constricted affect

    (7) Behavior or appearance that is odd, eccentric, or peculiar

    (8) Lacks close friends or confidants other than first-degree relatives

    (9) Excessive social anxiety that does not diminish with familiarity and tends to be associated with paranoid fears rather than negative judgments about self

B. Does not occur exclusively during the course of Schizophrenia, a Mood Disorder with Psychotic Features, another Psychotic Disorder, or a Pervasive Developmental Disorder.

Note: If criteria are met prior to the onset of Schizophrenia, add "Premorbid," e.g., "Schizotypal Personality Disorder (Premorbid)."

Note. From *DSM-IV-TR,* p. 701.

HISTRIONIC PERSONALITY DISORDER
"Make me the center of all your attentions."

—Millon (2004)

Individuals with histrionic personality disorder (HPD) are lively, overdramatic, and always calling attention to themselves. Their behavior is overreactive, with minor stimuli giving rise to emotional excitability such as irrational outbursts or temper tantrums. Individuals with HPD crave novelty, stimulation, and excitement and become quickly bored with normal routines. Though they are often creative and imaginative, they seldom show interest in intellectual achievement and careful, analytic thinking. Table 22-4 lists *DSM-IV-TR* criteria for HPD.

In relationships, these individuals are perceived as shallow and lacking in genuineness, though charming and appealing. They are quick to form friendships, but once a friendship is established, they become demanding, egocentric, and inconsiderate. Because of feeling helpless and dependent, they make continuous demands for reassurance and manipulative suicidal threats, gestures, or attempts. Typically attractive and seductive, people with HPD attempt to control the opposite sex or to enter into dependent relationships. Although flights into romantic fantasy are common, their sexuality is often constricted or unsatisfying. They experience periods of intense dissatisfaction and unhappiness, usually related to external changes such as a breakup with a lover.

This disorder is common and diagnosed more frequently in females than in males. The prevalence of HPD in the general population may be about 2–3% with rates of about 10–15% in inpatient and outpatient psychiatric settings. It occurs more frequently among family members than in the general population. A frequent complication is substance use disorder. A codiagnosis of narcissistic, dependent, or borderline personality disorder is common. Although the cause of histrionic personality is unknown, the disorder has been linked through family studies to somatization disorder and antisocial personality. Research has suggested that histrionic and antisocial personalities may be

---

TABLE 22-4

DSM-IV-TR *Criteria for Histrionic Personality Disorder*

A pervasive pattern of excessive emotionality and attention seeking, beginning by early adulthood and present in a variety of contexts, as indicated by five (or more) of the following:

(1) is uncomfortable in situations in which he or she is not the center of attention

(2) interaction with others is often characterized by inappropriate sexually seductive or provocative behavior

(3) displays rapidly shifting and shallow expression of emotions

(4) consistently uses physical appearance to draw attention to self

(5) has a style of speech that is excessively impressionistic and lacking in detail

(6) self-dramatization, theatricality, and exaggerated expression of emotion

(7) suggestibility, i.e., easily influenced by others or circumstances

(8) considers relationships to be more intimate than they actually are

Note. From *DSM-IV-TR,* p. 714.

---

sex-typed phenotypic variants of the same underlying genetic diathesis. It has also been suggested that histrionic personality is a sex-biased diagnosis that merely describes a caricature of stereotypic femininity.

> If one talks about personality *styles* rather than *disorders*, "hysterics" and "compulsives'" are cognitive opposites. Hysterics think in impressions, compulsives in facts. If Holly Go-Lightly, the Hysteric, and Carl Compulsive were to describe a person they recently met, Holly would exclaim, "He's just a darling, and such thrilling eyes. He must've murdered somebody. Either that or he's a poet. Did you see how he looked straight through me? I loved it." Carl would say, "He's about 5 feet, 11 inches tall, weighs 160 pounds, has black hair, bushy eyebrows, a Southern accent. . . . " Compulsives present exhaustive, and ultimately boring, details; hysterics make global comments that lack specificity and focus. Compulsives are too mired in detail to make hunches, whereas hysterics base all their decisions on hunches, eschewing logic and information. Most people invoke hunches as temporary hypotheses, but hysterics use them as final conclusions (Shapiro, 1999). Because they so complement each other, it's not uncommon for compulsive professionals to marry histrionic artists. Such a marriage offers drama for the compulsive and stability for the histrionic.

In clinical interviews, it is very difficult to get detailed information from patients with HPD. It's like trying to nail Jello to a wall. Asking a patient *how long* she has been feeling badly might evoke a response such as, "Forever, a very long time" (in reality, it started 12 days ago). If asked *how badly* she feels, the patient might say, "The worst ever. I can't take the pain." The patient is not deliberately creating a smoke screen or being passive–aggressive; she stores *impressions* in her brain, not details. To adapt to the histrionics' style, clinicians may fare better by using more global wording than usual (most clinicians tend more to the compulsive side). If medications are prescribed, the generalities about side effects may suffice, since the details will be lost anyway.

Interventions have not been clearly studied, but psychoanalytic psychotherapy has a long tradition in the treatment of this and related syndromes, and for that reason is considered by some the treatment of choice. However, others advocate a more supportive, problem-solving approach or a cognitive approach to deal with distorted thinking (i.e., inflated self-image) and to minimize the counterproductive effects of frequent excessive emotional outpouring. Interpersonal approaches tend to focus on uncovering conscious (or unconscious) motivations for seeking out disappointing lovers and being unable to commit to stable, meaningful relationships. Group therapy may be useful in addressing provocative and attention-seeking behavior. Because patients may not be aware of their behaviors, it can be helpful for others to point out these traits to them. A condition that may be related—*hysteroid dysphoria*, described in depressed women who have a history of sensitivity to rejection in relationships—is reportedly responsive to MAOIs (e.g., phenelzine).

NARCISSISTIC PERSONALITY DISORDER

"Please get me a tissue, I have a runny nose."

—Patient asking a nurse, who is attempting to resuscitate
a collapsed patient in the hallway.

Narcissus was the mythological Greek youth who fell so in love with his own reflection that he pined away and died. In 1898 Havelock Ellis used this myth to describe a case of male autoeroticism in his essay on Casanova. Twelve years after this, Freud introduced the term *narcissism*. Narcissism has been defined in many ways; in *DSM-IV-TR* the essential features for narcissistic personality disorder (NPD) include: (1) grandiose self-importance, (2) preoccupation with fantasies of unlimited success, (3) driven desire for attention and admiration, (4) intolerance to criticism, and (5) disturbed, self-centered interpersonal relations. Table 22-5 lists *DSM-IV-TR* criteria for NPD.

These patients' *grandiosity* manifests as an exaggerated sense of self-importance or uniqueness. Others call them "conceited." They greatly overestimate not only their accomplishments and abilities, but their failures as well. For example, at age 30, Isaac described himself as "the greatest actor since Edmund Kean." When he failed to land a part in a major motion picture, he insisted that "everyone in Hollywood will think I'm washed up."

Fantasies of fame substitute for actual achievements. Everyone daydreams, but true narcissists are preoccupied with brilliance, wealth, ideal love, beauty, copping an Oscar (or two), or whatever. In real life, most people enjoy reaching these goals, but narcissists don't. Their ambition is driven, their pursuit of recognition is a burden, their accomplishments don't satisfy. Isaac will perform in front of his own mirror, but not at an audition. He takes a role only if his agent gets him one, but even then, he loves the applause but hates the acting.

The narcissistic personality craves *attention* and universal admiration. Appearance is more important than substance. Being seen with the "right" people is more important than liking them. People with NPD are preoccupied with their physical image; they seek not merely to look attractive but to appear godlike. Isaac's home is a museum studded with photographs of Isaac, mostly in the nude.

TABLE 22-5
DSM-IV-TR *Criteria for Narcissistic Personality Disorder*

A pervasive pattern of grandiosity (in fantasy or behavior), need for admiration, and lack of empathy, beginning by early adulthood and present in a variety of contexts, as indicated by five (or more) of the following:

(1) has a grandiose sense of self-importance (e.g., exaggerates achievements and talents, expects to be recognized as superior without commensurate achievements)

(2) is preoccupied with fantasies of unlimited success, power, brilliance, beauty, or ideal love

(3) believes that he or she is "special" and unique and can only be understood by, or should associate with, other special or high-status people (or institutions)

(4) requires excessive admiration

(5) has a sense of entitlement, i.e., unreasonable expectations of especially favorable treatment or automatic compliance with his or her expectations

(6) is interpersonally exploitative, i.e., takes advantage of others to achieve his or her own ends

(7) lacks empathy: is unwilling to recognize or identify with the feelings and needs of others

(8) is often envious of others or believes that others are envious of him or her

(9) arrogant, haughty behaviors or attitudes

Notes. From *DSM-IV-TR,* p. 717.

Intolerance to criticism arises from the low self-esteem of these individuals. When their grandiosity is doubted, they respond with "narcissistic rage": cool disdain, anger, humiliation, extreme boredom, pessimism, negativism, and shame. Depressed moods result when they're rejected, neglected, or frustrated. When Isaac missed a key while playing the piano, he blamed the piano tuner for not doing his job correctly. At a party, Isaac was regaling his audience with show-biz stories, but when another actor joined in, Isaac became stone silent.

Interpersonally selfish, people with NPD act with a sense of entitlement, as if they are the masters and everyone else, servants. Arriving an hour late on the set, Isaac doesn't apologize ("Why should I? I rushed like hell to get here. If anything, they should thank me"). Narcissists do not sustain genuine, positive regard for anyone. Some alternate between idealization and devaluation ("splitting"), worshiping an individual one moment and despising him or her the next. While there may be many people in their lives, they are all "insignificant others."

Narcissistic and *histrionic personalities* are both self-centered, but the narcissist is more grandiose, egotistical, arrogant, vigorous, and selfish, whereas the hysteric is more overdramatic, flighty, and apprehensive. People with *mania* are grandiose, but episodically and often psychotically, whereas the narcissist's grandiosity is continual and nonpsychotic. Few patients with NPD become psychotic, and when they do, the episodes are brief. Wilhelm Reich (1949/1972) described the "phallic-narcissistic character" whose "penis is not in the service of love but is an instrument of aggression and vengeance" (p. 203). Indeed, some narcissism creates many a business tycoon, surgeon, trial lawyer, politician, movie producer, actor, and orchestra conductor. Great accomplishments require great egos.

At about 4 years of age, narcissism is quite normal. All boys are "Superman" (or some other hero) and want everybody to watch them do their next stunt. Girls are vying for the highest social standing, all wanting to be the queen or prima donna. The boy's parents either "pound it out of him, so he doesn't get too big for his britches," or the opposite, indulge his every whim so as "not to frustrate and upset him." The girl's parents might constantly tell her that she is pretty or cute, but pay little attention to her real accomplishments or ignore her because they really wanted a boy. Either approach can warp progress toward a normal narcissism that is healthy and has realistic limits on it: "I am unique and special, but so are others and I need to respect their rights."

NPD is probably more common in men. Estimates of prevalence are less than 1% in the general population and range from 2 to 16% in the clinical population. NPD may be associated with anorexia nervosa and substance-related disorders (especially cocaine). Individuals with NPD may have more trouble as they age and their body loses its youthful form and their role in society changes. Positive changes can occur as the person with NPD faces various life events such as experiencing achievements or enduring relationships (Ronningstam et al., 1995).

Patients with NPD seek treatment infrequently ("Why should I? There's nothing wrong with me"). But when they do, it's usually because depression or a medical illness threatens their grandiosity. Successful short-term management of these patients includes acknowledging their "specialness," setting some reasonable limits, and allowing them to conclude that their therapist or M.D. is also special and therefore able to appreciate their "special" problems. Long-term psychotherapy is usually recommended, even though its chance of inducing major change is low. When their invincibility is exposed, patients with NPD project their resentment onto their therapists, who should try to respect their patients' exaggerated self-importance while gently placing it into perspective. Group therapy should usually be avoided, because these individuals will monopolize the group until either everybody quits or group members run them out (Yalom, 2005).

ANTISOCIAL PERSONALITY DISORDER

"Why do I rob banks? Because that's where the money is."

—Willy Sutton, professional bank robber

In *DSM-IV-TR*, the essential features of antisocial personality disorder (ASPD) include (1) continuous and chronic antisocial behavior that violates the rights of others, (2) an onset prior to age 15, (3) a persistence into adulthood, and (4) several years of poor job performance. Table 22-6 lists *DSM-IV-TR* criteria for ASPD. This condition is also called "sociopathy."

Clinical Presentation

Although many sociopaths are charming and resourceful, they're without enduring or intimate relationships. Friendships, even with fellow crooks, are opportunistic alliances to be broken whenever it's convenient. With radar for people's vulnerabilities, people with ASPD can readily manipulate, exploit,

---

TABLE 22-6

DSM-IV *Criteria for Antisocial Personality Disorder*

A. There is a pervasive pattern of disregard for and violation of the rights of others occurring since age 15, as indicated by three (or more) of the following:

    (1) failure to conform to social norms with respect to lawful behaviors as indicated by repeatedly performing acts that are grounds for arrest

    (2) deceitfulness, as indicated by repeated lying, use of aliases, or conning others for personal profit or pleasure

    (3) impulsivity or failure to plan ahead

    (4) irritability and aggressiveness, as indicated by repeated physical fights or assaults

    (5) reckless disregard for the safety of self or others

    (6) consistent irresponsibility, as indicated by repeated failure to sustain consistent work behavior or honor financial obligations

    (7) lack of remorse, as indicated by being indifferent to or rationalizing having hurt, mistreated, or stolen from another

B. The individual is at least age 18 years.

C. There is evidence of Conduct Disorder with onset before age 15 years.

D. Occurrence of antisocial behavior is not exclusively during the course of Schizophrenia or a Manic Episode.

Note. From *DSM-IV-TR*, p. 706.

---

control, deceive, and intimidate. Unlike other criminals, these individuals enjoy "making suckers" of people. Their sexual relations are thrilling conquests and nothing more—and that includes marriage.

Emotionally shallow, people with ASPD seem incapable of shame, guilt, loyalty, love, or any persistently sincere emotion; although quick to anger, they don't even sustain hatred. One moment they'll proclaim how deeply they feel about someone, and momentarily, they might believe themselves. These feelings are at most fleeting. Expressions of guilt and remorse don't affect future conduct.

Like some addicts crave heroin, individuals with ASPD crave stimulation. Excitement alone medicates their allergies to boredom, depression, and frustration. They can't hold a job; it would be too dull. They are always on the move, "making deals," bumming around, picking fights, raping people, or killing them. They live solely in the present; the past is a dim memory and the future a fiction. Unconcerned with the consequences of their actions and unable to learn from experience, these individuals are not restrained by the threat of punishment. Rewards must come now, not later; gratification cannot be delayed. Sociopaths are said to have "superego lacunae," that is, they are virtually without conscience. Expediency, immediate pleasure, and "stimulus hunger" override all other restraints.

Clinical Course

Antisocial personalities have "always" been up to "no good"; they are not "good kids" who simply "fell into a bad crowd." *DSM-IV-TR* stresses that ASPD begins before age 15. In boys, it emerges during early childhood, in girls, around puberty.

As children, individuals with ASPD habitually lie, steal, skip school, and defy authority. They conceal feelings and talk to parents only when they want something. Exploiting parental affection, using siblings, running away from home, delighting in forbidden acts, and hanging around with older delinquents are common.

A mother describes her delinquent son: "He's always been different from my others, as if he's possessed. What kind of 5-year-old steals from his mother's purse? Once I caught him hammering a squirrel to death, and when I yelled at him to stop, he just smiled. He enjoyed taunting me."

As adolescents, these individuals abuse substances, gamble heavily, and display unusually early or aggressive sexual behavior. They mock rules, cut class, cause fights, and get expelled; their grades plummet. They're "pathological liars"—they lie without reason—and they delight in terrorizing others. A delinquent youth pulled out a pistol, aimed it at his teacher's head, and demanded he undress. Once the teacher was nude, the youth nudged the teacher's testicles with his gun and fired. The gun wasn't loaded. Only the youth laughed.

By age 30, the promiscuity, fighting, criminality, and vagrancy of people with ASPD tend to diminish. They "burn out." Some find they no longer have the energy required for a shiftless life and try to go "straight." Some succeed partially but few completely. Some end up on skid row, some are chronic substance abusers, some die by violence; in many prisons up to 75% of the inmates are sociopaths. Many subsist from one low-paying job to another and from one town to another. Only 2% of cases with full-blown ASPD remit after age 21.

Alcoholism and depression are the mental disorders that most often affect people with ASPD and, thus, the most common reasons they seek treatment. They often have conversion symptoms, especially when stressed or arrested. Many delinquent teenage girls develop somatization disorder as adults. Most sociopaths have low-to-normal IQs; a few have significant mental deficiency (IQ < 70). Early-onset conduct disorder (before age 10 years) increases the likelihood of developing ASPD in adulthood.

Complications

ASPD markedly impairs social and occupational functioning. Plagued by infidelity, jealousy, and child abuse, marriages usually end in separation and divorce. These individuals tend to marry young, beat their wives, and marry women with ASPD. Besides getting murdered, they have unusually high rates of venereal disease, out-of-wedlock pregnancies, injuries from fights and accidents, substance dependence, and gun wounds—which all lead to their shorter life expectancies. Major depression, suicidal threats, and gestures are common; about 5% commit suicide.

Epidemiology

In the general population ASPD affects about 5% of men and nearly 1% of women. Among psychiatric populations ASPD affects up to 15% of men and 3% of women. ASPD is more prevalent in lower socioeconomic groups and among urban dwellers.

Etiology and Pathogenesis

One should distinguish the "habitual" criminal (i.e., someone with ASPD) from the "occasional" criminal. Habitual antisocial behavior stems from genetic *and* psychosocial factors, whereas occasional antisocial behavior seems to arise more from psychosocial causes. This is a big generalization, but in large measure, habitual criminals are born whereas occasional criminals are made. This section only discusses the "habituals."

Psychosocial Factors

Sociological

Poverty contributes to ASPD, but it's hardly the sole cause. In a study of Philadelphia inner-city youth, 35% of males under 18 had at least one contact with the police, but only 6% caused half of all delinquencies and two-thirds of all violent crimes. These data confirm the distinction between habitual and occasional criminals. These data suggest that despite substantial economic deprivation, the vast majority of the poor do *not* develop sociopathic behavior.

Additional evidence demonstrates that factors other than poverty must be involved. First, ASPD also arises in middle and upper socioeconomic groups. Second, ASPD is becoming more prevalent worldwide, even where there is increasing wealth. Third, the childhood behaviors of adults with ASPD are remarkably similar regardless of economic class. Fourth, these childhood antisocial behaviors emerge so early, it's improbable that sociological factors are a primary cause.

Familial

Sociopaths generally grow up amid considerable parental discord (e.g., desertion, separation, divorce, custody fights) and family disruption (e.g., early deaths, frequent moves, brutal discipline). Mothers of children with ASPD often do not provide consistent affection or discipline (Glueck & Glueck, 1959; Rutter, 1981). Also common during their childhoods are maternal neglect, indifference, and alcoholism (perhaps leading to poor attachment). Instead of the mother, Robins (1966) found that the best predictor of ASPD was having a father with sociopathy or alcoholism. The children grew up to become delinquents whether or not their fathers had reared them. Was the father's absence or inconsistency the culprit? Or was sociopathy inherited from these fathers? The evidence is inconclusive. Many individuals with ASPD are also reared in stable families with loving parents and normal siblings. ASPD probably has multiple etiologies.

Biomedical Factors

On neuropsychological tests, individuals with ASPD frequently do better on performance than on verbal tests. When younger, they have trouble interpreting and abstracting verbal information. Tell a 6-year-old with incipient ASPD, "Do not get near the stove," and he will not understand *near* and continue approaching it from different directions until he is told *no*. He may appear to be "testing limits," but in reality he may be trying to figure out what was meant by *near*. It is not a coincidence that many fail reading and writing but excel at working on their cars or assault rifles.

> Studies of male felons, most having ASPD, revealed that 20% of their first-degree male relatives had ASPD and 33% had alcoholism. Among female felons, half being habitual criminals, a third of their male relatives had ASPD and half had alcoholism. Although most research demonstrates higher concordance rates for ASPD among identical (36%) than fraternal (12%) twins, these different rates are not as eye-popping as those with other mental disorders. One small study reported that the prefrontal lobes of people with ASPD had an 11% reduction in the gray matter volume and a lower autonomic response to social stress as compared with normal healthy controls (Raine et al., 2000). Adopted-away research suggests that genetic factors play some etiological role, but that environmental factors are also important.

Differential Diagnosis

ASPD should be diagnosed *unless* the antisocial behavior only occurs during the course of *schizophrenia* or a *manic episode*. Schizophrenia preempts ASPD because it's hard to know what is producing the antisocial conduct. Mania is easy to differentiate because its antisocial behavior is episodic, time-limited, and rarely occurs during childhood. People with ASPD often abuse drugs and alcohol, but a *substance use disorder* should be diagnosed only when the patient meets the full *DSM-IV-TR* criteria for it. Some people with substance use disorder displayed no antisocial behavior before they became addicted (Gerstley et al., 1990). After the addiction had taken hold, they lied, stole, and killed for their drugs. Treating the addiction in some cases may reverse this behavior.

Management and Treatment

No psychotherapy has been found to help these individuals. ASPD is ego-syntonic, and its bearers have no desire to change, consider insights excuses, have no concept of the future, resent all authorities (including therapists), view the patient role as pitiful, detest being in a position of inferiority, and deem therapy a joke and therapists as objects to be conned, threatened, seduced, or used.

A "tough love" approach reduces some of these problems by showing that the therapist cares but is not a patsy. It is important to remember that individuals with ASPD are human beings with feelings. Frequent confrontation is expected. They want to do things for themselves; they need to see that the way they are doing things isn't working. If they finally "burn out" or become depressed, they may find themselves willing to try the "straight" way.

Judges are as stuck as psychotherapists. They know that "rehabilitation" does not help the "hard-core criminal." Judges should know that sentencing individuals with ASPD to psychotherapy wastes everybody's time. Those made to enlist in the military can't tolerate the discipline, go AWOL, and are dishonorably discharged. So what can be done? Not much. But consider the following:

1. *Prevention* is the most important intervention medical and mental health professionals can make. Early detection of antisocial behavior in children and young teenagers should be treated promptly before it gets out of hand. Many teenage gang members are not sociopathic; they want the respect of other members. Youngsters with ASPD don't do well in gangs because they try to take advantage of their own fellow members. Getting the nonsociopathic members out of gangs and finding alternative ways for them to gain "respect" may prevent them from pursuing a life of crime.

2. *Family counseling* is critical. Therapists may not do much for individuals with ASPD, but they may help their families. Manipulated so often, family members swing from hate to guilt, never knowing what to feel. Because they are so close to the problem, common-sense guidelines from an objective outsider/professional can help them place matters into perspective.

3. *Treating substance misuse* is also critical, since antisocial acts increase during intoxication. Sociopathic behavior has gradations from milder to severe. Drug use may push someone with a milder ASPD into becoming a thief and murderer.

4. *Counseling should be independent of punishment and parole*, whenever possible. If sociopathic individuals know that therapists exert no influence on their sentence, they may be a bit more likely to use treatment constructively.

BORDERLINE PERSONALITY DISORDER

"Don't leave me, I hate you."

—Title of book on borderlines by Jerold Kreisman, M.D.

In *DSM-IV-TR* borderline personality disorder (BPD) is characterized by at least five of the following: (1) impulsivity, (2) unstable and intense interpersonal relations, (3) inappropriate or intense anger, (4) identity confusion, (5) affective instability, (6) problems being alone, (7) physically self-destructive acts, and (8) chronic feelings of emptiness and boredom. Table 22-7 lists *DSM-IV-TR* criteria for BPD.

In 1938 the term *borderline* was introduced to describe those patients who straddled the border between neurosis and psychosis. The diagnosis of "borderline schizophrenia," used widely until the mid-1970s, assumed that borderline disorders were a type of "latent schizophrenia." Most authorities now believe that borderline conditions are personality disorders. What nobody disputes is that people with BPD *look much better than they are*—a fact that continually deceives professionals as well as laypeople.

TABLE 22-7

DSM-IV-TR *Criteria for Borderline Personality Disorder*

A pervasive pattern of instability of interpersonal relationships, self-image, and affects, and marked impulsivity beginning by early adulthood and present in a variety of contexts, as indicated by five (or more) of the following:

(1) frantic efforts to avoid real or imagined abandonment. **Note:** Do not include suicidal or self-mutilating behavior covered in Criterion 5.

(2) a pattern of unstable and intense interpersonal relationships characterized by alternating between extremes of idealization and devaluation

(3) identity disturbance: markedly and persistently unstable self-image or sense of self

(4) impulsivity in at least two areas that are potentially self-damaging (e.g., spending, sex, substance abuse, reckless driving, binge eating). **Note:** Do not include suicidal or self-mutilating behavior covered in Criterion 5.

(5) recurrent suicidal behavior, gestures, or threats, or self-mutilating behavior

(6) affective instability due to a marked reactivity of mood (e.g., intense episodic dysphoria, irritability, or anxiety usually lasting a few hours and only rarely more than a few days)

(7) chronic feelings of emptiness

(8) inappropriate, intense anger or difficulty controlling anger (e.g., frequent displays of temper, constant anger, recurrent physical fights)

(9) transient, stress-related paranoid ideation or severe dissociative symptoms

Note. From *DSM-IV-TR*, p. 710.

Clinical Presentation

Feeling chronically bored and empty, people with BPD desperately seek stimulation: They might gamble, act out sexually, abuse drugs, overdose, instigate brawls, or attempt suicide. Many slash their wrists or douse lit cigarettes on their arms, not to kill or to hurt themselves, but to *feel* something ("I feel so dead, cutting myself is the only way I know I'm alive") or to relieve tension. Their moods are always reactive, intense, and brief; trivial problems mushroom into calamities. They have been well portrayed in movies such as *Fatal Attraction* and *A Streetcar Named Desire*.

The interpersonal relations of people with BPD swing between suffocating dependency and mindless self-assertion. They hate being alone and latch onto others to avoid feeling abandoned. For example, such an individual will call a recently made friend every day about a "disaster" needing immediate attention. Initially, the friend is flattered by the new friend's "idealization" of her, yet she soon finds herself sucked into a gooey, all-consuming relationship. When she tries to cool things, the person with BPD denigrates her ("devaluation") with a vengeance, pouring ink on her couch, demanding money, and accusing her of "being miserly," calling her at 3 A.M. to complain that she's a "bitch," etc. The digs contain just enough truth to fester under the friend's skin, which eventually leads the friend to apologize.

Borderline relationships, be they platonic or romantic, are all-or-nothing endeavors. People with BPD are in love with love, not people. Anything less than total love is hate; anything less than total commitment is rejection ("rejection sensitivity"). They expect—nay, *demand*—that others do for them what they cannot do for themselves. Chronically sad and demoralized, they adopt friends not because they like them but because they expect the friends to rid them of unhappiness. When the friends fail at this unknown and undoable task, the person with BPD dumps them, looks for another savior, and repeats the cycle. Unable to figure out who or what they are ("identity diffusion"), these individuals glom onto others so as to acquire an identity by osmosis. A 25-year-old with BPD said that she dresses like the rock star Madonna "to express my individuality." Whereas she's convinced that nobody ever does enough for her, others find her exhausting and draining—an "empty gas tank" in need of constant refueling.

People with BPD are notorious for *splitting*—that is, they view people as *all good* or *all bad*—and then get others to act out these roles. Everywhere they go, they set people against each other, create havoc, and walk away without anybody realizing until later who caused the chaos.

Mary Rae, an inpatient with BPD, superficially slashed her wrist, squeezed the blood, and showed it dripping to her psychiatrist. As anyone would have predicted, he canceled her weekend pass. This infuriated Mary Rae. She then "confided" in Nurse Peter:

"You're the only person who understands me. My doctor and everyone else here hate me. . . . When I cut my wrist I realized I should tell my doctor. So I did, and right away. I *thought* that was the right thing to do. So what does Dr. Jerk-ass do? He locks me up. I don't get it: Staff says we're supposed to be open with them. Well, I was! From now on, I keep everything to myself. I wasn't suicidal—I would hardly tell people if I was. Peter, if only *you* would have been here. Then I could have gone to you and never have cut myself at all. As it is, I'm stuck here all weekend: Just thinking about it makes me suicidal. Can't you help me?"

Flattered that Mary Rae had confided in him, Peter campaigns to restore her weekend pass. He doesn't realize that Mary Rae has similarly "confided" in five other staff members, each thinking they have a "unique and confidential relationship" with her, which must be kept secret. The unit's staff soon splits between those who feel Mary Rae has been victimized for "being honest" and those who think she's a manipulator and should be shipped to a state hospital. Very quickly, both sides cease squabbling about Mary Rae and instead attack each other as insensitive or naïve. Meanwhile, as if she's an innocent bystander, Mary Rae fiddles while the staff burns.

Patients with BPD may have many "neurotic" symptoms—panic attacks, phobias, anxiety, somatic complaints, conversion symptoms, dysthymia. Under stress, some become *briefly* psychotic. Highly characteristic of people with BPD is their ability to give sane answers on structured psychological tests (e.g., Wechsler Adult Intelligence Scale; WAIS), but bizarre, psychotic responses on unstructured tests (e.g., Rorschach). Where most people might see a bat or a butterfly on a Rorschach inkblot, one patient with BPD saw "the insides of a cow's stomach run over by a car."

BPD has a chronic, fluctuating course which, although it does *not* lead to schizophrenia, nonetheless significantly impairs social and occupational functioning. A 5-year follow-up showed that people with BPD function at pretty much the same poor level. Those with higher premorbid levels of functioning have better prognoses.

Epidemiology

Twice as many people with BPD are women than men. Using strict diagnostic criteria, 1.6–4% of the general population has BPD. The frequency of this diagnosis may be as high as 11% of psychiatric outpatients, and 19% of psychiatric inpatients. (Linehan, 1993).

Etiology and Pathogenesis

Kernberg (1975) hypothesized that people with BPD have a "constitutional" inability to regulate affects, which predisposes them to psychological disorganization under specific adverse conditions during childhood. Zanarini and Frankenburg (1997) describe a tripartite model of borderline development. They present a hypothesis embracing three elements: a labile temperament, early childhood trauma, and a triggering event.

BPD runs in families. First-degree relatives of people with BPD have 10 times the rate of BPD and three times the rate of alcoholism than do controls. These relatives also have higher rates of mood disorders but normal rates of schizophrenia and bipolar disorder. While the mode of this familial transmission is unclear, most investigations have focused on psychosocial determinants.

Mahler, Pine, and Bergman (1975) proposed that borderline conditions stem from a disturbance in the "rapprochement sub-phase of the separation–individuation" process—from 18 to 36 months. During this period, the child, having experimented with separating self from mother, tries returning to mother for approval and emotional "refueling." These mothers, however, have had their own difficulties with separation, and so they resent the child's "clinging," as if to say, "Before you wanted me, now you don't. So get lost!" These mothers experience their child's attempts at autonomy as abandonment (e.g., "How dare you leave me!"). As the child grows up, she replays these dependence–independence conflicts with others. This style of parenting sets up a vicious, out-of-control feedback loop. Fear of separation or abandonment is not met with comfort but rather rejection. Thus, fear becomes a cue for abandonment, which leads to more fear, and so on.

Along similar lines, Masterson (1976) contended that the essence of the borderline dilemma is a conflict between a desire for autonomy and a fear of parental abandonment. He claimed that mothers of children with BPD reward their children's regressive behaviors and discourage their individuation.

A majority of people with BPD were physically, sexually, and/or emotionally abused by their caregivers at times; at other times these caregivers may have been adequate or even nurturing. This vacillation creates the problem of both hating and loving the caregiver.

Splitting is a healthy and normal defense in 18- to 36-month-old children. For example, a 2½-year-old boy with a 6-month-old sister said to his father, "No like sister's daddy, like *my* daddy." Yes, this was the same daddy, but this splitting permitted the little boy to like his father while still feeling jealous that his sister was getting a lot of attention. Only later, when his mind is able to handle greater complexity, will this good–bad dichotomy diversify into more ambiguous shades of gray in which the good and bad coexist—the stuff of most adult experience. People with BPD don't accomplish this developmental task. Clinicians find themselves worshipped on an altar some days and vilified in an earthly hell on others. The clinician hasn't changed, but the patient's opinion has.

Strip aside everything people with BPD do and say and what remains is an underlying dread, or perhaps a conviction, of being *bad*—or as one patient remarked, "Underneath madness lies badness." These individuals typically disown this badness by projecting it onto others ("projective identification"), act out to escape feeling this "badness," employ reaction formation (as when romanticizing ideal love—e.g., Blanche DuBois), or may behave self-destructively. Similar defenses are used by people with BPD who feel that they are *nothing* inside, mere shells of humanity, scarecrows masquerading as people. Perhaps 10% of patients with BPD will commit suicide and 75% will engage in at least one episode of self-injurious behavior. Self-injurious behavior may decline over time, but the feelings of emptiness often persist (Zanarini et al., 2007).

Differential Diagnosis

Known as the "disorder that doesn't specialize," BPD presents with such variegated symptomatology that it appears in many patients' lists of differential diagnoses. BPD may coexist with *schizotypal, histrionic, narcissistic,* or *antisocial personality disorders.* What usually distinguish people with BPD are chronic feelings of emptiness and anger, self-mutilation, transitory psychoses, manipulative suicide attempts, intensely demanding relationships, and superficial intactness. The sadness common to people with BPD is short-lived and highly reactive. Still, *major depression* and *dysthymic disorder* can coexist with BPD or be confused with it. Because anger and irritability can be symptoms of major depression, some patients with depression may look like a person with BPD. However, they see their reactive behavior as different from usual for them, and friends usually confirm this observation. *Cyclothymic disorder,* like BPD, has roller-coaster mood swings, but BPD doesn't have true hypomanic periods. When briefly psychotic, people with BPD may be labeled *schizophrenic* but, unlike most with schizophrenia, they use logical sentences and demonstrate considerable affect in describing their psychotic experiences.

Management and Treatment

Clinicians working with patients with BPD must walk a narrow path between giving support without rescuing and encouraging independence without signaling abandonment. When patients with BPD are doing better, praise for their improvement is often interpreted as "You do not need to see me anymore"—another abandonment. With BPD, emphatic and supportive statements should be combined: "You still have a lot of pain, but you are handling it better. There is a lot of work still ahead, but I see progress." Structure and consistency are also very important. During a crisis, a scheduled phone check-in works much better than waiting for an emergency.

Only well-trained professionals should consider attempting to treat these most difficult of patients. *Long-term, psychodynamic psychotherapy* has demonstrated some positive impact and is the often- recommended treatment for BPD (Bateman & Fonagy, 2001). One approach starts with fostering the patient's trust in treatment so that exploration of unconscious wishes and fantasies can follow. Another approach stresses reality testing, providing structure, and avoiding overly stimulating "depth interpretations" that may induce psychological disorganization. A *cognitive–behavioral approach*, which stresses integrating adaptive coping skills with intense affective reactions and cognitively fusing opposites, has been successful when used over several years (Linehan, 1993). Linehan's therapy model, dialectical behavior therapy, DBT, combines manualized group training of patients with individualized therapy that focuses on empathy and validating the patient. DBT places the focus on stopping self-destructive behavior, whereas psychodynamic therapies focus on the underlying issues in hopes that once the psychic conflicts are resolved, then the suicidal thinking will subside. There is solid evidence demonstrating efficacy of DBT in reducing dysfunctional parasuicidal behavior, substance abuse, and hospitalization.

Drug treatment may utilize MAOIs for depression and rejection sensitivity and low doses of antipsychotics for brief reactive psychoses and irritability (Cornelius et al., 1993). Anticonvulsants such as divalproex sodium may decrease impulsive self-destructive behavior. Benzodiazepines may disinhibit behavior and create drug dependence and therefore are not usually recommended. Tricyclic antidepressants have a poor record in treating a BPD-related depression, *and* they are lethal in overdose. Lithium does help stabilize mood and reduce impulsive behaviors but is also dangerous in overdose. Selective serotonin reuptake inhibiters (SSRIs) may share the efficacy of MAOIs with a better safety and side-effect profile.

AVOIDANT PERSONALITY DISORDER

The essential feature of avoidant personality disorder (APD) is extreme social discomfort because of a pervasive fear of being judged negatively. More specifically, *DSM-IV-TR* lists these characteristics: (1) hypersensitivity to potential rejection, humiliation, or shame; (2) only entering relationships in which uncritical acceptance is virtually guaranteed; (3) social withdrawal; (4) a desire for affection and acceptance; and (5) low self-esteem. Table 22-8 presents *DSM-IV-TR* criteria for APD.

Schizoid and avoidant personalities are loners, but the person with SDPD doesn't want friends and the person with APD does. These are the painfully shy people, permeating Garrison Keillor's Lake Wobegon radio show. They want affection, but not as much as they fear rejection. Because they dread the slightest disapproval and will misconstrue people's comments as derogatory, they have few, if any, friends. Angry and upset at their own inability to relate, they'll try to prevent rejection by ingratiating themselves to others.

Children as young as 4 months of age have been described as fearful, withdrawn, and shy. These children with behavioral inhibitions possess the temperament most associated with APD in adults. A friendly, gentle, reassuring approach is the best way to manage people with APD. Most children and

---

TABLE 22-8
DSM-IV-TR *Criteria for Avoidant Personality Disorder*

A pervasive pattern of social inhibition, feelings of inadequacy, and hypersensitivity to negative evaluation, beginning by early adulthood and present in a variety of contexts, as indicated by four (or more) of the following:

(1) avoids occupational activities that involve significant interpersonal contact, because of fears of criticism, disapproval, or rejection

(2) is unwilling to get involved with people unless certain of being liked

(3) shows restraint within intimate relationships due to the fear of being shamed or ridiculed

(4) is preoccupied with being criticized or rejected in social situations

(5) is inhibited in new interpersonal situations because of feelings of inadequacy

(6) views self as socially inept, personally unappealing, or inferior to others

(7) is unusually reluctant to take personal risks or to engage in any new activities because they may prove embarrassing

Note. From *DSM-IV-TR,* p. 721.

---

teens with APD can't avoid becoming avoidant adults. Virtually all people with APD have social phobias, but a majority of people with social phobias do not have APD. Social phobias are responses to *specific* situations (e.g., public speaking), whereas APD pervades all social relations. APD may have started out as a social phobia that kept getting worse and involving more situations. One twin study strongly suggests that APD and social phobia share a common genetic vulnerability (Reichborn-Kjennerud et al., 2007). The prevalence of APD in the general adult population is estimated at 2.5%.

MAOIs are the most effective medication for social phobias and may also be indicated for APD. In one study, 75% of patients with APD who were treated for a year with MAOIs were so improved that they no longer qualified for the diagnosis. If this treatment proves to be effective, the diagnosis of APD may become obsolete. After all, part of the definition of personality disorder is an enduring pattern of behavior. SSRIs and selective serotonin and norepinephrine reuptake inhibitors (SNRIs) are also proving to have therapeutic benefit with social phobia and thus might be useful in the treatment of APD. The use of caffeine and other stimulants may heighten anxiety and actually interfere with the avoidant person confronting his fears—a necessary step for any clinical improvement. Cognitive–behavioral therapies are effective when they focus on assertiveness, desensitization in the situations, and cognitive change. Group therapy can also be helpful as patients with APD tend to be well liked and get much support in therapy groups. The use of alcohol (and benzodiazepines) can become a maladaptive coping behavior to free inhibitions and is best avoided.

DEPENDENT PERSONALITY DISORDER

In *DSM-IV-TR* the essential features of people with dependent personality disorder (DPD) include (1) passively allowing others to assume responsibility for major areas in their lives because (2) they lack self-confidence or the ability to function independently; (3) they then subordinate their needs to those of others, (4) become dependent on them, and (5) avoid any chance of being self-reliant. Table 22–9 lists the *DSM-IV-TR* criteria for DPD.

Everybody has dependent traits and wishes. What distinguishes the dependent personality is that the dependency is total, pervading all areas of life. People with DPD dread autonomy; they may be productive, but only if supervised. They are likely to view themselves as inept or stupid. When pressed to name redeeming qualities, they might reluctantly confess to being good companions, loyal and kind.

TABLE 22-9

DSM-IV-TR *Criteria for Dependent Personality Disorder*

A pervasive and excessive need to be taken care of that leads to submissive and clinging behavior and fears of separation, beginning by early adulthood and present in a variety of contexts, as indicated by five (or more) of the following:

(1) has difficulty making everyday decisions without an excessive amount of advice and reassurance from others

(2) needs others to assume responsibility for most major areas of his or her life

(3) has difficulty expressing disagreement with others because of fear of loss of support or approval. **Note:** Do not include realistic fears of retribution.

(4) has difficulty initiating projects or doing things on his or her own (due to a lack of self-confidence in judgment or abilities rather than to a lack of motivation or energy)

(5) goes to excessive lengths to obtain nurturance and support from others, to the point of volunteering to do things that are unpleasant

(6) feels uncomfortable or helpless when alone because of exaggerated fears of being unable to care for himself or herself

(7) urgently seeks another relationship as a source of care and support when a close relationship ends

(8) unrealistic preoccupation with fears of being left to take care of himself or herself

Note. From *DSM-IV-TR,* p. 725.

Ethel is prototypical. She refers to herself as "man's best friend." Her man is Mitch, a husband who schedules her days, tells her what foods to eat, picks her doctors, chooses her clothes, and selects her friends. Explains Ethel: "He likes to think, and I don't. Why should I decide things, when he'll do it for me?" This arrangement pleased both for years until Mitch announced he was going to China for 3 weeks on business. Ethel was frantic and sought treatment. Like most dependent personalities, she wanted help not for dependency, but for losing it.

Historically, DPD was known as "passive–dependent" personality, and dependent personalities were known as "oral characters." This label referred to their most striking clinical feature—the insistence on being "fed" or taken care of; it also suggested the etiology of overindulged or frustrated wishes during the oral stage of psychosexual development. More recently, the role of maternal deprivation during the oral stage has been stressed. Oral features include a constant demand for attention, passivity, dependency, a fear of autonomy, a lack of perseverance, dread of decision making, suggestibility, and oral behaviors (e.g., thumb-sucking, smoking, drinking). Oral traits are common in "normals," but even more so in psychiatric patients.

> The 1963 Midtown Manhattan survey showed that 2.5% of the residents had passive–dependent personalities. DPD is more prevalent in women and in the youngest sibling. Prolonged physical illness during childhood may predispose to DPD. *Histrionic, schizotypal, narcissistic, and avoidant personality disorders* often coexist with DPD, and *dysthymic disorder* and *major depression* are frequent complications. Although dependent traits are common in *agoraphobia*, the person with agoraphobia will *actively* insist that others assume responsibility, whereas the person with DPD *passively* abdicates control to others.

Management and Treatment

Patients with DPD will call the office incessantly asking for advice or clarifications and regularly to schedule extra appointments. From the start firm limits (e.g., no calls to home, clear expectations: "Let's schedule an appointment every 2 weeks") and information are important. If medications are being initiated, it is best to give out information sheets to reduce the calls with questions. If "emergency" appointments are happening too regularly, temporarily increase the frequency of scheduled visits. Sometimes knowing an appointment is coming soon is very reassuring to people with DPD, and they won't feel the need to call regularly. If clear limits are not established in the beginning, it is nearly impossible to establish them later without the patient experiencing a lot of anger or hurt.

More insightful patients may benefit from *psychodynamic psychotherapy*. Often addressed (in this sequence) are the patient's (1) low self-esteem and its origins, (2) fears of harming others by seeking autonomy, (3) dependency on the therapist, and (4) the experience of termination as it relates to dependency. Less psychologically minded patients or those not wanting psychodynamic therapy may benefit from supportive *group therapy* or *assertiveness training*.

OBSESSIVE–COMPULSIVE PERSONALITY DISORDER

"Are you sure there is a hyphen in *obsessive-compulsive?*"

—Anonymous medical student

In *DSM-IV-TR* the essential features of obsessive–compulsive personality disorder (OCPD) include (1) a restricted ability to express warm and tender emotions, (2) a perfectionism that interferes with the ability to grasp "the big picture," (3) an insistence that others submit to his or her way of doing things, (4) an excessive devotion to work and productivity to the exclusion of pleasure, and (5) indecisiveness. Table 22-10 lists *DSM-IV-TR* criteria for OCPD.

Wilhelm Reich called these patients "living machines." People with OCPD are highly productive but never enjoy what they produce. Everything is a chore, nothing is effortless. Every decision demands exhaustive analysis. Everything must be right, and nothing must be left to chance. They won't follow hunches, since hunches may be wrong. They are perfectionists: Carrots must be sliced exactly one-quarter wide or a meal is ruined. Cleanliness *is* Godliness. These individuals excel at concentrating, and they never stop concentrating (Shapiro, 1999). They can't skim a page; they must scrutinize every word. Their focus is sharp, yet narrow; they see the parts, but never the whole. They are interpersonally obtuse, boring, and annoying; they subject people to endless irrelevant details, refuse to make decisions, are moralistic and hypercritically self-righteous, insist on conformity (from others), and never get to the point.

TABLE 22-10

DSM-IV-TR *Criteria for Obsessive–Compulsive Personality Disorder*

A pervasive pattern of preoccupation with orderliness, perfectionism, and mental and interpersonal control, at the expense of flexibility, openness, and efficiency, beginning by early adulthood and present in a variety of contexts, as indicated by four (or more) of the following:

(1) preoccupied with details, rules, lists, order, organization, or schedules to the extent that the major point of the activity is lost

(2) shows perfectionism that interferes with task completion (e.g., is unable to complete a project because his or her own overly strict standards are not met)

(3) is excessively devoted to work and productivity to the exclusion of leisure activities and friendships (not accounted for by obvious economic necessity)

(4) is overly conscientious, scrupulous, and inflexible about matters of morality, ethics, or values (not accounted for by cultural or religious identification)

(5) is unable to discard worn-out or worthless objects even when they have no sentimental value

(6) is reluctant to delegate tasks or to work with others unless they submit to exactly his or her way of doing things

(7) adopts a miserly spending style toward both self and others; money is viewed as something to be hoarded for future catastrophes

(8) shows rigidity and stubbornness

Note. From *DSM-IV-TR,* p. 729.

Harold, a compulsive accountant, spent 8 years obsessing over whether to leave his wife and three kids for his mistress-secretary. "I stay only for the kids," he insisted, but in truth, he never saw them. Repeatedly calculating the pros and cons—even devising a mathematical formula—Harold would ask a friend for advice, promptly reject it, criticize the friend for not helping him enough, and cap it off by complaining that his friend doesn't donate enough money to the synagogue. Like most people with OCPD, Harold considered himself an intellectual, while others considered him rigid.

OCPD is diagnosed more often in men and in the oldest sibling. The prevalence in the general population is estimated at 1%; in psychiatric clinical populations around 6%. Frequent complications are major depression, dysthymia, and hypochondrias. Only 6% of patients with obsessive–compulsive disorder also have OCPD (Baer et al., 1990).

Laypeople call these patients "tight-assed"; psychoanalysts call them "anal characters" because, theoretically, they have arrested at the anal stage of psychosexual development. The anal character is known for having problems with control, authority figures, autonomy, shame, and self-doubt. OCPD runs in families, but it's unclear how much this results from the emotionally constipated climate of the anger-suppressing parents who often rear these patients or from heredity, as suggested by several twin and adoption studies.

Management and Treatment

Patients with OCPD prefer clinicians who are like themselves. To form an alliance with them, clinicians must demonstrate that they are careful and attend to detail. The patient with OCPD, like the patient with paranoia, must have complete explanations of what will happen during evaluation and treatment. These patients may require long-term therapy since they resist exploring their emotions and have trouble developing close relationships. They are lethal when they become suicidal because they will be sure to complete it with much planning and perfection. Though they are often bright, they do not use insight to instigate change, only to avoid it. Psychology is abstract, whereas patients with OCPD are concrete. They swamp therapists with details. Simply asking a person with OCPD if he's reviewed the want-ads can result in a critique of every ad in the paper. If interrupted, he becomes angry; if allowed to continue, 10 minutes later he will blame the therapist for wasting time. Consequently, therapy should focus on the here-and-now and stress feelings instead of thoughts. Cognitive–behavioral therapy may be effective since it focuses on the here-and-now. Psychodynamic psychotherapy will require long-term management, and will need to focus on the psychic defenses, soften the severe superego, and uncover unconscious conflicts. Progress should be measured in terms of changed behavior, not insight. Perry et al. (2005) have demonstrated that both cognitive–behavioral therapy and psychodynamic psychotherapy have beneficial effects on patients with cluster C personality disorders, including OCPD. Group therapy may help those with serious interpersonal problems.

Additional categories of personality disorders are described in the *DSM-IV-TR* (Appendix B) for further study, and will be considered for inclusion in the DSM-V, which is currently under development. For example, depressive personality disorder is defined as "a pervasive pattern of depressive cognitions and behaviors beginning by early adulthood." The passive–aggressive or negativistic personality disorder is described as "a pervasive pattern of negativistic attitudes and passive resistance to demands for adequate performance in social and occupational situations that begin by early adulthood." The apparent demarcation of clear boundaries defining the various categories is somewhat arbitrary. In reality, there is a continuum ranging between normal to abnormal personalities. For example, the ruthless but very successful businessman may have many antisocial traits but function exceptionally well in the modern-day competitive world. The detailed-oriented and hard-working physician is well-appreciated by her patients, yet he or she embodies many traits of an OCPD. This continuum will hopefully be addressed in the future DSM-V, perhaps through a dimensional model.

References

American Psychiatric Association. (2000). *Diagnostic and statistical manual of mental disorders* (4th ed., text rev.). Washington, DC: American Psychiatric Association.

Baer, L., Jenike, M.A., Ricciardi, J., Holland, A.D., Seymour, R.J., Minichiello, W.E., et al. (1990). Personality disorders in patients with obsessive–compulsive disorders. *Archives of General Psychiatry, 47,* 826–832.

Bateman, A., & Fonagy, P. (2001). Treatment of borderline personality disorder with psychoanalytically oriented partial hospitalization: An 18-month follow-up. *American Journal of Psychiatry, 158,* 36–42.

Colom, F., Vieta, E., Martinez-Aran, A., Reinares, M., Benabarre, A., & Gasto, C. (2000). Clinical factors associated with treatment amd noncompliance in euthymic bipolar patient. *Journal of Clinical Psychiatry, 61,* 549–555.

Cornelius, J.R., Soloff, P.H., Perel, J.M., & Ulrich, R.F. (1993). Continuation pharmacotherapy of borderline personality disorder with haloperidol and phenelzine. *American Journal of Psychiatry, 150,* 1843–1848.

Ellis, H. (1915). *Affirmations* (2nd ed., pp. 86–130). Boston and New York: Houghton Mifflin.

Gandhi, N., Tyrer, P., Evans, K., McGee, A., Lamont, A., & Harrison-Read, P. (2001). A randomized controlled trial of community oriented and hospital oriented care for discharged psychiatric population: Influence of personality disorders on police contracts. *Journal of Personality Disorders, 15,* 94–102.

Gerstley, L.J., Alterman, A.I., McLellan, A.T., & Woody, G.E. (1990). Antisocial personality disorder in patients with substance abuse disorders: A problematic diagnosis. *American Journal of Psychiatry, 147,* 173–178.

Glueck, S., & Glueck, E. (1959). *Predicting delinquency and crime.* Cambridge, MA: Harvard University Press.

Herbeck, D.M., Fitek, D.J., Svikis, D.S., Montoya, I.D., Marcus, S.C., & West, J.C. (2005). Treatment compliance in patients with comorbid psychiatric and substance use disorders. *American Journal of Addictions, 14*(3), 195–207.

Kahana, R.J., & Bibring, G.L. (1964). Personality types in medical management. In N.E. Zinberg (Ed.), *Psychiatry and medical practice* (pp. 108–123). New York: International University Press.

Kernberg, O. (1975). *Borderline conditions and pathological narcissism.* New York: Aronson.

Kessler, R.C., McGonagle, K.A., Ahzo, S., Nelson, C.H., Hughes, M., Eshleman, S., et al. (1994). Lifetime and 12-month prevalence of *DSM-III-R* psychiatric disorders in the United States. Results from the National Comorbidity Survey. *Archives of General Psychiatry, 51,* 8–19.

Koeningsberg, H.W., Kaplan, R.D., Gilmore, M.M., & Cooper, A.M. (1985). The relationship between syndrome and personality disorder in *DSM-III*: Experience with 2,462 patients. *American Journal of Psychiatry, 142,* 207–212.

Koerner, K., & Linehan, M.M. (2000). Research on dialectical behavior therapy for patients with borderline personality disorder. *Psychiatric Clinics of North America, 23*(1), 151–167.

Lenzenweger, M.F., Loranger, A.W., Korfine, L., & Neff, C. (1997). Detecting personality disorder in nonclinical populations. *Archives of General Psychiatry, 54,* 345–351.

Linehan, M.M. (1993). *Skills training manual for treating borderline personality disorder.* New York: Guilford.

Linehan, M.M., Armstrong, H.E., Suarez, A., Allmon, D., & Heard, H.L. (1991). Cognitive–behavioral treatment of chronically parasuicidal borderline patients. *Archives of General Psychiatry, 48,* 1060–1064.

Mahler, M., Pine, F., & Bergman, A. (1975). *The psychotherapy and the science of psychodynamics.* Boston: Butterworth.

Masterson, J.F. (1976). *Psychotherapy of the borderline adult: A developmental approach.* New York: Brunner/Mazel.

Millon, T. (2004). *Personality disorders in modern life* (2nd ed.). New York: Wiley.

Perry, J.C., & Bond, M. (2005). "Defensive functioning" in Gabbard's treatments of Psychiatric Disorders. In J. Oldham, A.E. Skodol, & D. Bender (Eds.), *American Psychiatric Publishing Textbook of Personality Disorders* (pp. 523–540). Washington, DC: American Psychiatric Association.

Pirkis, J., Burgess, P., & Jolley, D. (1999). Suicide attempts by psychiatric patients in acute inpatient, long stay inpatient and community care. *Social Psychiatry, 34*(12), 634–644.

Raine, A., Lencz, T., Bihrle, S., LaCasse, L., & Colletti, P. (2000). Reduced prefrontal gray matter volume and reduced autonomic activity in antisocial personality disorder. *Archives of General Psychiatry, 57,* 119–127.

Reich, J., Boerstler, H., Yates, W., & Nduaguba, M. (1989). Utilization of medical resources in persons with DSM-III personality disorders in a community sample. *International Journal of Psychiatry Medicine, 19*(1), 1–9.

Reich, W. (1972). *Character analysis* (3rd. ed.). New York: Noonday Press. (Original work published 1949)

Reichborn-Kjennerud, T., Czajkowski, N., Torgersen, S., Neale, M., Orstavik, R.E., Tambs, K., et al. (2007). The relationship between avoidant personality disorder and social phobia: A population-based twin study. *American Journal of Psychiatry, 164*(11), 1722–1728.

Robins, C.J., & Chapman, A.L. (2004). Dialectical behavior therapy: Current status, recent developments, and future directions. *Journal of Personality Disorders, 18,* 73–89.

Robins, L.N. (1966). *Deviant children grown up.* Baltimore: Williams & Wilkins.

Ronningstam, E., Gunderson, J., & Lyons, M. (1995). Changes in pathological narcissism. *American Journal of Psychiatry, 152*(2), 253.

Rutter, M. (1981). *Maternal deprivation reassessed* (2nd ed.). London: Penguin Books.

Shapiro, D. (1999). *Neurotic styles.* New York: Basic Books.

Svartberg, M., Stiles, T.C., & Seltzer, M.H. (2004). A randomized, controlled trial of the effectiveness of short-term dynamic psychotherapy and cognitive therapy for cluster C personality disorders. *American Journal of Psychiatry, 161*(5), 810–817.

Torgersen, S., Lygren, S., Oien, P.A., Skre, I., Onstad, S., Edvardsen, J., et al. (2000). A twin study of personality disorders. *Comprehensive Psychiatry, 41*(6), 416–425.

Trull, T.J., Tragesser, S.L., Solhan, M., & Schwartz-Mette, R. (2007). Dimensional models of personality disorder: Diagnostic and Statistical Manual of Mental Disorders fifth edition and beyond. *Current Opinions in Psychiatry, 20,* 52–56.

Whisman, M.A., Tolejko, N., & Chatav, Y. (1993). Social consequences of personality disorders, probability and timing of marriage and probability of marital disruption. *Journal of Personality Disorders, 7,* 44–62.

Yalom, I.D. (2005). *The theory and practice of group psychotherapy* (5th ed.). Basic Books: New York.

Zanarini, M.C., Frankenburg, F.R., Reich, B., Silk, K.R., Hudson, I., & McSweeney, L.B. (2007). The subsyndromal phenomenology of borderline personality disorder: A 10-year follow-up study. *American Journal of Psychiatry, 164,* 929–939.

23

Disorders Usually First Diagnosed in Infancy, Childhood, or Adolescence

Children have many disorders already discussed, such as mood, eating, and sleep disorders. But kids can have other problems too, and development may complicate their diagnosis. Behavior within the range of normal may become confused with psychopathology. Therefore, the best way to minimize this confusion is to have a good understanding of normal development, so that any deviations can be recognized and addressed. Many disorders of childhood occur when development deviates from normal, is in some way impeded or delayed, or regresses. This chapter does not focus on normal development, but an understanding of normal child development is an essential prerequisite for those who recognize and treat disorders of childhood. Table 23-1 lists a number of normal developmental milestones for children.

MENTAL RETARDATION

The diagnosis of mental retardation is not based on IQ alone but includes deficits in adaptive functioning. IQ tests mainly measure potential ability to perform in school and were not specifically developed to measure ability to perform life functions. Mental retardation is not a single disease, syndrome, or symptom, but rather a state of impairment that is identified by the behavior and abilities of the individual. Contrary to popular impression, many people with mental retardation are not immediately detectable. They can look, act, and talk normally. Table 23-2 lists the *DSM-IV-TR* criteria for mental retardation. The diagnosis, which is usually made before 7 or 8 years of age, describes an individual's current level of thinking and behavior, but does not necessarily give an accurate prognosis. People may be classified as retarded at one time during their lives and not at another. How a particular child will eventually turn out depends more on coexisting handicaps, resources, motivation, educa-

TABLE 23-1
Childhood Development

AGE	MOTOR AND COGNITIVE FUNCTIONS
1 month	Roots, sucks, and grasps
2 months	Social smile
5 months	Sits and grasps objects
7 months	Crawls (6–8 months)
8 months	Stranger anxiety
10 months	Object permanence (will look for an object hidden from view)
11 months	Walking (10–14 months)
15 months	Imitation
18 months	Talking (few words)
19 months	Preoperational thought
22 months	Toilet training (wide range of normal; 22–48 months)
6 years	Shift to verbal memory
7 years	Concrete operational thought
12 years	Formal operational thought, beginnings of abstract reasoning

M.R.

tional and training opportunities, and treatment than on the mental retardation itself. Indeed, people with mental retardation frequently have coexisting handicaps that are more incapacitating than the retardation.

The history of mental retardation is a checkered one. In Europe during the 14th and 15th centuries, those with mental retardation were regarded superstitiously as

TABLE 23-2
DSM-IV-TR *Criteria for Mental Retardation*

A. Significantly subaverage intellectual functioning: an IQ of approximately 70 (range 65–75) or below on an individually administered IQ test (for infants, a clinical judgment of significantly subaverage intellectual functioning).

B. Concurrent deficits or impairments in present adaptive functioning (i.e., the person's effectiveness in meeting the standards expected for his or her age by his or her cultural group) in at least two of the following skill areas: communication, self-care, home living, social/interpersonal skills, use of community resources, self-direction, functional academic skills, work, leisure, health, and safety).

C. The onset is before age 18 years.

Note. From *DSM-IV-TR,* p. 49.

blessed "infants of the good God." However, during the "Enlightenment" Martin Luther referred to the "feebleminded" as "Godless" and thought society should rid itself of them. It was not until Binet developed psychometric tests so that schools could "track" schoolchildren into special programs that the range of human intellectual capacity became evident. In spite of noble intentions, these IQ tests were often used to exclude many children from school and to identify "imbeciles" in need of sterilization so that mental retardation would not be propagated. Only with Folling's discovery in 1934 of phenylketonuria, a treatable cause of mental retardation, did the study and treatment of mental retardation become respectable.

Epidemiology

The adult prevalence of mental retardation is generally lower than in childhood. DSM-IV-TR lists the prevalence of mental retardation as about 1%, but estimates vary between 1 and 3% depending on criteria used. The vast majority of people with mental retardation are only mildly retarded. Most people with mild retardation can hold a job and live on their own, with perhaps some support from family members. Table 23-3 lists the levels of mental retardation by degree of severity in the adult population.

Different IQ tests are scaled with different standard deviations: This variation is reflected in IQ *ranges* rather than fixed points. Between 70 and 84 IQ is defined as borderline intelligence and not mental retardation. Individuals in this range may struggle with some aspects of independent living but generally are not considered mentally retarded. However, because of the range of error on standard IQ tests, a person with an IQ of 75 and significant adaptive deficits could be classified as mentally retarded. However, another individual

---

TABLE 23-3
Levels of Mental Retardation in Adults

CATEGORY	PERCENT OF MENTALLY RETARDED	IQ	MENTAL AGE (years)
Mild	89.0	50–55 to 69	8.5 to 11.0
Moderate	6.0	35–40 to 50–55	6.0 to 8.5
Severe	3.4	20–25 to 35–40	3.75 to 6.0
Profound	1.6	below 20–25	0 to 3.75

Note. 70–85 IQ is called *borderline intelligence* or *borderline intellectual functioning*—not quite "normal" but not mental retardation.

---

with an IQ of 75 who does not have adaptive deficits would be considered to have borderline intellectual functioning. People with mild mental retardation are considered "educable" and can master some school subjects such as basic reading and simple arithmetic. People with moderate mental retardation are termed "trainable" because they can learn simple basic tasks but usually cannot master most subjects taught in schools.

Intelligence in the general population does not follow a normal bell-shaped curve; rather, there are a larger number of cases than would be expected at the lower end of the IQ range. Specific pathological processes, such as major genetic abnormalities or brain injuries, probably cause this bulge at the lower end.

Etiology

The specific cause of mental retardation can be identified in only 25–50% of affected children. In general, the more severe the mental retardation, the more likely a specific cause can be found. In mild retardation there is usually a mix of cultural and multigenetic factors; such kids often have parents with borderline intelligence, and some may be raised in unstimulating environments or have neglectful early care. However, many children with mild mental retardation are born to parents of normal intelligence and receive good and loving care. In those cases, the cause of their delays may be due to genetic factors, prenatal insults, or birth complications. Most often, no specific cause is identified.

> A cause usually can be established more often in cases of moderate and severe mental retardation. The general frequencies of the known causes are (1) *prenatal* (includes genetic), 80–85%; (2) *perinatal* (most often asphyxia), 5–10%; and (3) *postnatal*, 5–10%. Public health measures have substantially reduced two main perinatal causes of mental retardation. Testing babies at birth for *hypothyroidism* (1 in 4,000 births) and *phenylketonuria* (PKU, 1 in 12,000), which is an inability to metabolize the amino acid phenylalanine, has essentially eliminated these causes. Newborn screening in the United States now tests for numerous rare but devastating metabolic disorders, thereby allowing these infants to be quickly identified and treated. Hypothyroid babies are treated with thyroid hormone, and PKU babies are put on very low phenylalanine diets.
>
> The three most common *chromosomal causes* of mental retardation are Down's syndrome, fragile X, and trisomy 18. The most common *genetic causes* are Prader–Willi syndrome and Wilson's disease.

Down's syndrome accounts for approximately 10% of the individuals institutionalized with mental retardation and is the most common genetic cause. It is usually the result of an extra 21st chromosome, and is also called trisomy

21. Its risk is higher with increasing maternal age and probably paternal age. People with Down's syndrome have a broad IQ range of a mean IQ of 47–50. They share numerous physical characteristics: high cheekbones, flat nasal bridge, large protruding tongue, microcephaly, small round ears, hypotonic muscles, and hyperflexibility. They are very susceptible to infections, particularly respiratory, and 30–50% have congenital heart defects. Many don't survive childhood, and few reach 50 years old. They generally have friendly temperaments and love music. Parents of children with Down's syndrome can contact the National Down Syndrome Congress, a parent organization, at www.ndsccenter.org or (800) 232–6372.

In *fragile X syndrome* mental retardation varies from severe to mild, with a few in the borderline IQ range. Children with fragile X tend to do particularly badly in math and block designs and have a specific developmental language disorder. Females are the carriers, and males are affected. Males are short with long ears, a long narrow face, and sunken chest (*pectus excavatum*).

Almost all of the chromosomal and genetic causes of mental retardation are associated with physical anomalies and most with short stature. Some have specific behavioral abnormalities, such as binge eating in Prader–Willi syndrome.

Prenatal brain and head malformations usually result in severe mental retardation. Many of these are caused by autosomal recessive genes. Approximately a third of the population carries one of these genes, but because each is rare, the chances of two parents both having the same gene is small.

Brain abnormalities include *anencephaly*, in which parts of the brain and skull are missing (usually fatal); *hydroencephaly*, in which the cranium is filled with fluid instead of with brain tissue; and *porencephaly*, characterized by large fluid-filled cysts in the brain. *Skull abnormalities* include *microcephaly*, which is an abnormally small head, and *hydrocephalus*, in which pressure from excess cerebrospinal fluid destroys brain tissue. Skull abnormalities can be caused by a variety of sources other than an autosomal dominant gene.

The most common *preventable cause* of mental retardation is *fetal alcohol syndrome*. The CDC estimates the prevalence of FAS at .2–1.5 per 1,000 live births (www.cdc.gov/ncbddd/fas). Other causes of mental retardation include *asphyxia* from maternal hypertension, toxemia, or placenta previa, and *intrauterine infections* such as cytomegalovirus (CMV) rubella, and toxoplasmosis (often acquired from cats). Anoxia during delivery can also lead to mental retardation.

Fetal alcohol syndrome (FAS) usually results in mild mental retardation with mean IQs in the 60s and a range of 25–120. The three hallmark signs of FAS are (1) CNS deficits (most often with lower IQ) and symptoms of attention-deficit/hyperactivity disorder (ADHD); (2) faces with narrow eye slits (cats eyes), flat cheeks, short nose, thin upper lip, and flat philtrum (the two vertical ridges between the upper lip and nose); and (3) growth retardation.

Children with FAS are often frustrating to their parents and teachers because they develop adequate verbal skills and sound normal but have serious attention and math deficits. They can often mimic words well but don't fully understand or comprehend their meaning. They can "talk a good line," but don't understand basic cause–effect relationships; hence, behavioral approaches utilizing positive and negative reinforcement don't work. When told to do a task, they may indicate that they fully understand but then perform disastrously because of very poor comprehension, judgment, and attention span. They do best with structure and repetition. Some mothers find that they must put up the same "to do" list every day for their grade-school children or they won't brush their teeth, get dressed, take a shower, and so on. Fetal alcohol effect (FAE), which is a milder variation of FAS, has only two of the three hallmarks and is more common (1 in 200 to 300 births) than FAS; these children have somewhat higher IQs. Very low social drinking levels during pregnancy (e.g., one drink a day) are associated with high frequencies of attention and math deficits.

> Parents desiring support and information about FAS can contact NOFAS (National Organization on FAS) at www.nofas.org or 800-66-NOFAS. Two books—*The Broken Cord* by Michael Dorris, a gripping account of raising a child with FAS, and *Fantastic Antone Succeeds: Experiences in Educating Children with Fetal Alcohol Syndrome* by Judith Kleinfell and Siobhan Westcott, a more upbeat "how-to" book for parents and educators—are must reading for parents with FAS children.

The most common *postnatal causes* of mental retardation are *meningitis*, *head trauma*, *encephalitis*, and *anoxia*. A child with physically abusive parents may be knocked unconscious and suffer enough brain damage to become mentally retarded.

Differential Diagnosis

In general, the more severe the retardation, the earlier the diagnosis is made. Children with mild retardation often do well enough that they aren't detected until they are in kindergarten or first grade. Typically it is a primary-care physician who makes the first professional assessment. Table 23-4 outlines key areas that should be evaluated in conjunction with the following helpful tips:

TABLE 23-4

Assessing a Child with Mental Retardation

Pregnancy Lack or loss of fetal growth, abnormal weight gain by mother, particularly minimal fetal movement, maternal drug or alcohol ingestion, illness during the pregnancy (particularly rubella, syphilis, and HIV)

Birth Low birth weight, birth complications, abnormalities at birth (floppy, unresponsive)

Infancy Head size or head growth too small or too large; delay in developmental milestones; abnormal muscle tone, reflexes, postures, and movements

1. When you see a child with some unusual features, don't immediately assume a mental retardation associated syndrome. Check both parents' appearances—they may have similar features with very normal IQs.
2. If the mother of a child with mental retardation has had multiple spontaneous abortions, then the child is more likely to be at risk for a chromosomal abnormality.
3. If the child has a selective delay in only one area, such as math or reading, it is not mental retardation but rather a *learning disorder*.
4. If the child progressed normally for some time and then stopped or slowed, a specific *medical cause* is more likely.

The Denver Developmental Screening Test is an excellent tool for identifying developmental problems in infants and preschool children. A child with *developmental delays* may not be retarded but instead have hearing or visual impairment. If this is suspected, an audiologist or ophthalmologist skilled in the evaluation of infants and difficult children should evaluate the child. *Chromosome studies* should be done if the child with developmental delays has any *congenital defects, multiple minor malformations, or a combination of minor and major defects.* Any child with developmental delays without a known specific diagnosis may have an *inborn error of metabolism* and should undergo appropriate metabolic studies.

Management and Treatment

Attempts should be made to make a diagnosis because the mental retardation may be treatable and, if not, a reasonable prognosis can still be established. If discovered early enough, the progression of some cases of mental retardation can be arrested, slowed, or partially reversed. The most dramatic examples of successful treatment are giving thyroid hormone to a hypothyroid infant, performing a shunt in a case of early hydrocephalus, and introducing a low-phenylalanine diet to a baby with phenylketonuria. Unfortunately, in most cases, the mental retardation doesn't have a specific cause or, if it does, it is not specifically treatable.

The clinician's ability to understand and provide direct management for these children and their parents may determine the child's eventual fate. Questions that parents frequently ask clinicians include (1) "Is our child retarded?"; (2) "What caused it?"; and (3) "What can we do about it?"

When told that their child is mentally retarded or developmentally delayed, parents might deny the retardation, which may lead to medical shopping—looking for a physician who will disagree with the original diagnosis or who will say the coveted words, "Your child will outgrow it." A second reaction, which is always present to some degree, is guilt. Since guilt is emotionally painful, parents may deal with it by projecting blame for the retardation on someone else, such as their spouse, their ancestors, their obstetrician, their pediatrician, or even on an event that occurred during the pregnancy. The guilt often results in frustrations for the parents and may be manifested by hostility directed toward the clinician. A third response is to rid themselves of the problem. Since this is socially and personally unacceptable, parents may hide these feelings from themselves and others by publicly demonstrating the opposite reaction of overprotection and oversolicitous care. Many parents of children with mental retardation become great advocates for their children and work effectively with schools and care providers to give their child every possible advantage. Support groups exist in many communities.

Clinicians caring for children with mental retardation must recognize the multifaceted problems facing the family and be able to deal with the parents at their level by helping them accept the diagnosis, cope with their feelings of guilt and disappointment, and by working with them to develop and implement a management plan for the child. Clinicians must avoid removing all hope for parents, and at the same time be realistic in terms of expectations for their child. Above all, clinicians should avoid making decisions for parents based on their own reactions and attitudes. For example, even though a clinician may feel that a baby would be better off if he or she succumbed at birth, the parents may not share this feeling. Most children with mental retardation have the best chance of reaching their full potential in a caring, supportive home wherein caregivers convey realistic expectations and provide training and care from specialists in mental retardation.

Because individuals with mental retardation have incurred some form of brain damage, it makes sense that they are more susceptible to other forms of mental illness than the general population. Specific accompanying diagnoses, such as ADHD, seizures (especially subtle partial seizures), and mood disorders should be vigorously treated. Anticonvulsants and lithium may improve aggression and impulse control. Children with mild retardation usually respond better to stimulants than children with severe retardation (Handen et al., 1992). Clomipramine and SSRIs may be helpful in reducing anxious, obsessional, or self-injurious behavior. Buspirone, starting at low doses 2.5 mg three times a day, has been used for agitation and aggression in children with mental retardation (Ricketts et al., 1994). Naltrexone, an opiate blocker, is prescribed in instances where there are repetitive harmful behaviors such as head-banging or self-mutilation. Sedating antipsychotics probably have been overused for behavioral control in this population.

LEARNING, MOTOR SKILLS, AND COMMUNICATION DISORDERS

These disorders, characterized by serious deficits in one or even two specific areas, do not imply mental retardation. Children with these disorders can function adequately in other areas. Three specific learning disorders are described in *DSM-IV-TR*: reading, mathematics, and written expression. Criteria for these disorders are listed in Table 23-5.

TABLE 23-5

DSM-IV-TR *Criteria for Learning Disorders: Disorders of Written Expression, Reading, and Math*

A. The particular area (reading achievement, mathematical ability or written skills) as measured by individually administered standardized tests (or as an alternative to a test for writing skills, functional assessments can be used) is substantially below that expected given the person's chronological age, measured intelligence, and age-appropriate education.[a]

B. The disturbance in Criterion A significantly interferes with academic achievement or activities of daily living that require this skill.

C. If a sensory deficit is present, the learning difficulties are in excess of those usually associated with it.

Note. From *DSM-IV-TR,* pp. 51–57.

[a]The category "Learning Disorder Not Otherwise Specified" is used for those who do not meet Criterion A for a specific learning disorder, but meet Criteria B *and* C. For example, a significant spelling deficit would be classified here.

Reading disorders usually start before age 7 with difficulties in learning to read and then include *spelling problems* by age 7 and *writing problems* by age 8. From 3–10% of schoolchildren have a reading disorder, and boys have it more often than girls. It is the most common type of learning disorder. Athough treatment can significantly help children with reading disorders, most will still have some problems in adulthood. Children given proper help and treatment can attain careers comparable to their normal classmates with similar IQs.

A *mathematics disorder* is often not detected until rote memorization and primitive counting strategies no longer work. About 5% of schoolchildren have this disorder with inconsistent gender differences. Some children may be diagnosed mistakenly with this disorder because of poor teaching in their schools. Early signs of a mathematics disorder include a failure to name and count numbers or to use or understand numbers in simple, everyday activities (e.g., unable to comply with instruction to "Give Jim two candies and Jennifer three candies").

Management and Treatment

Clinicians untrained in these areas too often assume that they can give professional advice about learning disorders. However, the causes of these disorders are myriad. One part of the brain may be functioning abnormally and the rest normally. Each of these abilities requires a complex integration of several subsets of abilities. Ideally, a child neuropsychologist or educational psychologist specializing in this area should evaluate children with these disorders to see which subset abilities are intact and which are not. Then a learning program can be prescribed that capitalizes on the child's strengths and circumvents the weaknesses. For example, a child with very good auditory memory and integration skills who has difficulties in complex visual integration might learn reading more easily by reading a book with a tape of the book playing in the background at the same time. Then the correct sounds are systematically paired with the words. More complex problems such as dyslexia may merit a variety of special interventions. Dyslexia is probably not a unitary disorder but caused by a variety of deficits that need to be individually assessed. Current treatment of mathematics disorders focuses on acquiring basic arithmetic skills and speed training. Giving attention primarily to underlying perceptual–motor–cognitive abilities has yielded poorer results.

Motor skills disorder is a separate category in *DSM-IV-TR*, and its only listing in this category is "developmental coordination disorder." The very clumsy child typically shows delays in gross motor skills (e.g., sitting and walking) and fine motor skills (e.g., self-feeding, zipping, or buttoning). The reported boy:girl ratio for this disorder varies between 2:1 and 4:1. These children break things often, though accidentally, and are called "destructive" or, refusing to attempt frustrating tasks such as writing, are called "lazy." Their peers have endless insulting names for them (e.g., "spaz," "klutz"). Academic performance is usually normal, but self-esteem is often affected. Kids with ADHD appear clumsy from excessive motor activity and inattention, and this disorder must be ruled out. The *DSM-IV-TR* criteria for developmental coordination disorder are listed in Table 23-6.

Communication disorders can be very specific and may not involve other areas of function. Unlike the learning disorders, they can be diagnosed as accompanying mental retardation if the language difficulties appear to be excessive for the level of retardation. Four main categories are defined: *expressive language disorder, mixed receptive–expressive language disorder* (developmental receptive language disorder), *phonological disorder* (articulation disorder), and *stuttering.*

Kids with *expressive language disorder* understand what they are told but can't express what they want to communicate. Those with *mixed receptive–expressive language disorder* have problems with both areas—understanding and communicating. *Phonological disorder* (articulation disorder) creates a problem with speech, but not necessarily a problem in communication or understanding. Disorders of speech pronunciation are best assessed by trained speech pathologists. Pronunciation difficulties are normal in young children

---

TABLE 23-6
DSM-IV-TR *Criteria for Developmental Coordination Disorder*

A. Performance in daily activities that require motor coordination is substantially below that expected given the person's chronological age and measured intelligence. This may be manifested by marked delays in achieving motor milestones (e.g., walking, crawling, sitting), dropping things, "clumsiness," poor performance in sports, or poor handwriting.

B. The disturbance in Criterion A significantly interferes with academic achievement or activities of daily living.

C. The disturbance is not due to a general medical condition (e.g., cerebral palsy, hemiplegia, or muscular dystrophy) and does not meet criteria for a Pervasive Developmental Disorder.

D. If Mental Retardation is present, the motor difficulties are in excess of those usually associated with it.

Note. From *DSM-IV-TR,* p. 58.

and are often defined as abnormal only if they persist past a certain age. Lisps and other kinds of pronunciation difficulties are often very treatable. Varying pronunciations due to regional accents or dialects are not considered disorders of speech. Dropping the *r* in water would be a problem in Seattle but normal in Boston. In *stuttering*, the sounds are accurately made, but the fluency and time patterning are frequently disrupted.

The sooner the more severe forms of these disorders are detected and treated, the better the outcome. Referral to a speech pathologist and therapist specializing in children's speech disorders is essential, and for the language disorders, a psychologist or neuropsychologist. The family and teachers should be educated about the diagnosis and taught how best to work with the child. Frequently, children with receptive language disorders are mistakenly accused of hearing but "not listening." Table 23-7 lists *DSM-IV-TR* criteria for the communication disorders.

Language disorders affect 3–10% of school-age children, while stuttering and articulation disorders each affect about 5%. Fortunately, these disorders usually are either outgrown or can be treated successfully. About 50% of children with expressive language disorder catch up to their peers before they reach school and do not need treatment. Those with more severe forms should get treatment before school-age. Many children who also have receptive language problems will eventually acquire normal language abilities, but some of the more severely affected do not. Children with language disorders often have other disorders suggesting developmental delay (e.g., enuresis, and/or phonological, coordination, and reading disorders).

With speech therapy almost all children recover from phonological disorder; the milder cases often recover by age 8 without speech therapy. Stutterers typically (80%) recover before age 16, 60% spontaneously. The disorder has strong biological and genetic association. Approximately 60% of those who stutter have a family member who stutters. The boy to girl ratio is about 3:1. Children with these disorders and their families often benefit from counseling to help them deal with the social repercussions from peers (teasing) and with low self-esteem from being criticized by parents and teachers.

PERVASIVE DEVELOPMENTAL DISORDERS: AUTISTIC DISORDERS AND ASPERGER'S DISORDER

Clinical Presentation

Children diagnosed with autism and pervasive developmental disorders may have intellectual delays but are more prominently delayed in areas of social

TABLE 23-7

DSM-IV-TR *Criteria for Communication Disorders:*
Expressive Language Disorder, Mixed Receptive–Expressive Language Disorder,
Phonological Disorder, and Stuttering

Common Criteria for Expressive and Mixed Receptive-Expressive Language Disorder

A. The difficulties with expressive (also receptive, if mixed receptive-expressive) language interfere with academic or occupational achievement or with social communication.

B. Criteria are not met for a Pervasive Developmental Disorder and, if only expressive, does not meet criteria for a Mixed Receptive-Expressive Language Disorder.

C. If Mental Retardation, a speech–motor or sensory deficit, or environmental deprivation is present, the language difficulties are in excess of those usually associated with these problems.

Additional Criterion for Expressive Language Disorder

D. The scores obtained from standardized individually administered measures of expressive language development are substantially below those obtained from standardized measures of both nonverbal intellectual capacity and receptive language development. The disturbance may be manifest clinically by symptoms that include having a markedly limited vocabulary, making errors in tense, or having difficulty recalling words or producing sentences with developmentally appropriate length or complexity.

Additional Criterion for Mixed Receptive-Expressive Language Disorder

D. The scores obtained from a battery of standardized individually administered measures of both receptive and expressive language development are substantially below those obtained from standardized measures of nonverbal intellectual capacity. Symptoms include those for Expressive Language Disorder as well as difficulty understanding words, sentences, or specific types of words, such as spatial terms.

Phonological Disorder

A. Failure to use developmentally expected speech sounds that are appropriate for age and dialect (e.g., errors in sound production, use, representation, or organization such as, but not limited to, substitutions of one sound for another [use of /t/ for target /k/ sound] or omissions of sounds such as final consonants).

B. The difficulties in speech sound production interfere with academic or occupational achievement or with social communication.

C. If Mental Retardation, a speech–motor or sensory deficit, or environmental deprivation is present, the speech difficulties are in excess of those usually associated with these problems.

Stuttering

A. Disturbance in the normal fluency and time patterning of speech (inappropriate for the individual's age), characterized by frequent occurrences of one or more of the following:

   1. sound and syllable repetitions
   2. sound prolongations

(*continued*)

TABLE 23-7

Continued

3. interjections

4. broken words (e.g., pauses within a word)

5. audible or silent blocking (filled or unfilled pauses in speech)

6. circumlocutions (word substitutions to avoid problematic words)

7. words produced with an excess of physical tension

8. monosyllabic whole-word repetitions (e.g., I-I-I see him)

B. The disturbance in fluency interferes with academic or occupational achievement or with social communication.

C. If a speech–motor or sensory deficit is present, the speech difficulties are in excess of those usually associated with these problems.

Note. From *DSM-IV-TR,* p. 69.

---

reciprocity and interest. These children often make poor eye contact, have limited interest in reciprocal social interactions, and may have very restricted repetitive interests that seem odd or obsessive to others. One father observed about his autistic child, "He lives according to a beat, but I have no idea what the beat is." Emerging between 6 and 30 months after birth, autistic symptoms do *not* include hallucinations, delusions, or paranoia, which partly explains why autism is not classified as schizophrenia but as a "pervasive developmental disorder."

> Soon after birth, children with autism develop abnormally. Within the first 3–6 months of their lives, their parents may note that they do not develop a normal pattern of smiling or responding to cuddling. As they grow older, they do not progress through developmental milestones such as learning to say words or speak sentences. Instead, they may seem aloof, withdrawn, and detached. Instead of developing patterns of relating warmly to their parents, they may engage in stereotyped behavior such as rocking, clapping, whirling, or head-banging. Children with this disorder are referred to as "autistic" because they appear to be withdrawn and absorbed into themselves. In the movie *Rain Man* Dustin Hoffman effectively portrayed most of the characteristics of high-functioning autistic disorder.

The impairment in social interaction is usually the first obvious sign of the disorder and persists throughout life. These children may struggle with not understanding social cues and expectations and may seem less interested in relationships than other children. Most children with autistic spectrum disorders do form attachments to parents and caregivers, but even within these attachments may show lack of social understanding and empathy. Interactions, when they occur, have a mechanical quality. When stressed, their behavior typically becomes strange, difficult, or overactive. Individuals on the autistic spectrum may be intensely bothered by changes in routine or schedule and may react to transitions with resistance, fear, and anger. Their verbal impairments range from the complete absence of speech to mildly deviant speech and language patterns. Their speech is often odd: These children may exhibit echolalia, misname objects, invoke words only known to family members, hum monotonous sounds, or have an unusual intonation to their voices. Some examiners have described a monotonous pattern of speech that lacks expression, but this characteristic is not universal.

> Even children who develop good facility in verbal expression produce speech that has a repetitive, sing-song, and monotonous quality to it. They may become obsessed with counting things or totally absorbed by spinning things (e.g., whirling fans, water fountains). There is an intense and rigid commitment to maintaining specific routines, and extreme distress if routines are interrupted.
>
> Higher-functioning individuals with autistic spectrum disorders and Asperger's disorder may have special skills (Treffert, 1988), though rarely. They may display a superb remote memory, remembering lyrics of songs heard years ago. They may recite schedules, TV programs, historical dates, math equations, and restaurant menus. At times, they may share this material out of context and inappropriately. Their savant skills—those islets of precocity or special capacities—can occur in music, drawing, calculating, and calendar dates. As preschoolers, a few can teach themselves to read (hyperlexia) without comprehending anything.

Children with autism may underreact or overreact to sensory stimuli. Sometimes smells enrapture them; they may ignore people speaking to them, suggesting deafness, but then respond to the tick of a watch or metronome. Because they might experience pain but react minimally, these kids occasionally can injure themselves and not cry. Table 23-8 lists *DSM-IV-TR* criteria for autistic disorder.

Most children with autism also have mental retardation: 40% score under 50, 30% between 50–70, and 30% can top 70. Only 20% have a normal nonverbal intelligence. "Elevated" IQs pop up, but often with inconsistent subscores, enormous "scattering," and considerable variation over time. In general, the lower the IQ, the worse the autism. Psychological tests show that verbal sequencing and abstraction are more disturbed than rote memory or visuospatial skills. These

TABLE 23-8

DSM-IV-TR *Criteria for Autistic Disorder*

A. A total of six or more items from (1), (2), and (3), with at least two from (1), and one each from (2) and (3):

    (1) qualitative impairment in social interaction, as manifested by at least two of the following:

        (a) marked impairment in the use of multiple nonverbal behaviors such as eye-to-eye gaze, facial expression, body postures, and gestures to regulate social interaction

        (b) failure to develop peer relationships appropriate to developmental level

        (c) a lack of spontaneous seeking to share enjoyment, interests, or achievements with other people (e.g., by a lack of showing, bringing, or pointing out objects of interest)

        (d) lack of social or emotional reciprocity

    (2) qualitative impairments in communication as manifested by at least one of the following:

        (a) delay in, or total lack of, the development of spoken language (not accompanied by an attempt to compensate through alternative modes of communication such as gesture or mime)

        (b) in individuals with adequate speech, marked impairment in the ability to initiate or sustain a conversation with others

        (c) stereotyped and repetitive use of language or idiosyncratic language

        (d) lack of varied, spontaneous make-believe play or social imitative play appropriate to developmental level

    (3) restricted repetitive and stereotyped patterns of behavior, interests, and activities, as manifested by at least one of the following:

        (a) encompassing preoccupation with one or more stereotyped and restricted patterns of interest that is abnormal either in intensity or focus

        (b) apparently inflexible adherence to specific, nonfunctional routines or rituals

        (c) stereotyped and repetitive motor mannerisms (e.g., hand or finger flapping or twisting, or complex whole-body movements)

        (d) persistent preoccupation with parts of objects

B. Delays or abnormal functioning in at least one of the following areas, with onset prior to age 3 years: (1) social interaction, (2) language as used in social communication, or (3) symbolic or imaginative play.

C. The disturbance is not better accounted for by Rett's Disorder or Childhood Disintegrative Disorder.

Note. From *DSM-IV-TR,* p. 75.

patients often have primitive neurological reflexes, "soft" neurological signs, mixed laterality of their hands, and physical anomalies.

Clinical Course

Parents may not recognize the first signs of autism, especially if the affected child is their first. Parents may blame the unusual behavior on deafness, until they see their child respond to music, echo sounds, or react to softly spoken words. In desperation, they may point to a particularly irrelevant event, such as a grandfather's death or a neighborhood fire, as the "cause" of their child's problems. Recently, there has been a great deal of controversy about whether or not childhood vaccinations may cause or contribute to autism in some cases. Many parents of children with autism advocate for this position, but the medical evidence has not been robustly supportive.

Although autism lasts the lifetime, slow gains can be made. A supportive home certainly helps. Even when socially awkward and egocentric, 15–30% of adults with autism can live alone and work, but only 2% reach a normal status and gainful employment. As these children become adolescents, depression may emerge. As the years continue, their speech and understanding may improve, despite continued perseveration, restricted interests, and stereotyped motor movements. Marriage is rare.

Medical illness, puberty, and major stresses can trigger temporary regressions. Over 25% of these children, especially those with IQs below 50, exhibit major or partial complex seizures. From 4 to 32% develop grand mal seizures in late childhood, which makes their prognosis very poor.

Epidemiology

The prevalence of all pervasive developmental disorders (i.e., autistic spectrum disorders) is estimated at 1%. Among kids under 15, the prevalence of classic autism is near 0.25%. Boys have it three times as often as girls. Mild autism outnumbers serious autism. Lower socioeconomic groups may produce more autism, but this finding may actually reflect inadequate research.

Autism has some genetic basis. Identical twins have 64% concordance rates; fraternal twins, 9% concordance rates. Other siblings are at a higher risk for cognitive and language problems. Fragile X syndrome may produce 2–5% of autism cases in kids; polygenetic factors may produce other cases. Parents of one child with autism have about a 4% risk of future children having autism. Some studies have shown even higher recurrence risks.

At birth, autistic children have more perinatal complications and congenital malformations. The disorder can also stem from specific diseases or conditions—e.g., tuberous sclerosis, anoxia during birth, intrauterine infections (rubella, cytomegalovirus herpes simplex), postnatal neurological infections, encephalitis, infantile spasms, untreated phenylketonuria, and drug exposure (thalidomide) during pregnancy. Neuroimaging studies in individuals with autism have demonstrated some regional brain size abnormalities with the most consistent finding being enlargements of temporal and frontal lobes. The increased size seems to be related to white matter versus gray matter and shorter versus longer neuron connections (Hazlet et al., 2006). This may account for the poor cognitive integration seen clinically with these patients. The underactivity of the amygdala, which has been implicated in autism, may also be related to this reduction in functional neuronal connectedness. Abnormalities in neurotransmitter systems have been discovered (especially dopamine, serotonin, and glutamate) and afflicted individuals more frequently carry polymorphisms of monoamine oxidase.

Differential Diagnosis

Children with mental retardation and without autism are more extraverted, act more like their age, and exhibit more normal language; they also demonstrate broad intellectual deficits without any of the savant's math, music, or other specialized skills. When both mental retardation and autism clearly coexist, diagnose both. The stereotyped movements that occur in *tic* and *stereotypic movement disorders* lack the numerous other features of autism.

Unlike patients with autistic disorders, patients with *hearing, language,* and *speech disorders* can read lips, perform sign language, relate to parents, and, over time, display emotional and social appropriateness. Children who are deaf, babble normally at birth but much less by 6–12 months, and if at all would respond only to loud sounds. In contrast, children with autism usually ignore both loud and normal tones, but will react to soft and low sounds. Auditory-evoked potentials can be used to diagnose deafness. Those children with *visual impairments* actively engage others, despite their poor eye contact and constant staring at people in motion.

Schizophrenia in children is extremely rare, and mental retardation or seizures do not typically accompany it. Development is usually normal prior to the onset of psychotic symptoms. Even for the most bizarre or shy person with autism, do not give adult diagnoses of *schizoid* or *schizotypal personality disorder.* From inadequate parenting, social isolation, or "hospitalitis," *psychosocial deprivation* can induce apathetic, withdrawn children who display delayed language and motor skills (*reactive attachment disorder*); yet, unlike autism, these patients markedly improve with an improved environment.

Management and Treatment

Two related goals guide treatment of autism disorders: reducing the child's symptoms and supporting constructive efforts. Initially, clinicians should assess patients' language, cognition, social interactions, and consider inborn metabolic disorders, degenerative diseases, EEGs, chromosomes, and psychological tests to determine if any treatable cause of symptoms exists.

Medications

Neuroleptics (e.g., risperidone) may decrease aggression, agitation, labile affect hyperactivity, and stereotyped movements (Parikh, MS). Social interaction, eye contact, anxiety, and learning may also improve with neuroleptics. If the autism is accompanied by hyperactive features, treatment with stimulants may be beneficial. Anticonvulsants curtail 35–50% of seizures, and lithium may reduce self-inflicted injuries. As with children with mental retardation SSRIs may reduce anxious, obsessional, and self-injurious behaviors but may more often have side effects in people with autism and are therefore used at very low doses (Kolevzon, 2006). Buspirone may reduce agitation and aggression (Buitelaar, 1998).

Social Therapies

Well-controlled studies suggest that structured classrooms and active behavioral programs encourage language, cognition, and appropriate behavior. Many children with autism benefit from picture schedules that visually reflect their daily activities and help them to mentally prepare for transitions. Parents should become adept at implementing these time-consuming behavioral techniques and providing highly structured routines. In addition, family life will be enhanced if parents pay attention to healthy siblings, collaborate with public agencies, and if necessary, arrange for long-term care. At some point, clinicians and family, working together, may want to evaluate whether well-supervised residential living would be better for the child with autism than living with parents.

Asperger's Disorder

Asperger's disorder is essentially a form of high-functioning autistic disorder. Kids with this disorder are impaired (although usually less severely) in social interaction and have the restricted, repetitive, and stereotyped behaviors and interests seen in autism, but without the delays in cognitive development and language. These children have normal intelligence and language skills but often demonstrate the lack of social reciprocity, restricted interests, and difficulty with transitions seen in children with more severe autism.

Childhood Disintegrative Disorder

In the rare *childhood disintegrative disorder* ("Heller syndrome"), afflicted children are normal in every way for at least 2 years and then disaster strikes in at least two major areas: (1) social interaction, communication, or restricted receptive language, and (2) stereotyped patterns of behavior. Some also lose bowel or bladder control. In its worse form, children with this disorder closely resemble children with autism. Most, fortunately, are less severely impaired.

Rett's Disorder

In *Rett's disorder*, seen only in girls, everything is normal for the first several months of life, but then they develop the stereotyped movements, poor social interaction, and impaired communication seen in autism. These girls have marked impairment of expressive and receptive language, severe psychomotor retardation, poorly coordinated gait or trunk movements, and deceleration of head growth. They may lose functional use of their hands (wringing and rubbing motions). Rett's syndrome is caused by a specific gene abnormality on the X chromosome.

ATTENTION-DEFICIT/HYPERACTIVITY DISORDER

Clinical Presentation

The cardinal features of attention-deficit/hyperactivity disorder (ADHD) are hyperactivity, short attention span, and impulsivity that are developmentally inappropriate and endure at least 6 months. Typically, this condition is recognized before or during early elementary school, although it can manifest from birth and perhaps before (some mothers report that their child was a nonstop womb kicker). Because younger children naturally have more ADHD features, kids diagnosed at age 4 are more likely to be "the little terrors" who wear out their parents. Historically ADHD was known as "minimal brain dysfunction," "hyperactive syndrome," and "minor cerebral dysfunction." The new name has been chosen because attention difficulties are prominent and virtually always present among children with these diagnoses.

Children with this diagnosis are a caricature of the "active" child. They are physically overactive, distracted, inattentive, impulsive, and hard to manage. In classrooms, these children can't pay attention; they fidget and fuss, fall off inanimate objects such as chairs, and disrupt conversations. Some even get expelled and require private tutoring. Their headlong dive into life seems determined *for* them and not *by* them.

Impatient and frustrated, even intelligent children with ADHD may get lower grades. They'll attack an exam but get bored or distracted after a few questions. They don't wait their turn; answers precede questions. When they zoom into a room, everybody notices them. Their world is a bang, not a whimper. They're constantly interrupting, screaming, and chattering. Minor events become major cataclysms.

Children with ADHD may exhibit a depressed mood with or without chronic "body anxiety." The constantly tapping foot is not driven by anxiety but rather by overactivity itself; ask the child why he does that and he might say, "I don't know—my legs just gotta move." Many children with ADHD also demonstrate social immaturity and/or impairments in motor, math, or reading skills. Although lacking overt vision or hearing difficulties, their hearing gets tested regularly, only to find that they hear well but listen poorly. They may have subtle impairments in copying age-appropriate figures; executing rapid alternating movements; making left–right discrimination; and showing reflex asymmetries, ambidexterity, and numerous "soft" neurological signs. In short, there's something wrong with these children, but nothing *that* wrong. Table 23-9 lists *DSM-IV-TR* criteria for ADHD.

Clinical Course

Half of the youngsters with ADHD present symptoms before age 4, whereas the rest do so in early elementary school. Gross agitation is more frequent in preschool children, finer degrees of restlessness, later on. The overall course of ADHD is unpredictable: Symptoms may continue into adulthood or remit at puberty. If any symptom disappears first, it is usually the disorder's major hallmark: hyperactivity. If ADHD subsides during adolescence, the kids may become productive, develop relationships, and launch serious adult plans.

TABLE 23-9

DSM-IV-TR *Criteria for Attention-Deficit/Hyperactivity Disorder*

A. Either (1) or (2):

(1) six (or more) of the following symptoms of inattention have persisted for at least 6 months to a degree that is maladaptive and inconsistent with developmental level:

Inattention

(a) often fails to give close attention to details or makes careless mistakes in schoolwork, work, or other activities

(b) often has difficulty sustaining attention in tasks or play activities

(c) often does not seem to listen when spoken to directly

(d) often does not follow through on instructions and fails to finish schoolwork, chores, or duties in the workplace (not due to oppositional behavior or failure to understand instructions)

(e) often has difficulties organizing tasks and activities

(f) often avoids, dislikes, or is reluctant to engage in tasks that require sustained mental effort (such as schoolwork or homework)

(g) often loses things necessary for tasks or activities (e.g., toys, school assignments, pencils, books, or tools)

(h) is often easily distracted by extraneous stimuli

(i) often forgetful in daily activities

(2) six or more of the following symptoms of hyperactivity-impulsivity have persisted for at least 6 months to a degree that is maladaptive and inconsistent with developmental level:

Hyperactivity

(a) often fidgets with hands or feet or squirms in seat

(b) often leaves seat in classroom or in other situations in which remaining seated is expected

(c) often runs about or climbs excessively in situations where it is inappropriate (in adolescents or adults, may be limited to subjective feelings of restlessness)

(d) often has difficulty playing or engaging in leisure activities quietly

(e) is often "on the go" or often acts as if "driven by a motor"

(f) often talks excessively

Impulsivity

(g) often blurts out answers before questions have been completed

(h) often has difficulty awaiting turn

(i) often interrupts or intrudes on others (e.g., butts into conversations or games)

B. Some hyperactive-impulsive orinattentive symptoms that caused impairment were present before age 7 years.

TABLE 23-9

Continued

C. Some impairment from the symptoms is present in two or more settings (e.g., at school [or work] and at home).

D. There must be clear evidence of clinically significant impairment in social, academic, or occupational functioning.

E. The symptoms do not occur exclusively during the course of a Pervasive Developmental Disorder, Schizophrenia, or other Psychotic Disorder and are not better accounted for by another mental disorder (e.g., Mood Disorder, Anxiety Disorder, Dissociative Disorder, or a Personality Disorder).

Note. From *DSM-IV-TR,* pp. 92–93.

About half of children with ADHD have a good outcome, completing school on schedule with acceptable grades. If childhood ADHD is severe, the chances of it persisting into adulthood are high. Around 60% of children with ADHD continue to have symptoms into adulthood. Adult ADHD symptoms mostly include inattention, disorganization, and failure to finish things. Other difficulties in adults associated with ADHD include frequent job changes, partner changes, and driving accidents.

ADHD commonly occurs with other psychiatric disorders, especially oppositional defiant disorder, conduct disorder, learning disorders, and substance use disorders. Kids with both ADHD and conduct disorder have a much worse prognosis than those with ADHD alone. Roughly 25% of adolescents with ADHD in combination with conduct disorder also develop antisocial personality disorder. These antisocial adults with ADHD complete fewer years of school, have a higher rate of substance abuse, more arrests, more car accidents, and more suicide attempts. Adults who had ADHD as children are more prone to mood disorders, perhaps secondary to both biological vulnerability and the constant assaults on self-esteem during childhood.

Hank got to school a little late. Getting ready for school that morning, he had spilled a glass of milk while gesturing with his hand, had fallen off the dining room chair twice, and while looking for a school book, had become distracted by five other things in his bedroom. Then he tripped a girl on the school bus as she was walking down the aisle because, for a moment, it seemed like a fun thing to do. He saw, he did, he thought—in that order.

At last Hank made it into the classroom, whereupon he dumped his books and homework into his messy desk. The class clown had arrived. While fidgeting at his desk, he chatted excitedly with his friend next to him, but the teacher was talking to the class and told him to stop. He tried paying attention to the teacher, and when the teacher asked the class a question, Hank answered it in the instant that five other hands went up. He thought, "Uh-oh, I got to remember to raise my hand next time," but at the next opportunity he blurted out the answer again. He was a smart kid who often knew the answer but got C's because he didn't finish assignments, lost homework, skipped items on exams, did 10 other things instead of studying for a test. The principal's office was all too familiar a place. He was sent there mostly for talking, but also for the stunts he performed to get laughs—he had learned to capitalize on his hyperactivity and impulsiveness by getting laughs from his friends. They liked him but also found him intrusive, annoying, and distracting.

Hank's parents were worn out by him and were reduced to hollow "don't-do-that-stop-that" interchanges that almost never netted the desired consequences. They regarded him like the family Labrador retriever: hyper, friendly—and untrainable.

Hank's fourth-grade teacher finally persuaded the parents to have Hank assessed. ADHD was diagnosed and in a week's time, he was responding to 30 mg/day of dextroamphetamine. His father was stunned by the rapid and very noticeable response. Hank's restlessness diminished, his concentration improved, and he began getting A's and B's. His parents were taught to deliver consistent, appropriate consequences for Hank's behavior. Hank remained the class clown, but slowly discovered that he could get positive attention in other ways—by helping someone out, doing well on a test or homework assignment, and working *with*, not against, other kids on a group project.

Epidemiology

DSM-IV-TR cites a prevalence rate of 3–7% in school-age children. Lower prevalence rates have been reported in several countries, which might be due to the use of different diagnostic criteria and cultural expectations. ADHD afflicts boys far more than girls, even though the precise ratios depend on the study. One investigation indicated that ADHD occurs six to nine times more often in boys than girls, whereas a community survey found a 3:1 ratio. The disorder is more common in firstborn boys. Among hyperactive ADHD kids 40% have oppositional defiant disorder. Depression and anxiety are also often co-morbid with ADHD (Elia, 2008).

Etiology and Pathogenesis

Despite the absence of specific brain damage, ADHD is mainly a *biological disorder*. In many cases genetics has a major role with heritability accounting for 75% of cases. In comparison to controls, the family members of these children have more ADHD; their brothers display ADHD three times more often. As mentioned above, other psychiatric disorders tend to travel with ADHD. The male relatives of children with ADHD have a higher incidence of substance abuse, alcoholism, and antisocial personality disorder, whereas their female counterparts have more somatization disorder and histrionic personality disorder. These various disorders are also more frequent in the biological parents of adopted-away children with ADHD. Newer evidence indicates that these other disorders may not be *genetically* linked to ADHD but are nonetheless linked: An adult with ADHD is more likely to marry a person with one of these other disorders (Faraone et al., 1991). Similarly, learning disorders (e.g., dyslexia) are more common in kids with ADHD and in their first-degree relatives, but this is due to the fact that a parent with ADHD is more likely to have married a spouse with a learning disorder (Faraone et al., 1993). Parents with *only* ADHD are more likely to have children with *only* ADHD, unaccompanied by conduct or learning disorder. Neurochemical studies of ADHD indicate multiple neurotransmitter involvement, including dopamine and norepinephrine. Structural brain imaging studies in children with ADHD found significantly smaller volumes in the prefrontal cortex, caudate, pallidum, corpus callosum, and cerebellum.

Possible *perinatal* risk factors for ADHD include poor maternal nutrition, maternal smoking, maternal substance abuse, birth complications, infections, and exposure to toxins such as lead. There is no specific neurobiological marker. Frontal lobe hypofunction may be a part of the pathology. Hyperactive parents of hyperactive children metabolize glucose in the brain at a level 8% lower than control parents. Chaotic families and child abuse may cause children to exhibit symptoms consistent with ADHD, but their cause may be trauma related. Some "experts" claim that food additives and sugar cause ADHD; yet after withdrawing these chemicals, in a placebo controlled fashion, mothers could not appreciate any change. Social class and ADHD appear unrelated.

Differential Diagnosis

Since many children seem fated to have at least some ADHD symptoms (especially high activity or low attention span), careful differential diagnosis is crucial. It is important to know what is normal at each age level and how children behave in a variety of environments. Inexperienced parents may conclude that their children's age-appropriate activity is highly pathological, but their children's teachers, who have experience with many children, may view the behavior as normal. The SNAP-IV Rating Scale, when completed by teachers, assists the clinician in diagnosis and monitoring treatment effectiveness. The scale is provided at the end of this chapter and may be reproduced without copyright infringement. A longer version covering more *DSM* diagnoses may be downloaded from www.adhd.net.

Separating ADHD from *conduct disorder* can be tricky. Children with conduct disorder alone are often misdiagnosed as having ADHD. Because they exhibit many bad and unacceptable behaviors, they may be labeled "hyperactive." However, most are no more active than their normal peers. In contrast, most kids with ADHD don't specialize in bad behaviors but rather exhibit *all* behaviors at high rates, including positive ones such as petting animals, joking with friends, and helping out little kids. Children with conduct disorders flaunt their meanness to people and animals; they intend bad outcomes and may not repent. Kids with ADHD can act in haste but tend to show remorse for wrongdoing.

Management and Treatment

The American Academy of Child and Adolescent Psychiatry has collected the latest evidence and clinical experience on ADHD and other childhood disorders in its published Practice Parameters (updated 2007 for ADHD). Because other conditions frequently occur with ADHD, referral for IQ, psychological, speech, language, and learning disabilities should be made if clinically indicated. Restlessness can also be caused by chronically used medications, such as anti-asthmatics, sympathomimetics, steroids, and decongestants. Some medications adults find sedating may cause a paradoxical response in children (e.g., phenobarbital or antihistamines).

Parent education, appropriate classroom placement, academic remediation, behavioral interventions, and medication are important components of treatment of ADHD. Stimulants and atomoxetine are FDA approved treatments for ADHD. Most children respond either to methylphenidate or D-amphetamine. Several long-acting preparations of stimulant medications are available with benefits of once/day dosing. Atomoxetine and buproprion are nonstimulants which improve ADHD symptoms less robustly than stimulants but without the risk of developing tolerance or dependency.

Medications

A child given separate trials of dextroamphetamine and methylphenidate has a greater than 90% chance of responding to one or the other. In trials of a single stimulant, roughly 30% of patients exhibited marked improvement, 40% received some benefit, and 10–30% were unaffected. If both drugs are equal, methylphenidate is preferred because of fewer cardiac effects (Sylvester, 1993). An EKG is now recommended prior to starting a stimulant. Optimal intellectual improvement and adequate behavioral control may be best at lower doses of methylphenidate. Methylphenidate's effects last from 3 to 6 hours; dextroamphetamine lasts somewhat longer. Stimulants diminish overactivity, impulsiveness, irritability, and emotional fluctuations; they increase vigilance, attention span, and general sociability. These medications don't facilitate learning per se, but when attention span lengthens and reduced criticism enhances self-esteem, learning accelerates.

These pharmacological agents can work immediately, but may require 1–2 weeks. Children with ADHD rarely develop tolerance and drug abuse, although stimulants might temporarily suppress growth slightly. If there is any question that the stimulant being used has little or no effect, the child should be placed on a different stimulant. While on these medications, blood pressure, pulse, height, weight, appetite, mood, and side effects (e.g., tics) should be regularly monitored. Common side effects of stimulants include loss of appetite, insomnia, headaches, stomachaches, and tics; less common but more serious side effects include psychosis, depression, suicidal ideation, and possibly stroke or sudden cardiac death.

Because children can grow out of ADHD, monitored trials of no medication should be conducted annually to see if they still need it. As alternatives to stimulants, antidepressants (e.g., imipramine, desipramine) help some kids with ADHD, particularly with depression, anxiety, and tics. However, these tricyclic antidepressants must be used very cautiously because they are more likely to cause cardiac arrhythmias in kids. Buproprion is an antidepressant that also has shown efficacy in ADHD. Atomoxetine is a nonstimulant medication that increases norepinephrine in the brain and is considered a first-line treatment for ADHD. Unlike stimulants, it is not a controlled substance. It carries a black box warning for possibly inducing suicidal ideation. In adults and adolescents with ADHD who are likely to abuse stimulants, atomoxetine or buproprion might be a good choice. Other medications that can be effective for hyperactivity and impulsivity in ADHD are the α-2 agonists, clonidine and guanfacine.

Environment

Medication, individual tutoring, family counseling, behavior therapy, and educational training may be helpful. Children with ADHD should be helped to understand that drug-taking does not mean that they're crazy, that *some* impaired behavior does not permit *all* poor behavior, that "unstructured permissiveness" is not good for them, and that genuine praise usually arises from jobs well done. They do best with a consistent, supportive, moderately structured environment.

The American Academy of Child and Adolescent Psychiatry recommends (1) family therapy if there is family dysfunction; (2) individual and/or group therapy for poor self-esteem and peer problems; (3) social skills training (including empathy training) and cognitive therapies for attention/impulsivity symptoms (one goal is to teach these children to verbalize/think *before* acting); and (4) parent behavior training to develop appropriate, consistent, limit-setting abilities and behavior modification programs for behavior problems. Too often, parents who are at their wits' end can no longer see anything positive about their children. Books such as *Raising Your Spirited Child* (1991, Mary Sheedy Kurcinka) and *Meeting the Challenge with Love and Logic* (2000, Jim Fay, Foster Cline, Bob Sorinson) help them recognize and harness their children's energy and "spiritedness" for positive purposes.

CONDUCT DISORDER

Clinical Presentation

Kids with conduct disorder violate norms and the rights of others. It's usually a boy's disorder, with about 9% of boys and 2% of girls having it. They're always into trouble, be it with parents, peers, or teachers. They're often informers on friends to try to place blame on others. Lying and cheating are typical. Some are called "pathological liars." Physical aggression and cruelty to other people or to animals is common, or they may destroy others' properties (e.g., setting fires). Stealing is common and can range from "borrowing" other people's possessions, to shoplifting, forgery, and breaking into someone's house. These children are often truant from school and may run away from home. Drug use is common, especially tobacco, liquor, or street drugs. They begin sex at an early age and often have multiple partners. Self-esteem is low, despite the image of "toughness" presented to the public. Poor frustration tolerance, irritability, temper outbursts, and recklessness are common. Table 23-10 lists *DSM-IV-TR* Criteria for Conduct Disorder.

Clinical Course

Onset is typically prepubertal for the "solitary aggressive" type. The group or gang delinquents often start at puberty. They usually show loyalty to the gang's members and norms but to no one else. Postpubertal onset is more typical of females who meet diagnostic criteria. Conduct disorder is the forerunner of adult antisocial personality disorder. Fortunately, only about half of all chil-

TABLE 23-10

DSM-IV-TR *Criteria for Conduct Disorder*

A. A repetitive and persistent pattern of behavior in which the basic rights of others or major age-appropriate societal norms or rules are violated, as manifested by the presence of three (or more) of the following criteria in the past 12 months, with at least one criterion present in the past 6 months:

Aggression to people and animals

    (1) often bullies, threatens, or intimidates others

    (2) often initiates physical fights

    (3) has used a weapon that can cause serious physical harm to others (e.g., a bat, brick, broken bottle, knife, gun)

    (4) has been physically cruel to people

    (5) has been physically cruel to animals

    (6) has stolen while confronting a victim (e.g., mugging, purse snatching, extortion, armed robbery)

    (7) has forced someone into sexual activity

Destruction of property

    (8) has deliberately engaged in fire setting with the intention of causing serious damage

    (9) has deliberately destroyed others' property (other than by fire setting)

Deceitfulness or theft

    (10) has broken into someone else's house, building, or car

    (11) often lies to obtain goods or favors or to avoid obligations (i.e., "cons" others)

    (12) has stolen items of nontrivial value without confronting a victim (e.g., shoplifting, but without breaking and entering, forgery)

Serious violations or rules

    (13) often stays out at night despite parental prohibitions, beginning before 13 years of age

    (14) has run away from home overnight at least twice while living in parental or parental surrogate home (or once without returning for a lengthy period)

    (15) is often truant from school, beginning before age 13 years

B. The disturbance in behavior causes clinically significant impairment in social, academic, or occupational functioning.

C. If the individual is age 18 years or older, criteria are not met for Antisocial Personality Disorder.

Note. From *DSM-IV-TR,* p. 99.

dren with conduct disorder go on to develop antisocial personality disorder. Those with milder forms, a later start, or simple peer-pleasing motives are less likely to become tomorrow's criminals.

Etiology and Pathogenesis

Some children have cognitive predispositions that lead them to conduct disorder. Despite normal IQs, they often are 2 or more years behind on academic (particularly verbal) skills and have difficulties with abstract reasoning (particularly, understanding complex directions and social interactions). However, they often have excellent, manipulative, problem-solving abilities. It is not a coincidence that many a delinquent has failed reading and writing in school but can work magic on cars or in picking a lock. Parents who decide that their child is inherently bad can send him down the road to jail; those who have the patience to view this child as having academic and educational problems can sometimes prevent a deteriorating course by working with the child and his school to help him overcome these problems.

Other risk factors for conduct disorder include family history of antisocial personality disorder or substance dependence; sexual, physical, or emotional abuse; a learning disorder that makes school an ordeal (especially reading problems); parenting issues such as a young mother, large family, inadequate supervision, inconsistent disciplining, or neglect; and/or an immediate environment that offers more temptations to get into trouble. These issues were discussed in more depth in Chapter 22 on antisocial personality disorder.

Differential Diagnosis

Conduct disorder continues over 6 months or more, so isolated acts of antisocial behavior don't count. Children with *oppositional defiant disorders* may look like a conduct disorder with their temper outbursts, violation of curfews, running away, playing hooky, being spiteful and vindictive, and generally showing disobedience and opposition to authority figures. However, they don't violate the basic rights of others or major age-appropriate societal norms or rules, as do kids with conduct disorders. Adolescents with *major depression* can suddenly engage in antisocial behavior, but they will also meet major depression criteria and, when asked why they behaved so badly, they will say for social approval or to distract themselves from pain. Kids with conduct disorders will answer "because it's fun" or "I don't know, I just felt like doing it." Children with *ADHD* or *specific developmental disorders* are more likely to develop conduct disorder. Each of these diagnoses should be given, if present.

Management and Treatment

Although conduct disorder is often difficult to treat, one intensive intervention, multisystemic therapy (MST), provides some evidence for effective treatment. The *multisystemic* part of the name refers to the capacity of the intervention to simultaneously address multiple risk factors for identified youths. Any coexisting problems such as ADHD, major depression, drug abuse, or learning problems should be addressed initially.

> MST is a coordinated effort to provide efficacious and evidence-based mental-health services throughout the continuum of care. Important principles include the therapist's assuming responsibility for the identified patient across the continuum of care, from residential facilities to acute hospitalization to therapeutic foster care and intensive home-based services, with the latter being the preferred venue. MST therapists work in teams of two to four clinicians and a supervisor. MST emphasizes accountability of clinicians to their supervisors, expert consultants, and patients. Therapists are available at times convenient for the patient, rather than the other way around. The typical duration of treatment is 3–5 months but may continue for as long as necessary to reach desired goals. Caseloads do not exceed six families and are usually three or four. MST is labor intensive, for example, requiring daily supervision during crisis stabilization.

Medications for aggression, hyperarousal, and behavioral dyscontrol, including lithium, anticonvulsants (e.g., carbamazepine), antipsychotics (e.g., risperidone), clonidine, hydroxyzine, and propranolol, are sometimes helpful adjuncts to treatment. Receiving tutoring for developmental problems may make it easier for these children to progress in school. If possible, children are removed from significantly abusive home environments. The parent(s) are coached to develop realistic rules and consequences and consistently enforce them. Too often these children are rescued from the consequences of their actions or, alternately, beaten and ignored. Commands should be clear but not hostile. When noncompliant, enforcing "time-outs" or loss of privileges is appropriate; when compliant and prosocial, give social rewards such as time with a friend or going on a recreational outing with the family. Objects and money (all too easily stolen) should not be the reward, and the punishment should not be too harsh and overwhelming. For example, grounding a child for 2 months almost never works.

Children who are truly led astray by the boy (gang) "down the block" can be helped to develop prosocial rather than antisocial alternatives by, for example, participating in community programs that structure their time in positive ways. No parent will admit that his or her child is the one who led others astray, but in this situation, even though the prognosis is much grimmer, prosocial programs can be attempted. Variations on "tough love" approaches have been touted to have some success. Ideally, all of these treatments should be implemented as soon as the symptoms appear and not years later, after the symptoms have become ingrained behaviors.

OPPOSITIONAL DEFIANT DISORDER

This disorder is displayed by the quintessential angry child who is chronically argumentative, volatile, spiteful, and vindictive. Children with this disorder ignore or openly defy adults' requests and rules, finding ways to annoy others. Some are more passive—"I wasn't doing anything"—and others more active—"You deserved it, hate you." They'll blame others for their own mistakes or difficulties. In spite of all these behaviors, they do not have a conduct disorder because they don't seriously violate the basic rights of others. They don't steal, destroy property, force people to do things, or engage in cruel activities. Table 23-11 lists *DSM-IV-TR* criteria for oppositional defiant disorder.

These behaviors are almost invariably present in the home, but not always at school or with other adults or peers. In some kids, the behaviors are displayed outside the home from the beginning, whereas in others, they start at home and later show them outside. Typically, these children reserve their awful behaviors for adults and peers they know well. Without a good history, children with this disorder are hard to diagnose because they often show little or no signs of the disorder in the clinician's office. When asked why they are so oppositional and defiant, they answer that they are merely responding to unreasonable rules, demands, and requests. Sometimes they are very convincing—so convincing that the naive clinician decides that the problem must be with the parents, and perhaps a "parentectomy" is in order.

Oppositional defiant disorder (ODD) typically begins by age 8 years and usually not later than early adolescence (Rey, 1993). With the right (or wrong, depending on how one looks at it) family environment, the child with a "difficult-child" temperament frequently goes on to become ODD (Maziade et al., 1990). Boys more often have this disorder before puberty, but after puberty the sex ratio is equal. These kids often have low self-esteem, mood lability, low frustration tolerance, and temper outbursts; they may abuse psychoactive substances, including tobacco, alcohol, and cannabis. Often ADHD is also

TABLE 23-11

DSM-IV-TR *Criteria for Oppositional Defiant Disorder*

A. A pattern of negativistic, hostile, and defiant behavior lasting at least 6 months, during which four (or more) of the following are present:

  (1) often loses temper

  (2) often argues with adult

  (3) often actively defies or refuses to comply with adults' requests or rules

  (4) often deliberately annoys people

  (5) often blames others for his or her mistakes or misbehavior

  (6) is often touchy or easily annoyed by others

  (7) is often angry and resentful

  (8) is often spiteful or vindictive

Note: Consider a criterion met only if the behavior occurs more frequently than is typically observed in individuals of comparable age and developmental level.

B. The disturbance in behavior causes clinically significant impairment in social, academic, or occupational functioning.

C. The behaviors do not occur exclusively during the course of a Psychotic or Mood Disorder.

D. Criteria are not met for Conduct Disorder and, if the individual is age 18 years or older, criteria are not met for Antisocial Personality Disorder.

Note. From *DSM-IV-TR,* p. 102.

---

present. Some kids with ODD later develop a conduct disorder, but most just maintain their ODD behaviors, no matter what happens.

The symptoms of ODD usually occur in *conduct disorder,* sometimes occur in the prodromal phase of *psychotic disorders,* and during the course of *mood disorders.* When this happens, diagnose these other disorders and not ODD.

Unfortunately, little is known about the cause or effective treatment of ODD, except that the outcome of treatment is usually poor. Sometimes family therapy can help. The therapist must work very hard at not assigning blame to the child or parents. Some clinicians have suggested the use of "paradoxical approaches." For example, the therapist assigns the child the task of having one temper tantrum next week, when asked to go to bed. In order to show defiance toward the therapist, the child may have to *not* have the temper tantrum next week. This approach should be used only by highly trained clinicians.

SEPARATION ANXIETY DISORDER

Separation is too gentle a word for this disorder—*abandonment* is closer to the real issue. These children are the clingers; they are scared and miserable when they are away from the important people in their lives and appeased when they are with them. These kids don't fully outgrow normal separation anxiety. For them, going to a friend's house or being left with a babysitter or in a preschool is an ordeal. They can't wait to get back home. At times, the children may be generally anxious and worry about separations even when with those they love. They may worry about significant family members getting sick, hurt, or dying. Often these children prefer to have a parent fall asleep with them at night, preferably with a night light on. Bedtime can turn into 1 or 2 hours of nightly misery. Fear of the dark is common. Mythical nighttime monsters may be under the bed or in the closet. Mere mention of a possible separation sets off physical symptoms of anxiety: Stomachaches, nausea, vomiting, and headaches are typical. Parents often say that the child is deliberately making up these symptoms to avoid separating. The truth usually lies somewhere in-between. Real anxiety is always there to set off these symptoms, but these children have also learned that reporting symptoms staves off separation. Adolescents, but not usually younger children, may also have cardiovascular symptoms, including palpitations, dizziness, and fainting. In short, these children are on their way to panic disorder. Although most are demanding and intrusive, some adapt by being compliant and eager to please.

Most children with separation anxiety are never brought to clinicians unless they develop "school phobia" or "school refusal" and completely stop going to school. They either never leave home or pretend to go to school and, when the parents are gone, sneak home. The symptoms of separation anxiety disorder include two types of worries (harm to, or separation from, major attachment figures), three types of behaviors (school refusal, daytime and bedtime clinging), and three categories of symptoms related to anxiety (anxiety itself, nightmares, and physical symptoms). The *DSM-IV-TR* criteria for separation anxiety disorder are listed in Table 23-12.

Etiology and Pathogenesis

Frequently this disorder manifests after a life stress such as the loss of a relative or a pet, an illness in the child or a relative, or a change in the child's environment (e.g., a move to a new neighborhood or a school change). It rarely starts in adolescence. Separation anxiety tends to wax and wane throughout child-

TABLE 23-12

DSM-IV-TR *Criteria for Separation Anxiety Disorder*

A. Developmentally inappropriate and excessive anxiety concerning separation from home or from those to whom the individual is attached, as evidenced by three (or more) of the following:

  (1) recurrent excessive distress when separation from home or major attachment figures occurs or is anticipated

  (2) persistent and excessive worry about losing, or possible harm befalling, major attachment figures

  (3) persistent and excessive worry that an untoward event will lead to separation from a major attachment figure (e.g., getting lost or being kidnapped)

  (4) persistent reluctance or refusal to go to school or elsewhere because of fear of separation

  (5) persistently and excessively scared or reluctant to be alone or without major attachment figures at home or without significant adults in other settings

  (6) persistent reluctance or refusal to go to sleep without being near a major attachment figure or to sleep away from home

  (7) repeated nightmares involving the theme of separation

  (8) repeated complaints of physical symptoms (such as headaches, stomachaches, nausea, or vomiting) when separation from major attachment figures occurs or is anticipated

B. The duration of the disturbance is at least 4 weeks.

C. The onset is before age 18 years.

D. The disturbance causes clinically significant distress or impairment in social, academic (occupational), or other important areas of functioning.

E. The disturbance does not occur exclusively during the course of a Pervasive Developmental Disorder, Schizophrenia, or other Psychotic Disorder and, in adolescents and adults, is not better accounted for by Panic Disorder With Agoraphobia.

Note. From *DSM-IV-TR,* p. 125.

hood with periods of remission. New stresses typically cause flare-ups. Boys and girls have an equal risk for this disorder. It is not a coincidence that kids with this disorder come from close-knit, caring homes. Such an environment is usually positive and creates strong bonds. On the negative side, however, children may have trouble forming bonds elsewhere. A general rule of pre-school teachers and day-care workers is that separation anxiety problems are as much the parents' as the child's problem. A mother may have trouble letting go of her "baby" and experience distress at leaving him in the care of others. She may be a little overprotective, not wanting him to experience unpleasant feelings. When he cries, she stays or returns soon to check on him. Even if he had just settled down, he may cry after spotting Mom, reinforcing her belief that she should never have left. Her hovering and attempts to ensure that he never feels distress reinforce his perceptions that something dangerous is always about to happen.

Clinical judgment and familiarity with *normal separation anxiety* is necessary to diagnose this disorder. The extreme narrowness of the source of anxiety—*separation*—distinguishes it from other anxiety disorders, such as *generalized anxiety disorder* and *panic disorder with agoraphobia*, and from disorders in which anxiety is but one symptom, such as *schizophrenia, pervasive developmental disorder*, or *major depression*.

A child brought in for school refusal can be asked, "Why don't you want to go to school?" If she has separation anxiety disorder, she may say, "I want to be home with my mommy." The child with *conduct disorder* might say, "I don't feel like it—it's not fun"; the child with *oppositional defiant disorder* might say, "Nobody can make me go to school if I don't want to." Kids without a specific disorder might say, "I'm afraid of failing and looking stupid in class" or "Someone bullies me there."

A variety of approaches are used to treat children who have never successfully separated. Children should be allowed to have transitional objects such as blankets, stuffed animals, and pictures of family members with them in the new setting. Stretching the length of separation very gradually from minutes to hours can help children master the sensations of separation anxiety. Since children pick up their parents' anxieties, counseling parents to help reduce *their* anxiety about separation is very often needed, and has demonstrated efficacy in reducing the child's anxiety.

For children who have successfully separated but are currently experiencing a separation anxiety disorder after the death or illness of a family member, more specialized approaches (such as grief work) are recommended.

SELECTIVE MUTISM

Children with this rare disorder typically talk at home but refuse to speak at school or in social situations. Children who have a speech disorder are socially withdrawn or are oppositional and more prone to this disorder. Selective mutism generally starts before age 5 and, in most, lasts only a few weeks. Major stresses such as immigration, hospitalization, or traumas before age 3 may predispose some children to mutism. Table 23-13 lists *DSM-IV-TR* criteria for selective mutism.

TABLE 23-13

DSM-IV-TR *Criteria for Selective Mutism*

A. Consistent failure to speak in specific social situations (in which there is an expectation for speaking, e.g., at school) despite speaking in other situations.

B. The disturbance interferes with educational or occupational achievement or with social communication.

C. The duration of the disturbance is at least 1 month (not limited to the first month of school).

D. The failure to speak is not due to a lack of knowledge of, or comfort with, the spoken language required in the social situation.

E. The disturbance is not better accounted for by a Communication Disorder (e.g., Stuttering) and does not occur exclusively during the course of a Pervasive Developmental Disorder, Schizophrenia, or other Psychotic Disorder.

Note. From *DSM-IV-TR,* p. 127.

REACTIVE ATTACHMENT DISORDER OF INFANCY OR EARLY CHILDHOOD

The profound disturbance in social relatedness of this disorder is usually associated with grossly pathogenic, neglectful care. In young children, social milestones such as smiling with pleasure by 2 months or shared laughter at 3 months are missed; they typically appear apathetic, staring vacantly and moving little. They often fail to gain weight but do get taller. Older children may exhibit indiscriminate sociability with strangers. Placement in a more positive environment may lead to normal physical growth, but may only partially correct the disturbed social relatedness. Attachment anxiety is associated with the child's inability to trust and is magnified in situations that promote intimacy. Table 23-14 lists *DSM-IV-TR* criteria for reactive attachment disorder of infancy or early childhood.

ELIMINATION DISORDERS

In contrast to reactive attachment disorder, elective mutism, and stereotypic movement disorder, elimination disorders are very common and are discussed in most pediatric and child-care books. Both *encopresis* (soiling of pants with stool) and *enuresis* (soiling of pants with urine) are more common in boys. They should not be diagnosed until the developmental age is 4 years for encopresis and 5 years for enuresis. One-fourth of children with encopresis also have enuresis. Physical causes for both disorders should be ruled out.

TABLE 23-14

DSM-IV-TR *Criteria for Reactive Attachment Disorder of Infancy or Early Childhood*

A. Markedly disturbed and developmentally inappropriate social relatedness in most contexts, beginning
   before age 5 years, as evidenced by either (1) or (2):

   (1) persistent failure to initiate or respond in a developmentally appropriate fashion to most social inter-
       actions, as manifest by excessively inhibited, hypervigilant, or highly ambivalent and contradictory
       responses (e.g., the child may respond to caregivers with a mixture of approach, avoidance, and
       resistance to comforting, or may exhibit frozen watchfulness)—Inhibited type

   (2) diffuse attachments as manifested by indiscriminate sociability with marked inability to exhibit appro-
       priate selective attachments (e.g., excessive familiarity with relative strangers or lack of selectivity in
       choice of attachment figures)—Disinhibited type

B. The disturbance in Criterion A is not accounted for solely by developmental delay (as in Mental Retardation) and does not meet criteria for a Pervasive Developmental Disorder.

C. Pathogenic care as evidenced by at least one of the following:

   (1) persistent disregard of the child's basic emotional needs for comfort, stimulation, and affection

   (2) persistent disregard of the child's basic physical needs

   (3) repeated changes of primary caregiver that prevent formation of stable attachments (e.g., frequent
       changes in foster care)

D. There is a presumption that the care in Criterion C is responsible for the disturbed behavior in Criterion
   A (e.g., the disturbances in Criterion A began following the pathogenic care in Criterion C).

Note. From *DSM-IV-TR,* p. 130.

Encopresis

Generally, the two types of kids that are more prone to *encopresis* are the
anxious and the oppositional. The anxious ones develop a vicious cycle: They
are afraid to use toilets in public places, develop constipation, and then may
develop involuntary overflow incontinence. Soiling almost always occurs during waking hours. For them, the encopresis does not feel under control. The
oppositional ones do it deliberately, don't usually have constipation, and to
rub their defiance in further, may smear their feces. Occasionally the anxious
ones smear their feces in a botched attempt to hide their accidents. Table 23-
15 lists the *DSM-IV-TR* criteria for functional encopresis. About 1% of 5-year-
olds have this disorder.

TABLE 23-15

DSM-IV-TR *Criteria for Encopresis and Enuresis*

Encopresis

A. Repeated passage of feces into inappropriate places (e.g., clothing or floor) whether involuntary or intentional.

B. At least one such event a month for at least 3 months.

C. Chronological age is at least 4 years (or equivalent developmental level).

D. The behavior is not due exclusively to the direct physiological effects of a substance (e.g., laxatives) or a general medical condition except through a mechanism involving constipation.

Enuresis

A. Repeated voiding of urine into bed or clothes (whether involuntary or intentional).

B. The behavior is clinically significant as manifested by either a frequency of twice a week for at least 3 consecutive months or the presence of clinically significant distress or impairment in social, academic (occupational), or other important areas of functioning.

C. Chronological age is at least 5 years (or equivalent developmental level).

D. The behavior is not due to the direct physiological effects of a substance (e.g., a diuretic) or a general medical condition (e.g., diabetes, spina bifida, a seizure disorder).

Note. From *DSM-IV-TR,* pp. 118, 121.

A history of constipation, developmental delays in other areas, ADHD, or coercive or premature bowel training each increases the risk for encopresis. Toilet phobia can also lead to encopresis and may develop if the available facilities are particularly gruesome or if fantasies about the toilet, such as being drowned or bitten by snakes, take over. Secondary encopresis (resumption of accidents after a period of successful toilet training) may begin with stressful events, often with separation themes such as birth of a sibling, starting school, or mom starting a full-time job. School-age children can successfully retain feces at school only to soil at home. The ones who don't are usually ridiculed by peers. Encopretic children usually can't explain their behavior.

To avoid the retention-leakage cycle laxatives, stool softeners are used to evacuate the colon. Children are then scheduled to have regular periods on the toilet for the purpose of muscle retraining and are given responsibility for cleaning themselves and any soiled clothing. The parents are helped to develop a matter-of-fact approach in helping their children.

Enuresis

Enuresis is a more biologically based disorder than encopresis, as 75% of these children have a first-degree relative who has had it. At age 5, 3% of girls and 7% of boys have enuresis. All but 1% of males and almost all females outgrow it by age 18. Nocturnal enuresis is much more common than diurnal (daytime) enuresis. Nocturnal enuresis usually occurs in the first third of the night. Very stressful events can trigger it in children who had previously been continent. When this happens, the enuresis is described as secondary enuresis.

> Children with enuresis should be evaluated for potential medical causes, such as urinary tract infection, minor neurological impairment, structural anomalies, and medical illness. If no medical problems are found, a variety of treatment options are available: (1) In *retention control* training, children drink a large amount of liquid and gradually delay the time to voiding. Token or social reinforcement can be used to amplify the rewards for success. This method works much better for daytime than for nighttime enuresis. (2) *Conditioning devices*, which set off an alarm when urine contacts the bed, can be highly effective, at least initially. Over 1–3 months, about 75% of children succeed with this approach, but about 35% relapse when it is stopped. Repeat trials are then used. (3) *Tricyclic antidepressants* (usually imipramine or an *antispasmodic* such as oxybutynin [Ditropan]), have also been used to treat this disorder. Although up to two-thirds of children have a reduction in wetting with 25–75 mg of imipramine, almost all relapse when the medication is stopped. Another useful medication is DDAVP (a synthetic version of antidiuretic hormone), but again, symptoms resume when treatment is stopped.
>
> A popular but unproven technique for nocturnal enuresis involves eliminating fluid intake after dinner, having children void before bedtime, and carrying the sleepy child to the toilet once during the night. This may keep the bed dry, but may not lead to enduring results.

TIC DISORDERS

Although anywhere from 5 to 24% of schoolchildren have some kind of tic, most fortunately don't have a tic disorder. A tic is defined as an involuntary, sudden, rapid, recurrent, nonrhythmic, stereotyped movement or vocalization. If they weren't normal, eyeblinks could be thought of as tics. Tics (like eyeblinks) are automatic, but can be voluntarily suppressed for varying lengths of time. Stress makes them worse; sleep and absorbing activities make them better. *Motor tics* may be simple (e.g., neck jerking, shoulder shrugging) or complex (e.g., facial gestures, grooming behavior). *Verbal tics* can also be simple (e.g., coughing or barking) or complex (e.g., words or whole phrases spoken out of context). The three tic disorders—*Tourette's, chronic motor or vocal tic disorder,* and *transient tic disorder*—are probably variations on the same genetic abnormality. Chronic motor or vocal tic disorder and transient tic disorder are partial forms of Tourette's. Chronic motor or vocal tic disorder meets all of the criteria for Tourette's, except only motor *or* vocal tics are seen, but not both. In transient tic disorder, a child has motor and/or vocal tics for at least 4 weeks but not longer than 12 consecutive months.

Boys have these disorders at least three times more often than girls. Half develop tics by 7 years and the majority by age 14. Tourette's, the worst form, is rare: 1 in 2,000. No other neurological or psychiatric disorder has the vocalizations heard in Tourette's and these related tic disorders. Three disorders that seem to occur together are ADHD, obsessive–compulsive disorder, and Tourette's. Over the past 10 years research has demonstrated that some cases of Tourette's disorder and other tic disorders may be related to streptococcal infections (pediatric autoimmune neuropsychiatric disorders associated with streptococcus—PANDAS). Children with these disorders should be screened for this cause of the illness, which is potentially treatable with antibiotics. Table 23-16 lists *DSM-IV-TR* criteria for Tourette's disorder.

TABLE 23-16
DSM-IV-TR *Criteria for Tourette's Disorder*

A. Both multiple motor and one or more vocal tics have been present at some time during the illness, although not necessarily concurrently. (A *tic* is an involuntary, sudden, rapid, recurrent, nonrhythmic, stereotyped motor movement or vocalization.)

B. The tics occur many times a day (usually in bouts), nearly every day or intermittently throughout a period of more than 1 year, and during this period, there was never a tic-free period of more than 3 consecutive months.

C. The disturbance causes marked distress or significant impairment in social, occupational, or other important areas of functioning.

D. The onset is before age 18 years.

E. The disturbance is not due to the direct physiological effects of a substance (e.g., stimulants) or a general medical condition (e.g., Huntington's disease or postviral encephalitis).

Note. From *DSM-IV-TR,* p. 114.

TABLE 23-17
DSM-IV-TR *Criteria for Stereotypic Movement Disorder*

A. Repetitive, seemingly driven, and nonfunctional motor behavior (e.g., hand shaking or waving, body rocking, head banging, mouthing of objects, self-biting, picking at skin or bodily orifices, hitting own body).

B. The behavior markedly interferes with normal activities or results in self-inflicted bodily injury that requires medical treatment (or would result in an injury if preventive measures were not used).

C. If Mental Retardation is present, the stereotypic or self-injurious behavior is of sufficient severity to become a focus of treatment.

D. The behavior is not better accounted for by a compulsion (as in Obsessive–Compulsive Disorder), a tic (as in Tic Disorder), a stereotypy that is part of a Pervasive Developmental Disorder, or hair pulling (as in Trichotillomania).

E. The behavior is not due to the direct physiological effects of a substance or a general medical condition.

F. The behavior persists for 4 weeks or longer.

Specify if:

With Self-Injurious Behavior: if the behavior results in bodily damage that requires specific treatment (or that would result in bodily damage if protective measures were not used)

Note. From *DSM-IV-TR,* p. 134.

STEREOTYPIC MOVEMENT DISORDERS

Unlike the tic disorders, the repetitive behaviors in this disorder are intentional. It occurs in 10–23% of institutionalized children with moderate or severe mental retardation. It is also more common in deaf or blind children. The child's primary goal may be to use self-stimulation as an antidote to an otherwise impoverished, low-stimulation environment. Table 23-17 lists DSM-IV-TR criteria for stereotypic movement disorder.

References

Cantwell, D.P., & Baker, L. (1989). Stability and natural history of DSM-III childhood diagnoses. *Journal of American Academy of Child and Adolescent Psychiatry, 28,* 691–700.

Faraone, S.V., Biederman, J., Keenan, K., & Tsuang, M.T. (1991). Separation of DSM-III attention deficit disorder and conduct disorder: Evidence from a family-genetic study of American child psychiatric patients. *Psychology of Medicine, 21,* 109–121.

Faraone, S.V., Biederman, J., Lehman, B.L., Keenan, K., Norman, D., Seidman, L.J., et al. (1993). Evidence for the independent familial transmission of attention deficit hyperactivity disorder and learning disabilities: Results from a family-genetic study. *American Journal of Psychiatry, 150*(6), 891–895.

Fay, J., Cline, F., & Sorinson, B. (2000). *Meeting the challenge with love and logic.* Golden, CO: Love and Logic Press.

Handen, B.L., Breaux, A.M., Janosky, J., McAuliffe, S., Feldman, H., & Gosling, A. (1992). Effects and noneffects of methylphenidate in children with mental retardation and ADHD. *Journal of the American Academy of Child Adolescent Psychiatry, 31*, 455–461.

Henggeler, S., Schoenwald, S., Rowlan, M., & Cunningham, P. (2002). *Serious emotional disturbance in children and adolescents: Multisystemic therapy.* New York: Guilford Press.

Kurcinka, M.S. (1991). *Raising your spirited child.* New York: HarperCollins.

Maziade, M., Caron, C., Côté, R., Mérette, C., Bernier, H., Laplante, B., et al. (1990). Psychiatric status of adolescents who had extreme temperaments at age 7. *American Journal of Psychiatry, 147*(11), 1531–1536.

Practice Parameters for the Assessment and Treatment of Children and Adolescents with Attention-Deficit/Hyperactivity Disorder. (2007). *Journal of the American Academy of Child and Adolescent Psychiatry, 46*(7), 894–921.

Rey, J.M. (1993). Oppositional defiant disorder. *American Journal of Psychiatry, 150*(12), 1769–1778.

Smalley, S.L., Asarnow, R.F., & Spence, M.A. (1988). Autism and genetics. *Archives of General Psychiatry, 45*, 953–961.

Strayhorn, J.M. (1988). *The competent child: An approach to psychotherapy and preventive mental health.* New York: The Guilford Press.

Swanson, J.M., Sandman, C.A., Deutsch, C., & Baren, M. (1983). Methylphenidate (Ritalin) given with or before breakfast, Part I: Behavioral, cognitive, and electrophysiological effects. *Pediatrics, 72*, 49–55.

Swanson, J.M., Lerner, M.A., March, J., & Gresham, F.M. (1999). Assessment and intervention for attention-deficit/hyperactivity disorder in the schools: Lessons from the MTA study. *Pediatric Clinics North America, 46*, 993–1009.

Sylvester, C. (1993). Psychopharmacology of disorders in children. *Psychiatric Clinics of North America, 16*(4), 779–791.

Volkmar, F.R., Bregman, J., Cohen, D.J., & Cicchetti, D.V. (1988). *DSM-III* and *DSM-III-R* diagnoses of autism. *American Journal of Psychiatry, 145*(11), 1404–1408.

SNAP-IV RATING SCALE

Name of child _____ Date____ Age__ Sex__ Grade___ Rating period_____

Completed by _____ Relation to child: Mother____ Father____ Teacher____ Other_____

Check the column that best describes this child:	Not at All	Just a Little	Quite A Bit	Very Much
1. Often fails to give close attention to details or makes careless mistakes in schoolwork, work, or other activities	—	—	—	—
2. Often has difficulty sustaining attention in tasks or play activities	—	—	—	—
3. Often does not seem to listen when spoken to directly	—	—	—	—
4. Often does not follow through on instructions and fails to finish schoolwork, chores, or duties in the workplace (not due to oppositional behavior or failure to understand instructions)	—	—	—	—
5. Often avoids, dislikes, or has difficulties engaging in tasks that require sustained mental effort (such as schoolwork or homework)	—	—	—	—
6. Often loses things necessary for tasks or activities (e.g., toys, school assignments, pencils, books, or tools)	—	—	—	—
7. Is often easily distracted by extraneous stimuli	—	—	—	—
8. Often forgetful in daily activities	—	—	—	—
9. Often fidgets with hands or feet, squirms in seat	—	—	—	—
10. Often leaves seat in classroom or in other situations in which remaining seated is expected	—	—	—	—
11. Often runs about or climbs excessively in situations where it is inappropriate (in adolescents or adults, may be limited to subjective feelings of restlessness)	—	—	—	—
12. Often has difficulty playing or engaging in leisure activities quietly	—	—	—	—
13. Is always on the go or often acts if driven by a motor	—	—	—	—
14. Often talks excessively	—	—	—	—
15. Often blurts out answers to questions before the questions have been completed	—	—	—	—
16. Often has difficulty awaiting turn	—	—	—	—
17. Often interrupts or intrudes upon others (e.g., butts into conversations or games)	—	—	—	—
18. Often stares into space and reports daydreaming	—	—	—	—
19. Often appears to be low in energy level, sluggish, or drowsy	—	—	—	—

20. Often appears to be apathetic or unmotivated to engage in goal-directed activities   —   —   —   —
21. Often engages in physically dangerous activities without considering possible consequences   —   —   —   —
22. Often shifts from one uncompleted activity to another   —   —   —   —
23. Often fails to finish things he or she starts   —   —   —   —
24. Has difficulty concentrating on school work or other tasks requiring sustained attention   —   —   —   —
25. Has difficulty sticking to a play activity   —   —   —   —
26. Frequently calls out in class or in other situations when silence is expected   —   —   —   —
27. Needs a lot of supervision   —   —   —   —
28. Moves about excessively (e.g., even during sleep, at home, or during quiet time at school)   —   —   —   —
29. Often acts before thinking   —   —   —   —
30. Often loses temper   —   —   —   —
31. Often argues with adults   —   —   —   —
32. Often actively defies or refuses adult requests or rules   —   —   —   —
33. Often deliberately does things that annoy other people   —   —   —   —
34. Often blames others for his or her mistakes or misbehavior   —   —   —   —
35. Often touchy or easily annoyed by others   —   —   —   —
36. Is often angry and resentful   —   —   —   —
37. Is often spiteful or vindictive   —   —   —   —
38. Often swears or uses obscene language   —   —   —   —
39. Often manifests provocative behavior   —   —   —   —
40. Often shows excessive stubbornness   —   —   —   —

Adapted from Swanson, Nolan, and Pelham (1983).

SCORING INSTRUCTIONS FOR THE SNAP-IV RATING SCALE

James M. Swanson, PhD, University of California, Irvine

The SNAP-IV Rating Scale, a revision of the Swanson, Nolan, and Pelham (SNAP) Questionnaire (Swanson et al., 1983), consists of 41 items. The first 18 items (#1–#18) are from the DSM-IV (1994) criteria for ADHD; the next 12 items (#19–#30) are from prior DSM definitions of ADD with and without hyperactivity (DSM-III, 1980), ADHD (DSM-III-R, 1987), and undifferentiated deficit disorder (DSM-III-R, 1987 and DSM-IV-Work in Progress, 1991); the last 11 items consist of the 8 items (#31–#38) from the DSM-IV (1994) criteria for oppositional defiant disorder (ODD) plus the 3 items from prior DSM definitions of ODD (DSM-III-R, 1987) and oppositional disorder (DSM-III, 1980).

The SNAP-IV is based on a 0–3 rating and scoring scale (Not at All = 0, Just a Little = 1, Quite A Bit = 2, and Very Much = 3) that has been used by many questionnaires (e.g., the Conners Questionnaire and the Satterfield Questionnaires from the 1970s). Subscale scores on the SNAP-IV are calculated by summing the scores on the items in the subset and dividing by the number of items in the subset. The score for any subset is expressed as the average rating per item, as shown below for hypothetical rating on the ADHD-inattentive (ADHD-1) subset:

	Not at All	Just a Little	Quite A Bit	Very Much	Item Score	
1. Makes careless mistakes	—	—	X	—	2	
2. Can't pay attention for long	—	—	—	X	3	Total of item ratings = 18
3. Doesn't listen	—	—	—	X	3	Average rating per item = 18/9
4. Fails to finish work	—	—	X	—	2	ADHD-I subscale score = 2.0
5. Disorganized	—	X	—	—	1	
6. Can't concentrate on tasks requiring great effort	—	—	—	X	3	
7. Loses things	—	X	—	—	1	
8. Distractible	—	—	—	X	3	
9. Forgetful	X	—	—	—	0	

The item numbers for the various DSM diagnostic classes are provided below, with items that have survived the three revisions printed in **bold** numbers on the same lines. By scanning across the rows, it is possible to determine which items were included and excluded in the progressive revisions of the DSM (III, III-R, and IV) concepts of ADHD and ADD.

		DSM-IV (1993)		DSM-III-R (1987)		DSM-III (1980)
Inattention	ADHD-I	**1, 2, 3, 4, 5, 6, 7, 8, 9**	ADHD	**2, 3, 4, 7, 8**	ADD	**3, 8,** 24, 25, 26
Hyperactivity	ADHD-HI	**10, 11, 12, 13, 14, 15**	ADHD	**10, 11, 13, 15**	ADD-H	**10, 11, 12, 14,** 29
Impulsivity	ADHD-HI	**16, 17, 18**	ADHD	**16, 17, 18,** 22, 23	ADD	**5, 17,** 23, 27, 28, 30
Undifferentiated ADD	UADD (1991)	1, 2, 3, 4, 5, 7, 9, 19, 20, 21	UADD	9, 19, 20, 21		
Opposition and defiance	ODD	**31, 32, 33, 34, 35, 36, 37, 38**	ODD	**31, 32, 33, 34, 35, 36, 37, 38,** 39	OD	**31, 32, 33,** 40, 41

Scoring templates for the two DSM-IV sets of ADHD symptoms and for the DSM-IV set of ODD symptoms are presented below:

DSM-IV subscales:	ADHD-I Item Rating	ADHD-HI Item Rating	ODD Item Rating
	#1 ____	#10 ____	#31 ____
	#2 ____	#11 ____	#32 ____
	#3 ____	#12 ____	#33 ____
	#4 ____	#13 ____	#34 ____
	#5 ____	#14 ____	#35 ____
	#6 ____	#15 ____	#36 ____
	#7 ____	#16 ____	#37 ____
	#8 ____	#17 ____	#38 ____
	#9 ____	#18 ____	
Total item ratings	= ____/9	= ____/9	= ____/8
Average rating per item	= ____	= ____	= ____

In general, scores over 1.65 are moderately high (M + 1SD) and scores over 2.0 are extremely high (M + 2SD).

24

Adjustment Disorders

Adjustment disorders are a large part of clinical practice and often the most rewarding conditions to treat. Using *DSM-IV*, clinicians diagnosed adjustment disorders in about 10% of adults and 32% of adolescents. Adjustment disorders can be disruptive and distressing, yet with time and treatment, they resolve; in fact, many patients emerge healthier and wiser.

Adjustment disorders are the most benign of mental disorders, but more severe than "normal" problems in living (e.g., uncomplicated bereavement, marital problems). Thus, adjustment disorders *are* psychopathology and their diagnoses *are* critical. When adjustment disorders are dismissed as normal problems in living, clinicians risk underestimating the seriousness of the patient's difficulties, such as truancy, financial disaster, or suicidal intent. On the other hand, when adjustment disorders are misdiagnosed as a more ominous condition, the patient may receive inappropriate medication, psychotherapy, or even hospitalization.

Clinical Presentation

Adjustment disorders, according to *DSM-IV-TR*, involve maladaptive reactions to psychosocial stressors occurring within the past 3 months; the disorders are self-limiting (less than 6 months) and are not due to another mental disorder. In other words, these are relatively benign, transient, but maladaptive situational reactions. Table 24-1 lists *DSM-IV-TR* criteria for adjustment disorders.

To qualify as maladaptive, a reaction must impair function, or it must be stronger or last longer than a "normal" person's reaction to the same stressor. These reactions constitute relatively persisting patterns of behaviors, not single acts. On watching his house burn down, a frightened man starts smashing his neighbor's windows. His reaction, although excessive, is limited to this outburst; subsequently, he experiences nothing but the expected sadness and frustration. This man does *not* have adjustment disorder.

TABLE 24-1
DSM-IV-TR *Criteria for Adjustment Disorders*

A. The development of emotional or behavioral symptoms in response to an identifiable stressor(s) occurring within 3 months of the onset of the stressor(s).

B. These symptoms or behaviors are clinically significant as evidenced by either of the following:

   (1) marked distress that is in excess of what would be expected from exposure to the stressor

   (2) significant impairment in social or occupational (academic) functioning

C. The stress-related disturbance does not meet the criteria for another specific Axis I disorder and is not merely an exacerbation of a preexisting Axis I or Axis II disorder.

D. The symptoms do not represent Bereavement.

E. Once the stressor (or its consequences) has terminated, the symptoms do not persist for more than an additional 6 months. The specific stressor can be specified on Axis IV.

Specify if:

Acute: if the disturbance has been present for less than 6 months

Chronic: if the disturbance has been present for 6 months or longer

Subtype (according to predominant symptoms):

With Depressed Mood

With Anxiety

With Mixed Anxiety and Depressed Mood

With Disturbance of Conduct

With Mixed Disturbance of Emotions and Conduct

Unspecified

Note. From *DSM-IV-TR,* p. 683.

Steve Walsh did have an adjustment disorder. Extremely bright and bored by school, at 16 Steve began to skip classes and to peddle marijuana and cocaine. Prior to these behaviors, he had been a good student and had never sold drugs. School officials and the police dragged in Steve, who dragged in his parents. While upstairs in his room one evening, Steve overheard one of his parents' many screaming matches. Steve says that his mother yelled at her husband, "My psychiatrist says I need tranquilizers because you're such a bastard," to which his father replied, "At least I didn't breed that delinquent bastard son of yours." Although Mrs. Walsh tried hushing her husband so Steve wouldn't hear, it was too late. Stunned at first, Steve turned up his stereo earphones to blast and empty his mind. At three in the morning, Steve quietly emerged, grabbed his mother's barbiturates, fled Dayton, drove to Cleveland, and began selling the barbiturates on the street. Steve hated living on the street, but had no place to go. He felt unloved and unwanted; Steve wanted his parents, but refused to call them. Five days later, his father tracked him down, scooped him up, and returned him to Dayton on the condition that the entire family would get therapy. Steve desperately wanted to get away from home and attend a challenging private school. The parents agreed, partly for Steve's sake, but also because they wanted to improve their relationship without Steve's acting up constantly (and "conveniently") distracting them. The plan worked.

Adjustment disorders present with *generalized* symptoms (e.g., disruptions of mood or conduct) as opposed to *specific* ones (e.g., hallucinations, delusions, phobias, and panic attacks). Depression and anxiety are the most frequent mood disturbances. Except for suicide attempts, depressive symptoms are more common in adults (87%) than adolescents (64%), whereas conduct (or behavioral) problems are more prevalent in adolescents (77%) than adults (25%). Suicidal thoughts are more often reported by adults (36% vs. 29%), but among those having these thoughts, adolescents (86%) attempt suicide more than adults (47%). Conduct problems among adolescents may include truancy, drinking, temper outbursts, vandalism, school suspension, persistent lying, and repeated arrests, among others.

The beginning clinician's most common mistake is to diagnose *adjustment disorders* with depressed mood when the person really has a *major depressive disorder*. If a patient meets criteria for major depression following a major stressor such as being fired from work, the diagnosis is still major depression. Even if it seems like the depression was entirely caused by the stressor, people with this form of major depression are more likely than normals to have major depression in their families, in their pasts, and in their futures.

> The stressor can be just about anything: It may be short-lived or ongoing, single, or multiple, affect individuals or groups; it may be associated with a specific event or a developmental stage. The stressor's impact varies according to its duration, timing, context, and meaning, and so the severity of any particular stressor depends on the particular individual. The nature of the stressor is indicated on Axis IV. For adults, the most common stressors are marital problems (25%), separation or divorce (23%), relocation (17%), finances (14%), and work (9%). For adolescents, they are school problems (60%), parental rejection (27%), substance abuse (26%), parental separation or divorce (25%), boyfriend–girlfriend problems (20%), and parental marital problems (18%). Death of a loved one affected a mere 3% of the adults and 11.5% of the adolescents (Andreasen & Wasek, 1980).

As seen in criterion E of Table 24-1, the diagnosis of an adjustment disorder requires an assumption, or a reasonable prediction, that the patient's symptoms will remit within 6 months after the stressor has ended. If not, a more severe diagnosis is presumably more appropriate.

Clinical Course

In most cases, once the precipitating stressor disappears, so does the adjustment disorder. In nearly every respect, adults fare better than adolescents. Adjustment disorders in adolescents are more severe, last longer, require more treatment, and ultimately are associated with more psychopathology and worse outcomes. Three- to five-year follow-ups revealed 59–71% of adults functioning well, but only 44% of adolescents doing so. Among those doing poorly in both groups, mood, antisocial personality, and substance use disorders were common, but suicide was rare (2–4%). Overall, the most reliable predictors of poor outcome were the chronicity of the adjustment disorder, being younger, the frequency of misconduct symptoms, and the number of stressors. Depressive symptoms did *not* predict outcome (Andreasen & Hoenk, 1982).

Epidemiology

Although adjustment disorders are common, few epidemiological studies have been conducted. In a study of 1,264 Operation Iraqi Freedom/Operation Enduring Freedom (OIF/OEF) service members evacuated from the theater of operations, 34.1% were diagnosed with adjustment disorders. They were also found to be more likely female, under the age of 31, and enlisted, i.e., without a college degree (Rundell, 2006). Adjustment disorders are more commonly diagnosed in younger persons and females, but the actual prevalence according to situation, gender, race, and class is unknown. However, clinicians may overdiagnose adjustment disorders because of their benign connotations. Their prevalence among various races and classes is unknown, but a 2:1 female to male ratio is common.

Etiology and Pathogenesis

When *normal* responses to stress are intensified, prolonged, or blocked, they produce either (the milder) adjustment disorders or (the more severe) mood or anxiety disorders. Responses to stress—normal or pathological—evolve in stages, as previously described (see Figure 4-5). A common adjustment disorder that follows this sequence is the classic "midlife crisis" (Getz, 1974). People may emerge from such a crisis better off than before depending upon inherent strengths of the person and availability of assistance in their crisis. They may develop greater maturity, ego strength, wisdom, or self-confidence.

It's unknown why some patients react to a stressor with an adjustment disorder, some with a more severe disorder, and some with no difficulties at all. Only a few clues exist: Neurological and personality disorders may predispose patients to developing adjustment disorders. Vaillant's (1971) lifetime study of Harvard graduates indicated that those who started with more primitive defenses (e.g., denial and projection) fared more poorly with life crises than those with more adaptive defenses (e.g., sublimation). Interacting variables of neurodevelopment, biological predisposition, early life experiences, delayed or arrested psychosocial development, temperament, and personality structure contribute to either resilience or vulnerability to psychopathology.

Differential Diagnosis

Adjustment disorder should not be diagnosed until "normal problems in living" and other mental disorders have been ruled out. *DSM-IV-TR* includes these normal problems in living under "Other Conditions That May Be a Focus of Clinical Attention," and they are outlined in Chapter 3. Adjustment disorders differ from these conditions either by impairing functioning or by exceeding the normally expected reactions to a particular stressor. These distinctions are relative and require clinical judgment.

Unlike *posttraumatic stress disorder* (PTSD), which has a delayed onset subtype, adjustment disorder must occur within 3 months of the stressor. The stressors producing adjustment disorder are "typical" (e.g., marital problems, retirement), whereas those that generate acute stress disorder and PTSD involve actual or threatened death or serious injury to self or others (e.g., 9/11, school shootings, suicide bombers, plane crashes, combat experience, earthquakes). Adjustment disorder is briefer and less severe than PTSD.

When a psychosocial stress exacerbates a medical illness, instead of adjustment reaction, the preferred diagnosis is *psychological factors affecting physical condition*. If a stressor aggravates a *personality disorder*, an adjustment disorder is diagnosed only when a new symptom appears that is not central to the personality disorder. For example, after her last child leaves home for college, a mother with a histrionic personality disorder becomes uncharacteristically withdrawn.

Management and Treatment

The main controversy concerning the treatment of adjustment disorders is whether to treat them at all. Although most patients recover fully with therapy, many do not. The arguments against treatment are that because (by definition) adjustment disorders are time-limited, treatment wastes the patient's time, money, and effort. Patients may be harmed by interfering with the natural recovery process (at least in theory). Additional problems might be generated: Patients may become "therapy addicts"; or they may be unable to cope with a newly discovered set of difficulties—how much they hate their fathers, how little they love their spouses; or, if therapy is a bust, they may terminate more discouraged than ever.

The arguments in favor of therapy contend that, because clinicians can never really know in advance whether patients will fully recover, if nothing else, treatment can minimize adverse consequences, such as preventing patients from making dumb, spur-of-the-moment, irreversible decisions. Therapy could also hasten recovery, stop patients from blowing matters out of proportion, and enable them to avert similar crises in the future.

Experts generally believe that treatment should be based on a crisis intervention model. Accordingly, the primary goal of treatment is to have patients return to baseline; the secondary goal, or possibility, is to capitalize on the emotional turmoil of the crisis to change some longstanding maladaptive patterns into more useful and self-satisfying ones. In this model, treatment is brief, time-limited, and focused exclusively on problems linked to the stressor. (About half the patients who enter brief psychotherapy for adjustment disorders finish in 4 weeks.)

The most frequently used treatment is *individual psychotherapy*, which identifies the stressor, examines how it affects the patient, and discusses how the patient could deal with it. The therapist typically supports defenses, reinforces existing coping skills, or suggests new strategies. *Family therapy* is the second most widely used treatment. When the family plays a major role in the adjustment disorder, family treatment can follow the same principles of crisis intervention. Supportive *psychotherapy groups* for common stressors are present in many communities. *Medications* might be used temporarily as long as there is a clear target symptom (e.g., insomnia, anxiety), which impairs functioning or slows recovery.

References

Andreasen, N.C., & Hoenk, P.R. (1982). The predictive value of adjustment disorders: A follow-up study. *American Journal of Psychiatry, 139*, 584–590.

Andreasen, N.C., & Wasek, P. (1980). Adjustment disorders in adolescents and adults. *Archives of General Psychiatry, 37*, 1166–1170.

Getz, W., Wiesen, A.E., Sue, S., & Ayers, A. (1974). *Fundamentals of crisis counseling.* Lexington, MA: D.C. Heath & Co.

Rundell, J.R. (2006). Demographics of and diagnoses in Operation Enduring Freedom and Operation Iraqi Freedom personnel who were psychiatrically evacuated from the theater of operations. *General Hospital Psychiatry, 28,* 352–356.

Vaillant, G.E. (1971). Theoretical hierarchy of adaptive ego mechanisms. *Archives of General Psychiatry, 24,* 107–118.

Glossary of Psychopathological Signs and Symptoms

Affect is the instantaneous, observable expression of emotion. It differs from mood (see below), which is a pervasive, subjectively experienced emotion. As the saying goes, "Affect is to mood as weather is to climate." Moods are symptoms; affects are signs. Commonly described affects are:

Blunted, flat, and constricted affects describe (in decreasing order of severity) patients who show almost no emotional lability, appear expressionless, look dulled, and speak in a monotone.

Broad affect is a normal range of affect.

Inappropriate affect is clearly discordant with the content of the patient's speech: A patient giggles while talking about his father's death.

Labile affect shows a range of expression in excess of cultural norms, with repeated, rapid, and abrupt shifts of emotion, as when a patient cries one moment and laughs the next. There are two types of labile affect: With "organic" etiologies, the lability of affect presents as a massive emotional overreaction to external stimuli, which is often part of a catastrophic reaction, and which the interviewer is usually unable to stop; With "functional" etiologies, the lability of affect is an overresponse to internal stimuli, which is less rapid and less extreme.

Alexithymia is a trait in which the patient has a constricted emotional life, diminished ability to fantasize, and a virtual inability to articulate emotions. Like anhedonia, alexithymia describes the absence of emotion, but in anhedonia, positive emotion seems blocked or stymied, whereas in alexithymia, it's as if no emotion exists. Patients will complain about anhedonia, but not about alexithymia. (See also Anhedonia.)

Ambivalence is having two strongly opposite ideas or feelings at the same time, which render the individual virtually unable to respond or decide.

Amnesia is a pathological loss of memory. There are two types:

Anterograde amnesia is for events occurring after a significant point in time.

Retrograde amnesia is for events occurring before a significant point in time.

Anhedonia is a mood (see below) in which there is a pervasive inability to perceive and experience pleasure in actions and events that are normally pleasurable or satisfying for the individual or most individuals. Anhedonia often begins with the person trying to carry out the activity, hoping the anticipated pleasure will materialize. When it doesn't, in time the person loses all interest in the activity and tends to avoid it: A football freak ignores the Super Bowl; a devoted father is totally bored by his children; a civil rights activist no longer cares. (Contrast "anhedonic" with "hedonistic"; see also Alexithymia.)

Anorexia is a loss of appetite.

Anxiety can refer to a symptom or a syndrome. As a symptom, anxiety is a mood (see below) of inner tension, restlessness, uneasiness, or apprehension. As a syndrome, anxiety combines this (internal) mood with (external) physiological signs, such as tremor, pounding heart, hypervigilance, dilated pupils, and agitation. Anxiety is pathological only when it chronically interferes with a person's functioning. Whereas *anxiety* implies the absence of a consciously recognized, external threat, *fear* implies that such a threat exists. Anxiety focused on an upcoming event is called *anticipatory anxiety*; unfocused anxiety is called *free-floating anxiety*. (See also Panic attack, Phobia.)

Autistic thinking is thought derived from fantasy: The person defines his environment based on internal fantasies instead of on external realities. Autistic thinking also refers to an individual's preoccupation with her own private world; social withdrawal into the inner world usually results.

Blocking is when a person's train of thought abruptly and unexpectedly stops. Blocking may or may not be pathological, depending on the degree.

Catatonia is manifest as extreme psychomotor agitation or retardation and minimal interaction with the environment. Catatonic patients seem driven, even when motionless; some appear frantic, others fanatical (see also Mutism, Posturing, Stereotypy). Examples include:

Catatonic excitement is extreme overactivity seemingly unrelated to environmental stimuli.

Catatonic negativism is an apparently motiveless and extreme resistance to all instructions or attempts to be moved. Three manifestations of this negativism are (1) *catatonic posturing*, in which a bizarre position is rigidly held for long periods; (2) *catatonic rigidity*, in which the patient resists all efforts to be moved; and (3) *waxy flexibility*, in which the patient resists having his body moved, but ends up with parts of his body being "molded" into odd positions, as if they were pliable wax.

Cataplexy is a sudden, unexpected, purposeless, generalized, and temporary loss of muscle tone.

Clanging is a type of language in which the sound of a word, instead of its meaning, dictates the course of subsequent associations (e.g., "ding, dong, dell . . .").

Clouding of consciousness is when the patient is awake and functioning, but has an incomplete or distorted awareness of the environment. It is a higher level of awareness than stupor (see below), in which an awake patient is unaware and unresponsive to the environment.

Circumstantiality is a pattern of speech, which although filled with detours, irrelevant details, and parenthetical remarks, eventually reaches its point; tangentiality (see below) is when the point isn't reached. Circumstantiality may or may not be pathological.

Coma is the most impaired end on a continuum of consciousness. Patients may be totally unresponsive to a (painful) stimulus, such as a pinprick, or may twitch but not display any further evidence of awareness. Slightly better on this continuum is stupor (see below), in which patients may rouse to their name, but their speech is not rational, they show little awareness of their environment, and they may promptly slip back into a coma.

Compulsions are repeated, stereotyped, overtly senseless actions or rituals that are performed to prevent anxiety. Compulsions are obsessions (see below) expressed in behavior. Obsessions are thoughts, compulsions are deeds. Lady Macbeth's hand-washing is a compulsion to wipe clean her obsession with Duncan's blood.

Concrete thinking is the inability to think abstractly, metaphorically, or hypothetically. Ideas and words are usually limited to a single meaning. Figures of speech are taken literally and nuances of language are missed and not used.

Confabulation is when a patient invents responses, facts, and events to mask an organic impairment.

Craving refers to urges and anticipation for using a habituating substance or performing a physical activity (e.g., bulimic episodes, gambling, jogging, weight-lifting). Craving is both physiologic (physical withdrawal) and psychologic (involving memory). Craving only exists when the habituating substance or activity is not in use and is only relieved when it is. Craving seems to be learned behavior that follows a classical conditioning paradigm. Craving is not necessarily associated with physical distress and may coexist with anxiety (see above), but they are different phenomena.

Déjà vu is a sense of familiarity when confronted by a situation or event that has not been experienced previously. Literally "already seen." Although it usually occurs in nonpathological states, it may be pathological.

Delusions are fixed, blatantly false convictions deduced from incorrect inferences about external reality; they are maintained despite enormous, obvious, incontrovertible proof to the contrary, and they are not widely believed in the person's culture or subculture. A false belief that involves an extreme value judgment is a delusion only when it defies credibility. Delusions differ from overvalued ideas (see below), which are unreasonable and persistent beliefs. To various degrees, delusions are systematized or unsystematized. In comparison to *unsystematized* delusions, *systematized* delusions are united by a common theme or event and belong to a complete and relatively well-organized network of beliefs; they develop more insidiously, cause less confusion and impairment, and last longer. (See also Folie à deux, Hallucinations, Ideas of reference, Mood-congruent, Mood-incongruent, Paranoia, Schneiderian first-rank symptoms.) Examples:

Bizarre delusions are patently absurd and weird.

Grandiose delusions involve an exaggerated sense of one's own importance, power, ability, or identity. "I am Christ."

Jealousy delusions involve suspicions about a rival (e.g., business rival) or about one's sex partner being unfaithful. Othello.

Nihilistic delusions involve themes of nonexistence (not "negativity"), either of the patient, others, or the world. "My insides are gone." "At 1:30 P.M., the world will evaporate."

Persecutory delusions are those in which the person is convinced others are trying to harm, cheat, attack, or conspire against him or her.

Reference delusions are beliefs that external events or people are sending messages or commands of great personal importance to the patient. These delusions are self-referential. A woman insisted that a man on TV was speaking to her specifically and instructing her to buy Ajax. (And she did— 1,280 cans!) (See also Ideas of reference.)

Somatic delusions pertain to the patient's body and are not consistent with cultural beliefs or with physiology or medicine. "My intestines are rotting." "My brain is turning black."

Depersonalization is when a person perceives her body as unreal, floating, dead, or changing in size. A person's arm may feel like wood or seem detached from her body. Depersonalization differs from derealization (see below), in which a person perceives his environment as unreal. Both phenomena often occur in nonpathological situations, with or without stress.

Derailment is a gradual or sudden deviation in a patient's train of behavior, speech, or thought onto a very different track. It may be hard to distinguish from flight of ideas and looseness of associations (see below). (See also Incoherence.)

Derealization is when a person perceives his environment as unreal. The individual feels removed from the world, as if he is viewing it on a movie screen. (See also Depersonalization.)

Disorientation is the inability to correctly identify the current time, place, and person's name.

Distractibility is when a patient's attention is frequently drawn to unimportant or irrelevant external stimuli.

Echolalia is a meaningless, persistent, verbal, repetition of words or sounds heard by the patient—often with a mocking, mumbling, staccato, or parrot-like tone. (Greek *echo* "an echo," and *lalia* "to babble.") Echolalia occurs in response to the same stimulus, whereas perseveration (see below) is repeated responses to varied stimuli.

Echopraxia is the repetitive imitation of another person's movements.

Ego-dystonic is a sign, symptom, or experience that the patient finds uncomfortable or doesn't want. For example, obsessions are ego-dystonic.

Ego-syntonic is a sign, symptom, or experience that the patient finds acceptable and consistent with her personality. Many, but not all, delusions, hallucinations, and overvalued ideas are ego-syntonic.

Flight of ideas is accelerated speech with many rapid changes in subject that derive from understandable associations, distracting stimuli, or play on words. In flight of ideas (FOI) the connections linking thoughts are understandable, whereas in looseness of associations (LOA) they are not. Nevertheless, extremely rapid FOI may be indistinguishable from LOA, and when there is a marked cultural gap between patient and interviewer, FOI is often misidentified as LOA. (See also Derailment, Incoherence.)

Folie à deux, or "madness for two," is when two closely related persons, usually in the same family, share the same delusions.

Fugue is a sudden, "purposeless," and unexpected flight or wandering away from home or work, during which the person assumes a new identity and has an anterograde amnesia (see above).

Guilt is a painful emotion directed inward, in which the person feels he has violated his own principles or conscience; the individual may feel bad, worthless, or in need of punishment. Whereas *guilt* is an affective state, *conscience* is a cognitive state consisting of ideas, beliefs, principles, values, standards, and norms. Both guilt and shame (see below) are emotions, but in shame the person feels embarrassed or ashamed before other people.

Hallucinations are false perceptions in the senses—hearing, seeing, touching, tasting, and smelling—based on no external reality. They differ from illusions (see below), which are false perceptions based on real stimuli. Hallucinations are disorders of perception; delusions (see above) are disorders of thinking. Delusions are always psychotic, hallucinations only sometimes: Some patients know their hallucinations are unreal (e.g., "My mind is playing tricks on me"); those who don't are described as giving a "delusional interpretation" to their hallucinations. Hallucinosis (see below) is a state in which the patient realizes her hallucinations are false. Except for dreams, hallucinations are pathological. *Hypnagogic* and *hypnopompic* hallucinations are dreams that occur on falling asleep or on waking up, respectively; if unaccompanied by other symptoms, they are merely variants of normal. Pathological hallucinations include:

Auditory hallucinations are false perceptions of sound, usually of a voice or voices.

Gustatory hallucinations are false, usually unpleasant, perceptions of taste. (Metallic tastes may be a side effect of medications or physical illnesses.)

Olfactory hallucinations are false perceptions of smell, such as the patient who kept smelling rotting flesh, as she viewed her "happily dead husband."

Somatic hallucinations are false perceptions of a physical experience inside the body. "I feel an orgasm running in my spleen."

Tactile hallucinations are false perceptions of touch. *Formication* is a tactile hallucination in which the patient feels that things, often insects, are crawling under his skin; it occurs most during withdrawal from alcohol, cocaine, or hypnosedatives.

Visual hallucinations are false perceptions of sight; they may consist of actual people or flashes of light.

Hallucinosis is when patients hallucinate following cessation or reduction of a substance, usually in a clear (or mildly clouded) consciousness. Most, but not all, hallucinosis is very unpleasant. Knowing these hallucinations are not real, the patient is less likely to act on them than on hallucinations she believes to be genuine.

Hypersomnia is a pattern of excessive sleeping.

Ideas of reference are overvalued ideas in which the patient is virtually, but not totally, convinced that objects, people, or events in his immediate environment have personal significance for him. A man felt that whenever a red car parked in front of his home, it probably was a well-disguised message from the FBI that he should be on the alert for dope addicts. With a delusion of reference, all doubt would cease. When they occur in a hypervigilant state, ideas of reference are not necessarily pathological: For instance, a man at a "swinger's bar" says, "All the chicks can't keep their eyes off me."

Illogical thinking involves conclusions that contain clear, internal contradictions or are blatantly erroneous, given the initial premises. A patient refuses to go to the movies because the tickets are green. Illogical thinking may or may not lead to a delusion or result from one. "I am a virgin, and therefore, I am the Virgin Mary."

Illusions are misperceptions of real external stimuli. During delirium tremens, alcoholics will misperceive the hair on their arms as bugs: These are illusions, not hallucinations, since they are based on a real stimulus.

Incoherence is a general term to describe incomprehensible speech arising from any kind of psychopathological thinking.

Insomnia is difficulty sleeping, either as *initial insomnia*, which is trouble falling asleep; *middle insomnia*, which is waking in the middle of the night and eventually falling back to sleep; or *terminal insomnia* (also known as "early morning awakening"), in which the person awakes early and cannot return to sleep; *paninsomnia* refers to difficulty sleeping throughout the night.

Looseness of associations refers to speech patterns characterized by leaps from subject to subject without the connections being clear or the patient being aware of his rapid shifts. "School is nice. I adore earlobes." (See also Derailment, Flight of ideas, Incoherence.)

Magical thinking is when a person is convinced that her words, thoughts, feelings, or actions will produce or prevent a specific outcome that defies all laws of cause and effect. Depending on how firmly the magical thinking is held, it may be a delusion or an overvalued idea, as in this example: "I know this seems odd, but when I move my third finger forward, I can make people walk faster; when I move my finger backward, they walk slower." Children, people in indigenous cultures, and patients with obsessive–compulsive and schizophrenic-like disorders use magical thinking.

Mood is a pervasive and subjectively experienced feeling state, as opposed to affect (see above), which is transitory and apparent to others. Unlike affect, mood colors the person's view of the world. (See also Alexithymia, Anhedonia.) Mood states include:

Apprehensive mood involves worried expectation or anticipation.

Dysphoria is any unpleasant mood, including irritable, apprehensive, and dysthymic moods.

Dysthymia is the mood of depression or pervasive sadness, including a subjective sense of heaviness or feeling "weighted down," blue, or down in the dumps. Dysthymia implies a mood that is more serious than "run-of-the-mill" unhappiness.

Elevated mood is more cheerful than normal for the person, but is not necessarily psychopathological.

Euphoric mood is an exaggerated sense of well-being and contentment; it implies psychopathology when elevated or expansive. (Elevated moods are "vertical"; expansive moods are "horizontal.") An elevated mood: "I feel wonderful, things are great!" An expansive mood: "I can do anything, bat .400, win every game single-handedly, and have all the fans worship me." A euphoric mood may be both elevated and expansive: "I'm flying, I'm on cloud nine, I feel like a god, I'm invincible."

Euthymia is a normal range of mood without dysphoria or elation.

Expansive mood refers to a lack of restraint in expressing feelings and an overvaluation of one's importance; it is often accompanied by an elevated or euphoric mood.

Irritable mood is a feeling of tension or nervousness; one feels prickly, easily annoyed, provoked to anger, or frustrated.

Mood-congruent delusions or hallucinations are consistent with the patient's dominant mood. A mood-congruent delusion in depression might be, "My body's rotting with cancer"; in mania, "I'm the Second Christ."

Mood-incongruent delusions and hallucinations are those that are inconsistent with the patient's dominant mood. Mood-incongruent delusions may be persecutory (e.g., "The Salvation Army is poisoning my tulips") or may involve Schneiderian symptoms (see below).

Mutism is an inhibition of speech; it is a frequent feature of catatonia.

Neologisms are distortions of words or new words that a patient invents for psychological reasons; neologisms may also be standard words given idiosyncratic meanings by the patient. A new or misused word is not a neologism when it arises for cultural or educational reasons (e.g., malapropisms).

Obsessions are unwanted and uncomfortable ideas, thoughts, images, or impulses that persistently invade one's consciousness. Unlike people with delusions or overvalued ideas, those with obsessions know that their beliefs are absurd and find them ego-dystonic. (See also Compulsions.)

Overvalued ideas are unreasonable and persistent beliefs, held with less than delusional intensity, which are not generally held in the patient's subculture. "The mob is tapping my phone—well, I think it is." Patients are more likely to act on delusions (see above) than on overvalued ideas. When patients recover from psychosis, they often go from delusions to overvalued ideas to "normality." Overvalued ideas may have a basis in reality, and some are not pathological, such as preoccupations that one's nose is too big, that only diet can cure cancer, or that "having a baby is the only way I will ever be happy." Ideas of reference (see above) are one type of overvalued idea.

Panic attacks are acute, terrifying, unexpected, and "senseless" attacks of anxiety, in which the person suddenly feels overwhelmed by an imminent sense of doom, despair, and destruction. The attacks include physiological signs of anxiety (see above) and usually end in several minutes.

Paranoia is not a symptom but a mental condition characterized by delusions of grandeur and persecution, suspiciousness, jealousy, and resentment.

Paranoid delusion is a delusion of persecution (see above). *DSM-IV* recommends using the term *persecutory delusion* because some patients have delusions of grandeur, believing that people want their money, ideas, etc., but do not feel persecuted.

Paranoid ideation is an overvalued idea (see above) that one is being persecuted.

Paranoid style is a character style in which people are unduly or excessively guarded, jealous, sullen, rigid, humorless, and hypersensitive to injustices allegedly being done to them. When a paranoid style substantially interferes with functioning, it becomes a *paranoid personality disorder.*

Perseveration is a persistent repetition of speech or movement to varied, usually internal, stimuli. It does not include repeated use of stock phrases, such as "you know" or "like." Echolalia (see above) and perseveration are often, but not always, found in dementia and delirium. (See also Stereotypy.)

Phobia is undue and irrational anxiety (see above) focused on an avoided object or place.

Posturing is the assumption of relatively fixed bodily positions, usually in catatonia.

Poverty of content of speech, sometimes called "poverty of content," is speech that conveys little information because it is vague, barren, or filled with empty repetitions or obscure phrases.

Poverty of speech is a striking lack of speech, so that replies to questions are brief or monosyllabic; some questions are not answered at all. Poverty of speech refers to an inadequate *quantity*; poverty of content of speech (see above) to inadequate *quality*.

Pressured speech is rapid, virtually nonstop, often loud and emphatic, seemingly driven, and usually hard to interrupt. It typically occurs in mania and in some drug-induced states and in severe anxiety states.

Psychomotor agitation, or simply "agitation," is repetitive, nonproductive motor activity usually associated with feelings of tension—e.g., pacing, fidgeting, constantly standing and sitting.

Psychomotor retardation describes slowed movements, reactions, or speech.

Psychosis is a mental state in which the person is unable to distinguish reality from fantasy.

Reality testing is the ability to distinguish reality from fantasy. The failure to test reality—what Lily Tomlin calls "man's collective hunches"—is the hallmark of psychosis.

Schneiderian first-rank symptoms (FRS) are specific types of delusions and hallucinations that involve themes of passivity. In 1939 Kurt Schneider originally claimed that FRS were pathognomonic for schizophrenia, but today, FRS are deemed only highly suggestive of schizophrenia. Patients with neurological disorders that produce pathological impulses or behaviors (e.g., unprovoked fighting, massive weeping) will commonly say, "This behavior isn't me," yet they will readily admit that they are responsible for the behavior. In contrast, patients with FRS deny responsibility for the strange behavior, claiming that "others made me do it." Specific FRS are:

Audible thoughts are auditory hallucinations in which the patient hears his own thoughts being spoken aloud by others. A patient says, "I will think about eating, and then I'll hear a man with a French accent repeat my very own words."

Being controlled (delusion of) reflects the patient's experience of her actions being completely under the control of external influences. She feels like an automaton, a totally passive observer of her own actions. "Andy and Barbara have placed an electronic bug in my brain that makes me run wild through Central Park. Blame them, not me." These are also called "made acts."

"Made" feelings are delusions in which the patient experiences emotions she insists are not her own, but have been imposed on her by others.

"Made" impulses are delusions in which the patient believes that powerful drives or urges have been forced upon him, compelling him to act. Although he disowns the impulse, he admits that it was he, and not others, who committed the act.

Somatic passivity are somatic hallucinations in which the patient is convinced that an external agent has caused her to be a passive recipient of unwanted bodily sensations.

Thought broadcasting are beliefs that one's inner thoughts are no longer private, have escaped from one's mind, and have become known to everyone. "Everyone in the hospital knows what I'm thinking." Telepathy is not thought broadcasting, since it is a culturally sanctioned belief and therefore not delusional.

Thought insertions are ego-alien convictions that thoughts have been placed into a person's mind, with the person believing that his thoughts are not his own.

Thought withdrawal is a patient's ego-dystonic belief that thoughts are being taken, or stolen from her mind or brain, and that she has fewer thoughts than before. "I was discussing Rome when suddenly my whole brain was sucked empty by the pope's vacuum cleaner."

Voices arguing are auditory hallucinations in which the patient hears two or more people arguing, typically about the patient, to whom they refer to as a third party.

Voices commenting are auditory hallucinations in which the patient hears people commenting on his actions while they are occurring: "He is standing up! He is walking!"

Shame is an emotion in which the person feels embarrassed or dishonored before others. (See also Guilt.)

Stereotypy is an isolated, repetitive, and purposeless movement. It appears most often in catatonic and drug-induced states. (See also Catatonia, Perseveration.)

Stupor is a state of foggy consciousness and nonalertness in which the patient may respond to noxious stimuli, but otherwise be oblivious to her environment. (See also Coma.)

Tangentiality is a disturbance of communication in which the person "goes off on a tangent," but unlike circumstantiality (see above), does not return to the point. Tangentiality may be viewed as repeated derailments (see above), which continually evade a central theme. It may or may not be pathological.

Thought disorder is a very general term to describe pathological thinking. Traditionally, thought disorder was divided into *disorders of thought content* (e.g., overvalued ideas, delusions), and *formal thought disorders*, which are abnormalities in the stream and continuity of thought (e.g., blocking, circumstantially, flight of ideas). Because the boundaries between the form and content of thought are often unclear, *DSM-III* suggested that both terms be avoided and that more specific descriptions and terms be used instead.

Vegetative signs are the biological (or physiological) signs of depression, such as insomnia, anorexia, weight loss, diurnal mood variation, constipation, and diminished libido. These signs are called *vegetative* because they primarily involve growth and nutrition; they're also called "hypothalamic signs" because they arise from disturbances involving the hypothalamic–pituitary axis.

Word salad is an apparently random and illogical mixture of words and sounds.

Index